Psychology, Adjustment, and Everyday Living

PSYCHOLOGY, ADJUSTMENT, AND EVERYDAY LIVING

Second Edition

Garry L. Martin
University of Manitoba

J. Grayson Osborne
Utah State University

Prentice Hall, Englewood Cliffs, New Jersey 07632

Library of Congress Cataloging-in-Publication Data

Martin, Garry
   Psychology, adjustment, and everyday living / Garry L. Martin and
J. Grayson Osborne.
      p.   cm.
   Includes bibliographical references and index.
   ISBN 0-13-735804-0
   1. Adjustment (Psychology)   I. Osborne, J. Grayson (James
Grayson)   II. Title.
BF335.M27   1993
155.2'4—dc20   92-22853
                                                         CIP

Editorial/production supervisor: Joan E. Foley
Acquisitions editor: Susan Finnemore Brennan
Editorial assistant: Jennie Katsaros
Interior and cover designer: Donna M. Wickes
Cover art: Georgia O'Keeffe, "Evening Star, III"
   (1917). Watercolor on paper, 9″ × 11 7/8″.
   Collection, The Museum of Modern Art, New
   York. Mr. & Mrs. Donald B. Straus Fund.
   Photograph © 1992 The Museum of Modern
   Art, New York.
Photo researcher: Rhoda Sidney
Copy editor: Nancy Savio-Marcello
Supplements editor: Sharon Chambliss
Prepress buyer: Kelly Behr
Manufacturing buyer: Mary Anne Gloriande

Additional acknowledgments appear on page 533 and
constitute a continuation of the copyright page.

© 1993, 1989 by Prentice-Hall, Inc.
A Simon & Schuster Company
Englewood Cliffs, New Jersey 07632

Printed in the United States of America
10 9 8 7 6 5 4 3 2 1

ISBN 0-13-735804-0

Prentice-Hall International (UK) Limited, *London*
Prentice-Hall of Australia Pty. Limited, *Sydney*
Prentice-Hall Canada Inc., *Toronto*
Prentice-Hall Hispanoamericana, S.A., *Mexico*
Prentice-Hall of India Private Limited, *New Delhi*
Prentice-Hall of Japan, Inc., *Tokyo*
Simon & Schuster Asia Pte. Ltd., *Singapore*
Editora Prentice-Hall do Brasil, Ltda., *Rio de Janeiro*

To Lee and Nancy: Respected colleagues, valued friends.

Brief contents

CONTENTS

BOXES

PREFACE

General Purpose of the Text

The second edition of *Psychology, Adjustment, and Everyday Living,* like its predecessor, has a threefold purpose: first, it is designed to teach students how psychology can help them understand their activities in everyday life—why they do, say, think, and feel what they do, say, think, and feel; second, it is intended as an easy-to-use guide to help students cope successfully with everyday problems of adjustment; and third, it introduces students to the broad range of traditional topics in the psychology of adjustment.

The style and organization of the book have been carefully crafted for students who have had no introductory course in psychology. We have tried to make the text enjoyable to read, easy to understand, well illustrated, engaging, and both comprehensive and practical. We provide a balanced discussion of topics found in most adjustment textbooks, such as personality, sexuality, marriage, stress, anxiety, prejudice, and discrimination. We also focus on areas that are of special concern to our readers, including developing a healthy lifestyle, developing interpersonal relationships, and successfully finding and keeping employment. Numerous questionnaires and behavioral checklists are provided to foster self-discovery. And specific guidelines show readers how they can successfully make adjustments in their own lives.

Learning Aids and Features

To promote understanding and facilitate learning, we've incorporated the following features into the second edition of the book:

1. **Chapter Outlines** at the outset of each chapter to help students organize the subject matter.
2. **Learning Objectives** at the start of each chapter to help students practice the question part of SQ3R.
3. Some **chapter opening dialogues** and/or case studies to capture student interest and awareness of the successful application of adjustment procedures.
4. A **marginal Glossary** that defines key terms and concepts that are discussed in the text. These will aid students in quickly locating important material and in preparing for exams.
5. **Comic strips and photographs** that have been chosen to illustrate points rather than simply to provide reader relief.
6. **Questionnaires and checklists** to increase self-discovery, raise self-awareness, and to focus on personal adjustment.

7. **Informative boxes** in each chapter to present material that is of special interest.
8. **Chapter Summaries** at the end of each chapter to help students review key points.
9. A **Memory Booster** section at the end of each chapter that lists important people, terms, and concepts from the chapter and that includes study questions to help organize student thinking about important issues.
10. **Interactive boxes** within and at the end of each chapter to help students define a personal problem in adjustment, and then accomplish self-adjustment of the problem.

Content and Organization

In keeping with our goal of balanced coverage, and to easily fit either the semester system or the quarter system, the second edition of the book is divided into five parts, each part comprised of three chapters. Part I is definitional and conceptual. In Chapter 1, we introduce the reader to psychology and the concept of practical adjustment. In Chapter 2, we present different views of personality, including trait, psychoanalytic, humanistic, and behavioral/social learning theories. In Chapter 3, we explore basic principles of learning including Pavlovian and operant conditioning, and observational learning. We recommend that the chapters in this section be covered in the order presented.

Part II begins a discussion of personal lifestyle adjustment. Chapter 4 is also necessarily definitional as it presents selected principles of psychology that relate to thinking and to the emotions. Application begins in earnest here with presentations of methods to adjust thinking and emotional behavior. Chapter 5 defines the concept of stress and our reactions to it and suggests ways to manage stress in our daily lives. Chapter 6 deals with ways to define and maintain a healthy lifestyle, particularly in terms of exercise, diet, and resisting drugs.

The focus of Part III is on the development and maintenance of interpersonal relationships. Chapter 7 begins this part with human sexual and reproductive anatomy, human sexuality, and sexual behavior. Gender development and some of its outcomes are also explored. Chapter 8 shows how and why relationships between humans commence and proceed via dating to love. In Chapter 9, one kind of human relationship—marriage—is explored, as are reasons for its dissolution.

Part IV looks at adjustment across the life cycle. Chapter 10 explores the development of thinking in children and adolescents, the psychological development of adolescents, and the progress of adult development from young adulthood to old age. In Chapter 11, we look at a unique topic—cooperative adjustments that may be required of us collectively if we are to survive as a society. Chapter 12 takes the reader into the world of work, providing tips on how to choose a career, get a job, and how to keep it.

Part V, the final part of the book, examines serious psychological disorders (Chapter 13) and their treatments (Chapter 14). These disorders are, for the most part, not problems in self-adjustment; but it is important for the student to recognize what they are and how they are dealt with. Chapter 15 explores how we can resolve harmful emotions such as anger, anxiety, loneliness, and grief.

Recommended Chapter Coverage

Obviously, for 15- to 16-week semesters, approximately one chapter per week must be covered. For 10-week quarters, approximately one and one-half chapters per week must be covered.

Our recommendations for the order of progress through the material are general in nature. Clearly, the foundational chapters of the book are the first four

(Psychology of Adjustment, Personality, Learning, and Thinking and Emotions). Many subsequent referrals are made to these chapters, so they should be covered first. Thereafter, order of procedure doesn't appear as critical except within some parts. With the definitional material in Parts I and II well in hand, the order of Parts III, IV, and V could be altered. Within Part III, some instructors may consider the biological background material (Chapter 7) essential to discussing relationships (Chapters 8 and 9), others less so. Within Part V, Chapters 13 and 14 should be covered in sequence—the former being definitional for the latter. The authors, however, have taught the material as ordered in the book and the students find this quite satisfactory.

Beginning with Chapter 3, we involve the student in a self-adjustment activity at the conclusion of each chapter, from defining a behavior to be adjusted to actually adjusting it and making the adjustment last. Instructors can easily capitalize on this feature by teaching the chapters in order. Alternatively, for instructors who wish to capitalize on this feature while at the same time altering the order of chapters, the self-adjustment boxes at the end of each chapter could be assigned in the order in which they appear, quite apart from the order in which the chapters are read.

Changes in the Second Edition

In preparing this revision, we wanted to retain the many features of the first edition that were positively received by professors and students. At the same time, we wanted to improve the book and to stay abreast of new developments in the field. To accomplish these goals, this edition differs from the first in several respects. At the outset, we opted to reorganize the text into the more traditional fifteen chapters (rather than the 30 chapters of the first edition) in order to make the text more amenable to typical semester and quarter length. We also made major revisions to many of the chapters and have provided additional coverage of cognitive, humanistic, and psychodynamic approaches. We organized principles of learning into a single chapter instead of scattering them throughout the text, as in the first edition. We added several new topics such as violence, drugs, AIDS, adjustment in adolescence, and personality assessment; and we provided updated and expanded information on most of the previous topics. Several new interactive boxes have been added to help students increase self-discovery and raise self-awareness. And we added a new section at the end of each chapter entitled, "Self-Adjustment for Students," which guides the reader through the steps of a self-adjustment project.

Student Study Guide

The study guide is designed to help students master the content of the text and to prepare for examinations. For each chapter, it contains a detailed chapter outline, a guide for studying important information, a fill-in-the-blanks review of key points in the chapter, and a self-test to assess mastery. It also prompts students to carefully study material from the Memory Booster section at the end of the chapter. We're confident that the study guide will be a very useful tool for students.

Instructor's Manual and Test Bank

Considering the extensive study aids incorporated into the text, we believe that the most helpful additional material we can give an instructor is a detailed answer key to the study questions contained in the Memory Booster section of each chapter. Such an answer key can be a tremendous timesaver for instructors who use the study questions on exams, and can facilitate accurate and consistent grading.

For instructors who prefer essay, multiple-choice, or true/false questions, we have provided a large pool of such questions on a chapter-by-chapter basis. The test items were chosen to be closely related to the Learning Objectives and to the material contained in the answers to the end-of-chapter study questions. This was deliberate so that students who master the textual material by learning answers to the study aids will perform well on the questions in the test bank.

Acknowledgments

The second edition of this book was made possible with the help of many individuals. We would like to acknowledge the following reviewers for their many valuable suggestions:

K. Robert Bridges, Pennsylvania State University—New Kensington
James O. Davis, Southwest Missouri State University
David R. Evans, University of Western Ontario
Charles W. Johnson, University of Evansville—Indiana
Nabil M. Marshood, Hudson County Community College
Ralph G. Pifer, Sauk Valley College
Gary W. Piggrem, De Vry Institute of Technology
Karen J. White, University of Notre Dame
Patrick S. Williams, University of Houston—Downtown

We take special pleasure in acknowledging Claudia Milton for her editorial assistance and Karen Ranson for her work on organizing the Instructor's Manual.

Finally, we express our appreciation to the very capable and enthusiastic editorial and production team at Prentice Hall. In particular, we want to thank Susan Finnemore Brennan, our editor, and Joan Foley, our production editor.

Garry L. Martin and J. Grayson Osborne

PSYCHOLOGY, ADJUSTMENT, AND EVERYDAY LIVING

chapter

1

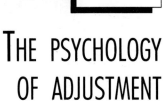

THE PSYCHOLOGY OF ADJUSTMENT

LEARNING OBJECTIVES

After reading this chapter, you should be able to:

- Describe problems of adjustment in everyday living.
- Discuss the benefits of viewing adjustment in terms of specific behaviors, thoughts, or feelings that need to be changed.
- Explain how knowledge of psychology's research methods and principles can help you cope with challenges to adjustment.
- Analyze your study habits and identify areas for improvement.
- Illustrate common misconceptions about time management.
- Implement a five-step program for improving your time management and study skills.
- Identify specific areas for adjustment in your own life, the accomplishment of which will be facilitated by studying this book.

"I'm a failure. I feel ugly and useless. I keep thinking that it was all my fault. I get really down and I don't want to do anything," Carol explained to the psychologist. "At work, when I start thinking of Fred, I go to the bathroom and cry. Sometimes I can't stop crying for a whole hour."

Carol is one of a number of people you will read about in this book. She and Fred were engaged for two years. But since their breakup three months before, Carol has suffered obsessive, disturbing thoughts about Fred, and particularly about herself.

Like Carol, many people face problems of adjustment. Of course, the specifics of the problems vary. Finding a job, shedding extra pounds, resisting pressure from peers to "do drugs," worrying about being the only virgin on campus, getting so nervous before tests that your hands shake and your mind goes blank—all are challenges to adjustment, challenges that many people face day in and day out, throughout their lives. Let's see how psychology helped Carol to cope with her problems.

Carol agreed to implement the following procedure. Each time she experienced a thought characteristic of those that caused her to cry, she would stop what she was doing, clasp her hands, close her eyes, and silently yell "stop!" to herself. This is called *thought stopping*. Then she would open her eyes and take some photographs from her purse. The photographs were arranged in a particular order and encircled by an elastic band. With a psychologist's guidance, she had written specific statements on the back of each of them. With the photographs facing down, she looked at the back of the first one and read, "I'm my own boss. My life is ahead of me. I can do what I want to do." She turned the photo over and looked at a picture of herself at the airport. The photo had been taken just prior to a trip alone during the previous year. She had had a great time. For the next five to ten seconds, she thought about how much she would like to travel again and about the fun that she had had on her previous trip. These are *positive thoughts*. Carol continued in this way with the remaining photographs. Following this entire procedure, which required approximately two to three minutes to complete, Carol recorded her thoughts on an index card and returned to her previous activities.

Carol used thought stopping to terminate disturbing thoughts, and photographs and written instructions to prompt positive alternative thoughts. (These techniques are described further in Chapter 4.) Did it work? Yes! Carol gradually

Do you practice a healthy lifestyle?

adjusted to life without Fred. At the beginning of her adjustment program, Carol still had some unhappy days. But during the next three weeks, her positive thinking gradually increased, and the unhappy thoughts of Fred occurred less and less. After two months, Carol decided that she no longer needed help (Martin, 1982).

The strategy that helped Carol illustrates an application of psychology to a problem of adjustment in everyday living. But what is adjustment? And what is psychology? In this chapter, we'll examine some dimensions of adjustment. We'll also discuss the nature of psychology. And we'll look at how psychology uses the scientific method to discover basic principles. Finally, we'll illustrate how psychology can help in an area of adjustment important to students—time management and study skills.

Adjustment and Everyday Living

behavior

Anything that a person says or does; common synonyms include *activity, action, performance, responding, response, reaction,* and *skill.*

adjustment

Changes in our ways of behaving, thinking, and feeling to meet the demands of our environment.

We judge the adjustment of others in terms of the behavior that we observe and its relation to the environment in which it occurs. It was obvious to Carol's boss, for example, that something was dreadfully wrong. His employees just didn't disappear for an hour each day and return with red eyes and a wrung-out look. In general, a **behavior** refers to anything that a person says or does. Some commonly used synonyms include *activity, action, performance, responding, response, reaction,* and *skill.* But from Carol's point of view, her problem involved much more than just behavior that was observable to her boss. Her obsessive *thoughts* about Fred, her *feelings* of loneliness, her loss of *self-confidence and self-esteem*—these were the private problems that her boss couldn't see. In our concern about adjustment, we have to consider more than just behavior that is observable to others. We all have thoughts, feelings, emotions, an inner self and an outer self, observable behavior, and "private" behavior unobservable to others. **Adjustment** refers to changes in our ways of behaving, thinking, and feeling to meet the demands of our environment.

The problems that we face in daily life can be thought of as problems of adjustment. Coping with relationships, family, school, work, the environment in which we live, the changing roles of the sexes, and cultural limitations on what we do—all of these involve problems of adjustment. This book will help you to understand and to deal effectively with challenges to adjustment—challenges such as those portrayed in the following situations.

Personal Lifestyle Adjustment

"I'm restless, anxious, irritable, I can't sleep, I get headaches, and I feel like barfing half the time," complained Jack. He and Stan were having their third cup of coffee in the Java House—a little hamburger joint just off campus.

"You ready for the exam?" asked Stan.

"If I'm not ready now, I'll never be." Jack drank the last of his coffee and glanced at his watch. "Must have drunk a gallon of this stuff last night," he thought to himself as he approached the refill area. "I guess one more cup before class won't hurt."

Like many college students, Jack drinks 12 to 15 cups of coffee per day. He is unaware that habitual daily intake in excess of 5 to 6 cups of coffee is considered a significant health risk (Greden et al., 1978). Jack's restlessness, anxiety, irritability, and many of his other complaints are symptoms of *caffeinism* (Kaplan & Shadock, 1981). Caffeinism is such a significant problem that it has been included as a separate classification in the *Diagnostic and Statistical Manual of Mental Disorders* (third edition, revised) of the American Psychiatric Association (1987). As with controlling your weight, exercise, smoking, drug and alcohol use, and other problems of personal lifestyle adjustment, caffeinism represents a significant concern. And like many concerns and challenges to adjustment, caffeinism has been effectively treated (James et al., 1985).

The caffeinism example raises questions about the critical components of effective adjustment. Are there reasonable steps that one can take to promote healthy living in such areas as dieting, exercising, smoking, and stress? The answer is yes! In Part II of this book, we discuss strategies for making personal lifestyle adjustments in everyday living.

Adjustment and Interpersonal Relations

"Women are usually sweet until they've caught a man, but then they let their true selves show." "A lot of men talk big, but when it comes down to it, they can't perform sexually." You might be surprised to learn that in a study of college students, approximately 40 percent of the men sampled agreed with the first statement, and approximately 40 percent of the women agreed with the second statement (Check et al., 1985); other studies have also indicated that a surprising number of persons have feelings of hostility toward the other sex. Interestingly, the men who score high on a scale measuring hostility toward women also tend to have traditional gender-role beliefs. They believe that a woman's place is in the home, that a woman should be a virgin when she marries, and that a wife should never contradict her husband in public. Such men are likely to agree with statements such as "I feel that many times women flirt with men just to tease them or hurt them" or "Many times a woman appears to care but just wants to use you." We hasten to add that this is not a one-way street. There are also a surprising number of women who feel hostility toward men. These women tend to agree with statements such as "When it really comes down to it, a lot of men are deceitful" or "I am sure I get a raw deal from the men in my life."

The foregoing suggests the challenge of relating openly with others, in this case with members of the other sex. What causes such hostility? If you feel hostile toward others, can you adjust so that you are no longer hostile? Does how you feel about the other sex influence your attraction to them, and vice versa? Challenges of relating well to others, regardless of their gender, are discussed in Part III of this book.

Adjustment Throughout Life

Susan was thinking about her courses while driving her 15-year-old sister to school. With two term papers due next week and a midterm exam at the same time, Susan was starting to panic. "How am I ever going to make it through my first year in college?" she wondered to herself. "Why didn't I start working on this stuff sooner?" Her thoughts were interrupted by the sound of her sister's voice.

"Sue, I've got a problem! I've been going with Brad for a month, and he wants me to go to bed with him. I don't know what to do."

Sue hit the brakes hard as a car cut her off in the heavy traffic. "Nice driving, you jerk!" Sue shouted out her window at the driver in front of her. Choking on the smog, she rolled up her window. She turned to her sister, wondering what she should say.

Living a well-adjusted life in today's society is not easy. We live in a changing world. We survive the challenges of adolescence to face the decisions of young adulthood. Gaining independence from our families, establishing careers, building relationships, facing the responsibilities of marriage and parenting—all this in a high-tech world with its ever-changing mix of progress, pressure, prejudice, and pollution. The diverse demands of our changing world require us to think of adjustment as a dynamic process, rather than as a static outcome. A well-adjusted young adult 20 years ago would be quite different than a well-adjusted young adult today. A well-adjusted young person during the 1990s might be quite different than a well-adjusted older person during that same period. Your view of "the good life" is influenced by the characteristics of your culture, your religious beliefs, and the values taught by your parents and expressed by your peers. In Part IV of this book, we examine adjustment throughout life. We'll explore human development from adolescence through old age. We'll focus on some important problems of living in today's society, such as violence, prejudice, and pollution. And we'll examine adjustment strategies in areas of vital importance to students—career decision making, preparing for employment, and adjusting in the world of work.

To live a well-adjusted life in today's society, one must be prepared to adapt to many challenges.

Coping with Maladjustment

"Flight CP 709, and it leaves at 8:15 A.M.? OK. Thank you very much. I'll pick up my ticket at the airport." As Barb put down the phone, her heart was pounding so hard she thought her husband might hear it in the next room. She had just made a reservation to visit her friend in Chicago. She kept telling herself, "This time I'm going through with it. This time I'm not going to cancel out at the last minute." Barb is an almost adjusted, healthy young woman with one quirk: She's terrified of airplanes. Even calling the travel agent a month in advance and making reservations is almost enough to make her panic.

Three weeks and six days later—one day before the date of her flight—Barb finished another conversation with the travel agent and put down the phone. "I've done it again," she thought to herself. "I know it's not rational, but I just can't help it. No one is going to believe that I canceled another trip."

Many people have such intense anxiety that they are virtually incapacitated. For example, a person might have such an intense fear of heights that he cannot walk up a single flight of stairs or look out a second-story window without acute anxiety. Or a person might be so terrified of crowds that she cannot bear to go into public places. Trying to convince these people that such anxiety is irrational rarely has a beneficial effect. They usually know that there is no rational basis for their anxiety and would like to control it; they cannot, however, because the anxiety is automatically produced by specific environmental events. Such intense, irrational, incapacitating anxiety is called a *phobia*.

As our example suggests, excessive anxiety can be personally debilitating. What causes excessive anxiety? Can an individual do anything to help him or herself if severe anxiety occurs? The answer is yes. In Part V of this book, we discuss the characteristics of major psychological disorders. We'll explore the most common and successful therapies for treating major psychological disorders. And we'll also explore psychological principles that you, yourself, can apply to control certain harmful emotions, such as anxiety, anger, loneliness, and depression.

What Are Problems of Adjustment?

As the above examples illustrate, problems of adjustment involve problematic behaviors, thoughts, and feelings. The people around us teach us to describe our behavior as good or bad, skilled or unskilled, and in numerous other ways. We're taught to describe our bodily sensations and feelings as satisfying or painful or somewhere in between. If we or others feel badly about our behavior, then a problem of adjustment exists until we and others feel good. What is it that makes us feel good, bad, or indifferent about ourselves? It's our consideration of specific behaviors, thoughts, and feelings in specific situations. That's what leads to judgments of adjustment or maladjustment. It was Carol's obsessive thoughts at work that caused her to seek professional help. It was John's excessive coffee drinking while studying that contributed to his caffeinism. It was Barb's feelings of fear about flying that led her to cancel her trip. If individuals have problems of adjustment, then they behave in ways that they or others consider deficient or excessive for some situation.

behavioral deficit

Too little of a particular behavior, thought, or feeling in a particular situation.

Consider, for example, the following **behavioral deficits** in particular situations:

1. Sally does not speak in her political science seminar, where 80 percent of her grade is based on class participation.
2. Jeff does not notice traffic signs while driving.

Box 1-1

COMMON PHOBIAS AND THEIR FANCY NAMES

There are many kinds of phobias that have been given fancy labels when they are published. You might like to see a few, and the titles they carry:

Acrophobia   Fear of high places
Agoraphobia   Fear of open places
Algophobia   Fear of pain
Astraphobia   Fear of thunder and/or lightning
Cardiophobia   Fear of heart attack
Claustrophobia   Fear of closed spaces or confinement
Hemotaphobia   Fear of the sight of blood
Hydrophobia   Fear of water
Lalophobia   Fear of (public) speaking
Monophobia   Fear of being alone

Mysophobia   Fear of dirt, germs, or contamination
Nyctophobia   Fear of darkness
Ocholophobia   Fear of crowds
Pathophobia   Fear of disease or illness
Peccatophobia   Fear of sinning
Phobophobia   Fear of fear
Pyrophobia   Fear of fire
Syphilophobia   Fear of syphilis
Thanatophobia   Fear of death
Toxophobia   Fear of being poisoned
Xenophobia   Fear of strangers
Zoophobia   Fear of animals (usually specific kinds)

More about dealing with these later!

---

behavior excess

Too much of a particular behavior, thought, or feeling in a particular situation.

Consider the following **behavioral excesses** in particular situations:

1. Janice watches a lot of television during final exam week.
2. John spends hours each morning in front of the mirror, making sure every hair is in place.

A practical approach to adjustment focuses on methods to strengthen behaviors, thoughts, and feelings that are deficient, and to weaken behaviors, thoughts, and feelings that are excessive in particular situations. There are two important benefits of viewing adjustment in this way. First, it helps us to avoid the *labeling trap*. When a person is labeled, we are likely to overemphasize problems and ignore that individual's positive attributes. This is what we mean by the labeling trap. To illustrate, what do you think of someone who is a "biker"? "Mentally ill"? A "convict"? A "drop-out"? A "punker"? A biker could be someone who rides a dirt bike in the hills on Sundays with his family. Maybe you thought of a "Hell's Angel." A mentally ill person could be someone who spent a couple of months in a hospital a few years back (yet you might have thought of characters from *One Flew over the Cuckoo's Nest*). Should we attach labels to people? Labels that imply maladjustment? Inevitably it seems that we do and there are definite dangers in doing so. Thomas Szasz, a psychiatrist, a third of a century ago declared: "There is no such thing as mental illness. We invent it! The majority of the people who are called mentally ill are mostly those who are too poor or too ignorant to defend themselves from such accusations" (Szasz, 1961). Szasz had become upset at the way psychiatrists made people with problems think of themselves as "patients" and as "sick," and he has continued to challenge the psychiatric profession about how they talk about and treat their "patients" (e.g., Szasz, 1989; 1991). Many people who seek counseling are simply having routine problems in daily life with family, love, work, stress, and the like. Labeling them, Szasz argued, leads to treatments that are often counterproductive. We agree with Szasz that many "psychiatric problems" are actually just problems in living. But we also need to recognize that there are individuals who are clearly a danger to themselves or others and are not capable of healthy functioning. While we need to avoid the labeling trap, we must also recognize that individuals with serious psychological disorders require professional help (discussed further in Chapters 13 and 14).

Just as no one is perfectly adjusted, neither is anyone totally maladjusted. If we think of adjustment in terms of behavior, thoughts, and feelings in situations, then we're more likely to focus on specific problems that are excessive or deficient for specific situations. Moreover, with this approach, we're more likely to recognize that so-called maladjusted individuals often behave in ways that are entirely appropriate for many situations. We may also be less likely to label them and thereafter treat them in inappropriate ways.

There is a second advantage to viewing adjustment in terms of specific behaviors, thoughts, and feelings in specific situations. During the past 30 years, behavioral scientists have investigated and developed practical programs for changing behaviors, thoughts, and feelings. Literally thousands of research reports in education, social work, psychology, rehabilitative medicine, and other areas have demonstrated the value of these programs for helping individuals in diverse settings. In situations where a person was motivated to behave differently, learn a new skill, develop persistence, eliminate a bad habit, change disturbing thoughts, or overcome troublesome emotions, psychological principles have been effectively applied (e.g., see Feist & Brannon, 1988; Martin & Pear, 1992). In later chapters, we'll introduce you to some of these principles. But first, let's explore the nature of psychology and the research methods used by psychologists to discover basic principles.

A Definition of Psychology

psychology
The scientific study and practical applications concerning the observable behavior and inner processes of organisms.

A proper definition of psychology has five parts to it. **Psychology** is the scientific study (part 1) and practical applications (part 2) concerning the observable behavior (part 3) and inner processes (part 4) of organisms (part 5). Let's examine these parts in more detail.

As part 1 of the definition indicates, psychology endorses the scientific method. No one disputes that science has been incredibly successful in uncovering laws of the universe—discoveries that have had wide-reaching effects on all of our lives. The scientific method is so important to psychology that we will discuss some of its characteristics in more detail in the next section.

In part 2 of our definition, we emphasize the *application* of psychological principles to the betterment of humankind. More than half of America's psychologists work in applied psychology (see Table 1-1). A proper definition of psychology must encompass all of the things that psychologists do—an increasingly broad spectrum.

Because of the emphasis in science that things studied be objectively measured, the third part of our definition focuses on observable behavior—such as walking, talking, working, playing, communicating, and socializing. But what goes on inside us is also important. The fourth part of our definition includes the study of things that people do that are private or covert, including thinking, imagining, sensing, and experiencing emotions. Psychologists study private activities by relying on an individual's verbal report of personal experiences, and by using special instrumentation (such as a pulse meter to record heart rate).

The fifth part of the definition indicates that psychologists do not just study human behavior. Psychologists study the behavior of all organisms—of cats, dogs, gorillas, even mosquitoes and flatworms. For some psychologists, animal behavior

TABLE 1-1
VARIETIES OF APPLIED PSYCHOLOGY

More than half of America's psychologists work in applied psychology. Here are some examples of the work that they do:

Clinical psychologists	Diagnose and treat behavioral and emotional problems.
Counseling psychologists	Advise people on job selection and career adjustments (vocational counseling), preparing for and improving marriage (marriage counseling), and dealing with a severe injury or illness (rehabilitation counseling).
Consumer psychologists	Conduct public opinion polls and market surveys, assess effectiveness of advertising, and determine consumer groups for potential products.
Child psychologists	Diagnose and treat emotional and behavioral problems with children.
Community psychologists	Assess, prevent, and treat psychological problems and promote mental health by working through community organizations.
Educational psychologists	Develop psychological tests for school psychologists and evaluate educational programs.
Engineering psychologists	Design equipment and machines, such as computer keyboards and airplane cockpits, to maximize human abilities and minimize human limitations of users.
Environmental psychologists	Examine how behavior is affected by architecture, housing projects, crowding, weather, noise, and space, with a view to helping people live with and adapt to an ever-changing environment while minimizing pollution and spoilage of natural resources.
Forensic psychologists	Evaluate mental competency of accused people, help in rehabilitation of convicted criminals, advise police on recruitment procedures and dealing with hostage taking and other crises, and help judges and lawyers to improve the reliability of witnesses.
Health psychologists	Examine psychological factors that determine stress, design programs to minimize the effects of stress on heart disease, and design and implement programs for helping people develop healthier lifestyles.
Industrial psychologists	Help in the selection, training, and management of employees, advise on management–union negotiations (for both managers and union), and evaluate ways of improving industrial productivity.
Medical psychologists	Design and evaluate psychological treatments for problems previously thought to have a medical origin (such as migraine headaches and asthma attacks), and advise medical personnel on strategies for improving medical staff/patient relations.
Sport psychologists	Provide strategies to help athletes learn new skills, increase motivation to practice, and improve concentration and confidence for competitions.
School psychologists	Administer psychological tests, assess and treat problem behavior of children in classrooms, and design and evaluate programs in special education.
University professors	Teach, conduct research, and perform some private consulting and independent practice.

is just as important and interesting as human behavior. For others, animal behavior is important because of what it can tell us about ourselves. But whether psychologists are basic researchers or practitioners, and whether they study humans or other animals, they all endorse the scientific method. Let's look at some of the characteristics of science as practiced by psychologists.

Psychology and the Scientific Method

It's 3:00 P.M. at a large urban university. In the counseling center, a psychologist is *describing* the results of psychological assessments to one of the students—trying to help the student to better understand herself. On the psychiatric ward at the university hospital, a patient is being restrained after physically assaulting a nurse. The patient had been progressing so well. How can such violent outbursts be *explained*? Downstairs in the behavioral sciences building, researchers are studying the effects of steroids on laboratory rats—examining *predictions* of such side effects as blocked arteries and liver problems. And in the university auditorium, a counselor is leading a weekly support group for students coping with obesity, helping them to *control* excessive eating and to follow a sensible diet. Each of these professionals faces very different tasks and challenges within the field of psychology. And yet at the same time, these people have something important in common—namely, the fundamental goals of psychology itself.

Description, explanation, prediction, and *control* are the four main goals of every science—including a behavioral science like psychology. Psychologists study what people do and say (description), search for causes of behavior (explanation), make informed guesses about future patterns of behavior (prediction), and help people to solve their problems (control). To pursue these goals, psychologists practice *the scientific method*, rather than relying on common sense, authority, or armchair reasoning.

Assumptions of the Scientific Method

In a general sense, the scientific method includes two basic assumptions. First, scientists assume that aspects of nature—living things, this planet, even the universe itself—follow certain broad natural laws of cause and effect. What happens to a lake when the temperature drops below zero degrees Celsius? The water freezes. What happens when you drop your shoe? It falls to the earth. These familiar natural occurrences are things that scientists have studied extensively and used as a foundation in formulating general laws of cause and effect—such as the law of gravity. Relatively few people would dispute that there is, in fact, a general law of gravity at work around us. But are there equivalent laws of cause and effect governing our own behavior, thoughts, and feelings? As behavioral scientists, psychologists would say yes. And the search for these broad behavioral laws—that is, for some general explanations of what leads to what in the behavior of living things—is at the heart of much psychological research.

The second assumption of the scientific method is that the best way to answer questions is by observation and experimentation. *The scientific method begins with observation of a phenomenon, something that catches the attention of the scientist.* Suppose, for example, that while visiting the state of Maine, a psychologist notices that there are not many places to buy sex magazines (like *Hustler, Penthouse,* and so on). Upon investigation, our visitor also discovers that Maine has a very low rate of rape relative to several other states. *The gathering of observations is often followed by the formulation of an **hypothesis**—*an educated guess about what leads to what. An hypothesis is usually phrased so that there is a choice, so that it can be confirmed or disproved. For example, if our visiting psychologist hypothesizes that an increase in the sale of sex magazines is associated with an increase in incidence of rape, then it should be possible to gather evidence that supports or

hypothesis

An educated guess or statement about the possible relationship between two or more variables.

36   Winnipeg Free Press, Wednesday, March 29, 1989

Women suggest but men dictate

When the war turns to words

By Stephen Nicholls
The Canadian Press

When the battle of the sexes becomes a war of words, the two sides brandish different weapons.

Men and women don't speak the same language, say the experts. Or, rather, they speak the same language, but differently.

"Over the last 15 years, there's been a fair amount of interest in gender differences (in communication)," says Deborah James, a professor of linguistics at the University of Toronto. "There are some interesting differences."

Men tend to order, for example. Women ask. Men dictate. Women suggest.

And, contrary to popular belief, men generally talk more than women.

Every day, you are bombarded with "pop" psychology on television, in newspapers, and in almost every magazine on the newsstand. How should you judge the latest article on "The Power of Self-Talk," "The Characteristics of the Ideal Mate," or "Sex Habits of College Sophomores"? The above article claims that "Men dictate. Women suggest." How valid is this claim? Some knowledge of the pitfalls and problems of the methods for gathering information can help you to sort fact from fiction in popular press reports about psychological issues. Also, an understanding of the methods of science can help you to think critically and to skeptically question—abilities that can be helpful in all areas of your life.

---

disproves that hypothesis. *The next step is to conduct research to evaluate the hypothesis.* Our psychologist might, for example, examine available statistics on sales of sex magazines and rapes in several states. *After conducting research, a scientist must interpret the results.* This is where the human element and most of the disagreements in science occur. It turns out, for example, that Nevada, with high sales of sex magazines, also has high rape rates, while Maine, with low sales of sex magazines, has low rape rates (Baron & Strauss, 1984). Does that mean that sale of sex magazines causes rape? Other interpretations are possible. All plausible interpretations of research results must be carefully considered. *The final step in the scientific process is for the researcher to communicate the results to other researchers,* such as by presenting at a scientific conference or publishing the results in a scientific journal. And why do psychologists accept and use this process? Because of its proven success in discovering principles and techniques that can be applied to the betterment of humankind. And that is one of the reasons why we want you to know about psychology's research methods (also see Box 1-2).

Psychologists conduct many different types of research studies, all of which draw on the assumptions of the scientific method. And all psychological research has another feature—it emphasizes *reliable* measurement. Before we can explain such things as anxiety, dreaming, depression, or loss of memory, we must be able to accurately describe and measure these phenomena.

Emphasis on Reliable Measurement of Variables

variable

A measurable event, characteristic, or condition that can vary and assume different values.

Objects of study, such as anxiety, are called **variables** because successive measurements of them can vary and assume different values. The variable of anxiety, for example, can vary from mild to moderate to extreme anxiety. The variable of height of college students can range from very short to average to exceptionally tall.

Scientists value experimental findings that are repeatable and therefore reliable. Experiments are not likely to be repeatable if they are based on imprecise descriptions of variables. Suppose, for example, that you wanted to study whether or not students are anxious when they take final exams. How would you measure their anxiety? One possibility would be to simply look at them during the exam (after all, can't you usually tell when someone is anxious?). But some students might feel anxious and yet not show it in any obvious way that you could readily detect. And your subjective notion of what an anxious person looks like might be quite different from someone else's perception of anxiety. Scientists solve the problem of defining variables to be observed by using **operational definitions**— definitions of variables in terms of the procedures used to measure them. For example, considering that anxiety is typically accompanied by a rapid heart rate, you might ask students taking an exam to wear a pulse meter. Their anxiety would then be operationally defined by unusually high heart rates (see Figure 1-1).

operational definition

Definition of a variable in terms of the procedures and actions (i.e., operations) that were followed to measure the variable.

Correlation vs. Causation

Psychologists are not content with just observing and measuring behavior reliably. What they really want to know is—what causes it? Why do people do and say what they do and say? Why do they think and feel what they think and feel? Why are some students extremely anxious when taking final exams while other students aren't? When we understand the causes of behavior, then we will be in a much better position to help people change their behavior, to help them adjust to the trials and tribulations of daily living, and to lead healthy and productive lives. In order for you to accurately recognize causes of behavior, thoughts, and feelings, you must appreciate the differences between two related, but different, aspects of "explanation"—correlation and causation.

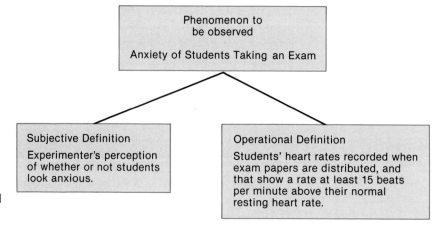

Figure 1-1

An example of a subjective vs. an operational definition

CORRELATION. What is your attitude toward minority groups? How do you behave toward them? For many people, their attitudes toward minority groups and the way they react to them are related: If they view minority groups positively, they treat them well; but if they have a negative attitude toward minority groups, they are likely to act in a prejudiced way toward them. If two variables—like attitudes and behaviors—are associated or vary together, they are said to be correlated (i.e., co-related). An example of a correlation mentioned earlier is the relationship in various states between the frequency of the sale of sex magazines and the incidence of rape. Where sales of sex magazines are high, so is the incidence of rape. Where sales of sex magazines are low, so is the incidence of rape. This type of correlation, in which two variables increase or decrease in value together, is called a **positive correlation.**

positive correlation

A correlation such that as the value of one variable increases, the value of a second variable increases, and vice versa.

Now consider a second type of correlation, one in which two variables are inversely related. That is, as the value of one variable increases, the value of the other decreases, and vice versa. This is called a **negative correlation.** In one study, for example, a group of students were given a test to measure the extent to which they were impulsive (i.e., their tendency to act on the basis of momentary urges rather than to think things through carefully before acting). Then their academic grade point average was examined at the end of their first year of college. Subjects who scored high on the test of impulsivity tended to have a lower grade point average, while those who scored low on a test of impulsivity tended to have a higher grade point average. In other words, a negative correlation was observed between scores on an impulsivity test and college grades (Kipnis, 1971).

negative correlation

A correlation such that as the value of one variable increases, the value of a second variable decreases, and vice versa.

Now consider a third scenario. Suppose that you select a group of 12 students. For each student, you measure two variables, the length of the student's big toe and the number of books that he or she read last year. It is quite likely that the size of each person's big toe is a poor predictor of the number of books he or she read. In this case, there would be neither an increase nor a decrease in the value of one variable corresponding to an increase or a decrease in the value of the other variable. This is called a *zero correlation,* or simply no correlation.

Statistical procedures have been developed so that correlational data can be summarized by a single number, a statistic called a *correlation coefficient.* The mathematics of correlation are set up so that the coefficients fall between +1, which represents the strongest positive correlation, to 0, which represents no correlation, to −1, which represents the strongest negative correlation.

Knowing that two variables are correlated is useful information. If we know what your attitude is toward minority groups, for example, we can predict how you will act toward them. However, the fact that two measures appear to be correlated (or to go together) does not necessarily mean that one causes the other. Both may be caused by a third variable. For example, while attitudes and behaviors are correlated, one is not likely a cause of the other. Rather, both are caused by an individual's socialization experiences (Altemeyer, 1988). If your parents and childhood friends showed a positive attitude toward minority groups and treated them like everyone else, then it's likely that you will do likewise—that is, show both a positive attitude and positive behaviors. Thus, causation goes one step beyond correlation.

CAUSATION. Let's suppose that we conduct a mini-experiment on the extent to which you perspire while sitting in a particular room. When the temperature in the room is low, we note that you do not perspire. When we increase the temperature to a high level, you perspire profusely. And your tendency to perspire is noticeable every time we change the temperature from a low to a high level. In our mini-experiment, we have demonstrated that one variable (temperature level) causes a change in another variable (perspiring). This little demonstration of causation goes

In psychological research, it is assumed that behavior, thoughts, and feelings are lawfully determined and that these causes can be demonstrated in research.

one step beyond correlation because rather than demonstrating that two variables are simply associated, we have demonstrated that one causes the other. We would refer to the increase in temperature as the *cause* and the occurrence of perspiration as the *effect*.

All psychological researchers accept the assumptions of the scientific method and strive for reliable measurement of variables. But they practice several different types of research methods. Some research methods relate more to psychology's first goal: They are descriptive. Other methods relate more to its second goal: They are experimental and lead to the discovery of explanations of behavior—cause-and-effect relationships—scientific laws. We'll look at both descriptive and experimental methods of psychological research.

Descriptive Research

Psychologists use a variety of techniques to systematically observe and describe their subject matter, including brief surveys of many people, naturalistic and laboratory observations of a small number of subjects, and the intensive study of an individual subject over a long period of time.

SURVEYS.   Have you ever been approached in a shopping mall by a person with a clipboard and pencil who asked you, "Excuse me, I wonder if you might have a few minutes to answer some questions for me?" Or perhaps you've received a telephone call from someone at Nielson Television Ratings who asked you what television channel you were watching. Or maybe you completed one of those checklists at a local restaurant—a card that listed several questions about the service and the food that you received. If so, you have participated in a survey.

A **survey** is a question or series of questions asked of a sample of individuals concerning one or more characteristics of interest. A **sample** is simply a group of individuals selected from a larger group and then used to estimate some characteristic about the larger group. A **population** is the entire group of individuals from which a sample has been taken. In this book, you will read about characteristics of left-handed versus right-handed populations, male and female attitudes toward premarital sex, characteristics that distinguish happy from unhappy marriages, the most common themes of dreams, and a host of other findings reported by survey researchers from their study of samples.

survey
A question or series of questions asked of a sample of individuals concerning one or more characteristics of interest.

sample
A group of individuals or subjects selected for study from a larger group.

population
The entire group of individuals or subjects from which a sample has been taken.

Problems with Survey Research.   Is survey research easy to do? Not as easy as you might think. First, the way that questions are phrased can greatly affect the kind of answers that are obtained. Suppose, for example, some American laborers were asked one of the following questions:

1. Should Canada, the United States, and Mexico sign a free trade agreement that will likely lower the price of goods for the average buyer?
2. Should Canada, the United States, and Mexico sign a free trade agreement even though workers' wages might decrease?

The phrasing of Question 1 could bias the reader to answer yes, while the phrasing of Question 2 could bias many readers to answer no. Questions should be phrased so as not to bias a reader to give a particular answer.

After questions have been appropriately phrased, the second problem in conducting surveys is to select a **representative sample** of people—a group of subjects chosen so that the characteristic of interest is reflected in the sample to the same degree that it is reflected in the population at large. Ideally, a **random sample** would be chosen for study, which means that each individual in the population has the same chance of being selected as any other individual. But random sampling is not easy to achieve when conducting a survey. Suppose, for example, that you wanted to survey American men and women concerning their views of the characteristics of the ideal man. Would the ideal man have the sensuality of *Cheers'* Sam Malone? The macho manliness of Sylvester Stallone's Rambo? Or perhaps some other qualities? How would you proceed? Ideally, you might obtain the names of every man and woman in the United States between certain ages, put them in a huge container, mix them thoroughly, and then randomly select a hundred or so, to whom you might submit your questionnaire. But of course, that's an impossibility. Another option would be to select several names from a phone book from each of several cities. But that would exclude those from the country, those who have unlisted numbers, and those who don't have phones. Another strategy was followed by the editors of *Psychology Today.* In the March 1989 issue, the editors asked their readers to complete a survey concerning the characteristics of the ideal man and to mail it in. (The results, published in the November 1989 issue of *Psychology Today,* make for interesting reading.) But the results of such a survey contain a *self-selection bias,* meaning that the sample selected themselves: Readers who felt (for whatever reasons) motivated enough to do so, *chose* to fill out the survey and mail it. The opinions of individuals who do not read *Psychology Today,* do not complete magazine surveys, or do not bother to return such surveys might be quite different.

Even if you have good questions on your survey and a representative sample, there is another problem with survey research. People like to present themselves in the best possible light. Due to actual distortions or honest memory loss, their answers may not be accurate. You can see that conducting quality survey research is not as easy as it might first appear.

NATURALISTIC OBSERVATIONS.   The survey method usually involves one-shot questioning of a large group of individuals, is intrusive—you stop "normal life" to complete it—and those surveyed might lie. In contrast to the survey method, **naturalistic observation** usually involves careful study of a smaller group of individuals as they interact with their "natural" environment.

Naturalistic observations have proven useful in providing us with some intriguing insights and in clarifying a variety of misconceptions. For example, it used to be common to talk about an "explosion" of language in human infants in the second through fifth years. It seemed like an explosion because, in just three short years, a child progressed from baby talk to speaking much like an adult. But

representative sample
A sample taken from a population such that the sample accurately reflects characteristics as they are distributed in the population.

random sample
A sample chosen such that each individual in the population has the same probability of being selected as any other individual.

naturalistic observation
Observation taken of subjects in the "real world" in such a way so as not to disturb the subjects being studied.

hundreds of hours of naturalistic observations have shown that the emergence of new language forms is not an explosion at all, but an orderly progression including, among other events, one-word labeling (for example, "doggie"), then two-word phrases in the proper order (for example, "doggie gone"), and then parent and child interacting as though they were carrying on a conversation (although the parent does most of the talking) (Brown, 1973; Snow, 1977).

Problems with Naturalistic Observations. A researcher obtaining observations in the natural environment faces the problem of remaining unobtrusive. To record observations *unobtrusively* means that those being observed should not notice the observer nor be exposed to anything that might disrupt their natural reactions. Unobtrusive naturalistic observations have been taken on such far-ranging subjects as the drinking habits of patrons in bars in a midsized American city (Sommer, 1977), the eating rates of people at McDonalds and other fast food restaurants (LeBow et al., 1977), and the posture of people waiting in a dentist's office (Lowther et al., 1978). But such studies raise another problem. Is it ethical to observe individuals without their consent? As long as no one individual or specific group can be identified in such reports, then the gain in scientific knowledge probably outweighs the concern for lack of consent by those being observed. Because of such concerns, however, the American Psychological Association (1985) has developed a set of ethical guidelines governing all types of experiments of psychological researchers.

LABORATORY OBSERVATIONS. Laboratory observation and naturalistic observation are similar in that their purpose is to describe behavior, not explain it. They are different in that it is possible to arrange and control conditions in the laboratory so as to more accurately observe behaviors that are difficult to observe in the real world. For example, naturalistic observations suggested that almost everybody dreams, but almost nobody dreams every night. But laboratory observations have shown this to be wrong. In the 1950s, researchers studying individuals in sleep laboratories were amazed to discover that, at various intervals during the night, a sleeper's eyes showed rapid coordinated movements, called rapid eye movement or REM (Dement & Kleitman, 1957). Curiously, when subjects were awakened during periods of REM, they invariably reported that they were dreaming. Subsequent laboratory observations have indicated that almost everybody dreams several times each night, but they may not remember their dreams by morning.

Robert Sommer (1977) and his students inconspicuously recorded drinking rates of patrons in a number of different bars in a midsized American city. They found that whether drinkers were in groups or drinking alone, they tended to imbibe at approximately the same rate. While such studies are interesting, they raise an important question. How would you feel about someone recording your activities in everyday life without your awareness of it? Is that an invasion of privacy? Ethical guidelines for conducting research are an important part of psychology's methods.

Problems with Laboratory Observations. It's definitely easier to study some things, such as dreams, in the laboratory than in the natural environment. But there's also the problem that the artificiality of the laboratory might affect the phenomenon being studied, making it different than what it would be in the real world. For example, William Masters and Virginia Johnson learned a great deal about the physiological changes that occur during sex by carefully observing volunteers having intercourse in their Washington University laboratory (Masters & Johnson, 1966; discussed further in Chapter 7). But is having sex in the laboratory under the watchful eye of the camera and with many wires attached to various body parts (to record physiological changes) the same as having sex in the privacy and comfort of one's own bedroom? We'll let you be the judge.

CASE STUDIES. The famous psychiatrist Sigmund Freud was just beginning his psychotherapy practice when he learned about a case referred to as "Anna O." Immediately following the death of her father, Anna suddenly became paralyzed and was confined to a wheelchair. Freud's colleague, Joseph Breuer, could discover no obvious medical cause for the paralysis. During therapy, and while under hypnosis, Anna began talking about how her symptoms first appeared. To Breuer's surprise, the symptoms disappeared while she talked about them. Anna was able to walk once again. This method of treatment, that came to be called the "talking cure," had a strong influence on Freud's development of psychoanalysis (Jones, 1953).

case study
An intensive investigation of a single subject.

The description of Anna illustrates a **case study**—an intensive investigation of a specific individual. Case studies are often reported by clinical psychologists based on their work with their patients. At other times, a case study might involve naturalistic observation of an individual over an extended period of time. For example, consider Hermann Ebbinghaus, who published a series of studies on memory and forgetting back in 1885, studies that are still important today. Over many years, Ebbinghaus conducted detailed investigations of the memory of only one subject—himself. His widely cited "forgetting curve" is a graph showing the rate at which he forgot memorized material over time.

Problems with Case Studies. While case studies can provide a rich source of ideas for future research, they have several drawbacks when considered by themselves. First, observations based on a single individual case may not easily be applied to others. The individual in the case study may be a rare person, quite unlike most others. Second, many case histories do not contain formal procedures to ensure that the observations reported are reliable. A psychologist with a pet theory might therefore see in a case history only those things that support the theory. Third, many case histories, such as the famous Anna O, rely on the patient's memory of past events. As Ebbinghaus and others have demonstrated, forgetting is a fact of life.

independent variable
The program, treatment, or condition that the experimenter manipulates in order to study its effects on a dependent variable.

dependent variable
The object of study; in an experiment, the variable that may be influenced by the independent variable; in psychology, usually some measure of behavior (or thoughts or feelings).

Experimental Research

The major drawback of surveys, naturalistic and laboratory observations, and case studies is that they do not demonstrate cause–effect relationships. To demonstrate a cause of behavior, psychologists deliberately change something to see if it will affect the subjects' behavior. If the subjects' behavior changes in a specific way each time a particular condition is introduced, then we can say that the condition caused the behavior to change. Then we will have demonstrated a cause–effect relationship.

In psychology, the condition that is manipulated to determine if it is a cause is referred to as an **independent variable.** The effect—some measure of the subjects' behavior, thoughts, or feelings—is referred to as the **dependent variable.**

Experiments always have at least one independent variable and one dependent variable. We'll look at two major categories of research, between-group experiments and single-subject experiments.

BETWEEN-GROUP RESEARCH.   Do students who set goals for studying study more than students who don't set goals? Steven Hayes and his colleagues examined this question with undergraduate volunteers who were interested in improving their study skills (Hayes et al., 1985). First, the researchers selected some material to be studied. Next, one group of students was given a goal-setting program. Each student set a goal concerning the amount he or she would study and the score that student hoped to receive on a test (to be given at the end of the program) of knowledge of the material studied. These students each announced their goals to other members of their group. A second group of students was not asked to set any goals. They were simply given the material to study for the same amount of time as the first group. The dependent variable in this experiment was knowledge of the material studied, and the independent variable was the goal-setting program. This type of research design is called a control group design.

control group design

A type of experiment that compares the average performance of two or more groups of subjects, one of which is exposed to the independent variable, and one of which is observed in the absence of the independent variable.

treatment or experimental group

The group in an experiment that is administered the independent variable.

control group

The group in an experiment that is studied in the absence of the independent variable as a control for possible extraneous influences.

   Control group designs typically compare the average performance of two or more groups of subjects, one of which is exposed to a treatment condition (independent variable) and is called a **treatment (or experimental) group,** and one of which is observed in the absence of treatment conditions and is called a **control group.** When examining the effects of a treatment (such as goal setting), it is necessary to have a control group because of the possible influence of *extraneous variables*. Extraneous (or uncontrolled or interfering) variables are conditions other than the independent variable that might influence the behavior under study, the dependent variable. For example, in the experiment by Hayes and his associates (1985), the subjects knew that they were going to receive a test at the end of the experiment. Perhaps this fact alone would cause an improvement in performance aside from any effects of goal setting. Having a control group enabled Hayes and his colleagues to control the effect of this and other possible extraneous variables. A control group provides the standard against which the effects of an independent variable applied to the treatment group can be compared.

   At the end of the experiment by Hayes and his colleagues, students in both groups were given a test to assess their knowledge of material that they had learned. The goal-setting group scored an average of 17 percentage points higher than the control group.

   Between-group experiments often have more than just one treatment group and one control group. In fact, in the experiment by Hayes and associates, another group of students (a second treatment group) practiced private goal setting. They set goals like the group described above, except that they kept them to themselves and didn't tell anyone about them. Interestingly, the private goal-setting group performed no better than the control group.

Problems with Between-Group Research.   There are many problems and pitfalls that await the unwary researcher. Let's consider two of the more common hazards.

Subject Expectations.   Suppose that your professor tells you of a new pill that will improve your memory with no harmful side effects. You and your classmates are asked to serve in a treatment group to test the pill. Control group subjects will get nothing. Would this be a fair test of this new memory enhancer? No, it wouldn't. You and others in the experimental group already have *expectations* about the outcome of the experiment before it's even done. You've been told that the pill will improve your memory. Your memory might not improve because of the pill but because you expect it to.

College students often serve as subjects in psychology experiments. But many college students are white, middle-class, and from approximately 18 to 24 years of age. Are results with this group likely to be characteristic of findings with other individuals? How do psychologists deal with this problem?

placebo effects

Effects observed in an experiment that are not due to the treatment, but rather to the subjects' expectations of the effects of treatment.

When subjects in an experiment change their behavior not because of the treatment itself but because of their own expectations of the effects of treatment, the results are called **placebo effects.** Placebo effects are common in drug studies where patients show improvement not because of the drug but because they expect to improve. To evaluate placebo effects in drug studies, a control group is often given a *placebo*—a fake drug that looks and tastes like the real thing. Subjects who receive placebos in such experiments do not know whether they are in the experimental group or the control group, a procedure known as a *single blind design*. In a *double blind design*, neither the experimenter nor the subjects know which is the experimental group and which is the control group, until after the experiment is completed.

Unrepresentative Subjects. Carin Rubenstein (1982) referred to social psychology as "the science of the behavior of the college sophomore." Rubenstein reported that approximately 77 percent of published research on topics of social psychology involved college students as subjects. But how representative of the general population are first- and second-year college students? The majority of college students are white, middle-class, and from approximately 18 to 24 years of age. While some of the findings with this select group no doubt apply to the general population, the fact remains that the unrepresentative samples on which many of psychology's cherished facts are based, may greatly limit their generality.

SINGLE-SUBJECT RESEARCH. Between-group experiments are the most common means used by psychologists to study causes of behavior. But is it possible to do a controlled experiment with a single individual? It is, indeed. Such studies are called single-subject experiments.

Consider, for example, the case of Annie, a nursery school child who typically played alone and did not interact with the other children. Annie's teachers, concerned about Annie's solitary behavior, conducted an experiment consisting of four phases. During the first phase, called a *baseline*, in which Annie was observed under normal conditions, she played with the other children only about 15 percent of the time. Her social play was the dependent variable. During the second phase, called *treatment*, the teachers implemented a program (the independent variable). When Annie approached other children, the teachers gave Annie and the other children lots of positive attention. But as long as Annie was engaged in solitary play,

Figure 1-2

Daily percent of time that Annie spent interacting with other children during morning sessions at the nursery school. During baseline sessions, Annie interacted primarily with the teachers. During treatment sessions, the teachers attended to Annie only when she interacted with other children. The results clearly demonstrated the effects of the treatment program for improving Annie's interaction with the other children. *Adapted from Allen et al., 1964.*

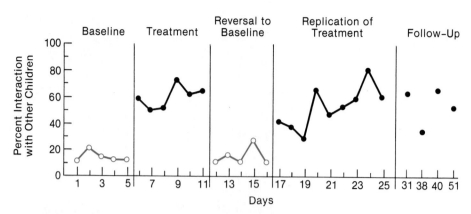

they ignored her (Allen et al., 1964). Over the next several mornings, Annie's interaction with the other children increased to approximately 65 to 70 percent of her playtime (see Figure 1-2).

The third phase in this design is a *reversal* back to baseline conditions. If the change during the treatment phase was really due to the treatment, then removing the treatment should result in a return of the dependent variable to the level observed during the baseline phase. During the reversal, the teachers no longer attended to Annie each time she interacted with the other children. Instead, they gave her attention only when she played alone. As you can see in Figure 1-2, Annie's social play quickly dropped to its original baseline level. The final phase in this design is a *replication* of treatment. To more convincingly demonstrate that the original improvement in the second phase was due to the treatment, and not due to some uncontrolled variable, the treatment is replicated. Once again, the teachers attended to Annie only when she showed social play, and they ignored her when she engaged in isolate play. Annie again showed an increase in social interaction with the other children. The teachers had demonstrated that their attention, given as a reward for social play, was the cause of Annie's improved socialization with the other children. After Day 25, the teachers gradually faded out their extra attention for Annie until all of the children were receiving the normal amount of attention.

reversal-replication design

A single-subject design that includes a baseline phase where the independent variable is monitored under normal conditions; a treatment phase; a reversal to baseline phase; and a replication of the treatment phase.

With this type of design, called a **reversal-replication design,** the subject is said to serve as his or her own control in the sense that behavior during treatment is compared with that individual's behavior during the baseline and reversal phases without treatment. Thus, single-subject designs include phases where behaviors are studied under controlled conditions, even though such designs do not involve control groups.

Problems with Single-Subject Research.   One problem with single-subject research is that it takes a great deal of time to cover all of the experimental phases. The study with Annie, for example, lasted for 51 school days, over three months in total. In contrast, even though between-group experiments involve many subjects, the data are often collected in a matter of days. Another limitation of single-subject research concerns the problem of generalizing results to other individuals. Is Annie typical of other children? Will the treatment program that was successful with Annie work with other children who show isolate play? The extent to which results can be generalized to other individuals requires that the treatments be replicated with different subjects in other settings.

We hope that this brief introduction to the scientific method will help you to more fully appreciate the examples of psychological research that you will encounter in the following chapters—research that provides the foundation for the psychology of adjustment. Now let's look at a detailed example of the application of psychological principles to an area of adjustment of great importance to all students—time management and studying.

An Important Area of Adjustment: Time Management and Studying

Many students frequently find themselves thinking the following:

- "I waste so much time doing trivial things, and the term is slipping away."
- "I'm overworked, stressed-out, and tired. I'm always on the go and I never seem to relax."
- "There's never enough time to do everything. I've just got to find more time."

If these thoughts have occurred to you, perhaps you need to learn something about time management.

time management

Learning to make the most of available time; learning to accomplish high priority activities that have highly valued consequences.

What is effective **time management**? Reports from successful individuals in different walks of life have revealed numerous commonalities (Turla & Hawkins, 1983). First, they plan and schedule important activities on a daily basis, knowing that an hour of effective planning and scheduling can save up to two hours in execution. Second, they have well-organized offices or study areas with some consideration given to economy of movement in order to obtain, use, replace, file, and store things. Third, they learn to minimize the amount of time wasted in the seemingly uncontrollable interruptions that plague many of us when we try to work or study. Finally, they learn to minimize personal time wasters and to maximize personal time savers. We'll describe how these practices can help you to do well at college. But first, let's examine some common misunderstandings about time management.

Some Misconceptions about Time Management

1. *Managing time better is essentially a matter of reducing the time spent in various activities.* This misconception fails to recognize one of the most important aspects of effective time management—distinguishing between high priority and low priority activities. Experts in time management tell us that "80 percent of our payoffs come from 20 percent of our activities" (Mackenzie, 1975). Although the accuracy of this statement remains to be proven, there is no doubt that some of our activities have a much higher payoff than others. Effective time management, therefore, is not simply a matter of reducing the time spent in all activities. Rather, you want to reduce the time spent on low priority activities and *increase* the time spent on high priority activities with high potential payoffs.

2. *People who concentrate on working efficiently are the most effective performers.* *Efficiency* involves the amount of time and the cost to do something. Somebody who can do a particular job correctly in less time than someone else is generally considered a more efficient performer. *Effectiveness*, however, is some-

thing very different. In time management, an effective performer accomplishes high priority goals and objectives. An ineffective performer spends most of his or her time on low priority goals and objectives. Some people are very efficient at performing lots of low priority activities. But an effective performer concentrates on high priority activities with high potential payoffs. As expressed by Leboeuf (1979), "Efficiency is doing the job right, whereas effectiveness is doing the right job."

3. *The busiest people are the ones who get the best results.* This is a misconception because it too fails to distinguish between high priority and low priority activities. People can be so busy accomplishing low priority activities that they never have time to do the really important tasks. The trick is to accomplish high priority activities.

prioritization

In time management, identifying the goals and activities with the highest payoffs.

Prioritization may be the most important variable in time management and therefore the most important change you can make in your behavior. It can have very powerful effects, as the following anecdote suggests.

One of the most frequently told stories in time management literature is that of the advice that Ivy Lee gave to Charles Schwab, then chairman of Bethlehem Steel Company. Around 30 years ago, Schwab asked Lee, a management consultant, "Show me a way to get more things done with my time, and I'll pay you any fee within reason." After some thought, Lee wrote the following advice:

- Every evening, write down the six most important tasks for the next day in order of priority.
- Every morning, start working on Task 1 and continue until you finish it; then start on Task 2, and so on. Do this until quitting time and don't be concerned if you have finished only one or two tasks.
- At the end of each day, tear up the list and start over.

When Schwab asked Lee how much was wanted for the advice, Lee told him to use the plan for several weeks and then to pay him what he thought it was worth. Several weeks later, Lee received a check in the mail for $25,000 (over $200,000 in today's money!) (Engstrom & Mackenzie, 1967).

4. *Most people can solve their time problems by working harder.* Not necessarily so. The trick is to work smarter, not harder. Working harder on a lot of low priority activities is not effective time management. You need to continually ask yourself questions such as "How can I obtain higher payoffs for my time and energy expended?" "How can I accomplish more high priority activities?" "How can I minimize the time spent on low priority activities with small payoffs?" As expressed by Lakein (1973), "What's the best use of my time right now?"

Effective Time Management

Effective time management means learning to make the most of available time. It means learning to work smarter, not harder. Time management skills increase the chances that you will perform activities leading to delayed but highly valued consequences, while such skills decrease the chances that you will perform only lower priority activities that have more immediate, although lower-valued, consequences. It is important for you to realize that effective time management, as with any skill, becomes habitual only after regular practice and frequent attention. You can't spray yourself with your "time management deodorant" in the morning and "be good for the whole day." It must be worked at constantly. Steps toward applying effective time management to studying include the following: (1) Evaluate your current time management and study skills; (2) identify your top priorities—your course requirements and deadlines; (3) estimate study requirements; (4) practice effective study habits; and (5) adopt an effective planning calendar to ensure that you spend at least some time each day working on your high priority activities.

Effective use of time is an important component of student success.

Steps to Effective Time Management and Studying

STEP 1. EVALUATE YOUR CURRENT SKILLS. The questionnaire in Box 1-3 is designed to help you determine the extent to which you apply good time management to studying. It is a quick, convenient way to prompt you to think of potential time savers and possible time wasters. More importantly, it will provide you with a "yardstick" to use later on; it will serve as a measurement of your progress at acquiring time management and study skills and as a source of reward for improving.

STEP 2. IDENTIFY COURSE REQUIREMENTS AND DEADLINES. Do you remember the words of the rabbit in *Alice in Wonderland*? . . . "I'm late! I'm late! For a very important date!" Unfortunately, those words also characterize the way some students deal with their course requirements. You don't want to find yourself in that position. Early in the term, therefore, you should prepare an overview of the deadlines for meeting the various commitments in all of your courses. What about exams? Essays? Term papers? Lab assignments? Practicum projects? When are they all due? These should be your high priority activities.

Box 1-3

A Time Management and Study Questionnaire for College Students

	Never 0	Sometimes +1	Often +2	Almost Always +3
Planning				
1. I keep, in writing, my short-term and long-term academic and personal goals.	0	+1	+2	+3
2. I update, in writing, my academic and personal goals.	0	+1	+2	+3
3. At the start of a term I record all the dates and due dates for exams, term papers, and so on in my planning calendar.	0	+1	+2	+3
4. At the start of each week, I carefully plan my study schedule for the week.	0	+1	+2	+3
5. I write out my daily activities on a to-do list.	0	+1	+2	+3
6. I prioritize the items on my to-do list and make sure that the priority items are done.	0	+1	+2	+3
7. I schedule my "most alert" times for studying (I avoid wasting my best times socializing, watching TV, and the like).	0	+1	+2	+3
8. I set reasonable deadlines for myself concerning studying, term projects, and so on.	0	+1	+2	+3
9. I begin and finish projects on time and meet my deadlines.	0	+1	+2	+3
10. I divide time-consuming projects into short steps or stages, each of which requires no more than an hour or two.	0	+1	+2	+3
11. When going to meetings or appointments, I always have something with me to read to take advantage of "waiting" time.	0	+1	+2	+3
My Desk and/or Study Area				
12. My desk top is clean and contains only the project on which I'm currently working.	0	+1	+2	+3
13. My desk faces a wall or corner to minimize distracting sights.	0	+1	+2	+3
14. I get a positive feeling when I approach my desk.	0	+1	+2	+3
15. I have a well-organized place for everything (books, notebooks, and the like).	0	+1	+2	+3
16. I put everything in its place.	0	+1	+2	+3
17. I can easily find items in my work area when I look for them.	0	+1	+2	+3
18. My work space is well-lit, quiet, and conducive to good work.	0	+1	+2	+3
19. At the place where I study, I only study. (I don't do other things such as write letters, read magazines, and so forth.)	0	+1	+2	+3
Obtaining Results				
20. I use a formal sign-out system for keeping track of books and other items that I lend to others.	0	+1	+2	+3
21. I review the subjects that I am going to study and I prepare, ahead of time, all the materials (papers, pencils, books) that I will need.	0	+1	+2	+3

	Never 0	Sometimes +1	Often +2	Almost Always +3
22. I set a goal in order to take a break, based upon some amount (such as reading a certain number of pages, writing a certain number of paragraphs, and so on) rather than on the basis of time (such as studying for one-half hour).	0	+1	+2	+3
23. Each goal that I set before taking a break never takes more than about an hour to complete.	0	+1	+2	+3
24. I take breaks for progress not for fatigue or daydreaming. (See the explanation of this item below.)	0	+1	+2	+3
25. I study the "tough" subjects when I am most alert. (For most students, this will be during the morning.)	0	+1	+2	+3
26. I try to arrange nonacademic activities and meetings during my "least alert" times. (For most students, these times are late in the afternoon and late in the evening.)	0	+1	+2	+3

Time Savers Involving Others

27. I politely resist requests from my friends to socialize or have coffee during my scheduled study time and especially during my "most alert" time.	0	+1	+2	+3
28. When doing a project with another student, I set appointments so that we can review a number of items at one time.	0	+1	+2	+3
29. When having coffee or socializing with friends during a study break, I suggest *at the start* of the break that we agree on a time to get back to studying, and I stick to our agreement.	0	+1	+2	+3
30. I am politely assertive about cutting off long-winded telephone callers and/or other instances where people just want to "shoot the breeze."	0	+1	+2	+3

Explanation of Item 24: Taking a break following progress and a feeling of alertness will reward you for making progress and feeling alert. If you do feel drowsy or begin to daydream, you should read at least one more page very carefully, or solve one or two easy problems, and then take a break, rather than taking a break after feeling drowsy or daydreaming and accomplishing relatively little for the preceding few minutes.

To Determine and Assess Your Score

Add your points together and compare yourself with the scale below.

60–90: You already manage your time very well.

45–59: You are on your way to being an effective time manager. However, you should increase the frequency with which you follow various time-saving strategies.

30–44: There is definite room for improvement in your time management skills. You need to take formal steps to implement some of the recommendations in this chapter in order to put more time into your life.

0–29: You're spending far too much time on low priority activities and time wasters. Take immediate steps to implement some of the recommendations in this chapter.

Box 1-4

Deadline Planning Page

IMPORTANT DEADLINES AND COMMITMENTS FOR THE TERM

Date	Month of:	Month of:	Month of:	Month of:
1				
2				
3				
4				
5				
6				
7				
8				
9				
10				
11				
12				
13				
14				
15				
16				
17				
18				
19				
20				
21				
22				
23				
24				
25				
26				
27				
28				
29				
30				
31				

When you collect relevant information on important examination dates and academic deadlines for each course, record it on the Deadline Planning Page in Box 1-4. Write the months of the term in the spaces in Box 1-4. Next, record all the exam dates (e.g., psychology exam) and deadlines (e.g., biology term paper) that you know about.

Of course, there are important things in life besides studying, such as football games, student council meetings, weekend ski trips, school dances, marathon running, and much, much more. On the Deadline Planning Page, list the various social and recreational activities that you have already planned for the term. As new activities arise, record them on that page. Having a one-page summary of all your "outside" activities along with exam dates and deadlines will facilitate your time management.

STEP 3. ESTIMATE STUDY REQUIREMENTS.   You have one more step in your early-term planning—you need to estimate your study requirements. Consider all of the exam dates and academic deadlines that you listed in Box 1-4. How much study and/or work will you have to do for each requirement and/or course? Here are some guidelines that might help:

- Numerous sources recommend that students should study two hours out of class for every hour in class. Surveys have indicated that relatively few students actually do this. The majority of students report spending approximately one hour out of class for every hour in class. Presumably, therefore, somewhere in the one- to two-hour range will be satisfactory.
- Allow one hour to read and underline twenty pages of textbook material.
- Allow two hours to review and study twenty pages of textbook material that has been previously read.
- Spend time on course requirements in proportion to their total course value. For example, one course may have only a single exam and a single term paper, each worth 50 percent of the grade for that course. Another course might have ten exams worth 10 percent each. Therefore, it might be necessary for you to spend approximately five times as long preparing for the single exam in the first course than you would spend for each of the ten individual exams in the second course.

On the basis of the above guidelines, review the course requirements for each of your courses and estimate minimal preparation time to meet each requirement. Remember, these are general guidelines. You should reevaluate your initial time estimates based upon your progress and success during the term. You should also allow for an increase in study time during the pre-exam period near the end of the term.

STEP 4. PRACTICE EFFECTIVE STUDY HABITS.   Most students can improve their study habits by examining three questions: Where is the best place to study? When and how much should you study? How should you study? Tips for answering the first two questions are contained in the Time Management Questionnaire (Box 1-3). As for "how to study," researchers have identified a variety of strategies that fall generally under the topics of reading, memorizing, and reviewing.

Reading.   Practice the SQ3R method, which stands for survey, question, read, recite, and review.

Survey.   When reading a chapter or a book, or reviewing your notes, you should briefly *survey* the material to get an overview of what it's all about. Examine its subheadings, pictures, and graphs. If the chapter has a summary, read the summary before reading the chapter. Surveying will help you to remember chapter content (Reder, 1985; Wilhite, 1988).

Question.   While reading material, try to think of many questions that you should be able to answer from the material to be studied. The questions might be provided at the end of the chapter, suggested by the professor, or made up from the headings and subheadings. Reading to try to answer questions is much more effective than just being a passive reader (Hamaker, 1986).

Read.   While reading, you should underline, highlight, or in some way identify material that will help you to answer the questions that you previously listed. For many students, reading is their *first* step in studying a chapter. But it should be their *third* step.

Recite.   At key points throughout the chapter, quiz yourself on the material just read, and recite answers to questions. Reciting is one of the most important parts of studying. When you are passively reading, it is kind of like watching someone else perform. It can be enjoyable, but you don't learn how to perform yourself. It is during the recitation of answers to questions that essential learning occurs. Simply reading and rereading is not as effective as combining reading with recitation (Orlando & Hayward, 1978).

Review.   After surveying, questioning, reading, and reciting, you should then review the material for additional learning and understanding. If you think back about some of the subjects that you took in high school, you can easily convince yourself of an important fact about remembering academic material—it generally operates on a "use it or lose it" mode. Many studies have demonstrated that periodic review of studied material will help you to remember it more fully (Higbee, 1988). And note that we're talking about reviewing *previously studied* material. Cramming just before an exam (by studying material for the first time) is not reviewing.

Memorizing.   Broader understanding produces better recall. Imagine walking into a supermarket and trying to find a can of soup if all the items were mixed up on the shelves. It would take a long time. It's much easier when you can simply walk to the section of the store that displays soup cans. The same is true for memory. That is, when studying complex material, first try to arrange the material into a meaningful organization with categories and subcategories. It's much easier to retrieve information from memory if it is a part of some larger, meaningful organization, rather than simply memorized in a helter-skelter fashion (Higbee, 1988).

Second, when learning a principle or definition, try to think of at least three examples of how it might be applied or used. Thinking of examples of a principle in action will increase the level at which that information is processed in memory as well as increase the chances of remembering it (Craik & Tulving, 1975).

Third, when learning a principle or definition, try to think of examples that apply to you personally. Linking new material to personally relevant material, called networking, will improve your memory of the new material (Dansereau, 1985).

Fourth, when trying to associate two things, such as a person's name with that person's face, try to relate them in an unusual image. Studies have indicated that we can easily remember thousands of pictures (Standing, 1973). Perhaps that's why "a picture is worth a thousand words." And relating items to be remembered to unusual images can enhance memory of those items (Paivio, 1986).

Fifth, when memorizing a series of several names or items, make up a word (called an acronym) from the list of first letters of words to be remembered, such as Roy G Biv. Acronyms constitute one of the most frequently used memory techniques (Harris, 1980), and they are especially useful for improving memory of lists of items (Wilson, 1987).

Reviewing.   Use your study hours wisely. We've given you some guidelines for initially reading and memorizing material. The following guidelines will help you to review for exams.

First, study by asking yourself questions; don't just read and reread the material. Suppose that the material that you must study for an exam will take approximately one hour to read. You have three hours to study. Is it better to read the material three times or to read it once and spend the rest of the time quizzing yourself? Several studies indicate that the latter is more effective (Higbee, 1988).

Don't fool yourself into thinking that, because you have read something several times, you know it for exam purposes.

Second, when faced with several hours of study to master a particular subject, space your studying across several shorter sessions. For example, if you allow three hours to study for a subject, you are much better off dividing your study time into three one-hour sessions with rest periods in between (called *spaced practice*), than studying for three hours in one sitting (called *massed practice*). Memory is typically much better after spaced practice than after massed practice (Rea & Modigliani, 1988).

Third, when studying two subjects back-to-back, try to study subjects that are quite different in content (such as Spanish and chemistry rather than Spanish and French). One of the main causes of forgetting is interference from other learning. And the more similar are two subjects being studied, the greater the likelihood of interference between them. If you must study two subjects that are quite similar, there will be less interference between them if they are studied on different days (Thorndike & Hayes-Roth, 1979) and in different rooms (Strand, 1970).

Fourth, when studying material, strive for "overlearning" rather than accepting minimal mastery. The more thoroughly you learn something, the more likely you are to remember it (Hayes-Roth, 1977). Even though you think that you know something after studying it briefly, keep studying to produce overlearning.

You will obtain best results if you follow the above strategies when reading, memorizing, and reviewing material. You will then face your exams with a high degree of confidence.

STEP 5. USE A PLANNING CALENDAR. Effective time managers use a daily planner or planning calendar. We strongly urge you to purchase a daily planner—one that contains a page for each day of the week. Effective planning requires that you take about a half an hour at the start of each week to plan for the week. In addition to weekly planning, you should take approximately ten minutes each morning to plan for the day. Finally, the Deadline Planning Page in Box 1-4 will help you to keep track of important meetings or deadlines scheduled more than a month in advance. Guidelines for using this system are as follows:

Planning for the Week

1. Using a weekly class schedule, write the course names or numbers in the appropriate time slots on your planning calendar.
2. Check your Deadline Planning Page (Box 1-4) for exam dates and social/recreational activities, and transfer dates for the week to appropriate time slots on your planner.
3. Now, consider "must study" time for the deadlines, due dates, or exams listed. Schedule *necessary* study time for the week. Try to use "waiting" or "dead" time, such as an hour between classes. Also, use your *most alert* time to study (for most students this is the morning and early afternoon).
4. As things arise that you would like to do later in the week such as going to the bank, doing laundry, and the like, record them on your planner.

Planning for the Day

1. At the start of the week you probably filled in many of the time slots for attending classes and studying. Review your Deadline Planning Page (Box 1-4) and other nonscheduled activities for the day and prioritize them.
2. Look at the time available in your day and schedule the highest priority activity in an available time slot. Continue scheduling activities until they are all scheduled or until you run out of time.
3. When you run out of time in your time slots, forget about the remaining activities. You are already taking care of your high priority activities, and the others can be postponed to another day.

4. As you complete each activity during the day, cross it off your list. This provides visual feedback on the proportion of your scheduled activities that you have accomplished.

Initially, you will not be able to accomplish all of your top priority activities each day. And usually you will have several things left over at the end of the day that you weren't able to do. It will probably require several weeks of careful time management practice before you'll be able to estimate accurately how much time each of your activities will require. The most important thing is to accomplish your high priority activities. As you progress, you'll become familiar with your limits and be better able to eliminate any unnecessary activities.

Design Your Study Area

In the Time Management Questionnaire (Box 1-3), Items 12 through 19 focus on your study area. Let's consider this important topic further.

First, the only things that should have a permanent place on your desk top are your planning calendar and a couple of material trays. Place your books in shelves nearby. Organize correspondence in letter carriers or in a drawer. Do not leave things on the top of the desk except for the project on which you're working.

Next, design the drawers in the desk for various storage purposes, and fill them according to purpose. Throw out or at least put out of sight (say on shelves) materials for low priority activities. Arrange your highest priority materials where they are easily accessed—but not on your desk top.

If you live in a dorm, make sure your desk faces a corner so that all the little knick-knacks, posters, yearbooks, and so forth are not immediately visible. Eliminating the many visual distractions that control daydreaming and fantasies is an important step toward designing your study area (Walter & Siebert, 1976).

Next, check the lighting in the room. Take whatever steps are necessary to ensure that you have a well-illuminated room with the main light source off to your side. Be sure that there are no lights immediately in front of you that will be reflected from the glossy pages of textbooks.

It's unlikely that you can create a completely quiet environment. The next best bet is to have some sort of background noise to mask distracting sounds. Some students turn on their hair dryers. Other students turn their radio to a spot between stations to produce steady static.

A well-organized study area is conducive to practicing effective study habits.

Finally, consider the location of your desk with respect to your bed. Some students claim that they study effectively while lying on the bed. As expressed by Green (1971), however, "If you study well on your bed you may develop trouble sleeping; if you sleep well in bed, you may find it hard to study there without becoming sleepy."

Additional Tips for Effective Time Management

If you practice the time management guidelines presented in this chapter, you should obtain additional rewards and satisfaction from the accomplishment of a high percentage of your academic goals. However, like all good advice, it won't help unless you follow it. A useful strategy to help keep you on track is to arrange your world to provide reminders and rewards for practicing good time management. We recommend that you practice the following.

1. *Work on one project at a time during uninterrupted work sessions.* As expressed by Bliss (1976), "The amount of time spent on a project is not what counts: it's the amount of *uninterrupted* time." Many successful authors, for example, take elaborate steps to ensure that they will be uninterrupted during writing sessions. It is said that Victor Hugo controlled his work habits in his study by having his servant take his clothes away and not bring them back until the end of the day (Wallace, 1971, pp. 68–69).

2. *When you're faced with major tasks that you keep postponing or avoiding, try the "pineapple" method.* A pineapple in its original state is somewhat unwieldy and unappetizing. But cut it into thin juicy slices and it's very manageable and appealing. The same thing can be true of major tasks that you've been postponing. If you break them up into small steps or "slices," you'll find it's much easier to get started.

3. *Protect your prime time.* Prime time is that time of the day when you're most alert and firing on all cylinders (Webber, 1980). If you use that time to drink coffee with your friends, read the newspaper, watch the soaps on TV, or do similar activities, then you're wasting the best part of your day. As much as possible, spend your prime time performing tasks that require you to concentrate, to learn, to be creative, to study, and to otherwise engage in productive activity.

4. *Reserve your work place exclusively for work.* Do you have a desk at which you typically do academic work? When at your desk, do you sometimes read magazines, write checks for bills, play with your cat, do crossword puzzles, or talk to friends on the telephone? If so, then you're strengthening all kinds of unproductive habits that interfere with effective academic work. If you reserve your desk exclusively for academic work, you're more likely to feel like studying every time you approach your desk. Thus, when doing things incompatible with studying while sitting at your desk, such as daydreaming, reading, or chatting, you should leave the study desk area (Spurr & Stevens, 1980).

5. *Deal with low priority activities in bunches.* All of us have low priority tasks that must be completed—paying the bills, running errands, answering letters, making telephone calls, shopping, getting the car washed, going to the bank, and the like. As much as possible, try to do several of these tasks at one time. This minimizes the extent to which low priority tasks will cut into the time for your high priority tasks (Scott, 1980).

6. *Give up waiting time forever.* How many times have you been kept waiting at the doctor's office? Dentist's office? Outside a professor's office? By a friend who's late? By a bus that's late? For many people, waiting causes anger and resentment. Rather than becoming angry or resentful look at waiting time as a gift—an opportunity to read something that you've been wanting to read but haven't gotten around to (Lakein, 1973). Always have something with you to do or read in any situation that might lead to waiting time.

7. *Arrange your world to reward your good time management behavior.* Once each month, complete the Time Management Questionnaire in Box 1-3. Each time your monthly evaluation shows an improvement, that is, a higher score, post the improved checklist in a conspicuous place near your desk. Show it to others when they visit your study area.

Try to think of additional ways you can reward yourself for accomplishing your high priority objectives. Incorporating rewards into your self-adjustment program is especially important to improve and maintain studying (Green, 1982; Heffernan & Richards, 1981). One way of doing this is to remind yourself, immediately after a successful period of studying, of the various benefits of obtaining good grades. Another strategy is to schedule enjoyable activities (such as watching your favorite TV program or taking a bubble bath) to occur as a reward for a productive evening of studying. Additional strategies for the development of self-reward programs are described throughout this book.

SUMMARY

- Adjustment refers to changes in our ways of behaving, thinking, and feeling to meet the changing demands of our environment. Problems of adjustment occur when behaviors, thoughts, or feelings are deficient or excessive in specific situations. Viewing adjustment in this way helps us to (1) avoid labeling traps, wherein the label influences us to overemphasize problems and ignore positive attributes of an individual; and (2) focus on proven, psychological principles and techniques for changing specific behaviors, thoughts, and feelings in specific situations.

- Psychology is the scientific study and practical applications concerning the observable behavior and inner processes of organisms. Psychologists endorse the scientific method because of its proven success in discovering principles and techniques that can be applied to the betterment of humankind. Two important characteristics of the scientific method include the assumption of lawfulness and the emphasis on reliable measurement of variables.

- Scientific research includes both descriptive and experimental studies. Descriptive studies include brief surveys of many people, naturalistic and laboratory observations of a small number of subjects, and the intensive study of a single case over a long period of time. While such studies yield useful observations, experimental research is required to identify causes of behavior.

- In an experiment, a researcher manipulates a treatment condition (called an independent variable) to see if it will affect the behavior, thoughts, or feelings (the dependent variable) of subjects. Between-group research designs typically compare the average performance of two or more groups of subjects, one of which is given the independent variable and is called a treatment group, and one of which is observed in the absence of treatment conditions and is called a control group. In a single-subject experiment, the subject's behavior in the absence of treatment is compared to that subject's behavior under treatment conditions.

- An area of importance to college students is time management and studying. The underlying theme of effective time management is to spend a part of each day working toward high priority goals and objectives. Steps college students can take for effective time management and studying include evaluating current time management and study skills, setting deadlines for meeting various course requirements, estimating study requirements for different courses, practicing effective study habits, and using an effective daily and weekly planning calendar to accomplish high priority goals.

- Living a well-adjusted life in today's society is not easy. This book will illustrate fundamental principles of psychology to help you to deal with challenges to adjustment in a number of areas, including physical health, stress, weight control, thinking, emotions, social interactions, the work world, today's society and environment, and coping with serious maladjustment.

Box 1-5

SELF-ADJUSTMENT FOR STUDENTS: HOW IS YOUR ADJUSTMENT?

It was about 20 years ago that Dr. George Miller, in his presidential address to the American Psychological Association, encouraged psychologists to "give it away." By that he meant that psychology has many proven practical techniques for helping people to meet the changing demands of everyday living, and that psychologists should help people to use these techniques. Strategies for applying psychological principles and techniques to adjustment in everyday living are described throughout this book. To further help you apply psychology to your own life, we conclude each chapter with a section on self-adjustment directed to you personally.

Let's start with an assessment of your current level of adjustment. Items in the following questionnaire in Table 1-2 focus on what you *do* or know, not on what you *should do* or should know. Take a few minutes to complete the questionnaire below. After you have done so, congratulate yourself for everything that you now do or know. Also, attend to the things that you don't do or know. As a first step to applying psychology in everyday living, this self-evaluation will give you a look at your own life in some areas where you may wish to make improvements. At this time, don't worry about pursuing any of the goals or needs that this questionnaire might uncover. In later chapters we will provide additional tools and knowledge to guide you through the steps of a self-improvement project.

TABLE 1-2
HOW IS YOUR ADJUSTMENT?

Check each statement to which you can reply with a "yes."

My Body

_____ I know my own medical history.
_____ I know my family's medical history.
_____ I have health insurance in addition to my Student Health Center coverage.
_____ I use prescription and nonprescription drugs only as directed.
_____ I have had a dental exam within the past year.
_____ I use dental floss and a soft toothbrush daily.
_____ I thoroughly understand the various birth control methods.
_____ My partner and/or I always use an effective birth control method.
_____ I know how to use an oral thermometer.
_____ My use of alcohol never interferes with my schoolwork, health, or personal relationships.
_____ I know what causes stress in my life.

_____ I understand how stress affects my physical and emotional health.
_____ I take definite action to maintain and/or improve my health.
_____ I consider my physical health to be: excellent_____ good_____ fair_____ poor_____
_____ I do not smoke.

FOR WOMEN

_____ I know the proper breast self-examination techniques and do an examination monthly.
_____ I have regular gynecological examinations and pap smears.

FOR MEN

_____ I know the proper testicular examination techniques and do an examination monthly.

Continued

TABLE 1-2 *(Continued)*

Eating

____ I try to have breakfast every day.
____ I avoid "junk" foods.
____ I am careful about selecting nutritious food at campus snack bars and cafeterias.
____ I consider my weight proportionate to my height and build.
____ I try to avoid artificial sweeteners and highly processed foods.
____ I eat two servings of milk/dairy products daily.
____ I eat four servings of bread/cereal products daily.
____ I eat two servings of protein daily.
____ I eat four servings of fruits/vegetables daily.

Playing

____ I take advantage of opportunities to add exercise to my daily routine (i.e., using stairs, walking).
____ Exercise or sports are a regular part of my life.
____ I do stretching exercise before physical activity.
____ I consider myself physically fit.

On the Move

____ I never drive while under the influence of alcohol or other drugs.
____ I will not ride with a driver who is under the influence of alcohol or other drugs.
____ If I ride a bicycle, I observe the proper safety measures.
____ I don't hitchhike.
____ I always use seat belts.
____ I consider myself a safe driver.
____ I keep my transportation vehicle in safe condition.

Where I Fit In

____ I read the student newspaper regularly.
____ I read a newspaper or listen to the news regularly.
____ I try to conserve energy whenever I can.
____ I am involved with at least one campus organization or activity.

____ I have emergency numbers near my phone.
____ I am currently certified to practice First Aid.
____ I have a current CPR certificate.
____ I know where and how to get the services I need on campus.
____ I feel like I'm part of my university.
____ I am registered to vote and vote regularly.

Hitting the Books

____ I usually accomplish what I set out to do each day.
____ I have a regular schedule of study time.
____ I sleep about the same number of hours each night.
____ I make extra efforts to stay healthy during exam time.
____ I am happy with my academic major.
____ I am content with my grade point average.

Day to Day

____ I am comfortable with meeting new people.
____ I have good communication with the people I live with.
____ I am content with my family relationships.
____ I am comfortable with my sexuality.
____ I have activities or hobbies that are rewarding to me.

Who Am I?

____ I know my strengths and weaknesses.
____ I usually resolve my problems to my satisfaction.
____ I consider myself to be open-minded.
____ I have a lot about myself that I am proud of.
____ I enjoy my own company.
____ I am optimistic about my life.
____ I can say "no" when I want to.
____ I often learn about myself from other people.
____ I know people who I can talk to about the good and bad things in my life.

MEMORY BOOSTER

■ IMPORTANT TERMS

Be prepared to define the following terms (located in the margins of this chapter). Where appropriate, be prepared to describe examples.

Behavior	Naturalistic Observation
Adjustment	Case Study
Behavioral Deficit	Independent Variable
Behavioral Excess	Dependent Variable
Psychology	Control Group Design
Hypothesis	Control Group
Variable	Experimental Group
Operational Definition	Placebo Effects
Positive Correlation	Reversal-Replication Design
Negative Correlation	Time Management
Survey	Prioritization
Sample	Psychology
Population	Hypothesis
Representative Sample	Variable
Random Sample	Operational Definition

■ QUESTIONS FROM IMPORTANT IDEAS IN THIS CHAPTER

1. Consider the definition of adjustment. Describe an area in which you would like to improve in your own life that illustrates all three aspects of that definition.
2. What is the definition of psychology? Why does the definition include an emphasis on both science and application?
3. Illustrate the four main goals of every science with examples that apply to psychology.
4. Describe the difference between correlation and causation.
5. How are surveys, naturalistic observations, laboratory observations, and case studies useful? And what are their limitations?
6. How can subject expectations and unrepresentative subjects affect experiments? What can experimenters do about them?
7. What steps might one follow in conducting an experiment with a single subject?
8. What is the distinction between efficiency and effectiveness? Why is this an important time management distinction?
9. What is the SQ3R method? How does it help you to remember more of what you read?
10. List five proven guidelines from psychological research for memorizing more effectively.

YOUR PERSONALITY: THEORETICAL VIEWS

CHAPTER OUTLINE

LEARNING OBJECTIVES

After reading this chapter, you should be able to:

- Discuss how consistency and distinctiveness are important to the definition of personality.
- Recognize distinctive features of the trait, psychodynamic, behavioral, and humanistic approaches to the study of personality.
- List some contributions and limitations of each of the four major approaches to the study of personality.
- Identify some uses and limitations of personality tests.
- Distinguish between projective tests and objective personality tests.
- Apply aspects of personality theories to better understand and make changes in yourself.

personality
A person's consistent and enduring ways of acting, thinking, and feeling across a variety of situations.

You've just had coffee with a bunch of your fellow students from psychology. One of them was really interesting—knew how to make the others laugh, laughed lots himself, too. Really a fantastic personality. Personality?

What is personality? Whatever it is, it's obvious that you think this person has lots of it. And it's this person's "person-ality" that makes him stand out—allows him to rise above the crowd. When you say this student has a fantastic personality, you probably mean that he has good social skills, good conversational skills, and perhaps a certain charm. At other times, you might use the term to refer to a dominant characteristic of an individual. You might describe a friend as having an outgoing personality, a bubbly personality, or a warm personality. What you're referring to is the consistent and typical way that that person acts in many situations. At still other times, you might think of personality as something within us that causes our actions (for example, you might say, "George gets into lots of arguments *because* of his aggressive personality"). You can see that *personality* has many meanings. We define **personality** as a person's consistent and enduring ways of acting, thinking, and feeling across a variety of situations.

Suppose that we wanted to study your personality. We would want to know about the *consistencies* that you show across situations. But we would also want to know what it is about your personality that makes you *distinctive*. What is it about your own special blend of thoughts, feelings, and actions that makes you *you,* different from everybody else? And how did you get that way—what factors influenced the development of your particular personality? To decide what makes you unique, we would need some way of assessing your particular characteristics, some test results to compare you to others. Personality tests have been developed to accomplish that task. But which of the many aspects of your personality should we examine? You'll find that different psychologists are likely to give quite different answers to this question. In this chapter, we review four major views of personality:

- *Trait theories* that study personality in terms of enduring ways of acting, thinking, and feeling across a variety of situations.
- *Psychodynamic theories* that look for unconscious forces within us that influence our personality.
- *Behavioral approaches* that study how our consistent and unique behavior patterns are a result of the learning principles discussed in Chapter 3.
- *Humanistic approaches* that emphasize how our personalities result from our unique capacities to grow as individuals and to lead fulfilling lives.

One's personality is often judged on the basis of dominant patterns of behavior that are shown.

Considering that each of these perspectives takes a different view of personality, it's not surprising that they also differ in their approach to personality testing. We discuss personality assessment within these different approaches including personality testing of traits, psychodynamic testing of the unconscious, behavioral assessment of specific behaviors in specific situations, and humanistic assessment of the self.

Finally, let's consider how this chapter differs from most of the rest of the book. Most of the other chapters focus on a variety of ways in which you can apply psychological principles to adjust in everyday living. This chapter is somewhat more theoretical. After all, it is a review of major theories of personality. Nevertheless, we believe that the current chapter can help you better understand yourself. When reading about the different theories of personality, think about whether or not you feel comfortable using them as a tool for understanding your own personality. And to help you further apply an aspect of each theory, we've added an application box after each of the four major views of personality.

Trait Personality Theories

Suppose that you want to describe your outstanding qualities to someone, to tell what kind of person you are (not how you look physically). You can use up to a dozen or so words, with each word describing one of your main characteristics. Which words would you choose? Intelligent? Friendly? Generous? Trustworthy?

It's relatively easy for most people to think of words that describe their distinguishing characteristics. The hard part is to keep the number of such words to just a few. When two psychologists counted words in an unabridged dictionary that could be used to describe peoples' distinguishing characteristics, how many of these words do you suppose they found? 40? 400? They found 18,000 (Allport & Odbert, 1936)! Psychologists who have approached the study of personality by identifying individuals' distinguishing characteristics are called trait theorists.

Some people think of traits as an inner determinant of behavior (for example, "Charlie gets into a lot of fights because of his aggressive personality trait"). We

trait

A consistent and enduring way that a person acts across a variety of situations.

believe that it is more useful to think of a **trait** as a consistent and enduring way that a person acts across a variety of situations, rather than as some *thing* that determines that person's behavior.

If a trait theorist were to study you and your friends, the theorist would try to identify each of your dominant characteristics and to determine the differences between you as individuals. But if there are 18,000 words that describe people's distinguishing characteristics, how can a trait theorist determine which are the most important? Let's look at how several trait theorists have approached this task.

Gordon Allport

From the 1920s through the 1960s, Gordon Allport laid much of the groundwork for modern trait theories. He observed that some people have a small number of behavioral characteristics that completely dominate their personalities. These he called *cardinal traits* (Allport, 1937; 1961). Consider Mike Tyson's aggressiveness, Abraham Lincoln's honesty, the Marquis de Sade's cruelty, or Mother Theresa's altruism. These words describe the behavioral characteristics shown by these well-known individuals in many situations and circumstances.

Do you have any cardinal traits? It's quite possible that you don't. According to Allport, only a small percentage of persons exhibit cardinal traits, and of those who do, they are likely to show only one or two.

The second level of traits identified by Allport are *central traits*—consistent behavioral tendencies. Some people are warm, outgoing, sociable, generous, and talkative. Others are characterized by a different conglomeration of central traits, perhaps as selfish, manipulative, untrustworthy, aggressive, and suspicious. According to Allport, most of us can be fairly accurately described by approximately five to ten central traits.

And finally, there are *secondary traits*—less consistent behavioral tendencies shown in particular situations or at particular times. John, for example, is generally very easygoing and mild mannered. But he becomes extremely aggressive when he feels someone is taking advantage of him. An aggressive reaction to being manipulated is one of John's secondary traits.

Unlike some of the other personality theorists, Allport did not develop a school of followers. Nevertheless, his work stimulated other psychologists, including Raymond Cattell, to study personality traits.

Raymond Cattell

One of the best-known trait theories is that of Raymond Cattell (1966, 1973, 1983). Cattell developed a list of word pairs and asked individuals to use the pairs to rate how well the words described close friends. Using a complex statistical technique called *factor analysis,* he reduced the list until 16 pairs of traits remained (see Table 2-1).

TABLE 2-1
CATTELL'S 16 PERSONALITY TRAITS *Adapted from Cattell, 1973.*

Outgoing	Reserved
More intelligent	Less intelligent
Stable	Emotional
Submissive	Dominant
Happy-go-lucky	Serious
Conscientious	Expedient
Venturesome	Timid
Sensitive	Tough-minded
Suspicious	Trusting
Imaginative	Practical
Shrewd	Forthright
Apprehensive	Self-assured
Experimenting	Conservative
Self-sufficient	Group dependent
Controlled	Uncontrolled
Tense	Relaxed

Cattell referred to the 16 traits in Table 2-1 as *source traits*—the foundation around which unique personality characteristics could be identified for each of us. The trait of being outgoing, for example, might be at the source of such characteristics as frequently telling jokes in groups, introducing yourself to strangers, and preferring the company of others to solitude. Cattell considered these latter characteristics to be *surface traits*—traits that show up on the surface as a result of an underlying source trait.

5-Factor Theory

Cattell suggested that our unique personalities could be adequately described in terms of various combinations of his 16 personality traits. But is it possible to reduce the number of basic personality traits even further, and still be able to adequately describe differences in personality from one person to the next? Based on studies of how individuals rate the personalities of their peers, several researchers have identified *five* major personality dimensions, namely neuroticism, extroversion, openness, agreeableness, and conscientiousness (Tupes & Christal, 1961; Norman, 1963; see Table 2-2). These factors have come to be known as the *Big 5* factors of personality.

Does some combination of the five factors or dimensions in Table 2-2 adequately summarize your main personality traits? Can those five factors distinguish between your personality characteristics and those of several of your friends, each of whom is quite different? Consensus is emerging among some personality researchers that they can (McCrae & Costa, 1987, 1989; Noller et al., 1987).

Hans Eysenck

Trait theorists like Allport and Cattell were primarily concerned with studying the different categories of traits that appear to make up each individual's unique personality. Hans Eysenck, a British psychologist, wants to carry the study of personality one step further. He also wants to know which traits might be due to genetics and which might be due to learning.

Eysenck (1947, 1967, 1982) identified three main dimensions of personality. One dimension is called introversion–extroversion. At one end of this dimension is a pure introverted personality type, and at the other end a pure extroverted personality type. A *type* is simply a clustering of traits. You probably don't know

TABLE 2-2
THE 5-FACTOR MODEL OF PERSONALITY *Adapted from McCrae & Costa, 1986.*

Dimensions	*Adjective Definers*
Neuroticism versus Emotional stability	Worrying versus calm, Insecure versus secure
Extroversion versus Introversion	Sociable versus retiring, Fun-loving versus sober
Openness versus Closed to experience	Imaginative versus down-to-earth, Preference for variety versus preference for routine
Agreeableness versus Noncompliance	Trusting versus suspicious, Helpful versus uncooperative
Conscientiousness versus Undirectedness	Well-organized versus disorganized, Careful versus careless

anyone who is a pure introvert because few such persons exist. But if you did, that person would be very reserved and cautious and would show considerable emotional control and a lack of sociability. At the other end of this dimension, a pure extrovert would be very daring in a wide variety of activities, would be very expressive, and would show a great deal of sociability.

Another dimension is the emotionally stable–neurotic dimension. At the stable end are even-tempered, calm, and reliable individuals. At the neurotic (unstable) end are moody, anxious, and rigid individuals.

Eysenck's third dimension of personality is an impulse control–psychotic dimension. Psychoticism is characteristic of someone who is insensitive to the feelings of others, solitary, and generally troublesome in society. At the other end of this dimension is the individual who shows great control over his or her impulses and who acts sensitively with regard to others' feelings. Thus, Eysenck's three dimensions of personality each represent a continuum with the ends of each continuum representing major personality types.

But the *type* is only one part of Eysenck's organization of personality. Eysenck argued that there are four levels of personality arranged in hierarchical fashion, including types, traits, habitual responses, and specific responses (see Figure 2-1). For example, an individual who is an extroverted *type* is likely to show several *traits,* such as sociability, liveliness, and impulsiveness. An individual with a trait of sociability is likely to show a number of *habitual responses,* such as going to parties and organizing group outings. Each habitual response (such as going to parties) is made up of a number of *specific responses,* such as telling jokes, dancing, and the like.

How does Eysenck combine heredity with learning as factors determining one's personality (Eysenck, 1967; 1982)? While habitual responses and specific responses that characterize personality traits are learned, Eysenck proposes that heredity plays a role in predisposing us to be a particular personality type. He believes, for example, that introverts and extroverts inherit differences in the way the brain functions. He proposes that extroverts generally show a low level of activity in a certain area of the brain, causing them to seek more stimulation. Thus, they show a tendency to be outgoing. Introverts, on the other hand, are thought to inherit a generally high level of brain activity, causing them to avoid extra stimula-

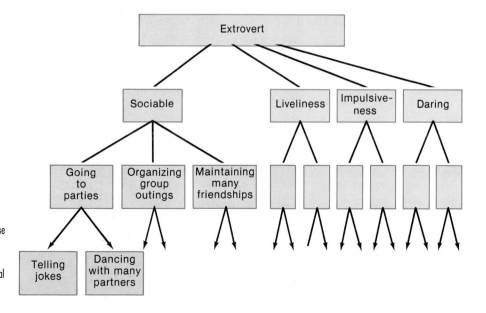

Figure 2-1

Eysenck's model for the structure of personality, showing the extrovert type. According to Eysenck, personality shows a hierarchical structure in which a particular type is made up of several traits, each trait is made up of several habitual responses, and each habitual response is made up of several specific responses. *Adapted from Eysenck, 1953.*

tion. Not surprisingly, therefore, they tend to be reserved and withdrawn and prefer a quiet environment.

Studies that have directly observed physiological reactivity of introverts and extroverts have yielded mixed results. Introverts and extroverts do *not* appear to show differences in their general level of physiological activity in the absence of specific stimulation, nor in their reactivity to high levels of stimulation (Stelmack, 1990). However, introverts *do* show greater physiological reactivity to medium levels of sensory stimulation than do extroverts (Stelmack, 1990). And evidence for a genetic influence on personality can be seen in studies of twins raised together in the same home versus those raised apart. Such studies suggest that genetically identical twins separated at an early age and raised apart are more alike in personality than are fraternal twins who are not separated (Eysenck, 1990). Although Eysenck's theory requires additional research, there is much to be admired in his scientific approach to the study of personality.

Personality Assessment: Measuring Traits

An important part of studying personality traits is to devise ways to measure them. One option is to ask a person how he or she behaves in particular situations. For example, when asked, "Do you trust strangers?" would you reply (1) never, (2) sometimes, or (3) practically always? Your collective answers to half a dozen or so similar questions might indicate that you show the characteristic of "trusting." Psychologists have spent a great deal of time developing combinations of such questions—questions that can be answered by yes vs. no, or always vs. never. When assembled into formalized tests, they're referred to as **self-report inventories,** or **personality inventories**—questionnaires that ask individuals a variety of questions about their behavior and feelings. One example is the 16 Personality Factor Questionnaire, described below.

16 PERSONALITY FACTOR QUESTIONNAIRE (THE 16PF). In Table 2-1, we listed the 16 personality traits developed by Cattell. Cattell and his colleagues developed a personality test, called the *16 Personality Factor Questionnaire (16PF),* to determine which of those traits you might show. He and his colleagues prepared test questions—such as "I like parties"—to which people answer yes, no, sometimes, or practically always (Cattell et al., 1970). The answers on the test

personality (self-report) inventories

Questionnaires that ask individuals a variety of questions about their behavior and feelings, and which are usually answered either "yes" or "no," or "true" or "false"; a type of personality test.

Many personality tests are paper-and-pencil, self-report questionnaires that ask individuals a variety of questions about their behavior and feelings. The person responds by checking yes vs. no, or always vs. never. In this way, a sample of the individual's behavior is obtained. A problem is—Does the questionnaire accurately reflect how an individual would behave in real-life situations?

Figure 2-2

Personality profiles from the 16 Personality Factor Questionnaire (16PF). Cattell applied the 16PF test to assess normal aspects of personality. The traits listed along the left and right sides of the figure are opposites. The airline pilots and the creative artists differed most on the tough-minded vs. sensitive dimension. *Adapted from Cattell, 1973.*

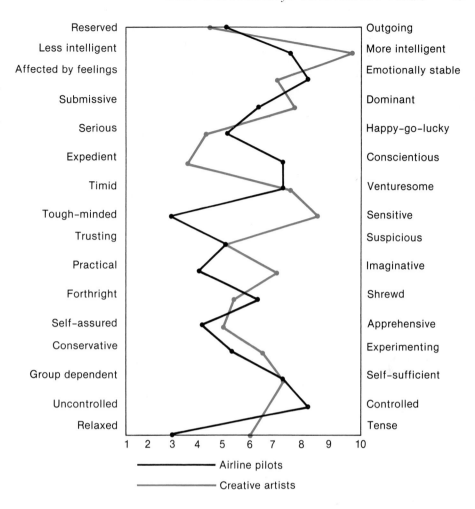

indicate which of the 16 items from Table 2-1 tend to predominate for a particular individual or group. For example, airline pilots tend to score as more self-assured and tough-minded than artists, while artists tend to show more sensitivity and imagination (see Figure 2-2) (Cattell, 1973).

A psychologist with experience in using tests like the 16PF typically combines the information from such a test along with other test scores and information in order to provide a detailed psychological analysis or profile of an individual or group. Such information, if properly used, might be of benefit to therapy, career counseling, and a host of other psychological services. For example, when screening applicants for pilot positions, the psychologist for an airline company might be hesitant to recommend someone who showed traits of being tense, apprehensive, or happy-go-lucky on the 16PF. However, as indicated in Box 2-1, personality tests also have their limitations.

Evaluation of Trait Theories

How useful are traits as descriptive terms for our consistent behavioral tendencies? Are they really predictive of behavior? If we identify someone as happy-go-lucky, is that person always happy-go-lucky? Of course, the answer is no. While particular traits may predict how a person will behave a certain percentage of the time, there will undoubtedly be many exceptions. In fact, personality theorist Walter Mischel

Box 2-1

CAN A PERSONALITY TEST ENABLE YOU TO MAKE AN
IMPORTANT CAREER DECISION?

There are literally thousands of personality tests on the market. They have been used widely to make decisions about placement of children in schools, hiring of people in business, promotion of people in government, and selecting lifetime careers. What are some of their limitations?

First, personality inventories are based upon what a person *says* about him or herself. But,

1. A person may not have accurate knowledge of his or her own beliefs and behavior.
2. A person may not be willing to disclose all information that he or she knows about him or herself.
3. The tests do not examine reasons behind the self-reports.
4. The tests do not allow individuals to expand beyond the yes or no in order to clarify their true response.

Perhaps the biggest problem of all is that the average person is likely to be very accepting of a personality description if it appears to come from a creditable diagnostician, even if that description has zero validity. Consider, for example, a study conducted by Roger Ulrich and his colleagues (1963). They gave college students a personality test. A week later, each student received his or her personalized interpretations of the results. Unbeknownst to the students, however, all interpretations were identical, except that the statements had been arranged in a different order. Students read, for example,

You have a strong need for other people to like you and for them to admire you. You have a tendency to be critical of yourself. You have a great deal of unused capacity which you have not turned to your advantage. While you have some personality weaknesses, you are generally able to compensate for them . . . (Ulrich et al., 1963, p. 832).

Amazingly, when questioned afterward, almost all of the students accepted the personality interpretations as an accurate description of their own personalities, saying such things as:

- "I agree with almost all your statements and think they answer the problems I have."
- "The interpretation is surprisingly accurate and specific in description" (Ulrich et al., 1963, p. 833).

When such personality interpretations are so broad that they are difficult to disconfirm, and when they imply positive attributes, they are often accepted as personal "insights" by the naive person. As expressed by Snyder and Shenkel (1975, p. 54): "They are oblivious to the fact that the interpretation is also correct for their mother-in-law, plumber, boss, or barber."

Most psychologists are well aware of the limitations of personality tests (Wade & Baker, 1977) and use them as only one source of information, along with many other sources, as an aid to clinical judgment. One should *not* use the results of a personality test as the sole basis for making important decisions.

(1968, 1984) has indicated that people's scores on personality tests are likely to predict only about 10 percent or less of their behavior in a given situation. In other words, a rating of "happy-go-lucky" is not closely related to how happy-go-lucky a person is at any given time on any given day. Thus, while we may see some evidence of consistency (that is, distinctive traits) shown by an individual across a number of different situations, such an observation is not particularly helpful to enable us to predict that person's behavior at any given moment in a particular situation.

Suppose that someone is considered to show an extroverted personality trait and is very sociable and outgoing at a party. Do you suppose that this same person will be sociable when awakened early the next morning? Probably not. In fact, personality traits can be considered useful mainly as general, not specific, descriptions.

Not all personality theorists, however, have agreed with the criticism of Mischel and others. Suppose that you have a friend who scores high on a sociability trait on a personality test. You would not expect such information to be particularly useful in predicting whether or not that individual will be in a good mood if you wake her up at 5:00 A.M. On the other hand, measures of personality traits can be useful to predict general behavior tendencies (Epstein, 1983). We *would* expect someone who scores high on sociability on a personality test to be an agreeable friend over the long run. Stated more generally, knowledge of a person's "average" way of behaving in many different situations will likely enable us to predict that person's "average" way of behaving in future similar situations (Kenrick & Funder, 1988).

Another criticism of some trait theories is that they do not address the question of how traits develop. Say you've identified a handful of your own distinguishing characteristics; these traits do offer some insights into your personality—but they also leave many questions unanswered. Where do these traits come from? Why did you develop these traits and not others? What causes them to change? It's one thing to try to determine an individual's distinguishing characteristics, but it's another to offer a theoretical explanation of their development. Psychoanalytic, behavioral, and humanistic theories of personality do just that.

Freud's Psychoanalytic Theory

Trait theorists attempt to describe, classify, and understand personality by looking at an individual's dominant characteristics—that is, by studying patterns of behavior. Sigmund Freud, on the other hand, was more concerned with explaining the underlying causes of behavior. Freud, the most famous and controversial personality theorist, believed that the mysteries of human personality could only be understood by exploring the unconscious—an enormous hidden dimension of ourselves where instincts, drives, and conflicts, he thought, determined much of our behavior.

When Freud proposed this theory in the early part of the century, it was revolutionary. At the time, many psychologists were studying human consciousness—yet Freud suggested the radical notion that our behavior was based largely on *un*conscious forces within us and long-forgotten childhood experiences. In fact, Freud believed that these experiences were not simply forgotten, nor were they irretrievable. His work with patients led him to believe that memories of painful and confusing experiences of childhood were actually repressed from consciousness but still exerted an influence on us and were therefore part of what he saw as the dynamics of personality.

Born in 1856, Freud lived most of his life in Vienna, where he earned a medical degree in 1881. He established a private practice in which he treated people with nervous disorders. But some of his patients' problems could not be explained medically. One patient compulsively washed her hands dozens of times each day, even though they were obviously clean. A young bride appeared to be paralyzed and was confined to a chair, yet Freud could find no evidence of physical disease or damage. Mysteries such as these influenced Freud to develop psycho-dynamic theory to explain their origins and psychoanalysis as therapy to treat them. Given his theory that a person's emotional problems are rooted in painful child-hood experiences, psychoanalysis (discussed further in Chapter 14) probes the past to help individuals understand how their problems are related to childhood conflicts. Gaining insight into repressed feelings might enable one to redirect his or her energies toward healthier relationships with important people in one's life.

During the first half of this century, psychodynamic theory was easily the dominant force in the study of personality, and psychoanalysis was the most common type of psychotherapy. Nowadays, Freud's theories are not particularly influential in psychology departments at universities, although they are still quite popular in schools of psychiatry. We'll discuss Freud's theory of personality in three parts: the structure of personality, the development of personality, and the dynamics of personality.

The Structure of Personality

id
According to Freud, one of the three theoretical subsystems within the personality; seeks to release energy in pleasurable activities, many of which have a sexual connotation; is fully unconscious.

Freud came to believe that human personality is composed of three powerful interacting subsystems: the id, ego, and superego. Only the **id** is said to be present at birth. The id is considered to be like a reservoir of all basic biological urges (to eat, sleep, have sex, and the like) that motivate the individual. While all basic urges are important, Freud placed greatest emphasis on our sexual and aggressive impulses. The id seeks to release the basic urges in pleasurable activities, many of which have a sexual connotation. Sexual pleasure for Freud, however, referred to physical pleasure in a general sense, not just satisfaction from copulation.

The id, according to Freud, operates totally unconstrained by society in order to produce immediate gratification. An infant's cravings for food and physical comfort are good examples of the id in action. The id operates according to the **pleasure principle**—seeking release of energy in activities that are immediately satisfying, and not worrying about the long-term consequences.

pleasure principle
Principle by which the id operates, seeking release of energy in activities that are immediately satisfying.

The impulsive behavior of very young children is a reflection of control by the id. But very early in life, society places restrictions on what individuals are allowed to do. Freud thought that these restrictions—placed upon a child by parents and others—contributed to the development of the second personality subsystem, the **ego.** By age two or three, as a child learns to delay gratification to cope with the real world, the ego develops to control basic urges of the id. Unlike the pleasure-seeking id, the ego was thought to operate according to the more practical, "law-abiding" **reality principle**—the tendency of the ego to satisfy the id's desires by acting within the constraints and demands of society's standards. Consider, for example, a three-year-old child playing in the front yard. The child might experience an id urge to play with his genitals. The reality-oriented ego, however, might influence the child to go into the bathroom where, under the guise of urinating, this behavior is acceptable. Thus, Freud saw the ego as a practical, socially minded system that controlled the more basic impulses of the id. While the id demands immediate gratification at any price, the ego seeks socially acceptable, alternative ways of reaching the same goals. Sexual and aggressive energies are channeled into trouble-free areas by the ego.

ego
According to Freud, the second of the three main theoretical subsystems within personality; attempts to channel id impulses to activities that are acceptable to the demands of society.

reality principle
Principle by which the ego operates; considers what is realistic in terms of society's standards.

At around age four or five, children begin to develop more abstract notions of right and wrong. They learn, for example, that they shouldn't tell lies or that it's wrong to "sneak a cookie" after Daddy has told them not to have any more. They

Figure 2-3

The conscious, preconscious, and unconscious, according to Freud. Freud postulated that the id is totally unconscious and we are unaware of the thoughts, wishes, feelings, and memories that are stored there. The id gains control of the outer world only through the ego and the superego. Much of our ego and superego are also largely unconscious. The preconscious area contains thoughts that are momentarily out-of-mind but which can be fairly easily retrieved into consciousness.

Adapted from Prentice Hall Transparencies for Psychology, Series 1, 1985.

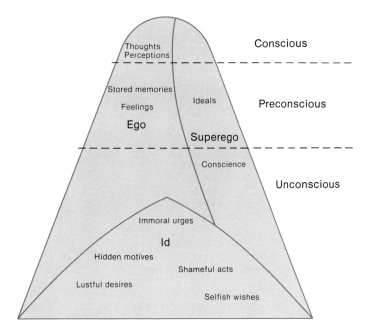

superego

According to Freud, the third subsystem of the personality; represents acquired values, morals, and ethics.

learn how one "ought" to behave. And they feel guilty if they don't behave that way. We say that they develop a *conscience,* that they acquire values, morals, and ethics. This led Freud to postulate the third subsystem of the personality—the **super-ego**—the part of our personality that embodies ideal standards of right and wrong. If you are about to do something that you were previously taught was wrong, and your conscience starts to bother you, Freud would say that you are experiencing the superego's influence (Hall, 1954; Kessler, 1966).

LEVELS OF CONSCIOUSNESS. Freud considered the id, ego, and superego to exist at three levels of conscious awareness—the conscious mind, the preconscious mind, and the unconscious mind (see Figure 2-3). Freud believed that the mind is like an iceberg; it's mostly hidden. Our *conscious* mind, the thoughts, feelings, and perceptions that we're aware of, is like the tip of the iceberg. Just below the surface is the *preconscious* mind, which consists of stored memories that we normally don't think of, yet can be recalled with a little effort. For example, you don't normally think of the specific clothes that you wore yesterday or the day before, but you could quickly remember them if you wanted to. Further below the surface is your *unconscious* mind, which consists of mental events which are more or less unavailable to conscious awareness. As can be seen in Figure 2-3, the id is entirely unconscious. The hidden desires stored there can be brought to consciousness only with great difficulty, if at all. The ego and superego are partly conscious and partly unconscious.

The id, ego, and superego form what for Freud was the structure of personality. The interactions among these three systems are expressed as personality. Let's see how, according to Freud, our unique personalities develop.

The Development of Personality

psychosexual stages

Five developmental stages in Freud's theory that parallel critical areas of child training, and during which children learn various personality characteristics; composed of the oral, anal, phallic, latency, and genital stages.

Freud's theory of personality has been called a developmental theory for two reasons. First, he stressed the importance of early childhood experiences to the development and functioning of personality in adulthood. Second, he stressed that children develop through a series of five stages called the **psychosexual stages.** As children progress from stage to stage, the basis of their sexual (physical) pleasure shifts from one source to another.

Freud's theory of psychosexual development includes the oral stage, anal stage, and phallic stage.

THE ORAL STAGE.   This stage lasts through approximately the first year of the child's life. During this stage, according to Freud, the id seeks outlet in sensual pleasures related to sucking, biting, and chewing. As parents introduce such demands as holding a bottle from which to suck, drinking from a glass, eating from a spoon, and eating according to a schedule, the child experiences collisions between the desires of the id and reality. This leads to the development of the ego.

THE ANAL STAGE.   This begins at approximately the end of the first year and lasts from about one to two years of age. During this stage, the child tries to balance satisfaction from expelling feces and urine with the control required of toilet training. On the one hand, urination and defecation are immediately satisfying, relieving pressure on the bowels and bladder. On the other hand, toilet training introduces demands on when and where these instinctive desires can be satisfied. As a result of such training, the ego undergoes further development.

Freud believed that conflicts and painful childhood experiences during the psychosexual stages had far-reaching effects for later personality development. If parents were overly strict during toilet training, for example, the child might vent anger by deliberately "letting go" when not sitting on the potty, and might later show personality traits such as destructiveness or disorderliness. Alternatively, the child might rebel by holding back his or her feces while sitting on the potty, and later show personality traits such as stubbornness, stinginess, and orderliness. As an adult, such an individual would be referred to as an *anal-retentive* personality type. You can see how Freud considered the development of one's personality traits to be firmly rooted in various childhood experiences.

THE PHALLIC STAGE.   This stage generally begins at about three years of age and lasts until approximately five or six years of age. During this stage, Freud theorized that children become preoccupied with genital stimulation, develop unconscious desires for the parent of the opposite sex, and experience feelings of jealousy and hostility toward the parent of the same sex. At this time, a male child is said to experience what Freud called the **Oedipus complex** (named after King Oedipus of the Greek legend, who unknowingly killed his father and married his mother). Male children who undergo the Oedipus complex feel sexual attraction to their mother and hostility toward their father. Female children experience opposite feelings, called the **Electra complex** (so named by later psychologists; Electra, also of Greek legend, plotted to avenge her father's death by killing her mother). Freud believed that children eventually repress sexual desires for the other-sex

oedipus complex
An experience that Freud attributed to male children in the phallic stage in which they develop an unconscious sexual attraction to their mothers along with feelings of jealousy and hostility toward their fathers.

electra complex
An experience that Freud attributed to female children in the phallic stage in which they develop an unconscious sexual attraction to their fathers along with feelings of jealousy and hostility toward their mothers.

parent and learn to identify with the same-sex parent. Also during this stage, children begin to acquire many of their parents' values and attitudes about right and wrong, which influence the development of the superego.

THE LATENCY PERIOD.   From the ages of five to twelve years, various sexual and aggressive impulses are more or less on hold, or latent. During this time, Freud believed that children generally identify with the same-sex parent and play mostly with peers of the same sex. At the same time, they are learning values that lead to further development of the superego.

THE GENITAL STAGE.   This begins at puberty and continues through adolescence and into adulthood. Young people begin to experience mature sexual feelings toward others, and move away from self-oriented stages of childhood toward more altruistic motives.

The Dynamics of Personality

Freud believed that safe, healthy passage through each of these psychosexual stages would result in the development of a normal personality. If children experience reasonable upbringing practices—not too permissive and not too severe—during the various psychosexual stages, then the superego would develop reasonable standards, the ego would develop productive, normal forms of control over the id impulses, and the individual would develop a healthy personality. If, on the other hand, during childhood, adolescence, or adulthood, societal demands are particularly permissive or severe, then the demands of the pleasure-seeking id would be in frequent conflict with the ideals of the superego. The ego would be under extreme pressure to balance these two opposing forces with external reality. When that occurs, the ego might resort to automatic and unconscious ego defense mechanisms to resolve the conflict between the desires of the id and the demands of the superego.

defense mechanisms

In Freudian theory, automatic and unconscious mechanisms that enable the ego to control id impulses so as to protect the individual from guilt and anxiety.

EGO DEFENSE MECHANISMS.   Suppose, for example, that an adolescent is chastised by his extremely strict father for masturbating, an act that the father considers "dirty and sinful." Now, each time the adolescent experiences a desire to masturbate, he also feels anger toward his father, both of which influence the superego to cause feelings of excessive guilt. In such situations, tension and anxiety might build within the individual. The ego might then resort to a **defense mechanism**—a strategy used by the ego to defend the individual against feelings of guilt and anxiety; the ego distorts the true id impulse and allows it to be released in a disguised manner so that the guilt and anxiety are relieved. For example, the young man described above might unconsciously convert his anger into exaggerated obedience to his father and develop a behavior opposite to "dirty masturbation," namely ritualistic, compulsive hand washing. The defense mechanism at work in this example is *reaction formation*. With this mechanism, individuals control unconscious, anxiety-producing desires by behaving in a manner opposite to their inclinations. The true desires of the adolescent are to masturbate and to feel anger toward his father. But instead, he displays compulsive cleanliness and obedience. If the compulsive hand washing persists, the individual might eventually be diagnosed as a compulsive neurotic. The compulsive cleanliness would be seen as a symptom of the underlying personality disturbance buried in the individual's unconscious.

We all experience conflicts between our basic desires and the demands of society. Most of these conflicts are appropriately dealt with in an acceptable way. But what happens when someone feels threatened by a conflict that just won't go away? Freud identified a number of defense mechanisms that people use to distort sources of threat to their idealized self-image. By distorting reality, anxiety experienced by an overwhelmed ego is unconsciously reduced. Let's look at how some of the more common ego defense mechanisms might operate in everyday life.

Repression is a mechanism in which the ego banishes awareness of unpleasant experiences or thoughts from the conscious to the unconscious mind so that we are totally unaware of them. Freud might hypothesize repression, for example, to explain a situation in which a man causes a car accident in which his entire family is killed, but he is unable to remember any of the details of the event.

A commonly used defense mechanism is *rationalization,* in which we offer justification or excuses for our behavior while the real, anxiety-evoking reasons remain hidden. For example, a parent might say to a child, "Just for spilling that milk on the floor, you're going to wash the entire kitchen floor!" The parent might rationalize, "It's for your own good! You've got to learn to be responsible for what you do." This rationalization, however, masks the real, underlying reason for the parent's overreaction to the spilled milk—unconscious hostility and resentment because the parents, unable to find a baby-sitter, had to miss a party at their friends' house.

Another defense mechanism is called *regression,* which occurs when a person reduces anxiety or guilt by reverting to behavior characteristic of an earlier age. Suppose, for example, that the parents of a young child frequently argued and fought bitterly with each other. To escape the sight of his parents fighting, and the anxiety felt about the possibility of his parents separating, the child developed a habit of going to bed shortly after the evening meal. Many years later, when married himself, the man began to experience frequent angry arguments with his wife. As a coping mechanism, the man developed a habit of going to bed shortly after the evening meal and sleeping until his wife went to bed later in the evening. The man had apparently regressed to a behavior characteristic of his childhood years.

Freud suggested that *displacement* is a defense mechanism in which individuals release unacceptable aggressive feelings toward someone by transferring them to a "safer" target. When someone is chewed out by the boss, that person might take out his or her hostile feelings (toward the boss) on a spouse upon arriving home in the evening.

In *projection,* the ego unconsciously attributes one's own disturbing thoughts and impulses to someone else. If a worker experiences unacceptable sexual impulses toward her or his boss, for example, the worker might interpret aspects of the boss's behavior as making sexual advances.

Freud believed that we all experience unconscious, unfulfilled wishes—id impulses distorted by our defense mechanisms— desires that would cause feelings of guilt and anxiety were they truly known or expressed. You might not know it, but deep in your unconscious might be buried a deep-seated hatred of a close relative or a secret lusting for your best friend's mate. Freud believed that our hidden desires are sometimes acted out in our dreams. Disguised release of hidden desires might also occur in *slips of the tongue.* Consider the case of a moderator of a hotly debated topic who, because of his role as moderator, could not express his strongly held views. Do you suppose that the moderator's slip of the tongue might have revealed an unconscious feeling when he stated, while thanking the participants, "I'd like to spank the adversaries in this debate"?

To summarize Freud's psychodynamic theory, our personality traits are determined by the interactions of the id, ego, and superego. The desires of the id seek release in activities that are pleasurable, often of a sexual or aggressive nature. The superego may influence the person to judge the impulse as "wrong," and cause feelings of guilt. The ego then channels the id energy to activities that are acceptable to both the real world and the ideals of the superego. When the id seeks outlet in actions highly disapproved of that influence the superego to cause excessive

---

Freud believed that defense mechanisms operated unconsciously to help us avoid anxiety about some of our true desires. If we were to recognize a selfish wish or an immoral urge, then a defense mechanism with respect to it would not be working. Thus, in the following examples, you might recognize in yourself the observable behaviors, but you're not likely to recognize the hidden motives. Neverthe-less, matching the following examples with one of Freud's defense mechanisms will help you better understand one aspect of his theory and may also help you appreciate hidden aspects of your own personality. Consider each of the descriptions in the left-hand column below, and match them to the appropriate defense mechanism listed on the right.

1. *Hidden motive.* You worry about whether or not you might be prejudiced against other races.
   Actual behavior. You frequently accuse others of being racist.

2. *Hidden motive.* Deep down you feel anger at your professor who asked you questions in class that you couldn't answer.
   Actual behavior. When you arrive home, you get into an argument with your roommate.

3. *Hidden motive.* You feel very attracted to another student but fear that getting involved may mean losing your independence.
   Actual behavior. When you interact with the student, you are quite argumentative and somewhat hostile.

4. *Hidden motive.* You fear some of your own desires for unusual sexual stimulation.
   Actual behavior. You are usually unable to remember the details of explicit sex scenes that you see in movies.

5. *Hidden motive.* You feel stress and anger from recent conflicts with your roommate.
   Actual behavior. You go home to visit your parents each weekend where they baby you and shower you with affection.

6. *Hidden motive.* You are worried about the repeated infidelity of your steady boyfriend or girlfriend.
   Actual behavior. You explain the infidelity by attributing it to other oversexed, overaggressive individuals who won't leave him (or her) alone.

a. repression

b. rationalization

c. displacement

d. regression

e. reaction formation

f. projection

(*Correct answers*: 1. f; 2. c; 3. e; 4. a; 5. d; 6. b)

---

psychodynamic approach
An approach in psychology that places great emphasis on unconscious drives and desires; strongly influenced by Freudian theory.

guilt, ego defense mechanisms bury the true id impulses in the unconscious and may lead to abnormal behaviors that are symptoms of the underlying personality conflict. Freud's approach to personality is described as **psychodynamic** in that it emphasizes the effects of unconscious mental (psychic) forces that determine our thoughts, motives, and actions. In Chapter 14, we will describe psychoanalysis, the form of therapy that Freud developed for helping people with disturbed personalities. But now let's consider how some of Freud's followers adapted and modified his psychoanalytic theory to explain the development of personality.

The "Neo-Freudians"

Followers of Freud, called neo-Freudians, were strongly influenced by many of Freud's ideas, such as the importance of the unconscious in personality development. Although initially disciples, many later developed their own varieties of psychoanalytic theory that differed from Freud's in significant ways.

CARL JUNG.   Carl Jung thought that Freud overemphasized the importance of sex drives in determining behavior (Jung, 1917). While Jung did not deny the existence of the sex drive, he placed greater emphasis on the ability of individual personalities to grow and change throughout life, and on the potential of individuals to be motivated by positive goals they set for themselves. This latter view has been pursued vigorously by modern-day humanists, as described later in this chapter.

Jung's version of the psychodynamic approach came to be called *analytical psychology* (Jung, 1968). Like Freud, Carl Jung believed that the unconscious is a powerful determinant of our actions. His notion of the unconscious, however, went beyond Freud's version. In addition to the personal unconscious of an individual emphasized by Freud, Jung proposed that each of us inherits a **collective unconscious**—a storehouse of images and memory traces inherited from our ancestors. The collective unconscious is not composed of individual personal experiences. Rather, it is thought to contain **archetypes**—meaningful and emotionally charged ideas and images passed on from generation to generation. The archetype of *mother*—nurturing and protective—is an idea with which a baby is born. Other important archetypes include birth, death, power, magic, God, and the wise old man. Jung believed that such universal ideas were frequently revealed in dreams and were therefore important in dream interpretation. He also believed that archetypes frequently characterized symbols in religion and art.

ALFRED ADLER.   Another of Freud's close colleagues, Alfred Adler, also broke with him over the importance of sexual motivation in determining human activity. Adler believed that the primary motivation for human action was a striving for power to overcome inferiority, rather than a need to satisfy sexual and aggressive impulses. Adler (1931) coined the phrase, **inferiority complex,** which refers to exaggerated feelings of inadequacy and insecurity. Because children are born weak and helpless in comparison to adults, Adler believed that they are motivated to acquire new skills and independence. They strive toward "superiority," but superiority over their own feelings of inadequacy, not over others. Because it is our interplay with others that leads to initial feelings of inferiority, Adler strongly emphasized social factors in the shaping of personality.

KAREN HORNEY.   Although Freud, Jung, and Adler were the early leaders of the psychoanalytic movement, Karen Horney assumed a leadership role some 20 years later, after moving to the United States. Born in Germany and trained by one of Freud's students, Horney moved to the United States just before World War II and had a major impact on the revision of psychoanalysis. Like Adler and Jung, she did not believe that sex and aggression are the primary drives motivating human behavior. Rather, she believed that people have a need for security, which arises out of "basic anxiety" from feeling alone in childhood. Children develop conflicts, she argued, not because of clashes between an unprincipled id and the ideals of the superego, but because children become anxiously insecure as a result of inadequate child-rearing practices. Adults also can suffer from basic anxiety as a result of insecurities in their relationships with others. To deal with basic anxiety, individ-

collective unconscious
In Jung's psychodynamic theory, the storehouse of images and memory traces inherited from our ancestors.

archetypes
Meaningful ideas and images passed on from culture to culture, and contained in our collective unconscious.

inferiority complex
Exaggerated feelings of inadequacy and insecurity;

uals are motivated to interact with others in a way that will produce feelings of safety and well-being. An individual might move toward others and seek approval and affection, move against others to achieve power or recognition, or away from others and become self-sufficient and independent. Horney maintained that our personalities typically represent a mixture of these three general courses of action (Horney, 1950). Neurotic tendencies, however, are likely to occur when an individual's personality reflects primarily one of these three courses of action to an extreme degree.

Projective Testing: Assessing the Unconscious

Though Freud's followers disagreed with him in important ways, all psychoanalytic psychologists agree that our unconscious thoughts and hidden desires influence our personalities. In the example described earlier in which a father chastised his adolescent son for masturbating, the adolescent's unconscious mind contained hatred and anger toward his father, hidden thoughts of which the adolescent was totally unaware. But if many of our thoughts and desires are unconscious and hidden, how can they be assessed? Personality inventories like the 16PF are inadequate to uncover such unconscious thoughts or feelings. If the adolescent's ego distorted his true id impulses and kept them hidden from his consciousness, then his true personality will not likely be revealed by simply answering yes or no to some straightforward questions. A better strategy, psychodynamic theorists argue, is to present a subject with some ambiguous stimulus like a drawing, photo, or design that could suggest any number of possible meanings. When the subject describes or makes up a story about that stimulus, hidden feelings and desires might be *projected* into the description or story. For this reason, personality tests to help psychodynamic theorists delve into the unconscious are referred to as **projective tests.** A commonly used projective test is the Rorschach Inkblot Test. It is somewhat misleading to refer to it as a *test*, in that there are no right or wrong answers.

projective tests

Personality tests, such as the Rorschach, that provide ambiguous stimuli, the description of which by subjects might contain hidden feelings and desires from the person's unconscious mind.

THE RORSCHACH INKBLOT TEST.   From 1910 to 1920, Hermann Rorschach examined thousands of inkblots. His use of inkblots was a bit like the game that children play when they look up at clouds to find pictures in the floating shapes. Rorschach asked subjects what they saw in his inkblots and then used subjects' answers to assess dimensions of their personalities.

Rorschach finally chose ten inkblots from all those studied, and published the *Rorschach Projective Test* in 1921 (see Figure 2-4). There aren't many rules to administering the Rorschach test. A subject is given the Rorschach cards one at a time in a particular order. For each inkblot, the subject is asked to describe what he or she sees. Subjects can look at the card from a variety of different angles and make one or more interpretations of the card. After all of the cards have been described, the examiner then goes over them one at a time and encourages the subject to describe which part of each inkblot led to his or her response. This is

Figure 2-4
An inkblot like those on the Roschach Test. On the actual test, five of the inkblots are black and grey, like the one shown here, two inkblots have patches of red on them, and the three remaining blots contain several colors.

essentially a strategy to encourage a subject to respond in more detail to ambiguous stimuli and to present additional opportunities for the subject to project unconscious thoughts and feelings into the descriptions.

Consider, for example, the inkblot in Figure 2-4. What do you see there? When shown this inkblot, one student responded, "It looks like two dogs playing tug-of-war over a piece of meat." When asked, "What part of the inkblot made you think of two dogs?" the student replied, "The part in the middle there. The two triangular shapes look like the top view of dogs' heads. Maybe they're trying to lick each other. Maybe they like each other." Obviously, the student was looking at the upper center part of the inkblot in Figure 2-4. But what do we make of such responses?

What does it mean, for example, if a subject focuses primarily on tiny portions of each inkblot? Is that person compulsive about orderliness? Highly individualistic and independent? Or is the person a stamp collector (who has learned to examine minute details of rare stamps)? The fact is, clinicians often disagree in their interpretations of the Rorschach, and it is not very useful for discriminating between groups or diagnosing different types of psychological disorders (Kleinmuntz, 1982). In spite of this fact, it is widely used in clinical practice by psychodynamically oriented clinicians (Lubin et al., 1984). Many clinicians believe that, in the hands of an experienced therapist, the Rorschach can provide useful information about a client's thoughts and feelings, thus helping the therapist gain insight into a client's personality.

Evaluation of Freud's Psychodynamic Approach

While Freud has had an important and powerful impact on psychology, many of his ideas have not been supported by research. But when we remember that he did not have access to the scientific data on human behavior that has since been gathered (about learning, emotions, motivation, and other areas described in later chapters), we can't help but admire the man's genius. Let's look at Freud's legacy to psychology.

Freud's views were based largely on talking to people with problems.

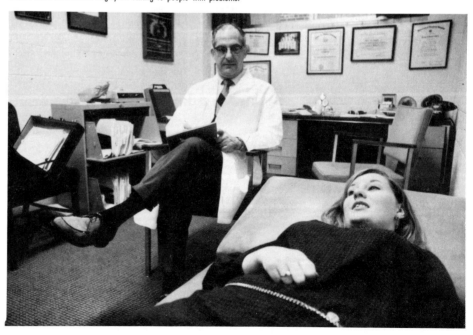

The foundation for Freud's theory has been criticized on two counts. First, it was derived from observations of a relatively small number of cases. As we discussed in Chapter 1, the case study method, while fruitful in terms of helping a researcher develop hypotheses, is not rigorous enough to allow researchers to prove cause-and-effect relationships. Second, Freud's work was based largely on the study of abnormal or maladjusted behavior—that is, his patients. But one cannot assume that all humans are like patients in therapy. A valid scientific theory of human behavior would be based on random study of all types of males and females, children and adults, "sick" individuals and "healthy" people. But Freud's theory was not based on those kinds of observations; therefore his theory is weak from a scientific viewpoint (Bachop, 1989; Bolles, 1967; Rothstein, 1980).

Another criticism of Freud's theory concerns his belief that the id and the ego have a biological basis. Freud's writings implied that the unconscious, preconscious, conscious, id, ego, and superego were not just abstract entities; and that counterparts to his mental apparatus would eventually be located in the brain. But this just hasn't happened. The id, ego, and superego are abstract ways of thinking about people's behavior. They have no biological reality in any part of human anatomy.

Even some of Freud's most enthusiastic followers have criticized Freud's heavy emphasis on the importance of sex as a driving force in an individual's life. And Freud's notion that sexual themes are common in dreams simply hasn't been supported. Less than 10 percent of reported dreams contain overtly sexual themes (Hall & Van de Castle, 1966). In Freud's defense, he would probably reply that the sexual nature of dreams would be distorted and would require expert interpretation to be revealed. Nevertheless, many psychologists consider this aspect of Freud's theory to be only weakly supported at best.

Implications of the inferiority of women in Freud's theory have come under especially heavy criticism. Karen Horney, one of the neo-Freudians, strongly challenged Freud's view that women feel inferior to men. In fact, Freud's views on the inferiority of women appear to be rather sexist beliefs, most likely shaped by the heavily male-dominated society in which he lived.

Critics have also questioned Freud's theory of psychosexual development. Cross-cultural studies seriously question the suggestion that all children proceed through a set series of psychosexual stages (Phares, 1991). And although some adults do show characteristics that Freud described as an anal-retentive personality (McAdams, 1990), it's simply not possible to obtain reliable observations that might tie such characteristics to specific childhood experiences, such as severe toilet training during the anal stage. Moreover, sufficient ambiguity exists in Freud's theory to explain any outcome. For example, if an adult is stubborn and stingy, Freud might say that the individual has fixated at the anal stage. However if that same person is cooperative and generous, then Freud might say that true tendencies to stinginess have been buried in the unconscious and the opposite behaviors have occurred through the defense mechanism of reaction formation. A good theory must be phrased so that it can be either confirmed or disproved. Freud's theory is just not stated in that way.

In spite of these criticisms, we must recognize that Freud has had a tremendous impact on the way that we think about ourselves in general, and on psychology in particular. He emphasized the importance of early environmental experiences in the determination of later behavior patterns, something most current psychologists still acknowledge as important. He emphasized that women, as well as men, experience sexual desires and, in a view that was revolutionary for his time, that women are not on earth solely for the pleasure of men. His emphasis on the unconscious contributed to our understanding of the fact that we are often unaware of both what we are doing and why we are doing it. And although Freud's view of the unconscious as something filled with selfish wishes or lustful drives is not widely accepted, his theories undoubtedly stimulated others to clarify different meanings of both consciousness and the unconscious. Perhaps most importantly, Freud emphasized that serious maladjustment could be changed. Rather than locking people away in asylums as was common in his day, Freud stressed that people could adjust to the problems of daily living, provided that they received proper counseling and guidance.

Behavioral Approaches to Personality Theory

Freud emphasized the hidden aspects of personality implied by the operation of the id, the ego, and the superego. The trait psychologists mentioned earlier focused on consistent observable behavior patterns. Like trait theorists, behavioral psychologists also emphasize the study of observable behavior patterns. Unlike the trait theorists, however, behavioral psychologists have focused more on how our personalities can change (as a function of learning experiences) rather than studying qualities that are relatively enduring.

In 1913, a brash young psychologist with a trenchant style of writing took psychology by storm when he published a paper entitled "Psychology as the behaviorist views it." John B. Watson was dissatisfied with the psychology of his day. He argued that the correct subject matter of psychology was observable behavior and observable behavior only. Consciousness, mental processes, and internal conflicts could not be objectively observed and they were not, therefore, the proper subject matter of psychology.

Known as the father of behaviorism, John B. Watson made important contributions to the psychology of adjustment. In particular, his emphasis on the idea that the external environment controls our behavior set the stage for the study of principles of learning that shape our personalities. But his brand of behaviorism also had serious limitations. Perhaps the most important of these was that it excluded inner thoughts and feelings as valid subject matter in psychology. Inner thoughts and feelings may be more difficult to study than observable behavior, but they are very important to the person who is thinking those thoughts or experiencing those feelings. Modern behaviorism (sometimes called radical behaviorism) has overcome the limitations of Watson's approach. We'll discuss personality within the context of the modern behavioral approach of B. F. Skinner, and the social learning perspective of Albert Bandura.

Skinner's Behaviorist Approach

As we describe further in Chapter 3, Skinner's research focused on principles of learning. For Skinner (1974), personality is simply the way that each of us behaves as a result of our own unique learning experiences.

While some trait theorists look for stable internal factors to explain personality, Skinner believed that our personalities are a result of external events, past learning, and our genetic makeup. Skinner emphasized that much of our behavior is determined by its consequences—behaviors that are rewarded tend to increase while those that are punished tend to decrease. Suppose, for example, that you are frequently reinforced by laughter for telling jokes, by the opportunity to socialize and dance for going to parties, and by positive reactions from your friends for organizing group outings. A trait theorist who observed your actions might conclude that you have the personality trait of sociability, but for Skinner you are simply showing behaviors that result from present patterns of reward (holding someone close feels goods), past learning (it felt good then, too), and your genetic makeup (with two healthy legs, you *can* dance).

Skinner believed that people show patterns of behavior because of learning experiences. If a particular pattern of behavior consistently pays off in particular environments, then that pattern of behavior will become highly probable. Others might call it a personality trait. Skinner viewed it simply as a pattern of behavior that is due to past and present environmental experiences, not due to psychological traits.

Skinner's approach to personality differs from trait theories in another way. Trait theorists look for stable, consistent patterns of behavior. Skinner did not assume that people will show a high degree of behavioral consistency. A person might be rewarded by attention for being happy-go-lucky with one group of friends and for being quite serious with another group of friends. Also, from Skinner's point of view, personality is not necessarily stable throughout one's lifetime. A reformed alcoholic who moves from a large city to a small country town, remarries, and becomes involved in community activities might change to such an extent that his old friends would describe him as "a completely different person"—as a totally different personality.

While Skinner's approach can explain why we show observable behavior patterns, what about that part of us that often can't be seen—our desires, thoughts, and feelings? After all, at the beginning of this chapter we defined personality as a person's consistent and enduring ways of acting, thinking, and feeling across a variety of situations. For Skinner, our inner thoughts and feelings are simply private or covert behaviors, no different in principle from our observable or overt behaviors. The application of learning principles to change aspects of our inner personality that we're unhappy about—things that we say to ourselves, think about, and feel emotionally—is a part of the area referred to as *behavior modification* or *behavior therapy,* and is discussed further in Chapters 3 and 14.

Like Freud, Skinner also used the term *unconscious* when discussing behavior. But Skinner's unconscious is something quite different than the unconscious of Sigmund Freud. For Freud, you will recall, the unconscious was something filled with selfish wishes and lustful drives (Maddi, 1980). For Skinner, unconscious simply refers to lack of self-awareness about what you are doing or why you are doing it (Skinner, 1989). You have probably had the experience of driving along the highway in a car during which you start thinking about something. Half a mile later, you realize that you have been driving without any awareness of what you passed during that entire distance. Skinner explained such events by saying that we are sometimes unconscious of our behavior and its causes. But he meant only that it was likely more rewarding for us to daydream (in that instance) than it was for us to attend closely to our driving or to the scenes along the highway.

Bandura's Social Learning Theory

Albert Bandura, like Skinner, believes that our personality is the sum total of the way that each of us acts, thinks, and feels as a result of our own unique learning experiences. Also like Skinner, Bandura believes that the behavior patterns that make up our personality are strongly influenced by their rewarding and punishing consequences. Unlike Skinner, however, Bandura sees our personality as determined not only by the consequences of behavior but also by our *beliefs* about those consequences and by our *expectations* of success and failure.

Bandura (1977, 1986) is one of the primary proponents of **social learning theory**—a theory that proposes that consequences of behavior *and* a person's expectations about those consequences are both important determinants of personality.

Bandura's approach is "social" in the sense that it places great emphasis upon the social contexts in which behavior is acquired and maintained. Bandura has strongly emphasized the importance of modeling and observational learning (discussed further in Chapter 3). He suggests that many of our personality characteristics are learned by watching other people act and by observing what happens to them. For example, if we see how popular our mother is because she is outgoing and witty, we are likely to learn to be that way ourselves.

social learning theory
An approach in psychology that combines learning principles with cognitive mediational processes as important influences on behavior, and that places great emphasis upon the social contexts in which behavior is learned and maintained.

This child looks like his father because of genetics. The child is dressed like his father because Dad dressed him and Dad wanted it that way. But Bandura would argue that the child's imitative behavior could occur solely from the effects of observing Dad.

Many situations in which you may find yourself might cause you to feel nervous, annoyed, or emotionally strained in some way. You might have serious concerns about your ability to perform in such situations. At the other extreme, you might feel totally confident about your ability to cope. To assess your self-efficacy, your degree of confidence that you can perform adequately at a particular task, consider the following situations. For each situation, try to imagine how you might feel, whether you might be relaxed or tensed. In the column on the right, estimate your degree of self-confidence that you could perform the tasks. Use a 1–9 scale where "1" means that you don't think that you could perform the task, "5" means that you have moderate confidence that you could perform the task, and "9" means that you are completely confident that you could perform the task.

Task	*Confidence Rating*
Go to a party where you don't know anyone.	___
Go to a party where you know only the host.	___
At a party, approach a group of people that you don't know, and introduce yourself.	___
At a party, join in the conversation with a group of strangers.	___

Task	*Confidence Rating*
At a party, discuss a controversial topic (such as AIDS, sexual harassment, religion, and so on) with people who strongly disagree with you.	___
Complain about consistently disorganized lectures given by a professor.	___
Complain about poor service to a waiter or waitress.	___
Send a meal back in a restaurant because the food was not appropriately hot when served.	___
Accept service by a salesperson who is very unfriendly.	___
While waiting in line at a movie, ask someone who cuts in line to go to the back of the line.	___
Ask people in neighboring rooms at the dormitory where you stay to stop making noise at night.	___
When returning a sales item with which you are dissatisfied, insist on seeing the manager.	___

Scoring: High ratings of self-efficacy tend to be good predictors of the relevant behaviors. On tasks for which you scored "5" to "9," it is likely that you would perform the behaviors.

Adapted from Bandura, 1986.

self-efficacy

An expectation or belief that one can perform adequately in particular situations.

According to Bandura, our *cognitions* or beliefs are also major determinants of our behavior. An important cognitive process, for example, is what Bandura calls **self-efficacy** (Bandura, 1982). Self-efficacy refers to a belief that one can perform adequately in a particular situation. If you really believe that you have the ability to get an "A" in a particular course, then you are more likely to study hard to achieve the "A" than if you believe such a grade is simply out of reach. Believing that you can influence your behavior—or personality—has a great deal to do with your success in doing so. In Bandura's words, "Given appropriate skills and adequate incentives . . . efficacy expectations are a major determinant of people's choices of activities, how much effort they will expend, and how long they will sustain effort in dealing with stressful situations" (Bandura, 1977; p. 194). Thus, like Skinner, Bandura considers personality to be simply the way each of us behaves. Unlike Skinner, however, he believes that our cognitions determine how rewards and punishers shape our personality characteristics.

Behavioral Assessment: Assessing Behavior in Situations

behavioral assessment

An approach that emphasizes objective description of behaviors in specific situations.

Personality tests, such as Cattell's 16PF, attempt to evaluate an individual's general behavioral tendencies or personality traits. Projective tests, such as the Rorschach, try to get at some of the underlying and hidden reasons that explain why people do and say what they do and say. The focus of behavioral assessment is quite different from both of these concerns. **Behavioral assessment** is concerned with what people do, say, think, or feel *in specific situations* (Bellack & Hersen, 1988). Behavioral assessment is useful *not* for making inferences about global personality traits or hidden motives but rather for changing some aspect of personality that is troublesome, such as in the case of Darren described below.

DIRECT ASSESSMENT PROCEDURES.   In direct behavioral assessments, an individual is observed in real or simulated situations characteristic of home, school, work, or other situations in which aspects of personality are likely to be revealed. Six-year-old Darren, for example, was extremely uncooperative with his parents. According to the parents, Darren virtually "ran the show," deciding when he would go to bed, what foods he would eat, when his parents could play with him, and so on. You might say that he had a "dominant" personality. To obtain direct observations of Darren's behavior, both cooperative and uncooperative, the psychologist who was assessing Darren asked his mother to spend some time with Darren in a playroom at the clinic. During the first two 20-minute sessions (called baseline sessions), Darren's mother was instructed: "Just play with Darren as you might at home," and Darren's "commanding" and "cooperative" behaviors were recorded.

Darren showed a very low rate of cooperative behavior during the baseline sessions (see Figure 2-5). His commanding behavior, on the other hand, occurred at an extremely high rate. Following the baseline sessions, Darren's mother was asked to be very positive and supportive to any instances of cooperative behavior shown by Darren. At the same time, she was instructed to completely ignore his commanding behavior. Over the next two sessions, Darren's cooperative behavior steadily increased.

Direct observation is a useful way to determine how an individual will behave in specific situations at home, at work, at school, or elsewhere. The observations

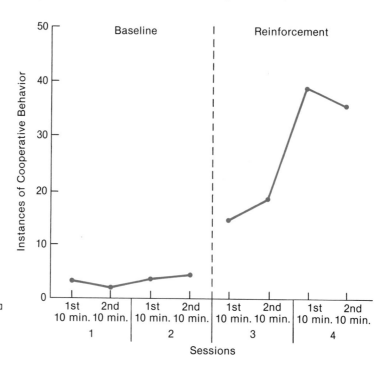

Figure 2-5

Data from direct behavioral assessment procedures. Each data point (dot) represents the total instances of Darren's cooperative behavior during a ten-minute interval within a session. Baseline refers to the observation phase prior to the reinforcement program.

Adapted from Wahler et al., 1965.

may have many uses, including helping a person to make personality adjustments (such as in the case of Darren), or selecting individuals with particular personality characteristics (such as hiring managerial staff for a large corporation), or in studying personality differences between individuals (such as aggressiveness vs. passivity in the face of threat). Often, however, psychologists frequently do not find it practical to directly observe individuals in real-life situations.

INDIRECT ASSESSMENT PROCEDURES.   An alternative to direct assessment is to gather information about the kinds of behaviors that occur in specific locations through situational interviews and behavioral checklists.

During a *situational interview,* an individual is asked how he or she would act in specific situations. Suppose, for example, that you applied for a job as a wading pool supervisor at a public park. In a situational interview, you might be asked how you would deal with children who remove their bathing suits, throw toys at one another, or try to drink the water in the wading pool. Situational interviews might reveal aspects of your personality that would be useful in predicting how you would behave in actual situations (Latham & Saari, 1984).

Behavioral checklists are questionnaires to help individuals identify particular behaviors that they would like to change. One type of checklist samples a wide variety of behaviors. An example is the adjustment questionnaire you completed at the end of Chapter 1. Another type of behavioral checklist focuses on a particular area and can enable you to assess the behaviors representative of a particular personality characteristic, such as assertiveness (see Chapter 15).

While behavioral assessments have many valid uses, we must remember that they, like personality inventories and projective tests, are only one of many possible sources of information about an individual. Whether the task is to assess an individual's personality broadly or to make accurate predictions about specific behavior in specific situations, experienced psychologists usually try to obtain information from a variety of sources.

Evaluation of Behavioral Approaches

The strength of the behavioral approaches lies in their experimental foundation. Literally thousands of research reports have demonstrated the value of these approaches in the improvement of a variety of behaviors of individuals in diverse settings. However, this has also led to the criticism that these approaches are overly concerned with changing specific behaviors in specific situations, rather than studying dominant personality characteristics such as those studied by trait theorists. Moreover, Skinner's approach, in particular, has been criticized for failing to consider the importance of cognitive factors in determining our personality. And while social learning theory includes the influence of cognitive factors (such as self-efficacy) in determining a person's individual behaviors, critics have argued that social learning theory does not indicate how all those individual behaviors "fit together" to make a total personality (Hall et al., 1985). Behavioral approaches nevertheless add an important dimension to the study of personality—namely, a proven set of techniques for helping people change those aspects of their personality with which they are dissatisfied.

Humanistic Approaches to Personality Theory

The humanistic approach to personality developed in the 1950s and 1960s as a result of dissatisfaction some psychologists felt with psychodynamic and behavioral theories. Humanists tend to see personality as an ideal self that all people seek to express. They emphasize the potential and inherent goodness of each individual, and they differ from Freudian and behavioral views in several ways. First, humanists characterize people as striving for increased self-awareness and fulfillment of their

Humanists emphasize the need for understanding, warmth, and sharing to help individuals lead fulfilling lives.

potential, rather than as resolving conflicts between a pleasure-seeking id and a restrictive society. Second, they believe that humans can make choices and are personally responsible for their behavior, rather than showing puppetlike learned responses. And third, their approach is *phenomenological,* emphasizing reality for an individual as that individual perceives it. To understand how someone's personality is reflected in the choices he or she makes, humanists argue, we must try to determine what the world looks like through that individual's eyes. This is in contrast with observing behavior objectively, as the behaviorists tend to do.

Humanistic theory has a number of contributors including Abraham Maslow, Carl Rogers, Virginia Satir, Rollo May, Fritz Perls, and Victor Frankl. We'll examine some of the key notions of Maslow and Rogers.

Abraham Maslow and Self-Actualization

self-actualization

The tendency to recognize what one is, what one can and should be, and the striving to be that person; a concept of humanistic psychology.

Abraham Maslow called the humanistic school the "third force" in American psychology, as distinguished from psychoanalysis and behaviorism. He was principally concerned with the development of the healthy personality. Maslow argued that we are born with needs, capacities, and tendencies that are essentially good and not evil. He argued that personality development involves "actualizing" these characteristics and fulfilling one's potential. Maslow (1970) indicated that the concept of **self-actualization** is extremely difficult to define. In a general sense, it involves recognizing what one is, what one can and should be, and striving to be that person.

Maslow suggested that we are motivated by a hierarchy of needs to achieve our potential. At the bottom of the hierarchy are our physical needs such as for food, water, shelter, and sex. Next are safety needs (such as the desire to feel secure), belonging needs (such as the need to be accepted and receive affection),

PEANUTS reprinted by permission of UFS, Inc.

TABLE 2-3
ACCORDING TO MASLOW, PEOPLE WHO ARE
SELF-ACTUALIZED SHOW CERTAIN
CHARACTERISTICS *Adapted from Maslow, 1970.*

People Who Are Self-Actualized:
Are realistic
Show acceptance of themselves, others, and reality
Are spontaneous and natural
Focus on problems rather than themselves
Have a need for privacy
Are independent and self-sufficient
Are capable of spontaneous rather than stereotyped appreciation of their environment and people in it
Have peak experiences
Identify with all of humankind
Have deep, intimate relationships with only a few people
Have a democratic attitude
Maintain strongly held values and ethics
Show a broad, unhostile sense of humor
Are creative
Are individualistic and resist conformity

and esteem needs (such as the desire to gain approval and recognition). At the top of the hierarchy is the need to self-actualize, to fulfill one's potential. He suggested that we pursue the satisfaction of higher level needs only after we satisfy more fundamental, lower level needs.

According to Maslow, those who reach the top of this needs hierarchy become self-actualized and are individuals with exceptionally healthy personalities. What are such people like? Who are they? In an effort to clarify the characteristics of self-actualization, Maslow studied exceptional historical and contemporary public figures as well as some personal acquaintances whom he considered to have reached their fullest potential. He eventually identified 38 people whom he considered self-actualized, including Albert Einstein, Abraham Lincoln, Albert Schweitzer, and Eleanor Roosevelt. Maslow described these people in the following way: "Such people seem to be fulfilling themselves and to be doing the best they are capable of doing. . . . They are people who have developed or are developing to the full stature of what they are capable" (1970, p. 150). More specifically, self-actualized people are those who show the characteristics listed in Table 2-3.

How many of us are self-actualized? Apparently not many. Maslow interviewed approximately 3,000 college students and found only one actualized person and one or two dozen "potentials" (Maslow, 1970). He concluded that less than 1 percent of all people are truly self-actualized.

In spite of the fact that few people are truly self-actualized, Maslow proposed that our society can encourage its members to strive for self-actualization. As students, for example, you should search for your own identities, choose your vocation based on your own deep-seated interests and concerns, and develop your own set of values.

Carl Rogers' Person-Centered Approach

As a practicing psychotherapist in the 1930s and 1940s, Carl Rogers came to the conclusion that he could best help his clients by trying to see things from the clients' point of view (he did not like the term *patients* because it implied illness).

By being an empathic listener, he could sensitively and nonjudgmentally reflect the person's feelings and meanings and help the person to identify his or her own true self, and to strive to become that true self. For these reasons, his method of psychotherapy became known as *client-centered* and *nondirective therapy.*

Rogers eventually expanded his notions about therapy into a general theory of personality. According to Rogers (1961, 1980), the core of one's personality is the self, or as it is known today, the **self-concept.** Your self-concept is the collection of beliefs, thoughts, and feelings that you have about yourself. It is your self-image—the way you see yourself.

self-concept

The collection of beliefs, thoughts, and feelings that you have about yourself.

Like Maslow, Rogers believed that we are all motivated to achieve self-actualization—to realize our capabilities and fulfill our potential. Rogers found that many of his clients who were unhappy typically encountered daily experiences that were less than fulfilling. A student who was quite bright in high school, for example, might develop poor study habits in college and, as a result, get poor grades. For such clients, their *real self* did not match up to their *ideal self*—their potential and capabilities that they visualized themselves as possessing.

Rogers believed that not only therapists but also people in general could nurture the growth of others in three ways: First, by being empathic listeners—by nonjudgmentally "mirroring" what people are saying to help them become more aware of their own thoughts and feelings; second, by self-disclosing—by being open about their own feelings and by sharing confidences; and third, by showing **unconditional positive regard**—by clearly showing people that they are accepted and valued no matter what their beliefs and failings. If you present your love to someone conditionally, that is, you indicate your acceptance and caring for them only when they do things that please you, then you are influencing them to meet your needs in order to be accepted by you. In order for them to be self-actualized and to pursue their own interests, you must show your regard for them unconditionally.

unconditional positive regard

Showing people that they are accepted and valued no matter what their beliefs and failings.

Humanistic Testing: Assessing the Self

A humanistic psychologist wants to help a client achieve self-actualization—recognizing what one is, what one can be, and striving to be that person. Many humanists believe that assessment of a person's real and ideal self can only come through empathic listening and the genuine openness and sharing that occur through intimate conversations. They would argue that it is not possible to determine the nature of a person's ideal self from a formal, objective paper-and-pencil test. Some assessment instruments, however, have been developed from the humanistic perspective.

THE SELF-IMAGE CHECKLIST.   Rogers (1980) suggests that, as we grow up, we acquire a self-image, a description of our behavioral characteristics as we see them, and that we also acquire an ideal self, a description of our behavioral characteristics as we would like them to be. Some questionnaires have been developed to help people get in touch with their own "self-image" and "ideal self." We have reproduced one such self-image checklist in Box 2-4.

Evaluation of Humanistic Approaches

By the common criteria of science—demonstrability, verifiability, replicability—humanistic theory does not fare well. Like Freud's id, ego, and superego, humanistic concepts like Maslow's self-actualization and Rogers' self-concept are difficult to define and measure. It has been argued that Maslow's study of famous persons represented nothing more than his impressions of his own personal heroes (Smith, 1978). Other theorists with different values might select a far different set of heroes

Box 2-4

A Self-Image Checklist

To help you get in touch with your own self-image and ideal self, we have reproduced below the Self-Image Checklist (Weiner, 1980). There is no specific score that you should strive for. If you find that very few of the items on the Self-Image Checklist match, so that you obtain a very low score, then changing certain aspects of your self might be an area to consider as a target for self-adjustment (as described in Box 3-3).

Read the adjectives listed below. Place an "X" in the column labeled "As I Actually Am" for each word that describes you as you see yourself now. Then, disregarding the marks you just made, go back and read through the list again. This time place an "O" in the column labeled "As I Would Like to Be" for each word that describes the way you would like to be if you could be your ideal person. Tally the number of "X"s and "O"s on the same lines and the number of lines that are left totally blank. How many of these matches did you have?

	(X) As I Actually Am	(O) As I Would Like to Be		(X) As I Actually Am	(O) As I Would Like to Be
Emotional	____	____	Cheerful	____	____
Opinionated	____	____	Envious	____	____
Humorous	____	____	Energetic	____	____
Independent	____	____	Considerate	____	____
Friendly	____	____	Quiet	____	____
Ambitious	____	____	Clever	____	____
Interesting	____	____	Bossy	____	____
Honest	____	____	Resilient	____	____
Attractive	____	____	Self-centered	____	____
Reserved	____	____	Fragile	____	____
Enthusiastic	____	____	Sincere	____	____
Average	____	____	Relaxed	____	____
Sensitive	____	____	Forceful	____	____
Dependable	____	____	Cynical	____	____
Intelligent	____	____	Impulsive	____	____
Lazy	____	____	Apathetic	____	____

and derive a far different description of self-actualization. Alternatively, researchers might look at the individuals identified by Maslow as being self-actualized and suggest other concepts to characterize their behavior. Willard Mittelman (1991), for example, proposed that individuals whom Maslow considered to be self-actualized were more simply characterized by the fact that they were very open—that is, in comparison to others, they were more receptive to information about the world, more able to see things clearly, and more able to appreciate what they saw. Whether or not openness is a better concept than self-actualization to describe the famous people studied by Maslow is debatable (for example, see Tobacyk & Miller, 1991). The main point is that both concepts (self-actualization and openness) are extremely broad, general terms and are therefore difficult to study scientifically.

Others have criticized the emphasis by humanists on *self*-actualization and *personal* satisfaction as encouraging self-indulgence, selfishness, and an erosion of moral restraint (Campbell & Specht, 1985; Wallach & Wallach, 1983). The encouragement of *self*-fulfillment might be interpreted by some as a license to do whatever they wish without regard to the feelings, thoughts, desires, and growth needs of others.

And even in cases where it is desirable to encourage individual self-fulfillment, it's quite another thing to provide the means to achieve it. What specific steps can one follow when there is incongruity between one's real self and one's ideal self? What about a step-by-step plan to achieve self-actualization? Humanistic psychology has fallen short when it comes to the development of specific self-adjustment techniques of proven effectiveness.

Nevertheless, humanistic ideas have had a considerable impact on psychology, counseling, education, and child rearing. Rogers' person-centered theory has stimulated a great deal of research on the interactions between client and therapist during therapy, research that has helped to clarify how therapists can best help clients achieve their goals. And therapist qualities emphasized by Rogers—being empathic, showing acceptance, and being genuine—are correlated strongly with successful therapeutic outcome (Gurman, 1977; Luborsky et al., 1985).

At the start of this chapter, we defined personality as our consistent and enduring ways of behaving, thinking, and feeling across situations. There are many theories of personality because different psychologists have focused on different parts of the many aspects of personality that we could examine. Trait theorists have objectively studied *behavioral consistencies* that reflect our personality. Other theorists emphasize the importance of *variables within each person* in determining our personality: Psychodynamic approaches stress the importance of unconscious and irrational forces within us; humanists focus on striving to self-actualize and achieve our potential; and at least some theorists, such as Eysenck, have focused on heredity to explain behavioral tendencies, like those of the introvert versus the extrovert. Behavioral approaches, on the other hand, have emphasized *situational variables*—those which serve as rewards and punishers—in shaping our personality. Each of these approaches has identified some of the pieces to the puzzle of personality. But no one approach has been able to put the puzzle together in a way that accounts for all of the research. Undoubtedly, personality researchers will continue to explore ways to account for consistency in individuals' behaviors across situations, differences in behavior patterns between individuals, and the prediction of individuals' behavior in specific situations (for example, Cantor, 1990).

SUMMARY

- The term *personality* has many meanings. In everyday conversation it sometimes implies social attractiveness. At other times it refers to a dominant characteristic of an individual, such as in an aggressive personality. For some psychologists, the term refers more to the underlying causes of behavior. We define personality as a person's consistent and enduring ways of acting, thinking, and feeling across a variety of situations.

- Several prominent personality theorists (for example, Allport, Cattell, Eysenck) have developed trait theories that focus on dominant behavior patterns which identify our distinctiveness and consistency. While knowledge of an individual's personality traits is not particularly useful to predict that person's specific behavior in specific situations, it is useful for predicting that person's "typical" way of behaving across a variety of situations.

- Freud's psychoanalytic theory considers personality to be the interplay of the id, ego, and superego. He believed that human personality could be understood only by exploring the unconscious drives and conflicts that determine much of our behavior. The unconscious desires of the id seek release in pleasurable activities. The superego may judge such impulses as wrong, causing feelings of guilt. The ego strives to channel id energy to activities that are both acceptable to reality and to the ideals of the superego. When an individual experiences excessive guilt, ego defense mechanisms bury the true id impulses in the unconscious and may lead to abnormal behaviors symptomatic of the underlying personality conflict. Although Freud made many significant contributions to psychology, his psychoanalytic theory is not stated in such a way as to be amenable to scientific tests. Moreover many of the neo-Freudians (e.g., Carl Jung, Alfred Adler, Karen Horney) were critical of specific aspects of Freud's theory, though their own personality theories were still based on the inner dynamics of personality.

- Behavioral approaches have focused more on how our personalities can change as a function of learning experiences rather than studying qualities that are relatively enduring. Skinner considered personality as simply the way that each of us behaves as a result of our own unique learning experiences. While emphasizing conditioning principles, Bandura also emphasized cognitive processes and observational learning as important influences on behavior. Because of their emphasis on the development of effective procedures for helping people change what they do, say, think about, and feel emotionally, the behavioral approaches are very useful for helping people change aspects of their personality that they're unhappy about.

- Humanistic approaches, such as those of Maslow and Rogers, focus on the capacity of the individual for personal growth and development. Although humanistic approaches do not meet common criteria of science, such as verifiability and replicability, humanistic ideas have had a considerable impact on psychology, counseling, education, and child rearing.

Box 2-5

SELF-ADJUSTMENT FOR STUDENTS: IDENTIFYING AREAS FOR IMPROVEMENT

In Chapter 1 we provided you with a questionnaire entitled "How Is Your Adjustment?" That type of questionnaire provides a useful starting point for adjustment. It's like casting a broad net to see how many fish you can catch. After you see what fish you have caught, you can then decide which ones you want to keep.

Another example of a "broad net" questionnaire is the Behavioral Self-Rating Checklist (Upper et al., 1975) shown in Table 2-4.

We encourage you to complete the Behavioral Self-Rating Checklist in order to further identify those areas that may be causing you particular difficulty. An advantage of using "broad net" questionnaires is that they require assessment in a wide variety of areas, and this often helps you identify areas for adjustment that might not otherwise come to your attention.

An alternative way of casting a broad net to help you identify areas for personal improvement and adjustment is to think about your *long-term goals.* These are specific career and/or personal goals that you hope to accomplish during approximately the next five to ten years. If you're like many individuals, you will have never seriously done any long-term planning. Completing Table 2-5 will help you to identify some long-term career and personal goals.

Continued

TABLE 2-4
BEHAVIORAL SELF-RATING CHECKLIST

Name_____   Date_____

Directions: The behaviors that a person learns determine to a large extent how well he gets along in life. Below is a list of behaviors that can be learned. Check the ones that *you* think you need to learn in order to function more effectively or to be more comfortable.

I need to learn:

_____ 1. to stop drinking too much.

_____ 2. to stop smoking too much.

_____ 3. to stop eating too much.

_____ 4. to control my feelings of attraction to members of my own sex.

_____ 5. to control my feelings of attraction to members of the other sex.

_____ 6. to overcome my feelings of nausea when I'm nervous.

_____ 7. to stop thinking about things that depress me.

_____ 8. to stop thinking about things that make me anxious.

_____ 9. to feel less anxious in crowds.

_____ 10. to feel less anxious in high places.

_____ 11. to stop worrying about my physical condition.

_____ 12. to feel less anxious in airplanes.

_____ 13. to stop stuttering.

_____ 14. to stop washing my hands so often.

_____ 15. to stop cleaning or straightening things up so often.

_____ 16. to stop biting my fingernails.

_____ 17. to take better care of my physical appearance.

_____ 18. to feel less anxious in enclosed places.

_____ 19. to feel less anxious in open places.

_____ 20. to feel less afraid of pain.

_____ 21. to feel less afraid of blood.

_____ 22. to feel less anxious about contamination or germs.

_____ 23. to feel less anxious about being alone.

_____ 24. to feel less afraid of the darkness.

_____ 25. to feel less afraid of certain animals.

_____ 26. to stop thinking the same thoughts over and over.

_____ 27. to stop counting my heartbeats.

_____ 28. to stop hearing voices.

_____ 29. to stop thinking people are against me or out to get me.

_____ 30. to stop seeing strange things.

_____ 31. to stop wetting the bed at night.

_____ 32. to stop taking medicine too much.

_____ 33. to stop taking too many pills.

_____ 34. to stop taking dope.

_____ 35. to stop having headaches.

_____ 36. to control my urge to gamble.

_____ 37. to be able to fall asleep at night.

_____ 38. to control my desire to expose myself.

_____ 39. to control my desire to put on clothing of the other sex.

_____ 40. to control my feelings of sexual attraction to other people's clothing, or belongings.

_____ 41. to control my sexual feelings toward young children.

_____ 42. to control my desire to hurt other people or be hurt.

_____ 43. to control my desire to steal.

_____ 44. to control my tendency to lie.

_____ 45. to stop daydreaming a lot.

_____ 46. to control my desire to yell at or hit other people when I'm angry.

_____ 47. to manage money better so that I have enough for what I really need.

_____ 48. to stop saying "crazy" things to other people.

_____ 49. how to carry on a conversation with other people.

_____ 50. to feel more comfortable carrying on a conversation with other people.

_____ 51. to stop bugging other people too much.

_____ 52. to be less forgetful.

_____ 53. to stop thinking about committing suicide.

_____ 54. to control my urge to set fires.

_____ 55. to hold down a steady job.

_____ 56. to feel comfortable on my job.

_____ 57. to stop swearing at other people.

_____ 58. how not to be upset when others criticize me.

_____ 59. to speak up when I feel I'm right.

_____ 60. to stop putting things off that need to be done.

_____ 61. to stop thinking so much about things that make me feel guilty.

_____ 62. to feel less anxious when my work is being supervised.

_____ 63. to feel less anxious about sexual thoughts.

_____ 64. to feel less anxious about kissing.

TABLE 2-4 *(Continued)*

_____ 65. to feel less anxious about petting.

_____ 66. to feel less anxious about sexual intercourse.

_____ 67. to be able to make decisions when I have to.

_____ 68. to feel at ease just being with other people in a group.

_____ 69. to feel at ease talking with other people in a group.

_____ 70. to feel less anxious about_____

_____ 71. to control my desire to_____

_____ 72. to feel less guilty about_____

_____ 73. to change my_____

How many did you check?_____

Which one that you checked is the one that you would most like to change?_____

From Upper et al., 1975.

TABLE 2-5
A GUIDE FOR IDENTIFYING LONG-TERM CAREER AND PERSONAL GOALS

The following subheadings will prompt you to think of long-term career and personal goals. If you are serious about long-term personal planning, then you should "brainstorm" goals in the following categories.

Categories	*List Your Goals for the Next Five Years*	*List Your Lifetime Goals*
Education: Extra courses		
Extra degrees		
Career: Target job or position		
Geographical location of work		
Target salary		
Target retirement date		
Special projects		

Continued

TABLE 2-5 *(Continued)*

Categories	List Your Goals for the Next Five Years	List Your Lifetime Goals
Health: Exercise program		
Dieting goals		
Family: Marital partner activities		
Child–parent activities		
Home style and location		
Vacations		
Financial planning		
Special projects		
Social: Relationships		
Friendships		
Personal improvement goals		
Other:		

To complete Table 2-5, start by listing some of your goals for the next five years within each of the categories listed. Each goal should be stated in two or three words. For example, under "Extra courses," what about that wine-tasting course you wanted to take? Perhaps you wanted to learn something about microcomputers for home use? During your first attempt at listing your goals, don't edit, and don't think about them too much. Rather, for each category write down what immediately comes to mind. Allow yourself two or three minutes to complete the entire first column (your goals for the next five years) and then two or three minutes for the entire second column. Also, don't be afraid to include far-out wishes under lifetime goals, such as taking a trip around the world or getting a law degree.

Your initial list might also include broad goals such as becoming a better person, communicating more clearly, or eating healthier. After brainstorming numerous goals in each of the two columns, leave your list alone for a day or two and then return to it. The second time you look at it, try to make some of the goals more specific. Eating healthier, for example, might translate into losing ten pounds and cutting back on salt and sugar intake. Becoming a better person might translate into taking a course on responsible assertiveness.

Of course, making a list of some long-term goals does not mean that you will accomplish them. But it is a step in the right direction. In the remaining chapters in this book we discuss further steps that you can take toward goal attainment, including setting priorities for your goals, setting deadlines, dividing projects into smaller units, learning to get help from others when you can't do it alone, learning to reward yourself, learning to increase your commitment to specific goals, and others. For now, we are interested in helping you identify some general areas for adjustment.

MEMORY BOOSTER

■ IMPORTANT PERSONS

You should know who these persons are and why they are important:

Gordon Allport	Karen Horney
Raymond Cattell	John B. Watson
Hans Eysenck	B. F. Skinner
Sigmund Freud	Albert Bandura
Carl Jung	Abraham Maslow
Alfred Adler	Carl Rogers

■ IMPORTANT TERMS

Be prepared to define the following terms (located in the margins of this chapter). Where appropriate, be prepared to describe examples.

Personality	Ego
Trait	Reality Principle
Personality (Self-Report) Inventories	Superego
Id	Psychosexual Stages
Pleasure Principle	Oedipus Complex

Electra Complex   Social Learning Theory

Defense Mechanisms   Self-Efficacy

Psychodynamic Approach   Behavioral Assessment

Collective Unconscious   Self-Actualization

Archetypes   Self-Concept

Inferiority Complex   Unconditional Positive Regard

Projective Tests

■ QUESTIONS FROM IMPORTANT IDEAS IN THIS CHAPTER

1. Describe two or three main characteristics of each of the trait, psychodynamic, behavioral, and humanistic approaches to the study of personality.

2. List some of the contributions and limitations of trait personality theories.

3. Discuss the role of conflict in Freud's approach to personality theory. What causes conflict and how is it resolved?

4. Describe how Jung, Adler, and Horney differed from Freud in their psychodynamic approaches to personality.

5. List some of the contributions and limitations of Sigmund Freud.

6. Distinguish among projective tests, objective personality tests, and behavioral assessments.

7. Discuss contributions and limitations of behavioral approaches to personality theory.

8. List some of the contributions and limitations of humanistic personality theories.

3

CHANGING HUMAN BEHAVIOR: PRINCIPLES OF LEARNING

CHAPTER OUTLINE

After reading this chapter, you should be able to:

■ Describe examples of reflexive learning in everyday life.

■ Illustrate how conditioned reflexes can be unlearned.

■ Distinguish between reflexive and operant learning.

■ Describe examples of operant learning in everyday life.

■ Illustrate how we are influenced by schedules of reinforcement.

■ Explain how our behavior comes under the control of cues in the environment.

■ Discuss modeling and observational learning and their importance to adjustment.

Does learning play a central role in your life? Most definitely! You were not born knowing how to read, write, dress yourself, turn on a TV set, or make breakfast. You were not born with a fear of muggers in a dark alley, a fondness for your close friend, or a hatred of your worst enemy. Every waking minute, our lives are filled with activities that we have learned—activities important to our survival and to our enjoyment of life. No wonder that learning is such an important topic in the psychology of adjustment.

learning
A relatively permanent change in behavior due to experience.

Most psychologists define **learning** in a general sense: a long-lasting change in behavior which is a result of experience. But let's examine this definition a little more closely. The "long-lasting change" referred to in the definition is important. Many examples of learning—like reading and arithmetic, which you learned in grade school, and skilled motor activities like riding a bicycle or driving a car—do stay with you throughout your life. However, long-lasting does not necessarily mean permanent. All of us have forgotten previously learned information, such as poems we had once memorized or rules for solving algebra problems. The replacement of "old learning" by "new learning" is also possible. The helping professions (clinical psychology, psychiatry, counseling, and the like) capitalize on this every day by guiding people to replace old, problematic behaviors with more effective new ones.

When we define learning as a "change in behavior which is a result of *experience*," we are not talking about temporary changes in behavior due to fatigue, maturation, disease, injury, or drugs. Any of these things can cause a change in behavior, but not all changes in behavior qualify as learning; learning results from experience.

In this chapter, we'll look at two kinds of learning—reflexive and operant learning—that underlie so much of what we do, say, think, and feel. We'll then describe a third type of learning, called observational learning, in which we acquire new actions by observing others. We'll also discuss applications of basic learning principles in everyday life.

Reflexive Learning

Suppose you're watching the science fiction movie, *Aliens*. Sigourney Weaver moves slowly down a dark passage, expecting an attack from an alien at any second. You begin to feel frightened, and the hair on your arms stands on end. What is the foundation of such a reaction? It represents a type of learning, but this *learning* involves your body's *unlearned* reflexes.

Many of us experience fear and excitement while watching a movie like *Aliens*. Such reactions to movies represent a type of learning that involves basic reflexes.

stimuli (plural of stimulus)

Events that can affect an organism's behavior.

unconditioned reflex

A stimulus-response sequence in which a stimulus elicits a response without prior learning.

Unlearned or unconditioned reflexes involve stimuli and responses. Events that can affect an organism are called **stimuli** (plural of **stimulus**); responses are an organism's reactions to stimuli. Sounds, smells, sights, tastes, and physical contact all can act as stimuli. An **unconditioned reflex** is a stimulus-response sequence in which a stimulus elicits a response without prior learning or conditioning. For instance, you are stirring up a pot of chili and decide it needs more spice. You pull a can of black pepper off the shelf, open it, inhale a small amount of pepper—and sneeze. The pepper was a stimulus; the sneeze was a response to the stimulus. The pepper and the sneeze together formed an unconditioned reflex. Such a reflex is inborn or *un*conditioned. Further examples of unconditioned reflexes in humans are shown in Table 3-1.

Learning a Conditioned Reflex

unconditioned stimulus

A stimulus that elicits a response without prior learning.

unconditioned response

A response elicited by a stimulus without prior learning.

conditioned reflex

A stimulus-response sequence acquired through Pavlovian conditioning; a learned reflex.

conditioned stimulus

A stimulus that elicits a response in a conditioned reflex.

conditioned response

A response elicited by a stimulus in a conditioned reflex.

Ivan Pavlov, a distinguished Russian physiologist, is generally given credit for discovering a type of learning involving unconditioned reflexes. In one of his experiments, Pavlov noted that a dog would salivate when food was presented, but it would not salivate when he presented a tone (by striking a tuning fork) (see Figure 3-1). A stimulus that elicits a response without prior learning or conditioning was referred to by Pavlov as an **unconditioned stimulus,** or US (for example, food). A response elicited by such a stimulus was called an **unconditioned response,** or UR (for example, salivation to food).

In the second part of his experiment, Pavlov paired the sound of the tone with food many times by placing a plate of food powder in front of the dog just after the tuning fork had been sounded for five seconds. Then, in the third part of his experiment, Pavlov sounded the tone for 30 seconds—but did not give the dog any food powder. The tone now caused salivation by itself (Pavlov, 1927). The salivation response to the sound of the tone seemed very much like an unconditioned reflex; after all, salivation was normally an automatic bodily response. However, it was obvious that the reflex had been learned and was not inborn. Pavlov therefore called it a **conditioned reflex** and referred to the stimulus in the conditioned reflex as a **conditioned stimulus,** or CS (for example, the tone), and the response in the conditioned reflex as a **conditioned response,** or CR (for example, salivation to the tone). This type of reflexive learning is also referred to as *classical, Pavlovian,* or *respondent* conditioning.

TABLE 3-1
A PARTIAL LIST OF UNCONDITIONED REFLEXES
Adapted from Baldwin & Baldwin, 1986.

Unconditioned Stimulus ⟶ Unconditioned Response

Digestive system
    food ⟶ salivation
    bad food ⟶ sickness, nausea
    object in esophagus ⟶ vomiting
Reproductive system
    genital stimulation ⟶ vaginal lubrication,
                    penile erection,
                    orgasm
    nipple stimulation ⟶ milk release (in lactating
                    women)
Circulatory system
    high temperature ⟶ sweating, flushing
    sudden loud noise ⟶ blanching, pounding
                    heart
Respiratory system
    irritation in nose ⟶ sneeze
    throat clogged ⟶ cough
    allergens ⟶ asthma attack
Muscular system
    low temperature ⟶ shivering
    blows or burns ⟶ withdrawal
    tap on patellar tendon ⟶ knee jerk
    light to eye ⟶ pupil constriction
    novel stimulation ⟶ reflexive orienting
Infant reflexes
    stroking the cheek ⟶ head turning
    object touches lips ⟶ sucking
    food in mouth ⟶ swallowing
    object in the hand ⟶ grasping
    head vertical, feet ⟶ stepping
      touching ground

reflexive learning

A type of learning in which two stimuli are appropriately paired, and the response elicited by one stimulus is transferred to the other.

Consider a plausible example of reflexive learning in everyday life. Let's suppose that a couple consistently make love by candlelight while playing soft music in their bedroom. On nights when they don't make love, they don't light the candles and they don't play soft music. The principle of **reflexive learning** states that if a neutral stimulus, or NS (the soft music and the candlelight in the bedroom), is closely followed by an unconditioned stimulus, or US (sexual stimulation), which elicits an unconditioned response, or UR (sexual arousal), then the previously neutral stimulus (candlelight and soft music) will also tend to elicit that response (sexual arousal). Now, when the couple light candles and turn on soft music in the bedroom, they begin to feel sexually excited.

Extinction of a Conditioned Reflex

reflexive extinction

Repeated presentation of a conditioned stimulus by itself until it loses its ability to elicit a conditioned response.

Once reflexive learning occurs, does it stay with us forever? No! Pavlov also discovered a process of "unlearning," which he referred to as **extinction.** When a tone (which had been established as a CS) was repeatedly sounded to one of his dogs without further pairings with food, the tone gradually lost its ability to elicit salivation. When a CS is presented repeatedly without further pairings with the US, the

Figure 3-1
The model for learning a conditioned reflex

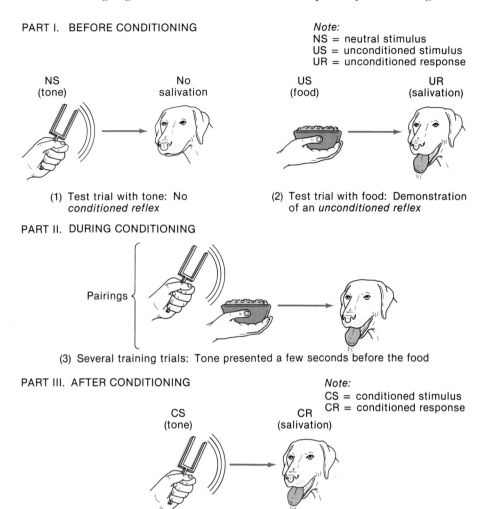

PART I. BEFORE CONDITIONING

Note:
NS = neutral stimulus
US = unconditioned stimulus
UR = unconditioned response

NS
(tone)

No
salivation

US
(food)

UR
(salivation)

(1) Test trial with tone: No
conditioned reflex

(2) Test trial with food: Demonstration
of an *unconditioned reflex*

PART II. DURING CONDITIONING

Pairings

(3) Several training trials: Tone presented a few seconds before the food

PART III. AFTER CONDITIONING

Note:
CS = conditioned stimulus
CR = conditioned response

CS
(tone)

CR
(salivation)

(4) Test trial with tone: Demonstration of a *conditioned reflex*

CS loses its ability to elicit the CR (see Figure 3-2). It's fortunate for us that such a process can happen. Let's suppose, for example, that a little boy reaches through the fence to touch a neighbor's large German shepherd just as the dog barks very loudly, scaring the child. As a function of several pairings of the loud bark (a US causing fear) with the sight of a big dog (previously a neutral stimulus), the sight of a big dog alone now causes the child to cry and tremble. Does this mean that the child will fear big dogs forever? Not necessarily. Let's suppose that the boy's parents take him to a dog show. Although there are lots of large dogs around, they've been trained to walk and sit quietly while on display. Repeated contact with these dogs helps the child overcome his fear of the sight of big dogs because reflexive extinction occurs. Many of the fears that we acquire during childhood—fear of the dark, of thunder, and so forth—undergo reflexive extinction as we grow older and encounter these events repeatedly without suffering any dire consequences.

Reflexive extinction is not limited to fears. Suppose, for example, that someone experiences numerous passionate sexual encounters with a partner who consistently uses a very distinctive perfume. After several such pairings, the perfume could become a conditioned stimulus eliciting pleasurable feelings and sexual arousal. Now let's suppose that the two people terminate their relationship. On the first few occasions that the man encounters someone wearing that particular perfume in a department store or elsewhere, the perfume might continue to elicit

Figure 3-2
The models of reflexive learning and reflexive extinction

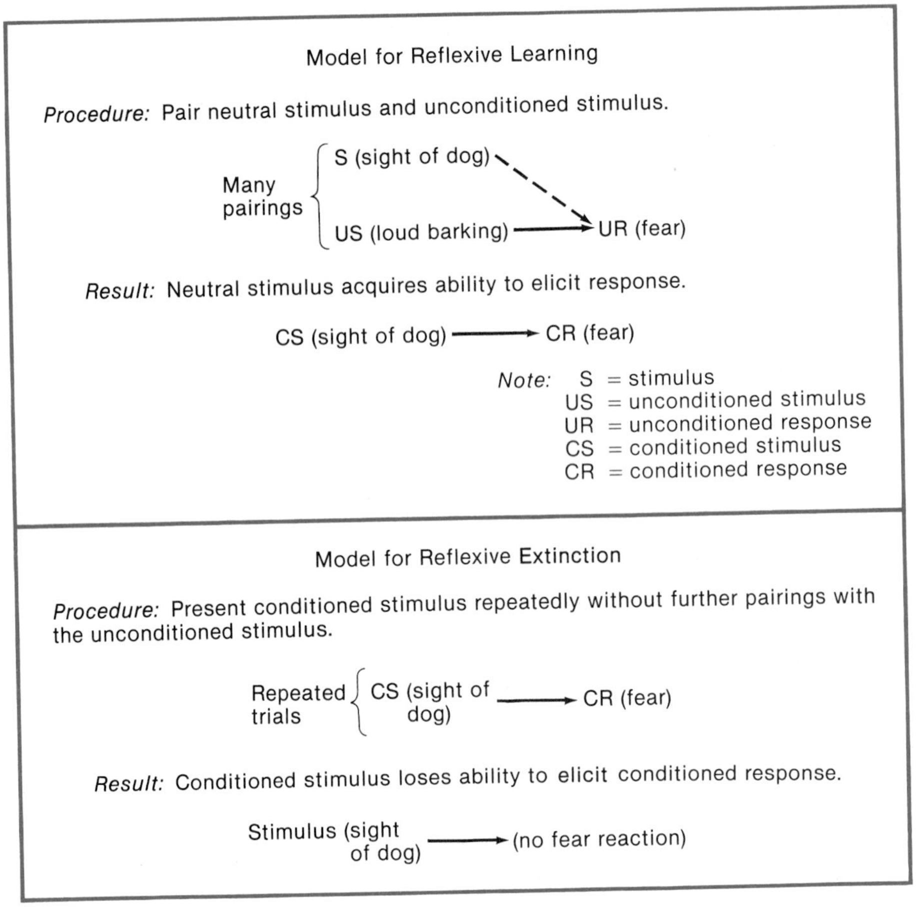

Model for Reflexive Learning

Procedure: Pair neutral stimulus and unconditioned stimulus.

Many pairings { S (sight of dog)
US (loud barking) ⟶ UR (fear)

Result: Neutral stimulus acquires ability to elicit response.

CS (sight of dog) ⟶ CR (fear)

Note: S = stimulus
US = unconditioned stimulus
UR = unconditioned response
CS = conditioned stimulus
CR = conditioned response

Model for Reflexive Extinction

Procedure: Present conditioned stimulus repeatedly without further pairings with the unconditioned stimulus.

Repeated trials { CS (sight of dog) ⟶ CR (fear)

Result: Conditioned stimulus loses ability to elicit conditioned response.

Stimulus (sight of dog) ⟶ (no fear reaction)

pleasurable feelings. After a few such occurrences—assuming that the man does not in this time have an enjoyable sexual experience with another woman who wears the same perfume—the perfume would lose its power to elicit arousal. Reflexive extinction would have occurred.

COUNTERCONDITIONING.   A conditioned response may be eliminated more effectively if a new (and very different) response is conditioned to the CS at the same time that the former conditioned response is being extinguished. This process is called counterconditioning. For example, Joseph Wolpe (1958, 1989) developed a procedure for helping people combat fear by teaching them to perform relaxation responses in the presence of situations that normally produced fear. (This procedure—systematic desensitization—is described in detail in Chapter 15.)

Counterconditioning occurs naturally in everyday life. Suppose that a child is knocked down several times by a large dog and learns to fear dogs. Then a new child moves next door and the two children become friends. The new child has an affectionate beagle that is always around when the children are playing. As the child plays with his friend and the friend's dog, some of the positive emotions elicited by the friend can become conditioned to the friend's dog. These positive conditioned emotional responses help counteract the negative conditioned emotional responses previously elicited by dogs, and thus more quickly and more effectively eliminate those responses.

Factors Influencing Reflexive Learning

Do you "shiver" in nervous anticipation at the sound of the dentist's drill? Experience "butterflies in your stomach" just before giving a talk to a group? Dread the thought of walking home alone on a dark night? Become sexually aroused watching movies that show lots of "skin"? Blush when told that your fly is undone (males) or that your blouse is unbuttoned (females)? All of these experiences are outcomes of reflexive learning. But there are a number of factors that influence the strength of a conditioned reflex in each instance. Here are several of the more important variables that influence the development of a conditioned reflex.

First, *the greater the number of pairings of a CS with a US, the greater is the ability of the CS to elicit the CR,* until the maximum strength of the conditioned reflex has been reached. Suppose that you frequently walk home at night past a small park that is not well-lit. If you are frightened several times by a stranger emerging from the dark park just as you approach, then approaching the park will elicit a stronger fear than if you had been frightened in its vicinity just once.

Second, *stronger conditioning occurs if the CS just precedes the US by up to a few seconds, rather than by a longer time or rather than following the US.* Conditioning in the latter case is difficult to attain. If a child sees a dog, and then is scared by the dog's loud barking, sight of the dog is likely to become a CS for fear as a CR. On the other hand, if the child hears loud barking, and a few seconds later sees a dog trot around the corner of a building, the fear caused by the loud barking is not likely to be transferred to the sight of the dog.

Third, *a CS acquires greater ability to elicit a CR if the CS is always paired with a given US, than if it is only occasionally paired with the US.* If our couple, for example, consistently light a candle in the bedroom just before having sex, and not at other times, then the candle is likely to become a CS eliciting sexual arousal. On the other hand, if they light a candle in the bedroom every night, but have sex there only one or two nights each week, then the soft glow of the candle in the bedroom will be a weaker CS for sexual arousal.

Fourth, *when several neutral stimuli precede a US, the stimulus that is most consistently associated with the US is the one most likely to become a strong CS.* A child, for example, may experience thunderstorms in which both dark clouds and lightning are usually followed by loud claps of thunder, which cause fear. On other occasions, the child sees dark clouds, but there is no lightning or thunder. The child will acquire a stronger fear of lightning than of the dark clouds because lightning is more consistently paired with the frightening thunder.

You can see that a variety of factors determine whether or not a conditioned response becomes attached to novel stimuli in a given situation. Additional limitations of reflexive learning are discussed in a later section.

Reflexive Learning Experiments with Humans

We've described some principles of reflexive learning and discussed how they might apply in everyday life. We've also looked at some of Pavlov's classic experiments with dogs. Now let's examine the details of two studies of reflexive learning with humans.

CONDITIONING OF EMOTIONS.   John Watson and Rosalie Rayner were interested in studying how an emotion, like fear, could be influenced by reflexive learning. They conducted a classic experiment with "Little Albert," an 11-month-old infant (Watson & Rayner, 1920). During preliminary observations, it was demonstrated that Albert was not afraid of a variety of items that were placed in his vicinity when he was playing on a rug on the floor. Watson then introduced a white rat (to which

---

Box 3-1

LIE DETECTION

An interesting application of counterconditioning underlies successful efforts of individuals to beat the "lie detector" test. The lie detector or polygraph became a fixture of U.S. law enforcement during the Chicago Gangland era of the 1930s (Biddle, 1986). It is used a million times a year or more in the United States (Lykken, 1981). In matters of national security alone, the Department of Defense and the National Security Agency conduct 21,000 lie detection tests annually (Smith, 1984). Lie detection is big business.

How Is It Supposed to Work? An underlying assumption is that lying is stressful and will cause anxiety. Another assumption is that the anxiety can be detected through appropriate physiological measures including respiration, perspiration, and heart rate. Thus, a polygraph indicates anxiety level by recording these three body reactions to specific questions.

Most polygraphists ask three types of questions: irrelevant questions ("Is today Tuesday?"), relevant questions (a suspected bank robber might be asked, "Were you in the First National Bank last Monday?"), and control questions that are likely to cause more anxiety than irrelevant questions ("Before the age of 20, did you ever take anything that wasn't yours?"). Many people may answer control questions with a little white lie, and it is assumed that they therefore will show a physiological reaction to such questions. Two comparisons can then be made. If physiological responses to potentially relevant questions are less intense than to the control questions, the examiner infers that the person

was telling the truth on the relevant questions. If physiological responses are approximately the same to the relevant and irrelevant questions, the examiner also assumes that the testee was telling the truth on the relevant questions.

How Well Does It Work? Several studies suggest that the reliability of the lie detector is not sufficiently strong to justify its widespread use. A 1983 study of polygraph validity for the Congressional Office of Technology Assessment (OTA) indicated that accuracy was nowhere near the 95 percent level claimed by many polygraphists (U.S. Congress, 1983).

Not only is there concern about the extent to which lie detector tests can detect liars. There is also the danger that they can lead to the false accusation of people who are telling the truth. That is, hardened criminals may be able to lie and remain relaxed, while innocent individuals might respond with increased nervousness to the implied accusation of the relevant questions. How often could this occur? Kleinmuntz and Szucko (1984) presented polygraph data from 100 individuals to polygraph experts. Fifty of the individuals were theft suspects who later confessed to being guilty, and the other 50 were suspects who were later proved to be innocent (by confessions of others). According to Kleinmuntz and Szucko, almost 25 percent of the guilty would have been declared innocent. More disconcerting is the finding that more than one third of the innocent suspects would have been declared guilty.

Can the Lie Detector Be Beaten? Yes it can.

Albert had previously shown no fear) and, while Albert was watching the rat closely, Watson banged a steel bar with a hammer just behind Albert's head. The loud noise caused Albert to startle, cry, and exhibit other fearful behavior. After a total of seven pairings of the loud noise within the sight of the rat, over two separate sessions approximately one week apart, Albert showed a very strong fear reaction to the rat. Whenever the rat appeared, Albert cried, trembled, and showed the facial expression for fear. When other "furry" items were introduced, to which Albert had previously shown no fear, Albert's fear had spread to these items as well. In particular, this fear generalized to a rabbit, a dog, a sealskin coat, and a Santa

Douglas G. Williams, a former police polygraphist who has conducted a personal campaign against lie detection, teaches people to beat the lie detector by helping them recognize the various types of test questions—relevant, irrelevant, and control—and then to alter their physiological responses to such questions (Biddle, 1986). In other words, he teaches them counterconditioning. Recommended strategies include breathing slowly and rhythmically to relevant questions and then departing from this breathing pattern when a control question comes along. To a control question, the subject might pant rapidly or hold his or her breath. Another strategy is to achieve a momentary elevation of blood pressure to control questions by tightening the sphincter muscles for several seconds. According to Williams, "If you can control your bowels, you can control your test results" (Biddle, 1986).

Claus mask. Unfortunately, Albert's parents removed Albert from the hospital (where the experiments were conducted) before Watson and Rayner could decondition the infant's fear. However, subsequent experiments by Jones (1924) followed up some of Watson's suggestions and clearly demonstrated that fear reactions like Albert's could be successfully eliminated by reflexive extinction. In our time, it would be considered cruel and unethical to subject infants to aversive stimuli for experimental purposes. Procedural questions about the Watson and Rayner study have also been raised (Harris, 1979). Nevertheless, the finding that fears and other emotions are influenced by reflexive learning is well established.

Box 3-2

Explaining Death by Overdose in Drug Addicts

In any given year, approximately 1 percent of all heroin addicts die from drug overdose (Maurer & Vogel, 1973). Mysteriously, however, the fatal dosage that causes many of these deaths is no greater than that used by the victims on many previous occasions (Reed, 1980). How can a drug dosage once tolerated by the body suddenly cause death? Let's see how Pavlovian conditioning helped scientists solve this mystery.

First, let's consider the physical effects of drugs like morphine and heroin. One immediate effect of such drugs is a temporary feeling of euphoria, the drug "high." But there is another effect—a protective mechanism that has developed through evolution. When a foreign substance enters the body, the body compensates by producing an "opposite" substance. For example, injection of an opiate such as heroin triggers a compensatory response—the production of anti-opiates (Snyder, 1984). It is common knowledge that in order to reproduce the same high, an addict must take larger and larger doses of heroin. The explanation for this seems to involve anti-opiates.

How is Pavlovian conditioning involved in this process? Psychologist Shephard Siegel reasoned this way. Injection of heroin (an opiate) as a US causes the production of anti-opiates as one of the URs. Aspects of the normal environment

(friends, a specific room) where the individual typically "shoots up" are paired with the heroin. These environmental cues become CS's eliciting the anti-opiate response as a CR. Now when the heroin addict enters the room where he or she usually takes the drug, the environmental cues (CS's) elicit the body's anti-opiate compensatory response (CR) even *before* the addict has a chance to "shoot-up." When the addict finally inserts the needle and takes the drug, the anti-opiate response is already well underway and therefore the drug produces less of a high. The next time, the addict is likely to take a larger dose.

Now let's consider what might happen if an addict takes heroin in a different, new environment. Even though the addict's dose might be the same as in the past, this new environment would not provide any CS's to elicit the body's strong anti-opiate reaction (which now occurs mainly in response to the familiar drug-taking environment) before the heroin gets into the bloodstream. The addict's standard dose (because it is not encountered by the anti-opiates it normally meets within the body) might have a much stronger effect on the body, perhaps causing death. In other words, stimuli previously associated with the drug (friends, a specific room) were not present to elicit an "anti-drug" or "tolerance" response to compete with the

---

MAKING WORDS "UNPLEASANT."   Have you ever wondered why some words "have a nice ring to them" while there are other words that you just don't like to hear? The answer might lie with reflexive learning. Consider the following experiment. A group of college students were asked to memorize a list of words that were presented to them one word at a time. The word *large* appeared several times on the list. After each presentation of the word *large,* subjects in the experimental group were given a mild electric shock or presented with a loud sound. The shock and the sound were US's that elicited mild anxiety. The anxiety was measured by a galvanic skin response (GSR), an increase in the electric conductivity of the skin that occurs during a sweat gland reaction. GSR was recorded by placing two electrodes on the palm of a hand. A control group received the same number of shocks and sounds, but these were never paired with the word *large*. At the end of the experiment, the word *large* was presented without shock or sound. With subjects

effects of the drug. In the absence of these stimuli (when the addict shot up in a new location), the tolerance response failed to occur; the addict's body was overwhelmed by an unchallenged stream of opiates, and, in some cases, the addict was killed by an amount of the drug that had previously been tolerated.

To test this view, Siegel (1984) interviewed heroin addicts who had experienced overdoses and been saved by emergency medical treatment. Seventy percent of those interviewed indicated that, while the dose taken was not unusually large, it had been taken in unfamiliar surroundings. Basic research with rats also supports this interpretation. Siegel and his colleagues (1982) gave repeated heroin injections to a group of rats. Injections were always given in the same room so that environmental cues might become CS's for a "tolerance" response. All of the rats were then given an "overdose," an amount that would normally kill a rat without prior heroin experience. Half of the rats were given the overdose injection in the same room as before. The other half received their overdose in a different room. Death due to overdose occurred twice as often among the rats that received the overdose injection in a different room.

in the experimental group, but not the control group, the word *large* had become a CS eliciting the GSR. Moreover, when subjects were asked to rate the unpleasantness of the meaning of several of the words, including the word *large,* experimental subjects rated *large* as much more unpleasant than did control subjects (Staats et al., 1963). Thus, you can see how reflexive learning might explain your reactions to certain words (like *cancer*) or even to a single letter (like a "D" on your term paper). These reactions may contribute to the meaning of words, at least on a personal level (Staats, 1963, 1968; Tyron & Cicero, 1989).

We have described just a few of the many applications of reflexive learning to humans. Additional applications involve conditioning of tastes, allergies, immune system function, reactions to drugs, sexual arousal, nausea, blood pressure, thoughts, and emotions, to name a few. Some of these applications are described in later chapters.

Limitations of Reflexive Learning

Can anyone be conditioned to respond to anything? Experiments by Pavlov and later followers seemed to indicate that just about any stimulus could be readily established as a CS in just about any species. But there are important exceptions. Some species have evolved to allow more rapid reflexive learning with certain types of neutral stimuli than with others (Garcia & Koelling, 1966). Rats, for example, are foragers. Because they will eat almost anything, the probability is high that they will eat something that might poison them. From an evolutionary point of view, rats that evolve with a great sensitivity to anything that makes them sick are rats that will be more likely to survive. Rats who are easily conditioned to taste as a CS are, then, less likely to be poisoned. And rats are more easily conditioned to the taste of food as a CS than to the sight of their food. Birds, on the other hand, rely greatly on their vision. It's not surprising that it is easier to condition them to the color of food than to its taste (Wilcoxin et al., 1971).

What about humans? Are we biologically predisposed to be more readily conditioned to some neutral stimuli than to others? The jury is still out on that one. However, some researchers say yes. Some experiments on learning fears, for example, have shown that humans are very quick to learn fears to stimuli that may have posed a threat to our survival during our evolution, such as snakes, insects, and heights, while we are much slower to learn fears to stimuli that were nonthreatening in our history, such as pictures of flowers (Hugdahl & Ohman, 1977; Ohman et al., 1984).

The type of learning studied by Pavlov involves reflexes—responses that are inborn and involuntary, like salivating in response to food or shivering in a cold wind. This type of learning can explain, for example, why the smell of your neighbor's steak sizzling on the barbecue might cause your stomach to growl. But while Pavlov opened our eyes to a very important form of learning, clearly many of our learned actions involve more than just involuntary responses. What about walking across the street? That's not a reflex. And what about reading, studying, talking on the phone, or driving a car? These behaviors are the result of an entirely different kind of learning, learning that has to do with voluntary behavior. This form of learning was referred to as operant conditioning by B. F. Skinner (1938).

Do you think birds of prey could be conditioned more easily to the *sight* of their food as a CS, or to the way their food *tastes*?

Operant Learning

operant behavior
Behavior that operates on the environment to generate consequences, and that is in turn controlled by those consequences.

operant conditioning
The modification of operant behavior by its consequences.

positive reinforcer
An event which, when presented immediately following a behavior, causes the behavior to increase in frequency.

positive reinforcement
Principle that states: If, in a given situation, a response is immediately followed by a positive reinforcer, then that response is more likely to reoccur in a similar situation.

Reflexes! That's what Pavlovian learning is all about—automatic responses to prior stimuli. But B. F. Skinner was interested in studying behavior that appeared to be voluntary rather than reflexive; behavior that was influenced by its consequences (rewards and punishers) rather than by prior stimuli (CS's and US's). Skinner (1953) referred to such activity as **operant behavior. Operant conditioning** is a type of learning in which behavior is modified by its consequences. One important type of consequence that influences our behavior is referred to as positive reinforcement.

Positive Reinforcement

An event which, when presented immediately after a behavior, causes the behavior to increase in frequency is called a **positive reinforcer.** Positive reinforcers play a central role in operant conditioning. In less technical terms, people sometimes think of a positive reinforcer as a "reward." In conjunction with the definition of positive reinforcer, the principle called **positive reinforcement** states this: If, in a given situation, someone does something that is immediately followed by a positive reinforcer, then that person is more likely to do the same thing again when she or he next encounters a similar situation.

Although everyone has a commonsense understanding of positive reinforcers, very few people are aware of just how frequently we are influenced by these reinforcers each day. Consider the following examples:

Response	*Naturally Reinforcing Consequence*
You *wave* to the driver in the next lane to pull in front of your car.	The driver nods "thanks" while turning into your lane of traffic.
A child in a department store *screams,* "I want that toy!"	The embarrassed parent buys the toy for the child.
When your ballpoint pen doesn't work while taking an exam, you *shake* it up and down.	Your pen starts working again.
At a party, your date ignores you. You become jealous and angry, and *leave* the party.	Your date immediately follows and showers you with attention.
A student *looks* out the window during a boring lecture.	The student sees a squirrel chasing another squirrel up a tree.

No one was deliberately applying the principle of positive reinforcement in the above examples. The reinforcing consequences just naturally followed the responses. In each of the examples above, it might take several repetitions before there would be an obvious increase in the reinforced response. That is, after shaking your ballpoint pen seems to get the pen working on several separate occasions, you markedly increase your pen-shaking whenever confronted by a ballpoint pen that doesn't work. Nevertheless, the effect is still there. Every time we do something, no matter what it is, there are consequences that "turn us on," "turn us off," or don't affect us one way or the other. Think about what you have done in the past hour or the past day, and think of the immediate consequences of some of those activities. Can you identify any positive reinforcers?

Conditioned and Unconditioned Reinforcers

We are influenced by some reinforcers naturally, without being taught, because of our genetic structure and our biological needs. These reinforcers are called *unconditioned (or primary) reinforcers,* and include such things as food for a hungry

Why is it that money is such a powerful generalized conditioned reinforcer?

person, water for a thirsty person, warmth, and later in life, sexual contact. Other events become reinforcers because of our learning experiences. These are things that we learn to like and appreciate. Particular types of books, favorite television programs, your taste in clothes and music, are what we call *conditioned (or secondary) reinforcers.* These are stimuli that acquire reinforcing power through their association with other reinforcers. If people consistently compliment you for wearing your hair in a short style, the appearance of short hairstyles will acquire reinforcing value for you. Any conditioned reinforcer that is paired with many different kinds of reinforcers becomes a *generalized reinforcer.* Early in life, for example, parents feed, wash, play with, and are otherwise associated with meeting their infants' needs. In this way, adult attention becomes a powerful generalized reinforcer. Similarly, money is a powerful generalized reinforcer. A $1 bill has value for us but it is certainly *not* an unconditioned reinforcer—as anyone can prove by trying to eat, drink, or build adequate shelter out of a $1 bill. Money acquires its value as experiences teach us that it can be exchanged for food, clothing, shelter, transportation, entertainment, and other reinforcers.

Learning without Awareness

An interesting thing about reinforcers is that they affect our behavior whether or not we are aware of them (Greenspoon, 1955). For example, a problem frequently reported by university students is that they get tired fairly quickly when they are studying at home or in the dorms. Such students usually report a typical pattern. The student sits down and begins reading or working on material for a class. After a certain period of time, the student begins to feel drowsy and decides to take a break. The break usually consists of making a cup of coffee and/or something to eat, watching a few minutes of television, or phoning a friend. After the break (which is sometimes very extended), the student returns to work. But after a relatively short period of time, the student becomes drowsy and the pattern repeats itself.

Let's examine this situation. What are the immediate positive consequences of the initial desirable behavior of working continuously in an alert fashion? None. Rather, the individual simply continues working until beginning to feel drowsy. On the other hand, what are the consequences of the individual feeling drowsy? Obviously, a very reinforcing break period featuring food, drink, entertainment, and friends! In other words, the student is following the worst possible course of action. Feeling drowsy in a study situation is being highly reinforced by food, drink, and entertainment, whereas working effectively does not lead to immediate reinforcing consequences.

Whether or not we recognize positive reinforcers at work affecting our actions, the positive reinforcers still exert control over us: In this case, the student feels increasingly drowsy at shorter and shorter intervals, keeps taking more breaks, and realizes the assignment at hand is not going to be finished on time—but the student has no idea what went wrong! Can we regain control of situations like this by identifying the positive reinforcers at work and applying them differently? Definitely. Once the student identifies the positive reinforcer in this situation (an enjoyable break) and the behavior it reinforces (drowsiness), the student can alter this pattern. An effective strategy here would be for the student to take a break earlier than usual. If the student can study normally for 15 minutes without feeling drowsy, then at about the 13-minute mark, *while still working effectively,* the student should take a brief break. The break, then, is used to reinforce effective work—not drowsiness. Over a period of time, the duration of the effective studying can be increased. By recognizing—and altering—what was once a hidden pattern of positive reinforcement, the student gains control over the situation . . . and has a better chance of getting the next assignment finished on time.

Operant Extinction

operant extinction
The withholding of a reinforcer following a previously reinforced response, and the subsequent decrease in the behavior.

Positive reinforcement is a powerful technique for strengthening behavior. But what happens when a response isn't followed by the usual reinforcer? Enter **operant extinction.** The operant extinction *procedure* refers to the withholding

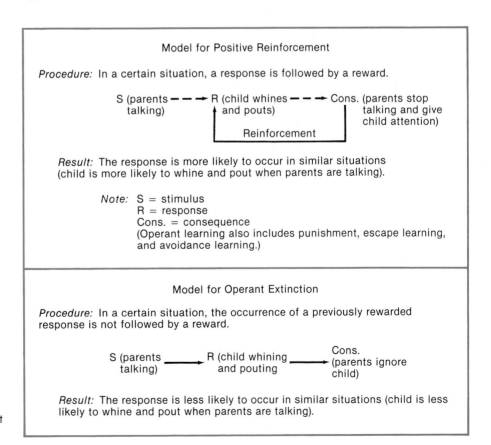

Figure 3-3
The models of operant learning and operant extinction

of a positive reinforcer following a previously reinforced response. The *effect* is that the response decreases in frequency when reinforcement for that response ceases. Of course, the effects of an operant extinction procedure are not likely to be noticed immediately. If you have been positively reinforced (by witty and funny jokes) for watching David Letterman's monologue over several months, then your Letterman-watching is not likely to be reduced after you see him do just one dull monologue containing only boring jokes. However, if the boring monologues continue over several nights, then your watching behavior may decrease. Poor David, in this case a victim of your operant extinction.

Shaping

shaping

The reinforcement of successive approximations to a final desired response.

If a behavior occurs once in a while, then it can be strengthened by following it with positive reinforcement. But what if you want to increase a behavior that doesn't presently occur, such as teaching a friend to play tennis? And if you have worked with beginners in any field, you will know that they rarely execute a skill perfectly the first time they try to perform. If you want to improve beginners' skills, you must be aware of their present level of skill and reinforce any small improvements. This technique is sometimes called **shaping** (see also Box 10-3). You reinforce "approximations" of, or increasingly close attempts at, correct execution, one small behavior at a time, until you have the desired response. Before you know it, your friend will be giving you serious competition on the court (Buzas & Ayllon, 1981).

Shaping is so common in everyday life that most people aren't even aware of it. Becoming a better dancer, learning to shoot a basketball more accurately, changing gears smoothly when driving a car with a stick shift—all involve shaping. Sometimes the shaping procedure is applied systematically, sometimes nonsystematically. Nonsystematically, for instance, the natural reactions of others gradually shape an immigrant's pronunciation of English words. Sometimes self-shaping occurs when, for example, you gradually perfect your method for making the world's best popcorn.

Chaining

In shaping, some aspect of the behavior (form, force, amount, speed) is gradually changed over time. In a procedure called *chaining,* an individual is taught to perform a series of steps that can be linked together, one after the other. An effective way to do this with humans is to have them practice each of the steps on every trial, and to provide a reward at the end of the entire sequence. David Test and his colleagues, for example, taught severely retarded adolescents to use the public telephone by proceeding through the steps of locating the telephone in the environment, finding the correct number, choosing the correct change, picking up the receiver, listening for the dial tone, and so on. Across trials in which each step was practiced, the teachers gradually faded out instructional help as the various steps in the sequence were mastered (Test et al., 1990). The result was a behavioral chain—a consistent stimulus-response sequence that terminated in a reinforcer. Many behavioral sequences that we perform in everyday life are behavioral chains. Playing a particular song on a musical instrument, following a shopping list at the local supermarket, and brushing your teeth in the morning are all behavioral chains. In a behavioral chain, each response provides the cues that lead to the next response. The final response in the chain produces a reinforcer. In the behavioral chain of making a sandwich, setting out all of the ingredients provides the cues for spreading some mayo on the slices of bread. Completion of that response provides the cues for laying on a slice of Swiss cheese and some bean sprouts. The next step is to lay the top slice of bread on the sandwich, which provides the cue for cutting it. The final response—eating the sandwich—produces the reinforcer.

Schedules of Reinforcement

We've discussed what happens when positive reinforcers are used continuously to shape behavior and to develop behavioral chains; we've also looked at what happens when positive reinforcers are withheld (operant extinction).

But what happens if you only reinforce a response every now and then? After all, it's often impractical to promptly reinforce each occurrence of a desired response. Real-life activities aren't reinforced this way; they are reinforced irregularly, sometimes late, and often not at all. You don't always get good grades after studying. You have to work for an hour before you earn an hourly wage, and you probably won't get your paycheck until the end of the week. Fortunately, we've learned that, sooner or later in such cases, our persistence generally pays off. Experiments on the effects of various strategies for rewarding behavior have been studied under the topic of **schedules of reinforcement** (Martin & Pear, 1992). In addition to a continuous schedule, in which every occurrence of a specified response is reinforced, there are many types of partial or intermittent schedules in which responses are reinforced only occasionally. Research on intermittent schedules of reinforcement has revealed two surprising results: (1) Individuals are likely to work much more consistently on certain intermittent schedules; and (2) a behavior that has been reinforced intermittently is likely to take much longer to extinguish than a behavior that has been continuously reinforced. If a behavior takes a long time to extinguish, we say that it is *resistant to extinction.*

One type of intermittent reinforcement is called *fixed ratio* reinforcement: Reinforcement occurs after a fixed number of responses. If an industrial worker, for example, is paid a certain amount of money for 25 completed parts (often called piece-rate pay), then that worker is being reinforced on a fixed ratio schedule. Psychologists would refer to this particular example as an FR (fixed ratio)-25 schedule. A student who writes 5 pages of a paper before listening to a favorite piece of music is performing on an FR-5 schedule, and so on. In general, fixed ratio reinforcement generates high rates of responding, and high resistance to extinction.

schedules of reinforcement

Arrangements between behavior and rewarding consequences.

Intermittent reinforcement is highly effective in maintaining persistent patterns of behavior.

A *variable ratio* is like a fixed ratio schedule, except that the number of responses required to produce reinforcement changes unpredictably from one reinforcer to the next. Slot machines and other gambling devices are programmed according to variable ratio schedules such that gamblers have no way of predicting how many responses they must make (that is, how many coins they must put in the slot) for reinforcement (hitting the jackpot). Casino managements may not know the term *variable ratio schedule,* but they definitely understand the principle—and how to profit from it. Examples of variable ratio schedules in everyday life can also be found in the behavior of commissioned salespeople. While good salespeople rely on skill, not luck, they still never know which client will "buy." An insurance salesperson who gets a sale about every 10 clients is working on what psychologists call a VR (variable ratio)-10 schedule. That is, although she can never predict exactly when she will make a sale, she knows that her average success rate is 1 in 10. Sometimes she makes 2 or more sales in a row. At other times, she may have to call on 20 or more clients before she makes a sale. Again, because success (reinforcement) can come at any time, the salesperson probably works long hours and hurries between clients. Each new client could be "the one."

Some reinforcement schedules require that you make only one response to be reinforced, but your response has to be made after a set, or fixed, time. These schedules are known, appropriately enough, as *fixed interval* (FI) schedules. Consider, for example, the behavior of catching a bus. City buses (giving rides as reinforcement) usually run on a regular schedule—say every 20 minutes (the fixed interval). An individual may arrive at the bus stop early, just before the bus is due, or just as it arrives—and be reinforced by catching the bus. However, the bus will wait only a limited time—perhaps 30 seconds. If the individual is not at the bus stop within this limited period of time, the bus goes on and the individual must wait for the next one. Technically, psychologists would call this an FI schedule with a limited hold: Behavior is reinforced only if it occurs after a fixed period of time, but it must also occur no later than another (brief) period of time.

Part of the fun in studying psychology is analyzing our own behavior—and finding hidden patterns—in everyday life. The week before writing this chapter, one of the authors had just returned from a trip and arrived at his home town airport. While waiting for his luggage to pop out of the luggage carousel, he looked around at the other passengers, all of whom were staring intently at the spot where the luggage would first appear. Suddenly it hit him—*variable interval* reinforcement. On a variable interval schedule, a response (looking) is reinforced (your luggage appears) after some period of time, but the period of time is unpredictable. The "looking" behavior, consequently, is very persistent. Telephoning a friend whose line is busy is also reinforced on a variable interval schedule. The line is busy but you keep calling over and over—after all, your friend could hang up at any moment and free the line. Watching television programs, movies, and sporting events are further examples of behavior reinforced on variable interval schedules (and in each case, with a limited hold—the enjoyable scene lasts only for a brief time).

It is fortunate for us that our behavior becomes quite persistent when reinforced intermittently. While you might be able to arrange for desirable behavior on an adjustment program to be rewarded each time that it occurs during the beginning of a program, it is often impossible or impractical to continue to reinforce each occurrence of a desired response. One solution to this problem lies in intermittent reinforcement. Once a particular skill or behavior has been mastered, or occurs at the desired frequency, then the schedule of reinforcement can gradually be made more and more intermittent. Not only is this more practical, but it will make the desirable behavior more resistant to extinction.

Stimulus Control

The operant conditioning procedures we've looked at so far explain how behavior is increased, maintained, or decreased. However, a newly acquired behavior is valuable only if it occurs at the right times and in the appropriate situations. For instance, at an intersection it is desirable if you stop the car when the light is red, not when the light is green. Executing a perfect double back-flip will earn you valuable points in a gymnastics routine, but it probably won't have the same effect in your first corporate-level job interview. As we acquire new behaviors, we also learn to produce those behaviors at the right time and place. How do we learn to do this successfully? A key factor in this process is something psychologists call *stimulus control.*

Let's consider how stimulus control comes about. Suppose that you have just moved into a dormitory and the person across the hall seems quite friendly. One day when returning from class, you notice that the person's door is partly open. You knock on the door, are asked to enter, and enjoy a very pleasant conversation. This happens several times. At other times, when your neighbor's door is closed (but you know the neighbor is in there), you knock on the door, seeking conversation. Your neighbor, however, very brusquely indicates that she wants to study. After several trials, you learn to knock on your neighbor's door to seek enjoyable conversation only when the door is partly open. This sequence of events is diagrammed below.

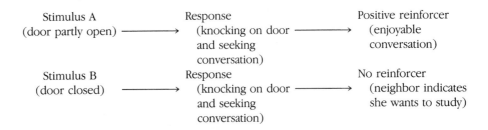

stimulus control

The tendency for a certain stimulus to be consistently followed by a certain behavior.

In general terms, when a behavior is reinforced in the presence of certain stimuli but not others, those specific stimuli begin to exert control over the occurrence of the behavior. When specific responses are linked to specific stimuli, we say that **stimulus control** exists. Put another way, stimulus control refers to events (stimuli) that direct, guide, or control our behavior toward particular consequences. You have just placed money into a vending machine and you are looking for your favorite candy bar. You see the name of that bar beside a particular button, and you press that button. The sign exerted stimulus control over your behavior.

While some stimuli are consistent predictors that a particular behavior will be reinforced, other stimuli are consistent predictors that a particular behavior will not be reinforced. An "out of order" sign on the vending machine is a cue that the behavior of inserting money into the machine will not be reinforced. Thus, stimuli not only guide what we do, but they also guide what we *don't* do.

What stimuli control some of your operant behaviors? What cues control your behavior of rising out of bed in the morning and getting dressed? (Perhaps daylight in the window? The sound of an alarm clock?) What are some of the cues that control your social interactions? A comment, a glance, a touch, a smile—all can exert stimulus control over the way you respond to others.

Stimulus Generalization

So far, things sound pretty mechanistic, don't they? A stimulus turns on; a behavior occurs. But we know that's not the way operant behavior works in the world at large. We do not respond like C3PO in *Star Wars:* Human beings are not robots. Rather, it seems that if we are operantly conditioned to one particular stimulus, we become more likely to respond to a whole range of similar stimuli. For example, an infant learns to say "doggy" to a furry, four-legged creature with floppy ears and a friendly bark. Later, the infant sees a different kind of dog and says "doggy." Still later, the infant sees a pony and again says "doggy." Both are instances of what is called stimulus generalization. **Stimulus generalization** occurs when a behavior becomes more probable in the presence of one stimulus or situation as a result of having been reinforced in the presence of other, similar stimuli. (With training, the child will learn to discriminate and tell the difference between ponies and dogs, a process called *stimulus discrimination*—responding differently to two different stimuli.)

stimulus generalization

When a behavior becomes more probable in the presence of a given stimulus, it also becomes more probable in the presence of similar stimuli.

Stimulus generalization is important to all of us in everyday living. Life would be very odd, not to mention dangerous, if you could not generalize newly learned behaviors: You would have to "relearn" the dangers of fire by touching every new candle, match, hot stove, or roaring campfire; when driving, you'd learn to stop safely at one red light and have to be told to stop at each new red traffic light; you'd learn to dance to one song but never realize that you could dance to others; you'd learn to order (and eat) a vanilla ice-cream cone but never realize you could also order chocolate chip, strawberry, or double mocha fudge. Stimulus generalization is also important to successful adjustment. Suppose that you get very nervous before exams. Following the procedures described in Chapter 15, you learn to practice relaxation exercises. Obviously, that accomplishment is valuable to you only if you can also apply the relaxation procedures in the classroom when taking an exam. That is, the relaxation response must be generalized, or show stimulus generalization.

Punishment

By this point, we've spent a fair amount of time examining operant conditioning in action, and emphasizing the important role that positive reinforcers (applied in any number of ways and schedules) play in this form of learning. There is, of course, a

Although punishment is often used, it can have serious side effects.

punisher
An event which, when presented immediately following a behavior, causes the behavior to decrease in frequency.

principle of punishment
A principle that states: If, in a given situation, a behavior is immediately followed by a punisher, then that behavior is less likely to occur again in similar situations.

flip side to the positive reinforcers that are used to encourage, or increase, certain behaviors: punishers, which are meant to discourage, or decrease the frequency of, specific behaviors. Like positive reinforcement, punishment has affected our learning throughout life. As infants, the bruises from a few falls helped to teach us better balance while learning to walk. A light swat on your behind from concerned parents may have taught you not to run into the street during heavy traffic. And we've all had our behavior affected by angry words, revoked privileges, or ridicule.

Technically, a **punisher** is an event which, when presented immediately following a behavior, causes the behavior to decrease in frequency. Associated with the concept of a punisher is the **principle of punishment,** which states: If, in a given situation, somebody does something that is immediately followed by a punisher, then that person is less likely to do the same thing again when he or she next encounters a similar situation. It is impossible for us to totally escape the influence of punishers in everyday life. But should punishment be *deliberately used* to decrease problem behaviors of individuals? Many people believe that punishment is used far too often in child raising, in formalized education, between peers and spouses, and as a form of societal control. As a behavior management technique, it leaves a great deal to be desired and has a number of troubling side effects. For that reason, we must be cautious about the deliberate use of punishment in everyday life.

WHAT ARE SIDE EFFECTS OF PUNISHMENT?　First, punishment can cause frustration and aggressive behavior on the part of the person being punished (Axelrod & Apsche, 1983). We should not be surprised to observe individuals who have just been punished attacking other individuals. Second, strong punishment can produce undesirable emotional side effects, such as crying and general fearfulness. Third, punishment teaches individuals to avoid or escape sources of punishment, and these tendencies may be more undesirable than the initial problem. Students may learn to cheat to avoid punishment for being wrong. People may lie to avoid the punishment that follows telling the truth. Fourth, punishment does not teach any new behavior. It tells us what not to do, rather than focusing constructively on what we should do instead. Fifth, if individuals see others administering punishment or showing aggression, they are more likely to exhibit aggression themselves, particularly if they see that there are rewards for behaving this way. And finally, punishment may become addictive to the user. Because it can result in quick suppression of undesirable behavior (and relieve the punisher's frustration or anger), it can tempt the user to rely heavily on it and to neglect the use of positive reinforcement for desirable behavior.

There is no doubt that punishment is an important principle of operant learning. It is obviously involved in teaching us to survive in everyday living. The immediate consequence of touching a hot stove, for example, teaches us not to do this again in the future. There are also situations where deliberate use of punishment by individuals to influence others is justified. For example, in a study in Minneapolis, overnight arrest of men who beat their wives was a relatively effective strategy for decreasing this offense (Sherman & Berk, 1984). Certainly most would agree that punishment should continue to be used in such cases. In areas of personal adjustment, however, because punishment is so easy to abuse, and because other learning principles (like reinforcing desirable behaviors) can be used to decrease problems, you should use punishment only as a last resort.

Escape and Avoidance Learning

In many situations, we have learned a response that enables us to escape from an aversive event. For example, in the presence of a bright light, we have learned to escape the intensity of light by closing our eyes or squinting. When a room is too cold, we escape the chill by throwing another log on the fireplace. When it's too hot, we escape the heat by turning on the air conditioner. If your roommate, while trying to study, frowns at you when you talk loudly on the telephone, you might talk more quietly to escape the frowning.

escape learning

Strengthening of a response because it leads to the removal of a punisher.

The principle of **escape learning** (or escape conditioning) states that we learn to do things that terminate aversive events, or that allow us to escape them. Note that escape learning is the opposite of punishment: In punishment, the likelihood of certain behavior is *decreased* as a result of *presenting* a punisher after past instances of that behavior. In escape learning, the likelihood of certain behavior is *increased* as a result of it having terminated or *removed* a punisher in the past. For example, aspirin ends your headache and you are now more likely to take aspirin for future headaches.

avoidance learning

Strengthening of a response because it prevents the occurrence of a punisher.

In addition to learning behavior that enables us to escape from an unpleasant event that has already occurred, we also learn behaviors that prevent unpleasant events from occurring at all. This latter type of learning is called **avoidance learning.** In many classrooms, children learn to give the right answers primarily to avoid the teacher's ridicule or anger and to avoid poor grades. Our legal system seems to be based largely on avoidance learning. We pay our taxes to avoid going to jail. We put money in parking meters to avoid getting a ticket. We pay parking fines in order to avoid a court summons. Avoidance learning refers to a procedure in which a response prevents the occurrence of an aversive stimulus. Responses acquired through avoidance learning often show great persistence. Why? Imagine that you are participating in an experiment on avoidance learning. You are in a room with two chairs and are told that you must sit on one or the other. A bell over your chair rings, five seconds pass, and you receive a mild electric shock. You move to the other chair. Now a bell rings over that chair, five seconds pass, and you receive another shock. You quickly realize that you can avoid these shocks simply by changing chairs each time that a "warning" bell rings. Half an hour later, each time the warning bell rings, you move to the other chair to avoid the shock. Or are you avoiding it? What you don't realize is that the electric shocks were discontinued 20 minutes earlier. You have been changing chairs to the sound of the warning bell for no particular reason . . . well, no reason except the persistence of avoidance learning. Avoidance learning is persistent, largely because it involves avoiding *anticipated* punishment—which may or may not actually be forthcoming.

Because escape and avoidance learning involve punishers or aversive stimulation, they suffer from many of the same disadvantages as punishment. An individual tends to avoid or escape any situation or person associated with the use of punishers. If a coach hollers at, criticizes, and ridicules athletes, the athletes may show improved skills primarily to avoid or escape the wrath of the coach, but they're also likely to avoid the coach away from the athletic field. And if the coaching tactics become too aversive, some team members might quit the sport entirely. As another example, you probably know people who often are quite antagonistic during conversations, negative in their outlook, and frequently in a bad mood. Chances are that you avoid such people.

To summarize this section, punishment, escape, and avoidance learning are categories of operant conditioning because they are additional ways (beyond positive reinforcement and extinction) that behavior can be modified by its consequences. Behaviors that are punished tend to decrease. Behaviors that enable an individual to escape or avoid aversive events tend to be strengthened. Deliberate use of punishment, escape, and avoidance learning (generally referred to as aversive control) may be defensible in certain cases, for instance, as a deterrent to crime. But these procedures also have a number of undesirable side effects. Therefore we should plan our adjustment strategies by emphasizing positive reinforcement for desirable behavior.

Observational Learning, Imitation, and Modeling

Pavlov studied reflexes—automatic responses to prior stimuli. Skinner studied voluntary behavior—the control of behavior by its consequences. And while both of these types of learning are important, there is a third kind of learning—a kind of learning that is especially important to humans—referred to as observational learning and studied extensively by Albert Bandura and his colleagues. Observational learning refers to the ability to learn by observing others, without being reinforced for doing so (Bandura, 1977; 1986). Let's examine this area further.

modeling
A procedure in which a sample of a given behavior is shown to an individual to induce that person to imitate the behavior.

Modeling involves person A performing a behavior to induce person B to imitate that behavior. Its effects can be quite powerful. You might want to try the following:

1. For an entire day, speak only in a whisper, and note how often people around you also whisper.
2. Yawn conspicuously in the presence of other people and note their frequency of yawning.
3. Stand looking in the window of a department store for an hour and note how many other people stop and also look in the window.

What determines whether or not we will imitate the behavior of a model? Consider a classic experiment by Bandura. Bandura showed nursery school children a film in which an adult beat up an inflatable, bottom-heavy "Bobo" doll (Bandura, 1965; see photo below). He also prepared different endings for the film. Some children saw an ending in which a second adult gave rewards of candy and soft drinks to "the champion" for beating up Bobo. Other children saw the aggressive adult being spanked, scolded, and called a "bad person." Still other children saw a third ending in which the aggressive adult was neither punished nor rewarded. Bandura then asked, "What will the children do if they are now given a chance to play alone with Bobo? Interestingly, the children who had seen the aggressive adult being rewarded were most likely themselves to beat up on Bobo.

Bandura's classic experiment on observational learning of aggression. After observing an adult attack Bobo, children imitated the aggressive behavior when given the opportunity to do so. *From Bandura et al., 1963.*

observational learning

The ability to learn from observing others' behavior, without necessarily being reinforced for it.

imitation

Performing a behavior acquired from observational learning.

Those children who had seen the adult being punished for abusing Bobo were least likely to abuse Bobo themselves. However, when Bandura offered these children some candy "to do everything that the adult had done," they were just as aggressive as the other children (Bandura, 1965). From such experiments, Bandura (1977, 1986) has argued that people are able to show **observational learning**— the ability to learn from observing others, without being reinforced for doing so. Such learning can occur without revealing itself in observable behavior. Later, if available rewards make it worthwhile, the newly learned behavior might be performed.

Performing a behavior acquired from observational learning is called **imitation.** The good news is that observational learning is a valuable strategy for producing a wide variety of desirable behaviors of humans (and other species, Robert, 1990). Parents, for example, teach caring, politeness, language, and other useful behaviors to their children through modeling and observational learning. The bad news is that antisocial, destructive behaviors can also be learned the same way. Just as children learned to beat up Bobo by watching an adult who was rewarded for doing so, boys who watch their fathers beat up their mothers are likely to batter their own wives later in life (McCall & Shields, 1986). Moreover, when parents tell their children, "Do as I say, not as I do," children are likely to learn to do both (Rice & Grusec, 1975; Rushton, 1975), or, even worse, to imitate what the parents *do* and *not* what they *say* (Bryan & Walbek, 1970).

Modeling and imitation are very useful tools in the psychology of adjustment. Consider, for example, the case of a male college student who had difficulty asking for dates over the telephone (Masters et al., 1987, pp. 100–101). The following excerpt from a therapy session illustrates how the therapist was able to combine instruction and shaping with modeling and imitation to help the student make a successful adjustment.

CLIENT: By the way (pause), I don't suppose you wanna go out Saturday night?

THERAPIST: Up to actually asking for the date, you were very good. However, if I were the girl, I think I might have been a bit offended when you said, "By the way." It's like your asking her out is pretty casual. Also, the way you phrased the question, you're kind of suggesting to her that she doesn't want to go out with you. Pretend for the moment I'm you. Now, how does this sound: "There's a movie at the Varsity Theater this Saturday that I want to see. If you don't have other plans, I'd very much like to take you."

CLIENT: That sounded good. Like you were sure of yourself and liked the woman, too.

THERAPIST:	Why don't you try it?
CLIENT:	You know that movie at the Varsity? Well, I'd like to go, and I'd like to take you Saturday, if you don't have anything better to do.
THERAPIST:	Well, that certainly was better. Your tone of voice was especially good. But the last line, "if you don't have anything better to do," sounded like you don't think you have much to offer. Why not run through it one more time?
CLIENT:	I'd like to see the show at the Varsity, Saturday, and, if you haven't made other plans, I'd like to take you.
THERAPIST:	Much better. Excellent, in fact. You were confident, forceful and sincere.

In this chapter, we have focused on principles of reflexive, operant, and observational learning. Work by Pavlov, Skinner, Bandura, and others has produced a valuable legacy of learning principles for helping us to understand our behavior. These principles also provide you with many tools for successfully adjusting in everyday life, as you will see in later chapters.

SUMMARY

- Learning is defined as a relatively permanent change in behavior due to experience. Two kinds of learning that underlie a great deal of what we do, say, think, and feel are reflexive and operant learning.

- Reflexive learning begins with an unconditioned reflex in which an unconditioned stimulus, or US (such as food), elicits an unconditioned response, or UR (salivation). When a neutral stimulus (such as a tone) predicts the US by being paired with it, the tone acquires the ability to elicit the response (e.g., salivation). The tone is then referred to as a conditioned stimulus, or CS, and the response is referred to as a conditioned response, or CR. A conditioned reflex does not necessarily stay with us forever. When a CS is presented without further pairings with the US, reflexive extinction occurs and the CS loses its ability to elicit the CR. Applications of reflexive conditioning described in this chapter include conditioning of emotions, reflexive reactions to words, and conditioning of a tolerance response in drug addicts.

- B. F. Skinner studied operant learning, the modification of behavior by its consequences (rewards and punishers). Important principles of operant learning include positive reinforcement, in which a behavior is strengthened when it leads to a positive reinforcer; operant extinction, in which a behavior is weakened when it no longer produces the usual reinforcer; shaping, in which new behaviors are developed by reinforcement of successive approximations; stimulus-response chaining, in which stimuli and responses are put together to form complex sequences of behavior; and schedules of reinforcement, in which different pay-off arrangements between behaviors and rewards lead to different patterns of responding.

- Punishment involves the presentation of an aversive stimulus following a response and is an effective strategy for decreasing behavior. While punishment plays a role in our learning in everyday life, it has a number of unfortunate side effects and its use should be strictly limited in formal educational and therapeutic settings. Aversive events can also lead to a strengthening of behavior, such as in escape learning, in which a response is strengthened because it terminates an aversive event, and in avoidance learning, in which a response prevents the occurrence of a punisher.

- From his classic study in which children watched adults "beat up Bobo," Bandura developed the concept of observational learning—the ability to learn by observing others, without being reinforced for doing so. Performing a behavior acquired from observational learning is called imitation. An understanding of reflexive, operant, and observational learning will provide you with many valuable tools for successfully adjusting in everyday life.

Box 3-3

SELF-ADJUSTMENT FOR STUDENTS: A MODEL FOR SELF-IMPROVEMENT

Have you ever been told things like, "If you had more willpower, you wouldn't have that extra dessert," or "If you had more willpower, you would spend more time studying"? Most of us have heard such advice many times. Unfortunately it's usually not very helpful because the person offering it almost always neglects to tell us how we can get more of this so-called willpower. Speculations about willpower do not constitute a useful starting point for self-improvement. A better approach is to learn to apply principles of learning.

Sooner or later, all of us would like to improve in some area of daily living. Perhaps you would like to improve your study habits, get on an exercise program, or say no more assertively (and stick to your guns) when friends nag you to go drinking at the local bar. In the psychological literature, problems of self-improvement such as these are referred to as problems of self-adjustment, self-management, or self-modification. Many people can solve such problems by consistent application of basic learning techniques.

In the self-adjustment box at the end of each of the following chapters, we will guide you through the steps of a self-adjustment project. Completing these steps not only will help you make a successful adjustment in everyday living but also will help you master the principles of learning described in this chapter. In the meantime, the following material will give you an overview of the model for self-improvement that you will learn to apply from the self-adjustment box in the following chapters. While studying this model, you may want to review the self-assessments you completed at the end of Chapters 1 and 2. The steps for a model for self-improvement follow.

STEP 1: SPECIFY THE PROBLEM

What is it that you would like to change? How will you know if you have succeeded? If possible, you should set goals for self-improvement in quantitative terms. For example, don't just say, "I want to study more." Set a goal for the specific amount that

you want to study, and identify the specific topics that you would like to master.

STEP 2: MAKE A COMMITMENT TO CHANGE

After picking an area for self-improvement, you should take steps to build your commitment to stick to the project. First, tell others about your program. Increasing the number of people who can remind you to stick to your program increases your chances of success. Second, give yourself frequent reminders of your goal such as notes on pieces of paper, pictures of famous people who serve as models, and so on. Third, plan ahead for temptations to quit the program, and figure out ways to deal with those.

STEP 3: OBSERVE, RECORD, AND GRAPH

For many self-improvement projects, a 3 × 5 card and a pencil will serve nicely for tallying instances of the problem as they occur throughout the day. Sometimes self-recording of the problem is all that is needed to bring about improvement. For example, McFall (1970) reported a study in which recording each urge to have a cigarette was sufficient to decrease not only the likelihood of having a cigarette but also the number of urges.

STEP 4: ANALYZE CAUSES

When recording a problem, try to determine its causes. For example, does the problem behavior lead to reinforcers that are maintaining it? If so, how can you control those reinforcers?

STEP 5: MANAGE THE SITUATION

Throughout your life, in certain situations, certain behaviors have certain consequences. You can look to each of these three variables—situation, behavior, and consequence—for ideas about self-improvement techniques for you to try.

In this step, we'll look at how you can manage the situation, how you can capitalize on stimulus control in your self-control program. Perhaps you can use some self-instructions. For example, if you get nervous when you enter a room to take an exam, you might tell yourself, "Take three deep breaths, relax, concentrate on what you know." Self-instructions have been used to increase exercise and study behavior (Cohen et al., 1980); reduce fears (Arrick et al., 1981); reduce nail-biting (Harris & McReynolds, 1977); and improve a variety of other behaviors (Dush et al., 1983).

Because numerous environments and occasions in our society control specific behaviors, it's possible to deliberately use particular environments in self-improvement programs (Martin & Pear, 1992). Having trouble sitting down and answering that letter you've been meaning to write? Place a pencil and paper on the desk, sit down at the desk, and place before you a picture of the person to whom you should write. Having trouble "getting up enough energy" to do your regular weight-lifting routine on Saturday afternoon? Place the weights in the middle of the room, turn on the television to the wrestling matches, and open your *Muscle Beach* magazine to the "Muscle Person" centerfold.

Step 6: Manage Consequences

Some rules of thumb for incorporating rewards into your program include the following: Make it possible for you to earn specific rewards on a daily basis; set up bonuses that can be earned for progress on a weekly basis; vary the rewards from one day to the next and one week to the next to prevent boredom with the whole system; consider the possibility of having other individuals dispense rewards to you for meeting your goals; and tell others about your progress.

Step 7: Change Complex Behavior

If the behavior that you want to improve is quite complex, such as learning to play a new sport or improving your essay writing, then you should break the behavior down into small steps. You should consider using the shaping and chaining procedures described in this chapter. Important rules of thumb for you to keep in mind include:

Start small, move on to a new step only after mastering the current step, and keep progressive steps small. Studies of dieters, for example, have reported that those who set small, gradual shaping steps for reducing calories are more likely to develop self-control of binge-eating than are dieters who set large steps (Hawkins & Clement, 1980).

Step 8: Review Your Program and Evaluate Progress

A problem has been identified, and a plan has been put into place. But is it working? An important step in successful self-adjustment is continually to compare current progress with the initial starting point and the long-term goal. In Step 1 you set a goal for yourself. In Step 3, you monitored your behavior at the start of your program. In subsequent steps, you initiated a plan. It's now time to evaluate your progress. You should also begin to think of the conditions under which you will end your program.

Step 9: Recognize Reasons for Relapse

Unfortunately, relapses are common in self-adjustment programs. Mary successfully dieted for three weeks, and then the sale at the local Baskin & Robbins caught her eye. John faithfully followed his exercise program for a month and a half, and then didn't exercise for two weeks straight while on a motor home trip. Relapses occur, but they don't have to signal failure. One step in preventing relapses is to recognize their common causes. Some of the more common reasons for failure at self-adjustment include: a drastic short-term change in living conditions; failure to continue recording and graphing problem behavior; negative self-talk about how slow progress seems to be; and feeling discouraged because others are progressing faster than you are in their adjustment projects. Examining your own self-adjustment program in light of common reasons for failure is an important step for relapse prevention.

Continued

STEP 10: TROUBLE-SHOOT AND PROBLEM SOLVE

If serious relapses occur, how can you get back on track in your self-adjustment program? To successfully self-adjust, you may need to learn to emphasize frequent improvements rather than occasional failures, to monitor and change negative self-talk, and to learn additional problem-solving strategies.

STEP 11: MAKE IT LAST

You've made considerable progress on your self-improvement program, and you're near your goal. But will your successful adjustment last? The final step in self-adjustment is to plan to maintain your gains. One strategy to maintain progress is to set specific dates for reviewing your progress. Another strategy is to set up a "buddy" system. Find a friend or relative with a similar problem and set mutual maintenance goals. Once a month, get together and check each other's progress. If progress is not satisfactory, reinstitute the program. One thing you can count on—the more you deliberately practice applying basic learning techniques to your own self-improvement, the more likely you are to continue to use them successfully.

MEMORY BOOSTER

■ IMPORTANT PERSONS

You should know who these persons are and why they are important:

Ivan Pavlov
B. F. Skinner
Albert Bandura

■ IMPORTANT TERMS

Be prepared to define the following terms (located in the margins of this chapter). Where appropriate, be prepared to describe examples.

Learning	Positive Reinforcement
Stimuli	Operant Extinction
Unconditioned Reflex	Shaping
Unconditioned Stimulus	Schedules of Reinforcement
Unconditioned Response	Stimulus Control
Conditioned Reflex	Stimulus Generalization
Conditioned Stimulus	Punisher
Conditioned Response	Principle of Punishment
Reflexive Learning	Escape Learning
Reflexive Extinction	Avoidance Learning
Operant Behavior	Modeling
Operant Conditioning	Observational Learning
Positive Reinforcer	Imitation

■ QUESTIONS FROM IMPORTANT IDEAS IN THIS CHAPTER

1. Using examples from your own experience, diagram the models for reflexive learning and reflexive extinction.

2. How can Pavlovian conditioning enable us to explain why a drug addict must take larger and larger doses of heroin to reproduce the same "high"?

3. Describe, using an example, how counterconditioning is involved in "beating" a lie detector test.

4. Using examples from your own experience, diagram the models for operant learning and operant extinction.

5. Define and give examples of four intermittent schedules of reinforcement.

6. Describe how you might apply stimulus control to improve your study habits.

7. Describe an example of the application of punishment in everyday life. List several reasons why we must be cautious about deliberately using punishment to decrease problem behaviors of individuals.

8. Describe four recent situations where you reacted in some way. Did your reactions involve responses that were learned via reflexive, operant, or observational learning? Explain your answer.

THINKING AND FEELING: THE INSIDE STORY

CHAPTER OUTLINE

LEARNING OBJECTIVES

After reading this chapter, you should be able to:

- Discuss different types of thinking.
- Explain how different types of thinking contribute to your self-concept or personal identity.
- Apply self-adjustment techniques to help you think positively, rationally solve problems, and stop unpleasant thoughts from occurring.
- Illustrate how reflexive learning is involved in determining our "feelings."
- Illustrate how operant learning is involved in the way we express our emotions.
- Describe four main causes of emotional reactions.
- Discuss cross-cultural studies of expression of emotions.
- Apply some cognitive and behavioral strategies to change troublesome emotions.

In the last chapter we described principles of reflexive, operant, and observational learning—principles that explain how learning affects our observable actions and that serve as valuable tools for changing behaviors that require adjustment. But what about that part of us that can't be seen—like the things we think about and the emotions we feel? What would your life be like if you couldn't imagine things that you had experienced, rehearse new knowledge, or think about your upcoming plans for summer vacation? And what if friends and family did not evoke feelings of love and happiness? Can you imagine winning without thrill or defeat without

What goes on inside us—such as our thoughts and feelings—is every bit as important as our observable behavior.

agony? Or poems, plays, movies, and soap operas without the emotions they evoke? Could you live even a single day without experiencing a multitude of thoughts and a range of emotions? The answer, of course, is no. What goes on inside us is every bit as important as our observable behavior.

In this chapter, we examine important components of "the inside story"—thinking and feeling. We'll look at different types of thinking and review several tactics for managing your thinking in order to achieve goals of personal adjustment. We'll also examine the characteristics of emotions. Finally, we'll review strategies to help you change emotions that are troublesome, and experience more of emotions that are pleasurable. But before continuing, we need to emphasize up front that it is impossible to do justice to these important topics in a single chapter. In this chapter, we explain important aspects of thinking and feeling, and describe some adjustment steps for coping with negative thoughts and troublesome emotions. But we want to emphasize that additional treatment of these topics will appear in later chapters. In Chapter 5 on stress, for example, we add further suggestions for changing your thinking when it is a source of stress. In Chapter 8 we examine the topic of love, an important emotion not discussed in the current chapter. In Chapter 11 we look at ways that prejudiced thinking comes about. And in Chapter 15 we examine further strategies for resolving harmful emotions, like anxiety, anger, loneliness, and depression. Thus, when reading ahead, please remember that the self-adjustment strategies presented in this chapter will be supplemented by additional useful tools presented in later chapters.

Thinking

Have you ever been on a long car trip alone? When you started to think about something, did you find yourself talking out loud? Thinking out loud is something that we all do at one time or another. Carrying on conversations with ourselves is a type of thinking that depends on our language abilities. But we also think by imagining things that have been experienced. And we mentally organize items into categories, called concepts. **Thinking** is the private manipulation of words and images, as in private self-talk, mental imagery, concept formation, problem solving, and decision making. Behaviorists, like B. F. Skinner, consider most thinking to be essentially private behavior. And when considered as behavior, thinking is subject to all the principles of learning presented in Chapter 3. Another word for thinking is *cognition,* and cognitive psychologists have made significant contributions to our understanding of how we think and solve problems. Let's see how different types of thinking come about.

thinking

The private manipulation of words and images, as in private self-talk, imagery, concept formation, problem solving, and decision making.

Thinking as Private Self-Talk

Language is fundamental to much of our thinking. Let's say you're tackling a tough spatial problem. You've got to plan how many skeins of wool it might take to knit a sweater, or how many cuts of a certain size you can make in a piece of plywood. How do you solve such problems? Chances are, you'll think out loud as you go over the possibilities. Carrying on conversations with ourselves is one of the ways that we think—one that depends on our language abilities.

Self-instructing out loud is something that we learn to do as children because it helps us perform tasks more efficiently (Luria, 1961; Roberts, 1979; Vygotsky, 1965, 1978). When children first attend school, they often say rules out loud to themselves to adjust to difficult tasks (Roberts & Mullis, 1980; Roberts & Tharp, 1980). When children are about five to six years of age, however, they also begin to whisper quietly to themselves—a type of thinking (Vygotsky, 1965). Children learn to talk quietly to themselves at a very early age because they encounter punishers when they think out loud (Skinner, 1957). For example, teachers in school require students to think to themselves because thinking out loud disturbs other students. Naturally distressed reactions from others also teach us to keep certain thoughts to ourselves. Upon being introduced to the hostess when you go to a party, you might say to yourself, "Wow, is that an ugly dress." But you're not likely to express that thought overtly.

RATIONAL AND IRRATIONAL SELF-TALK. Thinking as self-talk can play an important role in our emotional well-being. Albert Ellis, a noted psychotherapist, argued that many emotional problems stem from irrational statements that people make to themselves when conditions in their lives are not the way they would like them to be (Ellis & Bernard, 1985). People tend to "catastrophize," according to Ellis. They tell themselves that things are so horrible that they can't possibly "stand it." Ellis developed his rational-emotive therapy to help people identify irrational ideas or beliefs and replace them with realistic statements about the world. Suppose, for example, that a young man is emotionally upset because of a broken love affair. The man might be telling himself that he simply cannot live without the love of his former girlfriend. Ellis, working as the young man's therapist, would directly challenge such a belief. He might teach the man that, although his situation may be annoying and upsetting, it is not catastrophic, and, moreover, there are things that he can do to improve it. Ellis might further help the client change his irrational self-statements by giving homework assignments in which the client practices alternative ways of thinking about his past love affair and his potential for future love affairs. The client might be required, for example, to list all of his attributes, to act sociably toward other women whom he encounters during the day, and to consider making plans for a date with another woman. We discuss Ellis' therapy later in this chapter, and again in Chapter 14 (also, see Bernard, 1991).

While private self-talk is an important part of thinking, it is not the only part. We also think in terms of mental pictures, or images.

Thinking without Language

Try the following exercise: Ask a friend or two to sit back comfortably, eyes closed, and imagine that they're sitting on a lawnchair on a warm summer day. They look up and see the clear blue sky. A few white fluffy clouds are drifting slowly along. Now ask them to open their eyes. Did they have a clear image of the blue sky and the white fluffy clouds—so clear that they could almost see the colors?

All of us, at one time or another, have had the experience of thinking in images, not in words. And having a good imaging ability can be a valuable trait. Many people, including Albert Einstein, attribute many of their successes to their ability to think in images. People who score high on tests of creativity also tend to have a good imagination (Shaw & Belmore, 1983). And many highly successful athletes have learned to imagine specific aspects of their performance in considerable detail before they perform (Martin & Lumsden, 1987). Jack Nicklaus, for example, whom many consider to be the greatest golfer of all time, attributed much of his success to his ability to perform a mental picture of a golf shot just before hitting the ball (Nicklaus, 1974).

How is it that we learn to think in images? A part of the explanation may lie with reflexive learning. Consider the exercise mentioned previously where you ask a friend to close his or her eyes and try to imagine a clear blue sky. As illustrated in Figure 4-1, as we grow up, we experience many occasions on which the words *blue sky* are paired with actually looking at and "seeing" a blue sky. As a consequence, when you ask a friend to imagine looking at a blue sky (with white fluffy clouds), the words likely elicit activity in the visual system of your friend that makes it seem

conditioned seeing

Imagining that you are seeing an event when you encounter a stimulus that has been consistently paired with that event.

as though he or she is seeing the actual scene. We might refer to this as **conditioned seeing** (Skinner, 1953), or "seeing in the absence of the thing being seen" (Skinner, 1974).

In a broader sense, we might think of *conditioned sensing*. That is, just as we acquire, through experience, conditioned seeing, we also acquire conditioned hearing, conditioned smelling, and conditioned feeling. Let's suppose, for example, that you had experienced numerous passionate encounters with a partner who consistently used a very distinctive perfume or cologne. Then one day someone

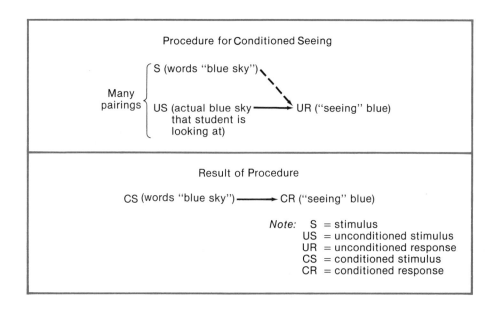

Figure 4-1

An example of conditioned seeing

walks by you in a department store wearing that same perfume or cologne. Chances are that you might immediately imagine that former partner (conditioned seeing), feel "tingly" all over (*conditioned feeling*), and you might even imagine that you hear that person's voice (*conditioned hearing*).

This sort of occurrence is also a big part of what goes on during fantasy (Malott & Whaley, 1983). To experience a fantasy as a result of reading or listening to a story is, in some sense, to be there. It's as though you can see what the people in the story see, feel what they feel, and hear what they hear. Perhaps we are able to do this because of many instances of conditioned sensing. Our long history in which we associate words with actual sights, words with sounds, words with smells, and words with feelings, enables us to experience the scenes that an author's words describe. The covert reactions that occur when we are thinking are real—we're really seeing or feeling or hearing when we respond to words (Malott & Whaley, 1983).

Concepts: Building Blocks for Thinking

concept

A grouping of objects, events, people, or qualities on the basis of shared common features.

We've described how we can think in words and how we can think in images. Much of our thinking involves a complex mixture of the two, a process called concept formation. A **concept** is a grouping of objects, events, people, or qualities on the basis of shared common features. For example, "chair" is a concept, something with legs and a back that you can sit on. Because you understand the concept of chair, you can recognize any chair instantly even though you have never seen it before.

We are able to manage massive amounts of information because we can organize the information into concepts and can arrange the concepts further into hierarchies. If you were a city planner, for example, you would be concerned with buildings. You might first divide buildings into businesses vs. family dwellings. Family dwellings might then be subdivided into apartment blocks versus houses, and so on. In this way, a single concept like "building" can be broken down into a hierarchy of concepts (see Figure 4-2). There is now evidence that children learn concept hierarchies (for example, that dogs and horses are animals), at least in a simplified sense, as young as three years of age (Waxman, 1990). As their ability to extend existing conceptual hierarchies increases (from a dog, animal hierarchy to a collie, dog, mammal, animal hierarchy), so does their capacity for thinking.

One way that we form concepts is to store them as a list of characteristics, such as the characteristics for "chair" mentioned earlier (Smith, 1988). When the characteristics of a concept are represented in our thinking, we are thereafter able to recognize instances of it and incorporate thoughts of it into our daily activities. Another possibility is that a concept is represented in our thinking in terms of a **prototype**—the most typical example of the category (Rosch, 1977). What, for example, do you think about when you try to imagine a bird? If you're like most

prototype

The most typical example of a category.

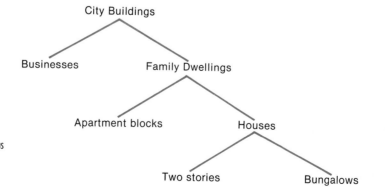

Figure 4-2

A hierarchy of concepts. Our ability to think in terms of hierarchies of concepts enables us to learn, remember, and use large amounts of information.

What do you think of when asked to think of a sport? Chances are that you did *not* think of Wrestlemania or the World Chess Championship. Baseball is a much more likely prototype—the best representative of a category.

people, you thought of a robin (Malt & Smith, 1984). You probably didn't think of a penguin even though penguins have wings, feathers, and lay eggs. A robin is simply a better prototype of a bird than is a penguin.

CONCEPTS AND PERCEPTION.   Do our concepts determine our perceptions? Or does what we see, hear, and smell determine our concepts? Linguist Benjamin Lee Whorf's studies suggested that our language influences our perception, an idea known as the **linguistic relativity hypothesis** (Whorf, 1956). Whorf pointed out, for example, that Eskimos have many words for snow, depending on whether the snow is falling, hard-packed, melting, and the like. According to Whorf, the Eskimo language influences Eskimos to perceive differences in snow that would not be noticed by people who just speak English. And this would make it easier for them to think about snow in the many different ways that are important to them in their world.

But does our language really determine the way in which we perceive the world? Are English-speaking people, for example, really limited in their ability to think about different types of snow? Probably not, at least not if different types of snow are important to them. Skiers, for example, readily perceive differences between "powder," "crusty," and "hard-packed." And research has contradicted Whorf's theory. People in cultures that have only a few color names, for example, can detect differences in color variations as well as English-speaking college students whose language has many color names (Heider & Olivier, 1972; Rosch, 1974).

Although language does *not* appear to determine how we perceive the world, our words *can* definitely influence our thinking (Hoffman et al., 1986). Even though *his, he, him, men,* or *mankind* can refer to humans or humanity, statements containing such words are often interpreted as referring primarily to males (Hyde, 1984; Sniezek & Jazwinski, 1986). For example, the statement, "A student must complete three years of medical school and a one-year internship before receiving *his* medical degree" refers to both males and females. Yet, because it uses the masculine pronoun *his,* it promotes the belief that it is more suitable for males to be doctors than for females. We must, therefore, be careful of how we say things, so as to encourage equal treatment of both sexes.

linguistic relativity hypothesis

The idea that our language influences our perception.

How does knowledge of concept formation and perception relate to the psychology of adjustment? For one thing, it can help us understand the basis for our individual self-concepts—the numerous ways that we see ourselves, our perceptions of our personal traits and characteristics. For another, it may help us change aspects of ourselves that we don't feel good about. Let's explore this area further.

Thinking and the Self

"Does my hair look okay?" "I wish I was taller." "What if I fail?" "I'm going to ace this exam." As illustrated by these examples, much of our thinking centers on ourselves. And the way that we see ourselves has been determined partly by the way that we have been taught to describe our physical appearance.

Self-Description of Our Physical Appearance

People around us teach us to describe our physical appearance at a very early age. Moms and dads might say things like, "You look so cute" or "Aren't you pretty?" We learn to describe our physical characteristics in a specific sense ("I have brown hair." "I have blue eyes") and in a comparative sense ("I'm tall." "I'm skinny"). As we learn to think about our bodies in particular ways, those thoughts also elicit imagining through conditioned sensing. Our self-imagining might be positive, to the extent that we see ourselves as a particular body type that is often associated with compliments and rewards, or negative, to the extent that we see ourselves as a particular body type that may be associated with unpleasant reactions from others.

Self-Awareness of Our Behavior

People around us also teach us to become aware of both what we are doing and why we are doing it. As kids, we experienced adults who entered rooms where we were playing and asked us, "What are you doing?" And that was often followed by another question, "What did you do that for?" We learn to describe some of our behaviors and to offer reasons to account for some of the things we do.

As the years go by, we also learn generalizations about our behavior patterns. If we frequently forget things, we learn to describe ourselves as forgetful. If we fail to do various chores or work tasks that others have asked us to do, we learn to describe ourselves as lazy. Such self-descriptions as honest, carefree, hard-working, unreliable, independent, selfish, incompetent, kind, graceful, unsociable, and the like, are acquired in a similar fashion.

Self-Concept

self-concept
A general term that refers to the broad range of self-descriptions that a person is likely to make about him or herself, and the associated imagining elicited by those self-descriptions.

identity
Another name for self-concept.

self-esteem
Liking oneself and seeing oneself as a worthy person.

By the time people have reached adulthood, they have acquired a large number of self-descriptions. Many of these self-descriptions will also elicit images. **Self-concept** is a general term that refers to the broad range of self-descriptions that you are likely to make, and the associated imagining elicited by those self-descriptions. Another term for self-concept is personal **identity.** Some people are said to have a very positive self-concept or identity. For these people, many of their self-descriptions have been associated with rewards and are likely to elicit very positive images and emotions. For example, Kelly is bright, witty, attractive, and she finished in the top 10 percent of her class at law school. She enjoys her budding career as a lawyer, and is engaged to marry a former Rhodes scholar who is also a lawyer. Her self-descriptions and associated images reflect all of these qualities. Kelly has high **self-esteem**—she likes herself and sees herself as a worthy person. Charlie, on the other hand, has a different self-concept. Charlie bounced around from subject to subject in college before dropping out halfway through his third year. He has worked at several jobs, although he has never stayed at one job for more than six

Box 4-1

How Big Is Your Body?

Do you see yourself the way others see you? Recent studies in which subjects were asked to estimate the size of their body parts suggest that many women see themselves as larger than they actually are. By projecting light beams on a screen, subjects were asked to adjust the width of the beam to correspond to their impression of the size of one of their body parts, such as the size of their waist. Results suggest that many women see themselves as having round cheeks, protruding tummies, and pudgy thighs and hips, even when no one else sees them that way. Specifically, more than 95 percent of the women overestimated their body size to an average of one-fourth larger than it really was (Thompson, 1986). Cheeks were overestimated the most, followed by waist, thighs, and then hips. While men, on the average, also overestimated the size of those body parts, they did so to a much lesser extent than did the female subjects. The research also indicated that the more inaccurate women were about their body size, the worse they felt about themselves. Another recent study indicated that 38 percent of the women and 34 percent of the men questioned were dissatisfied with their bodies (Cash et al., 1986). Perhaps a part of the dissatisfaction can be attributed to inaccurate self-descriptions of physical appearance.

These findings may have implications for your own self-adjustment. Specifically, if you are dissatisfied because you believe some of your body parts are too large, your first step should be to independently evaluate the accuracy of your self-description. A plausible strategy might be the following. Find two or three people whose judgment you trust. Then go to a public park, a sidewalk cafe, a shopping mall, or some other place that's good for people-watching. As specific individuals walk by

that have about the same build as you, ask your friends to rate specific body parts of those individuals relative to yours. They might indicate, for example, that your thighs are "about the same as," or "slightly larger than," or "slightly smaller than" those of particular individuals walking by. If you compare your own judgments to this type of feedback, you will learn to more accurately see yourself as others see you.

months. His rewards have never really pointed him toward any particular long-term goal or career. His self-descriptions do not show the kind of consistent patterns that were evident with Kelly. Moreover, many of his self-descriptions are followed by negative reactions (for example, "I'll never amount to anything" or "What am I going to do with my life?"). This type of learning history causes Charlie

identity crisis

A situation in which the self-descriptions that comprise one's self-concept do not show any consistent pattern, and have been associated with aversive experiences.

to have low self-esteem and to feel an identity crisis (Baldwin & Baldwin, 1986). An **identity crisis** refers to a situation in which the self-descriptions that comprise one's self-concept do not show any consistent pattern, and have been associated with aversive experiences.

Suppose that you sometimes feel like Charlie, and experience negative thinking about yourself. What can you do about it? Let's now turn to some strategies for changing troublesome thoughts.

Changing Your Thoughts to Achieve Self-Adjustment

Examples of changing your thought patterns in order to create personal adjustment are illustrated throughout this text. In this section, we briefly review four tactics aimed at the self-adjustment of your thoughts. These include thinking positively, imagery rehearsal to perform a skill, rational problem solving, and thought stopping to decrease unpleasant thoughts.

Thinking Positively

As a student taking an exam, you may have found yourself saying such things as: "What if I fail this test?" or "How come I'm the last to leave the exam? Everyone else must really know their stuff!" Not only is such negative thinking not likely to help you in any way, it may cause anxiety that can interfere with your problem-solving ability (Holroyd et al., 1978). *Negative thoughts* contain references to aversive events which elicit unpleasant emotional reactions (discussed later in this chapter). In most situations where negative thinking occurs, it is possible to learn to *think positively*—to think about events and activities that elicit pleasurable emotional responses. If you're the kind of person who thinks negatively when going into an exam, for example, you might practice positive thinking. In such a situation, you should first make a list of a half dozen alternative positive statements that you can rehearse to counteract the negative thoughts. For example, you might say, "There's no sense in worrying; worrying never helps anything." "One step at a time. I know I can handle this one step at a time." "I have studied, I know some things, and I'm simply going to relax and do my best." Your positive self-talk could be written on a 3 × 5 card, and practiced several times before going to the actual exam.

As another example, if you occasionally experience negative thoughts from arbitrary inference, then you might practice reality checking. *Arbitrary inference* is a term used by Aaron Beck (1976), a noted cognitive therapist, to refer to instances of drawing a conclusion on the basis of inadequate evidence; for example, misinterpreting a frown on the face of a passerby to mean that the passerby disapproves of you, or concluding that you're a "failure in psychology" because you obtained a "C" on an exam. One technique recommended by Beck for overcoming such thinking is that of *reality checking.* After a negative thought has been identified, you should treat it as an hypothesis rather than as a reality, and then test it experimentally. If, for example, you believe that everyone that you meet turns away from you in disgust, then you might devise a system for judging other peoples' facial expressions and body language so that you can determine objectively whether your negative thinking is indeed accurate. If you experience the thought that you're a failure in psychology because you obtained a grade of "C," then you might define failure as "not able to obtain a grade of 'B' or better after studying as long and hard as the average 'A' student." You are then in a position to test the negative thought and to prove it wrong.

Positive thinking can also be used in a general sense to influence your overall mood. For example, one person that we know frequently thinks about how he will spend the money he plans to win in a million-dollar lottery. High on his list are things like taking a trip around the world, buying a condo in Florida, buying another condo in Aspen, giving some money to some of his relatives, and buying a new house. These thoughts elicit pleasurable feelings (discussed later in this chapter) that put the person in a positive mood (especially for buying lottery tickets).

What thoughts might put you in a good mood? One strategy for mood control is to have handy a list of "good mood" topics to think about. Take a few minutes and make a list. Who are your five favorite people in the whole world? What are your three favorite vacation spots? What would your "dream house" look like? Who are your three favorite comedians? What specific activity are you most looking forward to during the coming year? When you prepare such a list, keep it handy, perhaps in your purse or wallet. Then when you would like to put yourself in a good mood, pick one of the items on the list and devote all your thinking to it for two or three minutes. Chances are you will feel much better afterward.

Premack Principle

For any pair of responses, the more probable one will reinforce the less probable one; developed by David Premack.

This strategy for improving your mood can be made even more effective by capitalizing on a technique referred to as the **Premack Principle.** This principle states: For any pair of responses, the more probable one will reward the less probable one (Premack 1959; 1965). In an interesting extension of this principle, Homme (1965) described ways in which the Premack Principle might be applied to increase one's happiness. The idea is to make a list of "good mood" thoughts, such as those described above, and then to use the Premack Principle to guarantee that they increase in frequency. Within the context of the Premack Principle, the happy thoughts would be considered the less probable response. You must next identify a more probable response—something that you do frequently during the day. Examples might include walking through doorways, turning light switches on and off, drinking sips of coffee, or answering the telephone. The final step in the procedure is to require yourself to think about one or more of the items on the "good mood" list before you permit yourself to engage in the more probable behavior. This strategy virtually guarantees that you will increase your frequency of happy thoughts and it can significantly alter your mood.

Johnson (1971) used this strategy to help a depressed 17-year-old college student increase the frequency of positive self-statements. The student was required to imagine a positive thought as prompted from a statement on an index card (a low-probability behavior) just before each instance of urinating (the high-probability behavior). After a few days of this procedure, the student spontaneously thought the positive self-statements just before urinating without the necessity of reviewing the index card. After two weeks of this procedure, the student reported that the depressive thoughts had completely disappeared.

Another strategy for thinking positively is to use self-instructions to engage in specific behaviors that will lead to actual reinforcing events. The technique of *positive self-instruction,* as illustrated in numerous examples throughout this book, is an effective strategy for increasing specific behaviors including asking for a date (Chapter 8), dieting (Chapter 6), exercising (Chapter 6), and improving time management (Chapter 1). A study of 69 separate research reports on self-adjustment projects indicated that individuals who use positive self-instructions improved more than control subjects who did not use such self-statements (Dush et al., 1983).

Imagery Rehearsal to Perform a Skill

imagery rehearsal

Imagining yourself performing a particular behavior by imagining how it feels and what you see and hear when that behavior is performed.

The positive thinking strategies described above strongly emphasize the importance of self-talk. But remember we also think in images. And we can use our imagination to improve specific skills. Have you ever watched Jack Nicklaus play golf? He takes forever standing over the ball before each shot! Have you ever thought about what he might be doing? Nicklaus claims that he goes through **imagery rehearsal** of every shot throughout an entire round (Nicklaus, 1974). Before hitting the ball, he imagines the execution of the swing that would produce

Many successful athletes practice imagery rehearsal.

a particular flight pattern. When he thinks of his swing, he imagines how it feels to him when he addresses the ball, how it feels on his backswing, the weight transfer from one foot to another on his follow-through, and so forth. Of course, we don't know for sure if this helps. What we do know is that many highly successful athletes have learned to imagine specific aspects of their performance in considerable detail before they perform (Harris & Harris, 1984).

Imagery rehearsal as a performance enhancement technique is not limited to athletics. For example, it has been used to help students improve exam-taking performance (Harris & Johnson, 1980), and to help individuals (on a drinking control program) resist social pressures to drink alcoholic beverages (Marlatt & Parks, 1982). It might also be used to help improve the performance of such varied activities as giving a speech, doing a dance routine, playing at a music recital, speaking up in class, and asking for a date. Guidelines for using imagery rehearsal to improve performance of a skill include the following:

- Use at least one imagery rehearsal just before performing the skill.
- The skill should be imagined in its entirety.
- When imagining the skill, imagine the feel of the action. Try to feel how your muscles feel when you are executing the skill and/or speaking, just as though you were actually doing it.
- Imagine performing the skill at approximately the rate or speed of the actual performance.
- Imagine performing the skill in the specific environment in which you will be performing it in reality.
- Imagine yourself as successful in the rehearsal.

Rational Problem Solving

rational problem solving

A form of problem solving that involves defining the problem precisely, identifying alternatives, and selecting the best alternative.

An important part of effective thinking is to learn to proceed through logical reasoning to satisfactory solutions of personal problems. This is called **rational problem solving.** D'Zurilla and Goldfried (1971) outlined the following five general steps in personal rational problem solving.

1. General orientation. Recognize problems and realize at the outset that it is possible to deal with them by acting systematically, rather than impulsively. As an aid, you might jot down on a 3 × 5 card a specific set of "coping self-statements" that you can use to prompt yourself to approach problems logically. Such statements might include:
   "I know I can work this out if I just proceed step-by-step."
   "Let me see how I can rephrase this as a problem to be solved."
   "I know I can solve this problem logically if I follow the five steps."

2. Problem definition. Describe the problem as precisely as possible and try to identify the specific situation in which the problem occurs. Often the initial problem definition is quite vague. In a case encountered by one of the authors, for example, a student described her problem as, "I've been very upset lately." After some discussion, it was discovered that what upset the student was that she shared an apartment with a very untidy roommate, and she couldn't stand the "mess" she felt forced to live in.

3. Generation of alternatives. After defining the problem precisely, "brainstorm" possible solutions. Let your mind "run-free" and think of as many solutions as you can, no matter how far-fetched. In the case of the student with the messy roommate, for example, possible solutions she thought of were to (a) move, (b) learn to accept messiness, (c) speak assertively to her roommate about keeping the place neat, (d) try to shape "neat" behavior in her roommate, (e) negotiate a behavioral contract with her roommate, (f) throw her roommate's things out the window, and (g) throw her roommate out the window.

4. Decision making. The next step is to examine the alternatives carefully, eliminating those that are obviously unacceptable, such as *f* and *g* above. You should then consider the likely short-range and long-range consequences of the remaining alternatives. Writing out the positives and negatives of various alternatives has been demonstrated to improve satisfaction with decision making, to increase the likelihood of sticking to decisions, and to lead to more productive choices and fewer regrets (Janis & Mann, 1977; Janis & Wheeler, 1978). On the basis of these considerations, you should select the alternative that seems most likely to provide the optimum solution, and devise a plan to accomplish it.

5. Verification. When the plan is in effect, keep track of progress to ensure that it solves the problem. If it doesn't, start the problem-solving sequence again and continue in this fashion until a successful solution is found

This approach to problem solving has been successfully applied to help individuals adjust to a variety of clinical problems (D'Zurilla, 1986).

Thought Stopping

The self-adjustment strategies described above illustrate ways that you can increase and improve various types of thoughts. But sometimes the opposite problem occurs. Sometimes you experience repetitive disturbing thoughts that you would like to get rid of. One strategy for doing so is called thought stopping.

Do you remember Carol from Chapter 1? She couldn't stop thinking about her former boyfriend. With help from a psychologist, she learned how to use thought stopping to terminate the disturbing thoughts, and to use photographs and written instructions to prompt positive alternative thoughts. The technique of thought stopping to eliminate unpleasant or self-defeating thoughts was developed by Joseph Wolpe (1958), a noted behavior therapist. The procedure involves learning to yell to yourself "stop!" in order to disrupt unpleasant thoughts. To teach yourself this technique, you might close your eyes and imagine a particular scene, such as sitting on the sand at a beach watching the waves gently roll up on shore. When you have the scene clearly in mind, yell "stop!" After a few minutes, repeat this routine. After several such occurrences, repeat the mental imagery again, except this time yell "stop!" silently to yourself. After several such attempts, you should find that you're able to temporarily disrupt any thought by saying "stop!" to yourself subvocally. When trying out thought stopping to eliminate some unpleasant or self-defeating thoughts, we recommend that you use two components: (1) say "stop!" immediately following the unwanted thought, and (2) immediately follow the thought stopping with the strategy of substituting a desirable alternative thought. In Carol's case, you may recall, she used photographs with written instructions on the back of the photos to prompt desirable thoughts (Martin, 1982). In other cases, the substituted thought has been simply the opposite of the unpleasant one (Cautela, 1983; Martin & Lumsden, 1987; Turner et al., 1983).

As indicated by some of the examples in the preceding pages, our thoughts can affect our mood—the way we feel at any given moment. And our feelings are a part of our emotions, the topic to which we now turn.

Emotions

Emotions, the second part of our "inside story," are a fundamental part of the experience of being human. And we humans are the most emotional of all the species (Hebb, 1980). In spite of their obvious importance, emotions have caused a great deal of difficulty for behavioral scientists. Emotions cannot easily be defined and measured, they can be classified in a number of different ways, and the terms commonly used to describe them are often so vague that psychologists are hard-pressed to talk about them precisely. We will try to make sense out of this important topic by discussing three characteristics of emotions: (1) the reaction that you feel inside during the experience of an emotion (such as the "queasiness" in the pit of your stomach when you feel nervous), (2) the way that you learn to outwardly express an emotion (such as talking fast in an animated fashion when nervous), and (3) how you become aware of and describe your emotions (for example, "I feel nervous" as opposed to "I feel sad"). Let's examine these characteristics in more detail.

The Reflexive Characteristic of Emotions: Our Feelings

Before discussing what you feel inside while experiencing an emotion, we need to review some characteristics of our nervous system. The brain and the spinal cord compose the *central nervous system*. The nerve pathways that fan out from the central nervous system into various parts of the body are labeled the *peripheral nervous system*. The peripheral nervous system is linked to all our sense organs, muscles, and glands. The peripheral nervous system consists of two components, the somatic and the autonomic nervous systems. The *somatic nervous system* controls our skeletal muscles, the muscles involved in what we say and do. The *autonomic nervous system* controls our internal functions, such as heart beat, respiration, digestion, and glandular activity. The organs and glands influenced by the autonomic nervous system are shown in Figure 4-3. Internal glands like the heart and stomach can act in two opposing ways: They can speed up (or contract) when they are aroused for action, and they can slow down after an emergency or exciting event has passed.

FEUDIN' AND FIGHTIN'.   Our physiological reactions during emotions include the activities of the various glands and organs shown in Figure 4-3. What happens inside you, for example, in a moment of great fear? Your body "clears the decks" for action. Your adrenal medulla (the inner core of the adrenal gland) secretes

Figure 4-3
The right side of the human autonomic nervous system. *From Kimble & Garmezy, 1963.*

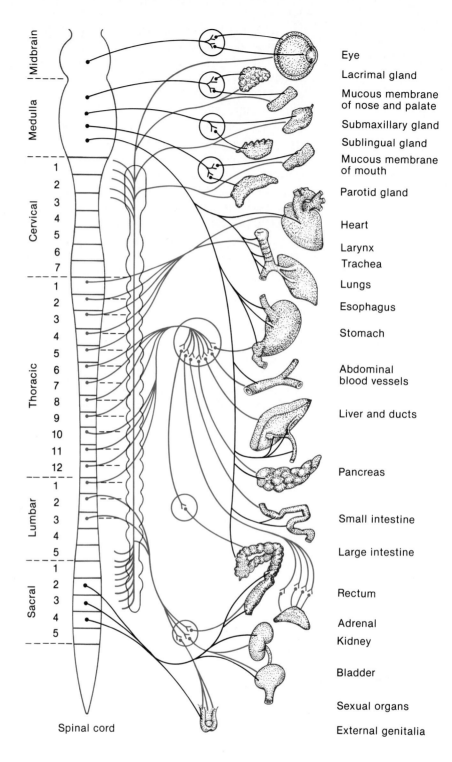

adrenalin (often called epinephrine) into your blood stream, releasing blood sugar for extra energy. Your heart rate increases dramatically. At the same time, increased respiration provides an increased supply of oxygen to the blood. This oxygen surges through your body with the increased heart rate and supplies more oxygen to your muscles. At the same time, you get that "queasy" feeling in your stomach because blood vessels to the stomach and intestines constrict and the digestion process is interrupted. Blood is diverted from your internal organs to your muscles. Your mouth dries as the action of the salivary glands is impeded. And if you're really afraid, bowel and/or bladder control may be lost temporarily. These internal reactions prepare you to fight or to flee. We have evolved this way over thousands of years.

Our emotions are accompanied by physiological arousal of the autonomic responses as described above. The results of autonomic responses can be visibly seen in many cases. Observable effects of autonomic activity include such responses as blushing, trembling, crying, piloerection of hair, and the like. Popular literature abounds with descriptions of such activity, for example, "My hair stood on end," "My hands were cold and clammy and shook like leaves," "I was quaking in my boots," "My breath caught in my throat and shivers ran up my spine."

EMOTIONAL "FEELINGS." Most of us learn to describe the physiological components of our emotions as our *feelings*. Popular literature would suggest that our feelings are distinct for each of the emotions. When people say, "I feel sad," as opposed to "I feel angry," they imply that what they feel in each case is quite different. Surprisingly, many researchers have been unsuccessful in demonstrating differences in physiological measures when subjects have reported feeling different emotions (Mandler, 1984). Experts, for example, could not distinguish measures of viewers' heart rates and respiration while they watched sad versus funny movies (Averill, 1969). Indeed, not only do heart rate and respiration increase during most emotions, they also increase during heavy exercise. But perhaps differences in the feelings experienced during different emotions are not dependent on any one physiological measure, like heart rate, but rather on the total pattern of bodily changes that may be involved, including facial expressions. Consider, for example, a study by Paul Ekman and his colleagues (1983) in which they asked experienced actors to make various facial expressions that simulated the expressions of various emotions, such as fear and anger. When the actors made the expression for anger, they showed an increased heart rate and skin temperature, while the expression for fear corresponded to an increased heart rate but a decreased skin temperature, and the expression for happiness was correlated with decreased heart rate and no change in skin temperature. Perhaps the specific combination of heart rate, skin temperature, and other physiological indicators is different for each of the different emotions. And perhaps there are cues other than what you feel inside that help you decide what emotion you are experiencing. You might decide that you are happy, for example, in part because others around you are laughing and having a good time. We'll examine this further when we discuss labeling of emotions.

EMOTIONS AT BIRTH. There is considerable debate regarding the number of emotions that babies are born with. This is due to the difficulty in identifying which of an infant's responses are evidence of emotion. In the early history of American psychology, Watson (1930), concluded from studies on newborn babies that there are three unconditioned emotional reflexes. They include *rage*, where the unconditioned stimulus is hampering an infant's movements and the unconditioned responses are crying, screaming, and body stiffening; *fear*, for which unconditioned stimuli include sudden loss of support, loud sounds, and a sudden push, and the unconditioned responses include sudden catching of breath, a clutching or grasping response, puckering of lips, and crying; and *joy*, for which unconditioned stimuli include tickling, gentle rocking, and patting, and unconditioned responses are smiling, gurgling, and cooing.

Other researchers have different views of the number of inherited emotions. Their studies suggest that, at birth, babies show an "excitement" response (Bridges, 1932), a neonatal smile, a startle response, and distress (in response to pain) (Izard, 1982). Expressions of anger and joy appear around three to four months, and

Infants show several basic emotions.

expressions of fear appear around six to seven months (Bridges, 1932; Izard, 1982). Expressions characteristic of all of the basic human emotions appear before age two (Bridges, 1932; Izard, 1977, 1982; Lazarus, 1991*a, b*). Thus, while researchers do not agree on the specific number of emotions present at birth, there is agreement that infants show a small number of emotions during the first few months.

EMOTIONAL FEELINGS AND REFLEXIVE LEARNING.   As described above, at least a part of the experiencing of an emotion is made up of the autonomic reaction. The autonomic component of such emotions as anger, anxiety, and joy are inborn in that stimuli exist that innately arouse them. A loud noise, for example, would cause an infant to feel afraid. And through reflexive learning, these feelings can be attached to new stimuli.

When experimenters have demonstrated reflexive learning of emotions, they have often relied on the visible signs of the physiological changes to demonstrate that learning has occurred. Do you remember the classic experiment with "Little Albert" described in Chapter 3? After a total of seven pairings of a loud noise when Albert was within sight of a white rat, he showed a very strong fear reaction to the rat. Whenever the rat appeared, Albert cried, trembled, and showed the facial expression for fear. All of us learn a variety of childhood fears through just such a process. A few painful falls while climbing trees or other high objects might establish the view from heights as a conditioned stimulus eliciting a fear reaction. The loud noise of a sudden clap of thunder paired with dark clouds and flashes of lightning might establish these latter stimuli as sources of fear.

The feelings associated with other emotions are also influenced by reflexive learning. When you party with good friends, for example, you experience the emotion of happiness. If you play your favorite cheerful music at those times, that music may become a conditioned stimulus eliciting "happy" feelings. Later, if you should play that music when you're by yourself, the music is likely to put you in a "happy mood."

PREPAREDNESS.   You may recall from Chapter 3 that all stimuli and responses are *not* equally conditionable. Indeed, attempts to replicate the Little Albert experiment (with other children) by Watson's contemporries failed (English, 1929; Bregman, 1934). They paired a loud noise with wooden and cloth objects instead of pairing the noise with a white rat. Perhaps the ease with which we can be conditioned to fear certain objects and events (such as rats and snakes) has to do with their evolutionary importance to us. That is, our ancestors might have been more likely to survive if they evolved so that they easily learned to fear things (like rats and snakes) that might harm them. Wooden and cloth objects weren't much of a threat to people in prehistoric times.

To describe the relative ease of conditioning some responses to some stimuli, Seligman (1972) has coined the term **preparedness.** His own personal experience involved a bout of stomach flu after a steak with Bernaise sauce. Seligman couldn't stand Bernaise sauce thereafter! Notably, he points out that he had no future aversion to the white plates he ate from, to the music that was playing at the time, nor to his wife who was also present. Apparently, only the taste of the Bernaise sauce became a conditioned stimulus for nausea. Thus, Seligman showed preparedness in the sense that he was easily conditioned to the taste of a particular food that made him sick. Having evolved this way greatly decreases the chances that one will continually consume food that causes illness (and perhaps death), while decreasing the chances of being inappropriately influenced by other stimuli that have nothing to do with the illness (such as white plates). In a similar manner, it is to our advantage to have evolved so that we may be more easily conditioned to fear things that might be harmful to us (like rats and snakes).

The Voluntary Characteristic of Emotions: Our Actions

As indicated above, when you experience an emotion-causing event, your body responds with an immediate physiological reaction and accompanying facial expression. But then what happens? That depends on how you've been brought up. In a situation that causes anger, for example, one person might shout, swear, and throw things. Another person in that same situation might simply count to ten silently. Fans at a hockey game in North America are likely to show their displeasure toward unsportsmanlike play by booing, while fans in Russia express their displeasure by whistling. After our initial reflexive reaction to an emotion-producing event, the different ways that we express our emotions are learned through operant and observational learning. Let's see how this comes about.

EMOTIONAL DISPLAYS AND OPERANT AND OBSERVATIONAL LEARNING.   You might recall from Chapter 3 that operant learning involves the modification of behaviors by their consequences (punishers weaken behaviors and rewards strengthen behaviors). Observational learning involves the ability to learn from observing the behavior of others. In any culture, individuals display their emotions in ways that have been modeled and rewarded in the past. Consider the following

preparedness

A predisposition of members of a species to be more easily influenced by reflexive learning with some stimuli than with others.

The different ways that we express our emotions are learned through operant and observational learning.

example. One of the authors grew up on a farm in a conservative community. He rarely saw his parents hug and kiss each other. Visits from aunts, uncles, and cousins were accompanied by greetings and the occasional handshake—but no other physical contact. The author learned to display his affection from these models. His wife, on the other hand, grew up in a close-knit, extroverted family in a city. Her family members displayed their emotions differently. Visits from relatives were always accompanied by hugging and kissing upon arrival, departure, and frequently in between. Affection was often openly expressed. And disagreements were often hotly and loudly disputed. When they were first married, the author's wife took pride in her emotional outbursts. She considered her husband to be unemotional. But the truth is that they simply learned to express their emotions in different ways.

To summarize thus far, an emotion-causing event occurs (for example, someone cuts in front of you after you have been waiting in line to buy theater tickets). The event causes an autonomic reaction (you feel "hot under the collar"), and the internal reaction has an immediate visible effect (such as a red face, clenched jaw, narrowed eyes, and so forth). This initial reaction is the reflexive component of emotion. After (or coinciding with) the initial reflexive reaction, a secondary display of emotion is likely to occur (you might shout angrily, "Go to the back of the line, I've been waiting for a half hour"). This secondary way of expressing your emotion depends on your operant and observational learning history. Both components of emotion—the initial reflexive component and the concurrent or subsequent operant component—are present in most instances of emotion. But there is a third part to the study of emotions that focuses on two interesting questions: How do we become aware of our emotions? And how do we learn to label them?

The Labeling Characteristic of Emotions: Our Awareness

Little Billy is playing with his favorite toy truck. His older brother, Ricky, grabs the truck and runs away. Billy runs after him screaming. Now Billy's mom comes on the scene. "Billy, why are you so mad?" she asks. From experiences like this, Billy learns to label some of his emotions as "being mad." Billy also learns other labels for other emotions. On his birthday, he plays with other children, opens presents, eats birthday cake, and listens while people sing, "Happy Birthday." Billy learns that on such occasions, he is "happy." One day, Billy goes to a funeral with his parents. People are crying. His parents tell him that Grandma has "gone away" and that he will never see her again. He learns that he feels "sad."

Like Billy, we all learn to label our emotions. By age nine, most children have learned to accurately label emotional expressions that accompany the majority of primary emotions (Izard, 1971). Yet, many emotions are not easily defined or described. (What's the difference, for example, between anger and annoyance? Or between liking and loving?) There are several reasons for this. First, there are so many different words that refer to emotions. Davitz (1969) counted over 400 of them in *Roget's Thesaurus*. Second, when people teach us a label for an emotion, the label may be produced by many events and not all of those events are present in all situations. Consider the example above in which Billy's mom asks him why he is mad. The label "mad" may be related to at least three sets of events: the outside setting (the sight of the older brother running away with a favorite possession), the inside pattern of autonomic activity (the feelings elicited by the loss of his toy truck), and the outside behavior (Billy running after his older brother screaming). The next day, when Mom is inside the house, she looks out the front window, and sees Billy running after his brother and screaming at him. Mom goes to the front door and shouts, "Now, Billy, don't get mad. You know how tired you get when you get upset." The external behavior of Billy that was called "being mad" in the second

Box 4-2

CROSS-CULTURAL STUDIES OF EXPRESSION OF EMOTIONS

In 1872, Darwin published *The Expression of Emotion in Man and Animals,* in which he proposed that there are some emotional expressions, such as smiles, frowns, and looks of disgust, that are innate and universal. For example, many animals bare their teeth and the hair on their neck becomes erect when they are angry and ready to attack. This has survival value for members of the same species because they can readily interpret it and avoid the angered animal. Darwin was also among the first to note the similarity of various emotional expressions across very different human cultures. Subsequently, a number of noted anthropologists and psychologists gathered volumes of cross-cultural data concerning expressions of emotion. These studies support our analysis of emotions into reflexive and operant behavioral components.

Reflexive Emotional Reactions May Be Universal. Infants appear to show a small number of distinct facial reactions to different emotion-producing stimuli. Cross-cultural evidence suggests that these reflexive reactions may be universal. Ekman and his associates (Ekman, 1972; Ekman et al., 1969) selected a group of photographs that they considered highly representative of facial expressions associated with one of six emotions: happiness, sadness, anger, fear, surprise, and disgust. A large number of subjects from Argentina, Brazil, Chile, Japan, and the United States were then asked to match each of the pictures to one of the six emotions. The subjects from the different cultures showed exceptionally high agreement in interpreting particular facial expressions as belonging to specific emotions. To determine whether or not the results might simply be due to high exposure of these modern cultures to American movies and television shows, the researchers asked members of a preliterate New Guinea tribe to show on their faces the appropriate expressions when told, "You friend has come and you are happy"; "Your child has died"; and "You are angry and about to fight." Videotapes of these subjects were later shown to American college students, who consistently identified the emotions portrayed as happiness, sadness, and anger, respectively. The expressions of one of the subjects are shown in the photos below.

Ongoing Display of Emotional Behavior Is Culture-Specific. After (or coinciding with) the initial reflexive emotional reaction, a secondary display of emotion is likely to occur. Because this is the operant component of emotions and its form depends on the individual's prior operant learning history, we would expect this behavior to vary from culture to culture. Cross-cultural evidence suggests that this is indeed the case. As indicated earlier, hockey fans in Russia express their displeasure by whistling, while North American hockey fans express their displeasure by booing. Numerous other examples of culture-specific displays of emotional behavior have also been recorded.

Expressions of happiness, sadness, and anger.

Box 4-3

Theories of Awareness of Emotions

Suppose that you are crossing the street when suddenly a car turns the corner and comes straight toward you. You jump out of the way. On the curb, your heart is pounding and you're trembling. Common sense suggests that you jumped and trembled because you were frightened. But American psychologist William James argued that it was the other way around. According to James, you felt afraid because you trembled. Instead of saying that you laugh because you feel happy or cry because you feel sad, James would say that you laugh and then feel happy, or cry and then feel sad. Let's take a closer look at some theories concerning how we experience and label an emotion.

James–Lange Theory. William James (1890) and Carl Lange (a Danish psychologist) argued that each different emotional state produces a unique pattern of physiological responses, and that we learn to label those unique patterns as they are experienced. Trembling combined with a queasiness in the pit of your stomach might be labeled as fear. A clenched fist, eyes narrowed, and feeling hot under the collar might be labeled as anger. And so on.

Cannon–Bard Theory. Walter Cannon and Philip Bard, two American physiologists, argued that a variety of emotions give rise to very similar physiological changes (for example, your heart rate

increases when you are afraid or angry). Therefore, the James–Lange assumption that differing bodily states give rise to different emotions seemed impossible. Rather, argued Cannon and Bard, experiencing and labeling an emotion occurs at the same time as physiological arousal—not one after the other, as proposed by the James–Lange theory. For example, when you see the car coming toward you, your brain sends messages causing you to feel afraid and to tremble at the same time.

Schachter Theory. In 1962, Stanley Schachter and Jerome Singer proposed a third theory of emotions. The theory has two factors: to experience an emotion, (1) you must be aroused, and (2) you must also have a cognitive reason for interpreting the arousal as an emotion before you will label it as such (Schachter, 1971). For example, if you have just finished riding an exercise bike, you will be physiologically aroused (rapid heart beat, heavy breathing, and so on), but you have no reason to say that you feel afraid. But if you jump out of the way of an approaching car, feel aroused, and realize that you might have just been killed, then you will interpret the arousal as feeling afraid.

Although Schachter and his colleagues conducted experiments that appeared to support their theory, other experimenters have criticized it (Denzin, 1984; Leventhal & Tomarken, 1986). At one ex-

---

case was the same as in the first case. But the outside setting (and maybe the pattern of autonomic activity) was quite different. What Mom didn't realize was that, on this occasion, Billy and Ricky were enjoying a game of tag. Thus, the problem of learning to label our emotions is that those who teach us don't always have access to the controlling events and our feelings. Often, all they see is our expression of emotions. But people can make the same overt response in quite different settings while experiencing different feelings in each setting. In fact, kids very quickly learn to "fake" emotions when consequences make it worthwhile to do so. They may fake "sadness" because such behavior leads to extra attention from Mom and Dad. They might fake "remorse" to avoid getting punished for performing a forbidden behavior. And of course, we all know how skillful actors can be at faking emotions.

Labeling your emotions is also difficult because you often encounter simultaneous events for several different emotions. For example, when riding the roller treme, for example, Richard Lazarus (1984a) believes that emotions can be produced by cognitive appraisals alone. At the other extreme, Robert Zajonc (1984) argued that cognitive appraisal of the reason for your feelings is not necessary for you to experience emotions. Only physiological arousal is necessary. As is so often the case with theories, the debate continues.

Facial Feedback Theory. Do you remember when you were a child and you used to run to Grandma after experiencing a fall or a bruise? And after comforting you, Grandma used to say, "Come on now, show me a big smile. There! Doesn't that feel better?" And it usually did feel better.

Maybe Grandma knew about the facial feedback theory of emotions. According to this theory, different basic emotions (anger, fear, happiness, and the like) are accompanied by different facial expressions (Izard, 1982). Secondly, when facial muscles show a particular expression, the nervous system feeds messages back to the brain and this information is used to label the emotion (Leventhal, 1982). This theory implies, for example, that you don't smile because you're happy, but rather that you're happy because you smile. And there is some experimental support for this theory, too. Ekman and associates (1983) found that heart rates rose faster when subjects put on an "angry" face

than when they put on a "happy" face. Also, subjects who were instructed to smile reported feeling happy (Kleinke & Walton, 1982).

Like the other theories of experiencing and labeling emotions, facial feedback theory has not been without its critics (for example, Matsumoto, 1987). While feedback from facial expressions may be one of the factors that can affect how we feel emotionally, other variables are far more powerful. Which do you think would make you feel happier, smiling for a few minutes or being told that you had just won a million-dollar lottery?

Summary of Theories of Emotion. So what do we conclude about all these theories? None of them can stand alone to explain all of the facts. And yet each has something to recommend it. As indicated earlier, we learn words for our various emotions through observational and operant learning. You may remember the case of Billy, described above, who learned that he felt "mad" when his brother took his toy truck, "sad" at his Grandma's funeral, and "happy" at birthday parties. What the different theories of emotions emphasize is that, after we have learned various words for our emotions, the specific words that we might use (such as "sad" versus "happy" versus "mad") to describe our feelings depend on a number of factors—physiological, situational, and cognitive.

coaster with a group of your friends, everyone is laughing and screaming. Although your heart is pounding, from events that would normally cause fear, you're not likely to say that you're frightened when you're laughing with the group. Moreover, because the group is likely to make fun of you if you let on that you're afraid, you may decide that your emotional response is one of excitement.

Some Basic Emotions and Their Causes

The characteristics of emotions that we have described thus far are summarized in Figure 4-4.

A key factor in the overview provided in Figure 4-4 is the emotion-causing event. What qualifies as an emotion-causing event? Let's examine some causes of some basic emotions.

Figure 4-4
A schematic of major components of emotions

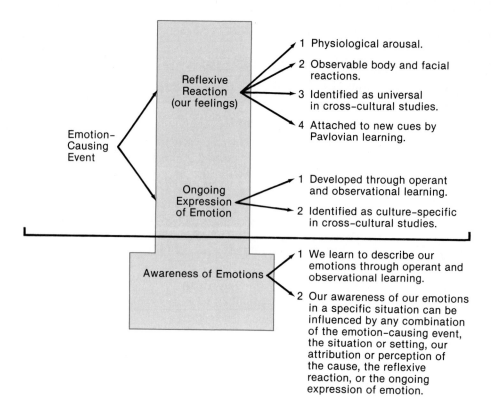

Happiness

What makes you happy? Getting an "A" on an exam? Receiving a compliment on your new hairstyle? Cashing in your paycheck? Watching a funny movie? We experience **happiness** when good things happen to us—when we encounter rewarding events and have rewarding experiences. Several lines of research support this contention. Setting and attaining goals, for example, enhances one's happiness (Diener, 1984). Goal-attainment generally involves rewards. Having a satisfying marriage and family life is highly correlated with reports of happiness (Glenn & Weaver, 1981). People in such a relationship experience many rewards on a daily basis.

In analyzing causes of happiness, we must keep in mind that events are rewarding to the extent that we are deprived of them. Your favorite cheeseburger is not likely to be a reward if you've just finished a big steak dinner with all the trimmings. A cold glass of water *is* likely to be a reward if you've just finished a long walk on a hot summer's day. What about winning a lottery? Would that make you happy? In the short run, probably yes! But what about after the initial surge of happiness—the initial spending spree—the initial "good times"? You would no longer be deprived of money (assuming that you have sense enough to invest some of it wisely). In fact, lottery winners do not experience a continued increase in happiness, and in the long run, their happiness is about the same as control groups of non-winners (Brickman et al., 1978). It seems that experiencing rewards today will make you feel happier today, but it will not guarantee your long-term happiness. Why is this? Maybe it has something to do with how we compare ourselves to others.

COMPARISONS TO OTHERS.   How you compare yourself to others affects your perception of whether or not you are well-off or hard-done-by. This in turn can affect your happiness. This might explain the finding that lottery winners tend to be no happier than non-winners. Initially, lottery winners are likely to compare themselves to those in their neighborhood, to feel lucky by comparison, and to feel happy. After a while, they tend to compare themselves to those at their new economic level or higher (by moving into a house in a richer neighborhood, by interacting with members at the country club that they join, and so forth). People have a tendency to compare themselves to those who are at or above their current economic, social, or professional level (Gruder, 1977), and this is likely to lessen their happiness (Diener, 1984).

An example of how comparisons to others can influence happiness can be seen with the seriously ill. People have been able to adjust satisfactorily to serious illness by thinking of someone else who is worse off. Women who have lumpectomies (that is, lump only removed) for breast cancer tend to pity women who have mastectomies (that is, complete removal of the breast). Women who have lost only one breast to surgery tend to pity women who have lost two. Older women who have mastectomies tend to feel sorry for young women who have them. And young women who have mastectomies with localized cancer enhance their personal feelings by feeling sorry for the women whose cancer of the breast has spread to other systems (Taylor, 1983).

THE HAPPINESS FORMULA.   So what is the magic formula for happiness? Maximize your social rewards (good friends, a happy marriage, supportive family, or all three). Seek challenging work with frequent feedback for accomplishments and a "job well done." Set lots of short-term goals and strive to achieve them. Congratulate yourself each time you do so. Pursue rewards that are consistent with your value system and moral standards, and those of your subculture. If you compare your circumstances to others, compare yourself to others who are less fortunate. And finally, as Bobby McFerrin says in the song—"Don't worry; be happy."

Anger

anger
An unpleasant emotion that is caused by withholding or withdrawal of rewards.

Do the following experiences make you mad: A vending machine that takes your money but doesn't produce the goods? Being kept waiting in the doctor's office? Having the ticket line close just before you get to the window to buy your ticket? Pens that stop writing in the middle of a quiz? Withholding or withdrawal of rewards causes **anger.** All of us have experienced such anger-causing events. Unpleasant occurrences, such as foul odors, high temperatures, and even disgusting scenes can also cause one to feel anger (Berkowitz, 1990). Some psychologists suggest that such experiences cause frustration, which in turn causes anger (for example, Rathus & Nevid, 1986). But this adds an unnecessary "middle man." It is simpler to identify the emotion-causing event, the emotional behavior that follows, and to then label the emotional behavior (as anger or whatever seems most appropriate).

ANGER DISPLAY.   The various ways that we learn to display anger are not always problematic. When people feel angry, they often experience a surge of vigor and energy, which can sometimes be channeled quite usefully—for example, by helping you to unscrew that frustratingly sticky top on the pickle jar. In other cases, however, anger is expressed in destructive ways and is often a contributing factor to physical and verbal aggression (Hazaleus & Deffenbacher, 1986), battered-wife syndrome and child abuse (Nomelini & Katz, 1983), personal injury and property damage (Hazaleus & Deffenbacher 1986), ineffective problem solving (Ellis, 1976), and various health problems (Gentry et al., 1982).

BOTTLING IT UP.   When you feel angry, should you "bottle it up"? Or should you "let it all hang-out"? Freud and others have suggested that release of pent-up emotions or catharsis is a healthy practice. Many people seem to feel that it is

Withholding or withdrawal of rewards causes anger.

especially bad to "bottle up" anger. On the other hand, not only does expressing anger not always get rid of it, it may prolong it and make it more intense (Averill, 1982; Tavris, 1984). Moreover, considering that anger is often a response to the perceived misdeeds of friends or loved ones (Averill, 1983), you should remember that expressing your anger today can cause you much regret tomorrow.

According to self-reports of individuals questioned by Averill (1983), most people become mildly to moderately angry at least several times a week, and in some cases, several times a day. Some people who cannot control their anger sometimes commit acts of violence. Such individuals may need special help in learning to control their anger (Deffenbacher et al., 1986; Hazaleus & Deffenbacher, 1986). Some guidelines for learning to control anger are presented later in this chapter and are described further in Chapter 15.

Anxiety

anxiety

An unpleasant emotion that is caused by the presentation of punishers or aversive stimuli.

According to the National Institute of Mental Health, anxiety is so distressing and persistent for one person in twelve that these people are said to suffer an anxiety disorder (Regier et al., 1984). **Anxiety** is the label given to our emotional experience when we encounter impending danger or aversive events. For example, consider the case of Kevin. When he was only four years old, he fell into the neighbor's swimming pool. Unable to swim, he almost drowned before he was hauled out. Since then, he has been deathly afraid of water. But he just *had* to go swimming with the other kids at the end-of-the-year class party. As he walked out onto the pool deck, the horrible experience came flooding back . . . the darkness, choking, wildly trying to claw his way to the top. With his heart pounding, his breath coming in short gasps, Kevin slumped into one of the deck chairs, trembling all over. Kevin was experiencing an anxiety attack.

Anxiety and fear are discussed further in Chapters 13 and 14. Some guidelines for controlling anxiety are presented later in this chapter and are described further in Chapter 15.

Relief

relief

A pleasant emotion that is caused by the withdrawal of aversive or punishing events.

Withdrawal of aversive events causes an emotion that we call **relief.** For example, imagine that you have just arrived at your winter cabin after driving for two hours in a blinding snowstorm. Without any place to stop along the way, you had to continue despite the ever-present danger of slipping off the road, or worse yet, having a head-on collision with a car that you couldn't see. Now, sitting safely in front of the fireplace, relief and relaxation slowly settle in.

How Many Basic Emotions Are There?

Presentation and withdrawal of rewards and presentation and withdrawal of aversive events: These are four major causes of emotions. Each of these causes and the emotions that occur range from very mild to very strong, as shown in Figure 4-5.

The basic emotions in Figure 4-5 are clearly distinguishable at the extremes. It's easy to tell if someone is experiencing ecstasy as opposed to terror. The emotions tend to merge, however, as we proceed along each continuum to milder versions of the emotions. A mild annoyance may seem quite similar to mild apprehension. Mild pleasure may seem similar to mild relief.

The model in Figure 4-5 implies that there are four basic emotions. However, leading researchers in this area suggest that there are anywhere from six to ten basic or primary emotions (see Table 4-1).

Why is there disagreement among researchers concerning the exact number of basic emotions? A part of the problem is that there is no agreed-upon definition for basic or primary emotions as compared to secondary emotions. Another source of disagreement concerns the role of cognitive appraisal in the experiencing of

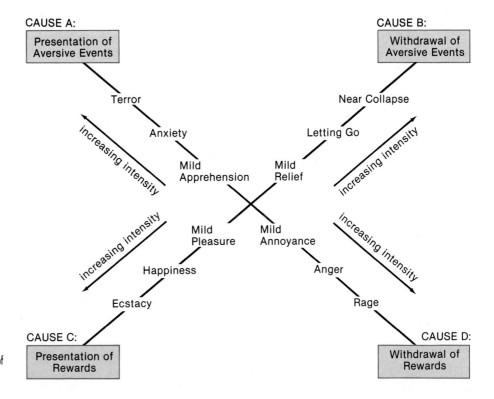

Figure 4-5

A schematic model of four major causes of emotions. *Adapted from Millenson, 1967.*

TABLE 4-1
WHAT ARE THE PRIMARY EMOTIONS?

	Paul Ekman (1980)	Carroll Izard (1977)	Robert Plutchik (1984)	Silvan Tomkins (1981)
Acceptance			X	
Anger	X	X	X	X
Anticipation			X	
Contempt		X		X
Disgust	X	X	X	X
Distress		X		X
Fear	X	X	X	X
Guilt		X		
Interest		X		X
Joy (Happiness, Enjoyment)	X	X	X	X
Sadness	X		X	
Shame		X		X
Surprise	X	X	X	X

emotions. Lazarus (1991*a, b*), for example, believes that emotions cannot occur without some kind of thought. Will the statement "You're ugly" cause you to feel anger? Perhaps it would if you interpret it as an insult by someone you don't like, but probably not if you interpret it as teasing by a friend. And if all emotions require some underlying cognition to be experienced, does that mean they're all basic? Others disagree with Lazarus' emphasis on the role of cognition (for example, Skinner, 1987).

Still another source of disagreement is that researchers have not always considered all components of emotions while studying them. For example, some researchers have classified emotions based primarily on the way emotions are expressed, such as by studying different facial expressions. But emotional expressions are only one of the components of emotions (see Figure 4-4). Perhaps a more reliable and valid analysis of basic emotions might be obtained by asking observers to classify distinctive emotions when they are given information about *both* the causes *and* the distinctive facial expressions controlled by those causes. Researchers might discover, for example, that what appear to be two different emotions are simply different places on one of the four continua presented in Figure 4-5. Consider a few examples. Cross-cultural studies of facial expressions suggest that disgust and anger are two different emotions. But if we were to study their causes, we might discover that both are caused by a withdrawal of rewards and that disgust might simply be a mild form of anger. As another example, cross-cultural studies of facial expressions suggest that surprise and fear are two separate emotions. But perhaps both are caused by the presentation of aversive events, and the facial expression for surprise may represent a very mild version of the facial expression characteristic of fear.

SOME COMPLEX EMOTIONS.   There's another reason why there appears to be more than four basic emotions. Perhaps some of what appear to be basic emotions are really combinations of simpler emotions.

Consider the case of a child who has been punished for taking cookies from the cookie jar. Now imagine that the child finds himself in the kitchen all alone and starts to reach for the cookie jar. At that point, the child thinks, "What if Dad comes and punishes me again?" This amounts to the presentation of an aversive stimulus,

guilt

A sense of wrongdoing; may be caused by a combination of events that produce both anxiety and happiness.

pride

A strong feeling of self-respect; may be caused by a combination of events that produce both happiness and anger.

sorrow

Strong emotional behavior elicited by the loss of someone close to you; may be based on a combination of anger, anxiety, emotional relief, and happiness.

causing anxiety. At the same time, the child thinks, "That cookie sure would taste good." This represents the presentation of a reward, causing happiness. The resulting combination of anxiety and happiness may be experienced as **guilt.**

As another example, consider the emotion of **pride.** Suppose a coach is giving a locker room pep talk to his junior high football team just before the big game. The coach might say, "This is the big one. One more to go and we've won the championship. Just think how good you're going to feel if you get to wear those championship jackets." This represents the presentation of rewards. The coach continues, "Are you gonna let their team take it away from you? Are you gonna let them win the championship?" This represents the withdrawal of rewards. While the players shout in unison, "Noooo," they're probably feeling a sense of pride . . . an emotion that may represent a combination of happiness from the presentation of rewards and anger from the potential withdrawal of rewards.

Sorrow may be the result of a mixture of all four causes of emotions (presentation and withdrawal of rewards and punishers; see Figure 4-5). First, the loss of a close friend involves the withdrawal of many rewarding experiences that were shared with that person in the past, causing some anger. Second, thoughts of the aversiveness of getting along without that person may cause some anxiety. Third, there might also be some relief in the sense that it's finally over, especially if death followed a long, drawn-out illness. And there might be some valued possessions that have been left for you, which may cause some small degree of happiness. All of these experiences might combine producing the emotion called sorrow or grief. (Sorrow and grief are discussed further in Chapter 10.)

Other complex emotions are described in later chapters. Now let's examine some strategies of emotional adjustment that you can use to induce particular emotions and to control others when you desire to do so.

Managing Your Emotions

There are steps that you can take to increase specific emotions. Earlier in this chapter, for example, we described what you might do to increase your happiness. In Chapter 8, we talk about liking and loving, emotions that many of us would like to increase in our lives. In Chapter 15, we review specific strategies for resolving harmful emotions like anxiety, anger, and loneliness. But there are some coping techniques that apply across a variety of situations—situations that evoke a whole range of emotions. These techniques include progressive muscle relaxation, controlled breathing, and rational thinking.

Progressive Muscle Relaxation

progressive muscle relaxation

A relaxation technique that involves alternately tensing and relaxing various muscle groups while thinking about how the muscles feel while they are tensed versus while they are relaxed.

An effective strategy to cope with a variety of troublesome emotions, including anger and anxiety, is to learn to relax (Lehrer & Woolfolk, 1985). One of the more widely used strategies for achieving a state of deep relaxation was developed by a Chicago physician, Edmond Jacobson, and described in his book, *Progressive Relaxation,* in 1938. The technique of **progressive relaxation** involves alternately tensing and relaxing various muscle groups while attending closely to the sensations you are feeling when your muscles are tensed versus when they are relaxed. You learn to become sensitive to the relaxed state of your muscles in contrast to the state of tension.

The instructions for achieving muscle relaxation that we provide in Box 4-4 will be maximally effective if they are recorded on a tape recorder. It would be best to have someone with a low, even, soothing voice record the relaxation instructions. You can then listen to the instructions as you practice this technique, rather than having to read them.

Box 4-4

RELAXATION INSTRUCTIONS FOR TAPING

The instructions on this tape will help you learn to relax. Included is a series of exercises in which you first tense various muscles, then relax them, while at the same time noticing the difference between how they feel when they're tense and how they feel when they're relaxed. Before you start listening to the instructions, find a comfortable place where you can sit or lie down and where you won't be disturbed for ten minutes or so. Listen closely to the instructions.

Each time I pause, continue doing what you were doing just before the pause. Now close your eyes and take three deep breaths. (p) (p)[a] Now squeeze both fists really tight and raise your fists up to your shoulders to make the muscles in your biceps tight. *Squeeze them tight. Note how they feel.*[b] Now relax. Just relax and think of the tension disappearing from your fingers. (p) (p) Once again, squeeze both fists at once and bend both arms to make them feel totally tense throughout. *Hold it. Keep them tight. Think about the tension you feel.* And now relax. Feel the total warmth and relaxation flowing through your muscles, (p) all the way down from your biceps, down to your forearms, and out of your fingertips. (p) (p)

Now wrinkle your forehead and squint your eyes very tight and hard. *Squeeze them tight and hard. Feel the tension across your forehead and through your eyes.* Now relax. Note how it feels in your eyes. They feel warm and relaxed. (p)

Now squeeze your jaws down tight together. Bite down hard and raise your chin. Stick your chin out to make your neck muscles hard. *Hold it. Bite down hard. Tense your neck. Squeeze your lips really tight together.* And once again, just relax. Just breathe deeply and relax. (p) (p)

Now squeeze both your shoulders forward as hard as you can, so that you feel your muscles pull tight across your back, especially between your shoulder blades. *Squeeze them. Hold it.* And relax. (p) Just breath deeply. (p) One more time, squeeze your shoulders forward again, but this time at the

same time suck in your stomach as far as you can, and make your stomach muscles hard. *Feel the tension in your stomach? Hold it.* And relax. (p) (p)

Now your legs. Bend your knees so that you can push down hard on your heels. *Push down hard. Raise your toes, make your calf muscles and thigh muscles tight. Hold it.* And relax. (p) (p) Just feel the warmth flowing down your legs, down to your ankles, down to your toes. (p) One more time with your legs. Bend your legs so you can push down hard on your heels, and squeeze your toes up toward your shins. *Make the muscles in your legs tight. Hold it.* And relax. (p)

Take three deep breaths. (p) (p) Now, when I call out the names of the muscles and the body parts, tense them just as you've been practicing. Ready? *Both fists—squeeze them tight. Bring your fists up to your shoulders: Make your arms tight. Wrinkle your forehead: Squint hard. Bite down hard with your jaw: Squeeze your lips together. Round your shoulders forward: Suck in your stomach. Push down hard on your heels: Squeeze your toes up. Hold it. Hold it.* And relax. (p) (p) Just breathe deeply, and notice how relaxed all your muscles feel. (p) (p)

Take three deep breaths. (p) (p)

One more time, as I call out the names of the muscles and the body parts, squeeze them the way you've practiced. Ready? *Both fists—put your fists up to your shoulders: Make your arms tight. Bite down hard. Wrinkle your forehead: Squint hard. Round your shoulders forward: Suck in your stomach, and push against your stomach. Squeeze down with your heels: Curl your toes up. Hold it. Everything tense. Hold it.* And relax. (p) (p) Just enjoy the feeling of complete relaxation. (p) (p) Breathe slowly and deeply. (p) (p) Now turn the tape off.

[a] *Each (p) represents a pause of 5 seconds.*
[b] *Each italicized phrase should be stated a little more loudly and quickly than the other statements.*

If you practice the relaxation exercises, you will become proficient at being able to relax in a matter of a few seconds. The amount of practice required before you get to that point will vary from individual to individual. Davis, Eshelman, and McKay (1980) recommend listening to the tape twice per day for one to two weeks. Neidhart and colleagues (1985), on the other hand, suggest that it takes from six to twelve weeks of practice to become really proficient at successfully using progressive muscle relaxation in high-stress situations. At a minimum, we recommend that you start out by listening to the relaxation tape and practicing the exercises just before going to sleep on at least five successive nights. Another benefit of this type of practice is that a number of authors have suggested that progressive muscle relaxation can improve insomnia (Neidhart et al., 1985). During the next phase of your mastering this technique, continue listening to the tape just before bedtime at least twice per week for the next three or four weeks. In addition, two or three times per day, practice total tensing and relaxing of all of your muscle groups as described in the last paragraph in Box 4-4. After two or three weeks of this practice, you should be able to relax totally in a minute or two in almost any situation. You should then find muscle relaxation exercises to be an effective way to combat the anxiety you might feel in a variety of stressful situations, such as having to give a talk in class, writing an exam, or perhaps going for a job interview. Just before entering such stressful situations, listen to the tape with your Walkman in a private setting, such as a nearby washroom. If that's not feasible, take a few seconds and go through the total tensing and relaxing as described in the last paragraph in Box 4-4.

Mastery of muscle relaxation techniques is a recommended component to deal with a variety of problems. In particular, it is recommended as a useful component of procedures to treat arthritic pain, tension headaches, migraines, bruxism (teeth grinding), insomnia, anxiety, sexual dysfunction, neck and back pain, high blood pressure, mild phobias, stuttering, and hypertension (Davis et al., 1980; Neidhart et al., 1985).

Controlled Breathing: Centering

An effective way of combatting mild levels of anxiety and anger is to practice **centering**—a martial arts procedure that emphasizes thought control, a particular way of breathing, and muscle relaxation (Martin & Lumsden, 1987). When centering, you should consciously relax and droop your neck and shoulder muscles, letting your arms hang down your side as low as possible. This can be done while standing or sitting. You should then breathe from very low down in the abdomen. An easy way to do this is as follows. Place your hands on your abdomen and inhale. Then, while exhaling, consciously push your abdomen in to force all of the air out of your body. Next, watch your hands move outward as you inhale, as your abdomen bulges while your lungs fill with air. Rather than your chest rising and falling while breathing, your abdomen should extend (when inhaling) and collapse (when exhaling). While you are exhaling, you should say slowly to yourself "relax." Breathing slowly in this manner for a half a dozen or so breaths can help you relax quickly. Also, because it takes some concentration to do it correctly, centering is an effective thought-stopping procedure.

Rational Thinking

Do you find yourself saying such things as: "I must be perfect at everything I do," "I'm such a klutz," "Why does the worst always happen to me?" Albert Ellis considers these overgeneralizations to be irrational (after all, the worst does not *always* happen to you) (Ellis & Harper, 1975). A problem with such irrational thoughts is that they can be quite stressful, causing considerable anxiety. As we mentioned earlier, Albert Ellis developed his **rational-emotive therapy** to help

centering
A breathing technique that helps one to relax and eliminate problem thoughts; involves breathing low down in the abdomen so that the abdomen extends when inhaling and collapses when exhaling.

rational-emotive therapy
A type of therapy in which clients are taught to counteract irrational beliefs (that cause emotional problems) by changing to rational beliefs; developed by Albert Ellis.

people identify irrational ideas or beliefs, and to replace them with realistic statements about the world. If you frequently find yourself making irrational generalizations that cause you to feel anxious, then you should follow the steps recommended by Ellis (for example, see Bernard, 1991). First, analyze your self-talk and write down the specific irrational, anxiety-evoking generalizations that you frequently make. Next, for each of the irrational statements, prepare specific alternative coping self-statements. Let's suppose, for example, that you are the type of person who overgeneralizes about the consequences of failing to carry out a particular assignment; you think such irrational thoughts as, "Why do I always screw things up?" "This is going to be terrible." Effective coping self-statements in such a situation might include:

- "I won't think about the consequences of failing; I'll concentrate on what I can do to be successful. That's better than getting nervous."
- "Everybody gets a little nervous once in awhile. But I have ways to manage it. I'll take three deep breaths, relax, slow things down, and practice positive thinking."
- "I'll just do my muscle relaxation, and calm right down. Then I'll start at the beginning."

There is no doubt that our emotions add greatly to the meaning and quality of our lives on a daily basis. But emotions also have a dark side. If you practice the strategies described in this chapter, you can increase emotional experiences that are pleasurable, and decrease or control emotions that have a negative impact.

SUMMARY

- Thinking is the private manipulation of words and images, as in private self-talk, imagery, concept formation, problem solving, and decision making. Thinking as private self-talk is influenced by operant learning while thinking in images is influenced by reflexive learning. Your thinking affects your self-concept, a general term which refers to the broad range of self-descriptions that a person is likely to make about him or herself, and the associated imagining elicited by those self-descriptions.

- Strategies to change your thoughts to achieve self-adjustment include thinking positively and using self-instructions; using imagery rehearsal to perform a skill by imagining how it feels and what you see when that particular skill is performed in real life; practicing rational problem solving which includes defining a problem precisely, identifying alternatives, and selecting the best alternative; and using thought stopping to eliminate unpleasant or self-defeating thoughts.

- Emotions have three important characteristics: (1) the autonomic reaction that you feel inside during the experience of an emotion (and which is typically accompanied by visible signs, such as frowns or smiles), which is influenced by reflexive learning; (2) the way that you learn to overtly express an emotion (such as shouting, running around, yelling, and the like), which is influenced by operant and observational learning; and (3) the way that you become aware of and describe your emotions.

- Four main causes of emotional reactions include: presentation of rewards, which causes happiness; withholding or withdrawal of rewards, which causes anger; presentation of punishers which causes anxiety; and withdrawal of aversive events, which causes relief. Other emotions may be complex mixtures of these basic emotions.

- As we grow up, we learn to label our specific emotions on the basis of several sets of events: the outside setting, the inside pattern of physiological activity, our appraisal of the cause of the emotion, and the outside behavior or emotional reaction. Because the people who teach us the various labels for emotions do not usually have access to all these events, our labels for emotional behavior can be inconsistent.

■ Strategies to manage emotions include practicing progressive muscle relaxation, learning a controlled breathing technique (called centering), and practicing rational self-talk.

Box 4-5

SELF-ADJUSTMENT FOR STUDENTS:
SPECIFY THE PROBLEM

In the self-adjustment box at the end of Chapter 3, we outlined for you a model for self-improvement. We suggest that you follow that model in completing a self-adjustment project. At this point, we suggest that you complete the first step in your project, *specifying a problem for change.* In the self-adjustment box at the end of each of the following chapters, we will guide you through the remaining steps of your self-adjustment project.

REVIEW YOUR QUESTIONNAIRES AND MAKE A LIST OF AREAS TO IMPROVE
The questionnaire that you completed at the end of Chapter 1 required you to focus on desirable behaviors that you currently perform. Now you should reexamine your answers to that questionnaire and identify several things that you are *not* doing that could be improved. Write them on a sheet of paper under the topic "Areas to Improve."

At the end of Chapter 2, we asked you to complete a Behavioral Self-Rating Checklist in which you identified things that you think you need to learn in order to function more effectively or to be more comfortable. Reexamine your answers to that checklist and identify several additional areas in which you might like to improve. Add them to your list.

Also at the end of Chapter 2, you identified some career and personal goals for yourself. Because those goals are long-term, it might not be possible for you to achieve any of them during the remainder of this course. But it might be possible for you to accomplish some subgoals to start yourself in the right direction. Reexamine your list of long-term goals from the end of Chapter 2. Try to identify subgoals that might be accomplished within the next few weeks. Add them to your list.

DO THE "AREAS TO IMPROVE" IDENTIFY SPECIFIC BEHAVIORS?
Many problems of self-adjustment can be easily specified in quantitative terms. It's relatively easy, for example, to set goals in the area of weight control and exercise. In contrast, other self-improvement goals are more difficult to measure. These include things like "having a positive attitude toward college," "becoming less nervous," or "improving a relationship." Mager (1972) refers to such vague abstractions as "fuzzies." A fuzzy is an acceptable starting point for identifying a self-adjustment problem. However, you must then "unfuzzify" the abstraction by identifying the performances that would cause you to agree that your goal has been achieved.

Consider, for example, the first item on your list of "Areas to Improve." For that item, what is it that you would like to change? How will you know if you have succeeded? That is, what would you take as evidence that your goals have been achieved? If your goals are outcomes (rather than something that you do) such as achieving a certain weight, accumulating a certain amount of money, or having a clean room, then make a list of specific behaviors that will help you achieve those outcomes. For each of the "Areas to Improve" that you have listed, ask the above questions and write out your answers to ensure that those areas are "unfuzzified."

Continued

Do Your "Areas to Improve" Involve the Strengthening of Desirable Behaviors?

Many of the items on the Behavioral Self-Rating Checklist at the end of Chapter 2 involve decreasing undesirable behavioral excesses, such as to stop biting fingernails, to stop saying "crazy" things to other people, or to stop putting off things that need to be done. And it is a common human tendency to focus more on what is "wrong" than on what we would like to be doing instead. While focusing on problematic behavioral excesses is a good starting point, your self-improvement project is more likely to be successful if you identify desirable alternative behaviors to replace the excesses that you would like to decrease. Suppose, for example, that you decide that you need to stop putting off things that need to be done. The desirable alternative behaviors would include aspects of time management described in Chapter 1. You might, for example, begin writing out a daily to-do list, prioritizing the items on your to-do list each morning, dividing time-consuming projects into short steps or stages, and so on.

Reexamine each of the items on your list of "Areas to Improve." For those that involve decreasing some undesirable behavior, identify several desirable alternative behaviors to strengthen in their place.

Prioritize the Items on the List of "Areas to Improve"

Now examine your revised list of "Areas to Improve." You now face the task of selecting a project to work on during the next few weeks. Therefore, on your list of "Areas to Improve," you should do the following:

1. Eliminate areas that appear to be so major that they will not likely be manageable within the next few weeks.
2. Eliminate areas that appear to be easily solved within a short period of time.
3. Eliminate areas that are not likely to be feasible at this time (perhaps because they have a monetary component that you can't afford, or because they require the cooperation of others that may be difficult to arrange, or for other reasons).
4. For the remaining areas, prioritize them in order of their personal value to you.
5. From the top few high priority "Areas to Improve," select one to work on during the remaining steps of your self-adjustment project.

MEMORY BOOSTER

■ IMPORTANT PERSONS

You should know who these persons are and why they are important:

Albert Ellis	Walter Cannon
William James	Philip Bard
Edmond Jacobson	Stanley Schachter
Carl Lange	Jerome Singer

■ IMPORTANT TERMS

Be prepared to define the following terms (located in the margins of this chapter). Where appropriate, be prepared to describe examples.

Thinking	Concept
Conditioned Seeing	Prototype

Linguistic Relativity Hypothesis	Anxiety
Self-concept	Fear
Identity	Phobia
Self-esteem	Relief
Identity Crisis	Guilt
Premack Principle	Pride
Imagery Rehearsal	Sorrow
Rational Problem Solving	Progressive Muscle Relaxation
Preparedness	Centering
Happiness	Rational-emotive Therapy
Anger	

■ QUESTIONS FROM IMPORTANT IDEAS IN THIS CHAPTER

1. When do children learn to think by talking silently to themselves? Why does this happen?
2. How is a single concept represented in our thinking?
3. How do we acquire a self-concept?
4. Using an example, illustrate how one might use positive thinking to counteract negative thoughts.
5. What are the basic steps in a rational approach to problem solving?
6. Briefly discuss the three main characteristics of emotions.
7. Cross-cultural studies indicate that emotions are both universal and culture-specific. How can we reconcile this apparent contradiction?
8. In two or three sentences each, summarize four theories concerning how we experience and learn to label our emotions.
9. Describe four main causes of emotional reactions.
10. Does your thinking affect your emotions? How can that cause problems? How can that be used in therapy?

chapter

5

COPING WITH STRESS

LEARNING OBJECTIVES

After reading this chapter, you should be able to:

- Describe environmental, psychological, and physiological sources of stress.
- Describe various effects that stress can have on our bodies and our lives.
- Identify many of the stressors in your own life.
- Take steps to alter some sources of stress in your life.
- Change your body's reactions to cope more effectively with stressors that can't be changed.

Fred Hansen bolted upright in bed, suddenly wide awake. He had slept through his alarm and was going to be late for class, again. Rushing to get ready, he cut himself while shaving. Unable to find a clean shirt, he hollered at his roommate in anger. His stomach knotted as he rifled through the pile of papers on his desk—frantically searching for his history notes. He rushed out the door without having breakfast, grabbing a pack of cigarettes from the counter.

Later, in the barely moving traffic, Fred yelled angrily at the motorist who cut into his lane. The smog and fumes caused him to cough and wheeze. Fred leaned on his horn in frustration, thinking, "Why does the worst always happen to me?"

We've all heard of stress causing ulcers and heart attacks. Fred Hansen is a likely candidate for both of these health problems. Why? First, there's his lack of sleep, as well as poor eating habits and nicotine addiction—three of the many physiological sources of stress. Second, he's surrounded by noise, crowds, and smog—three of the many environmental sources of stress. Third, he frequently thinks hostile, antagonistic, and self-defeating thoughts (about his roommate, other drivers, being late, the worst always happening to him)—examples of the many psychological sources of stress.

A certain amount of stress in daily living is a part of normal human existence. But excessive stress is associated with serious health problems, especially if, like Fred, we have difficulty coping with stress. For example, did you know that:

- During the seven months following the 1980 eruption of Mount St. Helen's, stress-related illness complaints doubled at a mental health clinic in the nearby town of Othello, Washington, when compared to the seven months prior to the eruption (Adams & Adams, 1984)?
- In general, studies of human-made (for example, nuclear accident) and natural (for example, earthquake) disasters are associated with a 17 percent increase in psychological problems reported by victims in comparison to control groups that did not experience various disasters (Rubonis & Pickman, 1991)?
- The greater the distance that employees at two California companies had to commute to work, and the worse the traffic, the higher was the workers' blood pressure when they arrived at work, the higher it remained later during the workday, and the worse were the employees' moods at work (Stokols et al., 1978)?
- For each 1 percent increase in the national unemployment rate, there is a 2 percent increase in heart disease and liver cirrhosis (Brenner, 1973)?
- Women who score high on life stress tests also report a high incidence of vaginal infections (Williams & Deffenbacher, 1983)?
- As students, your immune system is less capable of fighting diseases during high stress times such as exam week (Jemmot & Locke, 1984)?

You can see that there is overwhelming support for the association of stress with a variety of health problems.

But don't these sound like medical problems? And if they are medical problems, what role can psychology play in their successful resolution? Psychology's part in preventing illness and promoting health has emerged only recently, as health professionals discovered that many of the stresses and illnesses we face in life stem from our own behavior patterns. The man in our opening scenario, for instance, has poor eating and sleeping habits, ineffective time management practices; he smokes, is often hostile and quick to anger, constantly hurries, and tends to worry. All of these behavior patterns increase this man's risk of some serious diseases—including ulcers, heart attack, strokes, and lung cancer. If this man were to change his behavior, he could significantly lower his risk of serious illness. And when people need to change or better understand their own behavior, they turn to psychologists.

Psychology, then, as a science of behavior, plays an important role in solving medical problems that require people to change their lifestyles. As Thomas Stachnik, a health psychology researcher, put it:

> In short, the most serious medical problems that today plague the majority of Americans are not ultimately medical problems at all; they are behavior problems, requiring the alteration of characteristic response patterns, and thus fall squarely within the province of psychology (Stachnik, 1980, p. 8).

In this chapter, we introduce you to the topic of stress. We review different types of stressors and look at some effects of stress on human behavior and physical health. Finally, we examine strategies for coping successfully with stress and developing a healthier lifestyle.

There are many sources of stress, including natural disasters, a job with heavy demands and little control over what has to be done next, trying to do several things at once, uncontrollable delays, and environmental pollution.

Definition of Stress

Like death and taxes, stress is one of the things that you can be sure of encountering in life. To some extent, stress is an inevitable part of our existence. But there are many indications that this particular "part" of our existence often causes serious problems: Stress-related disorders and symptoms have become so common in Western society that they account for approximately two thirds of office visits to family doctors (Wallis, 1983). It's not surprising, then, that stress management is an issue of major concern in the psychology of adjustment. But exactly what is stress?

As you can see by the following quotes, the term *stress* is used in several different ways.

Stress as an Environmental Stimulus

- "Final exam week is a major source of stress for students."
- "The long winters in the north cause considerable stress for the people who live there."

Stress as a Response to Environmental Stimuli

- "I've been stressed out for weeks because of finals."
- "The most stress I ever felt was when my father died."

Stress as an Internal State That Can Cause Health Problems

- "After the stress of making it through finals, I always feel exhausted and run-down. In fact, I usually end up getting the flu."
- "Long-term stress is an important contributor to high blood pressure."

Stress, then, can refer to (1) challenging and potentially threatening events and situations; (2) our immediate reactions to those situations; and (3) our body's long-term physical reaction to continuing, threatening events and situations. It's no wonder that members at an institute of medicine concluded—following a review of 35 years of stress research—that "No one has formulated a definition of stress that satisfies even a majority of stress researchers" (Elliot & Eisdorfer, 1982).

Selye on Stress

Dr. Hans Selye studied stress for over 40 years. In his pioneering research with rats, he found that such stressors as excessive heat or cold, extreme hunger, and fatigue all led to the same physiological responses, such as rapid pulse, pounding heart, and tensing of muscles (Selye, 1982). And if the stressors were continued for a sufficient length of time, there were more permanent effects, such as the lymph glands becoming smaller and the stomach developing ulcers. As a result of this research, Selye considered stress to be a general response (the physiological reactions mentioned above) by an organism in reaction to any of a number of environmental events. He concluded that people react similarly to stressors, and he defined stress as the "rate of wear and tear within the body" (Selye, 1976). In terms of this definition, a certain amount of stress is perfectly normal. We all experience a pounding heart and tensing of muscles when we hear a car horn while crossing a busy street, or when we carry a heavy box of books up a long flight of stairs. Yet, when people are asked to describe stress, they most often choose words like *anxiety, overwhelmed, danger,* and *illness* (Patton et al., 1986). In other words, most people see stress as something beyond the simple wear and tear of daily living.

Lazarus on Stress

Selye was interested in stress as a physical reaction to events. Richard Lazarus and Susan Folkman (1984) focused on an individual's cognitive interpretation of a potentially stressful situation. In other words, nothing is *necessarily* stressful; things are only stressful if we fear we can't handle or survive them. Lazarus and Folkman argue that, when you first encounter an event, you engage in *primary appraisal*—a judgment of the event as irrelevant, benignly positive, or potentially stressful. In the first class at the start of the term, for example, you were probably given the course outline, examination schedule, and list of textbooks. Did you think that the course would be relatively easy for you? Or that you were in over your head? If an event is judged as potentially stressful (that is, potentially threatening, challenging, or harmful), then you engage in *secondary appraisal*—a judgment of your perceived ability to cope with the threat or the challenge. While considering the course outline, for example, you might have decided, "This course looks like a lot of work, but I've handled tough courses before. If I work hard, I'll do well." If you believe that you can cope with the situation, then stress is reduced. Finally, according to these authors, you might engage in *reappraisal* as new information becomes available. Reappraisal may lead to an increase or decrease in a situation's potential stress. If you did well on the first exam in the course, for example, your concerns about the course were likely reduced. Failing the first exam would have had the opposite effect.

For our purposes, we will distinguish between stressors and stress reactions. **Stressors** are conditions, such as excessive smog, a death in the family, and lack of sleep, that cause physiological and behavioral reactions that present coping difficulties for the individual. **Stress reactions** (sometimes called psychological distress) are the physiological and behavioral responses to stressors, such as fatigue, high blood pressure, anger, and aggression.

stressors

Conditions that damage the body beyond the normal wear and tear of daily living, and that cause physiological and behavioral reactions that present coping difficulties for the individual.

stress reactions

The physiological and behavioral responses to stressors.

Types of Stressors

We will discuss stressors under three broad categories: environmental, psychological, and physiological.

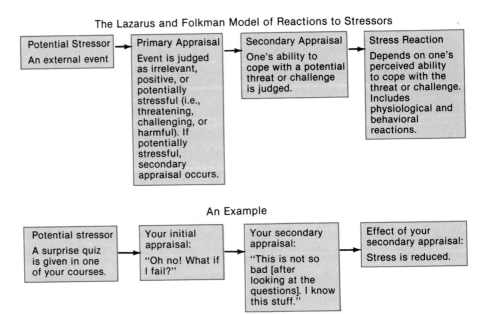

Figure 5-1

Experiences and judgments that lead to a stress reaction. *Adapted from Lazarus & Folkman, 1984.*

Environmental Stressors: Unhealthy Living Conditions

You are constantly bombarded by environmental stimuli to which you must adjust. Depending upon your living circumstances, you might have to endure pollution, noise, crowding, frequent bad weather or long winters, even natural or human-made disasters. When stressors like these are especially intense or prolonged, people often experience stress reactions. For example, at the Three-Mile Island disaster in Pennsylvania when the nuclear reactor released radioactivity into the environment, people living nearby reported much more stress than those living farther away (Baum et al., 1983). And it doesn't take a disaster to cause stress reactions. Each year in corporate America, there are mergers and acquisitions involving several thousand transactions, each causing considerable stress for the hundreds of thousands of employees whose jobs are affected (Ivancevich et al., 1990). Even daily events, such as excessive *noise*, can cause ulcers and other stress-related illnesses (Colligan & Murphy, 1982). A dramatic example of noise as an environmental stressor was reported by Cohen and his colleagues who found that children who attended school near a very busy airport with frequent overhead flights had higher blood pressure and lower scores on standardized tests than did a control group of children who attended school in a quiet neighborhood (Cohen et al., 1986).

Another source of environmental stressors is various life experiences: going through a divorce, making it through final exams, or being fired at work. What types of life events are stressful? And to what degree? These stressors were first studied systematically in the 1960s.

major life events

Changes in our life that can act as stressors.

MAJOR LIFE EVENTS AS STRESSORS. Thomas Holmes and Richard Rahe asked several thousand people from diverse backgrounds and occupations to rank **major life events** on a scale ranging from "very stressful" to "minimal stress" (Holmes & Rahe, 1967). When Holmes and Rahe compared the scores for each participant with their respective medical histories, they found an interesting correlation: the higher the stress score, the higher the incidence of disease. Moreover, a higher score appeared to predict a greater probability of illness during the next 24-month period. The Holmes and Rahe (1967) scale has been reproduced in Table 5-1. We have also included scale values for adolescents (Ruch & Holmes, 1971) and elderly people (Muhlenkamp et al., 1975).

According to Holmes and Rahe's study, it's not only negative life events that cause stress—it is any significant life change. Events such as a vacation, marriage, graduation, or changing to a new and better job are generally seen as positive. And

Major life events, whether positive or negative, are related to stress.

TABLE 5-1
HOLMES–RAHE STRESS SCALE *Adapted from Holmes & Rahe, 1967; Ruch & Holmes, 1971; Muhlenkamp et al., 1975.*

	Stress Value (or Life-Change Units)		
LIFE EVENT	ADULTS	ADOLESCENTS	ELDERLY PEOPLE
Death of spouse	100	69	73
Divorce	73	60	72
Marital separation	65	55	63
Jail term	63	50	73
Death of close family member	63	54	60
Major personal injury or illness	53	50	65
Marriage	50	50	50
Being fired at work	47	50	62
Marital reconciliation	45	47	35
Retirement from work	45	46	33
Major change in the health of family member	44	44	59
Pregnancy	40	45	47
Sex difficulties	39	51	36
Gaining a new family member	39	43	36
Major business readjustment	39	44	61
Major change in financial state	38	44	43
Death of a close friend	37	46	52
Changing to different line of work	36	38	42
Major change in the number of arguments with spouse	35	41	45
Taking out a mortgage or loan for a major purchase	31	41	61
Foreclosure on a mortgage or loan	30	36	61
Major change in work responsibilities	29	38	40
Son or daughter leaving home	29	34	43
Trouble with in-laws	29	36	31
Outstanding personal achievement	28	31	34
Spouse beginning or ceasing work outside the home	26	32	35
Beginning or ending schooling	26	34	34
Major change in living conditions	25	35	48
Revision of personal habits	24	26	39
Trouble with boss	23	26	28
Major change in working hours or conditions	20	30	27
Change in residence	20	28	39
Change to a new school	20	26	34
Major change in recreation	19	26	35
Major change in church activities	19	21	40
Major change in social activities	18	28	35
Taking out a small mortgage on your home	17	28	52
Major change in sleeping habits	16	18	36
Major change in number of family get-togethers	15	22	37
Major change in eating habits	15	18	45
Vacation	13	19	30
Christmas	12	16	34
Minor violations of the law	11	12	47

TABLE 5-1 (Continued)

Scoring for the Holmes–Rahe Stress Scale

To use the Holmes–Rahe Stress Scale, total your stress points for all of the life events experienced during the last 12 months. Holmes and Rahe suggest that scores between 150 and 199 indicate a slight probability of experiencing some form of illness within the following year, scores between 200 and 300 points indicate moderate risk for illness, and scores higher than 300 points indicate a high probability of suffering serious physical or emotional illness during the following year. If you score a high number of stress points, you can decrease your chances of suffering serious illness by becoming skillful with the stress management strategies described in this chapter. Your skill in dealing with stress is at least as important as the stressful events that occur in your life.

yet, Holmes and Rahe suggest that even these positive changes can act as stressors if they require significant readjustment in someone's life.

Some groups may face more stressors from life events than others. For example, Mexican Americans, especially immigrants, encounter higher levels of ongoing, day-to-day stressors from life events than do comparable groups of non-Hispanic whites (Golding et al., 1991). The additional stressors faced by Mexican Americans are often associated with greater economic strain from low household income, and more household strain from large household size.

Does the experience of major life events, such as death of a loved one, starting a new job, or a divorce, really increase one's risk of illness? A number of studies have indicated that scores on the Life Change Scale can predict susceptibility to illness during the coming year (Elliot & Eisdorfer, 1982; Holmes & Masuda, 1974). Moreover, a study commissioned by the National Academy of Sciences indicated that people who had been widowed, fired, or divorced during the past year were indeed more vulnerable to illness and more likely to develop heart disease than were persons who had not experienced such events (Dohrenwend et al., 1982). In another study, a group of college football players completed a modified version of the Holmes–Rahe Stress Scale at the start of the football season (Bramwell et al., 1975). When information about injuries was examined at the end of the season, 70 percent of the players who had a total of 300 or more points on the stress scale experienced at least one injury during the season. Of the 11 players who experienced multiple injuries, 9 were in the 300+ stress point group. Only a third of the players who scored 200 or fewer points experienced an injury.

Problems with Life Events Research.   Although research on the relationship of life events, stress, and future health problems is intriguing, we must interpret these findings with caution. First, in contrast to the research cited above, several studies have indicated that people's scores on life-change scales are not actually good predictors of their future health problems (for example, Krantz et al., 1985; Schroeder & Costa, 1984). Second, major events in life may have little negative effect on individuals who are skilled in stress management techniques—or on individuals who simply don't find these changes and events personally overwhelming. Third, some events on such scales are likely to be interpreted positively (such as an elderly couple moving from a house that demands a great deal of work to an apartment that is easily cared for); such positive gains may cancel out much of the stress involved in major change (Cohen & Hoberman, 1983). Fourth, people increase their risk of illness not simply by accumulating a high score of life events, but through unhealthy lifestyles. For instance, people are at greater risk for cardiovascular disease if their lifestyle includes a combination of poor eating habits, a high fat diet, smoking, lack of exercise, excessive alcohol drinking . . . and the experience of stressful life events (Farquhar, 1978). However, individuals who enjoy healthy eating habits and regular exercise, who don't smoke, and who drink alcohol only in moderation, may be able to experience a high score on a life-event inventory with little or no subsequent risk of illness.

DAILY HASSLES AS STRESSORS.   Fortunately, most of us do not have to handle major life events every day. And yet, we still experience stressors regularly. Where then is this stress coming from—and can it, too, affect our health? Some studies have suggested that the frequent hassles of daily life may be more stressful, and better predictors of future health problems, than major life changes.

daily hassles

Daily events and experiences that can act as stressors.

Daily hassles are "the irritating, frustrating, distressing demands that to some degree characterize everyday transactions with the environment" (Kanner et al., 1981, p. 3). Like most of us, you're probably quite familiar with these minor daily aggravations: misplacing keys or glasses, losing things, having too much to do and not quite enough time to do it all, the constant nagging of someone you live with, the checkbook that won't balance, and numerous other irritants and frustrations that occur regularly at home, at school, and at work.

Several studies have been conducted in which subjects first completed the Holmes–Rahe scale identifying the stressors which they had experienced from major life events during the past year. Then, on a monthly basis, they evaluated the hassles they experienced in everyday living, by completing a Hassles Scale developed by Kanner and colleagues (1981). After collecting data for a period from several months to a year, the researchers then examined the health and psychological problems experienced by their subjects. In general, health and psychological problems were found to be more strongly associated with the frequency and intensity of daily hassles than with scores on the major life-events scale (DeLongis et al., 1986; 1988; Lazarus & DeLongis, 1983; Lazarus & Folkman, 1984). The ten most frequently reported hassles are shown in Table 5-2.

Although research on the Hassles Scale has underscored the importance of daily stressors in human health, it, too, has its critics. After examining the Hassles Scale carefully, the Dohrenwends and their colleagues concluded that many of the items on the scale resembled symptoms of psychological disorders (Dohrenwend et al., 1984; Dohrenwend & Shrout, 1985). They argued that it was not surprising that a measure of stressors (the Hassles Scale) would correlate with measures of psychological problems if the measure of stressors already included many symptoms of psychological problems. In response to this criticism, Lazarus and his colleagues revised the Hassles Scale to eliminate items that were symptoms of psychological disorders. Using the revised scale, DeLongis and associates (1988) examined daily stress among 75 married couples during 20 assessments over a 6-month period. Overall, they continued to find an association between increases in

TABLE 5-2

THE TEN MOST FREQUENT HASSLES REPORTED BY A SAMPLE OF MIDDLE-AGED ADULTS. *From Kanner, 1981.*

1. Concerns about weight
2. Health of a family member
3. Rising prices of common goods
4. Home maintenance
5. Too many things to do.
6. Misplacing or losing things
7. Yardwork or outside home maintenance
8. Property, investments, or taxes
9. Crime
10. Physical appearance

daily hassles with a decline in health and measures of mood. However, there were large individual differences and many exceptions to this relationship. With approximately one third of the participants, *increases* in stress were in fact associated with somewhat *improved* health and mood. Thus, the complex relationship between experience of daily stressors and the occurrence of health and psychological problems requires additional research to be fully understood.

CONFLICTS AS STRESSORS.   A conflict is a problem of choosing between two competing opportunities, satisfying two competing motives, pursuing one of two alternative goals, or meeting one of two incompatible demands. As you've probably discovered in your own life, facing conflicts and making choices can be stressful. Psychologists identify four main types of conflicts based on two opposite tendencies: *approach* and *avoidance.*

In **approach-approach conflicts,** an individual must select just one of two appealing positive alternatives. Consider choosing between two potentially entertaining movies or choosing between an excellent Mexican or Chinese restaurant. Such choices demonstrate approach-approach conflicts.

Dealing with many approach-approach conflicts is not particularly stressful; either choice is attractive. Some approach-approach conflicts, however, require choosing between two life-altering courses, which can be very difficult. It's not always easy, for example, to choose between two excellent colleges, two great jobs, or between two interesting ways of spending the summer.

In an **avoidance-avoidance conflict,** an individual must choose between two negative outcomes or undesirable courses of action. For example, should a woman walk home in the rain or accept a ride from a stranger? Which of two dull textbooks will you choose to study tonight? When your teeth need fixing, do you choose the immediate experience of the dentist's drill or long-term tooth decay and loss of teeth? The degree of stress experienced when a person faces an avoidance-avoidance conflict depends on the degree of threat, pain, or unpleasantness implied by the choices. Choosing to experience the short-term pain of the dentist's drill in order to avoid long-term tooth decay is a relatively easy choice for most adults. Having to choose between jumping from the tenth floor of a burning building versus trying to escape down the burning stairs is much more difficult and stressful.

In an **approach-avoidance conflict,** the pursuit of a single course of action has both positive and negative outcomes; that is, the pursuit of a single goal both attracts and repels the person. For example, if a cigarette smoker lights up in a no-smoking area, she will enjoy the taste of the cigarette but may encounter the wrath of nonsmokers and possible prosecution. As another example, you might really enjoy the personality of the person whom you are dating but be disturbed by that person's religious beliefs. Approach-avoidance conflicts can be very stressful, leaving someone vacillating, unable to act decisively to resolve a given situation. Individuals who appear to be indecisive may well be in the middle of an approach-avoidance conflict.

In a **double approach-avoidance conflict,** an individual must choose between two alternatives, each of which has both pros and cons. Since this is true of most situations in life, double approach-avoidance conflicts are very common. If you must choose between two equally attractive colleges, for example, it is likely that each choice has both strengths and weaknesses. Suppose that you want to study medicine. College A has a good medical school but is a long way from your home town. Many of your friends are going to College B, which is nearby, but the medical school there is not as good. And so it goes. An effective approach to dealing with multiple approach-avoidance conflicts is the problem-solving strategy described in Chapter 4, and reviewed later in this chapter.

approach-approach conflict
An individual must choose between two attractive goals or incentives, only one of which can be pursued or obtained.

avoidance-avoidance conflict
An individual must choose between two negative outcomes or undesirable courses of action.

approach-avoidance conflict
An individual pursues a course of action or goal that has both positive and negative outcomes.

double approach-avoidance conflict
An individual must choose between two alternatives, each of which has both positive and negative consequences.

Psychological Stressors: Unhealthy Thinking and Feeling

Research suggests that many sources of stress actually lie within ourselves—in how we think, talk, and feel about the world around us, and in the ways we respond to life events. For example, some personality traits, like aggressive impatience and hostility, seem to increase people's stress reactions. Other traits appear to make for a "hardy personality," one that is highly resistant to stress, even in the face of difficult life situations. In still other cases, certain types of negative thinking can worsen an individual's stress reactions. Stress reactions may also depend on whether or not people feel they have control over the stressors in their lives. We'll consider each of these possibilities in more detail.

TYPE A PERSONALITY.   Do you frequently:

- Show a hurried, workaholic behavior pattern?
- Become angry and aggressively impatient because things aren't happening fast enough?
- Do several things at once (for example, dictating and driving)?
- Schedule more and more in less and less time and experience a "sense of time urgency"?
- Speak in a fast, loud, explosive style and display clenched fists and aggressive facial expressions when someone disagrees with you?
- Become aggressive and competitive in dealing with others?

If you answer yes to the above questions, then you are showing a Type A behavior pattern.

In *Type A Behavior and Your Heart* (1974), Meyer Friedman and Ray Rosenman described the implications of their classic nine-year study of more than 3,000 healthy men between the ages of 35 and 59 years. One group of men, classified as **Type A personalities,** were seen as very competitive, always in a hurry, highly motivated, ambitious, verbally aggressive, workaholics, easily angered, and very time conscious. Another group, referred to as **Type B personalities,** tended to be the opposite of Type A's. Specifically, Type B's were relaxed, easygoing, noncompetitive, happy in their jobs, understanding, and enjoyed lots of leisure time. Of the

Type A personality

A behavior pattern characterized by a sense of time urgency, hostile aggressiveness, and a tendency to become easily angered; associated with susceptibility to heart attack.

Type B Personality

A behavior pattern that tends to be the opposite of a Type A personality; noncompetitive, easygoing, and understanding; associated with low risk of heart attack.

Persons with a Type A personality are generally very competitive, highly motivated, aggressive workaholics who are easily angered and very time conscious. At least some of these characteristics may contribute to heart disease.

257 men of the original group who suffered a heart attack by the end of the study, 178 of them were Type A. Individuals with Type A characteristics were twice as vulnerable to heart attack as were individuals with Type B characteristics.

Since Friedman and Rosenman (1974) first described the self-imposed stressors inherent in the Type A behavior pattern, the concept of the Type A personality has proven extremely popular. Why? Perhaps because the original Type A research was directed at a topic that affects many of us in later life—coronary heart disease—and the findings hold for women as well as men (Baker et al., 1984); perhaps because its initial results seemed very clear in controlled research studies; and because almost everyone could immediately identify a friend or a relative as a Type A or Type B personality. For all of these reasons, the concept of the Type A personality took both psychology and medicine by storm.

Problems with the Type A Concept. In spite of its popularity, research suggests that the initial promise of the Type A construct has not been borne out. Some studies have reported a lack of a clear association between Type A behavior and risk of heart attack (e.g., Shekelle et al., 1985), and that Type A's even showed less risk of a second heart attack than Type B's (Ragland & Brand, 1988). Studies that have used self-report questionnaires to identify Type A individuals have not supported the earlier results between Type A behavior patterns and susceptibility to heart attack (Linden, 1987). The early Friedman and Rosenman (1974) study used a structured interview to classify persons as Type A or Type B, relying in part on the subject's general style for answering questions. So what do we make of these contradictory findings? Stephanie Booth-Kewley and Howard Friedman (1987) concluded, after analyzing 83 studies on Type A behavior, that there is at least a modest association between Type A behavior and coronary heart disease. They also found that some of the Type A characteristics are more closely linked to coronary heart disease than others. It appears to be the aggressive, anger-prone tendency (rather than the time consciousness or the hard-working characteristics) that provides the link with heart disease (Booth-Kewley & Friedman, 1987; Dembroski et al., 1985; Matthews, 1988). Perhaps Type A individuals should worry less about slowing down and more about controlling their anger and aggression. If you are a "high activity person," but you feel comfortable at what you do and the rate at which you do it, you may not have to worry about being classed as a Type A (and readers who are Type B's probably aren't worrying anyway, are you?).

THE HARDY PERSONALITY. Those with certain Type A personality characteristics, especially hostility and aggressive impatience, appear to be more susceptible to stress reactions. What about the opposite? Are there certain personalities that show high resistance to stress reactions? Research by Suzanne Kobasa suggests that the answer may be yes. She suggested that some people show **hardiness**—a personality characteristic that helps individuals cope successfully with life events and resist stress reactions. Kobasa (1979) studied middle-aged, mostly white, Protestant, business executives in what are generally considered to be high stress positions. As one might predict, many of the executives reported a high incidence of stress-related illnesses. Some of the executives, however, reported very few such stress reactions. They seemed to be a "hardier" lot. After testing both groups extensively, the hardy executives differed from the less hardy executives on three main characteristics: They showed a higher level of *commitment* on whatever they did; they viewed life-change events as *challenges* to be overcome rather than as threats to their existence; and they had a strong sense of *control* over their lives and the rewards and outcomes that they experienced.

While some studies have replicated Kobasa'a findings (for example, Kobasa et al., 1982; Oulette-Kobasa & Pucetti, 1983; Pines, 1984), others have questioned

hardiness

A personality characteristic that helps individuals resist stress reactions; characterized by a high level of commitment, viewing life change events as challenges, and feeling in control of one's life.

whether or not all the characteristics of hardiness identified by Kobasa are important in helping people to resist stress reactions (Funk & Houston, 1987). Hull and his colleagues (1987) believe that commitment and control are more important than viewing life as a challenge. There is also some evidence that this concept of psychological hardiness may not apply to females. The characteristics of hardiness, by themselves, did not appear to protect undergraduate college women against stress and illness (Ganellen & Blainey, 1984). Similar results have also been reported for a study of female secretaries (Schmied & Lawler, 1986). And a group of high hardy college men appraised an aversive task as less threatening than a group of high hardy college women (Wiebe, 1991). Whether or not some aspects of hardiness act as a buffer between stressors and stress reactions, and just why hardiness has not been shown to protect females from stress, awaits further research. Nevertheless, the findings of Kobasa and others add to the research indicating considerable individual differences in people's ability to deal with stressors.

IRRATIONAL SELF-TALK AS A SOURCE OF STRESS. Do you ever find yourself thinking: "I hate going to the library, I can never find any books that I need there!" or "I'm late for my first class, and I forgot my notes; my whole day's going to be a disaster!" or (after spilling coffee on yourself) "I've done it again! I'm such a klutz!" If so, such thoughts may be a source of stress for you.

These examples illustrate three of the many types of irrational self-talk described by David Burns (1989). The first example illustrates *overgeneralization,* seeing a single event as a never ending pattern of defeat (usually accompanied by "always" or "never"). The second example illustrates *jumping to conclusions,* predicting that your whole day will turn out badly because it started out badly. The third example illustrates *labeling,* a type of all-or-nothing thinking in which one incident leads to a negative label ("I'm such a klutz"). Such irrational self-talk can make you feel anxious and emotionally upset, and it is a source of stress for many individuals (Lazarus & Folkman, 1984). If irrational self-talk is a source of stress for you, we'll tell you how to change such behavior later in this chapter.

PERCEIVED LACK OF CONTROL AS A SOURCE OF STRESS. Another psychological factor that can affect stress reactions is the degree to which people have some control over a stressor. In general, uncontrollable stressful events are likely to be more damaging to a person's health than are controllable events (Stern et al., 1982). For example, exams are stressful for most students. But imagine how much more stressful they would be if a total stranger took your exams for you, and you had no control over whether or not that person attended classes or studied at all before the exams.

The increased health risks with loss of control can be clearly seen with the elderly placed in nursing homes. Rodin (1986) found that the health of elderly people placed in nursing homes without their consent declined more rapidly than did the health of those who had more control over their day-to-day activities.

A critical factor in lack of control as a source of stress appears to be how much people *think* they have control over a stressor, not how much control they actually

Excessive alcohol drinking, smoking, and late nights all tax the body. The average life expectancy of smokers has been estimated to be from five to eight years less than that of nonsmokers, and prolonged heavy alcohol drinking is associated with a variety of serious health problems.

exert. For example, in a study of subjects' performing a proofreading task in a crowded room, some subjects were told that they had the option of walking to a larger, uncrowded room to perform the task. Although they did not do so, such subjects did better on the task than did subjects who were not given the option of leaving (Sherrod, 1974). Studies of other stressors such as noise, mild electric shock, and demands for increased performance indicate that stressors have a greater negative effect on our performance when we think that we cannot control them (Cohen, 1980).

Physiological Stressors: Unhealthy Bodies

As these various studies have indicated, stressors in our lives come from such environmental sources as life events, daily hassles, and conflicts, and from such psychological sources as personality traits and irrational self-talk. But there is another important group of stressors that has been proven to take a dramatic toll on human health: physiological stressors.

Physiological stressors are unhealthy body conditions (such as obesity) resulting from activities that involve a significant element of free choice, such as unhealthy eating, smoking, and excessive alcohol drinking. Excess body weight has been associated with hypertension, gall bladder disease, toxemias of pregnancy, osteoarthritis of the knees and hips, low back pain, dermatological problems, high blood pressure, diabetes, and surgical difficulties (Kolata, 1985; LeBow, 1981). Smokers have a mortality rate of 1.7 times that of nonsmokers (Feist & Brannon, 1988). The average life expectancy of smokers has been estimated to be from five to eight years less than that of nonsmokers (Fielding, 1985). Prolonged heavy alcohol drinking (five drinks a day or more for several years) is associated with increased incidence of cirrhosis of the liver, cardiovascular and neural damage, and certain types of cancer (Feist & Brannon, 1988). Also, heavy alcohol consumption has a hazardous effect on the developing fetus during pregnancy (Pratt, 1982).

Some Common Reactions to Stressors

Physiological Reactions

What happens to your body when it is bombarded by stressors? And does your body react differently to some stressors than to others? Hans Selye devoted much of his life trying to answer these questions. He concluded that we have the same

general adaptation syndrome

A characteristic way that our bodies react to the continuing presence of stress; includes three basic stages of alarm, resistance, and exhaustion.

alarm or preparation stage

The first stage of the general adaptation syndrome; mobilization of physiological "fight or flight" resources to deal with a stressor.

resistance or fighting stage

The second stage of the general adaptation syndrome; the body draws on all of its available resources to cope with prolonged stress, thus taxing other bodily functions, resources, and overall health.

exhaustion stage

The third stage of the general adaptation syndrome; as stress continues unabated, the individual's defenses give out and he or she becomes especially vulnerable to diseases and tissue damage.

physical reaction to any type of stressor, and he called the reaction the **general adaptation syndrome** (Selye, 1976). While showing this syndrome, our bodies go through three stages of reaction to ongoing stressors: alarm, resistance, and exhaustion. Suppose, for example, that you just received your midterm marks, and they're so low that you're in danger of failing the year. How do you react?

The first stage, the **alarm or preparation stage,** occurs when you first encounter a stressor. When you first looked at your statement of grades and saw some "D"s and "F"s, your reaction likely included a rush of adrenalin and noradrenalin into your body, a rapid pulse, sweaty palms, a pounding heart, and tensing of leg and arm muscles. In other words, when faced with a stressor, our body goes into a *preparatory* state to prepare us to deal with the stressor through a "fight or flight" reaction.

Selye described the second stage of our reaction to stressors as the **resistance or fighting stage**—you mobilize your reserves to deal more effectively with the stressors. After your initial alarm at receiving such low midterm grades, you put in many hours studying and you cut back on your social and recreational activities. And your marks gradually begin to rise. Sometimes, however, people direct so many of their energies to dealing with an ongoing stressor during the fighting stage that resources are taken from other bodily functions, leaving them increasingly susceptible to illness. In fact, a number of studies have indicated that stress reactions may play a role in the onset of infectious diseases (such as the flu) and positive reactions to viruses (such as herpes) (Cohen & Williamson, 1991). You might find, for example, that long hours of late-night studying, excessive worrying, and perhaps the stress of continuing with a part-time job begin to take their toll. Suppose that, in spite of your best efforts, your grades rise only slightly by the end of the term. And now you must face the added stress of final exams. Unfortunately, you might enter the third stage of the general adaptation syndrome.

The third and final stage of the general stress reaction is **exhaustion.** During your final exams, after working so hard to raise your marks during the past two months, you may begin to experience inability to concentrate, irritability or frequent anger, disrupted digestion, and a lack of interest in lovemaking. During the exhaustion stage, an individual becomes especially vulnerable to diseases and tissue damage. There is an increased susceptibility to stressor-induced hormonal effects, diabetes, skin disorders, stomach ulcers, high blood pressure, asthma, susceptibility to cancer, and a host of other diseases (Allen, 1983; Bammer & Newberry, 1983; Selye, 1976). In the extreme case, resistance collapses, and you may be hospitalized.

While Selye's notion that our bodies show the same physical response to *any* form of ongoing stress has been very influential, it has not gone unchallenged. John

Figure 5-2

Selye's general adaptation syndrome in reaction to a stressor. During the alarm stage, resistance drops briefly as the body experiences brief shock in reaction to a stressor. Resistance then increases as the body prepares to deal with the stressor. During the resistance stage, resistance to that particular stressor is heightened as the body mobilizes its resources, and resistance to other stressors may be weakened. During the exhaustion stage, resistance collapses. *From Selye, 1980.*

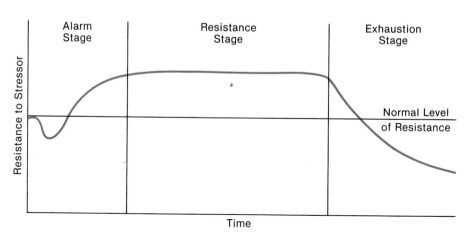

When faced with stressors, individuals react differently. Some become quite emotional, while others seem to be generally helpless.

Mason (1971, 1975) has argued, for example, that some stressors cause our body to produce certain hormones, while other stressors lead to other bodily reactions. Anis Mikhail (1981) has argued further that humans are highly individualistic in how they interpret events as stressors, and that Selye's model, developed using rats, is limited in its applicability. For some students, for example, asking the professor a question in class is far too stressful to contemplate, while for others, it's no different than asking a friend if they can borrow a pencil. While individual differences in physiological reactions to different stressors remains a topic for future research, there is no doubt that our behavioral reactions to stressors vary considerably from one person to the next.

Behavioral Reactions

Individuals react to stressful situations in a wide variety of ways, depending upon many things: their personality traits, upbringing, outlook, personal coping strategies, and perhaps even their biological makeup. And while many people learn to handle stress successfully, others learn to react to stressors in very unhealthy ways. In this section, we'll describe two problematic reactions to stressors: learned helplessness and task impairment.

learned helplessness

A tendency for an individual to act helpless and not try to escape or cope with aversive stimuli.

LEARNED HELPLESSNESS. For some people, stressors are seen as a challenge: "When the going gets tough, the tough get going." Others, however, seem to accept stressors passively as a defeating fact of life. Confronted with obstacles and stress, these individuals seem to give up easily, resigned to their fate. One explanation of this reaction to stressors is the phenomenon called **learned helplessness.** In the original set of experiments on this phenomenon, dogs that had experienced inescapable shocks while restrained in a hammock did not even attempt to escape shocks in a later experiment—even though escape could have been made easily by jumping over a barrier. The dogs had apparently learned to be helpless (Overmier & Seligman, 1967). And people who have been raped, victimized by other violent crimes, or who have been stricken with incurable or life-threatening diseases often face new problems with a kind of learned helplessness. After experiencing a situation in which we are helpless to end pain or solve a dilemma, we may then generalize this debilitating lesson, transferring it to other areas of our lives (Garber & Seligman, 1980; Seligman, 1975). It is as though we have learned that responding is likely to be useless. In such cases, therapists have stressed the importance of regaining some sense of control over our lives, learning that what we do *does* make a difference.

PERFORMANCE IMPAIRMENT.   Every day, we do things that are observed or judged by others. Your friends watch how you drive when you give them a ride somewhere. Your professor judges your performance on exams. Your playing partners watch your actions when you play tennis or bridge with them. If you feel pressure to perform these tasks well, the resulting stress may, ironically, impair your performance. For example, Roy Baumeister (1984) studied individuals at a video game arcade in a shopping mall. He surreptitiously observed individuals playing "Pac Man" or "Ms. Pac Man." After observing the score that a subject obtained in a game, he then approached the subject and asked if that person would like to participate in a video game experiment in which they could play a free game. He then said, "I want you to get the best score you possibly can, okay? I can only give you one chance, so make it the best you can." Under such conditions, subjects' performance (scores on the game) dropped by an average of 25 percent in comparison to their previous performance on games that had been observed surreptitiously.

Stress can also impair decision making (Janis, 1982). For example, Keinan (1987) asked undergraduate students from the University of Haifa to complete a multiple choice analogies test (e.g., "Butter is to margarine as sugar is to _____ [beets, saccarine, honey, lemon, candy, chocolate]"). Some of the subjects were also exposed to a stress manipulation. They were told that harmless but painful electric shocks might be administered while they were carrying out the test. This stressor appeared to affect the subjects' decision making in two ways: (1) They showed "premature closure"—a tendency to select an alternative before considering all possibilities; and (2) "Nonsystematic scanning"—a tendency to scan all alternatives in a nonsystematic, disorganized fashion. Although no shocks were administered in this experiment, the volunteer subjects were apparently distracted by the stress of anticipating possible shock, and their decision-making ability dropped.

Baumeister and Steinhilber (1984) have suggested that the apparent relationship between stress and performance impairment might explain a finding in professional sports—a tendency to "choke under pressure." In general, statistics indicate that the home team in professional sports wins the majority of games (Schwartz & Barsky, 1977). But when Baumeister and Steinhilber examined home win percentages in baseball during the World Series from 1924 to 1982, they found that the home team won 60 percent of Games 1 and 2, but less than 40 percent of the last game in the series. A similar effect was observed using National Basketball Association championship series betwen 1967 and 1982. Why? Baumeister and Steinhilber suggested that the extra pressure caused by playing the final game in front of home field fans caused the players to think so much about the details of how to play well that it interfered with them playing "naturally." In sports, this is referred to as "paralysis by analysis." Such effects did not, however, occur during the final game of championship series in the National Hockey League (Gayton et al., 1987). Extra pressure does not appear to impair performance in all activities. And where it does, psychologists can help individuals to more effectively cope with pressure so that it does not impair performance.

Long-Term Effects of Stressors

Psychophysiological Disorders

psychosomatic disorders
Genuine physical symptoms that are at least partly caused by psychological factors.

We've all heard stories about the worried business executive who developed ulcers from having to make so many tough decisions, or the harried air traffic controller whose constant worry about the safety of others caused frequent migraine headaches, or the professional athlete who got so nervous that she vomited before every important athletic contest. By the 1950s, the term **psychosomatic** was widely used to refer to genuine physical symptoms that are at least partly caused by psychological factors. When people suffer from psychosomatic ailments, the ailments are real. They are not "all in the head" of the afflicted.

Psychological causes of physical disorders were illustrated in a classic study by Joseph Brady (1958) titled, "Ulcers in 'Executive' Monkeys." In an experimental chamber, a monkey learned to press a lever to avoid a brief electric shock. Brady referred to the monkey as an "executive" because of the decision-making task the monkey was required to perform. Unfortunately, the executive monkey developed ulcers as a result of the stressful experience. But it wasn't just frequent exposure to shock that caused the ulcers. A companion monkey in the same chamber received the same number of shocks as the executive monkey, administered if the executive monkey failed to press the lever. But the companion monkey was not responsible for lever-pressing to avoid the shock, and the companion monkey did not get ulcers.

While Brady's research suggested that the necessity of business executives to make decisions may be what causes them to experience ulcers (and perhaps heart attacks, or other disorders), we now know this to be an oversimplification. Brady's "executive" monkeys were forced to attend closely to only one aspect of their environment for long periods of time (that is, when to lever-press), whereas business executives typically have a broad range of responsibilities. Brady may have been somewhat remiss in referring to his experimental monkeys as "executives." Their routine of having to respond continuously on the shock avoidance schedule for many hours straight might be more like that of a harried waitress working shifts in a busy diner, than of an executive. And, in fact, Smith et al. (1978) reported that waitresses had more stress-related illnesses than business executives. Moreover, the necessity of making decisions is not necessarily stressful. Weiss (1977) found that "companion" rats suffered from more ulcers than "executive" rats when exposed to an arrangement where an "executive" rat could turn off electrical shocks received while a companion rat received the same shocks but had no control over them.

We now know that repeated, prolonged contact with stressors is correlated with the presence of a variety of psychophysiological diseases including ulcers, hypertension, asthma, migraine headaches, and skin disorders (Kaplan, 1985). Additional research is needed, however, to identify the exact causal mechanisms between stress and such disorders. In recent years, researchers have begun to link stress with other physical disorders as well. We'll look at one such area: malfunctioning of the immune system.

Stressors and the Immune System

immune system

A complex system of specialized cells that defend us against invading foreign agents such as bacteria, viruses, and cancer cells.

Your **immune system** defends you against invading foreign agents such as bacteria, viruses, and cancer cells. When a foreign substance invades your body, your immune system calls into action specialized white blood cells known as *lymphocytes*. With amazing accuracy, these cells identify, disarm, and destroy invaders like viruses, cancer cells, parasites, and tumors.

How can stress interfere with the complex workings of your immune system? As described earlier, during the initial alarm stage in which you encounter stressors, your body deals with the situation through a "fight or flight" reaction. Substances flood into the bloodstream to generate emergency energy: from the adrenal gland come catecholamines (especially adrenalin) and corticosteroids (such as cortisol). One effect of corticosteroids, however, is to suppress the immune system, presumably so that all resources can be mobilized to prepare your body to cope with impending challenges. Thus, during stress, the number of lymphocytes in your body decreases, and their ability to proliferate and attack foreign substances is

It's a happy day for all of us when astronauts return safely to earth after a successful mission. But a trip to outer space can be quite stressful. In fact, right after returning to earth, astronauts' immune system function is suppressed, making them more vulnerable to various diseases.

reduced. In experiments with animals, for example, stressors such as electric shock, restraint, rapid rotation on a turntable, and crowding have been shown to impair immune functioning (Ader & Cohen, 1985), leaving the experimental subjects more susceptible to a variety of illnesses, including tumor growth.

Could the stress say, of final exams, affect the functioning of your immune system? It could indeed. In one study, medical students provided researchers with blood samples approximately a month before and also a day before their final exams. The activity of certain lymphocytes was significantly reduced at the second test just before finals (Kiecolt-Glaser et al., 1985). In another study, lymphocytes were measured in husbands of women who had terminal breast cancer. Shortly after their wives passed away, there was a significant decline in the activity of the mens' lymphocytes, leaving them much more vulnerable to various diseases (Schleifer et al., 1983). Similar results have been reported for individuals experiencing the stress of unemployment and marital separation (Arnetz et al., 1987; Kiecolt-Glaser et al., 1985), during stressful periods for first-year dental students (Jemmott et al., 1983), and right after returning to earth for astronauts (Kimzey et al., 1976).

By what mechanisms can psychological factors affect the functioning of our immune system? While we do not yet have a full answer to this question, Robert Ader and Nicholas Cohen (1982) demonstrated that reflexive conditioning procedures may play an important role. Over a number of trials, they paired saccharine-sweetened drinking water given to rats with injections of a drug known to suppress immune functioning (the drug also caused stomachaches, which they were studying at the time). After a number of trials, the rats developed a taste aversion for the saccharine (presumably because of its association with stomachaches). To eliminate the taste aversion to the saccharine, the experimenters force-fed the rats saccharine for several days. Unexpectedly, some of the animals died approximately 40 days after the study. Subsequent experiments indicated that the pairing of saccharine with the immune suppressive drug established saccharine as a conditioned stimulus eliciting immune suppression. Force-feeding the rats on this conditioned stimulus weakened the rats' immunity sufficiently that the experimental animals could no longer resist the invasion of pathogens. Other studies have since successfully demonstrated reflexive conditioning of various aspects of immune responses in other species (Ader & Cohen, 1985; Turkkan, 1989).

This exciting new area of research on the effects of psychological processes on the functioning of the body's immune system is called *psychoimmunology* or *psychoneuroimmunology*. Ader and Cohen (1985) have raised some fascinating questions concerning this new area. If it's possible to demonstrate that a neutral stimulus like saccarine can be conditioned to suppress immune system functioning, is it also possible to classically condition our immune system to be even more effective in battling invaders? If so, might such a procedure help our bodies fight cancerous growth and other diseases? Could this provide a mechanism for curing AIDS (Acquired Immune Deficiency Syndrome, discussed in Chapter 7)? Future research will address such questions.

Techniques for Coping with Stress

Stressors are a fact of life. We can't escape them. And frequent contact with them will inevitably take their toll, causing both physical and psychological stress reactions. What should you do about this dilemma? Learn some *coping strategies*—ways of controlling and reducing the effects of stressors (Monat & Lazarus, 1991).

The techniques described in this section have helped many people to lower the health risks caused by a wide variety of stressors, and to live a more peaceful, happier existence.

Changing the Sources of Stress

As a student, you face many problems that just won't go away, problems that can be quite stressful. If you're attending college away from home, you have to find a place to live. You might have to adjust to new roommates. You have courses to select, a major to choose, and maybe a part-time job to hold down. Perhaps you're considering applying for a job as a research assistant. Or you may be wondering about asking your boyfriend or girlfriend to move in with you—a heavy commitment. Difficult situations and problems like these are common, and sometimes very draining, sources of stress. By dealing actively with such stressors, you can often gain a significant measure of control over them—a situation that is ultimately far less stressful than passively sitting back and allowing stressors to exert control over *you*. Two ways of dealing actively with stressors include following the steps of rational problem-solving (D'Zurilla & Nezu, 1989) and practicing effective time management.

RATIONAL PROBLEM SOLVING. As we described in the previous chapter, the first step in rational problem solving is to recognize that you can minimize the effects of stressors by dealing with problems systematically, rather than impulsively. Don't make decisions impulsively just to get them over with. Second, you should define the problem as precisely as possible, and clearly identify the situations where you must deal with it. Third, generate as many alternative solutions as you can think of. Sometimes there are just two (you move in with your boyfriend or girlfriend, or you don't), but sometimes there are compromises and alternatives that can give you the best of several worlds. Fourth, examine the pros and cons and the potential benefits and costs of each of the alternative courses of action. Remember that there is no single, perfect solution to any problem; each solution will have its strengths and drawbacks. Select the alternative that seems to provide the optimum solution, and devise a plan to accomplish it. Finally, keep track of your progress at solving the problem. If things don't work out, repeat the steps of rational problem solving.

TIME MANAGEMENT.   How many of these characteristics apply to you?

- Frequently late for classes, meetings, or job.
- Typically rush from place to place in an effort to be on time.
- Often miss deadlines.
- Frequently indecisive about what to do next.
- Move on to a new task without finishing the one that you started.
- Feel dissatisfied at the end of the day about lack of accomplishment.

If these symptoms describe you, then you are a victim of poor time management (Douglass & Douglass, 1980). It's no wonder that poor time managers feel harried, frustrated, and continually under stress.

We believe that effective time management is a particularly important part of personal adjustment in everyday life—so important that we devoted a major section to it in Chapter 1. Moreover, it is also an effective stress management strategy (Neidhardt et al., 1985). We *don't* want to repeat here the content of Chapter 1 on time management. We *do* want to remind you that practicing good time management is an effective way of dealing with stress. We encourage you to reexamine frequently the content of the time management section in Chapter 1. In particular, regularly practice the time management principles of identifying priorities, scheduling some time each day to perform high priority tasks, and minimizing time wasters.

Changing Your Thinking

For some students, having to give a talk to a class is too threatening to even think about. For other students, it's an experience that might be eagerly anticipated. For many events, whether or not they are stressful depends upon how we appraise them. Strategies for changing one's appraisal of potential stressors are referred to as cognitive coping strategies, and include cognitive reappraisal and rational self-talk.

cognitive reappraisal

Changing the way you view an event, which may make the event seem less stressful.

COGNITIVE REAPPRAISAL.   Would having to give a talk to a class be a potential stressor for you? According to Lazarus (1984), that would depend upon whether or not you interpret the task as a source of threat (for example, "Will I make a fool of myself?"), and on your interpretation of your ability to cope with it (for example, "Do I know how to plan and give a good talk?"). One way of reducing the stressfulness of an event is **cognitive reappraisal**—changing the way you view that event. Consider, for example, a study of two groups of surgical patients. Prior to undergoing an operation, one group was given no special counseling. The second group of patients, however, was taught that it is often one's view of an event that causes stress rather than the event itself. These patients were encouraged to view surgery positively by concentrating on the improved health that they would experience afterward and on the fact that hospitalization would give them a break from outside pressures. Both groups of patients then underwent surgery. Afterward, the group that had received cognitive reappraisal counseling requested pain medication only a third as often as the control group, and they also recovered more rapidly (Langer et al., 1975).

Thus, if you really do have to give a talk to a class, think of it as a learning experience. Schedule time to plan and write out your talk. Then reduce it to cue cards, and practice it. Think of it as nothing more than telling a story to a group of friends. If you view it that way, and if you prepare adequately, it is less likely to be stressful.

RATIONAL SELF TALK.   Do you remember Fred Hansen from the start of this chapter? He frequently thought hostile, antagonistic, and self-defeating thoughts (about being late, the worst always happening to him, and so on). Not only are such thoughts irrational (after all, the worst did *not* always happen to Fred), they can also be quite stressful. As we described in the previous chapter, Albert Ellis developed his rational-emotive therapy to help people identify irrational thoughts and to replace them with realistic statements about the world (Ellis & Harper, 1975). If you experience stress from irrational thinking, then you should follow the steps described in the previous chapter to practice rational self-talk. For example, when Fred Hansen knew that he was going to be late for class, instead of thinking, "Why does the worst always happen to me?" he might have thought, "One class does not make a whole term. I'll talk to the professor after class and find out what I've missed."

Changing Your Body's Reactions

Suppose you experience stress that you can't escape, perhaps from major life changes or from pressure at work or from daily hassles. The stressors are there and you're experiencing stress reactions. What can you do about it? One possibility is to change your body's reactions to the stressors. Two techniques for doing so include muscle relaxation and biofeedback training.

PROGRESSIVE MUSCLE RELAXATION.   Mastery of muscle relaxation techniques is a recommended component to deal with a variety of stress reactions. In particular, it is recommended as a useful component of procedures to treat arthritic pain, tension headaches, migraines, insomnia, anxiety, anger, sexual dysfunction, neck and back pain, high blood pressure, mild phobias, and hypertension (Lehrer & Woolfolk, 1985). The technique of progressive relaxation, described in the previous chapter, involves alternately tensing and relaxing various muscle groups while attending closely to the sensations you are feeling when your muscles are tensed versus when they are relaxed (Neidhardt et al., 1985). You learn to become sensitive to the relaxed state of your muscles in contrast to the state of tension. Complete guidelines for practicing these exercises are described in Table 4-2. With practice, you can learn to relax your muscles within a few minutes. If you practice muscle relaxation in the presence of stressors, it will lessen their negative effects.

BIOFEEDBACK TRAINING.   Barbara, a university student, has been suffering from migraine headaches. She has agreed to try a type of treatment called biofeedback. At her first session, sensors (electrodes) are placed on the skin over the temporal artery on the most headache-prone side of her forehead. The sensors detect the blood-volume amplitude pulsing through the temporal artery. Any change in blood-volume amplitude is instantly processed by a computer and displayed on a screen that Barbara observes. The machine does not constrict the temporal artery, an effect that can lessen the pain of Barbara's headache. That is her responsibility. Rather, the machine gives Barbara instantaneous information on what her temporal arteries are doing (that is, dilating or constricting). With practice, Barbara can learn to control the pattern on the screen and thereby learn to voluntarily constrict the temporal arteries on her forehead (which are directly involved in migraines). Such a procedure has been shown to reduce migraines by approximately 50 percent (Lisspers & Ost, 1990).

biofeedback

A procedure in which information about a biological function of an individual is "fed back" to the individual.

   A **biofeedback** procedure is one in which information about a biological function of an individual is "fed back" to the individual. (You experience "biofeedback" when you take your own pulse.) The machine that Barbara used monitors blood volume amplitude. Other popular biofeedback machines monitor muscle tension (monitored by the electromyogram [EMG]), body temperature, the galvanic skin response (GSR, which measures skin conductivity or electrical resistance), and brain waves (monitored by the electroencephalogram [EEG]).

Box 5-1

HEALTH PSYCHOLOGY AND BEHAVIORAL MEDICINE

Traditionally, if you suffered from chronic headaches, respiratory disorders, or hypertension, you would see your physician. Beginning in the late 1960s, however, psychologists working with physicians began using behavior modification techniques to directly treat these and other medical problems—such as seizure disorders, chronic pain, addictive disorders, and sleep disorders (Doleys et al., 1982). This launched the field known as *behavioral medicine*, a broad interdisciplinary field concerned with the links between health, illness, and behavior. Psychologists practicing behavioral medicine work in close consultation with medical doctors, nurses, dieticians, sociologists, and others on problems that, until very recently, have been considered to be of a purely medical nature. Within the interdisciplinary field of behavioral medicine, *health psychology* considers how psychological factors can influence or cause illness, and how people can be encouraged to practice healthy behavior in order to prevent health problems such as heart disease (Feist & Brannon, 1988; Taylor, 1990). Health psychologists have applied behavioral principles in six major sub-areas.

DIRECT TREATMENT OF MEDICAL PROBLEMS

Do you suffer from headaches, backaches, or stomach problems during final exams? At one time it was thought that such problems were primarily psychological—existing mainly in the minds of those experiencing them. But the colds, headaches, and other symptoms and the accompanying pain are very real. Health psychologists are continuing the trend of the late 1960s of developing behavioral techniques to directly treat physical symptoms such as these (Feist & Brannon, 1988).

ESTABLISHING TREATMENT COMPLIANCE

Do you always keep your appointments with the dentist? Do you always take medication exactly as described by your doctor? As many as 50 percent of people don't (Sackett & Snow, 1979). But a drug that is 100 percent effective in curing a particular disease, for example, will be ineffective if the patient fails to take it as directed. Thus, an important part of health psychology is establishing treatment compliance with prescribed medical regimens. Since drug taking is a behavior, promoting compliance with medical prescriptions is a natural for psychologists.

PROMOTION OF HEALTHY LIVING

Do you exercise at least three times per week? Eat properly and minimize your consumption of cho-

Neal Miller (1985), a proponent of biofeedback, believes that it is an effective treatment for a variety of conditions including high blood pressure, speech disorders, motion and space sickness, epileptic seizures, and irregular heart beat. It has also been employed to treat tension headaches, asthma, ulcers, and facial tics (Blanchard & Epstein, 1977; Nigl, 1984). Others, however, have argued that supporting evidence for the effectiveness of biofeedback to treat clinical disorders is based on flawed research (Roberts, 1985; White & Tursky, 1982). Moreover, less expensive treatments, such as progressive muscle relaxation, appear to be equally effective (Nigl, 1984). But for individuals with access to suitable equipment, biofeedback continues to be a component of treatment programs for certain types of stress reactions.

lesterol and salt? Do you limit your consumption of alcohol, say to five drinks per week or fewer? Do you say no to tobacco and other drugs? If you can answer yes to these questions and can continue to do so as the years go by, then you can considerably lengthen your life span. An important area of health psychology involves the application of techniques to help people stay healthy, such as eating well-balanced meals and getting adequate exercise (Taylor, 1990).

Dealing with Aging and Chronic Illness

As an increasing percentage of the population is made up of the elderly, more and more individuals must deal on a daily basis with loss of skills that occurs with old age or with chronic illness. Habitual ways of performing daily routines at home or at work may no longer be possible. New routines must be developed and learned. Anxiety or fear about the possibility of failing to cope also might have to be dealt with. And new relationships might have to be developed with professional care staff. Health psychologists help the elderly and chronic care patients to solve such problems.

Management of Care Givers

Health psychologists are concerned not only with the behavior of the client or patient but also with the behavior of those who affect the client's medical condition. Thus, health psychologists deal with the behavior of the client's family or friends as well as with the various medical staff. Changing the behavior of nurses, psychiatric nurses, occupational therapists, and other medical personnel to improve service provided to patients is receiving increased attention (for example, see Reid et al., 1989).

Stress Management

As indicated throughout this chapter, an important area of health psychology concerns the study of stressors, their effect on behavior, and the development of behavioral strategies for coping with stressors.

Although the broad interdisciplinary field of behavioral medicine, and the sub-field of health psychology are very young, they have the potential to make a profound contribution to the efficiency and effectiveness of modern medicine and health care (Reed, 1990; Taylor, 1990).

Living a Healthy Lifestyle

If the stressors that you experience stem from your lifestyle activities such as lack of exercise, then the obvious strategy for stress management is to change your lifestyle. One possibility is to eat healthily, a topic addressed in the next chapter. Two additional possibilities are to exercise aerobically and to maintain a sense of humor.

aerobic exercising
Performing a moderately intense activity (such as rapid walking) over a sustained period (at least 15 minutes) so that you require large quantities of oxygen and your body improves its capacity to use it.

AEROBIC EXERCISING. *Aerobic* means "with oxygen." Aerobic refers to the ability of the body to take, transport, and use oxygen. Effective **aerobic exercising** requires that you perform moderately intense activity (such as rapid walking, jogging, cycling, or swimming) over a sustained period (at least 15 to 20 minutes) on a

During *biofeedback*, people can observe a visual pattern that provides information about their physiological responses, such as muscle tension or heart rate. By using such feedback, individuals can learn to voluntarily control processes that are normally thought to be involuntary.

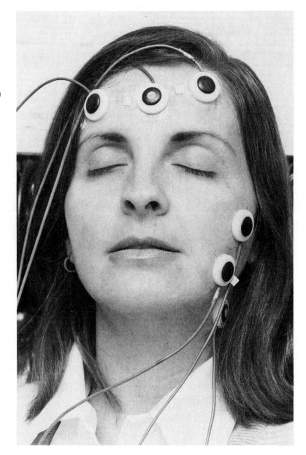

regular basis (three or four times per week) so that your energy systems require large quantities of oxygen and your body improves its capacity to use it. Aerobic exercising causes you to breathe deeper and harder and increases the ability of your body to use oxygen efficiently. When exercise improves the functioning of your cardiovascular system (heart, lungs, and blood vessels), a "training" or "conditioning" effect has occurred. Cooper (1982) lists the following beneficial effects that accompany effective aerobic training:

- The total blood volume increases so that the body is better equipped to transport oxygen; thus the individual has more endurance when engaging in strenuous physical activities.
- The capacity of the lungs increases, and some studies have associated this increase in "vital capacity" with greater longevity.
- The heart muscle grows stronger, is better supplied with blood, and the heart can pump more blood with each stroke (increased stroke volume).
- Beneficial high density lipoprotein (HDL) increases, the total cholesterol/HDL ratio decreases, and there is a reduction of developing atherosclerosis, or hardening of the arteries (Cooper, 1982, p. 113).

Are you surprised to find a discussion of aerobic exercising in a chapter on stress? Consider these examples. At the University of Nebraska, a number of students who experienced stress before and during written exams, were divided into two groups. One group was taught how to perform meditative relaxation exercises as a way of coping with exam-related stress. Another group participated in an aerobic exercise program. Both approaches led to reduced anxiety and the results were about the same with the two groups (Fuenning, 1981). Another study examined the relationship between physical fitness and stress management with a group of teachers and administrators in a school district in Dallas (Cooper, 1982). Approximately 100 subjects participated in an exercise and nutrition program for six months, and were compared to 60 non-exercising control subjects on several measures. Exercise participants were able to handle job stress significantly better than the control subjects. Still another study found that high blood pressure (a common symptom of stress) is much more likely to be found in both men and women who do not keep fit as opposed to those who do (Blair et al., 1984). Other researchers found that an eight-week aerobics program produced and maintained improvements in self-efficacy, anxiety, and coping in a group of stressed working women. These improvements were equivalent to those produced by an eight-week progressive relaxation program. Results were generally maintained in both groups at a 14-month follow-up (Long & Haney, 1988*a*, 1988*b*).

What is it that might underlie such findings? There are at least four possibilities. First, one effect of an aerobic exercise program is to significantly decrease the average resting heart rate. In a stressful situation, such an individual may be likely to remain calm and relaxed. Second, individuals who participate in aerobic exercising at the end of a very stressful day report that the exercising helps to dissipate the tension that they have accumulated during the day and to feel more relaxed during the evening (Cooper, 1982). A highly stressful day can lead to an internal buildup of adrenal secretions. As stated by Cooper, "Exercise apparently acts as nature's waste removal process, and helps your body return to a more relaxed state of equilibrium" (Cooper, 1982, p. 191). Third, regular exercise makes individuals feel in control of their lives, a belief that Bandura refers to as self-efficacy (see Chapter 2), and the belief that one can control events that affect oneself has been shown to reduce stress reactions (Rodin, 1986). Finally, focusing one's attention on physical fitness activities may redirect one's attention away from stressors in one's life (Brown, 1991). Whatever the explanation, there is no doubt that physical fitness makes one less vulnerable to the adverse effects of stress (Brown, 1991). Aerobic exercising will be discussed more fully in the next chapter.

MAINTAINING YOUR SENSE OF HUMOR.   When you exercise, you increase your physiological arousal. Afterward, however, you feel more relaxed. Laughter seems to work the same way (Robinson, 1983). Anecdotal reports indicate that many professional comedians learned to use humor as a strategy for dealing with stress in childhood (Fry & Allen, 1975). Carol Burnett, for example, reported using humor as a way of coping with tension between her parents who were both alcoholics and frequently fought. Martin and Lefcourt (1983) found that people who have a sense of humor and laugh easily are less disturbed by stressful life events. Perhaps we should change a well-known proverb to read, "He who laughs, lasts longer."

SUMMARY

- A major sub-area of the psychology of adjustment concerns the study of stress and stress management techniques. There is no widely accepted definition of stress. Some types of stressors are environmental, and include noise and air pollution; major life events, such as going through a divorce; and the numerous daily hassles that occur at home, at school, and at work.

- Some stressors are psychological in nature. For example, the Type A behavior pattern, characterized by a sense of time urgency, aggressiveness, and a tendency to become easily angered, has been associated with susceptibility to heart attack. For others, irrational self-talk or perceived lack of control in a situation can be sources of stress.

■ A third category of stressors relates to the state of the body and is referred to as physiological stressors. These include such things as obesity, fatigue, aging, unhealthy lungs from smoking, and cirrhosis of the liver from excessive alcohol consumption.

■ Individuals show both physiological and behavioral reactions to stressors. Selye described the characteristic way that our bodies react to the continuing presence of stress as the general adaptation syndrome. This includes an alarm stage in which our resources are mobilized to deal with the stressor, a resistance stage in which our bodies cope with prolonged stress by taking away resources from other bodily functions, and an exhaustion stage, in which our defenses give out and we are especially susceptible to disease and tissue damage.

■ Behavioral reactions to stress are likely to depend upon an individual's learning history. Some people react with aggression. Others show a behavior pattern called learned helplessness—a motivational, cognitive, and emotional deficit as a function of repeated exposure to inescapable aversive events. Still others react to stress by showing various degrees of performance impairment—an inability to perform up to their usual standard.

■ Repeated prolonged exposure to stressors can cause psychosomatic or psychophysiological disorders including ulcers, migraine headaches, and skin disorders. Stress can also affect the functioning of our immune system. Stress-induced suppression of the immune system has been demonstrated in a number of studies, such as during stressful periods for first-year dental students and right after returning to earth for astronauts.

■ There are a variety of techniques for helping individuals cope with stressors. You can deal with the source of stressors through rational problem solving and enhanced time management skills. Psychological strategies include various ways of changing how you think about stressors, such as analyzing irrational stressful statements that you make and substituting alternative rational statements to counteract them. You can change your body to make it more stress resistant by practicing progressive muscle relaxation or biofeedback. And you can minimize the stress from an unhealthy lifestyle by aerobically exercising and maintaining your sense of humor.

Box 5-2

SELF-ADJUSTMENT FOR STUDENTS: MAKE A COMMITMENT TO CHANGE

In the self-adjustment box at the end of the last chapter, you selected a specific problem for your self-adjustment project. Now we want you to take steps to build your commitment to stick to the project.

LIST REASONS FOR COMPLETING THE PROJECT
How will you (and/or others) benefit by the successful completion of your self-adjustment project?

Try to think of positive reasons for completing your project. If your project is to quit smoking, for example, and if you are successful, then you will have more energy and endurance for exercising and work, your senses of taste and smell will improve, you will be less likely to catch colds or flu, and the extra risk of heart attack due to smoking will be cut in half within a year after quitting. Write out at least five reasons for completing your project, and post them in a conspicuous place.

TELL OTHERS ABOUT YOUR PROGRAM

List the names of four friends and/or relatives whom you can count on to give you support in completing your project (see Table 5-3). These should be people whom you see and/or talk to on a daily or near daily basis. Each person should also be available in at least one of the settings in which you typically find yourself each day, such as home, school, work, and your neighborhood. One person may be someone who is also beginning a self-adjustment project so that the two of you could support each other on a buddy system. For example, Karol and Richards (1978) found that smokers who quit with a buddy and who telephoned encouragement to each other showed greater reduction of smoking in an eight-month follow-up than did smokers who tried to quit on their own. It is likely that the buddy system would benefit other types of projects as well. But if you don't have a buddy who is also on a self-adjustment project, generally increasing the number of people who can remind you to stick to your program increases your chances of success (Passman, 1977).

Contact each of the people on your list of supporters (Table 5-3). Tell them about your project and your goal and ask them to remind you to stick to the project each time that you see them. Ask them also to give you *positive* reminders and feedback for sticking to your project. Encountering a member of your support group should be a positive experience that gives you incentive to stick to your project. It should not be an aversive experience that simply makes you feel guilty.

PROVIDE FREQUENT REMINDERS OF YOUR GOAL

Arrange your environment to provide frequent reminders of your goal. You could state your goal on 3 × 5 cards and leave them in conspicuous places, such as taped to the door of your fridge or on the dashboard of your car. If your goal is to perform a particular skill well, you might think of famous people who already perform that skill and who might serve as models. Cut out pictures of them in an "action" pose and post them in conspicuous places. Your reminders should be phrased or structured in a way so that they are associated with the positive benefits of reaching your goal.

PREPARE COMMITMENT STATEMENTS

Write out a series of self-statements that you can rehearse to maintain your commitment. For example, you might think of the considerable time and energy spent in initially planning your project. On a 3 × 5 card you might write, "I've put so much into it, it would be a shame to quit now." Sometimes people feel overwhelmed when they think of facing several weeks of a self-adjustment project. In such cases, commitment statements might focus only on the moment, such as, "I'll take it one day at a time," or "I'll use my support group to make today a success. I'll worry about tomorrow when it comes." Rehearse your commitment statements at least once per day.

PLAN TEMPTATION RESISTANCE STRATEGIES

Because you will undoubtedly be tempted to quit your project, plan ahead for various ways to deal with temptations. Your temptation resistance strategies have to be tailored to your particular program. Consider George, who wanted to quit smoking. Initially George felt that he couldn't resist the temptation to smoke while playing poker with his friends on Friday nights. His temptation resistance strategy

TABLE 5-3
INDIVIDUALS WHO WILL SUPPORT MY SELF-ADJUSTMENT PROJECT

Name	*Phone No.*	*Setting Where We Usually See Each Other*

was to not play poker for the first month of his quit-smoking program. As another example, Sanchez wanted to lose weight. He found it especially difficult to control his eating at Sunday dinners at Grandma's house, and to resist visiting the Dairy Queen right beside the supermarket where he usually bought groceries. His temptation resistance strategies included an explanation to Grandma that he was on a diet and wouldn't be able to come to dinner for the next few weeks, and a change in the place where he bought his groceries so that he didn't have to walk by the Dairy Queen and resist his favorite sundae.

Think of the various situations during the next few weeks where you might be tempted to go off your program or to revert to earlier, problematic behavior patterns. For each such situation, write out at least one temptation resistance strategy.

Figure 5-3
A behavioral contract

A Contract for the Self–Adjustment Project of _____

My self–adjustment project concerns the problem of: _____
_____
_____
_____
_____

My specific goals for my self–adjustment project are: _____
_____
_____
_____
_____

The procedures that I plan to follow include: _____
_____
_____
_____
_____
_____

Rewards that I can earn for sticking to my project include: _____
_____
_____
_____
_____

Rewards that I can earn for successfully completing my project include:
_____
_____
_____
_____

I, ___(your name)___ , promise to explain each of the steps in my
project to ___(name of supporter)___ . I also agree to report my
progress to ___(name of supporter)___ during each day of my project
until my long–term goal is achieved.

Date _____

Signed _____   Signed _____
        (your signature)   (supporter's signature)

BEGIN A BEHAVIORAL CONTRACT

One way of building and maintaining commitment is to sign a contract that outlines your project and commits you to stick to it. A *behavioral contract* is a clear written statement of an individual's goal in a self-adjustment project, the procedures to be followed to achieve the goal, the rewards to be obtained if the goal is met, and how and by whom particular rewards will be delivered. You cannot yet complete an entire contract because you have not yet planned the procedures that you will follow in your self-adjustment project. That will come in later chapters. But you can begin your contract, and you can increase your commitment by having a member of your support group sign it with you. A sample contract is outlined in Figure 5-3.

MEMORY BOOSTER

■ IMPORTANT PERSONS

You should know who these persons are and why they are important:

Hans Selye

Richard Lazarus

Susan Folkman

Thomas Holmes

Richard Rahe

Meyer Friedman

Ray Rosenman

Suzanne Kobasa

■ IMPORTANT TERMS

Be prepared to define the following terms (located in the margins of this chapter). Where appropriate, be prepared to describe examples.

Stressors

Stress Reactions

Major Life Event

Daily Hassles

Approach-Approach Conflict

Avoidance-Avoidance Conflict

Approach-Avoidance Conflict

Double Approach-Avoidance Conflict

Type A Personality

Type B Personality

Hardiness

General Adaptation Syndrome

Alarm or Preparation Stage

Resistance or Fighting Stage

Exhaustion Stage

Learned Helplessness

Psychosomatic Disorders

Immune System

Cognitive Reappraisal

Biofeedback

Aerobic Exercising

■ QUESTIONS FROM IMPORTANT IDEAS IN THIS CHAPTER

1. Describe three different ways that the term *stress* has been used.
2. Discuss four problems with research on life events as stressors.
3. Discuss two criticisms of research on daily hassles as stressors.
4. What are the characteristics of a Type A personality that are linked to susceptibility to heart disease?

5. What characteristics of a hardy personality are associated with high resistance to the effects of stressors?

6. Illustrate with examples how irrational self-talk can be a source of stress.

7. Describe some research that indicates that exposure to stressors impairs the functioning of our immune system. What role might classical conditioning play in this process?

8. Briefly describe six sub-areas of health psychology.

9. Using an example, describe how you might use cognitive reappraisal to cope with stress.

10. Describe four possible explanations for why aerobic exercising can help one to cope with stress.

chapter

6

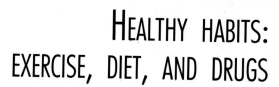

HEALTHY HABITS:
EXERCISE, DIET, AND DRUGS

CHAPTER OUTLINE

After reading this chapter, you should be able to:
- Contrast different types of fitness.
- List the physical benefits of an aerobic fitness program.
- Plan an effective exercise program.
- Describe some of the causes of obesity.
- Implement a program of healthier eating.
- Apply behavioral strategies for dieting.
- Differentiate between substance abuse and substance dependence.
- Describe some of the effects of major stimulants, depressants, and hallucinogens.
- List several ways to guard against drug abuse.

Do you exercise to the point of breaking a sweat at least three times per week? Do you eat properly and minimize your consumption of cholesterol and salt? What about alcohol drinking, do you limit it to five or fewer drinks per week? And do you say no to tobacco and other drugs? Unfortunately, few people can answer yes to all of these questions. Approximately 350,000 Americans die each year from heart disease. Another group of 500,000 suffer heart attacks that are not fatal. Americans, on average, are more overweight than the citizens of any other nation in the world. And millions of Americans are addicted to nicotine, alcohol, and other drugs. Unfortunately, a great many people practice *unhealthy* lifestyle habits. As we indicated in Chapter 5, an important area of health psychology involves the application of techniques to help people stay healthy. In this chapter, we examine the areas of exercise, diet, and drugs, and we review a variety of strategies to help you to develop and maintain a healthy lifestyle.

Exercising

Walking, jogging, weight lifting, swimming, cycling, dance aerobics, jazz aerobics—during the last decade, millions of Americans discovered fitness. If you have not already done so, should you consider climbing on the band wagon? Is it worth your while to participate in a regular exercise program? Should you deliberately force yourself to huff and puff and work up a sweat at least three times per week? Data from a number of studies indicate that there are many benefits of being physically fit.

What Is Fitness?

Exercise physiologists distinguish among several kinds of fitness. First (and most important) is *cardiorespiratory fitness.* As indicated in the previous chapter, this type of fitness is often referred to as **aerobic fitness,** and it refers to the ability of your cardiovascular system (heart, lungs, and blood vessels) to take, transport, and use oxygen during exercise. *Aerobic* means "with oxygen." Aerobic exercising requires that you perform moderately intense activity (such as rapid walking, cycling, or swimming) over a sustained period (at least 15 to 20 minutes) so that you require large quantities of oxygen and your body improves its capacity to use it. While you are aerobically exercising, fuel is provided by carbohydrates (and to a lesser extent, by fats) stored in the body, and oxygen is used in the energy conver-

aerobic fitness

The ability of your cardiovascular system (heart, lungs, and blood vessels) to take, transport, and use oxygen during exercise.

There are different types of physical fitness. What type is best for you?

sion process. Thus, swimming 400 yards, skiing cross-country for half an hour, and jogging three miles are all aerobic exercises. Guidelines for aerobically exercising are discussed later in this chapter.

A second type of fitness refers to *muscle strength and endurance*. Exercises that require relatively short, intense bursts of energy, such as weight lifting, running to catch a bus, or returning a punt in football, are referred to as anaerobic fitness activities. *Anaerobic* means "without oxygen." For intense muscular activity lasting from a few seconds to approximately two minutes, the fuel is provided by carbohydrates stored in the body and oxygen is not used in the energy conversion process. Beyond approximately two minutes of exercising, however, oxygen is increasingly required to provide energy.

A third type of fitness is *flexibility*—the range and ease of motion in a joint. Flexibility training involves muscles, tendons (which connect muscles to bones), and ligaments (which connect bones to bones). Flexibility is developed through a series of slow stretching exercises such as bending down and pulling on the ankles with legs straight, and applying increasing pressure for 10 to 15 seconds. While flexibility fitness is important, flexibility alone does not constitute an adequate fitness program.

The fourth type of fitness refers to *body composition and weight.* Guidelines for healthy dieting and weight control are described later in this chapter.

IMPLICATIONS OF DIFFERENT TYPES OF FITNESS FOR EXERCISING. The *specificity principle of training* suggests that training of specific muscles and a particular type of fitness will primarily affect those muscles that are exercised. In other words, specific training produces specific results. A downhill ski racer might concentrate on an anaerobic fitness program. A cross-country skier, on the other hand, requires aerobic fitness. In softball or baseball, players are required to produce bursts of speed of only a few seconds duration. Their fitness programs therefore typically emphasize anaerobic training (wind sprints, and the like). Whatever the reasons for emphasizing a particular type of exercise program, it is important to remember that a superior score in one type of fitness test does not necessarily mean that you will perform well in some other fitness test. A few years ago, the winner of the "Mr. Texas" contest had well-developed muscles, but his aerobic fitness scored below the 15th percentile (Cooper, 1982). An even more dramatic example of the specificity principle of fitness training was the case of Hasely Crawford, who won the gold medal for Trinidad in the 100-meter dash at the Montreal Olympic Games. Running the 100-meter dash, which requires approximately 10 seconds of all-out effort at that level of competition, draws on anaerobic fitness. When Crawford was later tested at the Cooper Clinic, his outward appearance was that of an excellent physical specimen, tall, lean, muscular, and only 9 percent body fat. When tested aerobically, however, he was in very poor shape (Cooper, 1982).

Why Be Fit?

The first obvious benefit of exercising regularly is that participants report that they feel better—physically, emotionally, and mentally. Benefits of a regular exercise program include (Cooper, 1982; Feist & Brannon, 1988; Patton et al., 1986):

- More energy.
- More enjoyable and active leisure time.
- A greater ability to handle domestic and job-related stress.
- Less depression, less hypochondria, and less "free floating" anxiety.
- Fewer physical complaints.
- More efficient digestion and fewer problems with constipation.
- Better self-image and more self-confidence.
- More attractive, streamlined body, including more effective personal weight control.
- Bones of greater strength.
- Slowing of the aging process.
- Easier pregnancy and childbirth.
- More restful sleep.
- Better concentration at work and greater perseverance in daily tasks.
- Fewer aches and pains, including back pains.

A second reason for being fit is that it can save you money in medical bills. Much of the data supporting this contention comes from studies of medical costs for employees in business and industry. For example, Gettman (1983) testified before the House Ways and Means Select Revenue Measures Subcommittee that:

> Fitness programs are related to lower medical costs, lower absenteeism rates and increased productivity. In 1982, Mesa Petroleum employees who did not participate in the fitness program averaged $434 per person in medical costs, paid by Mesa. However, employees who participated in the fitness program averaged only $173 per person.

A third reason for pursuing physical fitness is not one that young people tend to think about. It concerns how long you will live (or how soon you will die). Statistically, individuals who maintain a lifetime of physical exercise tend to live longer than those who don't. In a longitudinal study of 16,936 Harvard alumni dating back to 1916, exercise was clearly linked to increased longevity (Paffenbarger et al., 1984). There was a particularly strong relation between exercise and a lower risk of cardiovascular disease among those middle-aged and older men who burned off more than 2,000 calories per week in various physical activities (Paffenbarger et al., 1986).

IMPORTANCE OF AEROBICS.   Regardless of your reasons for exercising, fitness experts strongly recommend that an exercise program should include approximately one and one-half hours per week, distributed across three or four sessions, for aerobic exercising. There are a number of reasons for this. First, the data supporting many of the physical, emotional, and mental benefits of a regular exercise program listed earlier in this chapter are derived mainly from individuals who participated in aerobic fitness programs. Second, people who do various aerobic exercises regularly are less susceptible to heart attack later in life (Feist & Brannon, 1988). Third, because it can involve the burning of fat (especially if done at a slow pace so as not to draw primarily on stored carbohydrates), aerobic training can be beneficial in reducing excess body fat and excess body weight (as discussed later in this chapter). Fourth, if you are a weekend sport enthusiast (a game of tennis, volleyball on the beach), a reasonable level of aerobic fitness will enable you to participate more strenuously and enjoy those sporting activities more fully with less danger to yourself. Even if your sport draws heavily on the anaerobic system (for example, if your tennis rallies last only a few seconds), the aerobic energy system will still contribute approximately 10 to 20 percent of the energy that is used.

Important Characteristics of a Regular Aerobic Fitness Program

As stated previously, *aerobic* means "with oxygen." When aerobic exercising improves the functioning of your cardiovascular system (your heart, lungs, and blood vessels), we say that a "training" or "conditioning" effect has occurred.

HOW INTENSE SHOULD THE AEROBIC ACTIVITY BE?   There are several rules of thumb that can be used to help you monitor whether your aerobic exercise activity is sufficiently vigorous to produce a training effect. A formula described by Cooper (1982) requires you to determine your predicted maximum heart rate (PMHR). For men, PMHR = 205 − ½ of age; for women PMHR = 220 − age. An aerobic-training effect is achieved if the exercise routine causes heart rate to exceed 80 percent of the PMHR for approximately 20 minutes. A second rule of thumb is that you should be aerobically exercising vigorously enough to feel "almost tired" during the last half of the aerobic exercise session (Farquhar, 1978). A third rule of thumb is that you should be breathing heavily but you should still be able to talk while exercising (Farquhar, 1978).

HOW LONG SHOULD THE AEROBIC WORKOUT LAST?   This depends, in part, on your level of fitness at the beginning of the program. In general, many authorities recommend that minimal training effects require continuous activity of at least 20 minutes, producing an elevated heart rate and also causing you to sweat. Another consideration is whether you are also using aerobic training to lose weight. It is important to remember, as will be discussed later, that total caloric expenditure is closely related to the total duration of exercise.

HOW OFTEN SHOULD YOU TRAIN PER WEEK?   Research has shown that the best frequency for most individuals is three or four sessions per week (Cooper, 1982; *Coaching Theory Level III,* 1989). More than four sessions per week brings into play a sort of law of diminishing returns. That is, more than four training sessions per week appears to lead to additional gains in aerobic fitness at a much lower rate over and above that derived from three or four sessions per week. Once you have achieved a particular level of fitness, a number of beneficial training effects can be maintained for several months with two sessions per week. Fewer than two sessions per week will mean loss of fitness. If you achieve a particular level of aerobic fitness, and then stop exercising aerobically altogether, there is some evidence that aerobic fitness will be lost at approximately the same rate that it was gained. That is, the gains made in two months of aerobic exercising three to four times per week would be lost in approximately two months of no aerobic exercising (*Coaching Theory Level III,* 1989). Thus, once a certain level of aerobic fitness is attained, a maintenance program should be put into effect.

WHAT TYPE OF AEROBIC ACTIVITY SHOULD YOU PERFORM?   At this point you might be asking, "You mean to tell me that the only way I can achieve all those wonderful benefits of aerobic fitness is to get into a cycling, running, or swimming program?" Definitely not. As long as you don't overdo it, every little bit of exercising can help. A game of tennis, a walk in the park, a round of golf (assuming that you don't drive a cart), a 20-minute handball game—all can contribute something to aerobic fitness. Each might contribute a little differently, depending upon how long the activity lasts, and to what extent it requires you to huff and puff and work up a sweat.

Is there a way to put together different types of aerobic activities in different combinations for different weeks and still have some means of calculating how those activities will contribute to the development of a desired level of fitness? There is indeed. During the past 25 years, Cooper (1968, 1970, 1978, 1982, 1985) has developed an **aerobic points system.** Cooper and his colleagues examined a wide variety of activities in terms of the energy expended while performing them. They collected all the air expired from subjects who performed various exercises at certain intensities over certain periods of time. They discovered, for example, that "walking on a treadmill for a distance of one mile in 20 minutes required an average oxygen consumption of about 3.4 calories per minute over and above a resting state. Therefore, walking one mile burned 68 calories" (Cooper, 1982,

aerobic points system
A system developed by Cooper to enable persons to judge the extent to which various activities contribute to aerobic fitness; involves converting durations of various activities of particular intensities to a standardized point system.

TABLE 6-1
SOME EXAMPLES FROM COOPER'S AEROBIC POINT SYSTEM *Adapted from Cooper 1982.*

Activity	Distance	Time (Min:Sec)	Point Value
Walking	1 mile	12:00–15:00	2
	2 miles	24:00–30:00	5
	3 miles	36:00–45:00	8
Jogging	1 mile	6:41–8:00	5
	1 mile	8:00–10:00	4
	2 miles	13:21–16:00	11
	2 miles	16:00–20:00	9
	3 miles	24:00–30:00	14
	3 miles	30:00–36:00	11
Swimming	500 yds	8:21–12:30	4.2
	1000 yds	16:41–25:00	10.3
	1000 yds	25:00–33:20	8.3
	2000 yds	33:21–50:00	23.7
	2000 yds	50:00–1:06:40	19.5
Cycling[a]	3 miles	9:00–12:00	3
	6 miles	18:00–24:00	7.5
	6 miles	24:00–36:00	4.5
	9 miles	27:00–36:00	12
	9 miles	36:00–54:00	7.5
Handball, squash, racquetball}		30:00	4.5
		45:00	6.75
		1 hour	9
Golf	18 holes		3
Tennis, badminton}		1 hour	1.5
		2 hours	3
Cross-country skiing		30:00	9
Volleyball		30:00	2
		30:00	7.5
Minitrampoline		40:00	10
		20:00	4
Aerobics dancing}		30:00	6

[a] *Stationary cycling is awarded approximately ½ points for regular cycling, providing that resistance is sufficient so that the pulse rate immediately after cycling equals or exceeds 140 beats per minute.*

Box 6-1

WEIGHT TRAINING: ANOTHER KIND OF FITNESS

Whether you want to develop the "body beautiful" or to simply tone up a few flabby muscles, you should *not* casually walk into a gym and start swinging weights around without some prior knowledge. Because barbells and dumb bells are more likely to be available to the average person, the following guidelines are based on research into strength building methods using these free weights. They should also be reasonable guidelines for variable resistance equipment (for example, Nautilus) (Rasch, 1983; Sanders, 1980; Wolf, 1984).

1. Strength training should be carried out approximately three times per week, or at most, every other day.

2. During the first few days of weight training, use lighter weights so that each exercise can be performed with a minimum of 10 to 15 repetitions.

3. After the first few days, use that amount of weight for a lift that will enable you to do a maximum of 6 to 9 repetitions. Increase the amount of weight when you can do 10 or more repetitions.

4. During workouts, do two sets for each muscle group.

5. During workouts, a sequence of exercises should be planned to alternate muscle groups used.

6. A weight training program of approximately eight weeks can produce considerable gains, with more gradual gains after that.

7. Once a particular level of strength is achieved, that level can be maintained with two workouts per week.

8. What you train is what you get. Therefore, if you want strength for particular activities (such as strong wrists and grip for tennis), make sure that you exercise the muscle groups needed for those particular activities.

p. 122). Once these values were established, they then developed a numerical point system so that different activities could be compared to each other. Let's consider some examples. According to Cooper's point system, running 2 miles in under 20 minutes 3 times per week would give you a total of 27 aerobic points. Running 2 miles in under 16 minutes 3 times per week would give you 33 aerobic points. Eighteen holes of golf, on the other hand, would give you 3 aerobic points. Swimming 1,000 yards in 25 minutes or less would give you approximately 10 aerobic points. A 30-minute pickup volleyball game would be worth 2 aerobic points while a half hour of aerobic dancing would be worth 6 points. Detailed tables listing the point values of a variety of exercises performed at a variety of speeds can be found in Cooper's books, cited above. Some examples of common activities are listed in Table 6-1.

How many points should you earn per week to keep yourself in "reasonably good shape"? Cooper suggests that most of the benefits of aerobic fitness can be maintained by a man who acquires approximately 35 aerobic points per week, and by a woman who attains approximately 27 points per week.

Warm-Ups and Cool-Downs

At the beginning of exercise sessions, you should go through a series of slow stretching exercises. For each exercise, such as bending down and pulling on the ankles with legs straight, you should apply increasing pressure for 10 to 15 seconds. Some people have a tendency to "bounce." Bouncing should definitely be avoided. Stretching should progress through the larger and lower muscle groups, especially the lower back, hamstrings, and groin. Stretching should also emphasize those body parts and joints that are likely to be stressed in your exercise program. After stretching, you should perform vigorous activities, such as running in place, sit-ups, leg raises, and other calisthenics, to increase body temperature and circulation.

In addition to warming up at the beginning of exercise sessions, you should also perform light cooling-down activities immediately after exercising. Fox and Mathews (1981) outlined two important physiological reasons for this practice: (1) Lactic acid built up during intense muscular activity will decrease more rapidly during mild exercise than during total rest. Thus, a mild exercise cool-down period will promote faster recovery from fatigue. (2) Mild activity during cool-downs keeps the blood circulating and prevents it from cooling in the extremities, which reduces the possibilities of muscular stiffness and decreases the tendency for fainting and dizziness. Fox and Mathews (1981) recommend that your cool-down should be done in reverse order of the warm-up. That is, do some slow jogging or light calisthenics, and then finish with some stretching exercises.

Steps in a Program of Regular Exercise

The following material is presented on the assumption that you do not participate in a regular aerobic exercise program. If you are already an aerobic exerciser, the following material might give you some useful ideas to maintain your program and make exercising even more enjoyable and beneficial than it already is. If you are not an aerobic exerciser, the following material will help you launch a successful program.

In Box 3-3 we outlined a number of steps for you to follow to carry out a successful self-adjustment program. Before proceeding further, we encourage you to review those steps and to apply them in setting up your exercise program. The following suggestions should be added to the guidelines for successful self-adjustment, and are specifically related to exercising.

CONDUCT SOME PRELIMINARY ASSESSMENTS.   Are you physically fit enough to start an aerobic exercise program? The questionnaire in Box 6-2 is a physical activity readiness tool to identify individuals who might be at risk by beginning an aerobic exercise program. If you answer yes to any of the items, then you should obtain medical clearance prior to participating in the vigorous-exercise assessments designed to determine your current level of fitness.

12-minute fitness test

The test developed by Cooper to assess one's current level of fitness; involves comparing, to a set of standards, the greatest distance that you can cover in 12 minutes while performing either running and walking, swimming, or cycling.

If you were able to answer no to all of the questions in Box 6-2, or if you have medical clearance to do so, then Cooper's **12-minute fitness test** is an excellent way to assess your current fitness. You can conduct the test by selecting a combination of running and walking, or by swimming, or by cycling. Whichever activity you select, you should do some preliminary stretching and warm-up exercises as described previously. Then, for the chosen activity, simply cover the greatest distance that you can in 12 minutes. Don't go out and work yourself into a state of total exhaustion. But do put out what you consider to be a "good solid effort." You should be breathing heavily and sweating at the end of your test. Also, if you feel any unusual symptoms during the test (such as dizziness, nausea, or heart palpitations), then stop immediately and go into your cool-down exercises. Assuming that you complete the test appropriately, continue with several minutes of cool-down exercises. Then, by comparing the distance that you cover in 12 minutes to the information in Table 6-2, you can obtain a rough idea of your level of fitness.

MAKE A COMMITMENT.   Review the guidelines in Box 5-2 for making a commitment to an adjustment program. You might also enlist the aid of an exercise partner. Having a regular exercise partner or a supportive spouse has been reported by exercisers who have maintained their program sufficiently long to experience significant health benefits (Heinzelmann & Bagley, 1970; Lawson & Rhodes,

Box 6-2
PRE-EXERCISE SCREENING QUESTIONNAIRE

Yes   No

1. Has a doctor ever said you have heart trouble? ____ ____

2. Have you ever had angina pectoris or sharp pain or heavy pressure in your chest as a result of exercise, walking, or other physical activity, such as climbing a flight of stairs? (Note: This does not include the normal out-of-breath feeling that results from vigorous activity.) ____ ____

3. Do you experience any sharp pain or extreme tightness in your chest when you are hit by a cold blast of air? ____ ____

4. Have you ever experienced rapid heart action or palpitations? ____ ____

5. Have you ever had a real or suspected heart attack, coronary occlusion, myocardial infarction, coronary insufficiency, or thrombosis? ____ ____

6. Have you ever had rheumatic fever? ____ ____

7. Do you have diabetes, high blood pressure, or sugar in your urine? ____ ____

8. Do you have or does anyone in your family have high blood pressure or hypertension? ____ ____

9. Has more than one blood relative (parent, brother, sister, first cousin) had a heart attack or coronary artery disease before the age of 60?

10. Have you ever taken any medication to lower your blood pressure? ____ ____

11. Have you ever taken medication or been on a special diet to lower your cholesterol level? ____ ____

12. Have you ever taken digitalis, quinine, or any other drug for your heart? ____ ____

13. Have you ever taken nitroglycerin or any other tablets for chest pain—tablets that you take by placing them under the tongue? ____ ____

14. Have you ever had a resting or stress electrocardiogram that was not normal? ____ ____

15. Are you overweight? ____ ____

16. Are you under a lot of stress? ____ ____

17. Do you drink excessively? ____ ____

18. Do you smoke cigarettes? ____ ____

19. Do you have any physical condition, impairment, or disability, including any joint or muscle problem, that should be considered before you undertake an exercise program? ____ ____

20. Are you more than 35 years old? ____ ____

21. Do you exercise fewer than three times per week? ____ ____

Adapted from O'Donnell & Ainsworth, 1984.

1981). Examine how you can rearrange your environment to provide frequent prompts for participating in your exercise program. Have comfortable running or walking shoes readily available. Buy a sweat suit or exercise outfit that you feel comfortable wearing. Post pictures of your favorite celebrities participating in jogging, dance aerobics, or some other form of exercise. Enlarge a picture of yourself participating in an exercise program, perhaps from a favorite vacation spot.

Try preparing counterarguments for all of the reasons you might think of for not exercising. You say you can't jog because of bad knees and you don't like to sweat?—then try a swimming program. You say you can't swim?—then how about water jogging? Jogging in a pool (either in place or on the slope going to the deep end) is an efficient way to achieve cardiovascular conditioning without putting pressure on your knees, and while keeping cool at the same time (Castronis, 1976). You say you don't like exercising alone?—then check the yellow pages for hiking

TABLE 6-2
FITNESS LEVELS OF COOPER'S 12-MINUTE TEST Adapted from Cooper, 1982.

12-Minute Walking/Running Test—Distance (Miles) Covered in 12 Minutes

FITNESS CATEGORY		Age (years)					
		13–19	20–29	30–39	40–49	50–59	60+
I. Very poor	(men)	<1.30[a]	<1.22	<1.18	<1.14	<1.03	< .87
	(women)	<1.0	< .96	< .94	< .88	< .84	< .78
II. Poor	(men)	1.30–1.37	1.22–1.31	1.18–1.30	1.14–1.24	1.03–1.16	.87–1.02
	(women)	1.00–1.18	.96–1.11	.95–1.05	.88– .98	.88– .93	.78– .86
III. Fair	(men)	1.38–1.56	1.32–1.49	1.31–1.45	1.25–1.39	1.17–1.30	1.03–1.20
	(women)	1.19–1.29	1.12–1.22	1.06–1.18	.99–1.11	.94–1.05	.87– .98
IV. Good	(men)	1.57–1.72	1.50–1.64	1.46–1.56	1.40–1.53	1.31–1.44	1.21–1.32
	(women)	1.30–1.43	1.23–1.34	1.19–1.29	1.12–1.24	1.06–1.18	.99–1.09
V. Excellent	(men)	1.73–1.86	1.65–1.76	1.57–1.69	1.54–1.65	1.45–1.58	1.33–1.55
	(women)	1.44–1.51	1.35–1.45	1.30–1.39	1.25–1.34	1.19–1.30	1.10–1.18
VI. Superior	(men)	>1.87	>1.77	>1.70	>1.66	>1.59	>1.56
	(women)	>1.52	>1.46	>1.40	>1.35	>1.31	>1.19

[a] < Means "less than"; > means "more than."

12-Minute Swimming Test—Distance (Yards) Swum in 12 Minutes

FITNESS CATEGORY		Age (years)					
		13–19	20–29	30–39	40–49	50–59	60+
I. Very poor	(men)	<500[a]	<400	<350	<300	<250	<250
	(women)	<400	<300	<250	<200	<150	<150
II. Poor	(men)	500–599	400–499	350–449	300–399	250–349	250–299
	(women)	400–499	300–399	250–349	200–299	150–249	150–199
III. Fair	(men)	600–699	500–599	450–549	400–499	350–449	300–399
	(women)	500–599	400–499	350–449	300–399	250–349	200–299
IV. Good	(men)	700–799	600–699	550–649	500–599	450–549	400–499
	(women)	600–699	500–599	450–549	400–499	350–449	300–399
V. Excellent	(men)	>800	>700	>650	>600	>550	>500
	(women)	>700	>600	>550	>500	>450	>400

[a] < Means "less than"; > means "more than."

The Swimming Test *requires you to swim as far as you can in 12 minutes, using whatever stroke you prefer and resting as necessary, but trying for a maximum effort. The easiest way to take the test is in a pool with known dimensions, and it helps to have another person record the laps and time. Be sure to use a watch with a sweep second hand.*

12-Minute Cycling Test—3-Speed or Less, Distance (Miles) Cycled in 12 Minutes

FITNESS CATEGORY		Age (years)					
		13–19	20–29	30–39	40–49	50–59	60+
I. Very poor	(men)	<2.75[a]	<2.5	<2.25	<2.0	<1.75	<1.75
	(women)	<1.75	<1.5	<1.25	<1.0	<0.75	<0.75
II. Poor	(men)	2.75–3.74	2.5–3.49	2.25–3.24	2.0–2.99	1.75–2.49	1.75–2.24
	(women)	1.75–2.74	1.5–2.49	1.25–2.24	1.0–1.99	0.75–1.49	0.75–1.24
III. Fair	(men)	3.75–4.74	3.5–4.49	3.25–4.24	3.0–3.99	2.50–3.49	2.25–2.99
	(women)	2.75–3.74	2.5–3.49	2.25–3.24	2.0–2.99	1.50–2.49	1.25–1.99
IV. Good	(men)	4.75–5.74	4.5–5.49	4.25–5.24	4.0–4.99	3.50–4.49	3.0 –3.99
	(women)	3.75–4.74	3.5–4.49	3.25–4.24	3.0–3.99	2.50–3.49	2.0 –2.99
V. Excellent	(men)	>5.75	>5.5	>5.25	>5.0	>4.5	>4.0
	(women)	>4.75	>4.5	>4.25	>4.0	>3.5	>3.0

[a] < Means "less than"; > means "more than."

The Cycling Test *can be used as a test of fitness if you are utilizing a cycling program. Cycle as far as you can in 12 minutes in an area where traffic is not a problem. Try to cycle on a hard, flat surface, with the wind (less than 10 mph), and use a bike with no more than 3 gears. If the wind is blowing harder than 10 mph take the test another day. Measure the distance you cycle in 12 minutes by either the speedometer/odometer on the bike (which may not be too accurate) or by another means, such as a car odometer or an engineering wheel.*

Box 6-3

GETTING "HIGH" ON EXERCISE

Can you really experience a "high" from exercise? The answer appears to be yes. And we're not talking about running to Denver, the mile-high city. Many people have reported that they experience an incredible feeling of euphoria just after completing an exercise session. The explanation of this experience appears to lie in an understanding of hormones called endorphins. *Endorphins* are substances like morphine, but about 200 times more powerful at comparable doses. A number of studies have indicated that endorphins are released from the pituitary gland in a variety of situations, including exercise, and that they are responsible for a phenomenal feeling of euphoria that can last for 30 minutes to an hour after vigorous exercise (Cooper, 1982; Moore, 1982).

or walking groups such as the Sierra Club. Local community colleges and YMCAs frequently provide a variety of exercise classes for individuals of all ages. Similarly, the Amateur Athletic Union sponsors age-grouped running programs and swim masters programs with sufficient variety for you to join with others of your age group in such activities. Whatever reasons you might come up with for not exercising, there are usually solid counterarguments in favor of exercising. Preparing those ahead of time can help your commitment.

Record Data and Set Goals.   An important step of a self-adjustment program is to collect data on the target behavior—when, where, and how often it occurs. There are a variety of measurements one could record with respect to an exercise program—number of miles run per week, number of hours exercising per week, number of times exercising per week.

Probably the most versatile data to plot are the number of aerobic points earned per week. As we learned earlier, such data allow you maximum flexibility for earning your points in a variety of activities of varying durations and intensities. Moreover, they readily lend themselves to realistic and personalized goal setting. For example, Keefe and Blumenthal (1980) described a study of three males aged 47, 51, and 56 who were all considerably overweight for their height and age, and all of whom had chronic problems in exercise maintenance. Following preliminary assessments, each subject began a walking program with goals of earning a minimum of 10 aerobic points per week. Each week, they increased their exercise goals to a value which was not greater than a 10 percent increase over the distance covered in walking during the preceding week. All subjects were able to maintain their exercise over the 1-year period of the study, and all subjects eventually shifted to a jogging program. Aerobic points also lend themselves to maintenance goal setting, at the values mentioned previously of 35 aerobic points for men and 27 for women.

Short-term goal setting is especially important at the onset of exercise programs because initial stages of exercising often result in performance *decreases*. Comparisons with more fit companions, muscular soreness from initial exercise sessions, and full realization of the long-term process that you face to get into really good shape, often lead to setbacks for beginning exercisers. For these reasons, we recommend that initial short-term goals focus simply on participating in an exercise program rather than on making gains. Additional short-term goals might relate to familiarization with various exercise facilities and activities that may be new to you, becoming acquainted with companion exercisers, and monitoring your heart rates and level of exertion. After the first two weeks of an exercise program, your short-term goals could vary from 5 to 10 percent improvement per week during the initial months of your fitness program (Patton et al., 1986).

ENSURE SUPPORT FOR YOUR PROGRAM.   In the self-adjustment box at the end of Chapter 9 (Box 9-4), we describe a variety of strategies for managing consequences to ensure support for self-adjustment programs. In studies by Kau and Fischer (1974) and Keefe and Blumenthal (1980), subjects initially signed contracts that enabled them to earn various rewards for participating in their programs. Keefe and Blumenthal suggested that, if possible, the reinforcers should be relevant to exercise itself. One subject, for example, earned a new warm-up suit. Another subject earned a new pair of running shoes. Rewards for exercising don't necessarily have to be related to exercising, however. One person we know "loves his beer." One of the most pleasing parts of his day was arriving home after work when he could settle down to two or three cold brews. When he went on an exercise program, he decided that having a cold beer was one of the most powerful reinforcers that he could have. Therefore, although it may have appeared to some to defeat the purpose, he postponed his beer time until he completed a half-hour brisk walk. There are many ways to structure your fitness program so that exercising leads to natural rewards in your daily activities. The more that you're able to do this early in your exercise program, the more likely you are to capture some of the intrinsic rewards of being fit, and to establish regular exercising as a lifetime habit.

Dieting and Weight Control

Why is it that millions of Americans are overweight? Why is nutrition so important to everyday activities? If you want to lose a few pounds, what is a sensible, potentially successful approach to dieting? In this section, we address these questions. First, we will discuss some of the causes of obesity. Next, we review some facts about the seven major nutrients that make up a healthy diet: carbohydrates, fats, proteins, vitamins, minerals, water, and fiber. Finally, we describe steps that you can take to achieve a healthier diet and approach an ideal weight.

Are You Overweight?

Someone who is obese is someone who is excessively fat, someone who is overweight for their height and body structure. But how heavy does one have to be to be considered overweight? The answer is quite arbitrary, and depends on prevailing social standards. Before 1920, for example, to be plump was to be attractive, and to be thin was to be unattractive. Nowadays, "thin is in," at least in the fashion industry.

How can you determine if you are overweight? By studying many individuals, experts have prepared tables to give you a general idea of ideal weights for individuals of a particular height, age, sex, and frame size. Two such tables have been reproduced in Table 6-3.

First you must decide whether your body frame is small, medium, or large. By your frame, we are generally referring to your bone size and structure, not your current waistline measurement. Assessing your frame size is a subjective undertaking, so give it your best guess. Next, check the information in Table 6-3 to get some idea of your ideal weight. Keep in mind that weight charts represent averages that specific individuals may only approximate. You might also consider how comfortable you have felt in the past at a particular weight. Considering all of this information, you can decide whether or not you need to lose a few pounds. Many experts

TABLE 6-3

A. DESIRABLE WEIGHTS FOR DESIGNATED HEIGHTS AND BODY BUILDS: WEIGHTS OF PERSONS 20 TO 30 YEARS OLD

HEIGHT (WITHOUT SHOES)	SMALL FRAME	MEDIUM FRAME	LARGE FRAME
Weight in Pounds (Without Clothing)			
Men			
5 feet 3 inches	118	129	141
5 feet 4 inches	122	133	145
5 feet 5 inches	126	137	149
5 feet 6 inches	130	142	155
5 feet 7 inches	134	147	161
5 feet 8 inches	139	151	166
5 feet 9 inches	143	155	170
5 feet 10 inches	147	159	174
5 feet 11 inches	150	163	178
6 feet	154	167	183
6 feet 1 inch	158	171	188
6 feet 2 inches	162	175	192
6 feet 3 inches	165	178	195
Women			
5 feet	100	109	118
5 feet 1 inch	104	112	121
5 feet 2 inches	107	115	125
5 feet 3 inches	110	118	128
5 feet 4 inches	113	122	132
5 feet 5 inches	116	125	135
5 feet 6 inches	120	129	139
5 feet 7 inches	123	132	142
5 feet 8 inches	126	136	146
5 feet 9 inches	130	140	151
5 feet 10 inches	133	144	156
5 feet 11 inches	137	148	161
6 feet	141	152	166

B. 1983 METROPOLITAN HEIGHT AND WEIGHT TABLE FOR MEN AND WOMEN, 25 TO 59 YEARS OLD[a]

FT.	INCH.	SMALL FRAME	MEDIUM FRAME	LARGE FRAME
Height				
Men				
5	2	128–134	131–141	138–150
5	3	130–136	133–143	140–153
5	4	132–138	135–145	142–156
5	5	134–140	137–148	144–160
5	6	136–142	139–151	146–164
5	7	138–145	142–154	149–168
5	8	140–148	145–157	152–172
5	9	142–151	148–160	155–176
5	10	144–154	151–163	158–180
5	11	146–157	154–166	161–184
6	0	149–160	157–170	164–188
6	1	152–164	160–174	168–192
6	2	155–168	164–178	172–197
6	3	158–172	167–182	176–202
6	4	162–176	171–187	181–207
Women				
4	10	102–111	109–121	118–131
4	11	103–113	111–123	120–134
5	0	104–115	113–126	122–137
5	1	106–118	115–129	125–140
5	2	108–121	118–132	128–143
5	3	111–124	121–135	131–147
5	4	114–127	124–138	134–151
5	5	117–130	127–141	137–155
5	6	120–133	130–144	140–159
5	7	123–136	133–147	143–163
5	8	126–139	136–150	146–167
5	9	129–142	139–153	149–170
5	10	132–145	142–156	152–173
5	11	135–148	145–159	155–176
6	0	138–151	148–162	158–179

[a] *Weights at ages 25–59 based on lowest mortality. Weight in pounds according to frame (in indoor clothing weighing 3 lbs., shoes with 1" heels).*

suggest that an individual is overweight if he or she exceeds the ideal weight in the weight chart by 20 percent or more (LeBow, 1989).

Causes of Obesity

Recent studies suggest that one out of five Americans is overweight, and that approximately a third of American adults need to be treated for obesity (LeBow, 1989). Why are so many Americans overweight? Were they born that way? Do they simply eat too much? Let's examine some of the causes of significant problems of long-term weight control.

GENETIC CAUSES.   Perhaps some people really are "born that way." Kids whose parents are both overweight have an 80 percent chance of being overweight themselves (Haney, 1983). But is this due to genetics or simply due to obese parents overfeeding their children, thereby teaching their offspring to be "big eaters"? Some answers can be found in studies of twins. In general, weights of identical twins raised apart are more similar than weights of fraternal twins raised in the same environment, suggesting that genetics does influence degree of obesity in adults (Stunkard et al., 1986).

So what exactly is it that we inherit that may determine our future body weight? Two leading candidates are the rate at which your body metabolizes food and your number of fat cells.

The rate at which your body converts food into body tissues and energy is referred to as your **metabolic rate.** For some people, their metabolism seems to run at "90 miles per hour." That is, their heart rate and bodily functioning are such that they can consume a lot of food, but they seem to burn that food off very rapidly and not convert it to fat. Others have a much slower metabolism. Some overweight people eat the same amount of food as control groups of average weight (Stunkard, 1980). Perhaps the overweight people in these studies have simply inherited a slower metabolism (Bogardus et al., 1986; Bouchard et al., 1989).

Another candidate for a genetic link to obesity may be our *fat cells*, in which our body fat is stored. The number of fat cells that you have at birth is inherited (Bogardus et al., 1986). And throughout your life, the number of fat cells you have won't decrease, but fat cells can increase in number and size from certain eating patterns. Once fat cells are present, dieting can reduce their size, but not their number (Zeman, 1991).

One theory suggests that our metabolic rate when we diet is linked to our fat cells. Suppose, for example, that you decide to lose a few pounds. Theoretically, burning off approximately 3,500 calories more than you consume in food translates into one pound of weight loss. Thus, if you consume 500 fewer calories per day than you burn off, and you do so for one week, you should lose a pound. But for some obese people, it doesn't seem to work that way. In one study, obese patients burned off far in excess of the 450 calories per day that they consumed and still had lost very little weight at the end of 24 days (Bray, 1969). How come? One theory is that we each have a physiological **set point** for the amount of fat in our bodies (Keesey & Powley, 1986). The assumption is that when people go on a starvation diet, the set point clicks in. The body's metabolic rate slows down to conserve energy, to ensure that vital functions will be performed. For those who want to lose weight, it just doesn't seem fair.

LEARNING EXPERIENCES.   Learning also plays an important role in our long-term eating habits and the likelihood of our being overweight (LeBow, 1991). As kids, for example, many of us were told, "Clean off your plate if you want dessert." Now, as

---

metabolic rate

In general terms, the rate at which your body converts food into body tissues and energy; your metabolism refers to the rate at which you burn calories.

set point theory

The notion that a "set point" regulates the amount of fat in our bodies, and when people go on a starvation diet, the set point causes their metabolic rate to slow down so as to conserve energy, making it difficult for them to lose weight.

Learning plays an important role in our long-term eating habits. Eating patterns acquired as children and teenagers often carry over into adulthood.

adults, we tend to eat the food that is placed before us, even though we are satiated. Research indicates that obese people tend to take larger mouthfuls, chew their food less, and eat more rapidly than normal weight people (LeBow et al., 1977), and these response patterns were probably learned as kids (LeBow, 1991).

Other learned habits that affect our long-term weight control relate to our overall level of activity. Many overweight people consistently eat the same or less than normal weight people; the difference is that many overweight people are much less active (DeLuise et al., 1980). Who, among your friends, for example, is most likely to gain weight over the next few years? A good way to decide is to consider their activity levels. Those with low levels of daily energy expenditure are most likely to gain weight (Ravussin et al., 1988).

Eating habits can also be influenced by advertising. Food displays always look so tasty in the magazines and the television commercials. Stanley Schachter (1971) suggested that overweight people may be more strongly influenced by external cues, such as the appearance and taste of food, than by internal cues (the physiological mechanisms that control hunger). In one study, for example, obese people in a restaurant were more likely to order dessert than non-obese people when the dessert was given an appetizing description by the waitress (Hermann et al., 1983). Although subsequent research has suggested that overweight people may not be as sensitive to external cues as Schachter believed (Rodin, 1981), you will likely be doing your children a favor if you encourage them to eat primarily at mealtimes, and to resist the temptation to get a snack every time they see a food commercial (LeBow, 1991).

MISUNDERSTANDINGS ABOUT NUTRITION. Some cases of obesity may stem from basic misunderstandings about nutrition. Many people, for example, think that "starchy" foods (such as potatoes and pasta) are fattening. Yet, foods with a high fat content are more readily converted into body fat than are foods high in carbohydrates (such as starchy foods) (Gurin, 1989).

Unfortunately, most people have experienced deficient nutritional education programs as well as considerable misinformation about nutrition. How about you? How would you answer the following questions?

1. *Is it true that whole milk is good for everybody, especially for young kids, in order to help build healthy bones and teeth?* False. People need to know that the high fat content of whole milk and other dairy products is a major cause of the development of cholesterol deposits in arteries, and a major contributor to heart attacks (Hamilton et al., 1991). People also need to know that they can obtain calcium from skim milk just as well as from whole milk without, at the same time, consuming excessive fat.

2. *Is it true that the more protein in the diet, the heathier it is, especially for athletes who want progressive muscle development?* False. Many athletes believe that large amounts of protein from the "meat group" and the "dairy group" contribute to big muscles because muscles are made of protein. This represents several misunderstandings. First, you don't have to eat muscle to make muscle. Lots of herbivores have large, strong muscles from eating nothing but grass. In the grueling Hawaii "Iron Man" triathalon in 1982 there were 850 contestants. The first, second, and fourth places were won by men who ate high-carbohydrate, low protein diets (Pritikin, 1983). Second, the traditional meat and dairy sources of protein in the American diet are laden with saturated fat, which contributes to the risk of heart attack. Third, high-protein diets are not only not needed for muscle development, they can be very dehydrating. Approximately 50 to 70 percent of a person's body weight is water. **Dehydration** can disrupt the fluid balance in tissues, body fluids, and the blood, which can cause serious medical complications and even death (Lemon, 1984). Finally, there is no evidence to suggest that athletic

dehydration

A condition in which water contained in the human body is lost to the point where there is disruption of the fluid balance in tissues, body fluids, and the blood, which could cause serious medical complications and even death.

performance can be improved by protein supplements over and above the protein available through a balanced diet (*Coaching Theory Level III*, 1989).

3. *Is it true that bacon and eggs, orange juice, and a large glass of milk is an ideal breakfast, especially for active people?* False. The bacon is loaded with saturated fat. The egg yolk is loaded with cholesterol. From a nutritional point of view, it would be best to eat the white and throw the yolk away. Whole milk has a high fat content. Even the orange juice is calorically high for its weight. Better nutrition would result if you consumed a whole orange instead, because it would contain fewer calories (by weight) and would additionally provide a source of fiber or bulk.

4. *Is it true that soft drinks and candy bars can provide you with lots of sugar to give you quick energy?* It's partly true and partly false. They certainly provide you with lots of table sugar. Table sugar (discussed in a later section) is a concentrated or refined carbohydrate that has no nutritional value. It certainly doesn't give you quick energy. The table sugar in such sweets stimulates increased insulin which causes the blood sugar level to become dangerously low (a condition called hypoglycemia). This results in a greater need to rely on muscle carbohydrate as an exercise fuel. Such a situation can hasten exhaustion, rather than postponing it. Moreover, table sugar tends to draw fluid from other parts of the body into the stomach. This can contribute to dehydration, a problematic situation when sweat loss is excessive. Thus, if athletes (or others) eat chocolates and other sweets just before strenuous activity, the practice not only does not help, it is likely to be harmful (Lemon, 1984).

5. *Is it true that starchy foods (such as potatoes, breads, and pastas) make you fat?* Partly true and partly false. Of course, too much starchy food when combined with too little exercise can contribute to obesity. Starchy foods, however, are potentially less fattening than meat or dairy products (Hamilton et al., 1991). As will be indicated later in this chapter in our discussion of carbohydrates, the complex carbohydrates contained in starchy foods are the major source of energy for muscular activity. Moreover, the majority of people in the world are on a diet of more than 70 percent complex carbohydrates and, in many of these populations, obesity is rare (Pritikin, 1983).

6. *Is it true that megadoses of vitamin and mineral supplements should be a part of everyone's diet?* False (Whitney & Cataldo, 1987). As will be seen later in this chapter, a well-balanced diet adequately meets our daily needs for vitamins and minerals. Moreover, excessive vitamin intake can be hazardous, especially fat soluble vitamins and minerals (Farquhar, 1978; Pritikin, 1983).

Nutrition for Healthy Living

To have some effective nutritional knowledge, at a minimum you need to know about the three main food groups: carbohydrates, fats, and proteins. You must have some understanding of the vitamins and minerals necessary to help regulate the chemistry of the body. And you should also appreciate the importance of drinking lots of water and consuming fiber.

CARBOHYDRATES, FATS, AND PROTEINS. **Carbohydrates** form an extremely important part of our diet. Foods commonly considered starchy, such as potatoes, whole-grain products, beans, rice, and corn, contain **unrefined carbohydrates** (also called natural or complex carbohydrates). Table sugar, on the other hand, is a concentrated or **refined carbohydrate.**

Unrefined carbohydrates provide the major fuel used to supply energy during intense exercise. Unrefined carbohydrates are stored in the body as glucose (a form of sugar) in the blood, and as glycogen (which contains glucose units) in muscle and the liver. Although unrefined carbohydrates are the major fuel used in

carbohydrates

The major source of fuel for the brain and muscle tissue; refined carbohydrates, such as table sugar, provide empty calories, while unrefined or complex carbohydrates, such as starches, are an important source of fuel.

unrefined carbohydrates

Also called natural or complex carbohydrates; an excellent source of fuel for the brain and muscle tissue; includes such foods as potatoes, whole-grain products, beans, rice, and corn.

refined carbohydrates

Provide "empty" calories that appease hunger but do not have nutritive value; includes such food as table sugar.

intense exercise, the body's store of it in the forms of glucose and glycogen will last for only a limited period of time—approximately two to three hours with moderately intense exercise and substantially less with very intense exercise.

Fats provide a source of fuel during low to moderately intense exercise, or after intense exercise has consumed all of the carbohydrate stores. As a source of fuel during exercise, fat requires oxygen in order to be metabolized. As a part of cell membranes, fats also help control which substances leave and enter the cells.

Our body contains several different classes of fats, and cholesterol falls into one of these classes. **Cholesterol** is a fat substance present in foods of animal origin. A certain amount of cholesterol is needed for healthy functioning. However, a person's blood level of cholesterol is the best dietary-related predictor of chronic heart disease (Hamilton et al., 1991). Excess cholesterol is the major component of the plaques that clog our arteries and cause atherosclerosis (hardening of the arteries). These plaques can also break loose, block heart valves, and cause heart attack and death. Because cholesterol is fat soluble, and therefore doesn't mix well with blood, it's carried in water soluble protein "containers" called lipoproteins. Of these, there are several different types. The low-density lipoproteins (LDLs) are the ones that carry the cholesterol that form dangerous deposits on the walls of blood vessels. High-density lipoproteins (HDLs), on the other hand, are believed to serve two important functions: (1) They scavenge deposits of cholesterol from various parts of the body and take them to the liver for breakdown and excretion into the bile, and (2) they prevent the buildup of fatty deposits on artery walls (Hamilton et al., 1991). The total amount of cholesterol in your body is equal to the total HDLs + LDLs. Your goal should be to keep the ratio of your HDLs high in comparison to your total cholesterol in order to minimize the risk of heart attack.

Interestingly, the main food factor associated with a high blood cholesterol level is a high saturated fat food intake (Hamilton et al., 1991). Thus, contributors to high blood cholesterol are the saturated fats contained in the layer of fat on steaks and chops, the marbled streaks of fat in red meats, dairy products made with whole milk, and fried foods. While foods high in cholesterol (such as egg yolks) also contribute to blood cholesterol levels, they do so to a lesser extent than foods high in saturated fats. Recommended dietary steps to lower your cholesterol level include using polyunsaturated fats and monounsaturated fats, and limiting your dietary cholesterol to 300 milligrams per day (Hamilton et al., 1991).

When we compare the relative proportion of carbohydrates and fats consumed in the typical North American diet, we see that most people consume too many fats and not enough carbohydrates. The diet of the average North American contains an estimated 45 percent carbohydrates and 40 percent fats. Modern nutritionists, however, now maintain that it would be much healthier if the average North American diet consisted of at least 65 percent carbohydrates and less than 30 percent fats (Hamilton et al., 1991; Pritikin, 1983). This would provide much more energy for daily activities with much less risk of heart attack.

Protein provides what are referred to as the building blocks of the body. These building blocks, called **amino acids,** are essential for growth, development, and tissue repair. While a number of the amino acids can be manufactured by the body, some of them must come from our diets. The minimum daily requirement of protein is about 10 to 12 percent of total calories consumed, and there is no nutritional advantage to exceeding this amount (Farquhar, 1978). This is true in part because protein is recycled in the body quite efficiently (Pritikin, 1983). Common sources of the amino acids that we need in our diet include dairy products, meat, fish, eggs, and poultry. People who strive for a large muscle mass (such as football players or weight lifters) often consume extra protein. It is important, however, to ensure that the extra protein is not taken at the expense of a high-carbohydrate diet.

fats

A food substance that helps to control transfer of substances across all cell membranes; a source of fuel for low to moderately intense exercise; can increase the risk of heart disease when taken in the form of saturated fats and cholesterol.

cholesterol

A fat substance present in foods of animal origin, and especially dairy products; a person's blood level of cholesterol is the best dietary-related predictor of chronic heart disease.

protein

Formed from chemical components called amino acids; essential for growth, metabolism, healing, and upkeep of our bodies.

amino acids

Called building blocks, they are essential for growth, development, and tissue repair.

vitamins

Food substances that are essential to the body for normal daily functioning, but that cannot be manufactured by the body.

water soluble vitamins

Vitamins that are water soluble, and that can therefore be washed away in the urine.

fat soluble vitamins

Vitamins that are fat soluble (not water soluble); excessive fat soluble vitamins in the body can be poisonous.

minerals

Food substances that are essential to normal daily functioning and that cannot be manufactured by the body.

VITAMINS AND MINERALS.   The body needs a number of vitamins and minerals daily to perform at maximum efficiency. **Vitamins,** for example, help cause chemical reactions that make it possible for carbohydrates to provide fuel for muscle activity.

It is important to distinguish the two kinds of vitamins: **water soluble vitamins** and **fat soluble vitamins.** The water soluble vitamins are washed away in the urine. Thus, water soluble vitamins are not retained in the body. While excessive intake of them may not necessarily enhance physical performance, neither is it likely to cause a decrease in performance. Fat soluble vitamins such as vitamins A, D, E, and K are a different story, however. These are retained in the body, and it is this retention that may allow them to approach poisonous levels (Lemon, 1984).

The benefits and risks of vitamin supplements have been at the center of controversy for some time. Linus Pauling (1971, 1980), for example, has argued that megadoses of vitamin C are valuable to combat the common cold. Other suggestions range from supplemental doses of vitamin B12 for athletes in endurance sports, to supplemental doses of vitamin E to make people sexier and keep them from aging. However, there is little or no evidence that such nutritional excesses are beneficial (Whitney & Cataldo, 1987). On the contrary, fat soluble vitamins and minerals can be poisonous when taken in excess (Lemon, 1984; Pritikin, 1983). Even a water soluble vitamin like vitamin C can be problematic if taken in excess, causing an increased risk of heart attack by increasing the tendency of the blood to clot, possible uterine bleeding in pregnant women, and precipitating attacks of gout (Pritikin, 1983).

The body also requires a number of minerals. **Minerals** are important components of hormones, bones, teeth, hair, nails, enzymes, blood, and other body fluids. They also play a role in the function of nerves and muscles and help regulate the body's water and acid-base balance. Like the fat soluble vitamins, minerals are also stored in the body; excessive intake of them can prove harmful. Cases of iron poisoning in young children who ingest an excess of mineral supplements are not uncommon, and cases of selenium poisoning have also been recorded (Pritikin, 1983).

So what does this mean as far as recommending vitamin and mineral supplements? Since vitamins and minerals are only required in trace amounts, most people will adequately supply their daily needs of vitamins and minerals if they eat several daily servings from each of the four main food groups listed in Table 6-4. Also, if you begin to habitually assume that you are meeting your daily vitamin and mineral requirements through supplements, you might also slip into eating a nutritionally poor diet. Having said that, we encourage you to take modest supplements just to "be on the safe side." In particular, people who consume excessive

TABLE 6-4
GUIDELINES FOR A HEALTHY DIET *Adapted from Farquhar, 1978.*

1. Eat several servings each day from *each* of the four main food groups:
   Breads and Cereals (3–5 servings daily)
   > Serving Examples: 2 pieces of toast
   >   1 bowl of cereal

   Meat and Meat Alternatives (2 servings daily)
   > Serving Examples: 1 piece of fish
   >   1 piece of chicken

   Dairy Products (3–4 servings daily)
   > Serving Examples: an 8-ounce glass of skim milk
   >   a ½ cup of yogurt
   >   a ½ cup of low-fat cheese

   Fruits and Vegetables (4–5 servings daily)
   > Serving Examples: one large carrot
   >   a salad
   >   an apple
   >   an orange

2. Eat sufficient unrefined carbohydrates (for example, bread, pizza, cereals, pancakes, pasta) to constitute approximately 65 percent of your diet.

3. Limit your intake of cholesterol, sweets, fats, salt, and greasy foods.

4. Limit your intake of junk food to a maximum of 1 or 2 servings (not meals!) per week.
   > Serving Examples: 1 chocolate bar
   >   1 soft drink (with sugar)
   >   1 slurpee
   >   1 small bag of salted chips
   >   1 order of french fries (greasy and salted)
   >   1 pack of sweetened gum
   >   1 piece of cake
   >   2 cookies
   >   1 piece of pie

5. If you supplement your diet with vitamins and minerals, take only a multiple vitamin with iron.

6. Be careful not to consume excessive fat soluble vitamins (A, D, E, and K) and minerals.

junk foods, or those on food restriction programs because of dieting, might be encouraged to take a multiple-vitamin supplement.

WATER AND FIBER. Water is absolutely essential to bodily functioning. An individual can survive as much as four times as long without food than without water. While a loss of approximately 50 percent of the body's protein and over 90 percent of the reserve carbohydrate and fat stores can occur without danger, a loss of 10 percent of water in the body can be serious. Thus, you must be continually sensitive to losses of body water because of vigorous activity or living in a hot, dry climate. When exercising, you should ensure that water is continuously available. Everyone should drink several glasses of water per day.

Fiber is dietary roughage that improves digestion, prevents constipation and other colon problems, and may even lower cholesterol levels (Hamilton et al., 1991). One of the changes in the 1990 *Dietary Guidelines for Americans* is the increased emphasis on the selection of vegetables, fresh fruits, beans, and whole-grain products in one's diet to ensure adequacy of fiber and complex carbohydrates in the diet (U.S. Department of Agriculture, 1990).

Healthier Eating and Successful Dieting

Is dieting the great American pastime? Each year, Americans spend billions in the "battle against their bulges" (Toufexis, 1986). There are literally hundreds of diet books and programs that you can follow. It seems that almost every week some newly published diet and fitness guide is on one of the best-seller lists. The fact is, however, that fad diets and crash weight loss programs simply don't work well in the long run (LeBow, 1981). Here's the bottom line: *The only way to lose weight is to use more calories than you consume. And, once you have reached it, the only way to maintain your ideal weight is to use about the same number of calories you consume.*

If you wish to lose weight, you should review the guidelines for successful self-adjustment described in Box 3-3, and in the self-adjustment section at the end of each chapter. Additional guidelines are described below.

STEP 1. ASSESS THE PROBLEM.   How much do you weigh? How much should you weigh? Use the information presented in Table 6-3 to determine your ideal weight, and to decide whether or not you need to lose a few pounds.

STEP 2. LEARN ABOUT CALORIES AND NUTRIENTS IN FOODS.   The next step is for you to become an expert concerning the calories and nutrients contained in various foods. Convenient calorie counters are available in most pharmacies. We encourage you to purchase one of them. Alternatively, you may want to look at the tables contained in such books as those by LeBow (1989, 1991), and most cookbooks.

The Alternative Food Pattern.   Becoming an expert on the calorie content of various foods is only a part of the knowledge required to help you genuinely adopt an alternative food pattern. You must also acquire some information concerning which foods are low in cholesterol and saturated fat, low in table sugar, and low in salt. You need to ensure that the foods you eat contain sufficient carbohydrates for maximum energy, and sufficient vitamins, minerals, and fiber for healthy living. Try to follow the guidelines for a healthy diet provided in Table 6-4.

STEP 3. LEARN ABOUT CALORIES EXPENDED IN VARIOUS ACTIVITIES.   Another area in which you should become an expert concerns the calories expended in various types of activities. Table 6-5 lists the calories expended in typical daily activities, as well as the calories used performing specific sports and exercises. You say you just went for a walk for an hour? And afterward you just had a cup of black coffee and a small doughnut? Are your calories minus or plus after that exchange? When answers to questions like these come readily to mind, you are in a much better position to proceed with the remaining steps of the weight control program recommended below.

STEP 4. REALISTIC GOAL SETTING.   What's that you say? You want to lose 15 pounds by next weekend to get ready for the staff party at the boss's house? Then forget it. This plan is not for you. We're talking serious and effective weight control here, not crash diets. If a crash diet is what you want, save your money and go to one of those expensive fat farms. Or try one of the other fad diets on the market—those that frequently end in long-term failure. We don't recommend any of them.

A realistic goal is to lose 1 or 2 pounds per week. If you are really serious about a weight loss program, and if you are considerably overweight (at least 20 pounds according to the weight charts), then you might set a goal of 4 or 5 pounds

TABLE 6-5
TOTAL CALORIES EXPENDED PER HOUR OF VARIOUS ACTIVITIES

Activity	Approximate Total Calories Expended per Hour of Activity
Sleeping	60
Restful activities such as reclining in a chair and reading, or watching TV	75
Activities performed while seated or standing such as typing, driving a car, or playing cards	95
Light exercise or physical work such as walking at a medium pace, shopping, playing golf, and certain types of dancing	250
Moderate exercise or physical work such as walking fast, bicycling at a medium speed, playing tennis, and aerobic dancing	400
Heavy exercising or physical work such as cross-country skiing, jogging, swimming, or playing handball	650

The above calorie expenditures are approximate values only. For more precise values, consult appropriate tables in LeBow (1981).

weight loss for the first week of your program. Thereafter, however, a goal of 1 or 2 pounds weight loss per week is realistic and has a good chance of long-term success (Brownell, 1989; Brownell & Wadden, 1991).

STEP 5. WHEN YOU EAT IT, COUNT IT—WHEN YOU LOSE IT, COUNT IT. As we indicated earlier, there's really only one way to guarantee that you will lose weight. You must use more calories than you consume. Most overweight adults, let alone overweight teenagers, underestimate the calories they consume in foods and at the same time overestimate the calories that they expend in exercise. If you have seriously followed the previous steps, then you have already gathered some important information about weight loss. You probably already know, for example, that a large-sized sugared doughnut has approximately 450 calories. You probably also know that walking an extra 4 miles daily burns about 250 calories.

A worthwhile strategy for losing weight is to count the calories consumed and the calories burned off each day. For most people, a deficit of 500 calories per day will enable them to lose approximately a pound a week. A deficit of 1,000 calories

Set goals to counteract the many cues that influence your eating.

per day will enable them to lose approximately two pounds per week. Although keeping track of calories consumed and utilized involves considerable effort, those who do so find it to be an effective motivational strategy (LeBow, 1989).

STEP 6. MAINTENANCE.   When you have reached your desired weight, you don't have to continue to count calories in and calories out on a daily basis. But you should weigh yourself once per day. Weighing yourself once per week was sufficient during your weight program because your goal was to lose one or two pounds per week, and at that rate there's not much weight loss to notice on a daily basis. During maintenance, however, you need to be especially sensitive to any gain in weight—hence our recommendation to weight yourself once per day. In addition, you should regularly review the behavioral strategies described in the next section.

Additional Self-Adjustment Strategies for Losing Weight

Can you really lose weight by following a self-adjustment program such as the one just described, especially if you are seriously overweight to begin with? Indeed you can. Researchers have estimated that from 29 to 55 percent of obese people have been able to return to normal weight after following self-adjustment programs (Jeffrey & Wing, 1983; Schachter, 1982). Others have been able to lose weight through the use of self-adjustment procedures with minimal therapist contact (Pezzot-Pierce et al., 1982). In addition to following many of the steps outlined above, many successful weight loss programs have involved other behavioral strategies (Brownell & Wadden, 1991).

CHANGE THE BEHAVIORS THAT CAUSE EXCESSIVE WEIGHT.   Overweight people don't eat the same way as people of normal weight. Overweight people are likely to eat many times each day; eat when they are emotionally upset; eat rapidly during individual eating episodes; eat while participating in other enjoyable activities such as while watching television or reading; eat leftovers to avoid wasting food; pile more food on their plates than individuals of normal weight; keep many fattening foods around the house; exercise infrequently; weigh themselves infrequently; and starve themselves and then overeat (LeBow, 1981, 1989). To lose weight successfully, you should try to change each of these behaviors if they apply to you. List

Goal setting and charting your weight can motivate you to maintain your diet.

specific alternative behaviors that you can engage in. For example, at mealtime, try to have less food on your plate at the start of the meal than most other people sitting at the same table. Deliberately chew your food slowly while eating. Put down your utensils after each mouthful until that particular mouthful has been chewed several times and swallowed.

EMPHASIZE FREQUENT IMPROVEMENTS RATHER THAN OCCASIONAL FAILURES. A common mistake of people who try to lose weight is to dwell on the few occasions when they go off their diet rather than emphasizing the many occasions when they have stuck to it (Ferguson, 1975). Refer to your self-monitoring sheets frequently concerning "calories in" and "calories out." If, at the end of a particular day, you have consumed more calories than you have expended, chalk it up to a bad day. But don't dwell on it. Instead, review the previous days of that particular week when you recorded a calorie deficit. Use your successes to set new goals and to make a renewed commitment to stick to your newly developed alternative food pattern.

USE COPING SELF-STATEMENTS TO FIGHT "AUTOMATIC EATING." For some overweight people, their eating behaviors automatically occur at certain times or in certain situations independent of whether or not they're hungry. Have you ever heard yourself saying, "I just can't resist chocolate eclairs," or some other such statement about your favorite sweets? If so, then the sight of chocolate eclairs automatically stimulates you to eat, whether you're hungry or not. People who are overweight are also likely to be slaves to time. They feel ready to eat if they think it's lunchtime or dinnertime, independent of what time it actually is or whether or not they have just eaten (Schachter & Gross, 1968). If you find that your eating is under the control of the clock, or that it occurs when you observe others eating, or when you see and smell your favorite foods, then prepare some coping self-statements to help control your eating. Actually write out several examples and practice them. For example, when faced with that chocolate eclair, you might say to yourself, "That thing represents almost 500 calories. If I eat that it will kill my calorie deficit for the day. I know I can resist it if I work at it."

ATTEMPT GRADUAL CHANGE. Change your eating habits gradually and slowly, but consistently. For example, two years ago one of the authors drank his coffee with two spoons of sugar and thick cream. Over a period of three months, he gradually faded out the sugar by adding a little bit less in each cup. Then less and less cream was added, so that he now uses only a couple of drops. He can't really taste the difference, but he likes the color. Similarly, you might gradually move to healthier foods over a two- to three-year period. Bringing about a total overhaul in your eating patterns all at once is too much to expect of yourself. Gradual change can help you to meet your long-term goals and at the same time enable you to enjoy frequent rewards and success along the way.

ARRANGE CONTRACTS WITH SUPPORTIVE OTHERS. An effective strategy can also involve setting up a contract with supportive friends or relatives (Dubbert & Wilson, 1984; Murphy et al., 1985). For example, Lutzker and Lutzker (1977) described a program in which a husband managed rewards and punishers for a wife who was trying to diet. If his wife lost a half pound or more each week, the husband provided several rewards (for example, going to a movie). Alternatively, if she gained weight, then she had to do specific household chores that were normally done by her husband. The contract was very effective.

Getting adequate exercise, eating well-balanced meals, controlling your intake of fats, cholesterol, salt, and refined sugar, and maintaining your weight at a reasonable level are important components of healthy living. Another important component is understanding and controlling your use of drugs, the topic of the next section.

Do you remember the case of Jack from Chapter 1? He was the college student who drank 12 to 15 cups of coffee per day. If you told Jack that he was a "druggie," he would deny it vehemently. He rarely has more than a few beers on weekends. He hasn't touched marijuana since trying a few joints in high school. And, unlike some of his friends, he has never taken uppers to stay awake to study. However, Jack's restlessness, anxiety, irritability, and many of his other complaints were symptoms of caffeinism, a significant health problem. And yet Jack's "drug problem" is clearly less devastating for him than use of drugs is for many others. Because drug use and abuse is so prevalent in our society, we conclude this chapter on healthy living with a discussion of the effects of three major groups of drugs: stimulants or "uppers," depressants or "downers," and hallucinogens.

Stimulants, like caffeine, speed up nervous system activity, making you feel like you have more energy and can stay awake longer. Depressants, on the other hand, slow down body functions, causing relaxation, slowed reaction time, and possibly sleepiness. Hallucinogens get their name because they can cause you to hallucinate—giving you dreamlike, distorted images and perceptions.

When does the use of any of these drugs become drug abuse? *The Diagnostic and Statistical Manual of Mental Disorders* (3rd edition, revised, 1987) defines **substance abuse** as persistent use of a substance that contributes to a social, occupational, or physical problem that persists for at least one month. For example, if a student gets drunk on several weekends in a row and consistently misses Monday morning classes because of being hung over, then the student has a problem of substance abuse. A more serious problem is that of **substance dependence.** When substance abuse is combined with increased tolerance for the substance (more of it is needed to produce the usual effect), and withdrawal symptoms occur when use of the substance is stopped or delayed, then substance dependence is defined. Let's now review some examples of stimulants, depressants, and hallucinogens.

Stimulants—The "Uppers"

CAFFEINE.   We tend to associate **caffeine** with coffee, but it's also found in tea, cola drinks, chocolate, and many nonprescription painkillers and cold remedies. As illustrated in the case of Jack, it can cause a variety of health problems. Additional problems related to excessive caffeine use in women include the development of breast cysts, links to miscarriages during pregnancy and possible birth defects in children carried to full term (Grady, 1986).

NICOTINE.   What is the nation's #1 preventable cause of death? If you guessed cigarette smoking—you're right (Feist & Brannon, 1988). The scientific link between tobacco smoking and cancer is now firmly established (Reif, 1981). The U.S. Surgeon General estimates that smoking is responsible for nearly 400,000 deaths in the United States each year, which is approximately 15 percent of *all* yearly deaths (U.S. Department of Health and Human Services, 1990). Yet, approximately 30 percent of the people in the United States aged 20 and older are smokers, and they consume enough cigarettes each year to average in excess of 3,000 cigarettes per person for everyone over the age of 18 (Feist & Brannon, 1988).

Tobacco contains nicotine, a natural stimulant, and it's the most widely used psychoactive drug next to caffeine (Julien, 1988; Murray, 1991). Statistics on smokers in America show both good news and bad news. The goods news is that the

---

substance abuse

Persistent use of a substance when it contributes to a social, occupational, or physical problem that persists for at least a month.

substance dependence

The condition that exists when substance abuse is combined with increased tolerance for the substance, and withdrawal symptoms occur when use of the substance is stopped or delayed.

caffeine

A stimulant found in coffee, tea, cola drinks, chocolate, and many cold remedies; excessive use can lead to a variety of health problems.

Social situations are one of the environments in which substances are used and abused.

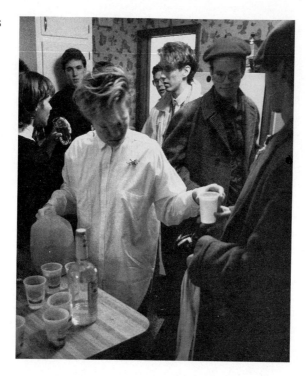

percentage of both men and women who smoke has been steadily decreasing (American Cancer Society, 1986). The bad news is that an estimated 55 million Americans continue to smoke (Taylor, 1986). Moreover, although the percentage of women smokers is declining, there is a greater number of women smoking, and they are smoking more than they have in the past, causing lung cancer death rates for women to rise (American Cancer Society, 1986).

Are you a smoker? Do you want to quit? Once again, there is both goods news and bad news. The goods news is that millions of Americans have quit—by 1985, an estimated one quarter of all U.S. adults were former smokers (Feist & Brannon, 1988). It is estimated that 95% of those who have quit did so on their own, without the help of formal quit-smoking programs (Feist & Brannon, 1988). For those who need help, quit-smoking manuals (for example, Shipley, 1985) and quit-smoking clinics are readily available. The bad news is that for smokers who quit with the help of quit-smoking programs, from 70 to 80 percent of them were smoking again a year later (Feist & Brannon, 1988). If you are a smoker, and you would like to quit, the guidelines in Box 6-4 may be helpful to you.

AMPHETAMINES. "Uppers," "bennies," or "speed" are street names for powerful synthetic stimulants called **amphetamines.** They are sold under trade names like benzedrine, dexadrine, and methadrine. Like all stimulants, the amphetamines speed up the central nervous system, causing people to stay awake, experience improved energy levels, and generally feel good (Blum, 1984). They also suppress appetite and have been prescribed for people who want to lose weight. When the users "come down," however, they usually feel tired and irritable. There may also be more serious aftereffects, such as headaches and depression.

If you're tempted to try some form of amphetamines to help you study, it's important to remember that these drugs don't make you smarter, and they don't create energy. They simply mask the symptoms of fatigue. Because you might therefore go beyond your normal level of endurance, their effects can be dangerous.

amphetamines

Powerful stimulants that are sold under trade names like Benzedrine, Dexedrine, and Methedrine; they cause the nervous system to speed up, which influences people to stay awake and experience improved energy levels and a loss of appetite; excessive use can cause serious aftereffects such as headaches and depression.

Box 6-4

GUIDELINES FOR QUITTING SMOKING

If you have decided to quit smoking as your self-adjustment project, carefully follow the guidelines at the end of each chapter. In addition, consider the following steps.

Step 1. Identify Some Reasons for Quitting. Examine the list of reasons for quitting smoking listed in Table 6-6. Beside each of them, place a checkmark in the appropriate column indicating their relative importance for you. If you can think of additional reasons for quitting, add them to the list. Finally, read the entire list to a friend or relative and indicate your evaluation of the items' importance to you as you read them.

Step 2. Identify Your "Triggers" for Smoking and Some Alternatives. For most smokers, getting a cup of coffee is an automatic cue for lighting up. The same is true for watching television, talking on the phone, or having a beer or cocktail. The Ameri-

can Lung Association (1980) refers to these cues as *"triggers" for smoking.* Identify your own smoking triggers and list them in Table 6-7. Careful and accurate identification of the cues controlling smoking will help you apply some powerful procedures to quit.

Some triggers for smoking can be simply avoided, at least during the first week or two after you quit smoking. However, you will continue to experience many of the triggers. For example, the simple act of finishing a meal is a trigger that you will encounter daily. You should therefore prepare a list of alternatives to smoking that you can perform in the presence of smoking triggers that you encounter. Keep in mind that the activities involved in smoking a cigarette provide stimulation to your hands and your mouth, and it often gives you something to think about or talk about. Smoking can

TABLE 6-6
REASONS FOR QUITTING SMOKING

	Importance for Me		
	NOT AT ALL	SOMEWHAT	VERY
1. If I continue smoking, I will have far more wrinkles on my skin than nonsmokers at a comparable age.	___	___	___
2. If I continue smoking, the chance of my dying from heart disease is nine times greater compared to nonsmokers.	___	___	___
3. If I continue smoking, the chance of my dying from lung cancer is eight times greater compared to nonsmokers.	___	___	___
4. The risk of heart attack falls dramatically after a smoker quits; the extra risk of heart attack due to smoking is cut in half within a year after quitting. Within five to ten years after quitting, I can reach the lower cardiovascular and lung cancer risk level of a person who has never smoked.	___	___	___
5. If I am a female, quitting smoking can increase the chances of my having a healthy baby.	___	___	___
6. If I quit smoking, I will have more energy for exercising and work.	___	___	___
7. If I quit smoking, I will set a good example for children, friends, and relatives.	___	___	___
8. My senses of taste and smell will improve if I quit smoking.	___	___	___
9. I will be less likely to catch colds, flu, and other diseases.	___	___	___
10. I will save approximately $1,000 per year.	___	___	___
11. _____	___	___	___
12. _____	___	___	___
13. _____	___	___	___

TABLE 6-7
MY TRIGGERS FOR SMOKING

Possible Triggers	*Is This a Trigger for Me?*	*Is This an Especially Strong Trigger for Me?*
Drinking coffee	☐	☐
After a meal	☐	☐
Getting in the car to drive somewhere	☐	☐
Upon waking from sleep	☐	☐
Taking a work break	☐	☐
Upon taking or sipping an alcoholic drink	☐	☐
Arriving at a party or social function	☐	☐
While reading	☐	☐
While waiting for bus, train, subway, or plane	☐	☐
During intermission at a sporting event	☐	☐
When someone else lights up	☐	☐
After sex	☐	☐
In smoky places, such as bars or bowling alleys	☐	☐
In a favorite "smoking chair" at home	☐	☐
With specific friends who almost always smoke	☐	☐
_____	☐	☐
_____	☐	☐
_____	☐	☐
_____	☐	☐
_____	☐	☐

relieve boredom, make you feel less awkward in a social situation, provide an opening line for meeting someone or starting a conversation, or provide you with temporary relief from tension. Your substitute activities should also serve these functions. Thus, something to chew or suck on can include carrot or celery sticks, unbuttered popcorn, sugarless gum, toothpicks, and the like. Things to occupy your hands could include squeezing a rubber ball, playing with a "worry stone" or marbles, doodling with a pencil, and so on. Alternative activities that give you something else to do and think about include centering, muscle relaxation, taking a shower or bath, working on a hobby, playing solitaire, working on a crossword puzzle, stretching, and doing calisthenics. An alternative to smoking that has proven helpful in some cases is that of chewing nicotine gum (Oster et al., 1986). However, the gum itself would eventually have to be faded.

Step 3. Announce Your Quit Date.   Identify some friends and/or relatives who will support you in your quit smoking program. Ideally, they will include individuals at home, school, and work. Announce to them the day that you will be quitting, and ask for their support. The day before you quit, get rid of all your cigarettes. If you have any pockets, briefcases, or other nooks and crannies in which a cigarette or two might be hiding, find them and throw them out. On the morning of your quit day, you want to start the day in complete control of potential triggers for smoking.

As a smoker, you might have asked yourself the question, "Should I quit cold turkey, gradually cut back on cigarettes smoked over a period of time, smoke cigarettes with less tar and nicotine, or some combination?" For the following reasons, we

Continued

recommend quitting cold turkey. First, the great majority of successful ex-smokers have quit cold turkey (Burton, 1986). Second, several studies have found that smokers who switch to brands that are lower in tar and nicotine tend to either increase their rate of cigarette consumption to compensate for the decreased nicotine levels per cigarette (Benowitz et al., 1983), increase the number of puffs per cigarette (Schachter et al., 1977), or increase their puff volume (Kumar et al., 1977). Third, in a controlled experiment that directly compared quitting cold turkey versus cutting down gradually, quitting cold turkey was more effective (Flaxman, 1978).

Step 4. Reward Yourself. We have no doubt that your friends (particularly your support group) will compliment you daily during the first week or two of your quit smoking program. After a while, however, they will naturally stop commenting on it. When that happens, you yourself can continue to give your accomplishment the attention it deserves. Approximately once a day, say to a friend or neighbor, "I haven't had a cigarette in X days. I'm really happy about it." Regardless of how long you have been off cigarettes, you are a nonsmoker. Enjoy the identity.

cocaine

A powerful stimulant that is highly addictive; excessive use can lead to a variety of serious health problems including heart and lung damage and immune system impairment.

COCAINE.   Extracted from the leaves of the coca shrub found in Bolivia, Colombia, and Peru, **cocaine** is a powerful stimulant. Approximately a hundred years ago, cocaine was cheap, easy to obtain, and a common ingredient in many patent medicines. It became even more popular when introduced as a stimulant soft drink in 1886, called Coca-Cola. As evidence of its harmful effects accumulated, however, its popularity as a patent medicine cure-all declined. (Because of the dangers of cocaine use, it has not been an ingredient in Coca-Cola since 1906.)

The effect of cocaine is much briefer than that of amphetamines but also much more powerful. Snorting (sniffing) or freebasing (smoking) cocaine almost immediately produces a euphoric rush, a sense of well-being, and increased energy and alertness that lasts about 20 to 30 minutes. Thus, regular users take the drug often—a very expensive habit. Cocaine is highly addictive, and cocaine abuse leads to a variety of serious health problems including heart and lung damage and immune system impairment (McCarthy, 1985). As demonstrated by the death from cocaine overdose of superstar basketball player Len Bias, in 1986, its effects can be tragic.

crack

A cocaine derivative that is becoming increasingly popular on the streets and in the schools, and that is highly addictive; chronic crack users experience a variety of health problems.

In 1985, **crack** hit the streets. Crack is prepared from a mixture of coke (the crystalline derivative of the coca leaf) with ammonia or baking soda and water, which is then heated. Apparently, the baking soda causes a crackling sound when heated—hence the name "crack." It is cheaper than cocaine and is becoming increasingly popular on the streets and in the schools. It produces a briefer, more intense high than cocaine, and even small doses can be fatal.

Some ghetto areas in major cities have been devastated by the crack epidemic. And even more tragic is the high incidence of fetal cocaine addiction found among children of chronic crack users. Such children show alarming learning disabilities and emotional problems and appear to suffer from permanent brain damage.

Depressants—The "Downers"

SEDATIVES.   Drugs that decrease central nervous system and behavioral activity are called sedatives. More commonly known as "sleeping pills," sedatives include *barbiturates* (such as Nembutal), and *benzodiazepines* (such as Valium). Over the years, sedatives have been a widely abused strategy for helping people relax during the day and fall asleep at night. While they do have those effects, they can also cause memory lapses and reduced ability to concentrate. If taken in sufficient quantity, they can also cause death. Many well-known personalities, such as Marilyn Monroe and Judy Garland, have died of barbiturate overdoses.

opiates

Powerful depressants derived from poppy seeds, including opium, morphine, and heroin.

OPIATES. The opiates are drugs derived from poppy seeds, including opium, morphine, and heroin. The **opiates** can have powerful effects in reducing pain and anxiety, producing a lethargic blissfulness (Wallace & Fisher, 1987). They are, however, highly addicting. While cocaine and crack are replacing heroin as the most commonly purchased of the powerful street drugs, heroin addiction is still a significant problem. Moreover, sharing of needles among heroin addicts has become a major cause of the spread of AIDS.

ALCOHOL. More than 200,000 alcohol-related deaths occur each year. Alcoholism is still the nation's #1 drug problem and its third largest health problem. It is estimated that chronic alcoholism costs the economy a whopping $42 billion a year in poor job performance and absenteeism (Taylor, 1986). Over 90 percent of high school seniors in the United States have used alcohol, and 57 percent had used alcohol within a month of a major survey in 1990 (Freiberg, 1991). Clearly, alcohol abuse is a major problem.

Factors related to excessive alcohol drinking by young adults are complex and many. For example, in a study of over 8,000 persons ages 20 and 21 years, the group showing the highest rate of alcohol use consisted of white males from higher socioeconomic backgrounds, living in urban or suburban areas (as opposed to the inner city), and having a weak family orientation (Martin & Pritchard, 1991). Another study of a nationally representative sample of young adults (aged 19 to 26 years) indicated that joint alcohol and cocaine abusers tend to show a high level of delinquent activity, high rates of unemployment, a high degree of marital instability, and long-time drug abuse (Windle & Miller-Tutzauer, 1991). Obviously, isolating the causes of alcohol abuse is not an easy task.

Alcohol affects different people in quite different ways. While it is a central nervous system depressant that slows activity in brain centers, it appears to have the behavioral effects of decreasing good judgment and removing inhibitions. Thus, someone with aggressive tendencies might be prone to violence under the influence of alcohol, while another person who normally keeps "silliness" in check might become boisterous and childlike when drunk. In other words, low levels of alcohol consumption might influence a person to do what that person would otherwise resist (Steele et al., 1985; Steele & Southwick, 1985).

Large doses of alcohol consumption act like a sedative (Niaura et al., 1988). Large doses also cause increased impairment of reaction time, coordination, and judgment (Ward & Lewis, 1987). What does this mean for your drinking and driving? If you have five or six beers, or five or six 1.5 ounce shots of 80 proof alcohol (or more) over a couple of hours (producing a blood alcohol content that reaches 10 percent), your chances of having an accident may be several times greater than normal.

The most successful alcohol abuse treatment programs are those that contain components to (1) decrease the rewarding properties of alcohol drinking; (2) teach alcoholics new skills to take the place of alcohol abuse; and (3) provide rewards for work, social, and recreational activities that do not involve alcohol (Feist & Brannon, 1988). Average success rates with such programs are approximately 40 percent. However, success rates across studies vary tremendously. They depend upon individuals' socioeconomic status, the availability of a regular job, an intact family, and the circle of friends of the alcoholic. Those whose environments contained such additional support showed recovery rates as high as 68 percent,

Box 6-5

AA—ALCOHOLICS ANONYMOUS

AA was formed in the mid-1930s. Its originators were alcoholics who found that they could manage their drinking through public confession, striving toward moral perfection, and the social support of others like themselves (Curlee-Salisbury, 1986). The sole requirement for joining is a desire to stop drinking. Individuals who join are encouraged to immerse themselves totally in AA—to attend meetings and confess their drinking problems to other alcoholics, and to stay completely sober. AA members believe that alcoholism can be managed but never cured. While there is no denying the popularity of AA, or that it has helped many individuals to overcome alcoholism, the degree of success of AA is difficult to evaluate, because no membership lists are kept (it is anonymous). AA itself maintains that approximately three quarters of its members have stopped drinking through AA (Wallace, 1985). Critics believe that the claim of AA is probably on the high side because it appears to be based on those who remain in treatment, and a very high percentage of those who initially attend AA drop out after the first few meetings (Brandsma et al., 1980; Robinson, 1979). However, many psychologists see programs such as AA as valuable additions to other programs to treat alcoholism (Buie, 1987).

whereas studies of individuals without such support showed success rates of approximately 18 percent or less (Feist & Brannon, 1988).

Hallucinogens

The hallucinogens are drugs that can cause you to hallucinate, distorting your perceptions, your sense of time, and causing vivid and sometimes scary images.

LSD. Created by chemist Albert Hoffman in 1943, LSD (lisergic acid diethylamide), or "acid," has caused people to report severe perceptual distortions in colors, shapes, forms, and time dimensions. During the 1950s and early 1960s, researchers examined it as a potential technique for treating a variety of emotional disorders (Neill, 1987). Unfortunately, its effects remained largely unpredictable, causing interest in the drug to decline. During the 1960s and 1970s, LSD was a popular street drug for those who, in the words of Timothy Leary, wanted to "turn on, tune in, and drop out." During the last decade, however, its popularity in the streets has declined. As a "mind expanding," "spiritual inducing," "source of ecstasy," LSD has become a "bad trip."

MARIJUANA. By the late 1970s, *marijuana* ("pot," "grass") was second in popularity only to alcohol among high school seniors and college students. Over half of the college students surveyed by the American Council on Education in 1977 thought that marijuana should be legalized. After corn, the nation's second largest cash crop was not wheat—it was marijuana.

Marijuana is composed of the leaves and flowers of the hemp plant *cannibus sativa,* which is also used to make ropes. Its general immediate effects are relaxation, a mild high or feeling of well-being, and an altered sense of time. It can also produce mild perceptual distortions. Marijuana has been used for a number of medical purposes: to help treatment of asthma and glaucoma (a disease that can cause blindness), and to help lessen the severe nausea associated with chemotherapy.

Although use of marijuana is still popular among some college students, research indicates that its long-term use may be more damaging to the lungs than cigarette smoking and that long-term users show more health and family problems than non-users.

There is also a "dark side" to marijuana use, especially if the use is regular and long-term. Long-term use may negatively affect the reproductive systems of both sexes—such as disrupting the menstrual cycle in females and decreasing testosterone levels in males (Relman, 1982; Smith et al., 1983). Long-term use is more damaging to the lungs than cigarette smoke (Wu et al., 1988). A study of long-term users of marijuana indicated that they had more health and family problems than non-users (Newcome & Bentler, 1988). Perhaps because of such studies of the dangers of long-term use, and perhaps for other reasons, views on marijuana use have changed since the late 1970s. Now, less than 20 percent of new college students support the legalization of marijuana and the percentage of high school students reporting use of marijuana is at its lowest point since 1975 (Freiberg, 1991; Johnston et al., 1988; also see Figure 10-5).

Guarding against Drug Abuse

Now that you are familiar with some common drugs and their effects, are you susceptible to becoming a substance abuser? To help you decide, consider the following questions.

Are you aware of the long-term effects of drugs that you take? Do you know, for example, that long-term frequent use of alcohol can cause considerable liver, heart, and brain damage? Do you know about the long-term effects of regular marijuana use described earlier? If you consume any substance in excess, educate yourself about its long-term effects.

Are your friends drug abusers? One of the best predictors of a person's drug use is whether a person's friends are drug users (Marlatt et al., 1988; Schultz & Wilson, 1973). If your friends are drug abusers, maybe you should consider finding new friends. At the very least, you might want to raise your level of assertiveness. Learn to say no without being preachy.

Do you use drugs to escape from stress, to avoid coping with problems, or because your life seems meaningless? Many regular users of alcohol, marijuana, and cocaine take drugs to relieve depression, anxiety, or a feeling that their life is directionless (Feist & Brannon, 1988). If you find yourself turning to drugs to cope with life, or in response to stress, frustration, anger, depression, or a similar factor, try to substitute other activities whenever you have the urge. Run, swim, cycle, or relax your way out of it (see Chapter 5).

Do you associate drug taking with having a good time? When Brown and associates (1985) interviewed heavy and light drinkers concerning their expectations about the effects of alcohol on relaxation, sexual performance, and generally having a good time, the heavy drinkers had far more positive expectations than did the light drinkers. In other research, both males and females reported feeling sexually aroused when they thought they were drinking vodka even though they were actually drinking tonic water that tasted like vodka (Abrams & Wilson, 1983; Marlatt & Rohsenow, 1981). If you think of drugs as an easy way to get high and enjoy yourself, consider strengthening your ability to produce natural highs. Exercise can work in this way, naturally producing the same feelings associated with opiates (see Box 6-3, "Getting 'High' on Exercise").

Do your job and social activities require you to be where alcohol is served? Half of all Americans drink alcohol. It is the first thing to be offered at a dinner party, the "ice breaker" at a cocktail party, and a "night cap" to end the day. Whether you are at weddings, business luncheons, baseball games, or having a candlelit dinner for two at your favorite restaurant, you will likely be surrounded by alcohol drinkers. It's likely impossible for you to totally avoid places that serve alcohol. But you can be prepared to engage in alternative behavior (for example, non-alcoholic wine, Perrier, and so forth).

It's not easy to recognize when social use of alcohol or drugs has turned into abuse. And many people who are at the stage of substance abuse deny having an alcohol or drug problem. You may be suffering from drug abuse if you frequently experience hangovers, go to work or class while high, think about liquor or drugs most of the time, always get high to have a good time, miss class or work because you are high, or get high in situations when you are alone. Drug and alcohol abuse or dependence are serious problems, and they are extremely difficult to cure without help.

SUMMARY

■ Exercising that improves your cardiovascular system draws on the aerobic energy system. Aerobic exercises require you to perform a moderately intense activity over a sustained period of time so that you require large quantities of oxygen and your body improves its capacity to use oxygen. While strength training and flexibility training can be beneficial, the majority of physical, emotional, and psychological benefits demonstrated to accrue from a regular exercise program have been associated with aerobic exercising. General principles of exercising include the following: (1) do warm-up exercises at the start of each session; (2) gradually increase the extent of your exercising across sessions until the desired level of fitness is achieved; (3) individualize your program in terms of your pre-exercise fitness level; (4) remember that specific training will bring specific results; and (5) develop a maintenance program for long-term fitness goals.

■ Obesity refers to the condition of being approximately 20 percent or more in excess of an individual's ideal weight for a particular height, age, sex, and frame size. Some individuals who are overweight may have a slower metabolism and may have a larger than normal number of fat cells. For others who are overweight, their condition may be primarily due to long-term eating habits and a general lack of exercise. Also, some cases of obesity may stem from misunderstandings about nutrition.

■ Experts on nutrition suggest that (1) complex carbohydrates such as potatoes, whole grains, beans, rice, and corn are valuable sources of energy, while refined carbohydrates (sugar) are unhealthy; (2) most North Americans have a saturated fat and cholesterol intake that's far too high; (3) there is little value in consuming protein in excess of the minimal daily requirement; (4) needed vitamins and minerals can be obtained in adequate supply in a balanced daily diet; and (5) people should drink lots of water and consume lots of fiber.

■ Successful weight loss programs all have one common ingredient: More calories are used in daily activities than are consumed in eating. Steps in a program to healthier eating and to reach your ideal weight include the following: (1) assess your current weight in comparison to weight charts; (2) learn about the calories in certain foods, and which foods are low in cholesterol and saturated fat, low in sugar, and low in salt; (3) learn about the number of calories expended in various daily activities; (4) set realistic goals for weight loss, such as one or two pounds' weight loss per week; (5) monitor calories consumed as well as calories expended and work toward a calorie deficit of 500 to 1,000 calories per day until you reach your ideal weight; and (6) practice various self-adjustment strategies for weight loss and to maintain your ideal weight.

■ Drug use and abuse is prevalent in our society. Substance abuse is persistent use of a substance when it contributes to a social, occupational, or physical problem that persists for at least one month. Substance dependence is substance abuse combined with increased tolerance for the substance, and the occurrence of withdrawal symptoms when use of the substance is stopped or delayed.

■ Three major groups of drugs include stimulants, depressants, and hallucinogens. Stimulants, such as caffeine, nicotine, and amphetamines speed up nervous system activity, and make you feel like you have more energy and can stay awake longer. Cocaine (and its derivative, crack), a powerful stimulant, is highly addictive. Depressants, such as sedatives, opiates, and alcohol, slow down bodily functions, and cause relaxation, slowed reaction time, and possible sleepiness. Alcoholism is still the nation's #1 drug problem and its third largest health problem. Hallucinogens, like LSD and marijuana, get their name because they can cause one to hallucinate, causing dreamlike, distorted images and perceptions. Use of LSD and marijuana peaked in the 1960s and 1970s and appears to be on the decline now.

■ To avoid becoming an abuser of substances may require staying away from settings where substances are heavily used, developing alternative behaviors (for example, drinking non-alcoholic beverages), and producing natural "highs" through, for example, regular exercise.

Box 6-6

SELF-ADJUSTMENT FOR STUDENTS: Observing, Recording, and Graphing

In the self-adjustment box at the end of preceding chapters, you selected a specific problem for improvement, and you strengthened your commitment to stick to the project. The next step is to take data on the occurrence of the problem—when, where, and how often or how long it occurs.

Reasons for Recording and Observing the Problem
There are several reasons for accurately observing and recording the occurrence of the problem before beginning a specific adjustment program. First,

Continued

accurate observations will sometimes indicate that what you thought was a problem is actually not a problem. Consider the following example from Greenspoon (1976, p. 177):

> The reliance on casual observation led a woman to complain to a psychologist that her husband rarely talked to her during meal time. She said that his failure to talk to her was becoming an increasing source of annoyance to her and she wanted to do something about it. The psychologist suggested that she prepare a chart and record on the chart the number of times that he initiated a conversation or responded to the verbal behavior that she emitted. She agreed to the suggestions. At the end of a week, she called back to inform the psychologist that she was surprised and pleased to report that she had been in error. It turned out that her husband both initiated conversation and responded to her verbal emissions at a very high rate.

Second, observing and recording may help you determine the causes of the problem. Does your problem behavior lead to reinforcers? If so, how can you control those reinforcers? These and other questions will be addressed later.

Third, accurate observations will enable you to judge whether or not your adjustment program (when it is applied) is leading to improvement. You wouldn't want to prematurely terminate an effective program that you mistakenly thought to be ineffective, nor continue with an ineffective program that should be abandoned or modified.

Fourth, recording and graphing a behavior may lead to adjustment apart from any other program (Maletzky, 1974). Students who monitor their own study behavior (for instance, by keeping a graph of the daily number of paragraphs or pages studied, or the amount of time spent studying) may find that their study behavior increases.

You can see that there are a number of reasons for accurately observing and recording your problem behavior. The kind of records that you should keep depends to some extent on the nature of the problem.

RECORDING FREQUENCY

The frequency of a behavior is the number of instances of a behavior in a particular period of time. Recording frequency is especially appropriate for excessive behaviors that you wish to decrease and for which each instance of the behavior is relatively brief. Examples include swearing, puffs on a cigarette, nervous twitches, biting fingernails, and interrupting others during conversations. For many self-control projects, a 3 × 5 card and a pencil may serve nicely for tallying instances of the problem as they occur throughout the day. Another strategy is to use a counter, such as the relatively inexpensive wristwatch-type used by golfers to record their score. With these counters you can count up to 99 simply by pressing a button for each instance of the behavior. Another easy recording technique is to transfer an item, such as a bead, from one pocket to another. At the end of a day, the number of beads in the second pocket can be counted and recorded to give you a measure of the frequency of the behavior for that day. Adequate ways of monitoring behavior that require little of the observer's time can almost always be found.

RECORDING DURATION

Sometimes it's not the frequency of behavior that's important, but rather how long each instance of the behavior lasts—its duration. For behaviors like watching television, talking on the telephone, taking coffee breaks, or studying, timing the duration of the behavior may be most appropriate. One strategy for monitoring duration is to simply write down the time at which the particular behavior begins and ends. Alternatively, many inexpensive wristwatches now have a stopwatch function that makes it easy to monitor the total duration of some behavior as it occurs off and on throughout a day.

Sometimes, both frequency and duration should be recorded. Dieters, for example, have monitored the frequency of mouthfuls during meals, the number of calories consumed per day, and the length of time that it takes to eat each meal (LeBow, 1981; 1989).

RECORDING QUALITY OR INTENSITY

Often an evaluation of quality—whether or not you are good at something or poor at something—involves a measure of frequency or duration. For example, if you are a good student you are most likely someone who shows a high duration of studying and a high frequency of answering test questions correctly. Sometimes, however, quality is assessed by developing a rating scale. Consider, for example, Carol's case from Chapter 1. You might remember that Carol was very upset about her former boyfriend leaving her. Carol and her psychologist rated each of her days with respect to her thoughts about her former boyfriend. If Carol couldn't stop thinking of Fred for a long period of time, felt very unhappy, and cried for a total of an hour or more, she assigned that day a score of 5, a very bad day. On the other hand, if she thought of Fred only fleetingly during the day, and such thoughts were not particularly disturbing, the day was assigned a score of 0, a very good day. Specific guidelines were also agreed upon for scores of 1, 2, 3, and 4. During her first week of using the recording system, Carol's ratings averaged 4.2—a very unhappy week (Martin, 1982). The observation system helped Carol and her psychologist monitor Carol's progress during her adjustment program in subsequent weeks.

Other psychologists have used rating scales to help individuals assess the degree of anxiety felt in certain situations. For example, Wolpe and Lazarus (1966) developed a "suds" (subjective units of discomfort) scale (discussed further in Chapter 15), which ranges from 100 (the situation in real life elicits extreme panic) to 0 (the situation in real life elicits essentially no anxiety). Such a ranking is useful in developing a program to treat extreme anxiety (see Chapter 15).

Rating scales are not limited to unpleasant emotions (such as Carol's reaction to loss of her boyfriend or someone's fear of heights). Happiness, self-satisfaction, sexual arousal, and feelings of affection can also be recorded with rating scales. If you decide that a rating scale is most appropriate to assess your particular problem of study, then the number of points on your scale might vary from 5 (such as was the case with Carol) to 100 (such as the suds scale). The trick is to have enough units on your scale so that you can monitor improvement on a day-to-day basis.

Selecting a Recording and Graphing System

After reviewing the different strategies for observing and recording, which recording strategy is most suited to your particular problem behavior? Make your choice and then complete the behavioral con-

tract in Figure 6-1. Also, at the end of each day of your adjustment program, you should transfer your records to a graph. Your graph should indicate a measure of behavior on the vertical axis, and a measure of time (hours, days, and so on) on the horizontal axis. A data sheet that also serves as a graph is shown in Figure 6-2. John, a student of one of the authors, completed a self-adjustment project to decrease the frequency of his self-put-downs (for example, "I'm not as smart as the rest of the students," "Don't ask questions, you'll make yourself look stupid," and the like) that often occurred while he was on campus. As you can see from Figure 6-2, instances of put-downs were recorded up the side of the graph and the days of the program were recorded across the bottom of the graph. Each time John thought self-put-downs, he simply added an "x" to the total number of "x"s that were already on the chart for that particular day. His treatment program was similar to Carol's in that it involved thought stopping for the self-put-downs followed by positive coping self-statements that identified his strengths. You can see by Figure 6-2 that his program was quite successful.

Helpful Hints for Recording and Graphing

1. If your recording system is time-consuming and cumbersome, you are less likely to use it consistently. Keep your recording system as simple as possible, provided that it enables you to obtain accurate data on your problem behavior.

2. If possible, try to make it rewarding for yourself to keep accurate records. For example, you might give control of some of your spending money to one of your supporters, who in turn will monitor your behavior and return your money contingent upon consistent data-taking.

3. If the problem that you have chosen is an undesirable behavior to decrease, consider ways in which you can record desirable behaviors as well as the problem behavior. If your goal is to go on a diet, for example, don't just record total calories consumed each day. Keep a separate record of calories consumed in healthy foods such as salads and whole-grain cereals. If, like Carol, your goal is to decrease unhappy thoughts of a particular type, then you should also consider recording frequency of happy thoughts during a day. Keeping records of positive behaviors will help to offset possible discouragement from self-recording

Figure 6-1
A Behavioral Contract

A Contract for the Self—Adjustment Project of _____

My self—adjustment project concerns the problem of: _ _____
_____
_____
_____

I will monitor this problem by recording its (frequency/duration/
intensity/quality) by (describe details of recording system):
_____
_____
_____
_____
_____
_____
_____
_____
_____
_____
_____

At the end of each day, I will update a graph that displays the results
of my recording.

Date _____

Signed _____   Signed _____
      (your signature)   (supporter's signature)

Figure 6-2
John's self-put-downs. Each "x" represents one put-down.

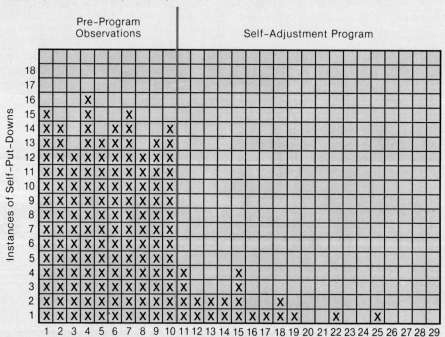

only negative behaviors. It may also be useful later in designing your self-adjustment program.

4. Make a pledge to your supporter that you will record the problem behavior as soon as it occurs. If you record instances of your problem behavior sometime after they occur (such as at the end of the day), then your records are much less likely to be accurate.

5. Keep your recording materials with you at all times. This, of course, is easiest when your recording materials consist of a wrist counter or a stopwatch you can wear. Having your recording apparatus with you provides a reminder for you to take data and increases the chances that you will record the problem behavior immediately.

MEMORY BOOSTER

■ IMPORTANT TERMS

Be prepared to define the following terms (located in the margins of this chapter). Where appropriate, be prepared to describe examples.

Aerobic Fitness	Amino Acids
Aerobic Points System	Vitamins
12-minute Fitness Test	Water Soluble Vitamins
Metabolic Rate	Fat Soluble Vitamins
Set Point Theory	Minerals
Dehydration	Substance Abuse
Carbohydrates	Substance Dependence
Unrefined Carbohydrates	Caffeine
Refined Carbohydrates	Amphetamines
Fats	Cocaine
Cholesterol	Crack
Protein	Opiates

■ QUESTIONS FROM IMPORTANT IDEAS IN THIS CHAPTER

1. Using an example, illustrate the specificity principle of training.
2. In two or three sentences, explain what we mean by aerobic fitness.
3. Explain the basis of Cooper's aerobic point system.
4. What is the best dietary-related predictor of chronic heart disease, and what food substances contribute to this condition?
5. Briefly describe some common misunderstandings about nutrition.
6. Identify three behavioral strategies for losing weight that emphasize stimulus control as a major ingredient. Defend your choices.
7. Describe three behavioral strategies for losing weight that emphasize consequence management as a major ingredient. Defend your choices.
8. Do you know individuals who abuse substances? How can you tell that they are substance abusers?
9. What are some of the effects of long-term use of cigarettes? Of marijuana? Of alcohol?
10. List five questions you can ask of yourself to assess potential drug abuse.

SEXUALITY, GENDER ROLES, AND SEXISM

LEARNING OBJECTIVES

After reading this chapter, you should be able to:

- Identify the male and female sexual and reproductive anatomies.
- State the kinds of behaviors that comprise safer sex practices.
- Discuss the major complaints that women and men have about their sex partners.
- Discuss some facts and fictions about AIDS.
- Describe processes by which gender role socialization occurs.
- Differentiate among masculinity, femininity, and androgyny; instrumentality, and expressiveness.
- Differentiate between gender typing and cross-gender typing.

Joel and Marcia have been living together for about 6 months. They feel pretty good about their sexual interactions. Joel began masturbating when he was 11 years old, and he still does occasionally. He feels vaguely guilty about this. Joel doesn't know it, but every once in a while Marcia also masturbates. Marcia's masturbatory fantasies don't include Joel! She also doesn't attain orgasm very often when she and Joel have intercourse. Marcia considers Joel to be a little selfish in their sexual interactions but she's not quite sure what to do about it. To Joel, Marcia is a little slow to excite. He feels he really has to work hard to bring her to orgasm. Both feel that the frequency of their sexual intercourse is about right.

Why do they both masturbate if they have a good sexual relationship together? What about the fact that sexual intercourse with Joel rarely brings Marcia to orgasm? Is this typical? Or is it a problem for these two people? This topic—human sexuality and sexual behavior—is important to human adjustment. Behaving sexually can feel great. Ultimately, it can also make us feel bad.

When they decided to live together, Joel and Marcia were already lovers. In a lighthearted way, they casually discussed a few ground rules preparatory to sharing an apartment. Marcia didn't want the responsibility for doing the cooking, cleaning,

Many young, unmarried couples live together.

and laundry to be hers alone. As they were each going to college, they decided to share many household duties.

Several months later, however, Joel hasn't kept his end of the agreement. He finds it easier to sit and read the paper while Marcia does most of the cooking and cleaning. On the few occasions that he does help, his "heart's not in it" and he usually does a sloppy job.

Marcia is more than a little peeved. The household arrangements aren't working out. She's doing little but keeping house for Joel. Joel seemed so considerate before they began living together. What happened? And what should Marcia do about it? So far, she keeps telling herself that things will get better.

Why does Joel not live up to his end of the bargain? Why does Marcia accept it? Why doesn't Joel share more of himself with Marcia? Doesn't he love her? Is the behavior of these two typical of people who live together?

In this chapter we examine the separate and overlapping biologies of the human male and female. We then discuss some of the problems humans may have with their sexual behavior. Moreover, we talk about gender roles and examine some of the more typical ones in our culture. We provide you with a means for determining whether you behave according to any particular gender role. We discuss erotica and its influence on sexual behavior. And we discuss homosexuality. We approach all of these areas in terms of gender-role behavior.

The Biology of Sex

primary sexual characteristics

The parts of our bodies that identify us as males or females; the genitals.

secondary sexual characteristics

Changes that occur in the genitals and elsewhere in the body as a function of hormonal development, usually during adolescence; for example, appearance of pubic hair.

ovaries

The two female reproductive organs that release eggs and female sex hormones.

uterus

An organ of the female that contains the environment for nourishing a fertilized egg through its development prior to birth.

Each of us is unique because the combination of individual genes that gives us our physical characteristics is unique. Our genes also determine our biological sex, identified in one way by our **primary sexual characteristics,** the parts of our bodies that identify us as either male or female (that is, our sex organs). Prenatal sexual development appears due to *hormones*. These are minute chemical compounds that are very important to growth and development, and may possibly relate to behavior as well. Hormones also determine when we begin to develop **secondary sexual characteristics** and what these will be. These latter characteristics develop during adolescence. Among others they are the development of breasts, hips, and pubic hair in females, and the growth of the testes, scrotum, the penis, and pubic and facial hair in males. (See also Chapter 10.) Let's continue our study of the biology of sex by examining human female and male sexual and reproductive anatomies.

Female Sexual and Reproductive Anatomy

For the most part human females are smaller than human males, a relationship that holds true for many but not all species. And, of course, females have a distinct sexual and reproductive anatomy as well. Human female sexual and reproductive anatomy is portrayed in Figure 7-1. There are two ovaries, but because of the side view in the figure's top panel, only one is shown. The **ovaries** release an egg approximately once every 28 days in the mature female. The egg travels out of the ovaries via the *Fallopian tubes* to the **uterus,** where it lodges in the walls of the uterus. If it is unfertilized by male *sperm*, it is disposed of during *menstruation*, when the nutrients awaiting the possibility that the egg will be fertilized are shed. The tube that joins the uterus is the *vagina*. The neck of that tube is the cervix. Anterior to the vagina in Figure 7-1 is the bladder where urine is stored prior to urination. The tube leading from the bladder is called the *urethra*. Posterior to the vaginal opening is the *anus* which is the posterior opening of the alimentary canal. Above the anus is the *rectum*, the last 8 or so inches of the alimentary canal.

In the lower panel of Figure 7-1, a frontal view of the female sexual anatomy called the *vulva* is depicted. Most anterior is the *mons veneris*, a fleshy cushion

Figure 7-1
Female reproductive system

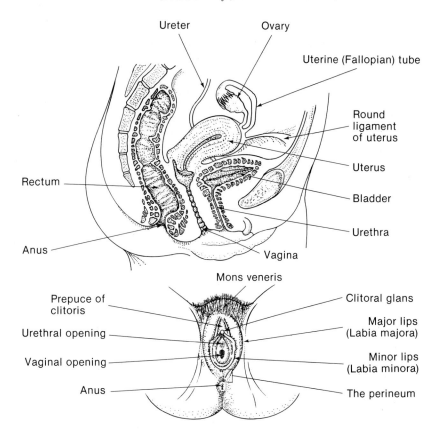

Ureter • Ovary • Uterine (Fallopian) tube • Round ligament of uterus • Uterus • Bladder • Urethra • Rectum • Anus • Vagina

Mons veneris • Prepuce of clitoris • Clitoral glans • Urethral opening • Major lips (Labia majora) • Vaginal opening • Minor lips (Labia minora) • Anus • The perineum

covered with pubic hair which can cushion the female during sexual intercourse. Below the mons is the *clitoral glans*. It is usually covered by a fleshy hood called the *clitoral prepuce*. The clitoris is a major center of pleasure for the female during sex, and sensation is its only known function. Whether the clitoris is the only center of female sexual pleasure is the subject of some controversy. The outer rim of the vaginal opening is comprised of lips called the *labia majora* (major lips). More central to the vaginal opening are the *labia minora* (minor lips). The apex of the labia minora is the clitoris and clitoral prepuce. Slightly posterior to the clitoris is the urethral opening, and posterior to that is the vaginal opening. Further posterior is the anus. The region between the vaginal area and the anus is the *perineum*.

Male Sexual and Reproductive Anatomy

A lateral view of the human male's sexual and reproductive anatomy is depicted in Figure 7-2. The externally visible organs are the *penis* and the *scrotum*, which contains the *testicles* or testes. The penis is the major sexual sensory center for the male; however, it also functions to deliver semen and to excrete urine. The major parts of the penis are the *glans* which is the head, the *prepuce* or foreskin which may or may not cover the glans, and the **corpus cavernosum** and **corpus spongiosum,** the erectile tissues comprising the mass of the penis itself. The tube leading from the penis is the urethra. It connects to the urinary bladder to allow urination. The testes in the scrotum are connected by the *vas deferens* to the *seminal vesicles* and the *prostate gland*, repositories for the spermatozoa produced in the testes, and the fluids that help transport the sperm called *semen*. These latter structures are also connected to the urethra.

corpus cavernosum
Spongy tissue on the upper side of the penis containing spaces that are filled with blood during the erection of the penis.

corpus spongiosum
Spongy tissue on the lower side of the penis, partially responsible for the erection of the penis.

Figure 7-2
Male reproductive system

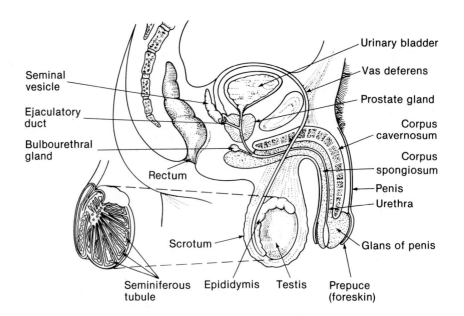

Reproduction

During sexual intercourse, the male's penis (made rigid by sexual stimulation) can be inserted into the vagina. Male orgasm usually results in the *ejaculation* of sperm into the vagina near the cervix. The sperm then swim into the uterus and/or the Fallopian tubes (depending on how far the egg has traveled) to contact the egg. Only one spermatozoa penetrates the egg, at which point the egg is fertilized and the female becomes pregnant.

TROUBLE GETTING PREGNANT?   Fertilization and pregnancy are more likely during some parts of the female reproductive cycle than during others. Biological signals from the cycle, if accurately gathered and used, can either promote fertilization or avoid it. The mature egg is ready for fertilization somewhere around the middle of the cycle (approximately 13 to 14 days after the start of menses). The egg lives for only a day or so, while sperm can live up to about 3 days. Couples practicing birth control using only this information can abstain from sexual intercourse from around Day 10 to Day 17 of the cycle. Couples wishing to conceive, of course, can have intercourse during this time. The time of ovulation can be fairly accurately recorded for the individual woman by taking repeated basal body temperature readings—say, each morning before one becomes active. Basal body temperature stays fairly even until just before the start of ovulation, then basal temperature decreases, to later rise above normal after the egg is released. There are drawbacks with this method because menstrual cycles of a large proportion of women are not that regular. Temperature can also change due to infection. Drawbacks notwithstanding, women should certainly know how their bodies work, particularly with regard to this most important function.

Sexual Response in Males and Females

sexual response cycle
A four-phased response by males and females to sexual stimulation that includes excitement, plateau, orgasm, and resolution.

There are a variety of views on what constitutes the **sexual response cycle** in humans. Most likely, the sexual response cycle is multidimensional. For example, there are cognitive factors involved in the recognition and appraisal of erotic stimuli. And there are emotional components involved in the reactions one has to such stimuli. Finally, of course, there are the tremendous physiological responses of the body to erotic stimulation. The physiological responses have been the most fully studied of these various dimensions, thanks to the pioneering work of Masters and Johnson (for example, Masters & Johnson, 1966). In some senses, however, the focus on the physiological has permitted the neglect of the other possible dimensions of the sexual response. Research now shows that there are very complex interactions among the cognitive, emotional, and physiological dimensions of the response (Rosen & Beck, 1988).

One question is how many phases there are to the sexual response cycle. Early researchers suggested that there were only two, that is, excitement and orgasm (for example, Ellis, 1906; Beach, 1956). Kaplan has suggested three phases: desire, excitement, and orgasm (Kaplan, 1977; 1979), but has not well operationalized how it is that desire is measured or coupled with the other two phases in her model (Rosen & Beck, 1988). The best-known and best-researched model, that of Masters and Johnson, contains four phases: excitement, plateau, orgasm, and resolution (Masters & Johnson, 1966). Masters and Johnson's model emphasizes the physiological responses to erotic stimulation.

EXCITEMENT.   For both sexes, in this first phase there is increased heart rate and blood pressure elevation. Blood flow to the genitals increases, leading to the lengthening and tumescence of the penis which produces penile erection in males, and nipple erection, vasocongestion of the labia and lower vagina, and tumescence of the clitoris in females. Further, in females the vagina begins to expand and vaginal lubrication occurs quickly. There is often flushing of the skin (for example, on the breasts) due to increased blood flow.

PLATEAU.   In this phase for both sexes there are further increases in heart rate and blood pressure. In the female the lower vaginal area including the labia minora becomes further engorged with blood and the clitoris retracts. Skin flushing may be more widespread. In the male there is often a deepening of the color of the corona, that is, the rim of the glans of the penis due to further engorgement with blood. Testicular elevation and tightening of the scrotum that began somewhat in the first phase continue along with the enlargement of the testes.

ORGASM.   In this phase, there is continued elevation of heart rate and blood pressure for both sexes as well as continued skin flushes. Orgasm consists of involuntary contractions of a variety of muscle groups for both sexes as well as the regular contraction (about 5 to 12 per orgasm) of the orgasmic platform of the vagina (the lower third) in the female, and ejaculatory contractions of the entire length of the penile urethra for several seconds in the male. Orgasm terminates this phase.

RESOLUTION.   In this phase there is a return to resting levels in all systems. Skin flushes cease. Heart rate and blood pressure return to normal levels. With reduced blood flow to the genitals normal coloring returns to the vagina and the labia, nipple erection disappears, and the clitoris retracts to its normal position in females, while in males detumescence quickly reduces the penis to about 50 percent of its erect, orgasmic length, followed thereafter by a gradual return to its resting size. There is further loss of scrotum tension and loss of increase in the size of the testes which descend into the relaxed scrotum.

Variations in the Sexual Response Cycle

refractory period
The period of time after an orgasm for males during which another orgasm cannot occur.

For males the sexual response cycle is pretty invariant. There is a rapid transition to the plateau phase from the excitement phase, and the plateau phase is usually fairly short before orgasm occurs. Immediately after orgasm is the **refractory period.** Additional orgasm is impossible for the male during this period. During resolution the events described above are the most likely. However, occasionally in the reso-

Box 7-1

STDs (Sexually Transmitted Diseases)

Sexually transmitted diseases (STD's) used to be called *venereal diseases*, in reference to Venus, Roman goddess of love. There are about 20 of these diseases, and they are transmitted through sexual activities of all types. Here are some very common STD's, how they are usually transmitted, and their symptoms. Notably, STD's most frequently diagnosed among college students are chlamydia, gonorrhea, genital herpes, syphilis, and pubic lice (Payne & Hahn, 1989).

1. *Bacterial vaginosis.* A bacterial infection of the vagina caused by bacteria that are transmitted by coitus (sexual intercourse). Produces a smelly discharge in women that is like flour paste in consistency and gray in color. Men show no symptoms.

2. *Candidiasis.* Also known as *thrush*, this is a yeast (fungal) infection which may be stimulated by changes in the balance of chemicals in the vagina caused by unusual stressors such as pregnancy, sexual activity, birth control pills, and antibiotics. This fungus produces a cottage-cheeselike discharge, white in color; vaginal and vulvar tissues also become irritated. It is rarely reported by men and can be successfully treated with prescribed antibiotic and antifungal medications.

3. *Trichomoniasis.* This is a parasitic infection transmitted mostly by genital sexual contact but it can also be transmitted via toilet seats, bathtubs, and towels used by those who are infected. It produces a white or yellow vaginal discharge and vulvar soreness. It is rarely reported by men and is successfully treated with prescribed medications.

4. *Chlamydia.* This bacterial infection is transmitted primarily by sexual activity. The most prevalent STD in the United States at this time (Payne & Hahn, 1989), it can be spread from one body site to another via the fingers. When the urethra is infected in men, it may lead to a discharge and burning urination. If the testicles are infected there may be heaviness in the affected area, inflammation of the scrotum, and swelling at the bottom of the testicles. Failure to treat can result in sterility, arthritis, and heart complications. Most women report no symptoms; however, without treatment chlamydia may lead to pelvic inflammatory disease which includes disrupted menstruation, abdominal pain, fever, nausea, vomiting, and headache with sterility and peritonitis (chronic infection of the lining of the abdominal cavity). It is successfully treated with prescribed antibiotics.

5. *Gonorrhea.* Also known as "clap," this is a bacterial infection transmitted via sexual contact (oral, anal, and genital). It is probably the second most frequent STD in the United States at this time (Payne & Hahn, 1989). Infected men produce a cloudy discharge from the penis and experience burning urination; however, about one in five men show no symptoms. If untreated there are many complications including testicular and scrotal swelling. Infected women produce a green or yellowish vaginal discharge. However, there are no overt symptoms in about four of five women. If untreated it can lead to pelvic inflammatory disease. It can be successfully treated with prescribed antibiotics.

6. *Syphilis.* This bacterial infection is transmitted from open breaks in the skin during sexual contact. A painless sore in the genital area is the

lution phase, it may be possible for some males to move back into the orgasmic phase and attain another orgasm. This is most likely in young males, and then only in a portion of those. It is also possible to prolong the plateau phase for a much longer period of time to await the female's orgasmic phase. This is accomplished only through practice (see below).

While the female sexual response cycle contains the same phases as the male, it contains no refractory period. Several variations on the usual cycle may be possible. For example, after experiencing excitement, plateau, and orgasm, further first indication, then the sore disappears and a general skin rash appears, possibly accompanied by sore throat and patchy loss of hair. Individuals are highly infectious during this stage. Then the rash disappears and there are no observable symptoms for an extended time. In the final stage (maybe 15 to 25 years later!), if untreated, there can be cardiovascular, central nervous system, eye, and skin damage with death resulting. Syphilis can be successfully treated with prescribed antibiotics.

7. *Pubic lice.* Lice are easily spread through virtually any body contact or through sharing beds or clothes. As they attach to the base of the pubic hair, they produce itching that won't go away. The lice may actually be seen. Lice are successfully treated with prescription and over-the-counter creams and lotions.

8. *Herpes.* Herpes are a family of over 50 viruses, some of which are responsible for chicken pox and mononucleosis. Genital herpes approximately rivals chlamydia and gonorrhea in frequency in the United States (Payne & Hahn, 1989). The virus that produces genital herpes is transmitted by genital sexual contact and usually displays in the genital area. Oral herpes, the second of the two sexually transmitted herpes viruses, is often transmitted by kissing and usually displays in the mouth area. In the active stage of herpes, a blister or series of blisters appear, causing minor irritation and itching. The blisters enlarge until they rupture, becoming painful ulcers which take up to six weeks to heal. Some people may show only a single active phase after which the virus remains dormant in the body. Others may have several active phases. The virus is extremely contagious in the active phase. There is no successful treatment at this time.

9. *Viral hepatitis.* This is a viral infection transmitted by blood, semen, vaginal secretions, and saliva. Anal contact is associated with both forms (Hepatitis A and B) of this virus. The symptoms vary from nonexistent, to mild flulike, to high fever, vomiting, and abdominal pain. There is no successful treatment at this time.

10. *Genital warts.* A virus spread through genital or anal contact. The warts are hard, yellow-gray in color where skin is dry, and soft, pink, and cauliflower-shaped where skin is moist. They can be treated by various removal methods.

11. *Human Immunodeficiency Virus (HIV).* A virus spread by contact with an infected person's body fluid, especially semen and blood. The virus attacks parts of the body's immune system, thus weakening the body's defense against infection. (See Box 7-2 for a more complete discussion.)

NOTE: The vagina is a warm, dark, and moist environment, virtually perfect for growing a variety of organisms. Normal hygiene can keep it in appropriate chemical balance. However, certain behavioral practices can make vaginal infection more likely. Wearing tight pantyhose (without cotton panels), which can raise vaginal temperature, and using commercial vaginal douches, which can raise the acid level of the vagina (Payne & Hahn, 1989), are two such practices.

stimulation may lead directly to another orgasm. In this variation, a series of orgasms may be possible for some women. A second variation contains no orgasm: The plateau phase is reached and this phase waxes and wanes in intensity before resolution begins. In a third variation, the plateau phase may be skipped entirely. Here there are periods of waning sexual response briefly interrupting an otherwise quick rise to the orgasmic phase where the woman quickly achieves orgasm. The several types of sexual cycle may occur in the same woman on different occasions. There is much that is still not known here (Morokoff, 1978). Indeed, we need to

Figure 7-3
Male (upper panel) and female (lower panel) sexual response cycles

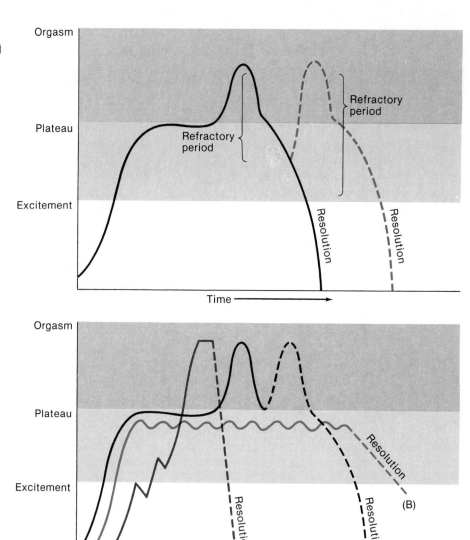

emphasize that the information we have presented on the sexual response cycle is essentially biological. Yet as humans we know that a large part of "good sex" depends upon those not well researched cognitive and emotional components of the response. In common terms these are the psychology of the moment—how we feel about ourselves, how we feel about who we are with, and what the background circumstances are.

Some Varieties of Human Sexual Adjustment

Homosexuality

Most of us channel our sexual energy toward members of the other sex. But, in all societies, a minority of individuals channel their sexual energy toward members of the same sex. In 1948, Alfred Kinsey and his associates astounded the world with their finding that a substantial portion of their male interviewees reported at least one homosexual contact in their lives. This finding began the modern-day discussion of the varieties of human sexual adjustment.

Most of us tend to think of individuals as either heterosexual or homosexual. But, two-category classifications can be overly simplistic. We also tend to simplify in another way that is erroneous, that is, that one is defined as homosexual or heterosexual based solely on copulatory behavior. Sexual behavior takes place on many levels, including the all-important cognitive and emotional levels. These levels should also be included in any comprehensive definition of sexual orientation.

Let's see how homosexuality is formally defined, at least in terms of sexual behavior. Feldman and MacCulloch (1980) define **homosexuality** as "sexual behavior between members of the same sex, accompanied by sexual arousal, carried out recurrently and despite the opportunity for heterosexual behavior" (p. 149). This definition excludes individuals in prisons, but it includes individuals who may also engage in heterosexual activities. Feldman and MacCulloch further define individuals as **primary homosexuals** if they have never experienced arousal from heterosexual activity at any point in their lives. **Secondary homosexuals** they define as those who have experienced substantial heterosexual arousal. Feldman and MacCulloch do this because the variety of individuals who are homosexual runs the gamut from those who are exclusively homosexual to those who are both homosexual and heterosexual, that is, **bisexual.**

The Feldman and MacCulloch definition—which references sexual behavior directly—fails to mention cognitive and emotional variables. This is probably a conscious omission on their part. There has been very little formal study of how cognitive and emotional variables relate specifically to sexual orientation. We consider definitions of sexual orientation as incomplete until they also contain cognitive and emotional variables.

homosexuality

Sexual behavior (with arousal) between members of the same sex when there is opportunity for sexual behavior (with arousal) between members of the other sex.

primary homosexual

Homosexual individual who has never experienced heterosexual activity at any point in life.

secondary homosexual

Homosexual individual who has experienced considerable heterosexual arousal.

bisexual

An individual who experiences sexual arousal in contact with members of either sex.

Homosexuality is more open in today's society than it was years ago. This is in part due to the fact that gay and lesbian groups have learned how to represent themselves politically and to stand up for their rights as citizens. But at the same time, a lot has not changed. Imagine how you might feel if you were threatened because you openly expressed your feelings toward someone of the other sex. This is how many homosexuals feel living in a society that remains largely disapproving of same-sex relationships. Faced with personal or professional discrimination, many gays and lesbians feel that they must hide even simple expressions of their love and sexuality. Some things have changed in our society regarding homosexuality—but much has not.

No single cause of homosexuality (or, for that matter, heterosexuality) can be acceptably pinpointed. The most popular explanations—genetic, hormonal, structural, and environmental—all fail in one way or another. There is evidence that identical twins can both be homosexual (for example, Kallman, 1952a, 1952b; but see Kallman, 1953), or that one twin can be heterosexual while the other is homosexual (Klintworth, 1962; Parker, 1964; and Rainer et al., 1960). Recent evidence suggests that identical twins (52 percent) are more likely to *both* be homosexual than either fraternal twins (22 percent), or adoptive brothers (11 percent) (Bailey & Pillard, 1991). These data imply a genetic component to homosexuality, but they fail to explain the remaining identical twin (48 percent) and fraternal twin (78 percent) cases where one twin is homosexual and the other is not. Thus, no conclusions regarding genetic factors should be made at this time.

There are some minute hormonal differences between homosexual males and some heterosexual males (Masters & Johnson, 1979), and some minute differences in brain structure (LeVay, 1991) but these may be the result of the homosexual lifestyle rather than the cause of it (Sandler et al., 1980). Therefore, a positive conclusion is not possible about the role of hormones or brain structure in sexual orientation either.

Although Freud receives credit for pointing childhood as a place where adult sexual behavior is learned, Freudian theory was written far too casually to prove that specific childhood experiences produce homosexuality. No one, in any case, has been able to identify such experiences. However, many social scientists think that, in general, a homosexual orientation may have its roots during these formative years. In general, the jury is still out on what causes homosexuality.

Premarital Sex

For quite a few years researchers have been interested in sexual attitudes and behavior. The first major survey of such behavior by Alfred Kinsey and his associates in 1948, *The Sexual Behavior of the Human Male*, raised a furor. Since that time, however, we have become used to reading and hearing the results of such surveys. Now, data on sexual attitudes and behavior are often gathered through volunteer responses to questionnaires in magazines, for example, *Playboy* and *Redbook*. Some of these surveys have produced as many as 100,000 respondents. We've come a long way.

One of these surveys has now been repeated a fifth time on college students in the United States. It details some interesting changes in college students' attitudes and behavior with regard to premarital sex.

ATTITUDES TOWARD PREMARITAL SEX AND THE WOMEN'S SEXUAL REVOLUTION.   We present the results of this series of surveys because they show some interesting changes in attitudes toward premarital sex and promiscuity. Table 7-1 contains the data.

- Men have always reported higher frequencies of premarital sexual intercourse and heavy petting than women, although women's reporting of premarital sexual intercourse and heavy petting have caught up substantially in the 20 years of these surveys.
- From 1965 to 1985 both men's and women's reported frequencies of premarital intercourse and heavy petting increased although both activities may be leveling off for both sexes.
- A majority of women are again considering a man with experience with many women to be immoral. This is a dramatic shift in women's attitudes since the 1970s and marks a return to an attitude of the 1960s.
- Men are much less likely than women to consider themselves immoral for having multiple relationships, although for men, too, consideration of the immorality of multiple relationships for their own sex is on the rise.

TABLE 7-1
SURVEY OF COLLEGE STUDENTS' ATTITUDES AND BEHAVIOR REGARDING PREMARITAL SEX *Adapted from Robinson et al., 1991.*

	1965		1970		1975		1980		1985	
	MEN	*WOMEN*	*MEN*	*WOMEN*	*MEN*	*WOMEN*	*MEN*	*WOMEN*	*MEN*	*WOMEN*
Percent reporting premarital intercourse	65.1	28.7	65.0	37.3	73.9	57.1	77.4	63.5	79.3	63.0
Percent reporting heavy petting	71.3	34.3	79.3	59.7	80.2	72.7	84.9	72.9	81.2	74.1
Percent who agreed that "a man who has had sexual intercourse with a great many women is immoral"	35.0	56.0	15.0	22.0	19.5	30.1	26.5	38.9	31.7	51.8
Percent who agreed that "a woman who has had sexual intercourse with a great many men is immoral"	42.0	91.0	33.5	54.0	28.5	41.0	41.8	49.6	51.4	64.2

■ About two out of three women are now likely to consider members of their own sex immoral for having multiple relationships. While a lower figure than in the 1960s, this figure, too, represents a dramatic change from the 1970s and is at the highest point since these surveys were begun in 1965.

■ More men than since the beginning of these surveys now consider it immoral for a woman to have had multiple relationships.

The Old Double Standard. In the first of these surveys in 1965, the investigators (King et al., 1977; Robinson & Jedlicka, 1982; Robinson et al., 1972; Robinson et al., 1968) turned up evidence for the double standard. That is, both men and women were less inclined to criticize men as immoral or sinful for having experienced multiple sexual relationships, and both men and women were more inclined to criticize women for having had multiple sexual relationships. In other words, there was one standard of sexual behavior for men and another standard for women (Table 7-1). In 20 years this has not changed, reports of more liberal premarital sexual behavior notwithstanding (Robinson et al., 1991). However, with respect to the issue of multiple partners both men and women appear to be getting more conservative.

The fear generated by sexually transmitted diseases, particularly the spread of HIV, will likely contribute to a decrease in premarital sex. Women are now also reporting dissatisfaction with the "casual sex" touted by the so-called sexual revolution of the 1970s. This may mean a trend toward celibacy—having no sexual relations—or it may mean having full sexual relations only in the context of deep, potentially lifelong relationships with another. Given that the revolution in sexual behavior in the 1970s appears to have been largely a women's revolution—and possibly only in reporting—we can speculate that it will again be a change in women's behavior if there is to be any movement away from the new premarital sex norms.

Masturbation

As late as the last century it was thought that masturbation caused physical illnesses and could lead to insanity, since it was observed that mental patients masturbated (Colp, 1985). Early in this century that view changed: Masturbation, it was claimed, could lead to an impairment of character. Jokingly, it was even said that masturbation would grow hair on the palms of your hands! This did not stop young men from masturbating; it just hid the practice. At the same time no one discussed the possibility that women masturbated, too, because it was not thought that women had sexual desires (Colp, 1985). Much has changed since then. Kinsey and his associates (1948) reported that over 90 percent of the men they interviewed masturbated. Subsequently, Kinsey and others (1953) reported that over 60 percent of the women they interviewed masturbated. Kinsey was the first to say that masturbation caused no harm and, indeed, might be helpful to sexual development. Masturbation has also become the basis for some sex therapies (see below). It has been said about masturbation that in some ways it may be the best kind of sex, in the sense that the person doing the stimulating is identical to the person being stimulated (for example, Masters & Johnson, 1970).

In the sense that most people do it, masturbation can be considered normal sexual behavior. It becomes problematic only if it is one's preferred outlet in a situation where sexual intercourse is the norm, such as in an intimate relationship between two people.

Thus, Joel and Marcia are not unusual. Masturbation is sometimes continued by couples after their relationship begins. It's not known why this should be—perhaps simply because it is a strongly rewarded behavior and is easily engaged in. Perhaps masturbation offers a fantasy outlet not provided within the context of a particular relationship; it may help match couples where sex drives are quite different; or, it may provide sexual satisfaction where the relationship does not. For each of these speculations, self-adjustment is desirable if masturbation per se is used to avoid dealing with sexual problems within the relationship.

Sexual Problems and Adjustments

It's Saturday night and Joel and Marcia have just returned from the movies. They're getting ready for bed. Joel grabs Marcia and says, "Hey, I'm horny!"

"God, you don't have a romantic bone in your body!"

"What'd I do, ask for the moon? All I wanted to do was make out a little!" And Joel grabs Marcia and they wrestle on the bed.

Afterward, there is a period of brief recrimination.

"Joel, you're just not considerate when we make love. I end up feeling frustrated."

"Geez, babe, you're just so slow," mumbles Joel, rolling over and closing his eyes. "Let's talk about it in the morning."

And in the morning, of course, they don't talk about it.

In this hypothetical conversation, several problems are apparent between these two people. We'll point them out below.

Males

Male sexual problems and adjustments center around erectile failures and ejaculation (usually premature, but occasionally delayed or absent). Erectile insufficiency refers to chronic erection difficulty resulting in either the failure to attain orgasm or to ejaculate into the vagina (Feldman & MacCulloch, 1980). Premature ejaculation refers to the fact that orgasm occurs before, or immediately upon, vaginal penetration. Delayed or absent ejaculation refers to the fact that ejaculation occurs either not at all or long after one's partner's orgasm.

Failure to achieve and maintain an erection can be either organically or psychologically caused. In the former case medical help should be sought. Organic causes of this dysfunction include a low androgen level, early undiagnosed diabetes, stress, fatigue, alcohol abuse, and side effects of medication (Kaplan, 1974). Where erection failure has a psychological source, as we will see for the problems of both sexes, the causes lie in our social learning histories. Where these problems are severe, professional help is necessary. Where they are not, however, self-adjustment is possible and desirable.

If a man has never had an erection, or has had very few, this is a strong sign that the erection failure is organic. Morning erections and those during sleep (not necessarily sexual in nature) and erections produced by self-masturbation all indicate that physical capacity for erection with a partner exists (Karacan, 1977).

If erective failure is nonorganic, then adjustment toward producing erection with a partner is possible. What is important is an understanding of the precipitating conditions. Is the failure due to fear? An inability to relax? Anger? Frustration? Thoughts that sex is dirty and degrading? All of the foregoing? Each of these possibilities and the numerous others not mentioned must be treated before direct work on the erection begins.

ERECTILE INSUFFICIENCY. One way to create conditions in which an erection is at least possible, is to produce relaxation. Methods already discussed in this book such as Jacobsonian relaxation and centering (both in Chapter 4) can be employed. It is unlikely however that these relaxation procedures alone will cure erectile failure, so adjustment efforts do not stop there (Kockott et al., 1975). Indeed, a partner can be an important part of the relaxation process. Masters and Johnson's sensate focus (Feldman & MacCulloch, 1980) is essentially a sexual variation of the relaxation process. **Sensate focus** begins with an understanding that one partner completely forsakes all sexual demands on the other. During sensate focus one partner touches (massages, strokes) another, while the other enjoys being touched. Intercourse is forbidden. Touching begins in nongenital areas and then gradually proceeds to the genitals. During this time the partners learn how to express their joy at particular touches and to gently express how other touches are not as pleasing. They also learn to focus on what they are feeling during this time. This is

sensate focus

A relaxation technique developed by Masters and Johnson that promotes the development of attention to stimulation of various parts of the body.

Preeminent researchers and therapists of human sexual behavior, William Masters and Virginia Johnson.

not a quick process! Proceeding too quickly—at the first sign of erection, for example, attempting intercourse, or even masturbation by one's partner—may be premature. Both partners need to be very understanding and patient.

When erection occurs frequently during sensate focus it may be permissible to attempt gentle masturbation with the assistance of one's partner. Orgasm is not the immediate goal! Continuing to feel good is. Once the partner can produce orgasm through manipulation of the penis, and this has become a regular occurrence, intercourse may be attempted. The woman can masturbate the man to the point of ejaculatory inevitability, followed by rapid insertion of the penis into the vagina. (The female superior position is good for this.) Across several encounters, the penis can be inserted earlier in the sequence.

PREMATURE EJACULATION.   Perhaps the most successful technique of sex therapists have been for premature ejaculation. There are a number of variations of the basic theme: that ejaculation is a reflex and, like other reflexes, can be controlled (LoPiccolo & LoPiccolo, 1978; Sandler et al., 1980). In the **Semans technique,** the male masturbates almost (but not quite) to the point of ejaculatory inevitability, then stops until the feeling of inevitability passes, then begins again until the same point is reached, and so on, until it is possible to maintain a high level of sexual excitement without orgasm, though orgasm is approached a number of times (Semans, 1956). A variant of this technique involves one's partner in the activity; however, this should probably not happen until a measure of control develops, particularly if this is initially too exciting. In the Masters and Johnson variation of the Semans technique, called the **squeeze technique,** the female orally or manually stimulates the penis to just before ejaculatory inevitability and then firmly (but gently) squeezes the glans between two fingers for a few seconds. If the squeeze is applied correctly it will cause a partial loss of erection, which can be recovered quickly. This procedure can be repeated until both partners determine that sufficient progress has been made.

More explicit feedback to determine progress in sustaining an erection may be gained by counting and recording. For example, the male can count the number of strokes to just before the point of inevitability. Or either partner can note the elapsed time from beginning the activity to the point of inevitability. In this manner the partners can observe increases in total strokes or total time to orgasm as signs of progress.

After some control has been attained in the masturbatory exercise, **nondemanding intromission** can be attempted. This is best accompanied in the female superior position, in which the penis is held in the vagina without movement by either partner. If ejaculatory inevitability is approached, it should be communicated by the male; the female withdraws and applies the squeeze technique.

Solving the problem of premature ejaculation is not a quick process. Masters and Johnson asked their patient/couples to practice their procedures for as long as six months after initial therapy was concluded (Sandler et al., 1980). Various aspects of the techniques for treating premature ejaculation would seem to be valuable even where there is not a severe problem. For example, couples could practice aspects of the technique to adjust orgasmic timing.

Females

Problems of female sexual response also fall in two categories: vaginismus and orgasmic dysfunction. **Vaginismus** refers to spasms of the lower third of the vagina (Feldman & MacCulloch, 1980). It is painful and can prevent intromission by the male. **Orgasmic dysfunction** refers to the absence of orgasm, but the definition must be subdivided into **primary orgasmic dysfunction**—if females have never experienced an orgasm—and **secondary orgasmic dysfunction**—if fe-

---

Semans technique

Masturbation of the male almost to the point of ejaculatory inevitability, pausing, then repeating the process to promote delay of ejaculation.

squeeze technique

Squeezing the glans of the penis between the fingers to delay ejaculation when ejaculatory inevitability is almost reached.

nondemanding intromission

The insertion of the penis into the vagina with no pelvic thrusting by either partner thereafter.

vaginismus

Painful spasmodic contractions of the lower third of the vagina which often prevent sexual intercourse.

orgasmic dysfunction

The absence of orgasm.

primary orgasmic dysfunction

Refers to females who have never experienced an orgasm, although they have tried.

secondary orgasmic dysfunction

Refers to females who have experienced orgasm but never during sexual intercourse.

males have experienced orgasm but never during sexual intercourse (Feldman & MacCulloch, 1980). This latter is not thought a dysfunction by everyone.

VAGINISMUS. Vaginismus is thought to be caused primarily by unfortunate early experiences in which intercourse was painful or unwanted, although a variety of organic causes are also possible (Kaplan, 1974). It is fairly rare when compared with orgasmic dysfunction. Nonorganic vaginismus is treated by deconditioning the unwanted vaginal spasms. This involves the gentle insertion of graduated catheters into the vagina until dilation is eventually tolerable (Fuchs et al., 1973; Kaplan, 1974). The phobic component is treated by systematic desensitization (see Chapter 15). We don't suggest self-adjustment for this problem.

PRIMARY ORGASMIC DYSFUNCTION. For orgasmic dysfunction that is primary, there are at least two basic ways to proceed with self-adjustment. First, masturbatory and premasturbatory exercises can be practiced. The female must be free of thoughts of anger, frustration, demeaning self-talk, and so on. Being relaxed is important, so that relaxation techniques (or sensate focus) may be employed to produce such a state. LoPiccolo and Lobitz (1972) suggest beginning practice after a nice, warm bath. Women who have not done so may need to get in touch with their bodies by observing and manipulating their genitals (LoPiccolo & Lobitz, 1972). Observation can be accomplished through the use of a mirror. If you don't already, learn to think positively about your genitals—men do! Discover which manipulations produce the most intense sensations, and use those manipulations to produce orgasm. If orgasm is not produced in this way, you can intensify the frequency and duration of masturbation by using a vibrator. Use whatever fantasy stimulates you to help the process. Eventually, involve your partner in the process. During the sensate focus exercises, diplomatically report what you like him to do. Be just as gentle when suggesting what not to do. You can guide or shadow your partner's hands in such a way as to show him what pleases you the most. A first goal might be to develop enough trust to allow him to masturbate you to orgasm. Once this outcome is reached in most sessions, concurrent intromission can also be effected. After intromission, focus on the pleasurable sensations of the penis in the vagina. Begin with the female in the superior position, and avoid thrusting. Simply concentrate on the fullness and deep touch that is produced. If it is desired and does not interfere with vaginal sensations, your partner can also continue to manipulate your clitoris in a way that heightens sexual tension. In fact, this manipulation can be carried on until the orgasmic phase is reached. At this point thrusting will probably produce orgasm.

A second way to improve female orgasm is to strengthen the muscle that is presumably related to it (Kassorla, 1980; Sandler et al., 1980). This is the *pubococcygeous muscle*, a sphincter muscle running along either side of the vaginal opening. Awareness of this muscle occurs during urination—it is the muscle that stops and starts the flow of urine. This muscle can be exercised just like any other muscle to increase its tone. First, to avoid problems with urinating, tensing and relaxing exercises can be performed on the commode. Initially start the flow of urine by pushing out, then stop it in midflow. Repeat this procedure until the bladder is empty. Then try several cycles with the bladder empty. When confidence in control builds, successive relaxation and tensing of this muscle can be practiced anywhere, and considerable practice is suggested.

Kassorla (1980) calls these your "magical push muscles." After becoming initially aware of the muscle, she recommends daily practice in the following sequence: (1) relax; (2) push out (in attempt to hold your vagina open); (3) experience the nice feeling of being open; (4) hold for just a moment; (5) relax once more; (6) start again. A perineometer, a device available only on prescription that is inserted in the vagina, can also be used. Contraction of the pubococcygeous muscle forces air out of the perineometer which provides feedback on the pressure exerted. This is biofeedback—that is, feedback regarding one's biological functioning—and it may help in the evaluation of gains in strength that otherwise may be difficult to detect.

SECONDARY ORGASMIC DYSFUNCTION.   Who said that this was a problem? It may or may not be. And if it is a problem, whose is it? First, regular orgasms for women via intercourse alone are not the norm. Only 25 to 30 percent of women report regular orgasms as a result of intercourse (Hite, 1976; Hoch et al., 1981). Second, the absence of orgasm during intercourse may just as easily be due to the technique (or lack of technique) of the woman's partner. Finally, lack of communication—admitting that there is a problem and discussing it—may involve one or both partners. If either this type of communication or the new ways of behaving that may be necessary to produce orgasm are difficult for either partner, therapy for the relationship may be indicated (McGovern et al., 1975).

Enjoying Sex

orgasmic timing

Matching the sexual response cycles of the male and female so that the orgasms of both occur at similar times.

A major complaint of one sex about the other's sexual techniques tends to involve **orgasmic timing** (Feldman & MacCulloch, 1980). Women complain that their male partners often attain orgasm too quickly, before they themselves can successfully attain orgasm (Kassorla, 1980), or that American men simply hurry all of sex in general. On the other hand, men complain that their female partners are too slow to reach orgasm.

It may help if stimulation during foreplay is directed toward and for the female. Intromission may be delayed unless the male is able to withhold orgasm until his partner's orgasm is imminent (see Kassorla, 1980). Since this isn't a sex manual per se, we'll leave the details up to you. But the foregoing section on delaying male orgasm provides some useful guidelines that Joel and Marcia, in the earlier example, might have attended to.

A second major complaint which each sex has about the other is their respective failure to stimulate their major sensory areas appropriately (Penney, 1982). Women complain that men are not sensitive enough in their "touch," particularly when stimulating the clitoris, the head of which can be painful because it is so

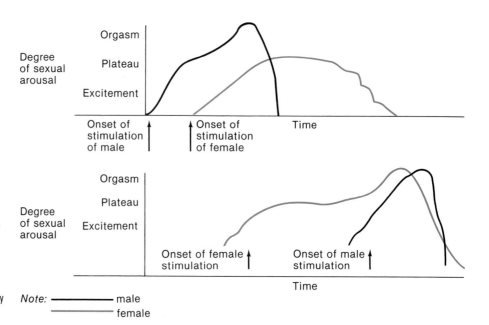

Figure 7-4

Improving orgasmic timing. In the upper panel, where stimulation of the male begins first, the male reaches orgasm while the female is still in the plateau phase. In the bottom panel, where onset of female stimulation is first, the likelihood of female orgasm is increased and orgasmic timing may be synchronized.

Note: ———— male
        ———— female

sensitive. The major preference here appears to be for stimulation of the shaft of the clitoris, or for the area around the clitoris. Men complain similarly about their partner's technique of penile stimulation. Stimulation of the shaft here may also be performed if the fingers are used. The shaft of the penis can be grasped very firmly. It may be that men like **fellatio,** that is, oral stimulation of the penis, partly because the mouth and tongue of their partners are soft and well-lubricated when contacting the glans of the penis. Women enjoy **cunnilingus,** that is, oral stimulation of the vaginal area for similar reasons.

fellatio
Oral stimulation of the penis.

cunnilingus
Oral stimulation of the vulva.

Intimacy, Romance, and Communication

Are American men capable of intimacy in the same way women are and in the way that women want them to be (McGill, 1985; Rubin, 1983)? It has been said that "foreplay starts in the morning" (Penney, 1982), meaning that intimacy starts a long time before the act itself. Many women like to be romanced for a long time before the sex act itself commences. For women, most men can be more romantic and intimate than they usually are. Joel may have been aware of this, but in his interactions with Marcia he was not practicing it. Later in this chapter we present some reasons why the behavior of American males may account for the failure of intimacy in some cases.

Improved communication within couples would help most of them become aware of the problems discussed in this chapter. However, communication should be positive. Criticism should be muted, because many sexually related responses are so fragile. Marcia might have been more gentle in her critique. Better yet, she might have asked Joel to help her attain orgasm before he went to sleep. She then could have expressed her appreciation for his cooperation. Try praising a partner for the things he or she does correctly—for example, "I just love it when you do that to me"—and you'll be surprised to find that most of them will do "that" more often. In turn, be a good listener and your own skills will improve.

Finally, good sex depends largely on how good the relationship with your partner is in other, nonsexual ways. Many sexual dysfunctions can be secondary to other difficulties inherent in a relationship. All of this chapter's advice needs to be understood in that context.

Safer Sex

Sex is always risky, if only because it involves very important social interactions, which can include emotional and cognitive commitments. Naturally, the act can also lead to conception, and often does when neither partner intends it. In fact the figures today suggest that the United States is in the middle of an explosion of

Box 7-2

ACQUIRED IMMUNE DEFICIENCY SYNDROME (AIDS): FACTS AND FICTION

AIDS is a sexually transmitted disease for the most part, so we include it here in this chapter. Over 100,000 people in the United States have died as a result of AIDS, and many more will die in the next decade. Here are some facts and fiction about AIDS.

FACTS

AIDS is caused by a virus.

The virus is called human immunodeficiency virus (HIV).

HIV does not destroy the immune system: It selectively attacks and destroys one type of blood cell in the immune system.

HIV does infect some of the body directly, for example, the central nervous system and the colon, and maybe more as more is known about it.

The highest risk behaviors with respect to getting HIV are to engage in homosexual or heterosexual anal or vaginal intercourse with transmission of semen with an infected individual; to engage in needle sharing (injection implied) among infected individuals; to receive contaminated blood via transfusion; or to be a newborn of an infected mother (Centers for Disease Control, 1987).

HIV is not very infectious or very contagious. It's difficult to transmit and doesn't survive well in the body after transmission (Batchelor, 1988). *However, the fact that HIV is spreading suggests the importance of understanding what risky behavior is with respect to it.*

The fear of casual contagion is the major issue facing the public and professional alike (Batchelor, 1988).

HIV can be killed by soap, alcohol, bleach, detergent, hand soap, heat, and drying (Centers for Disease Control, 1987).

HIV is most easily gotten from semen and/or blood.

At this writing there is no cure, and because HIV changes fairly easily, a cure will be difficult.

Homosexual and bisexual males and intravenous drug users are most at risk to get AIDS because together they constitute most of the population that has AIDS (over 80 percent).

FICTION

You can get AIDS from sitting on a toilet seat used by someone who is HIV+. Unlikely; HIV doesn't live long outside the body.

You can get AIDS from sharing a drinking glass with someone who is HIV+. Unlikely; there is not much HIV in clear bodily fluids (see below), and the virus doesn't live long outside the body.

You can get AIDS from kissing someone who is HIV+. This is a little more controversial—particularly the matter of deep kissing—but again the likelihood is low because of the low concentration of HIV in clear bodily fluids. But what if the person has bleeding gums? This is much more problematic.

People die from HIV itself. Actually they die from secondary "opportunistic" diseases to which they are no longer immune.

You are likely to get AIDS from heterosexual sex. Not at this time. Only about 4 to 6 percent of cases in the United States are currently transmitted this way (Centers for Disease Control, 1988). However, note that this figure is not zero and is increasing. Moreover, Earvin "Magic" Johnson's situation shows that it is certainly possible.

You can get AIDS from clear body fluids (sweat, urine, saliva, tears). Not in normal contact quantities. In the infected person the virus is present in these fluids in very small amounts. Directly injecting a quart of clear body fluid into your veins could do it (Batchelor, 1988).

SAFER SEX PRACTICES with RESPECT TO AIDS

Know your sex partners and limit their numbers.

Use latex condoms.

Avoid contact with body fluids, semen, and feces.

Avoid using substances that impair good judgment.

Avoid sex with known IV drug users, those with AIDS, and those at some risk for AIDS.

Get regular checkups for STD's.

Keep foreign objects out of the rectum.

Maintain proper hygiene.

teenage pregnancies, many of which may be unwanted. A third level of risk lies in the acquisition of a sexually transmitted disease (STD).

How can you manage your level of risk against STD's and unwanted pregnancy? Let's deal first with STD's.

REDUCING STD RISK.   There are three principal adjustments you can make to reduce your risk of acquiring an STD: (1) You can abstain from sex. And for those who don't want intimate (sexual) relationships with others for any of a number of reasons (religion, handicap, protection of virginity) this is a perfectly acceptable adjustment. (2) You can have sex with only one uninfected partner who is mutually faithful with you. This is a somewhat difficult adjustment to manage if your relationships are casual, particularly since people may be unlikely to disclose their health status if the relationship is not truly intimate (that is, a communicative one). This adjustment emphasizes the development of a truly intimate relationship first, before full sexual relations begin. (3) You can properly use a latex condom, spermicide, and/or diaphragm. The combination of condom and spermicide together is better than either one alone. Condoms protect against bacterial infections transmitted by an infected penis and infected semen as well as protect the penis from vaginal infection, but condoms don't protect against open sores that are not on the penis but are in either partners' genital area; nor do they protect against pubic lice. Condoms and spermicide together protect against STD's that may be transmitted via semen or blood (for example, HIV, see below). Of course, none of the foregoing protect against STD's that can be transmitted by mouth-to-genital contact (for example, gonorrhea of the throat) and no protective method is 100 percent safe.

Finally, for those of you who are sexually active it would be a good adjustment to see your physician for regular checkups. Remember that most physicians are pretty conservative, so if you want a checkup for an STD you will have to explicitly ask for it. This means being frank.

It is worth noting that your risk of acquiring an STD rises with the number of sexual partners you have. That is, the more partners you have, the greater your risk of acquiring an STD.

If you are sexually active, it is also a good idea to examine your genital and anal areas and how you feel about the function of these organs, regularly. Look for any of the symptoms described in Box 7-1—sores, small painless ulcers, warts, rashes, growths that may be felt but not seen; discharges that are other than normal color, consistency, or smell; and changes in function such as painful urination, abdominal pain, pelvic pressure, or bleeding between menstrual periods.

REDUCING PREGNANCY RISK.   One reduces the risk of pregnancy in a large variety of ways which grouped together are *methods of contraception* (*contra* = against; *ception* = conceiving). None are totally effective, but some are nearly so. Their effectiveness is again a problem in adjustment—how compulsive are you willing to be? We present these methods in roughly the order of their effectiveness in Box 7-3.

Explicit sexual behavior is one aspect of human sexuality. But more general behavior patterns are also important. How do we get to feel the way we do about ourselves as sexual beings? About the way that we relate to members of our own and the other sex? Let's now examine the roles that we play as males and females.

Gender Roles

sex role or gender role
Society's expected behavior patterns for individuals based on their biological sex.

In all cultures there are very clear expectations concerning how males should talk, act, and dress. The same is true for females. In Western cultures, as children, boys are traditionally expected to dress in long pants, roughhouse, and play with toy trucks and guns. Girls are expected to wear dresses, be gentle, play with dolls, and play house. As adults, Western males are expected to be logical, competitive, aggressive, domineering, and ambitious. On the other hand, females are expected to be sensitive, emotional, dependent, and talkative. These stereotypes are referred to as **sex roles** or **gender roles**—society's expected behavior patterns for individuals based on their biological sex.

Box 7-3

CONTRACEPTIVE METHODS

1. *The Intrauterine Device (IUD).* This is a device that can be semipermanently inserted in the uterus. Its mechanism of action is unknown but it probably changes the chemical balance in the uterus. It is inexpensive and can be easily checked. Given that it is already in place, it need not interrupt lovemaking. Plastic IUD's that can be inserted on a one-time basis are now available. There are several important side effects: Insertion may cause discomfort, there may be an increase in menstrual cramps and flow, the uterus may reject the IUD, IUD's require medical supervision, and they may increase the possibility of pelvic infection or aggravate an already present infection. The use of an IUD suggests a commitment to full sexual relations and this may inhibit their use by young, unmarried women. They are about 95 to 98 percent effective. They may fail if not checked before intercourse, and there is the occasional pregnancy with the IUD in place, for reasons as yet unknown (Chilman, 1983).

2. *The Minipill.* This is the pill of old with less hormone. It gives the most protection against pregnancy and its use does not interfere with lovemaking. It may also regulate menstruation and reduce menstrual cramps and flow. However, it does require initial medical supervision and a commitment by the female. There is some risk of blood-clotting problems especially in women over 35 and in heavy smokers. Prolonged use (greater than 5 years) is related to circulatory disease. It can fail for two reasons: Occasionally there is not enough hormone for some women, and—more frequently, an adjustment problem—the pills are not taken regularly (Chilman, 1983). The pill is greater than 95 percent effective (Payne & Hahn, 1989).

3. *The Condom.* This is a latex rubber sheath which fits over the erect penis. With its advent in the late nineteenth century, it became the first casually available birth control device. Today condoms are available in the pharmaceutical section of virtually any large grocery store in the United States as well as at pharmacies. Their advantages are their inexpensiveness, their availability (no prescription), lack of side effects, and their use in the prevention of STD's (see above). Typically, condoms have been the male's responsibility, although sexually active females may be changing this. Their disadvantages are that they may interrupt lovemaking to be put in place, they may decrease sensation for some men, and they require planning (that is, they have to be bought ahead of time). The only great risk to pregnancy is the failure to use them every time and the failure to use them properly. They are about 80 to 90 percent effective (Chilman, 1983; Payne & Hahn, 1989).

4. *The Diaphragm (with Jelly/Cream).* This is a latex device which fits over the neck of the cervix. It should be initially fitted by a gynecologist but thereafter requires no medical supervision. The jelly/cream used with it can be spermicidal and increase its effectiveness as well as provide additional lubrication during intercourse. Insertion can be interruptive of lovemaking, although that can be made part of foreplay (Chilman, 1983). Diaphragms can aggravate the bladder and may cause cystitis. There is also the occasional allergic reaction to jellies and creams. Diaphragms fail primarily through inattention—using too little jelly or cream, having a second intercourse without adding more jelly or cream, not being refitted after pregnancy or weight change, not using it every time, and not leaving it in place for 6 to 8 hours after intercourse. This method is about 80 to 90 percent effective (Payne & Hahn, 1989).

5. *Contraceptive Foams or Suppositories.* This

Sex Assignment

At birth an event almost as significant as the birth itself occurs: Someone on the birthing team says, "It's a boy" or "It's a girl." This sex assignment is based primarily on viewing the newborn's genitals. These and other labels (girl–boy; Joan–John;

method involves the vaginal insertion of commercially available spermicidal foams or suppositories just before intercourse. The method is inexpensive, no prescription is needed, and there are virtually no side effects. Use of foams or suppositories is highly effective if combined with the use of a condom. However, their use can interrupt lovemaking, can be messy, and can provide too much lubrication. Moreover, they must be used every time. Occasionally there is an allergic reaction by one or the other partner. This method fails moreso if the foam is inserted more than 30 minutes before intercourse. Foam or suppositories by themselves are about 75 to 80 percent effective. When used with a condom the combination is 95 to 99 percent effective (Chilman, 1983).

6. *Periodic Abstinence (the Rhythm Method).* As we discussed above, in this method the woman monitors her menstrual cycle and intercourse hypothetically takes place only during "safe" times. The method is complicated by the facts that many women's menstrual cycles are not all that regular and that sperm live for several days. This can mean considerable abstinence for a couple. Its advantages are that it costs nothing, involves no mechanical devices, and has no side effects. Its disadvantages are that it requires considerable self-adjustment not only in terms of abstinence but also in monitoring basal temperature daily, vaginal mucus (which changes during the cycle), and menstrual cycles. Moreover, it should be taught by a professional or experienced user. Its biggest failure is due to lack of self-control—an adjustment problem. Reportedly it can be as much as 70 to 80 percent effective but only when carefully practiced (Payne & Hahn, 1989).

7. *Sterilization.* This involves either the male or the female having surgery to preclude reproduction. Sterilization need not impair sexual performance. This is unusually effective but is usually not reversible. It provides maximum freedom during intercourse because there are no interruptions. There are risks of any surgery and this is a surgery. Sterilization is virtually 100 percent effective as a contraceptive method.

8. *Other Methods.* The male can withdraw prior to ejaculation. This is relatively ineffective (only 75 to 80 percent) because of mistiming, and because there are sperm in the male's lubrication fluid.

While woman are breast-feeding they do not ovulate, but they become fertile again before their periods resume, so breast-feeding is not a very effective indicator of infertility (maybe 60 percent).

9. *Ineffective Methods.* Regarding douching, Chilman (1983) says, "Sperm travel faster into the uterus than a woman can travel to her douche" (p. 267). And the force of the douche can actually push sperm into the uterus. Not good.

Some women apparently think that holding back—not having an orgasm—will preclude pregnancy. It won't. The position during intercourse is also irrelevant.

Finally, sperm are so intent about going about their business that even sperm deposited near the vaginal opening can impregnate a woman. Thus, it is possible to remain a virgin technically and still become pregnant.

Use this information for what it is—an overview. If you are making any decisions regarding contraception, it is a very good idea to seek some professional advice and to do some detailed study.

Adapted from Chilman, 1983; Payne & Hahn, 1989.

male–female) set the occasion for a great deal of differential treatment throughout life. That differential treatment starts right at the point of sex assignment, with the swaddling of females in pink blankets and males in blue, with naming, and with differential handling of each sex by their parents and others. Such differential treatment leads to the development of a gender identity and a gender role.

Gender-role behavior is learned very early in life. It is probably strengthened in play.

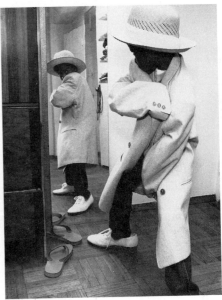

Gender-Role Socialization

gender identity
The sense of being male or female; the biological sex that one's behavior is most related to; an inference based on observations of one's behavior by oneself and by others.

In our society, children by approximately the age of three begin to acquire a sense of being male or female (Kohlberg & Ullian, 1974). This is referred to as **gender identity.** They also begin to learn the roles expected of them for their gender. The process begins with labels. An infant is called a boy or a girl. An infant may be dressed primarily in pink or in blue. Later, the young child may be expected to behave as little boys do (be aggressive, explore, be outgoing, play football, play with trucks, and weapons), or as little girls do (be passive, be introverted, play house, play with dolls). In our own society, by age six, girls and boys successfully identify which activities are expected of girls and boys (Weitzman, 1979).

Adults who teach children such things may not even be aware of what they are doing or of the long-term effects. Fathers may simply play more gently with their daughters than they do with their sons, or speak to the former more gently than to the latter (Weitzman, 1979). The entire process is called **gender-role socialization.** Such experiences, products of our social environment and culture, influence how we eventually behave with respect to who and what we think we are as boys and girls, women and men, fathers and mothers.

gender-role socialization
The differential reinforcement of social behavior that is characteristic of one sex only—for example, not crying by males.

As yet there is no clear agreement on how gender-role socialization happens. Some think it is solely a result of our biology (Gadpaille, 1972; Imperato-McGinley et al., 1979; MacLusky & Natfolin, 1981), while others think it is an interaction between biological and social factors (Diamond & Karlen, 1980).

In fitting with the adjustment model of this book, we believe that the gender-role socialization process involves an interaction between biological and social factors. Others treat you as a person based on how you look (your biology is involved here) and how you act (social factors are involved here). Parents and significant others reward their children for behaving in accordance with their sex assignment and reprimand them when they do not. Traditionally, in our society, boys are rewarded for playing aggressively, for being independent, and for not showing emotions. They are criticized if they do show emotions ("Stop crying Joey, you're not hurt!"), if they are passive and dependent, or if they engage in non–gender-typical activities. Girls, on the other hand, are rewarded for staying close to adults and their homes, for cooperating with one another in play and other activi-

Box 7-4

HERMAPHRODITES AND GENDER IDENTITY

Relevant to the development of gender identity is the work on hermaphrodites by John Money and his associates (1961, 1965, 1972). Hermaphrodites are very rare individuals born with all or part of the sexual and reproductive anatomy of both sexes. In such cases, determination of biological sex can be accomplished chromosomally, gonadally, or hormonally. These individuals, however, indicate they are happiest behaving as the "biological sex'" they were taught to be while growing up (Weitzman, 1979).

Biologically, the developing female and male embryo are essentially identical up to about six weeks of gestation (Money & Ehrhardt, 1972). After

that point and up until birth there is differentiation in biological development, which owes primarily to the presence or absence of a Y chromosome. The Y chromosome influences the development of the testes, producing testosterone, which in turn produces male genitalia. If at any time during the embryonic stage the production of testosterone by the testes is limited, or if the external reproductive organs are absent, the embryo will develop as a female (Sandler et al., 1980). Therefore, early sex differentiation is essentially genetic and biological. However, after birth, the gender identities of hermaphrodites suggest that much subsequent "sexual" development is *psychosocial*.

ties, and for relating to others emotionally. They may be especially encouraged to nurture other children. They are criticized if they behave aggressively ("Andrea, don't get your pretty dress all dirty!").

Children also learn through observation of their parents, relatives, and peers (Bandura, 1977). Noting that mommy puts on makeup in front of a mirror may lead to similar "dressing up" like adults by children of both sexes. Dressing up may be followed by positive attention from the adults who say how much the kids look like their parents. On the other hand, cross-sex dressing may be admonished. If imitated behavior leads to a reward, the children will be more likely to perform this behavior again under similar circumstances. If the behavior is not rewarded, it may be less likely to occur again.

Moreover, if a child sees a model rewarded for a particular behavior (for example, cigarette smoking), that behavior is more likely to be imitated than a behavior which is unrewarded or punished. Individuals are particularly likely to be imitated if they are perceived to be warm and dominant—that is, they are high-status individuals whose behaviors are frequently reinforced (Bandura, 1977). Think for a moment who the most warm and dominant adults were in your own youth. Do you exhibit any of their characteristic behavior?

Our culture communicates that our sex is important in life. If you are a large, athletically inclined male you may be able to play football in the National Football League or basketball in the National Basketball Association. You cannot play football or basketball in these leagues if you are a female—at least, not yet. In response to many implicit communications of this sort, children develop a readiness to classify social reality in terms of gender. In doing so they develop gender-related schemas. A schema is a way of imposing meaning on a portion of the world. Children (and later, we as adults) behave in the contexts of these gender-related schemas. As their gender identity develops, children's behavior lines up more and

Weight lifting, once a sport in which only men participated, now includes women. However, the gender-role issue is not dead. Judges cannot decide the winning criteria for the sport. Traditionalists want women to look smooth (as in the beauty pageant), others want them bulked up, with their muscles defined just like men.

more with what they see as appropriate for their sex. They reject ways that are not congruent with the way they expect their sex to respond (Bem, 1985; 1987). Males who have never seen another male wash the dinner dishes may feel funny doing so and may actually attempt to avoid the activity altogether. Females who have never thrown a football may feel funny doing so and may attempt to avoid the activity also.

Gender Norms

gender norms

A society's beliefs regarding sex-appropriate behavior.

Eventually we live up to **gender norms.** Gender norms are a society's beliefs, attitudes, and behavior toward what is sex-appropriate and sex-inappropriate for its citizens.

In our society, there have traditionally been two fundamental gender norms for women. One is the *motherhood mandate* (Russo, 1976), the idea that women's purpose is to have, to raise, and to nurture children (Bernard, 1974; Contratto, 1984; Hardin, 1974; Peck & Senderowitz, 1974). The other is the *marriage mandate*. Marriage has traditionally been the institution through which a female gains independence from her parents and her family (Doyle, 1985).

Men have traditionally been socialized to respond to four or five gender norms which include: antifeminism, success and status, self-reliance, aggression, and sexual prowess (Brannon, 1976; Doyle, 1989).

HAVE THESE NORMS CHANGED?   The large change in our society's thinking across the years about the (working) role of women suggests that traditional gender norms for women have changed. One major indicator of change in these norms is the proportion of women in the work force, which today is near 50 percent. The increasing numbers of women in business careers suggest the possible addition of a career norm for women. How much the addition of a career norm has modified marriage and motherhood norms for today's women is not clear; most college women now assume that they can combine a career and family (Christy, 1990).

Men's and women's attitudes about women having careers have changed. In 1938 only about 20 to 25 percent of people approved of a married woman working if she had a husband who could support her. In 1986, about 75 percent of people approved (Simon & Landis, 1989).

Men's gender norms also appear to be undergoing change, but it is not clear how many men these changes involve. The changes in men's behavior seem to be in response to the demands of women for change in all aspects of power sharing between the sexes. Astrachan (1986) suggests that only 5 to 10 percent of men genuinely support women's demands for independence and equality and that 35 percent of men are accepting for pragmatic reasons, for example, they are in a marriage where their spouse provides a share of the income for the partnership.

"NEW WOMEN." "New women" appear to want both careers and marriage. Moreover, they want equality between the sexes in all areas of life. They want equal pay for equal work, careers open to everyone independent of sex, equal educational opportunity, full sharing of household duties, and full sharing of parenting.

"NEW MEN." Where there are "new men," the newness is seen in the abandonment of some of the traditional norms. New men may be more sensitive, more capable of intimacy, more capable of commitment to a mate, friends, family, and community. They also have a vision of equality among women and men and an equality among men (Ehrenreich, 1984). The new man doesn't insist on being the dominant wage earner, is not always a slave to his job (although he is still competitive), believes that he is just as emotional as women are, expresses his feelings, and can discuss his problems and weaknesses (Astrachan, 1986).

Sexism

sexism

A negative attitude toward members of a given sex, and/or institutionalized discriminatory practices that place members of that sex in an inferior role.

Does gender-role socialization have any benefits? Myers (1986) suggests that it "serves to grease the social machinery." It makes it easier to deal with socially awkward moments, such as who opens a door and who enters a building first. Unfortunately, it also leads to **sexism**—the domination of one sex by another, economically and socially. Technically, sexism can apply to both sexes. In practice, however, it has primarily been women who have suffered. Until recently, men have monopolized powerful and prestigious positions in business, politics, governments, and religions within Western societies. Within the family in many societies, "Dad is the boss."

During the past 20 years, the women's movement in the United States has achieved considerable success in fighting the deeply rooted tradition of sexism. For example:

- In 1973, the U.S. Supreme Court outlawed sex-segregated classified advertisements for employment.
- In 1978, more women entered college than men for the first time in U.S. history (Rubin & McNeil, 1985).
- In 1981, Sandra Day O'Connor became the first female justice of the U.S. Supreme Court.
- A Gallup report in 1984 indicated that 63 percent of Americans supported the Equal Rights Amendment to the U.S. Constitution.
- In 1984, Geraldine Ferraro became the first woman nominated by a major political party to run for Vice-President of the United States.
- In 1984, 44 percent of the women entering college intended to pursue such traditionally male-dominated careers as law, business, medicine, and engineering—double the percentage of 1970.

Notwithstanding these changes, inequities still exist between men and women in the work force, at home, and in our nation's schools.

Sexism in School

Unfortunately, major areas where sexism still exists include our nation's schools and work places. The schools may be the biggest problem because that's where children spend their formative years. When girls start school, they are more ready to read than boys and more ready to compute; but when they leave school, boys are ahead of girls (Sadker & Sadker, 1985). These facts clearly imply preferential treatment for boys in schools. This problem is not as simple as that of sexism in our language (for example, the use of the masculine pronoun "he" as the generic case). Much of the sexism in our language has been corrected through consciousness-raising activities; today sexism in language is less a problem than it was even a few years ago. Yet something more serious is wrong in our schools.

Sadker and Sadker (1985), for example, have shown in a study that teachers interact with girls and boys in the classroom in a biased way, one that gives boys an advantage in the teaching/learning environment. Consider some of the following findings:

1. When teachers evaluated which students participated most in class, they tended to think girls participated far more than they really did. That is, the teachers didn't recognize the extent to which boys *over*participated, even when boys outtalked girls three to one (Sadker & Sadker, 1985)!

2. Teachers typically respond to students' answers to questions with either praise, mild criticism, neutrality ("Ummm, Yes"), or with revision prompts ("Well, that answer is correct as far as it goes, but can you tell me where. . . .?"). Sadker and Sadker found that teachers responded more often to boys with revision prompts than to girls, who tended to receive the neutral outcome. In fact, boys received more interactions with the teachers overall (Sadker et al., 1984). In essence, the boys got more instruction.

3. Boys also tend to get more attention from talking without permission. While teachers tolerate this from boys, they appear to criticize girls who talk without permission (Sadker & Sadker, 1985; Sadker et al., 1984).

Happily, these investigators were able to show that a few days of training of the teachers to recognize the inequities in their responses to students was sufficient to reduce this bias. But what of all the teachers who have not had such training? Or all the parents? Or all the employers?

This kind of study is important for us to know about because it affirms what we have said above: First, gender roles are largely acquired through operant, reflexive, and observational learning. Second, the learning is largely incidental; that is, adults are not consciously disposed, for the most part, to develop sexism in children and the children are unaware of what is happening to them. Clearly, this does not lessen the likelihood that sexism will result.

What can we do about it? We can talk about it at every opportunity, in order to increase others' awareness of sexism. We can consciously attempt to avoid sexist practices. And we can lobby politicians at all levels to pass the legislation that is needed. While we cannot predict what changing our traditional practices will mean for cultural survival in the long term, change toward equality of the sexes is consistent in the short term with Western principles of fairness and the goal of equal opportunity for all. Sexism is discussed further in Chapter 11.

Masculinity, Femininity, and Androgyny

When Joel was growing up he never saw his father wash the dishes. Several nights a week Joel's dad went to the corner tavern for a beer with the other men who were there. Joel's mom only occasionally went to the tavern; she was usually busy with homemaking. Joel and his dad never kissed and rarely embraced. In Marcia's family, on the other hand, her dad always helped her mother. Marcia feels it's only right that Joel share in the housework, especially since Marcia contributes half the funds to their household account. She also doesn't like it when Joel insists on going out with the guys without her. After all, she likes some of the same activities—having a beer, shooting some pool, joking around. While Joel recognizes some of this, he doesn't do anything about it.

masculinity

Observation that a person has empathy with the feelings of males and not the feelings of females.

femininity

Observation that a person has empathy with the feelings of females and not the feelings of males.

androgyny

Observation that a person has empathy with both the feelings of males and females.

gender typing

Observation that a male behaves primarily in a masculine way and/or a female behaves primarily in a feminine way.

cross-gender typing

Observation that a male behaves primarily in a feminine way and/or a female behaves in a masculine way.

Empathy with the feelings attributed primarily to one gender role and not the other has been labeled **masculinity** or **femininity,** while empathy with the feelings of both sexes has been labeled **androgyny.** One is **gender-typed** if one's feelings lie primarily with those stereotypical to one's sex. That is, one is masculine if one is male and identifies with the feelings and attitudes of men, and feminine if one is female and identifies with the attitudes and feelings of women. One is **cross-gender typed** if one identifies with the feelings and attitudes of the other sex. One's gender-role orientation can also be described as *traditional* (i.e., male-oriented) or *nontraditional* (i.e., person-oriented).

These feelings can be measured and summarized as a gender-role orientation, and the feelings are real! For example, males who are highly gender-typed will actively avoid behavior appropriate to the other sex (for example, picking up and cuddling a baby), and if they engage in such behavior they report feeling less comfortable about it than do androgynous individuals (Bem & Lenney, 1976).

Is it better to be masculine, feminine, or androgynous? Is this a sensible question? After all, we are what we are, right? Yes and no. In the early research on androgyny, androgynous individuals appeared more flexible, more ready to adjust, more fully in touch with individuals of both sexes (Bem, 1977), and more loving (Coleman & Ganong, 1985). They appeared more ready to draw on the strengths of both masculine and feminine behavior without being limited by the rigidity of one extreme or the other. But other research did not support the notion that androgyny is more strongly associated with psychological well being (Taylor & Hall, 1982).

An alternative approach is to do away with the concepts of androgyny, masculinity, and femininity by developing gender neutral terms to talk about human characteristics. Rather than masculinity or femininity, we might talk about *instrumentality* (showing skills and providing services) and *expressiveness* (showing emotions and empathy). With this approach, the notion of androgyny disappears because its definition depends on the existence of the concepts of masculinity and femininity (Deaux, 1984). Were we to do this, individuals would be rated on how instrumental and expressive they are, not whether they are masculine, feminine, or androgynous. As parents, you may want to teach your children of either sex both instrumental and expressive behaviors.

Cultural changes also have a hand in gender-role socialization. Currently both partners of most couples must work outside the home to provide for their families; this fact means some reshaping of roles in the home. Many young couples are now also much more aware of sexism, given the consciousness-raising activities of the American women's movement. And tomorrow's generation may very well be different in their gender-role development from today's.

Gender Identity Problems

If you are genetically a male and yet you feel strongly like a female and not at all like a male, or if you are genetically a female yet you feel strongly like a male and not at all like a female, you may have a gender identity problem. Gender identity problems affect more males than females (Money, 1986). Very difficult gender identity problems are seen where individuals have some of the biological characteristics of both sexes (that is, they are hermaphrodites).

Other forms of gender identity problems exist as well. Take the young man portrayed in the recent movie, *Dead Poets' Society.* The son of a very militaristic father, he could not become the image of his father and instead developed into a sensitive artist, with disastrous consequences.

TRANSSEXUALISM. Transsexualism is usually evidence of a gender identity problem. Transsexuals are individuals who seek to become members of the other sex because that is where their gender identity lies. They have a strong sense of being

Box 7-5

GENDER-ROLE ORIENTATION

Read the following statements and circle one of the preceding pairs of letters that describes your response. The letters mean: SA = Strongly agree; MA = Moderately agree; AS = Agree slightly more than disagree; DS = Disagree slightly more than agree; MD = Moderate disagree; SD = Strongly disagree.

Scoring for this inventory can be found below.

SA MA AS DS MD SD 　1. It is more important for a wife to help her husband's career than to have a career herself.

SA MA AS DS MD SD 　2. The idea of young girls participating in Little League baseball competition is ridiculous.

SA MA AS DS MD SD 　3. The relative amounts of time and energy devoted to a career on the one hand, and to home and family on the other hand, should be determined by one's personal desires and interests rather than by one's sex.

SA MA AS DS MD SD 　4. It is more important for a woman to keep her figure and dress becomingly than it is for a man.

SA MA AS DS MD SD 　5. The old saying that "a woman's place is in the home" is still basically true and should remain true.

SA MA AS DS MD SD 　6. A woman should refrain from being too competitive with men and keep her peace rather than show a man he is wrong.

SA MA AS DS MD SD 　7. A woman whose job involves contact with the public, for example, a salesperson or teacher, should not continue to work when she is noticeably pregnant.

SA MA AS DS MD SD 　8. The husband should take primary responsibility for major family decisions, such as the purchase of a home or car.

SA MA AS DS MD SD 　9. In groups that have both male and female members, it is appropriate that top leadership positions be held by males.

SA MA AS DS MD SD 10. Unless it is economically necessary, married women who have school-aged children should not work outside the home.

SA MA AS DS MD SD 11. If there are two candidates for a job, one a man and the other a woman, and the woman is slightly better qualified, the job should nevertheless go to the man because he is likely to have a family to support.

SA MA AS DS MD SD 12. Marriage is a partnership in which the wife and husband should share the economic responsibility of supporting the family.

SA MA AS DS MD SD 13. A woman should not accept a career promotion if it would require her family to move and her husband to find another job.

SA MA AS DS MD SD 14. A married woman who chooses not to have children because she prefers to pursue her career should not feel guilty.

SA MA AS DS MD SD 15. Unless it is economically necessary, married women who have preschool-age children should not work outside the home.

SA MA AS DS MD SD 16. It is generally better to have a man at the head of a department composed of both men and women employees.

SA MA AS DS MD SD 17. A husband should not feel uncomfortable if his wife earns a larger salary than he does.

SA MA AS DS MD SD 18. It is all right for women to hold local political offices.

in the wrong-sexed body, a feeling that usually begins in childhood. Such individuals often live all or part of the time as members of the other sex. They may even seek sex-change surgery.

Sex-change surgery is neither casually sought nor casually administered. Currently, any individual seriously considering sex-change surgery is given a two-year,

SA MA AS DS MD SD   19. A male student and a female student are equally qualified for a certain scholarship; it should be awarded to the male student on the grounds the he has greater "career potential."

SA MA AS DS MD SD   20. The use of profane or obscene language by a woman is no more objectionable than the same usage by a man.

SA MA AS DS MD SD   21. It is certainly acceptable for boys, as well as girls, to play with dolls.

SA MA AS DS MD SD   22. Girls should primarily be counseled to enter "feminine" vocations such as nursing, public school teaching, library science, and the like.

SA MA AS DS MD SD   23. Women should not feel inhibited about competing in any form of athletics.

SA MA AS DS MD SD   24. Parents should encourage just as much independence in their daughters as in their sons.

SA MA AS DS MD SD   25. Women should be able to compete with men for jobs that have traditionally belonged to men, such as telephone lineman.

SA MA AS DS MD SD   26. It is OK for a wife to retain her maiden name if she wants to.

SA MA AS DS MD SD   27. There is no reason why a woman should not be President of the United States.

SA MA AS DS MD SD   28. Career education for boys should have higher priority with parents and teachers than career education for girls.

SA MA AS DS MD SD   29. Even though a wife works outside the home, the husband should be the main breadwinner and the wife should have the responsibility for running the household.

SA MA AS DS MD SD   30. In elementary school, girls should wear dresses rather than slacks to school.

SA MA AS DS MD SD   31. It is acceptable for a woman to become a member of the church clergy.

SA MA AS DS MD SD   32. It is acceptable for women to hold important elected political offices in state and national government.

SA MA AS DS MD SD   33. It is not a good idea for a husband to stay home and care for the children while his wife is employed full-time outside the home.

SA MA AS DS MD SD   34. The only reason girls need career education is that they may not marry or remain married.

SA MA AS DS MD SD   35. There is no particular reason why a man should always offer his seat to a woman who is standing on a crowded bus.

SA MA AS DS MD SD   36. Men should be able to compete with women for jobs that have traditionally belonged to women, such as telephone operator.

Adapted from Brogan & Kutner, 1976.

SCORING THE GENDER-ROLE ORIENTATION SURVEY

Score the gender-role orientation survey as follows: For Items 1, 2, 4, 5, 6, 7, 8, 9, 10, 11, 13, 15, 16, 19, 22, 28, 29, 30, 33, and 34, score SA = 1; MA = 2; AS = 3; DS = 4; MD = 5; and SD = 6. For items 3, 12, 14, 17, 18, 20, 21, 23, 24, 25, 26, 27, 31, 32, 35, and 36, score SA = 6; MA = 5; AS = 4; DS = 3; MD = 2; SD = 1. Add your scores up to get a total across all 36 items. The result will be a score between 36 and 216. The closer your score is to 36, the more traditional is your gender-role orientation; the closer your score is to 216 the more nontraditional your gender-role orientation is.

real-life test of living as an individual of the other sex, including appropriate hormone treatment. Of major importance to sex-change surgery is to determine if people who desire a sex-change operation have other, severe psychological problems. Such individuals may be confused about who they are (and a lot of other things), but they may not have a gender identity problem.

Dr. Richard Raskin was an eye surgeon with a gender identity problem. He sought and received sex-change surgery and changed his name to René Richards. René Richards competed for a while on the women's pro tennis circuit. There were objections that René had an advantage over the other women players, although the quality of her tennis play never really bore this out.

Erotica and Gender Roles

From earliest times we have captured sexual behavior in whatever media were available—statues, illustrations, paintings, print, photographs, movies, and today the ubiquitous videotape. Today, the trade in sexually stimulating materials is a billion-dollar business.

We'll call materials that are sexually stimulating to both sexes *erotica* (Byrne & Kelley, 1984), without regard to the value judgments necessary to subclass them as pornography. We'll call *pornographic* those erotic materials that degrade the status of either sex (cf. Longino, 1980) or that lead to socially inappropriate behavior.

Many men love to watch, read, or listen to erotica. Some women do, too. More women than men do not like erotica. What's the problem with it? This appears to depend very much on your point of view.

Why include such a discussion in this section on gender roles? First, by definition erotica is sexually stimulating to both sexes, whether it be in the form of print, audio recording, or picture (Byrne & Kelley, 1984). Second, there may be effects of exposure other than sexual stimulation that we should know about. Third, much of today's erotica places women in a subordinate role and is, therefore, pornographic. In most pornographic films, the plot portrays them as instantly available sexually to men, and suggests that they are interested in virtually any kind of sexual activity. A typical scene may portray a woman as reluctant to engage in sex, then being coerced to engage in sex, then finally, enjoying the act(s). This type of fantasy appeals to many men, the major consumers. It's obvious why it may not

With the advent of films such as *Deep Throat* and *The Devil in Miss Jones,* pornography became big business in the United States. Erotica has been around for all of recorded history, however, and it occurs in many forms.

appeal to women, particularly women who don't share the "feelings" of the women in the films, given the unreality of these feelings for many women and the false gender-role stereotype that is presented about women. At least one study indicates that men who are highly gender-typed are more likely to find such depictions arousing (Check & Malamuth, 1983).

What are the effects of erotic stimuli on individuals? By definition, of course, such stimuli are sexually arousing, that is, they start the sexual response cycle. Do they do more than that?

Benefits of Erotica

Those who believe that the experience of erotica is beneficial usually point to its use in helping individuals with sexual problems. Such materials might be used by a sex therapist, for example, to demonstrate some therapeutic procedure, or by a normal couple to heighten sexual stimulation.

catharsis hypothesis
The idea that viewing or imagining sexual activities that are not available in one's environment will satiate one's desires to perform such activities.

There is also the **catharsis hypothesis**—that is, that erotic stimulation allows potentially inappropriate sexual behavior to occur harmlessly, for example, in fantasy-induced masturbation. There is little supportive evidence for this hypothesis.

A U.S. Commission on Obscenity and Pornography, asked to study the effects of erotica by then President Lyndon Johnson, concluded that the effects were minimal, short-lived, and were not related to sex offenses (U.S. Commission on Obscenity and Pornography, 1970; but see Cline, 1970). A more sweeping test of the societal effects of erotica took place in Denmark in 1967 and 1969. The Danes removed criminal penalties for the production and distribution of erotica, with some surprising results: The overall incidence of reported sex crimes in Denmark decreased and continued to decrease. Was this liberalization a far-sighted move?

Undesirable Effects of Erotica

Since the late 1960s the content of erotica has become more violent. For example, the number of rape scenes in American paperback sex novels doubled from 1968 to 1974 (Smith, 1976) and the victim—almost always a woman—was usually portrayed as enjoying the act. This is one example of what is called a **rape myth.** The conclusions of the first U.S. Commission on Obscenity and Pornography were made in the absence of studies which found that sex and violence were associated (Malamuth, 1984; Malamuth & Donnerstein, 1982). Further, the outcomes of the Danish experiment have been challenged on a more specific level. While the incidence of many sex crimes decreased—exhibitionism, peeping, statutory rape,

rape myth
False verbal behavior (mostly male) about why rape occurs and what happens during it; for example, "When she says no, she means yes."

Eroticism has long been a theme of some great artists. Picasso explored it frequently, as in this reproduction.

verbal indecency, and child molesting, as examples—the levels of rape in Denmark either stabilized or increased (Baron & Strauss, 1984). Moreover, the violence in erotica has almost totally been directed toward women, a fact that feminists find illuminating in regards to the value that our culture places on women (Brownmiller, 1975; Steinem, 1980). Should we be concerned about the exposure of young people to the combined messages of violence and erotica? What are the facts?

Sex and Violence Together

Is it possible that our society produces "compulsive masculinity" in men (see Toby, 1966) by rewarding them for aggressive behavior toward women, by teaching them to consider women as sex objects, by teaching them to dominate women, and by teaching them to believe in rape myths? This would certainly be extreme gender-role behavior.

First, we're a very violent society. The media reflect this, and some would say, promote it. We know in general that violence observed on TV or in the movies tends to make violence more attractive to the viewer (Bandura, 1965; Bandura et al., 1963a, 1963b; Leyens et al., 1975; Liebert & Baron, 1972; Liebert & Schwartzberg, 1977; Parke et al., 1977). However, there is no unequivocal evidence that such portrayed violence will lead to violence by the viewer, under *all* circumstances, for *all* viewers. In fact, most of us have watched thousands of violent scenes on television and in the movies and have not thereafter been violent ourselves. Most of us know that Rambo is not real. Most of us know that Rambo-like activities in our local shopping mall will land us in jail.

Yet the evidence about the effects of pairing sex and violence is disconcerting at best for anyone who considers humankind basically good. For example, in a series of studies, men who were shown movies with and without aggressive content became more aggressive, as inferred from their questionnaire responses and self-reports, if the movie contained violence. They became even more aggressive if the victim of the violence was a woman and if the movies contained sexual content (Donnerstein, 1984; Malamuth & Donnerstein, 1982). The men were particularly likely to be more aggressive if the event portrayed the involuntary arousal of the woman and if there was any suggestion that the experience was reluctantly enjoyed—a rape myth again.

Donnerstein (1984), however, did not find similar outcomes where explicitly sexual but nonviolent materials were shown. These materials may be sexually arousing but they do not promote violence. In other words, the culprit that promotes aggression toward women may be primarily the portrayed violence. Such aggression occurs whether there is sex or not, yet it certainly appears to be heightened by any juxtaposition with sex.

SUMMARY

■ With sufficient hormones our primary sexual characteristics begin observable development during the embryonic stage of gestation. Our prenatal sexual development appears to be largely biological, that is, genetic and hormonal. Our primary sexual characteristics permit our global identification as males and females, set our different sexual and reproductive processes in motion, and provide a background for our eventual socialization as girls and boys and women and men.

■ Sexual processes are observed in the sexual response cycle, which has four stages. There are different variations of these stages possible for males and females, particularly the fact that females can experience repeated orgasms without the intervention of a refractory period.

■ There are many varieties of human sexual adjustment. While sexual energy is usually channeled toward members of the other sex, in every society there are homosexuals whose sexual energy is channeled toward members of the same sex. There are no proven causes of this sexual adjustment.

■ Another sexual adjustment is the more liberal reporting of premarital sex by college students who have been surveyed over the last 20 years. However, with the advent of serious sexually transmitted diseases such as human immunodeficiency virus (HIV), the liberal sexual trends of the 1970s appear to be waning.

■ There are fairly standard sexual problems for both sexes. For males typical problems are erectile insufficiency and premature ejaculation while for females typical problems are vaginismus and orgasmic dysfunctions. There are effective sex therapies for all of these problems when it has been determined that they are not organically caused.

■ There are a variety of ways to make sex safer from disease and from pregnancy—if the latter is not desired—that typically involve contraceptive methods, restriction of the number of partners, and abstinence.

■ Sexual behavior involves more than just sex. It also involves how we feel about ourselves and how we act as males and females. These behaviors, collectively called gender roles, appear to be due to gender-role socialization processes. In turn gender-role socialization processes are based on our biology and social factors such as rewards and punishments and observational learning of gender-related behavior. Our current ways of gender socialization appear to lead to sexism in all aspects of life, and they may occasionally lead to gender identity problems.

■ An outcome of our current gender-role socialization practices may be the juxtaposition of violence and erotica. This combination appears to affect men's aggressive behavior toward women especially if the men are highly gender-typed.

Box 7-6

SELF-ADJUSTMENT FOR STUDENTS:
Analyzing Causes

By now, you have focused on some behavior that you want to increase, decrease, or get to occur in the correct circumstances; you've made a public commitment to the change; and you're prepared to record the occurrence of the behavior. Well and good! But now what?

Behavior Analysis

Now you need to engage in some analysis of the behavior. When, where, and why does it occur? Actually, if you figure out when and where a behavior occurs, you'll often be able to make an informed guess about why it occurs. Let's see how to do this.

Construct yourself an ABC sheet. Or simply record the same facts on a 3 × 5 card that you can carry in your pocket.

A = Antecedent. An antecedent is a stimulus, setting, or time that appears just before the behavior you are counting. In this section of your sheet, you need to record what was happening just before you responded (or failed to respond).

Let's hypothesize that you're trying to deal with binge snacking. You find yourself snacking without being aware that you are doing it. While you are snacking, try to recapture what was happen-

Continued

ing just before you began the snack. Record an estimate of the time, where the snack was taking place, what day it was, who was present, what you were doing (watching football on television), what anyone said that seems relevant ("Care for a Twinkie?"), how you felt (strong craving), when you last ate, what the snack food was, what else was going on (Twinkie commercial on television), what you said to yourself ("I'll just have one"), and so on.

Antecedent stimuli are often the triggers or cues for the occurrence of behavior that we want to change. As such they may be *proximal causes,* that is, causes that are near in space and time to the response we want to self-adjust. If you faithfully record antecedents you may eventually see patterns emerge that relate to the occurrence of your behavior. For example, perhaps you have the urge to snack only at 5:30 P.M. when you come home from school or work. No urges on the weekends. Or perhaps you snack only when there are certain foods in your home (Twinkies!).

But it is also important to understand your state, that is, how you feel, at the time of your behavior. Sometimes how you feel may be a *distal cause,* that is, a cause lurking in the background. With respect to Twinkies other distal causes may be your propensity to be reinforced by foods that are sweet (perhaps inherited) and your history of experience with sweet foods. Perhaps you never snack if you have a well-balanced meal at lunchtime because you don't have cravings for food later on. In this case, feeling sated or not having food cravings could be thought of as the absence of the distal cause for enjoying a Twinkie. Distal causes are often hard to do something about, particularly if they are buried in the past.

Your learning history is also sort of a distal cause of current behavior, but not one about which you can do much except to be aware. Maybe it was your mom who always used to bring home a package of Twinkies when she went shopping. Perhaps it was an evening ritual in your past to sit in front of the television and have a snack of some kind. However, knowing about distal causes may assist in determining how ingrained your problem behavior is.

B = Behavior. We won't deal with this anymore here, because we have done so earlier. By now you will have this nicely defined so that you can record its occurrence validly and reliably.

C = Consequence. A second source of events to analyze is what happens after you behave (or fail to behave). As you know from Chapter 3, consequences for behavior such as rewards, punishments, and their absences can be powerful changers of behavior. Consequences for behavior are clearly proximal causes of behavior. What happened when you ate the Twinkie? Did you enjoy its taste or its texture? Did you feel more relaxed? Did you feel more guilty? Did something enjoyable happen on the television (your team scored)? Did your significant other join you in the snack? Consequences for your behavior also need to be faithfully recorded on your ABC sheet to determine what the behavior's relation is to them.

WHY ANALYZE CAUSES?

Having analyzed some causes of your behavior, you'll find that the exercise leads you to potential adjustment strategies. If you snack only when there are Twinkies in the house, then one strategy would be to never have them in the home. If eating while watching a particular television program is problematic then you could watch another program or, failing that, you would at least be aware that the possibility that you are going to snack is high and you can plan to deal with that possibility accordingly.

In sum, before you attempt to self-adjust a behavior, find out as much as you can about what happens immediately before and after the behavior occurs. Do this for sufficient time (at least a week or so in most cases) to see whether there are commonalities of time, place, people, rewards, punishers, and so forth. Only then will you be in a position to consider strategies to manage the behavior.

MEMORY BOOSTER

■ IMPORTANT PEOPLE

You should know who these persons are and why they are important:

Alfred Kinsey

William Masters

Virginia Johnson

John Money

■ IMPORTANT TERMS

Be prepared to define the following terms (located in the margins of this chapter). Where appropriate, be prepared to describe examples.

Primary Sexual Characteristics	Primary Orgasmic Dysfunction
Secondary Sexual Characteristics	Secondary Orgasmic Dysfunction
Ovaries	Orgasmic Timing
Uterus	Fellatio
Corpus Cavernosum	Cunnilingus
Corpus Spongiosum	Sex Role or Gender Role
Sexual Response Cycle	Gender Identity
Refractory Period	Gender-Role Socialization
Homosexuality	Sexism
Primary Homosexual	Masculinity
Secondary Homosexual	Androgyny
Bisexual	Femininity
Sensate Focus	Gender-Typing
Seman's Technique	Cross-Gender Typing
Squeeze Technique	Gender-Role Orientation
Nondemanding Intromission	Rape Myth
Vaginismus	Gender Norms
Orgasmic Dysfunction	

■ QUESTIONS FROM IMPORTANT IDEAS IN THIS CHAPTER

1. Describe the symptoms of the three most common STDs among college students.
2. Describe variations in the human sexual response cycle for females and males.
3. Briefly describe four explanations of homosexuality, and show how each may be incorrect.
4. Describe how premature ejaculation and erectile insufficiency in males are treated.
5. State how the conditions of vaginismus and of primary and secondary orgasmic dysfunction in females are treated.
6. What is a gender identity, and how do we acquire one? Explain with examples.

7. Describe three ways that teachers have treated boys and girls differently in the classroom.

8. What is the difference between erotica and pornography?

9. State the general and specific outcomes of the legalization of the production of pornographic material in Denmark.

chapter

8

FRIENDSHIPS, DATING, AND LOVING

After reading this chapter, you should be able to:

- Discuss the effects of a number of variables which relate to attraction.
- Explain what it means to be an "opener."
- Describe intimacy and suggest how it develops.
- Describe methods to decrease the fear of dating.
- Describe ways to increase your chances that your date will like you.
- Discuss two different kinds of love.

Jill and Jack have been dating for about three months. "Hey," said Jill while reading the newspaper, "professional wrestling's in town on Saturday night. Wanna go?"

"Are you serious?"

"I'll go if you want to," replied Jill.

"How about that new film at the Bijou that we haven't seen? It has a good rating. Whattya say?"

"I guess that'd be better than wrestling," said Jill. "Let's go."

In their relationship, Jack usually suggests some weekend activities to Jill by Thursday. This week, he has not done so. Jill may be indirectly calling his attention to this. She may be unaware why she suggested professional wrestling; in fact, if questioned she would probably say she proposed it "as a lark." Jack may likewise not notice this reminder. But, if we look at their past encounters together we might see that, indeed, by Thursday Jack has usually asked Jill to go out. What we see in this **dyadic** interaction is evidence of a relationship.

How do relationships develop? Why are we initially attracted to others? How and why do we become acquainted with others in general or best friends with someone in particular? Is how we look important? Is what we talk about important? These are some of the most interesting issues in the psychology of adjustment because they affect all of us most of our lives. In this chapter we examine such questions as: How do relationships among humans begin? How does relationship development relate to personal adjustment? Are first impressions important? When in a relationship should one disclose information about oneself? What are some of the characteristics of intimate behavior, and how can one overcome a fear of intimacy?

But we're ahead of ourselves. If Jill and Jack are already dating, how did they start? What made them want to keep on dating each other? If they've been dating steadily for several months what does this mean? Are they in love?

Dating patterns have changed over the years, in a number of ways, and they're still changing. In this chapter, we also discuss various aspects of dating patterns in North America. We then offer some guidelines for those of you who may be unhappy with your current dating activity. More specifically, we focus on steps for getting a date, overcoming fear of dating, and what to do on a date—at least initially.

Discussions of dating lead naturally into discussions of love, so we have a good look at love, too. We try to answer what love is and how people can know if they are in love. We discuss how long the various forms of love can last. When we finish, some of the mystery will be gone, but not the delicious feelings that come with it. Are you ready for this?

dyad
A pair of individuals, usually in a socially significant relationship.

The Development of Relationships

relationship
A special circumstance between people such as that brought about by familiarity with the other person.

A **relationship** is "a series of interactions between two individuals known to each other . . . where the interaction is affected by past interactions or is likely to influence future ones" (Hinde, 1981; p. 2). Individuals who have a relationship bring with them their histories with each other and with similar others. Like Jill, they expect the other in the relationship to act in ways particular to their past interactions together (Chelune et al., 1984).

What Starts a Friendship?

Relationships proceed from casual to intimate. They do so in part because of societal expectations about the way relationships develop (Gergen & Gergen, 1981). That is, we expect relationships to become more intimate with time, and, at least in part, they may do so because we expect them to. But they also develop for other reasons such as propinquity, exposure, first impressions, and self-disclosure.

propinquity effect
Dynamic that makes relationships more likely to develop between individuals if they are close to each other in space and time, such as either living nearby or working at the same establishment.

PROPINQUITY.   The term **propinquity** basically means closeness or nearness in space and/or in time. Simply being nearby may relate to individuals becoming friends (Gergen & Gergen, 1981; Johnson, 1989). Consider the following example.

The house of the Jackson family faces the house of the Newton family on the corner of a street. Glen Jackson was out cutting his lawn when Don Newton came out to trim his shrubs. It's only natural that they stopped to chat for a while. Glen's wife, Susan, who came out to check the mail, joined the conversation. While Don's wife, Emily, was making some lemonade for Don, she noticed the three of them chatting on the front lawn and brought enough glasses and lemonade for everyone. "Say," suggested Don, "why don't you guys come over for a few drinks after dinner?"

"Sounds good to me," replied Glen. "How 'bout you, Hon?"

"Love to," replied Susan.

Mike Johnson's house is down the street. It faces a church and is shrubbed heavily on both sides. When Mike cuts his grass, no one really sees him. Mike and his wife haven't made too many friends in the neighborhood.

Some evidence of the propinquity effect. Neighbors whose yards adjoin one another are more likely to become friends with each other than with those who live farther away.

The friendship formed between the Jacksons and the Newtons illustrates the propinquity effect. For the Johnsons—no propinquity and fewer friends. In general, the evidence indicates that:

- We are much more likely to know and be friends with the people who live next door than we are with those who live even one residence farther away.
- People are more likely to make friends if their houses face one another.
- People whose houses face away from other houses have about half as many friends as those in houses facing other houses.
- These findings are not unique to separate family dwellings. Similar outcomes occur in apartment buildings. Friendships are much more likely between individuals living close to one another in apartment housing as well (Festinger, 1951; Festinger et al., 1950).

The propinquity effect even holds generally for those relationships that eventually end in marriage. You're much more likely to marry someone who lives nearer to you than farther away. Just-married couples were interviewed in Columbus, Ohio, and it was found that more than half resided within 16 city blocks of one another at the time of application for their license. About the same proportion resided the same distance away when they first met and began courting (Clarke, 1952), proving that this finding did not result from couples moving closer together after they began courting.

The propinquity effect may in large part be mediated by other events that are more difficult to measure. Perhaps, for example, proximity results from similar interests and values (Johnson, 1989). Perhaps people with similar personal, leisure, and business interests are attracted to each other because of their similarities. Nevertheless, the propinquity effect has implications for personal adjustment. For example, if you wish to meet someone who is a skier, it would be better to reside in Vail, Park City, Banff, or Sun Valley than somewhere else. At the very least, the probability of meeting someone and thereafter developing a friendship is raised considerably by propinquity.

MERE EXPOSURE. "I wonder where the hosiery section is?" thought Mary to herself as she wandered through the department store. "I really do need some new nylons." When she arrived at the hosiery section, she approached one of the clerks. "Do you carry 'Vek' nylons?" she asked.

"What kind was that?"

"Vek."

"I'm sorry," replied the clerk, "but I've never heard of that particular brand. Are you sure you have the correct name?"

In fact, Mary does have the correct name but it is indeed a brand the clerk has never heard of. Mary participated in an experiment on *attraction* (Becknell et al., 1963). Attraction describes the pull that people feel toward one another in a developing relationship. What has this to do with 'Vek' nylons? Mary and some other women were shown slides of landscapes, advertisements, and nonsense syllables. The nonsense syllable is usually a three-letter combination of consonant, vowel, and consonant (called CVCs), such as "gif" or "roq." It is used in psychological research when the researchers want to employ a languagelike event against which to measure a person's reaction, but where the event should not carry the multiple meanings of our regular language. The landscape and advertising slides Mary saw were dummies. Interspersed among them were four nonsense syllables which appeared 1, 4, 7, or 10 times. Afterward, the women were individually invited to choose between packages of nylon stockings; the "brand" names of these stockings were the nonsense syllables they had been exposed to. Asked which "brand" they preferred, the women chose the packages bearing the nonsense syllables they had been most frequently exposed to (Becknell et al., 1963). "Vek" was the most common.

The same effect occurs with exposure to people. Simply being exposed to them may be sufficient to begin attraction. Zajonc found that people shown photographs of strangers rate more positively those photographs that occur the most frequently in the sample they are observing (Moreland & Zajonc, 1982; Zajonc, 1968). In fact, simple exposure to many different kinds of events produces the same effect (Gergen & Gergen, 1981).

First Impressions

Simon, who attends a southwestern college, is doing his weekly grocery shopping. He's nattily attired in pressed (and faded) Levis, deck shoes (no socks), and a rugby shirt. He's also freshly showered and shaved. While feeling tomatoes for ripeness, he turns and bumps into Sue. Sue is in his botany class at the college, but she usually hangs out with other people and she sits pretty far away from Simon—it's a large class. She has just had her hair done. She's wearing fairly snug Levis, a blouse, and sandals.

"Excuse me," said Simon. "I didn't know somebody was behind me."

"That's ok, I guess I snuck up on you."

"Say, don't you take botany at the college?"

"Yes," replied Sue. "I'm in the 10:30 section."

"I thought I recognized you. See you next class."

This looks like an ordinary interaction between two people who have never met. But is the dialogue all that went on? Probably not. Let's tune in on Simon and Sue's thoughts while they walk away from each other.

Simon (while still selecting tomatoes): "Definitely a dynamite lady. Just the right height. What a bod! And that tan . . . I wonder where she got it? I wonder if she'd go out with me? . . ."

Sue (on her way to the checkout stand): "Don't remember seeing *him* in botany. I'll have to look a little closer next class. He's sort of cute. Wonder what kind of after shave he was wearing? Maybe he'd be interested in getting together. Hmmm . . . How could that be arranged? . . ."

These two people meeting for the first time have formed a first impression of each other. She thinks he's cute. He thinks she's got a "great bod." First impressions can be very important to the possibility of a relationship developing between two persons. **Impressions** are attitudes or beliefs that are formed about another, perhaps as a result of a first encounter. A number of variables that have been studied are known to influence both first impressions and subsequent attraction to someone. Let's look at several.

PHYSICAL APPEARANCE.   Does how we look have anything to do with attraction? (Do *Playboy* and *Playgirl* sell millions of magazines each month?) Common sense dictates that physical appearance is related to attraction, yet there remains the difficulty of defining what kind of physical appearances produce attraction. That is, what is beauty?

Beauty appears to be relative to culture. In some cultures thin is in. In others thin may denote malnourishment. Within cultures, beauty may be relative to the age, social history, socioeconomic status, and other attributes of the beholder (Adams, 1982). Take a look at the latest fashion models and designer clothes in *Vogue* magazine. Do they appeal to you or do they seem extreme? Would you wear those clothes or have your hair done in similar styles? At least in part your response will be due to who you are, where you live, how old you are—that is, your own social and biological history. If you live in New York City and attend functions

---

impressions

Attitudes or beliefs that are formed about another person upon encounter with them or with information about them.

Beauty is in the eye of the beholder. The individuals portrayed here are considered beautiful by members of their own cultures.

where high fashion is common, the clothing, the hairstyles, and the makeup in *Vogue* may be just right. If you live in a rural area, these clothes may be wildly impractical in your life, and may appear quite extreme. People who differ greatly from the norm in your life may also not be attractive to you (Adams, 1982). Thus, what may physically attract some may not attract others.

PHYSICAL APPEARANCE AND ATTRACTION.   What is known about physical appearance and attraction? We know that individuals considered to be good looking receive more favorable treatment than those who are not: Attractive people are thought to be of better character, more self-confident, more kind, more poised, more flexible, better employed, more sociable, more outgoing, and more likable (Adams, 1982). They're also thought to have more desirable personality characteristics, such as being more curious, more pleasure seeking, and more outspoken (Miller, 1970). They win credit for good deeds that others have worked harder for (Adams, 1982; Huston & Levinger, 1978). In other words, we tend to stereotype those who are "handsome" or "beautiful." Dion et al. (1972) had male and female college students rate photographs of people to discover whether detailed impressions could be formed with very few cues. People in the photos who were rated most attractive were also rated more highly on personality, occupational status, marital competence, social and professional happiness, and total happiness. Finally, they were seen as more likely to be married.

Being beautiful, however, may not be without its drawbacks. It is perceived, for example, that the physically attractive may be egocentric, snobbish, and vain (Dermer & Thiel, 1975). In a courtroom, attractive people may be treated more leniently when found guilty, but not if they are perceived as having used their beauty in the commission of the crime (Adams, 1982). Punishment is more harsh in the latter case.

Of course, many of us would put up with what seem to be minor irritations in order to be physically attractive. Huge industries such as those that produce cosmetics or fads such as tanning salons exist as validation of this statement. Clearly, physical attractiveness is a factor in first impressions, in getting breaks in life in general, and in school and the work place in particular—although being too beautiful may work against women in certain jobs (Adams, 1982).

Would you like to increase your attractiveness? Here's one way: Wear higher status clothing (Hill et al., 1987). College students rated other-sex models more attractive who wore clothing associated with upper rather than lower socioeconomic status, so long as physique was not emphasized. Enhancing your physique by wearing tighter and more revealing clothing may enhance your attractiveness as a sexual partner, but it appears to decrease your attractiveness as a marital partner (Hill et al., 1987).

MATCHING UP. Doug was standing by the fountain in the college student center when Lori approached. "What a lady," thought Doug to himself. "Homecoming queen, drives her own Corvette, straight-A student . . . incredible. Maybe if I offered to hold the fountain for her? Nah, don't be a jerk," he reprimanded himself as he walked away from the fountain, "You're not in her league."

Doug considers himself plain. He's a little overweight and doesn't pay much attention to how he dresses. At one level, he knows he would love to get to know Lori and to go out with her. At another level, he feels that they would be mismatched. "No way she'd even consider going out with someone like me," he thought to himself.

Are you likely to be attracted to someone more handsome than you are? It's possible. The very attractive, however, are often thought unattainable by those of us who are less attractive. **Matching** is the process by which we tend to be attracted to people who are about as attractive as we ourselves are; the parties on both sides see themselves as well matched (Berscheid & Walster, 1969). It's not clear that this is a conscious process, although that seems to be part of rationalizations such as that of Doug's, above.

You may be thinking, "So where does that leave me? I'm not about to enter any beauty contests." Or perhaps you think you're too tall, or too short, or too heavy. Maybe you think your muscles are too puny, or maybe you worry about having small breasts? What to do? First, understand that we're all the same on this score. We all worry about aspects of ourselves, from our bodies to our behavior. Second, do what you can to help yourself. Lift weights a little (see Chapter 6). Control your eating (see Chapter 6). Work on your complexion. Have your hair styled. Wear higher status clothing. Third, don't despair. Continue working on yourself until you're happy with who you are. But be realistic. When you've done what you can, you'll be more relaxed—and this relaxed state of yours will make you more attractive. Fourth, think about your strengths. What are they? Write them down. Review them often and make the most of them. Finally, remember that there are others out there similar in attractiveness to you with whom you would be well-matched.

matching
Dynamic in which people seek relationships (or relationships are more likely to develop) between and among people who have similar personal characteristics and interests.

Self-Disclosure

Fred and Mary have been dating for several weeks. They've engaged in heavy petting, but they haven't had sexual intercourse. Although they haven't really talked about it, it's obvious that Mary is pushing toward sexual intercourse and Fred is resisting. One night, in a moment of passion and in a partial state of undress, Mary whispers, "I *really* want to make love to you."

"We'd better not."

"Why not? We have really strong feelings for each other."

"I'm afraid to," replied Fred. "If you get pregnant, I'd be really upset if you had an abortion. And, with a child you'd probably never finish your degree. Besides, all that stuff about AIDS and herpes is really beginning to get to me. And I'm not the kind of person who has sex casually. Sex is a big commitment to me."

"But I really don't want to see anyone else anymore, except you," said Mary. "I want to be with you all the time. I want to have you beside me at night, I want to wake up with you each morning. You know what I'm saying. I want to move in with you."

"Let's talk about it," replied Fred.

You can put whatever soap opera ending you'd like to the above dialogue; the point is that Mary opened up to Fred about her feelings. And Fred disclosed back to Mary. Such disclosures can have very powerful effects on relationship development.

self-disclosure

Telling about your own behavior to another person, such as your likes and dislikes; self-disclosure statements begin with "I."

Self-disclosure is the process by which one person lets another know about himself or herself, usually in terms of statements that begin with "I" (Derlega, 1984; 1988). When in a relationship should you disclose personal information? Friends disclose information about themselves that they would not disclose to strangers. And a measure of the depth of a relationship might be the amount and/or kind of information disclosed (see below, on intimacy). Precisely why people disclose to one another is not known, but there are a number of speculative reasons that seem plausible (Derlega, 1984; 1988). Self-disclosure may acknowledge the interdependence that is developing in a relationship between two individuals. It can reduce the ambiguity of a new relationship by focusing on the ambitions of the parties involved. It may also occur to gain feedback about oneself. Revealing opinions may be offered between two people, and agreement tends to confirm one's desires, self-concept, and self-worth.

TIMING AND CONTENT OF DISCLOSURE.   Do you seem more attractive if you disclose early in a relationship? Will "telling all" enhance your attractiveness to the person to whom you disclose? Jones and Gordon (1972) evaluated the timing and content of disclosure as well as the responsibility of the discloser for the type of news disclosed. College women rated an "interview" between a "student" and his "college adviser" in which the student disclosed why he had to leave his prep school early. Different groups of subjects rated different disclosures (good news and bad news; responsible and not responsible; early disclosure versus late disclosure). In the good news disclosure, the student was leaving to go to Europe; in the bad news disclosure, he was expelled or left because of his parents' divorce. He was obviously not responsible for his parents' divorce, but he was responsible for the prep school expulsion—he was caught cheating. He had either earned a scholarship to go to Europe (good news, responsible) or had inherited money (good news, not responsible). Finally, he disclosed one of the foregoing combinations of events either early or late in the interview. Table 8-1 summarizes the results.

You can see from the table that timing and content of self-disclosure can affect the impressions you make on someone. The same will also affect impressions made on you.

TABLE 8-1
THE CONTENT AND TIMING OF SELF-DISCLOSURE *Adapted from Jones & Gordon 1972.*

1. Good fortune disclosure is more attractive than bad fortune disclosure.
2. Good fortune disclosure is more attractive when disclosed late.
3. Good fortune disclosure is more attractive when disclosed late, especially if the good fortune was unearned.
4. Bad fortune disclosure is more attractive when disclosed early if the discloser was responsible for it.
5. Bad fortune disclosure is more attractive when disclosed late if the discloser was not responsible for it.

DISCLOSURE IN YOUR OWN LIFE.   How should you handle disclosure in your own life? It's probably wiser to be a reluctant discloser than an eager one. However, that does not mean not disclosing at all, in which case people may be less likely to be friendly and less attracted to you. Too much self-protectiveness could stifle a budding relationship. Clearly, if someone discloses to you, you have the opportunity to disclose back to them. Reciprocal disclosure is more appropriate than not reciprocating (Strassberg et al., 1988). This type of reciprocation may be important to the development of a relationship (Cozby, 1972; Jourard, 1959; Jourard & Landsman, 1960). A gentle rule of thumb is to disclose at the same level and on the same subject matter as the person who has just disclosed to you. If you are in a discussion with someone where you feel like disclosing, do so. But keep the content fairly mild (that is, not socially shocking) and don't necessarily start disclosing too early in a relationship. But, do disclose. Lastly, don't get so caught up in disclosing that you overdo it. You may be thought maladjusted (Cozby, 1972).

Self-disclosure is related to liking and this is the reason for a positive stance on it. In fact, more is disclosed to people who are more liked than those who are less liked (Worthy et al., 1969). And those who disclose neither too much nor too little may be liked better than those who disclose either not enough or too much (Cozby, 1972). However, the implied happy medium is difficult to specify with any precision.

"OPENERS" AND SELF-DISCLOSURE.   There are some people to whom others naturally bare their innermost secrets. People to whom others are more likely to disclose have been dubbed **openers** (Miller et al., 1983; Purvis et al., 1984; Shaffer et al., 1990). People who score high as openers also tend to be thought of as attractive. Miller and others (1983) have developed a scale which measures how much of an opener a person is (see Table 8-2). People who are shy score low as openers. People who are sociable score high. How did you score? If you are a high opener, your average score would probably be greater than 2.5. If you're average as an opener, your average score will be around 2.0. If you're a low opener, your average score will probably be less than 2.0.

Are there some specific behaviors that you can learn to improve your score as an opener? Yes, indeed! Individuals who promote self-disclosure use an identifiable set of behaviors to do so (Purvis et al., 1984): They are more likely to interject comments in disclosure if they are men; affix their partner with their gaze if they are women; and they appear more interested, comfortable, and attentive regardless of their gender.

To summarize, research reviewed on the development of relationships thus far suggests the following guidelines for establishing relationships:

- Be where people are (propinquity).
- "Expose yourself" to others.
- Look as good as you can, and feel good about yourself.

openers
People whose behavior makes it more likely that others will disclose to them. They usually are very attentive to the person disclosing.

TABLE 8-2
THE OPENER SCALE *Adapted from Miller et al., 1983.*

	Almost Always	Sometimes	Almost Never
For each statement, circle the number that best applies to you.			
People frequently tell me about themselves.	4	2	0
I've been told that I'm a good listener.	4	2	0
I'm very accepting of others.	4	2	0
People trust me with their secrets.	4	2	0
I easily get people to "open up."	4	2	0
People feel relaxed around me.	4	2	0
I enjoy listening to people.	4	2	0
I'm sympathetic to people's problems.	4	2	0
I encourage people to tell me how they are feeling.	4	2	0
I can keep people talking about themselves.	4	2	0

TOTAL (sum of circled numbers) = ____

$$\text{Average Score} = \frac{\text{Total}}{10} = \frac{}{10} =$$

- Disclose things about yourself at about the rate you are disclosed to.
- Practice behavior characteristic of the opener.

Intimacy

intimacy

Interactive behavior between or among people which is unique in terms of its characteristics; it is usually private and involves a strong relationship such as love.

After a relationship is established, its further development may lead to intimacy. How does a relationship become intimate?

Characteristics of Intimate Behavior

Intimacy describes a constellation of behavior emitted by two (or more) people. Most of these behaviors also occur in nonintimate interactions, but less often. People who are intimate disclose aspects of their own behaviors that they would

Being close and face-to-face are two factors that contribute to intimacy.

not disclose to those with whom they are not intimate; listen carefully to those who are disclosing to them; care deeply about one another; and feel good being close (Hatfield, 1984). Moreover, their interactions are frequent, diverse, and face-to-face; they may have a unique communication system, synchronized goals and behavior, and substantial influence on each other's lives; and they may see their separate interests as being tied into the relationship in such a way as to be essential to its goodness (Levinger & Snoek, 1972). They also have knowledge of the innermost being of one another, mutuality, interdependence, trust, commitment, and caring qualities (Chelune et al.,1984).

Let's take conversation as one example of intimate behavior. What might mark the disclosures in conversations as more or less intimate? And how might conversation become more intimate across time? Early conversations between female strangers are characterized by their relative absence of disclosures of private facts by either party and by the relative absence of disclosures of feelings and opinions (Hornstein & Truesdell, 1988). As the parties become acquaintances, disclosures of feelings and opinions occur more frequently, but disclosures of private facts do not occur more frequently. Finally, as the parties become friends, they disclose both more private facts and personal feelings and opinions (Hornstein & Truesdell, 1988).

Developing Intimacy

Good human relations turn on intimacy. Have you never been intimate with someone? It's a social skill you *can* develop. What behaviors are involved? A whole constellation, some of which we have alluded to above. In addition, intimate behavior tends to be subtle behavior. Winks are more intimate as a form of communication than a slap on the back. Quiet conversation is more intimate than boisterous shouting. Intimacy also relates to physical space. For the most part, the closer that two or more individuals are, and the more private the setting, the more likely they are to be intimate. Sharing a table for two for dinner in a quiet restaurant is more intimate than a gathering in a German beer hall at Octoberfest.

While intimate behavior can be developed like any other skill, the process may be long. To begin with you can carefully study the material in this chapter. **Behavioral rehearsal** is also a good way to practice the skills of behaving intimately. Actual rehearsal of skills may be the most important aspect of overcoming social skills deficits (Galassi & Galassi, 1979). It is well known that these are difficult to strengthen on your own. If doing so seems impossible to you, professional help can be sought. On the other hand, this book's adjustment model provides an alternative way of proceeding.

behavioral rehearsal

The practicing of a particular way of behaving (for example, assertively) prior to the situation in which the behavior will eventually be tried.

TOUCHING. Eight times a day the average man touches someone. For the average woman, it's 12 touches. After analyzing more than 3000 individuals over a 4-year period, Jones and Yarbrough (1985) found that people liked touching and that most people would like to do more of it and get more of it. Woman are more comfortable with touch than men (Fromme et al., 1989).

Touching is important in intimacy in part because it may produce a much more potent emotional response than words. When you speak to someone, you can either deny what you said or claim that you were misinterpreted. But that's almost impossible to do with a touch. It's very difficult for you to touch another and then argue that no meaning was intended.

Jones and Yarbrough contend that there are 17 meanings of touches. Of these, 5 deal with communicating positive emotions and can be very important for intimacy. These include:

Box 8-1

INTIMACY AND HELPING

Are we more liable to help people with whom we are more intimate? Does this apply in the fairly extreme case of interacting with strangers? Let's see.

Goldman and Fordyce (1983) enlisted a graduate student who stopped men and women on a midwestern college campus. The 160 people were divided into several groups, each of which was exposed to a different combination of conditions. The student asked if the person who had stopped would take two or three minutes to react to some statements regarding college athletics. If the person agreed, the student asked a series of opinion questions. These were asked in two explicit ways: either the student employed a monotone when talking—previously practiced and perfected—or he talked in a warm, natural, expressive tone. He also did two other things systematically. He either made eye contact with the person while asking questions and listening to answers, or he did not. And, just before delivering the final question, when he said, "Okay, this will be the last statement," he either touched the person simultaneously on the forearm, or he did not. Then, as the final act, he "accidentally" dropped 30 questionnaires that he had been carrying under a clipboard.

The investigators wanted to see whether people with whom the student had acted intimately—those whom he touched, or with whom he made eye contact, or with whom he had used an expressive voice—would be more likely to pick up the "accidentally" dropped questionnaires.

The outcome showed no sex differences. More people of both sexes were likely to help if they had been spoken to warmly—about 60 percent versus 40 percent. And more were likely to help if the student touched them and/or made eye contact than if he hadn't done either.

But most importantly, there were subtle interactions between two of these variables—eye contact and touching. The most helping occurred only if the student either made eye contact *or* touched, but not both; it was almost as though eye contact and touch together were too much for such a casual encounter. However, absence of both touch and eye contact were less intimate than the situation would tolerate. Possibly there is some sort of happy medium for intimacy in a particular situation, a sort of equilibrium (Argyle & Dean, 1965).

We should observe that to our knowledge these results have not been replicated. They may be very specific both to the locale in which the experiment took place and to the character of the student who performed the encounters, to mention just two possible variables. Nevertheless, there may be a moral here. "All is not what it seems in the casual encounter on a college campus."

- *The support touch,* such as holding hands or putting your arm around someone's shoulder when they are distressed and need to be comforted.
- *The appreciation touch,* which is usually accompanied by an expression of gratitude for something that another person has done.
- *The inclusion touch,* indicating togetherness or closeness, such as when people are sitting together and their knees are touching for several minutes.
- *The affection touch,* such as touching a mate on the arm or back, which does not necessarily have a sexual connotation.
- *The sexual touch,* which can involve several areas of the body.

While people like touching, research such as that described in Box 8-1 indicates that touching with strangers must be done with caution.

personal space

That area around us that others cannot enter without us feeling discomfort.

WHEN CAN YOU BE CLOSE? In certain situations the usual prohibitions regarding personal space may be in abeyance. **Personal space** is that area around us that others cannot enter without us feeling discomfort (Hayduk, 1978, 1983; Mishra, 1983). Parties, singles bars, and dances are obvious places where one can be physically closer to others than ordinarily is the norm. Where it is acceptable to be physically close, the skills necessary to behaving appropriately in these environments may be important. If you want to hold a person close at a dance, then you had better be somewhat skilled at dancing. A particular behavioral repertoire—to be able to dance—provides an entree. However, even with the repertoire the entree may be insufficient. Other circumstances may militate against success. Personal space may be more easily entered if one is smiling, rather than frowning. Your request for a dance may be more acceptable if you are well-groomed and dressed appropriately (see above on impressions).

There are some locales (subways, elevators, streets) that necessitate physical closeness because of extraneous circumstances, but psychologically speaking, personal space is maintained in these locales. People tolerate the close physical proximity only because of their mutual need to get somewhere. They are not more likely to be intimate in these situations. In fact, the barriers are up! People don't talk freely; they avoid eye contact; they ignore verbal interactions. In all ways there is no intimacy.

Presumably, one purpose of social gatherings is to allow social behavior to occur. While you would not expect to behave socially with strangers on the street, you can expect to behave socially with a stranger at a party. At a party if you see a stranger who looks interesting, then eye contact, a smile, and a warm, "Hello! My name is . . ." are quite acceptable. In various situations look for the openness of people whom you meet. You might do a rough sample in various environments by seeing how many make eye contact. You will probably note that very few make eye contact on the street in a major American city, whereas more may do so in a small community. Some environments may be perceived as more safe than others and eye contact may be more likely therein. How about your campus? Is it an example of a relatively safe locale?

Before you become intimate with someone you have to know him or her pretty well. How can you get to know someone that well? Propinquity in terms of where you live, work, and play can certainly help to set the occasion for the beginning of a relationship; so can exposure and self-disclosure. Alone, however, these strategies may be insufficient to demonstrate your interest in someone. So what's the next step? In the United States, that step is dating.

Dating

When Do People Start?

free dating

Dating that is unrestricted in societal terms; the participants are able to ask one another for a date without fear of societal sanction.

That depends. In the United States they start in their teens. Elsewhere, they may not start at all. That's right, **free dating** began as an American phenomenon (Duvall & Miller, 1985). In many other cultures, relationships between prospective couples may still be formally arranged by parents and/or community elders. To preclude informal relationships from beginning, adolescents in other cultures may be closely supervised by their elders when in contact with the other sex, or even socially isolated from the other sex during adolescence. In fact, even in the United States dating is a relatively recent phenomenon. It began with college students during the 1920s and 1930s and spread downward thereafter to the junior high school student. Inventions (automobile, telephone), urbanization, and industrialization probably contributed to the rise of dating (Duvall & Miller, 1985). The automobile and telephone contributed strongly to additional personal freedom, and urbanization and industrialization brought greater numbers of young people together than ever before. Dating patterns are still evolving (Miller & Gordon, 1986). The "traditional" date wherein the male asks the female, picks her up at her residence at a prearranged time, pays for the evening, and returns her at yet another prearranged time is being supplemented by other kinds of dating. More casual get-togethers are now the rule for some teenagers (Murstein, 1980).

Getting a Date

Some people do not date nearly as much as they would like to. The suggestions in this section are directed primarily at such persons.

SELECTING SOMEONE TO ASK.   Do you remember the concept of propinquity from earlier in this chapter? It implies closeness or nearness in space and/or time. Besides a factor contributing to the development of friendships, it also contributes to whom you date.

A majority of college students meet their eventual dates through friends, at parties, at work, or in class (Knox & Wilson, 1981). But maybe your life is structured in such a way that you do not meet many others who are potential candidates for a date. What do you do then? Some people have turned to dating services.

Dating services attempt to match people from their "data banks" with one another. There is excellent reason to believe they are not very successful. The problem is that we all have so many requirements for the people we want to date that it isn't easy to find another who meets them. In fact, to satisfy only certain minimum requirements—a human of the other sex, who is neither too short nor too tall, who lives in the same locale, who is about the same age, and who perhaps is of the same race, religion, socioeconomic class, and educational level—it may take a data bank of over 1 million people to find someone like that. No computer service has such a data bank (Hatfield & Walster, 1978). In essence, a date through one of these services may be little different from a blind date. You are more likely to find a person with many of the qualities that interest you in your daily environment.

ASKING.   It may sound glib to say all you have to do to get a date is ask, but there is an essential kernel of truth here.

John, a student in range science, is just back from six weeks away from the campus on a project in the field. He's unshaven and grubby, and anyone downwind can smell him from a hundred yards away. As he brings his Land Rover to a halt in front of the Range Science Building, he sees an incredible vision of loveliness coming down the steps. After six weeks' deprivation of the other sex, and forgetting for a moment how he looks and smells, he jumps from his vehicle and blurts out, "You look fantastic. Can I take you out to dinner tonight?" The young woman who's aghast that such an animal would have the audacity to speak to her, says, "Beat it, creep, or I'll call Security," and hurries away.

Well, maybe you have to do a *little* more than just ask. First, it would obviously have helped if the individual whom John asked on the date was known to him, and he to her. If you don't know a person and you're driven to ask him or her, you need an opening line. Both sexes agree that cute, flippant opening lines are less desirable than inoffensive direct opening lines (Kleinke et al., 1986). But the best rule still is to confine your requests to someone you know and who knows you. In turn this implies another rule. One needs to know people to ask. We'll assume that this is not a primary problem and that you have enough friends so that selecting a date is possible.

Traditionally in Western society, men have asked women for dates. The women's movement, however, is beginning to change that. In recent surveys, most men—even men with traditional gender-role attitudes—indicated that they would respond positively if a woman they wanted to date asked them out (Muehlenhard &

Miller, 1988). So whether you're a man or woman, if you want to date a particular person, ask.

HOW TO ASK.   You don't want to end up as John did. So what to do? Practice, practice, practice. If you are unpracticed you may make errors. **Indirect asking** is probably better than making your request sound like a demand.

Table 8-3 illustrates some ways of asking for a date. Note that the correct ways involve the conditional mood (could, would, might, should) rather than the imperative (must, will).

Let's examine some of the obvious problems with the incorrect examples in Table 8-3. In the first incorrect example, the language employed suggests that the potential date is an afterthought. The asker states only his or her own feelings and leaves little room for the potential date to express any opinion other than a yes or no, and we would probably guess a no. Second, the asker doesn't specify a date or time. This request, in essence, requires a much larger commitment from the potential date. The question, "Whaddya think?" is so open ended that the most appropriate reply might be, "About what?"

In the second example, the phrasing of the question suggests to Jeannie that she probably doesn't want to go out with the asker. The third request suffers from being too broad. An equally broad reply might be, "Yeah, I am." While a day is specified, neither a time nor an activity is. In the fourth example the phrasing, "if you don't have anything better to do," makes Marnie sound as though she doesn't have much to offer.

HOW TO GET OTHERS TO ASK YOU.   Getting dates is a problem for many people, but especially for women (Klaus et al., 1977). If you are a woman, and if you are reluctant to ask a man for a date, it's important to learn ways to communicate that you are available and would accept an invitation. Muehlenhard and colleagues (1986) studied different verbal and nonverbal cues that women may use to convey interest in dating. The effectiveness of such behaviors was rated by college men who viewed videotapes of women engaging in them. Examples of verbal behaviors that received high ratings involved the woman complimenting the man, asking the man questions about himself, and making it clear that she had noticed him in the past. Examples of nonverbal behaviors that received high ratings involved the woman looking at the man almost constantly, smiling almost constantly, standing

indirect asking

Phrasing a question (such as asking for a date) in such a way as to make a "yes" response most likely; usually involves providing a context for the questions.

TABLE 8-3
INCORRECT AND CORRECT WAYS OF ASKING FOR A DATE

Incorrect

1. "Hi, Jeannie. I'd like to see that show that's playing at the Orpheum. Whaddya think?"
2. "Hi, Jeannie. I don't suppose you want to go out Saturday night?"
3. "Hey, Joe, this is Marnie. Are you doing anything Saturday?"
4. "Hi, Joe, this is Marnie. My sorority is having a dance this Saturday night. Would you like to come as my date, if you don't have anything better to do?"

Correct

1. "Say, Jeannie, I've got some tickets for a show on Saturday night. I was hoping, if you weren't busy, you might like to see the show with me?" (Pause for response.) If positive, then ask about options: "Would you like to go to the early show or the late one? I thought maybe we could get a bite to eat afterward, how does that sound to you?" If positive: "Shall I pick you up at 7:30?" If negative, be polite: "Gee, that's too bad. Well, maybe some other time then. Would you like me to call again?"
2. "Hi, Joe? This is Marnie. Yeah, I'm fine. Hey, my sorority is having a dance this Saturday night. It'll be pretty informal, we're having it at the house. I was wondering if you'd be my date for that?"

close (about 18 inches) rather than farther away (either 4 or 7 feet), and touching the man while laughing.

GROUP DATES.   It may be that in your circle of friends, dating is rather rare. Instead one may go on **group dates.** The dynamics of such groups can produce the friendly relations that result in more relaxed meetings between the sexes. In a group date, everyone agrees to a common activity that all members of the group are similarly interested in; for instance, everyone goes to a football game together. At such activities you will likely encounter opportunities to ask one of the group on an individual date. Such times usually occur when the group is together for a particular activity, for example, studying.

Fear of Dating

A fear of dating may stem from any number of problems people may have in social relationships. Problems might include starting and continuing conversation with a date, being a good listener, giving and receiving compliments, giving and receiving affection, dealing with sex, expressing personal likes and dislikes to the partner, finding out about the partner's likes and dislikes, dealing with criticism, apologizing for gaffes, and maintaining relationships (Spence, 1983). One of the biggest problems for both sexes, however, is asking for dates (McFall & Dodge, 1982).

Your first step in dealing with dating fear should be some self-assessment. You may want to review some of the strategies described in Chapters 1 and 2 toward assessing problems of adjustment. It may be that your difficulties stem from *perceived social inadequacies.* Perceived inadequacies run the gamut from lack of self-confidence in general to specific problems, for instance, not being able to dance or converse well. You may need to improve proficiency in such areas as a way of reducing these fears and changing your self-image. Suppose, for example, your fear of dating stems largely from perceived inadequacies in starting and maintaining a conversation. To deal with such a situation, you might use shaping (see Chapter 3). The first step would be to create an opportunity to talk with a person of the other sex on a topic in which you have much in common, such as talking with a classmate about coursework. You could then progress to other topics such as movies, personal philosophies, politics, and so on.

In some cases, fear of dating may be strong enough that it is impossible for an individual to engage in initial shaping steps. A strategy that may be effective in such cases is behavioral rehearsal. Recall that with this technique, you rehearse playing a particular role. For example, when you're by yourself, imagine approaching a person whom you know and in whom you have an interest. Imagine that you are going to initiate conversation. Then practice responses that involve various aspects of the probable conversation. Talk out loud while watching yourself in a mirror. Behavioral rehearsal can help decrease your initial fears and help give you confidence to approach the person whom you'd like to date.

In some cases, fear of approaching a member of the other sex may stem from **negative self-talk.** Do you recall Doug? Doug was standing by the water fountain in the campus student center when Lori, the homecoming queen (super-popular, super-smart, super-lovely, and so on), approached. Doug thought of operating the fountain for Lori or saying something to her, but his negative self-talk stopped him ("Nah, don't be a jerk; you're not in her league"). To determine if this might be a part of your problem, keep track of what you think and say to yourself when in the vicinity of the person whom you would like to approach for a date. If you detect negative self-talk, then write out specific positive **coping self-statements** to counteract the negative self-talk. Doug, for example, could think to himself when he next encounters a similar situation, "Smile, be polite. You're not being offensive; Doug-boy; you're showing common courtesy that most people would appreciate."

---

group dates

Social occasions attended by an approximately equal number of males and females, for the purpose of enjoying a particular activity and the social relationships it permits.

negative self-talk

Talking to oneself about one's own behavior in a derogatory way.

coping self-statements

Self-talk or statements that you can say to yourself to counteract irrational statements or problem thinking.

If fear of dating is quite strong, then you may want to consider a formal program of self-desensitization. As indicated in Chapter 15, it would require making up a formal hierarchy of anxiety-provoking situations and using relaxation procedures to work your way through the hierarchy. Professional help might be sought for this.

Effective Dating Skills

Most of you already know what behavior is expected on a date. When asked to list the content and sequence of actions on a date, both sexes agree on the parties' roles (Rose & Frieze, 1989). These roles suggest that women are more concerned with appearance, conversation, and the control of sexuality, while men are more concerned with planning, paying for, and orchestrating the date (Rose & Frieze, 1989). In other words, traditional gender roles prevail.

GETTING TO KNOW YOU.   In the words of the famous song, dates are mainly about "getting to know you" (your date) . Who is this person you are with? What does he or she enjoy? If the dating relationship is to develop, it's time for self-disclosure. You look for things you both have in common, at first as agreements such as about current events, later, deeper insights about lifestyles and important philosophical issues (for example, religion, birth control). Presumably, if you have both agreed to go on the activity that is the occasion for the first date, you have at least that activity as a common interest! There may also be sexual interest by both parties.

reciprocal reinforcement
Reinforcing the behavior of those who reinforce your behavior.

BEING LIKED BY YOUR DATE.   What can you do to help your date like you? Byrne (1971) provided considerable documentation for the principle of **reciprocal reinforcement** in interpersonal relations. In general terms, this principle implies that people like you to the extent that your behavior is rewarding to them. Being liked is an important first step to romantic relationships, to being loved, and to satisfying sexual relationships—in short, to a quality of life that is indeed fulfilling. You may be thinking, "I'm me. I am what I am. If people don't like me for what I am, there's nothing I can do about it." Wrong. Others will like you to the extent that you are associated with various rewarding experiences for them. (And conversely, they may dislike you according to the extent that you are associated with punitive experiences for them.) In fact, Miller and Siegel (1972) argued that you will be loved by a person if you become a **generalized reinforcer** for him or her. What that implies is that someone will love you if you provide a variety of rewards for that person in a variety of contexts.

generalized reinforcer
A stimulus that has the power to reinforce a response independently of a specific (biological) state of deprivation; money and social attention are good examples of such stimuli.

"Hey, wait a minute," you say, "I'm just looking for some advice on dating, not love, at least not yet." And you're right. We're getting ahead of ourselves. But let's consider the principle of reciprocal reinforcement as it applies to dating. If others like you, they're more apt to have fun on a date with you. If they're more apt to have fun, then you're more apt to have fun. If you both have fun, you'll get to know each other better, and the date will be successful. Perhaps more important for your current point of view, you'll acquire increasingly positive dating skills. Let's examine various ways in which your behavior can be rewarding for your date.

1. *Practice being a good listener.* Most people find it rewarding if someone is interested in what they have to say.
2. *Be an active listener.* When people say things or express opinions, paraphrase what they say. A useful phrase is, "You seem to be saying that. . . ." Paraphrasing indicates that you value what others are saying. Abruptly changing the topic of conversation indicates something quite different.
3. *Watch for body language.* Facial expressions and slight movements often communicate that the other person is nervous, upset, happy, or is experiencing other emotions, independent of what they actually say. When you sense feelings from

An activity that is mutually rewarding is a good dating activity

body language

Facial expressions, body postures, and movements that communicate emotions and attitudes.

closed-ended question

A question that is likely to evoke a very brief reply, such as a yes or no.

open-ended question

A question that is likely to evoke a lengthy reply; one that stimulates further discussion.

someone's **body language,** let that person know. You might say something such as, "I sense that you're feeling. . . ." If you are responsive to his or her feelings, it will enhance your status as a sensitive person.

4. *Ask open-ended questions.* "Do you have a computer?" is a **closed-ended question.** It can be answered yes or no. The question "What do you think about people having microcomputers in their homes?" is an **open-ended question.** Open-ended questions are provocative of further discourse. They give the other person the opportunity to disclose.

5. *Give sincere approval.* Sincere approval is always appreciated. Insincere approval is often detected. It's an act, and it will be treated accordingly. Also, remember about touching. Touching or other positive body language (smile, nod, eye contact) can assist in the acceptance of your sincerity.

6. *Self-monitor unrewarding habits.* The foregoing behaviors can make you rewarding to your date. On the other hand, some behaviors can have the opposite effect. Lack of eye contact during conversation or frequent shifting of your eyes during conversation is unrewarding to many people. Nervous habits such as fiddling with your glasses, frequent frowning, or verbal redundancies ("eh," "you know," and so on) can also be unpleasant. You may be unaware of various unpleasant habits that you show. A fruitful exercise is to ask a friend to keep track of the frequency with which you show various nervous habits during a conversation. You can then target them for change.

Breaking Up: Is It Hard to Do?

What keeps a dating relationship together? Some togetherness relates to commitment. If the couple has equal involvement in the relationship, if they've been dating for a long time, if they are dating exclusively, if they think they are in love, and if they visualize their relationship as culminating in marriage, all of these variables predict staying together (Hill et al., 1976). Those involved in a dating relationship also perceive other-sex individuals as less physically and sexually attractive, helping to maintain the dating relationship they are in (Simpson et al., 1990). It may also help relationship maintenance if those in the relationship perceive that there are relatively few other members of the other sex on their campus for them to date (Jemmott et al., 1989).

However, many long-term dating relationships don't end in marriage. The parties may break up the relationship, with or without mutual consent. Loss of interest is the main reason given for breaking up among college students (Hill et al., 1976), although other factors such as the perceived transitoriness of the relationship, control external to the relationship, and the instability of the relationship itself also contribute to the dissolution of a dating relationship (Hortascu & Karanci,

---

Box 8-2

STEADY DATING AND SEXUAL RELATIONSHIPS: ARE THEY RELATED?

There is pretty clear evidence that dating patterns relate to sexual permissiveness (for example, Miller et al., 1986). In a sample of 836 New Mexico and Utah high school students gathered in 1983, those who answered that they were dating steadily in the ninth grade were more likely to have engaged in sexual intercourse than those who had never dated in the ninth grade (Table 8-4). A similar finding occurred when these students reported on their current dating status. Those who were engaged to be married were most likely to have engaged in sexual intercourse (overall about 65 percent), while those who were not currently dating were least likely to have engaged in sexual intercourse (overall about 20 percent). Students who dated early, and those who dated steadily or who were engaged (that is, one partner exclusively), also had the most permissive attitudes toward full sexual relations.

TABLE 8-4
PERCENT OF HIGH SCHOOL SCHOOL STUDENTS WHO HAD SEXUAL INTERCOURSE, BY NINTH-GRADE DATING STATUS[a]

Ninth-Grade Dating Status	*Male*	*Female*
Never Dated	15.8	18.3
Occasionally Dated	51.9	34.5
Several Partners	57.9	55.6
Mostly One Partner	62.5	38.5
Dated One Steadily	70.0	63.6

[a] *The question was "Which of the items listed below best describes your dating behavior in the ninth grade?"*

1987). Individuals who are close to their former partners, who have dated their former partners for a long time, and who believe that they cannot easily find an alternative partner are most distressed upon relationship breakup (Simpson, 1987).

Dating relationships dissolve much more easily than marital relationships, given the latter's greater complexity (Cupach & Metts, 1986). Interestingly, breaking up by college couples seems to occur most often at the academic breaks in the year, for instance, graduation or term break. Does this suggest that such premarital relationships contain a lower degree of commitment than marriage?

As we indicated earlier in this chapter, there are many reasons for dating. Regardless of your initial reasons, an inevitable outcome of dating for many people is the development of friendship and love. An important component of fulfillment in life is the experience of a loving relationship. It is to that topic that we now turn.

Love

Love is funny, or it's sad,
Or it's quiet, or it's mad,
It's a good thing, or it's bad,
But beautiful . . .

Love is tearful, or it's gay,
It's a problem, or it's play,
It's a headache either way,
But beautiful . . .

J. Burke & J. Van Heusen, "But Beautiful"

The above lyric from an old movie song is only one of thousands that we could have chosen to introduce this section. More has been written about love than any other human relationship. As the lyric so eloquently suggests, love has many facets. These facets have been explored across centuries by composers of plays, novels, poems, music, and even self-help manuals. What is love? How does it happen? How should one deal with it? These are issues of interest to the serious student of adjustment.

What Is Love?

In the movie *Love Story,* love meant "never having to say you're sorry." Harold Bessell, author of *The Love Test* (Bessell, 1984), claims that *love* is a combination of two separate but equally important parts: romantic love or "chemistry," and emotional maturity. In spite of the attention it has received, there is currently no generally accepted definition. When Leo Buscaglia, a guru of love, was asked if he could define love, he said, "Noooo! But if you follow me around I'll try to live it" (Buscaglia, 1982).

SUBFACTORS OF LOVE.   Isn't it possible to compare the many definitions of love and identify common characteristics? That was the approach taken by Sternberg and Grajek (1984). With the help of some very complicated statistics, Sternberg and Grajek concluded that love is comprised of a large number of subfactors; for example, the personal benefits that one receives from the relationship, compatibility of the partners, sharing between the partners, emotional support received from the relationship, communication within the relationship, and more. According to Robert Sternberg's *triangular theory of love* (1986), the various subfactors of love fall into three main categories: passion, intimacy, and commitment. Feeling passionately toward someone is associated with feeling some arousal and romance. Being intimate with someone gives rise to feelings of warmth and caring, and makes you want to share your innermost secrets. The commitment component can be expressed in a variety of ways, including making promises, being honest with each other, and living together.

These categories might combine in various ways, depending upon the type of love relationship being experienced. The love that you feel for a brother or a sister, for example, might involve heavy doses of emotional support and sharing. Romantic love would obviously involve additional subfactors. Let's look at two types of romantic love, passionate and companionate love (Berscheid & Walster, 1974; Hatfield, 1988).

Passionate Love

"Oh, Will," said Melinda. "You're the most important thing in my life. I can't stop thinking about you. Each day that we're apart I love you more and more."

"I feel the same way! It's really hard to concentrate on my work because I'm always thinking about you. I'm not interested in anything else. I don't want to spend time with my friends anymore. I don't want to watch the football games on television. I just want to be with you."

passionate love
Love associated with acute biological urges to be in intimate contact with the loved one.

Passionate love is a state of all-consuming, intense absorption in someone. Passionate lovers can't stand to be apart. They may be unable to help how they feel. And they are strongly sexually attracted to each other. In terms of Sternberg's triangular theory of love, passionate love is made up largely of the components of passion and intimacy. Such a relationship may only happen to people a couple of times in their lives. A sample of 85 men and women ranging in age from 18 to 70 years reported an average of 2.8 love relationships in their lives, with a range of 1 to 15 love relationships (Sternberg & Grajek, 1984).

Passionate love may very well start the way other relationships do between

Box 8-3

On Measuring Love and Liking

Rubin (1974) has differentiated between loving and liking. These distinctions probably equate fairly well with the difference between passionate and companionate love (Hatfield & Walster, 1978). He developed two short scales of around ten items each that differentiate between those in love and those "in like." We present below three items from each of the two scales for your perusal. These three items from the love scale are indicative of the three components of love relationships as defined by Rubin. For example, Item 8 is about caring, Item 2 is about intimacy, and Item 7 is about attachment. On the other hand, the items in the liking scale reflect an evaluation of another on different dimensions—adjustment, maturity, judgment, intelligence, and similarity to oneself.

Sample Items From Rubin's Love Scale

2. I feel I can confide in _____ about virtually everything.

7. If I were lonely, my first thought would be to seek _____ out.

8. One of my primary concerns is _____'s welfare.

Sample Items From Rubin's Liking Scale

2. I think that _____ is unusually well-adjusted.

5. I have great confidence in _____'s good judgment.

9. I think that _____ is one of those people who quickly wins respect.

individuals. But the speed with which such a relationship blossoms suggests some additional cause at work. It's possible that biological variables are involved, because a strong sexual attachment is usually characteristic of passionate relations (Berscheid & Walster, 1974). However, environmental variables undoubtedly also play a role. For example, in many passionate relationships the individuals spend most of their time together for weeks or months. There is ample opportunity during such time for repeated pairing of one's own and one's partner's behavior with powerful rewards in such massive doses that strong feelings and attachment can result (see the discussion of emotions in Chapter 4).

Passionate love is thought not to last longer than a few years, and often much less (Berscheid & Walster, 1974). It may thereafter grow into companionate love (about which more below). In the same way that steak is unappealing after one has just eaten a steak, or if one has eaten steak very often for several years, so, similarly, passionate love may wane for the biological reason of *satiation*. The notion that passionate love appears to wane, fits well with the biological constructs of deprivation and satiation. People may be ready biologically for a passionate relationship—all other things equal—if they haven't had one for quite a while, or ever.

There may also be a novelty effect. Initially, many rewarding aspects of a passionate relationship can stem in part from the novelty of it all. But after spending all of their time together for several weeks or months, a couple can run out of fresh activities, things they haven't done or discussed before, many times.

When Do People Decide They Are in Love?

Melinda and Will discussed their feelings for each other (see above) and concluded that they were probably in love. What is it that made them reach such a conclusion? There appear to be three necessary ingredients: strong feelings, displays of "loving

Box 8-4

On Playing Hard to Get

Is playing hard to get the way to start a relationship? Walster and colleagues (1973) gave male students at a midwestern college who had come to a computer dating center five folders containing information on five women with whom they had ostensibly been matched by a computer. In reality, the folders contained information on five fictitious women.

The information was fixed to give the impression that one woman was uniformly hard to get; she rated all five males (including the subject) with a +1 or a +2 (on a scale of 10). A second woman appeared uniformly easy to get; she rated all five males from +7 to +9. A third woman rated the subject highly (+8) and the remaining males much lower (+2 or +3). Thus she appeared easy for the subject to get, but hard for the others to get. The last two were women who "hadn't been in yet," so there was no date-selection information in their folders. Having digested this information, the men were asked to fill out first-impression question-naires on each of the five women and to decide which one they would like to date.

Far more men wished to date the selectively hard-to-get woman, the one easy for him to get but hard for the others. This particular woman was also better liked than either the uniformly easy or the hard-to-get women. Moreover, the men considered the selective woman to have the best characteristics of the most elusive woman (popular, friendly, warm) and none of the worst characteristics ascribed to the uniformly easy-to-get woman (unpopularity, lack of selectivity).

Desirability may be heightened, then, if a woman's behavior suggests that she is hard to get for others but interested in a particular man—particularly if that man is you. We don't know whether the reverse works in terms of men. In any case, it would seem that playing hard to get across the board is not conducive to starting a relationship. In fact, it will probably preclude such a start.

behavior," and an environment that leads to labeling the feelings as love (the three characteristics of emotions in Chapter 4): That is, the biological sensations are felt, the love is expressed, and the situation lends itself to partners describing it as passionate love. In fact, attraction may be heightened by the generation of strong feelings. The feelings of men about women may be enhanced if the man considers the woman hard to get—that is, easy for him, hard for others (Walster et al., 1973).

People who have fallen in love appear to note frequently that someone is interested in and likes them and that that person has desirable characteristics. Less frequently, they may also perceive similarities with themselves and the fact of the other individual's propinquity (Aron et al., 1989). But there are other circumstances that can heighten attraction. Read on.

DANGER HELPS.   For example, more men interviewed by an attractive college coed on a high, swaying suspension bridge tried to contact her (she prompted this) than men who were interviewed by the same coed on a regular bridge over the same river (where she also prompted). Further, the interviewees' answers—responses to a psychological projective test—by the men on the suspension bridge contained more sexual content (Dutton & Aron, 1974). The presence of the attractive female interviewer apparently was sufficient for the males on the suspension bridge to label the arousal produced by the height and sway of the bridge as sexual attraction (see Schachter & Singer, 1962). There were fewer responses to a male interviewer on either bridge.

Passionate love contains a healthy dash of biological (sexual) attraction.

Even more irrelevant or punitive feelings can be interpreted as sexual attraction. Men who were threatened with shock as part of an experiment for which they had volunteered (Brehm et al., 1970; as cited in Berscheid & Walster, 1974) rated themselves as more attracted to a coed, to whom they were briefly introduced, than did men who weren't threatened with shock. Physiological arousal from any source—an air raid siren during wartime, a death-defying leap by Evel Kneivel over the Grand Canyon, anxiety just before taking a final exam—in conjunction with meeting someone attractive might translate into feelings of passionate love for that person. Does this happen often? It may, given the plethora of ways in which Americans are taught to label events as love or love-related (Berscheid & Walster, 1974; Rubin, 1974). The romantic heroes of the movies, the continuing travails of soap opera stars on television with their daily and weekly passions, the huge industry of romance fiction (primarily targeted at women), all may build expectations that love, when it occurs, is passionate. Moreover, the expectation may be reinforced that it should occur for everyone and should be a prerequisite to marriage (Simpson et al., 1986).

FRUSTRATION HELPS. There is also some evidence that romantic feelings may be heightened by frustration. Driscoll et al. (1972) assessed parental interference and depth of romantic love in dating couples. They found that the greater the parental interference, the deeper the romantic feelings. In fact, in a follow-up experiment it was confirmed that where parents had resigned themselves to the relationship, the couples reported a decrease in passionate feelings. The authors called the heightened feelings from the parental interference the **Romeo and Juliet Effect.**

Romeo and Juliet Effect

Enhancement of the feelings of love in a couple by the attempts of their parents to keep them apart.

BELIEVING IS FEELING.   The simple belief that one has been aroused, even if erroneous, may also contribute to feelings of attraction. Men who were shown slides of seminude women from *Playboy* photographs, rated as more attractive those photographs that were associated with changes which they thought had occurred in their heart rates. In fact these "heart rates" were bogus sounds which they were led to believe were their heart beats (Valins, 1966). Apparently, our feelings may not even have to exist as physiological facts. The simple belief that they do may heighten attraction.

Companionate Love

After ten years of marriage, Melinda and Will were talking early one Sunday morning.

"Hey!" said Will. "We're still pretty good together, aren't we?"

"Yeah," Melinda laughed, "if we can keep the kids at bay, it still happens. Do you remember when you couldn't keep your hands off me?"

"Whaddya mean, 'remember'?" joked Will. "I still feel great with you, but now, somehow, it's more. I mean there's the kids, all the stuff we do together as a family, all the stuff we've collected. Even the dog."

"Even the dog? It really *is* everything about us isn't it? When I think about it, I never think of us separately. I always think of us together."

"You mean like this?"

"No, silly, but don't stop."

Melinda and Will are still in love, but it's different than it was at the beginning. What they have now is companionate love—the embers that are left when the fires of passion are somewhat banked. The passion is not necessarily gone, it just doesn't drive the relationship the way it did once. Hatfield and Walster (1978) suggested that **companionate love** "is a steady burning fire, fueled by delightful experiences but extinguished by painful ones" (p. 128). Brehm (1985) characterized companionate love for a person as feeling that the person is one of the most likable people you know, the sort of person you would like to be, and a person in whose judgment you have great confidence. In terms of Sternberg's triangular theory, companionate love is made up largely of the components of intimacy and commitment.

> While it is useful to distinguish between passionate and companionate love, it is important to remember that this distinction is far from sharp. As suggested by Brehm (1985), it's helpful to think of a continuum of love. Passionate love and companionate love exist at the extremes, and various combinations of the two are found as one moves along the continuum toward one extreme or the other. We must also be careful about trying to make sharp distinctions between companionate love and friendship. While there are differences in the kinds of feelings that in-love couples have in their relationships versus those found in friendship pairs (Pam et al., 1975), the differences between companionate love and friendship are minimal (Dion & Dion, 1976; Steck et al., 1982). Both companionate love and friendship are based upon two people having a lot in common—opinions, values, attitudes, likes and dislikes.

REQUIREMENTS FOR COMPANIONATE LOVE.   Our requirements are numerous. We generally want someone who is about as good looking as we are, about as smart as we are, about our own age, who professes the same religion, who will provide for us, and who will nurture us. Last but not least, males want someone who is not as tall as they are and females want someone who is taller. All in all, we do not want just anybody. In fact, very few will fill the bill.

Actually, the requirements we have for companionate love are even more numerous. Hatfield and Walster (1978) interviewed several hundred couples, in-

companionate love

Love that remains when passion is not the major reason for intimate contact with another; composed of a large number of subfactors (for example, friendship).

Companionate love is comprised of its own collection of factors to which friendship is a large contributor.

cluding dating couples, newlyweds, and couples long married. They attempted to ascertain what the individuals in those relationships expected to give and to get in the relationship. The answer was an astounding array of traits. Couples expected their partners or themselves to be: socially graceful (relaxed, friendly); intelligent and informed; physically attractive, well-groomed, exercised, and healthy; emotionally expressive; understanding of their partner's emotional needs; accepting of role flexibility; appreciative of their partner; openly affectionate (touching, hugging, kissing); sexual—both in terms of working to make that aspect of the relationship fulfilling and of being faithful; respectful of their partner's freedom; committed to their partner and the future of the relationship; contributive to the day-to-day management of the relationship through mundane duties (shopping, cleaning, maintenance); a contributor to the relationship's finances; sociable—a good companion as both talker and listener; someone who fits in; someone able to make decisions and be responsible; and someone who remembers important occasions (birthdays, anniversaries, and so on.) Hatfield and Walster conclude aptly that we all seem to want a great deal out of a companionate love relationship.

SUMMARY

■ Relationships are "a series of interactions between two individuals known to each other . . . where the interaction is affected by past interactions or is likely to influence future ones" (Hinde, 1981; p. 2). Relationships develop for a number of reasons, but especially because of propinquity, exposure, and self-disclosure. *Propinquity* essentially means closeness or nearness in space and/or time. Attraction is more likely to develop between people who are physically near to each other. Mere exposure is another factor influencing the development of friendships. Simply being exposed to someone may be sufficient for you to feel some attraction to that person. First impressions are also important in the development of relationships; first impressions are strongly influenced by one's physical appearance.

■ Two additional factors influencing interpersonal attraction are self-disclosure and "opening." A reasonable guideline on disclosure is to self-disclose at the same level and on the same matter as the person who has just disclosed to you. Because individuals who are openers are rated highly on measures of interpersonal attraction, another strategy is to practice behaviors characteristic of the opener. While all of these factors are important, overall, we tend to be attracted to people who are about as attractive as we ourselves are.

- After a relationship is established, its further development may lead to intimacy. While intimacy describes a constellation of behaviors, physical closeness, touching, and eye contact are three of the more important ones. Five types of touches important for intimacy include the support touch, the appreciation touch, the inclusion touch, the affection touch, and the sexual touch. Finally, when seeking intimacy, it is important that you be careful not to be misinterpreted.

- Dating is a recent, still-evolving phenomenon that promotes socialization among youth. Dates occur for a variety of reasons, from getting to know more about the other sex to just being friends. The toughest part of dating may be the initial asking, which exposes the asker to potential rejection. Practicing asking in the correct manner may assist those who have trouble in getting enough dates. But other parts of the dating game are important, too: These involve being a good listener, a good conversationalist, knowing how to have fun, and being a natural dispenser of rewards. It also helps to be thought attractive by others.

- Love seems to emerge from dating. It is a unitary phenomenon which means that our love for anyone is basically the same; it only differs because of whom it's focused on. We seem to label our feelings as "love" when they're strong and when the environment cues us that love is a good label. Love can be viewed as a continuum with passionate love and companionate love at the extremes. The former appears biologically driven, although it most surely has environmental components as well. Passionate love may only happen a couple of times in the average person's life, and it seldom lasts forever. Companionate love seems to result from the meeting of many interpersonal requirements that make two people very similar in their likes and dislikes. Each type of love necessitates rewards from each partner to the other in large quantities. The nature of the rewards may differ somewhat in each, although there is likely to be considerable overlap.

Box 8-5

SELF-ADJUSTMENT FOR STUDENTS:
MANAGING THE SITUATION

Remember, no behavior occurs in a vacuum; all behavior occurs in situations. In fact, often it seems as though the situation *controls* the behavior (see discussion of stimulus control in Chapter 3). Because this is so, it is possible for you to capitalize on the stimuli that exert control over your behavior when planning self-adjustment programs.

DISCOVER GENERAL SITUATIONS THAT CONTROL YOUR BEHAVIOR
Suppose that you want to decrease an undesirable behavior, such as drinking too much beer. One strategy is to limit your access to situations that make the behavior more likely (called potentiating situations). To manage excessive beer drinking, for example, you may want to limit the number of times you attend sporting events, go to bars, or associate with friends who drink a lot of beer. Another strategy is to increase your access to situations that inhibit the undesirable behavior (called inhibiting situations). To decrease beer drinking, for example, you might spend more time in your college library, or your parent's home, or in other situations that inhibit the behavior that you want to decrease.

If your goal is to *increase some desirable behavior,* then you want to increase your access to potentiating situations and decrease your access to inhibiting situations for that behavior. Suppose that you want to increase exercising. Your probability of exercising will be higher if you attend an exercise class—a strong potentiating situation. Conversely, perhaps you shouldn't fix your automobile when it breaks down, making it more likely that you will ride your bicycle or walk. The automobile, of course, is a great inhibiting situation with respect to walking or bicycle riding.

Thus, one way to manage your own behavior is to manage the general situations in which it occurs. This means planning to be in inhibiting situations that lower the likelihood of undesirable behavior, and in potentiating situations that raise the likelihood of desirable behavior. At the same time, you want to avoid potentiating situations for undesirable behavior and inhibiting situations for desirable behavior. What are the potentiating and inhibiting situations for the behavior that you would like to manage? Make a list.

Change Specific Stimuli within General Situations

Another way of capitalizing on stimulus control is to focus on specific stimuli, such as instructions, modeling, features of the environment, and other people, that can be altered within general situations.

Instructions. As we indicated in Chapter 4, self-instructions have been used in a variety of self-adjustment projects. To use self-instructions, review the behaviors that you want to perform to achieve self-adjustment, and then think of how you might instruct yourself to perform them. Write the instructions on 3×5 cards and rehearse them at various critical times, or post instructions to yourself in conspicuous places.

Modeling. Modeled behavior is another class of stimulus events that is useful in self-adjustment programs. For example, do you want to improve your skills at introducing yourself to an attractive person at social gatherings? Find someone who's good at it, observe that person's behavior, and try to imitate it.

Rearrange the environment. One way to increase desirable behavior or decrease undesirable behavior is to introduce into situations specific stimuli that already exert control over the behavior. Do you want to increase your tendency to write a letter to your parents, for example? Try placing a picture of them in the middle of your desk. Would you like to promote improved and more persistent studying? Try improving the lighting over your desk, clearing your desk of irrelevant material, having the desk facing away from your bed, and place a sign on the desk listing the dates of upcoming exams.

Other people. As we indicated above, modeling other people is one way of providing strong prompts for you to engage in some behavior. Another strategy is to simply change the people around you. Suppose, for example, that you want to decrease your beer drinking. You know that you will be attending a social event on Friday evening, so you can't avoid that potentiating situation for drinking. But will there be people there in whose presence you tend not to imbibe (whether they do or not)? Perhaps, for example, you could be the designated driver for those people. Because you've learned to behave in one way with some people and in another way with others, being around certain people in a situation can be an effective stimulus control tactic.

Make a list of the specific stimuli that you can rearrange within situations in order to alter the likelihood of your undesirable and desirable behavior. Remember, situations and controlling stimuli can be anything—people, places, times, days, events, and objects. Then ask yourself the following questions:

> What controlling stimuli can I really manage in my program?
> What steps do I need to take to manage those stimuli appropriately to control the desirable behavior and/or the undesirable behavior?

Be Realistic

Sometimes, managing the situation is all that's necessary to bring about successful self-adjustment. Perhaps that will be true in your case. In some programs, however, managing the situation is just a first step for successful self-adjustment. The next step, managing consequences for your behavior, is discussed at the end of the next chapter.

MEMORY BOOSTER

■ IMPORTANT TERMS

Be prepared to define the following terms (located in the margins of this chapter). Where appropriate, be prepared to describe examples.

Dyad	Group Dates
Relationship	Negative Self-Talk
Propinquity Effect	Coping Self-Statements
Impressions	Reciprocal Reinforcement
Matching	Generalized Reinforcer
Self-Disclosure	Body Language
Openers	Closed-Ended Question
Intimacy	Open-Ended Question
Behavioral Rehearsal	Passionate Love
Personal Space	Romeo and Juliet Effect
Free Dating	Companionate Love
Indirect Asking	

■ QUESTIONS FROM IMPORTANT IDEAS IN THIS CHAPTER

1. Cite some evidence that mere exposure to someone or something is sufficient to strengthen attraction to that person or thing.
2. List at least four outcomes of "being beautiful."
3. What behaviors do people show that make them openers?
4. How do timing and content of self-disclosure affect attraction?
5. Describe the kinds of behaviors that characterize intimacy.
6. What factors should you consider to increase your chances of successfully getting dates, or to make it more likely that you may be asked?
7. Name and briefly describe four strategies for overcoming a fear of dating.
8. Describe several general ways in which your behavior can be rewarding for your date.
9. How are companionate and passionate love similar? How are they different?

MARRIAGE AND ITS ALTERNATIVES

CHAPTER OUTLINE

LEARNING OBJECTIVES

After reading this chapter, you should be able to:

■ Describe recent trends in marriage and divorce in the United States.

■ Answer some marriage readiness questions.

■ Describe three relationship phases in mate selection.

■ Discuss common stages that marriages go through.

■ Describe several features that distinguish happy and unhappy marriages.

■ Describe several common myths about family violence.

■ Discuss changes that have occurred in traditional marriages during the last two decades.

■ Describe some correlates of divorce and the kinds of adjustments that are necessary when divorce occurs.

Carl and Monica have been married for seven years. Carl, who was intimate with quite a few women prior to his marriage to Monica, is beginning to tire of their relationship. In his work he meets many women. He likes to flirt with them and they reciprocate. He thinks more and more about going to bed with someone other than his wife. He's bugged by his kids when he comes home. It seems to him that there's never any peace and quiet. Carl also notices that they're having trouble paying their bills. He enjoys going out with his buddies for a beer more than he does going out with his wife. It annoys him that most of his paycheck goes to his family and that there's little left for himself.

Monica is also unhappy. She wishes Carl were a little more romantic. She wishes there were more money because she knows there are things their children need. She feels a little trapped. She recalls fondly when she taught school and had her own income. She wonders if she should go back to work. Housework is certainly boring enough. But she feels the children need her at home still, and she feels vaguely guilty about leaving them to go back to work.

The traditional church wedding—if a reflection of the couple's commitment to a religion—is associated with greater longevity of the marital relationship.

marriage
The contractual union of a man and woman as husband and wife.

Carl and Monica had a lovely church wedding—something their parents really wanted. As we use the term throughout this chapter, **marriage** will mean the contractual sanction of the union of a male and female pair of humans by civil (and possibly religious) authority. This sanctioning of marriage by society is a legal formality and as such gives special force to the contract to which the parties agree to abide.

What chance does a marriage have of survival in today's hectic world? Does living together accomplish the same thing as marriage? Are *you* thinking of marriage? Are you ready for it? How can you tell? Do some of your married friends seem like Carl and Monica? What can you expect from marriage? Are there many divorced among the people you know? We discuss these and other questions in this chapter.

Marriage: Temporary and Western?

First, the Bad News

polygyny
A human social-sexual relationship that involves the union of one man (husband) concurrently with more than one woman (wife).

polyandry
A human social-sexual relationship that involves the union of one woman (wife) concurrently with more than one man (husband).

monogamy
A human social-sexual relationship that involves the union of one man (husband) with one woman (wife).

Notwithstanding their initial love and commitment to one another, it's possible that Carl and Monica's marriage will not survive. In fact, in the United States the divorce rate numbers above 40 percent of marriages in a given year, and the number of divorces increases with each passing year. In Table 9-1, the top section shows that the total number of divorces and the rate of divorces in the United States have increased steadily in the last 20 years. The bottom section shows that the duration of marriage has steadily shrunk. (However, this statistic may have leveled off and may even be increasing again.) What's going on? Isn't marriage a permanent institution? That is, isn't it the preferred mode of bonding a deep relationship between two people? Hasn't it always been?

Well, no, it hasn't always been. And marriage may be peculiar to our Western heritage. There does seem to be some form of sanctioned coupling of men and women in every society. These vary from **polygyny** (one man, more than one woman), to **polyandry** (one woman, more than one man), to **monogamy** (one woman, one man), and are marked by formal or informal cultural rituals. Thus, we must not think that our form of marriage is unique.

TABLE 9-1
SOME RECENT TRENDS IN MARRIAGE AND DIVORCE

	1965	1970	1975	1980	1985
Divorce					
Total[a]	.48	.71	1.04	1.20	1.19
Rate[b]	2.5	3.5	4.8	5.2	5.0
Marriage					
Total[a]	1.80	2.16	2.15	2.39	2.41
Rate[b]	9.3	10.6	10.0	10.6	10.1
Median Age at First Marriage					
Male[c]	22.5	22.5	22.7	23.6	24.8
Female[c]	20.4	20.6	20.8	21.8	23.0
Median Duration of Marriage					
Years	7.2	6.7	6.5	6.8	6.8

[a] *In millions.*
[b] *Rate is per 1,000 population.*
[c] *Age is in years.*

Then, the Good News

More couples are marrying than ever before (see Table 9-1). Both totals and rates of marriage have risen over the past 20 years—with some leveling off during the 1970s. Marriage is still important to us!

But people are waiting longer until they marry. The median age of males and females at their first marriage is increasing more rapidly recently (Table 9-1). This may be due to two factors: that more education is required for youth to find employment today, and that lack of employment binds today's youth to their parents' home for a longer time.

The changes in these figures over the years suggest the continuing evolution of marriage as a social phenomenon. Its form is likely to change with changes in our society. It could even evolve out of existence to be supplanted by other forms of relationships. Of course we don't mean that men and women will not continue to develop intimate relationships. Marriage probably will exist in some form or other because people seem to come back to it. Remarriages of divorced women, for example, have steadily increased over the past 20 years.

Are You Ready for Marriage?

Deciding to marry is one of life's big decisions. Yet it may be accomplished in the heat of passion with very little thought. The decision is such a weighty one that it ought to be taken only after much rational evaluation and discussion. A substantial commitment is about to be made. Among other things, a person about to be married generally commits to one sexual partner—the same person for life; shared resources—giving up some or all of one's earnings to the common good of the relationship; potentially having children and facing all the years of nurturance and self-denial that feat demands; potentially sublimating oneself in favor of one's partner; and on and on.

How do you know if you're ready for marriage? No one really ever does, not completely. But it should feel very comfortable; it should be what you most want to do *rationally*. Thinking about marriage should really occur long before any overt discussion between prospective partners. In other words, you should have examined and interpreted your own and your partner's actions and feelings throughout the development of your relationship. Then when the time comes to decide, you'll feel pretty comfortable with your decision.

Answer Some Marriage Readiness Questions

To help you decide if you're ready for marriage, we present some important factors to think about in the form of questions (adapted from Kirkendall & Adams, 1971). Answer each question with a yes or no after thinking about it. No peeking at what we say about the question until you've thought about your answer! The questions assume that you have someone in mind as a possible partner, but many of the questions are about you yourself, and can be answered without a potential partner. You may want to think of answers in terms of past relationships if you aren't in a current one. There are no right or wrong answers to these questions. Their primary purpose is to make you think about some important variables that contribute to successful marriage. Nevertheless, the questions can contribute to your sense of self-knowledge. We suggest the intent of the question in parentheses after each one.

1. Even though you may accept advice from your parents, do you make important decisions yourself? (Yes) (No)
   (If you don't make your own decisions such as what to eat, how to dress, what to do with your money, and what your life is about, then you're probably not ready

to leave home. Essentially you need to be independent before you think seriously about marriage.)

2. Are you often homesick when you're away from home? (Yes) (No)
(If you get homesick, you're not ready to leave home either. It may be a good idea to have some fairly extended time away from home to find out about your feelings on this.)

3. Do you ever feel embarrassed or uneasy in giving or receiving affection? (Yes) (No)
(Giving and receiving affection is a necessary component of a successful marriage. You needn't be heavily involved with someone to answer this one: How much giving and receiving affection occurs within your own family? Does it embarrass you?)

4. Are your feelings easily hurt by criticism? (Yes) (No)
(Like it or not, criticism occurs in marriage. You need to be able to take it, to an extent, and deal with it in regard to your own adjustment.)

5. Do you enjoy playing or working with small children? (Yes) (No)
(While children are not necessary in a marriage, they generally are part of it. If you don't know your response to this, volunteer at a preschool, or volunteer to look after the children of some of your friends. If your answer is no, you may want to consider some arrangement other than marriage, or at the very least determine whether there is agreement between you and your fiancé(e) about not having children.)

6. Do you feel embarrassed or uneasy in conversations about sex with older persons or members of the other sex? (Yes) (No)
(If you're not relaxed about sex matters, then trouble may lie ahead. Excellent communication with another about one's sexual relations is necessary for them to be successful.)

7. Do you have a clear understanding of the physiology of sexual intercourse and reproduction? (Yes) (No)
(You should be able to answer yes to this if you have thoroughly read Chapter 7. You should also know the way your own body varies within the norms presented in that chapter.)

8. Do you understand the psychological factors determining good sexual adjustment? (Yes) (No)
(That is, can you learn what pleases someone else? Is this a natural part of your repertoire? It should be. Do you know what pleases you? Can you communicate that diplomatically?)

9. Have you had the experience of using some of your earnings to meet the expenses of others? (Yes) (No)
(The question contains two sets of implications: First, have you ever worked? Are you successful at it? Are you prepared to? This is an important skill to bring to a marriage. Second, have you shared, without rancor, your earnings for a common good? If you have, you've experienced one of the common occurrences of a marriage. A yes signifies your willingness to share yourself with a common goal. This sharing should probably be something you actually feel like doing with your intended spouse. If you have reservations about this, heed them.)

10. In an argument do you lose your temper easily? (Yes) (No)
(Are you rational? Can you work things through with someone else when you are very upset? For instance, your fiancé(e)? Your parents? Your brother or sister? This is also an important quality for a successful marriage.)

11. Have you and your fiancé(e) ever worked through disagreements to a definite conclusion agreeable to both of you? (Yes) (No)
(Do you know the person you are thinking of marrying well enough so that you know how he or she reacts to disagreements between you? Think of at least one such occurrence and examine the outcome. Has anything changed?)

12. Can you postpone something you want for the sake of later enjoyment? (Yes) (No)
(Can you put off things that you want for yourself in order to get things that are for the two of you together [for example, the kids, the house] or that are for your partner alone [for example, her or him finishing school]? There's a great deal of putting-off in many marriages, sometimes a lifetime of it.)

13. Are you normally free from jealousy? (Yes) (No)
(How often if ever do you lose control over another person flirting with your fiancé(e)? What if your fiancé(e) flirts with someone else? Do you envy others, someone smarter than you? Someone more handsome? Someone with more money? Jealousy and envy are unusually destructive emotions and should be largely absent or controllable for one to be well enough adjusted to attempt marriage. For one thing they suggest that you are unsure either of your fiancé(e)'s or your own allegiances, and this you shouldn't be.)

14. Have you thought carefully about the goals you will strive for in marriage? (Yes) (No)
(Do you have any goals for a potential marriage? If not, why not? If so, are they realistic [for example, attainable in five years]? Have you discussed these goals with your fiancé(e)? Do you agree with his or her goals? Does he or she agree with yours? Are your goals similar right from the start? Goals can be good motivators capturing the joint efforts of a couple. They need to be realistic, attainable, agreed to, and then worked toward with a sense of purpose. Any evidence in your life that you are capable of defining some goal and then meeting it? For example, have you ever been able to save a long time for something you wanted? Any of this kind of evidence in your fiancé(e)'s life?)

15. Do you sometimes feel rebellious toward facing the responsibilities of marriage, occupation, or family life? (Yes) (No)
(If you answer yes to this one, or you are unsure, then you may not want to plunge into marriage immediately. Everyone has these feelings now and then, so that's normal. If such thoughts happen to you fairly often, however, you might want to wait.)

16. Have you been able to give up something gracefully that you wanted very much? (Yes) (No)
(There is much giving-up in successful marriages. This is an indirect measure of how committed you are to the other person and to the institution of marriage itself.)

17. Do you think of sexual intercourse as chiefly a pleasure experience? (Yes) (No)
(There are at least three facets to this question: First, it is good if you do think of sexual intercourse as a pleasurable experience, for that is what it should be. If it has not been for you, then perhaps marriage should be put off until you do find sexual intercourse pleasurable [see Chapter 7]. Second, ask yourself if you enjoy seeing the pleasure you can bring to your partner as much as feeling your own pleasure. If not, then maybe you aren't in love enough to put off your own gratification a little. Finally, sexual intercourse is also reproductive behavior, and it produces children with amazing regularity! Thus sexual behavior must also be responsible behavior. In essence, it can lead to other goals that are not immediately pleasurable, indeed perhaps in the eyes of some, never pleasurable. Are you ready for that responsibility?)

18. Do you find it difficult to differ from others on matters of conduct or dress, even though you disagree with what they think? (Yes) (No)
(In a different way this question asks about how independent you are, how much social approval you can do without. Many marriages may have to exist without societal or familial blessing, for example, interracial or interreligious marriage. The lack of these supports is usually, but not always, fatal to the marriage. Could you get along without them? Be realistic!)

19. Do you often have to fight to get your way? (Yes) (No)
(A yes to this question suggests a potentially aggressive approach to the way that you deal with others. Your views may be very strongly held, and you may not often negotiate. Successful marriages balance on the negotiation skills of the partners. In turn, successful negotiations turn on compromise. Could you pursue some self-adjustment in this area?)

20. Do you often find yourself making biting remarks, or using sarcasm toward others? (Yes) (No)
(Biting remarks and sarcasm may suggest another inappropriate way of dealing with others. They may disguise feelings of dislike for those to whom the remarks are made. Do you do this with your potential partner?)

21. Do you find yourself strongly emphasizing the glamourous aspects of marriage, for example, the announcement, congratulations, showers, the wedding? (Yes) (No)

(If yes, then you are probably not thinking of the important things necessary to evaluate your readiness for marriage and the likelihood of its success. In fact, if this is a major motivator of your behavior, stop the wedding!)

22.   Have you and your fiancé(e) associated with each other in a variety of situations outside of dates and other forms of social entertainment, for example, caring for children, in a work project, in time of stress? (Yes) (No)
(Here, we really ask how well you both get along in tough situations—approximations of the ones you will inevitably face when you are married. We also ask whether you know your potential partner well enough to have experienced some of these situations and whether you have evaluated the experience. Well, have you? If you haven't, do so. As a trial experiment, baby-sit your friends' kids one night when you'd both rather go to the movies.)

23.   Have you and your fiancé(e) discussed matters which might cause marital conflict? For example: Religious differences? Plans for having children? Attitudes toward sex? Differences in family background? Financial arrangements in marriage? Basic values in life? Your parents? (Yes) (No)
(How well do you and your partner-to-be communicate? How deep is your relationship? If you have not discussed some of the big issues listed in this question, either you aren't communicating well enough or your relationship is not intimate enough or both. Postpone the wedding date until you have satisfactory answers to *all* the questions listed above.)

By the way: Few individuals ever feel totally ready. When you approach marriage, your life is changing and such situations should be approached cautiously. So don't overly worry if you don't feel totally ready. This is fine. It simply means that you need to do your homework on knowing yourself and your partner-to-be. Then, you take your best shot.

Getting to Marriage: Mate Selection

Perhaps your answers in our marriage readiness section tell you that you are ready for marriage. How do you decide whom to choose? There are at least three stages to this process which we'll call "getting to know you a little," "getting to know you a lot," and "thinking of marriage" (cf. Murstein, 1986).

GETTING TO KNOW YOU A LITTLE.   In the first stage the variables that lead to the development of any relationship are important. That is, your attractiveness will determine who is drawn to you, and others' attractiveness will determine to whom you are drawn. As we have already mentioned (Chapter 8), attraction depends in part on such variables as propinquity and exposure. There may also be "love at first sight," that is, the passionate love which drives a relationship from the beginning.

Most to-be-marital relationships start with dating, so the variables that relate to someone else liking you pertain. If a to-be-marital relationship is to progress, however, and in many cases if it is even to start, a great many implicit requirements must be met. Many of these requirements are the same as they are for close friendship and companionate love (Chapter 8). One of these requirements can be described as **endogamy,** which is the tendency of people to marry within their own social group (Buss, 1985). Specifically, we are more likely to marry someone who professes the same religion and is of the same ethnic group, race, and social class. In part, this may just be because these are the individuals to whom we have the most propinquity and the greatest exposure. A second requirement is **homogamy,** which is the tendency of people to marry others who have similar characteristics such as the same attitudes, values, age, height, and attractiveness (Folkes, 1982; Honeycutt, 1986).

GETTING TO KNOW YOU A LOT.   If a to-be-marital relationship progresses beyond the first stage, comparability of attitudes and values assumes more importance. The partners may reexamine their mutual suitability, for example, in terms of politics, religion, sex, careers, goals, and leisure (Levinger & Huston, 1990).

endogamy
The tendency of people to marry within their own social group.

homogamy
The tendency of people to marry others who have similar characteristics.

THINKING OF MARRIAGE.   Finally, people begin to view their relationship partners as marriage partners and to examine how well they fit that role. Are they good companions? Do they share? Are they even tempered? Do they know how to negotiate fairly? Do they keep bargains they make? Are they emotionally supportive? Not everyone consciously asks all of these questions, but most everyone asks some. Indeed, many of the questions in our marriage readiness test above relate to how much of this type of homework you have done. Our suggestion is that you do a lot of this type of analysis when you start thinking of marriage.

The Stages of Marriage

It is possible to think of marriage as traversing some common stages for many couples. Before we start discussing these stages, proposed in this case by Carter and McGoldrick (1988), we need to say that such stages don't necessarily exist for all marriages and that there should be no implication from our discussion below that a couple has to pass through all of these stages to have a successful marriage. At best these stages should be thought of as capsule descriptions of the events that characterize many marriages.

1. *Newlyweds.* In this first stage you find yourself newly married. No longer are you between families; you're part of a new one. During this stage the two of you have a chance to explore your new roles as husband and wife. For many marriages it's one of two general times of maximum happiness—the time before children. It's a time when you may decide when to or whether to have children. More couples now do not have children right away, making this stage longer. It's a time when relationships with others—your family and friends—change because of your new status. For a number of marriages this period can be tough if you have different role expectations of each other.

2. *Children Arrive.* Oh happy day! Your roles change as you take on parenting responsibilities. Space and time in your lives now are taken up by your children. Marital satisfaction usually dives during this period, not to rise to its former heights until the children have grown and left home. This period involves a major transition that can be troublesome if you expect that things will continue as they used to. They don't. However, a strong commitment to children and realistic expectations—especially by the new mother who typically shoulders most of the initial childcare burdens—ease this transition.

3. *The Kids Become Adolescents.* Oh woe, now the kids are adolescents, typically a time of low marital satisfaction. This stage can be a time of family conflict

These two couples, one newly married, the other married many years, span the stages of marriage.

as your children lurch toward young adulthood and the balance of power in the family shifts. Moreover, many of you may be simultaneously dealing with midlife yourselves, reexamining your values, your careers, and your lives in general. In addition, you may be looking toward the time when your children have left home, and what that means.

4. *The Children Leave Home.* "Are they really gone?" Perhaps not. It may take several attempts and approximations to successfully leave home, prolonging this stage as your children win and lose jobs, succeed and fail in college, marry and divorce, and otherwise face life's trials and tribulations. You may also inadvertently increase their difficulties by not making it easy for your children to leave.

Then you find that you are left with "the empty nest." And you may feel lonely, perhaps wandering around in a home that is suddenly too big. But, there is also a sense of relief that child-rearing is over, and that you can now devote more of your time to yourself, your spouse, and your career. In other words, this may not be a difficult transition. Typically, marital satisfaction rises during this period. Friends of one of the authors joked about how they could again make love in their home in an unrestricted fashion.

5. *Alone Again Together.* During the final period of this cycle, you and your partner again share many friendship experiences because you can wholly attend to each other once again. This is not a time without stress, however, as physical illness and even death sometimes intervene. For most, though, it is a time of high marital satisfaction.

Marital Adjustments

After you're married, of course, there are adjustments to make. You and your new spouse must confront many new issues. These include but are not limited to communications, finances, work, relatives, sex, children, housekeeping, leisure, infidelity, and physical abuse. Actually, these issues are those that unhappy couples most frequently bring to family counseling (Beck & Jones, 1973). All of these interact with your expectations with respect to your marriage. If your expectations are too high then trouble is more likely than if they are realistic (Sabatelli, 1988). Let's look briefly at some of these areas.

COMMUNICATIONS. Poor communication is the most frequent complaint brought to marital counseling by unhappy couples (Beck & Jones, 1973). Poor communication also differentiates satisfied from dissatisfied couples (Fowers & Olson, 1989). Obviously then, you need to communicate well. As we discussed previously, this may mean self-disclosure at the same rate as your partner's. But it also means a high frequency of positive messages, a low frequency of negative, critical messages, and listening very carefully to your partner's messages.

WORK. This is a complex topic, because today many more families exist where both spouses must work outside the home. Indeed, most college women today want careers. Yet they also want children (several), and they want egalitarian marriages. However, most college men cannot define what an egalitarian marriage is (Machung, 1989), let alone live it. Women know, however. This is clearly an area where gender expectations differ in many marriages and, hence, can be a source of difficulty. We'll discuss dual careers further below.

How do children develop in families where both parents work? There appear to be few difficulties. Working mothers and their offspring easily form strong attachments. Child development appears to cruise along quite normally if both parents are happy about their own and their spouse's roles at work and in the family. Well-adjusted children result (Easterbrooks & Goldberg, 1985), more than likely, because the parents are happy and well-adjusted themselves.

FINANCES.   These are usually most troublesome where the family is poor. Under such circumstances the occasion is set for husbands' self-esteem to decrease and for wives to complain. In turn, communication suffers. However, finances can also be problematic where there is enough money but there is not enough discussion about how it should be used (Schaninger & Buss, 1986). Couples should thoroughly understand what kind of lifestyle is possible for them given their skill levels and their earning capabilities before they decide to marry.

SEX.   This is a chicken-and-egg problem area. If there are problems with a couple's sexual interactions these are known to lower marital satisfaction. But, just as clearly, other problems in the marriage (for example, poor communication), which themselves account for lower marital satisfaction, can increase the likelihood of sexual problems. Again, it is wise to understand each other's expectations and roles in this area before marriage.

CHILDREN.   We saw above how children change the roles, tasks, and relationship of a married couple. Raising children is another area for clear communication and consistent behavior. Have you agreed upon goals for them? Have you agreed upon disciplinary procedures? Have you agreed on a division of labor with respect to them? Great stress awaits many new parents who overestimate the benefits of children and underestimate their costs (Belsky, 1985).

PHYSICAL ABUSE.   Unfortunately, a towering problem for married couples is the possibility of physical abuse, either spouse abuse, child abuse, or both. Within this framework also lie the subclasses of sexual abuse of spouses and children, and child neglect. Such problems are not the province of a few cruel or mentally ill families—they are commonplace. Here are a few ugly facts (Strauss, 1991):

- A man is 20 times more likely to be assaulted by his family than by someone outside his family.
- A woman is 200 times more likely to be assaulted by her family than by someone outside her family.
- Incidence rates show that men and women in marriages are equal in their violence toward one another. However, women are much more likely to suffer the effects of such violence.
- Among women who report a familial assault, the average is 5 assaults per year; among women in battered women's shelters as many as 60 assaults per year have been reported.

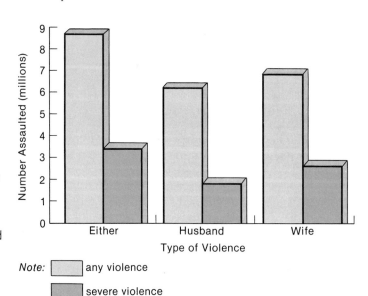

Figure 9-1
Estimated annual incidences of spousal violence in the United States by type of violence. Violence incidence estimates are for the 1984 American population. Severe violence = kick, punch, stab, and so on. Any violence = slap, push, and the like. Either = violence by either spouse; Husband = violence by husband; Wife = violence by wife. *Data are from the 1985 National Family Violence Survey of 6,002 current married or cohabiting couples (see Strauss, 1991).*

Box 9-1

EIGHT MYTHS ABOUT FAMILY VIOLENCE

Here are eight common misstatements about family violence (Gelles & Cornell, 1990):

Myth 1. It's Rare. You've seen from Figure 9-1 that it is anything but rare and that the perpetrators are of both sexes.

Myth 2. It's Mostly Mentally Disturbed People. Bizarre cases make headlines, but they're not representative. Less than 10 percent of family violence owes to persons with psychiatric disorders (Strauss, 1980).

Myth 3. It's Mostly the Lower Classes. More family violence is reported in the lower classes, but it occurs in all classes. Moreover, people in the lower classes stand a greater chance of being reported falsely if their children have injuries, for example.

Myth 4. Social Factors Don't Count. They most certainly do. Though violence is seen in all classes, it is still seen primarily in the poor, notwithstanding the potential for biased reporting.

Myth 5. Abused Children Become Abusers Themselves. It's a myth to think that they all do. But, as with all stereotypes there's a grain of truth here. The facts show that abused children don't necessarily become abusers. However, there is a higher likelihood that they will than someone who has not been abused.

Myth 6. Battered Wives Like Being Hit, Otherwise They'd Leave. This myth turns on the assumption that women who are battered and don't leave actually have a functional choice when, in reality, the fact that they don't leave suggests just the opposite. This point of view, which is highly middle-class, neglects all of the data (some of which we explore below in Box 9-2) about why people stay in bad marital relationships.

Myth 7. It's Caused by Alcohol and Drug Abuse. There is a pretty good association between substance abuse on the part of both offender and victim and subsequent family violence, but that's all it is—an association. There is no strict causation. If there were, anyone who drank alcohol would always become violent. With few exceptions (amphetamines may be one such class), violent outcomes after substance use are mediated by a web of individual, situational, and social factors that may interact with substance ingestion.

Myth 8. Violence and Love Don't Exist Together. Unfortunately, more often than not, they do. Violent families are not violent all of the time. And violent individuals can be very loving—often during periods of remorse following violent acts. In fact, in violent families, violence is often confused with love, and a child may learn that this is how dad and/or mom expresses love for me.

- Over 30 percent of couples report a violent incident over the entire course of their marriages.

(All of these figures should be considered low estimates; the actual figures are probably much higher.)

Intra-family violence is clearly a problem that requires professional help. If it happens in your marriage chronically, seek that help, because it is unlikely that you can successfully deal with it on your own.

Let's say that you've made many of the important adjustments. Now, what is it that's likely to make your marriage last?

What Makes a Marriage Endure?

It is well known that both satisfaction with marriage and amount of love in marriage decline with time, even if the marriage endures (Rollins & Cannon, 1974; Swensen et al., 1981). Then what makes a marriage continue? Clearly, long-term marriage is

---

Box 9-2

ENHANCING YOUR MARRIAGE: SOME TIPS

1. Surprise your spouse in as many ways as you can think of. Invite her or him to lunch when you don't usually do that. Schedule a weekend away together without the children. Buy a gift for no special occasion. Take the humdrum out of your shared existence.

2. Count the number of critical remarks you make to anyone in your family. Keep a daily chart of them. Reduce these remarks to zero.

3. Count the number of praise statements you make to all of your family. Increase this number; it will undoubtedly be too low. (You may need to develop new ways to praise.)

4. Develop your skills as a listener (Chapter 8). When your spouse talks, devote your entire attention to whatever is being said.

5. Make time for your spouse as a top priority item. This time can be spent however you want to. It might just be an informal regular bedtime session, for example, pillow talk; or it could be an exchange of news when you both arrive home for dinner and neither of you is concurrently engaged in some other activity. (Men: This is not necessarily a time just for sex!) (Women: This could be a time when you let him know that you're available.)

6. Be romantic and intimate. Increase the number of hugs you give your spouse; kisses, too. People derive a great deal of contentment from just being held, so do it.

---

related to the degree of commitment of the partners involved in the relationship. Where there is "personal commitment" in the relationship, the marriage is the most stable—more stable and with fewer problems than if the commitment is to the *institution* of marriage itself (Swensen & Trahaug, 1985). However, commitment to the institution of marriage helps, too. What has probably changed in today's unsuccessful marriages is the degree of commitment to one's partner as a person. It's also possible that in unsuccessful marriages, there's little companionate love.

Lauer and Lauer (1985) completed a survey of couples who had been married for 15 years or more. The questions explored what it is that helps marriages survive in today's world. Each husband and wife responded individually to a questionnaire, which included 39 statements and questions about marriage. The questions ranged from agreement about sex, money, and goals in life to attitudes toward spouses and marriage in general. Some of the results are shown in Table 9-2.

You can see that the first four reasons given by men and women with regard to what keeps a marriage going pertain to one's spouse as friend and person, and to the importance of the institution of marriage. It may be of interest that sexual matters are well down the list.

Destabilizing Factors in Marriage

What factors make a marriage unhappy? Table 9-3 suggests some of the perceived differences between couples in unhappy and happy marriages. Drawn from a lengthy questionnaire, these are items on which there were the greatest differences between unhappy and happy couples. They are ranked in order of the greatest difference (Mathews & Mihanovich, 1963). Of the first 50 of these problems, the largest number were from the area of personal needs (for example, Items 4, 5, 6, and 7), the second most from the area of personal interaction (Items 1, 2, and 3), and the third most from the area of personality complaints (Items 13 and 18). Only one sexual item showed sufficiently different scores to be ranked in the first 50

TABLE 9-2

REASONS GIVEN FOR AN ENDURING MARRIAGE (15 YEARS) LISTED IN ORDER OF FREQUENCY

Men	*Women*
My spouse is my best friend.	My spouse is my best friend.
I like my spouse as a person.	I like my spouse as a person.
Marriage is a long-term commitment.	Marriage is a long-term commitment.
Marriage is sacred.	Marriage is sacred.
We agree on aims and goals.	We agree on aims and goals.
My spouse has grown more interesting.	My spouse has grown more interesting.
I want the relationship to succeed.	I want the relationship to succeed.
An enduring marriage is important to social stability.	We laugh together.
We laugh together.	We agree on a philosophy of life.
I am proud of my spouse's achievements.	We agree on how and how often to show affection.
We agree on a philosophy of life.	An enduring marriage is important to social stability.
We agree about our sex life.	We have a stimulating exchange of ideas.
We agree on how and how often to show affection.	We discuss things calmly.
I confide in my spouse.	We agree about our sex life.
We share outside hobbies and interests.	I am proud of my spouse's achievements.

TABLE 9-3

ITEMS THAT DISTINGUISH UNHAPPY FROM HAPPY MARRIAGES[a] *Adapted from Mathews & Milhanovich, 1963.*

Problem
1. Don't think alike on many things.
2. Mate has little insight into my feelings.
3. Say things that hurt each other.
4. Often feel unloved.
5. Mate takes me for granted.
6. Need someone to confide in.
7. Mate rarely compliments me.
8. Have to give in more than mate.
9. Desire more affection.
10. Can't talk to mate.
11. Mate does not enjoy many things I enjoy.
12. Often feel neglected.
13. Keep things to myself.
14. Can't please mate.
15. Don't confide in each other.
16. Mate is not open to suggestion.
17. Can't discuss anything with mate.
18. Mate is stubborn.
19. Mate can't accept criticism.
20. Mate magnifies my faults.

[a] In rank order of difference between unhappy and happy marriages. Thus Item 1 reflects the largest difference between unhappy and happy marriages.

Box 9-3

MARRIED AND UNHAPPY: WHY STAY?

Some married couples seem to stay together even though they appear to be very unhappy. Why? A number of variables that can also be thought of as barriers to divorce are known:

- The pool of potential, attractive mates declines with age (Thornton & Rodgers, 1987), so the longer you are in a marriage the more this factor can become important.

- The longer a couple remains married, the more they have accumulated (which may be intangible and/or otherwise hard to divide) and the more experiences they have shared (Huber & Spitze, 1980).

- People may stay in marriages because they are concerned about their children (Glenn & McLanahan, 1982; Heaton, 1990). Within this framework, male children may tend to keep fathers around because fathers play a larger role in rearing sons (Morgan et al., 1988).

- People who need a marital partner for socioeconomic reasons may be more likely to stay in an unhappy marriage because they have fewer economic alternatives and the picture outside of marriage may look impoverished (Heaton & Albrecht, 1991).

- People who have never divorced may have inertia that keeps them from divorcing because they have never experienced it, so those who have married only once—and expect it to last a lifetime—may tend to stay married more than those who have already divorced (McLanahan & Bumpass, 1988).

- Religious norms may keep some unhappy couples married, particularly among Catholics, conservative Protestants, and Jews where their peer groups may reinforce staying together and working things out (Larson & Goltz, 1989).

- Promarriage attitudes may keep some unhappy couples together, even though approval of divorce is much higher now than it used to be (Thornton, 1985).

- If the couple's labor is specialized—wife does the housework, husband does the breadwinning, for example—ending a marriage may involve a greater change in lifestyles for each than if the division of labor is egalitarian (Heaton & Albrecht, 1991).

- If social contacts outside the marriage are few, there may be less perceived support for ending a marriage (Heaton & Albrecht, 1991).

- If a partner feels unable to control his or her life he or she may feel incapable of changing an unhappy marriage (Heaton & Albrecht, 1991).

- Some people may stay in unhappy marriages if they perceive that the consequences of terminating the marriages are worse than remaining in them (Heaton & Albrecht, 1991).

- The consequences of dissolving an unhappy marriage may be greater for women than they are for men, hence, women may be more likely to tolerate a bad marriage than are men.

- Finally, the longer you are in a marriage, the more likely it will continue (Heaton, 1991).

items. Characterizing the items in this way suggests the important problem areas in marriages that contain unhappy partners.

Changes in Traditional Marriage: The Women's Movement

If there is a revolution in marriage, it is a female revolution (Olson, 1972). Role expectations of young women entering marriage are changing. Young women often expect not to be housewives. They may expect that each partner will contribute equally to all facets of the relationship. They may not want to bear many children, and definitely not any immediately when their careers are just underway. They may also expect that important decisions affecting any business of their families are made conjointly. Where these expectations are not met, either because of resistance on the part of society in general, or on the part of their husbands in particular, there is conflict. Such conflict can either be troublesome or it can provide the grounds for growth and change (Olson, 1972).

Figure 9-2
Women in poverty. Women are several times more likely to be poor if they are widowed or divorced and many times more likely to be poor if they are separated than if they are married and living with a spouse. This may be one reason that women are more likely to tolerate a bad marriage than men are. *Data from U.S. Bureau of the Census, 1989.*

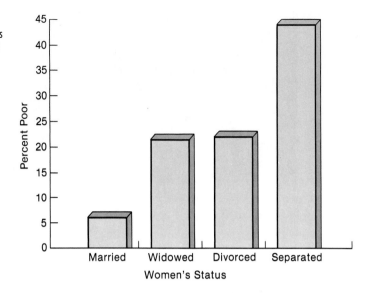

Has the women's movement produced changes in traditional marriage? Let's examine some data from dual-career families and see.

Dual Careers

Today's marriages are not like those of your parents or your grandparents. One reason is that over half of wives with school-aged children work outside the home (Bryson & Bryson, 1978), and this number is increasing as it becomes more and more difficult for many couples to exist on one income. What goes on in dual-career families? Let's look at some of the facts.

EARNINGS AND MARITAL POWER.   Who gets to make the decisions in a marriage? Typically it is the husband who brings the most earnings to the relationship (Blood & Wolfe, 1960; Blumstein & Schwartz, 1983). Women not employed outside their homes tend to be relatively powerless, at least in part because homemaking pays no salary. In cases where it looks as though the wife is making important decisions for the family (for example, the purchase of furniture), it is often found that she has been delegated this responsibility by her husband (Blumstein & Schwartz, 1983). Thus, women working outside the home should have more power in their marriages than women who are solely homemakers. But is this the case? Let's look at housework for answers.

HOUSEWORK.   It's there and it remains there all of the time. On the positive side, it can be done whenever one chooses to do it (Doyal, 1990), and it is easier now than it was in past generations, given labor-saving devices such as washing machines and vacuum sweepers. On the negative side, however, there is no time off from it because it is repetitive and neverending. Indeed in our larger modern living spaces there may be more of it!

In traditional marriages wives stayed home, cooked meals, tended the children, cleaned the house, and did all of the shopping. Housework alone was thought to require 50 to 60 hours per week (Levant et al., 1987). What do women do now if they have a career? Both spouses agree that in two-earner households, housework should be divided more equally. Yet the actual division of housework does not at all reflect this expectation (Hochschild, 1989). Women do spend less time on housework if they are employed outside the home, but their husbands don't spend more time on it (Thompson & Walker, 1989). Moreover, women's housework tends to be fixed and daily in nature, binding them more closely to the

While this looks egalitarian, it doesn't represent many modern marriages; the so-called new generation of househusbands is more myth than fact.

home, whereas men's housework tends to be less regular or binding, permitting them more freedom. If there are children the extra hours of child care most significantly affect the woman's time. Typically, women put in three to four times the time that men do in housework, and this difference does not change significantly if women are employed outside the home.

But what about the new generation of househusbands? In reality, the existence of this group is more myth than fact (Pleck, 1983). First, they are very small in number, and second, where they do exist, they are found to be men who either work at home or who are temporarily out of work (Johnson & Firebaugh, 1985).

Thus, it looks as though the division of labor in dual-career marriages is relatively unchanged from that of traditional marriages. The absence of relief from household chores is not what women expect (St. John-Parsons, 1978). Egalitarianism is not the norm (Weingarten, 1978). Perhaps this is why women in dual-career

The Amish maintain a traditional separation of roles in marriage.

marriages are less well-adjusted than housewives on two global measures: wishing they had married someone else and thinking about divorce (Staines et al., 1978). Dual-career marriages are less stable than those in which only one partner works outside the home.

To this point we've pretty much assumed that you'd like to get married. But maybe you're not thinking about marriage, at least not yet. Are there alternatives other than marriage? If so, how good are they? Also, so far we've assumed heterosexual relationships at the core of our discussion. If you're gay or lesbian these relationships may not suit you at all. What alternatives are there for you?

Alternatives to Marriage

Cohabitation = Living Together

cohabiting
Living together with someone to whom you are not married.

Since 1970, the number of couples living together without marriage, that is, **cohabiting,** has risen to 2.6 million, suggesting that cohabiting appeals to Americans. Most couples enter such an arrangement with a strong, affectionate relationship between them and a "let's-see" attitude (Macklin, 1972). The pros of this type of arrangement relate to the absence of its legal basis and the freedom to maintain a good relationship because it can be easily dissolved. These casual arrangements may also be thought of as a way to measure one's compatibility with another—a sort of **trial marriage.** Kafka and Ryder (as cited in Olson, 1972) found that such couples were more oriented to the present, had fewer traditional role expectations, were interested in working out any difficulties, worked toward increased openness and intimacy, and played down materialistic goals.

trial marriage
An informal arrangement between a man and a woman who practice most of the aspects of a marriage without a formal contract.

Most cohabiting relationships are of short duration—of the order of two years or less (Blumstein & Schwartz, 1983). At the end of a cohabiting relationship, cohabitors either break up or get married. Most cohabiting relationships are childless, although some may contain children from a previous marriage. And, the cohabitors are reluctant to have children without first marrying (Blumstein & Schwartz, 1983). Over 50 percent of cohabitors have never been married; however, about a third have been divorced.

While there are the benefits of this type of relationship that are mentioned above, there are also some serious drawbacks. A cohabiting relationship provides no basis for splitting up possessions or products that the partnership may have produced, there is no machinery in place to see that an equitable arrangement is reached, and no legal claim by offspring to the property of their parents should the relationship dissolve. Since a formal contract is absent, the arrangement may be entered into more casually, making what happens in the relationship somewhat different from the situation of partners who formally marry (see Berger, 1971). Women may wonder if this is just another easy way for men to get sex. Men may wonder whether this is just another way for women to gain security.

Does premarital cohabiting increase one's chance of a successful marriage? Clearly, the answer is no. In fact, at first glance, premarital cohabitation appears to lessen the chance of a successful marriage. For example, women who cohabit premaritally have much higher marital dissolution rates than those who don't (Bennett et al., 1988; Teachman & Polonko, 1990). However, when both the married and cohabiting time of a couple are summed, there is no difference in marital disruption when compared to those who have not cohabited (Teachman & Polonko, 1990).

While society is more accepting now of cohabitation, it is clear that this acceptance is for heterosexual cohabitation. Gay or lesbian cohabitation is still stigmatized, and the legal problems raised as a result of cohabitation may be increased for gay and lesbian couples.

In a communal living arrangement, the participants' roles may differ quite sharply from what their roles would be in regular society.

Communal Living

communal living

Any of a number of living arrangements that involve people living together under rules that are mutually agreed upon; such arrangements are often nontraditional.

utopian society

A society that purports to be ideal in terms of its government, laws, and culture.

Although in some communal arrangements it's possible to be married as well, communal living offers another alternative to marriage. In **communal living** a number of people live together under sets of rules they fabricate themselves. These rules may vary from little more than boarding-house regulations to complex societal structures. People may choose to live communally when they dislike a society's standard living arrangements and contingencies. The commune is typically a place where society's regular values are changed to ones the group perceives as more equitable. In essence, it is a mini-society. Such mini-societies propose that life will be better for their members than were the members to participate in regular society. These societies are called **utopian,** meaning that conditions in the society strive to be virtually ideal. Ideas for utopias have occurred with regularity for many years. One was proposed by Sir Thomas More in 1516, who first used the term in this context. Another example is the book *Walden II* (Skinner, 1948).

Single and Loving It?

More young people are staying unmarried longer as we showed you in Table 9-1. Does this mean that there are more people opting to remain single forever? No one knows at this time but probably there are not. There are nearly twice as many men and more than two and one-half times as many women who are single now between the ages of 25 and 29 than there were in the 1960s. But with the median age of first marriage for men and women being between 23 and 25 years, it stands to reason that there may be as many singles above those ages as below. So maybe all that these data reflect is the longer time to first marriage. Moreover, given higher divorce rates now, there have to be more people between 25 and 29 who are single *again*, who have been married for the average length of time of first marriages in this country (that is, about 6.8 years), and who have subsequently divorced. Add to this the fact that most young people still plan to marry (Cargan & Melko, 1982), and you can see that singlehood is probably temporary for most.

Being single means to not be treated all that well in the United States. Singles essentially find themselves the victims of one or two stereotypes: either as casual swingers who are sexually promiscuous or as hermits who can't get dates and have missed the chance to get married. As with all stereotypes these two don't accurately represent the rich variety of single people. Governments also discriminate. They are interested in the production of new taxpayers, so they provide tax breaks for those who are married and have children; moreover, historically, governments have sent married people with families to war later than they have singles. It may also be harder for singles to get jobs (they are perceived as less stable) and to establish and maintain social networks because so much socializing among us is done on a couple basis. In these and many other subtle ways, singlehood may be discriminated against.

Finally, singles are thought to be less happy than those who are married (Glenn & Weaver, 1988). This discrepancy may be changing, however, as married people have been rating themselves as less happy over the past decade while singles have been rating themselves as happier.

Single-Parent Families

The single-parent family is usually an outcome of divorce. While not strictly an alternative to marriage, the single-parent family is now a fact of life in the United States, especially for minority families. Overall, the United States has gone from 11 percent in 1970 to 23 percent of households with single-parent families in 1989. Currently, for hispanics 30 percent and for Afro-Americans 54 percent of households have a single parent (U.S. Department of Commerce, 1990). Some 86 percent of these single-parent families are headed by women. For these families a primary problem is poverty, for they constitute the majority of families in poverty with children under 18 years.

Divorce leaves women more likely to be impoverished than it does if they are married (see Figure 9-2 again). Often families have few assets to divide after

Single-parent families, mostly headed by women, are frequently poverty stricken.

houses, automobiles, and attorneys are paid for. Additionally, no-fault divorce and inadequate child-support laws make poverty more likely (Jacob, 1989; Kamerman & Kahn, 1988; Weitzman, 1985). Moreover, women who are homemakers may be unskilled for good-paying jobs. Even women who have had careers, may find their resumés badly outdated.

Clearly, impoverished single-parent families may constitute environments that are neither healthy for child-rearing nor good for the well-being of parents either. However, where resources are plentiful, being a single parent may be a viable alternative to remaining in an unhappy marriage or even to marrying in the first place.

Toujours Gai

By writing a separate section on gay and lesbian relationships we run the risk of implying that gay and lesbian relationships are fundamentally different from heterosexual relationships. With the exception of the fact that the participants are of the same sex, this is not true. Gay men and women form and maintain relationships with one another for basically the same reasons that heterosexual men and women do: They are attracted to one another and they have mutuality of interests and goals. Thus, much of what we have said about the commencement of heterosexual relationships and their long-term maintenance applies to gay and lesbian relationships as well.

Here are some common stereotypes and misunderstandings about gays and their relationships:

heterosexist

The view that heterosexual relationships are superior.

- *Most gays are unhappy being gay.* They're not. Such thinking is **heterosexist,** the view that heterosexual relationships are inherently superior because they reflect some sort of natural plan (Renzetti & Curran, 1992).
- *Most gays wish they were members of the other sex.* They do not. Most gays are quite happy with their sex and their gender identity, and they are not at all confused about either one.
- *Gay adults frequently try to seduce young children.* Wrong. In fact, about 90 percent of child molesters are heterosexual men (Gelles & Cornell, 1990).
- *Gays can't be parents because the children they raise will have confused gender identities.* There is no evidence of this (Bozett, 1988).
- *Gays are notoriously promiscuous.* Not really. This is painting with too broad a brush. It is true that some gay men are promiscuous, but the AIDS epidemic has begun to decrease that. In fact, most lesbian relationships and about 50 percent of gay male relationships are sexually exclusive.
- *Intimate gay relationships are short-term.* Not any shorter than, say, cohabiting relationships between heterosexual couples. And lesbians expect their relationships to last a long time (Macklin, 1987). In fact, lesbian relationships appear to last longer than either male gay relationships or male–female heterosexual relationships (Blumstein & Schwartz, 1983). While longer relationships exist between straight people who are married, that fact may depend on the availability of a formal marriage contract binding the straight couple in their relationship and the nonavailability of such a contract in the gay relationship.

Divorce

"Carl," Monica said, "I got a phone call today from someone who wouldn't give me his name. He said he saw you in the Black Rooster with Joyce Barnes. What's going on?"

"Oh, I just took her to lunch. We've been told we should pay more attention to the staff."

"Well, how come you told me you went to lunch with Barney?"

"Uh, well . . . at the last minute Barney couldn't go. He was supposed to be with us," lied Carl.

Drawing by M. Stevens; © 1985 The New Yorker
Magazine, Inc.

"Now, you wait right here while I go ask my wife for a divorce."

"You liar. I've had it with you fooling around! I called Barney to see if he knew where you were. He didn't know anything about lunch with you. Pack your bags and get out. I'm calling a lawyer!"

divorce

The legal dissolution of a formal marriage contract.

   Divorce is one of life's most stressful events, nearly as stressful as a death in the family. The parallel with a death is a fair analogy. When death of a loved one occurs, a relationship is irrevocably terminated. In divorce, too, a relationship is terminated, also usually forever. In fact, in divorce several relationships may change at the same time: relationships with children of the marriage, relationships with both sets of parents, and relationships with friends. In addition, divorce is financially taxing, adding to the overall stress. Moreover, lifestyles of the partners change: One must start cooking or begin eating out; one must face dating new partners years after courting skills have last been practiced. One of the partners may not have been employed before the divorce and may not be very employable after it. (Women suffer the most here: A plurality of U.S. families on welfare are headed by single or divorced women.) So, all in all, divorce is a very painful experience.

   There are a number of variables that appear related to whether one divorces, including marriage at a young age, divorce or unhappiness among one's relatives, religion, education, race, and, perhaps, whether one has another partner waiting.

Correlates of Divorce

AGE WHEN MARRIED.   If you marry in your teens, your marriage is twice as likely to end in divorce than if you marry in your twenties. This is true regardless of whether the teen marriage occurred because of premarital pregnancy (Glick & Norton, 1977; Yoder & Nichols, 1980). Yet the relationship appears to be curvilinear, since women who are over 30 when they first marry are also more likely to divorce than the national average. Apparently they are less tolerant of a bad marriage (Albrecht et al., 1983).

PARENTS' AND GRANDPARENTS' DIVORCES.   The more divorce there is in your family history the more likely you are to divorce (Bumpass & Sweet, 1972; Landis, 1956; Pope & Mueller, 1976). This may relate to faulty role learning. After all, if your parents and/or your grandparents didn't make their marriages survive, what did they inadvertently (or consciously) teach you about it?

RELIGION.   The likelihood of a divorce appears directly related to religion. Included here are several variables such as religious identification (what religion you profess) and religious practice. The strongest religious determiner, however, is whether or not your marriage occurred in a religious setting (synagogue, church, or temple). If you belong to a religion where marriage is sanctified (perhaps eternally as for the Mormons), if you are actively religious, if you actively identify with a particular religion, if you marry someone of the same faith, and if the wedding takes place in a religious setting, the likelihood of divorce in such marriages is lower (Albrecht et al., 1983; Bahr, 1981; Bumpass & Sweet, 1972).

EDUCATION.   For men, the higher the educational level, the lower the likelihood of divorce. For women, the same is true up to the highest educational levels, then the likelihood of divorce rises again (Glick & Norton, 1977). Glick and Norton speculate that this latter finding may be due to conflicts produced by the careers of such women. Such women may also have greater financial independence (Albrecht et al., 1983).

RACE.   Afro-Americans are slightly more likely to divorce than whites (Carter & Glick, 1976) and they are very much more likely to be separated (Glick & Norton, 1977). These data, however, must be interpreted cautiously because they only reflect a population's status at the time of the census on which they are based (Albrecht et al., 1983).

Adjusting to Divorce

Obviously, major adjustments are necessary when divorce occurs. Here are some problem areas commonly experienced by those undergoing a divorce:

THE INITIAL CRISIS.   This is a crisis of change: a radically altered lifestyle, disrupted social networks, and some loss of identity are all possible. It is probably a good idea not to make far-reaching decisions during this period, for example, to change jobs or to move to another city, as these may compound stress. As with grief, waiting it out and working through it may be all that are possible. Bad habits such as smoking or drinking may be more problematic during this period. Watch out for retreating into self-pity, rebounding too quickly into the marriage market, yearning for your former spouse, and harboring unreasonable resentment (Cox, 1979). Life goes on and you must also.

EMOTIONS.   Your emotions are likely to seem as though they are on a roller coaster running the gamut from anger with the former spouse and shame and guilt with yourself and your family to residual love for your spouse. You may also feel lonely. To be forewarned about this roller-coaster ride is in some ways to be forearmed for it, but, for the most part, these feelings have to be experienced repeatedly in order to be neutralized. You will probably be helped by being able to confide in someone during this period. Don't be afraid to seek professional help if you feel you need it. Many people do.

CHANGING YOUR LIFESTYLE.   There are many things you'll have to do differently. Much depends on what you did during your marriage. You will almost surely have to work if you weren't already working. If you have no marketable skills, you will need to consider training. You may have much more to do with child care. And you may have to start looking after yourself in terms of food, laundry, and housework. New social relationships and social networks have to be built also. It is a time for rebuilding.

Remarriage

One fact that may help you get through a divorce are the statistics on remarriage (Glick, 1984*b*): A majority of men and women remarry after divorce within three years. So a comeback is possible. These figures also suggest the continuing desirability of the marriage relationship even to people who have had trouble with a prior marriage.

SUMMARY

■ Marriage is still the preferred relationship between women and men. While both sexes are waiting longer to get married, the total numbers of people getting married continue to increase each year. The length of first marriages—which has decreased for the past 20 years—may have stabilized. Divorce rates—which have also increased over the past 20 years—may also have stabilized.

■ Mate selection for marriage seems to fall into three phases. The first phase in which a couple meet owes to the same variables that assist in the formation and development of any relationship—attractiveness, propinquity, exposure, and love at first sight—among other variables. The second phase involves attitude and value comparisons and matching. If everything compares and matches well, a couple may enter the third phase, thinking of the partner as marriage material, and examining how well the partner fits the role of spouse, lover, and lifetime companion.

■ Marriage itself can be divided into at least five common stages: being a newly-wed and starting a new family; having and raising children; getting through the children's adolescence; getting through the adult children's leave taking; and being alone again together. Each stage has its common occurrences and their effects on marriage satisfaction, which is lowest during the child-rearing years.

■ Marriage itself requires a large number of personal adjustments in significant areas such as communications, work, finances, sex, children, and the possibility of physical abuse, to name a few. Enduring marriages have at their core the acceptance of one's spouse as best friend and the inherent commitments to the spouse as a person, and to the institution of marriage. On the other hand, marriages are destabilized when spouses don't think alike and have little insight into each other's feelings and needs.

■ Modern marriages are highly likely to be characterized by both spouses working outside the home. Women in these marriages expect to share in breadwinning. But they also expect that women's chores from traditional marriages (such as housework and child rearing) will be equitably shared. Alas, this does not appear to happen to as great an extent as women would like and is a source of friction.

■ There are viable alternatives to marriage including cohabiting, communal living, remaining single, and parenting singly. All these arrangements seem temporary to the extent that most people plan to marry (or remarry). Overall there seems to be somewhat higher satisfaction with marriage than other relationships.

■ Gay and lesbian relationships, which can also be considered alternatives to heterosexual marriage, develop and maintain in the same way as heterosexual relationships, though there is still considerable institutional discrimination against them. They may be less stable than heterosexual marriage in part because they are by necessity informal in nature.

- Divorce is a very stressful life event evoking some of the same grief and emotional upset that occurs with the death of a loved one. Social relationships are disrupted, emotions are entangled, and considerable changes in lifestyle often result. Most people who are divorced remarry within a few years suggesting that marriage is still the preferred type of relationship between heterosexual adults.

Box 9-4

SELF-ADJUSTMENT FOR STUDENTS:
Managing Consequences

We know beyond a shadow of a doubt that what happens after a behavior occurs—particularly if the behavior is directly responsible for what happens after it—is very important to the future occurrence of the behavior. Recall from Chapter 3 that consequences for behavior that have the effect of increasing or maintaining the future likelihood of the behavior are called *positive reinforcers* and those that decrease the future likelihood of behavior are called *punishers*.

Identifying Consequences

It is as important to identify consequences for behavior as it was to identify the situations in which behavior occurs (Chapter 8). The correct identification of consequences can help you pinpoint the environmental events that are helping to maintain undesirable behaviors and those that are inhibiting the occurrence of desirable behaviors.

Look for the following kinds of reinforcers that may maintain undesirable behavior. They may also be scheduled (by you or someone else for you) to get desirable behavior to occur more frequently:

1. *Consumable reinforcers.* Anything that can be consumed may function this way including regular foods, junk foods, sweets, drinks, cigarettes, etc.
2. *Activity reinforcers.* Any activities that you enjoy including sports, hobbies, crafts, and leisure (for example, watching television, reading, listening) may function this way.
3. *Manipulative reinforcers.* These often cross with activity reinforcers but involve any activity in which the manipulation of objects or games itself is reinforcing. Putting together puzzles, working on a favorite car, and art painting would qualify.
4. *Possessional reinforcers.* These are reinforcers, the owning (and therefore the using) of which may be reinforcing. Clothes, luxury items, virtually any object that you want, but don't have, will qualify.
5. *Social reinforcers.* These are potentially the most important kind of reinforcers for us. They are characterized by almost any kind of contact with another person: a smile, a hug, a verbal statement of praise, sexual contact, etc.
6. *The Premack Principle.* A high probability behavior (HPB) will reinforce a low probability behavior (LPB) if the high probability behavior is restricted until the low probability behavior occurs. In other words, if we can't do what we want to do (HPB) until we do what we have to do (LPB), we'll do what we have to do (LPB). Remember, your mother used to say, "Eat your spinach because when you get finished you can go outside to play." And you ate your spinach, didn't you?

From the last chapter, review the list of situations and stimuli that control your behavior to be adjusted. In those situations, try to determine if any of the above reinforcers are maintaining the problem behavior.

Managing Consequences

In order to make consequences effective for your behavior, they must be managed. Managing them means scheduling them to occur or preventing their occurrence immediately after behavior occurs.

Scheduling Positive Reinforcers for Desirable Behavior. Select as large a variety of positive reinforcers as you can to strengthen a new, weak positive behavior. This is called a reinforcement survey. Schedule one of the reinforcers to occur immediately after each occurrence of a desirable behavior. If you cannot exert the self-control to deny yourself these reinforcers until you exhibit the new behavior, give your control over them to a friend or family member.

You will be able to judge that some reinforcers are much more desirable to you than others, the difference, say, between an ice-cream cone and a banana split. Divide your reinforcers into those that you can earn for each instance of a behavior (or for a day's instances) and those that become available only after a larger number of instances, say a week's worth of the new behavior. Schedule the more desirable reinforcers only after a lot of behavior is exhibited (a week's worth).

After the new behavior occurs fairly regularly, reduce the reinforcement for its occurrence so that it requires two or three instances of the behavior before reinforcement becomes available. Also solicit social reinforcement for your successes from others.

Preventing Positive Reinforcers for Undesirable Behavior. This is a trickier proposition because often these reinforcers occur naturally. Drinking too much beer makes you feel relaxed and uninhibited (the reinforcers), but it may also impair your judgment. What to do? One way is to attempt to dissociate the undesirable behavior from the myriad of situations in which it occurs and is reinforced. Maybe this means slowly cutting down the number of environments in which you drink beer. You will also need to schedule other reinforcers for behaviors that successfully control your propensity to drink beer. Let's say, for example, that you go to a movie (a reinforcing activity for you) on Friday night instead of to the bar.

Scheduling Mild Punishers for Undesirable Behavior. You can also schedule mild punishers for yourself to be applied immediately upon the occurrence of an undesirable behavior. Thought stopping seems to work this way. You shout "no!" to yourself upon the occurrence of an undesirable behavior and then follow that punishing response by making yourself engage in a low probability be-havior for a few minutes. A low probability behavior is something that you don't want to do and that you don't do very often. Let's say the undesirable behavior is nagging. You catch yourself in the act, silently shout "no!," and then announce to the naggee that you are sorry about nagging and you'll try not to do it again. If apology is a low probability behavior for you, it and the silent shout should suppress future nagging.

Students of the authors have also used elastic bands around their wrists which they snap against their skin upon the occurrence of some undesirable behavior. A related technique is simply to record each instance of the undesirable behavior when it occurs. In many cases the recording itself acts as punishment sufficient to reduce the frequency of the undesirable behavior. This happens for a combination of reasons—recording may interfere with the usual reinforcement for the response, it may break up a sequence of behavior, it may raise awareness of habitual, automatic responses, and it may force you to be public about what you are up to.

Getting Rid of Punishers That Stop Desirable Behaviors. This usually involves making some prior responses to make sure that your response to-be-adjusted can occur without being punished. If you want to do electrical work around your home, for example, turning off the electricity entirely will allow you to take apart a receptacle without being shocked. If learning to dance is your to-be-adjusted behavior and public embarrassment is the punisher that stops you from trying, you could set up conditions so that you could practice in private.

If it is impossible to get rid of a punisher for a desirable response you may be able to increase the reinforcement for making the response in the face of the punishment. Perhaps this involves getting lucky—you ask the most beautiful girl at the dance whether she will guide you through the steps and she does.

In sum, managing consequences first requires their identification to help you zero in on what's causing or maintaining some behavior or stopping other behavior from getting started. Then it requires the adroit scheduling of positive and/or negative consequences (reinforcers and punishers) immediately after your targeted behavior occurs. Good luck!

MEMORY BOOSTER

■ IMPORTANT TERMS

Be prepared to define the following terms (located in the margins of this chapter). Where appropriate, be prepared to describe examples.

Marriage

Polygyny

Polyandry

Monogamy

Endogamy

Homogamy

Cohabiting

Trial Marriage

Communal Living

Utopian Society

Heterosexist

Divorce

■ QUESTIONS FROM IMPORTANT IDEAS IN THIS CHAPTER

1. In a sentence or two each, describe six areas in which some adjustment is typically necessary to sustain marriage.

2. What two types of commitment help to make a marriage endure?

3. According to surveys of happy marriages, what are the reasons that marriages endure happily?

4. Describe how the women's movement and dual careers have changed women's expectations of roles in marriage.

5. Many of the problems that characterize unhappy marriages can be categorized into three general areas. List those three areas.

6. List several reasons why people are likely to stay in unhappy marriages.

7. List five variables that relate to the likelihood of divorce. For each, state the relationship between it and the likelihood of divorce.

GROWING UP AND GROWING OLD

CHAPTER OUTLINE

After reading this chapter, you should be able to:

■ Describe how language, thinking processes, and moral reasoning develop in children.

■ Describe what are thought to be several tasks of adolescence.

■ Show how midlife may discriminate against women, and discuss what should be done about it.

■ Discuss difficulties faced by men and women during their middle years.

■ Discuss some of the physical and cognitive changes that occur with aging.

■ Understand the kinds of personal adjustments that people must make during the process of dying.

Many of the adjustments we make are associated with particular times of our lives. As children most of us are informally socialized to obey our parents and other adults, and to behave as boys or girls. We all may have reasonably similar experiences as teenagers and as young adults. And the adult years may have their similarities also. As young adults our adjustments are different than our adjustments are during childhood, adolescence, midlife, or after midlife. In part, our bodies dictate the similarities of our experiences as they grow, sexually mature, and then begin the long, slow decline to death. But also in part, our environments, which are filled with the behavior of others, play their roles. In the late teenage years it is commonly expected that a large portion of the teenage population will go on to college. Most young adults eventually expect to get married. Adults in midlife find themselves reevaluating their careers, and dealing with their adolescent children, their aging parents, and their changing physical capacities. Each of these times can be considered a phase, a stage, or a period during which characteristic events, changes in our bodies, and our responses to them occur.

Life-span developmental psychologists have cast their theories in terms of these stages and we can now say something about each phase of the life cycle. Yet the validity of theories of life-span development is still an open question. First, there is wide variability in behavior across all people who are the same age. Second, some people show some, all, or none of the behaviors common to a particular age or stage. While the validity of stage theories of development is still open, they are useful teaching devices because they impose a certain order to life—the life cycle. So, in this chapter we'll briefly examine some of the stages of the life cycle and the adjustments associated with them.

Prenatally Speaking

There wasn't much you could do to adjust to the prenatal conditions that were foist upon you. But some knowledge of what went on at that time can help those of you who plan to have children.

Prenatal development is primarily genetic and hormonal. It takes place via incessant cell division as the fertilized egg or zygote becomes two cells, those two become four cells, and so on. The first two weeks of development of the zygote are called the **ovum stage.**

ovum stage

The first two weeks after conception.

TABLE 10-1
SOME POTENTIAL EFFECTS ON THE
NEWBORN OF VARIOUS AGENTS
EXPERIENCED DURING GESTATION
Adapted from Zamula, 1989.

Agents	Potential Effects
Alcohol	Mental retardation
	Alcohol dependence
Heroin	Heroin addiction
Rubella	Mental retardation
	Deafness
	Blindness
Cigarettes	Premature delivery
	Fetal death
Thalidomide	Limb changes
Streptomycin	Hearing impairment

embryonic stage
Three to nine weeks or so after conception.

fetal stage
Ten to forty weeks or so after conception.

The developing embryo is most vulnerable during the **embryonic stage,** the next six weeks or so, when much of our nervous systems are being formed. After the eighth week or so the **fetal stage** begins and lasts to the end of the gestation period, about 32 weeks more, for a total of about 40 weeks' gestation. There are large changes in growth during the fetal stage.

Pregnant women should do nothing to upset the delicate biological environment that exists in the uterus during gestation. They must be careful, for example, of chemicals that pass through the placental barrier, such as drugs, that can produce developmental difficulties in newborns (for example, fetal alcohol syndrome; the "crack" baby) (see Table 10-1). Even cigarette smoking, which raises the level of carbon monoxide in the mother's bloodstream and partially starves her of oxygen, also partially starves her fetus of oxygen.

Infants and Children

There are many adjustments that infants and children make. Foremost is birth itself, but that event is quickly followed by attachment to significant adults, the acquisition of language, socialization, emotional development, and the changes in children's thinking processes across childhood. We'll briefly examine a few of these.

Attachment and Independence

Infants and toddlers become attached or bonded to those who care for them early in life. By attachment we mean that the infant seeks out a significant caretaker for comfort, for security, and as a base from which to safely learn about the world. The attachment process appears to begin with nursing. A well-bonded infant of eight or nine months will be distressed if its mother—a significant caretaker—leaves it in the presence of a stranger. Given pain or other difficulty, it may be soothed only by its mother. Such behavior is called **attachment behavior** (Bretherton, 1985), an important part of social development.

attachment behavior
Any behavior that is evidence of an emotional tie by an infant to a caretaker adult.

Imbedded in the attachment process are the seeds of autonomy, for it is from the secure base of the significant caretaker that the infant explores new environments, at first briefly, returning as though for reassurance, only to strike out again, perhaps farther. Individuation and autonomy are thought to develop from this process.

Language Development

Of course, one of the great accomplishments of most young humans is that they learn to talk. This process seems to start at about six months and is largely finished by about five years. Most children start off with a word at a time (but some say more); progress to two words at a time in special constructions (such as "Doggie gone," "Daddy gone," "Mommy gone"); conversational turn taking along with a myriad of different meanings for their two-word utterances (such as location: "Daddy here"); and then learn to use connectives such as "and," "because," and "what." It's an extraordinary accomplishment in a short time so that it looks like an explosion, but it really isn't. It's quite orderly—just fast.

Cognitive Development: Thinking

Thanks to the early work of Swiss psychologist Jean Piaget there has been much interest in how children think at different times of their lives. Piaget carefully observed his own and other children and ran simple but elegant demonstrations with them to probe how they thought. The result of his work was the division of children's thinking into four different stages. Piaget thought that children biologically matured into these stages of thinking (Table 10-2).

CRITIQUE OF PIAGET'S THEORY.   While Piaget made valid inferences about child cognitive development we now know a lot more. For example, newborns are not just reflexive beings as Piaget thought they were. Rather, we know that children can be engaged in operant learning in the first few hours of life (Siqueland & Lipsitt, 1966) and that something akin to imitation can be observed then also (Meltzoff, 1988; Reissland, 1988). And Piaget's division of cognitive development into stages is

TABLE 10-2
LEVELS OF COGNITIVE DEVELOPMENT ACCORDING TO PIAGET

Age	Level	Behavior
0–2 yrs.	*Sensorimotor*	Automatic actions and sensory feedback are important; slow development of awareness.

Example: Objects are grasped, mouthed, flung, pushed, pulled, examined, touched, tasted, listened to. Presented two beakers of colored water, child grasps and spills them.

2–6 or 7 yrs.	*Preoperational*	Words and images are developed and used but adult logic is not; complexities of systems are not understood; self-centered communication.

Example: Child is shown two equal-sized beakers equally filled; colored water is poured from one to a taller, thinner beaker. Child states that there is more water in the taller beaker.

6 or 7–11 or 12 yrs.	*Concrete operational*	Logical thinking observed; no hypothetical thinking; case-by-case reasoning.

Example: Child shown the liquid conservation demonstration above states that the amount of water is the same in the taller beaker, but cannot abstract the underlying principle.

11 or 12 yrs.	*Formal operational*	Abstract thinking appears; broad reasoning.

Example: Child shown liquid conservation demonstration above states that the amount of water is the same in the taller beaker and that the amounts remain equal regardless of the size or shape of the container.

not thought to be as fixed as he thought it was. Children can be in one stage on one task (for example, conservation of liquid) and in another on a related task (for example, conservation of weight). We also know that training can accelerate children's cognitive development, which Piaget did not think was possible. Yet Piaget's theory still provides a decent framework with which to describe how children think at different ages.

Cognitive Development: Rule Acquisition

A more recent way to think about the development of thinking by children conceptualizes Piagetian tasks as problems to be solved. We can then ask, "How many rules are there that can be used to solve a task?" We can then see which rules children use and whether the rules change with age.

Figure 10-1
A balance beam. Washers can be inserted on the pegs while the beam is locked and a child asked to guess which end of the beam will descend when the lock is released. *From Siegler, 1986.*

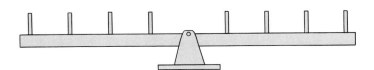

Let's use a balance beam task as an example. The child is shown a small balance beam, which is locked, and asked which end will go down when metal washers are placed on the rungs on either side of the center of the beam. You can see that both weight (the number of washers) and their distance from the center of the beam may have to be figured. In fact there are four possible rules in this situation (Table 10-3). The psychologist can manipulate weight or distance separately or together and infer what rules the child's behavior seems to demonstrate.

TABLE 10-3
RULES IN THE BALANCE BEAM TASK *From Siegler, 1986.*

Rule 1. Total weight on each side is all that matters. Distance from fulcrum is not accounted for.

Rule 2. Total weight on each side is used, and distance is ignored except when total weight on each side is the same. Distance is considered at this time only.

Rule 3. Weight and distance are considered equally. When one dimension is unequal to the other that dimension is used to predict. When both dimensions are unequal (different weights and different distances) but predict the fall of the same side, this rule works. But if the dimensions are unequal and favor the descent of different sides, this rule does not work. Children using this rule guess at these last examples.

Rule 4. Torque is computed for both sides. This is the distance from the fulcrum multiplied by the weight at that distance. Side with greatest torque descends. This rule always works since it is a physical law that accurately describes nature.

Psychologist Robert Siegler has worked with all of the Piagetian tasks, including the balance beam, from this rule development perspective (Siegler, 1986). Siegler suggested that children's cognitive development might be better thought of as the use of more and more complex rules rather than as a progression through different stages. In other words, very young children may exhibit no rule-governed behavior at all, then control by simple rules, and finally control by more complex rules. The results of Siegler's experiments support his theory. In the balance beam task, for example, children under five don't seem to use any rule, unless specifically taught portions of it. Then they use Rule 1 (Table 10-3). Thereafter, the older they get, the more they use Rules 2, 3, and 4. Generally speaking, the older the child, the more advanced the rule.

Siegler's theory is a good example of an information-processing account of child cognitive development. In one way it, too, can be criticized. We might ask whether all thinking is problem solving. Both Siegler and Piaget treat cognitive development as primarily problem solving. But, as we described in Chapter 4, we can also think in images.

Cognitive Development: Morals

Psychologists have also been interested in studying the way in which moral reasoning develops in children. This follows from the observation that we are socialized in ways that supposedly lead us to behave morally. How can moral development be examined and described?

The best known theory of moral development is that of Lawrence Kohlberg (1969). Kohlberg presented small vignettes that posed moral dilemmas and then examined the kinds of responses that children made to these vignettes. A moral dilemma occurs when, to do something that appears to be inherently correct, a law must be broken. Let's take Kohlberg's most famous vignette as an example (Kohlberg, 1969, p. 379):

> In Europe a woman was near death from a special kind of cancer. There was one drug that the doctors thought might save her. It was a form of radium that a druggist in the same town had recently discovered. The drug was expensive to make, but the druggist was charging 10 times what the drug cost him to make. He paid $200 for the radium and charged $2,000 for a small dose of the drug. The sick woman's husband, Heinz, went to everyone he knew to borrow the money, but he could only get together about $1,000, which was half of what it cost. He told the druggist that his wife was dying and asked him to sell it cheaper or let him pay later. But the druggist said: "No, I discovered the drug and I'm going to make money from it." So Heinz got desperate and broke into the man's store to steal the drug for his wife.

After hearing the vignette, the child is asked a series of questions: Should Heinz have done it? Was it right or wrong? Did the druggist have the right to charge that much? From the answers he got over 20 years to vignettes such as this, Kohlberg developed a theory which contained three levels and two stages at each level of development (Table 10-4). Kohlberg found that children's moral reasoning seemed to advance with their age. It was also related to their intelligence. Younger children produced more stage 1 and stage 2 reasoning. 10- to 13-year-olds produced more stage 3 and stage 4 reasoning, but less stage 4 reasoning than 16-year-olds. Kohlberg found little stage 5 or stage 6 reasoning in adolescents. Stage 5 reasoning doesn't seem to appear commonly until the twenties. Stage 6 is even fairly rare in adults (less than 5%) (Kohlberg, 1981).

A KOHLBERG CRITIQUE. Moral reasoning doesn't necessarily translate into moral behavior. And individuals don't appear to progress smoothly through Kohlberg's stages. Moreover, the stages aren't universal across cultures. Finally, as do other developmental theorists in many areas, Kohlberg left out women in his treatment of moral dilemmas (Modgil & Modgil, 1985). His vignettes involved only men (Gilligan, 1982). And Kohlberg's scoring system (which was also controversial) often located women at Stage 3 and not above.

THE DEVELOPMENT OF MORAL REASONING IN WOMEN. Gilligan (1982) has reasoned that women—having considerably different socialization than men—should reason differently—not in an inferior way, just a different way. She proposed that young women are socialized to be care givers. They are taught the importance of maintaining relationships between individuals and avoiding isolation. They tend to see dilemmas in terms of conflicting responsibilities rather than conflicting rights, and to make decisions pragmatically rather than abstractly. In Gilligan's three levels of women's moral development, Level 1 moral reasoning

TABLE 10-4
KOHLBERG'S LEVELS OF MORAL DEVELOPMENT *From Kohlberg, 1981.*

The Preconventional Level

Stage 1. Punishment and Obedience.
Stage 2. Individual Instrumental Purpose and Exchange.

This is the level of young children who answer on the basis of the immediate external consequences of the action in the dilemma. Stage 1: "You could get caught and go to jail." Stage 2: "You'd save your wife."

The Conventional Level

Stage 3: Mutual Interpersonal Expectations, Relationships, and Conformity.
Stage 4: Social System and Conscience.

This is the level where moral reasoning is partially internalized. Older children abide either by parental standards or by society's rules. Stage 3: "Your family wouldn't think much of you." Stage 4: "You'd be breaking the law."

The Postconventional or Principled Level

Stage 5: Social Contract or Utility and Individual Rights.
Stage 6: Universal Ethical Principles.

At this level morality is completely internalized. Personal moral codes are adopted after consideration of alternative moral choices. Stage 5: "You'd probably feel pretty guilty if you let your wife die." Stage 6: "If you don't take it you'd be okay in society's eyes, but not in your own."

involved concern for self and survival; Level 2 involved being responsible and caring for others; and Level 3 involved concern for self and others as being interdependent. Gilligan's theory of women's moral development is new enough that it hasn't received much validation as yet. However, it is clear that she has located a considerable omission on the part of developmental theorists.

After getting through early and middle childhood we develop into adolescents. Who are adolescents? And why do they act the way they do?

Adolescents/Adolescence

Who Are They?

Adolescents are people in transition between childhood and adulthood. The adolescent stage of development appears to occur primarily in developed countries. In undeveloped countries children go right into adulthood with all of its responsibilities. In our culture one reason for adolescence is the time necessary for young people to separate from their families. In turn, this feat rests upon the adolescent successfully traversing high school and in many cases college. During this period our society contains physiologically mature people who lack the rights of adults—a confusing state at best.

Age isn't a very good marker for the boundaries of this stage, but we often rely on it. Take Bill and Gene for instance: They're both 12 years old. When they were both 11, Bill and Gene were the same height. Now Bill is 4 inches taller than Gene, his voice is changing, and he's growing pubic hair. None of this has happened to Gene yet.

Or consider Kathy and Juanita. They're both 20. Juanita lives at home where her parents pay for her to attend a local college. She has no job; her parents provide her with life's essentials. Kathy is married and has two children. Her

Age is not a very good indicator of the beginning of adolescence. The onset of puberty would seem to be better. The photo shows all 13-year-olds from the same seventh/eighth grade class. The obvious differences in size suggest that within this group of students there is wide variation in the age at which puberty begins.

husband has left her. She works full-time in a supermarket and shares an apartment with her children. Has adolescence ended for either of these two? We would argue that it has for one of them. While Juanita can still act like an adolescent, Kathy cannot. She has all the responsibilities of a young adult. Perhaps the best we can do is say that adolescence is the period begun by puberty (see below) and ended when the adolescent behaves mostly as a young adult, with a young adult's responsibilities and independence.

The Big "P"

puberty

The time period during adolescence when rapid growth and the development of secondary sexual characteristics occur.

The big physical marker of adolescence is called **puberty.** That's where your genetic program—again in concert with the environment (for example, nutrition)—starts flooding the body with hormones. The whole event involves the secretions of several glands including the pituitary, the adrenals, the thyroid, the testes (males), and the ovaries (females). Among other events such as the development of secondary sexual characteristics, this hormonal activity produces a growth spurt (Figure 10-2). For each sex the pubertal growth spurt lasts about two years.

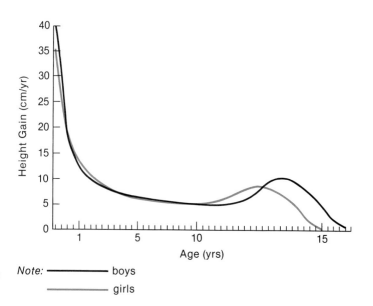

Figure 10-2

Height gain at various ages. After the rapid growth of the first two years of life there is a steady decline in growth until puberty. Early in puberty there is a growth spurt. *From Tanner et al., 1965.*

Girls grow about 3.5 inches per year during this time and boys grow about 4.0 inches per year.

Secondary Sexual Characteristics

sex hormones

Hormones that produce the primary and secondary sexual characteristics.

During puberty in males there is an increase in levels of testosterone (an androgen) and in females an increase in estradiol (an estrogen), so-called **sex hormones** that are responsible for the development of secondary sexual characteristics (see Chapter 7). The secondary sexual characteristics appear in very regular order. For males, there is an increase in the size of the testicles and the penis, the appearance of straight pubic hair, minor voice changes, the first ejaculation, the appearance of curly pubic hair, a period of maximum growth, the growth of hair in the armpits, larger changes in voice, and finally, the growth of facial hair (Faust, 1977).

menarche

The first menstruation.

For females, this hormone flood produces either breast enlargement or the growth of pubic hair; followed by hair growth in the armpits; growth in height; widening of the hips; development of fatty tissue in and around the breasts, shoulders, and hips; and the first menstruation called **menarche** (Faust, 1977).

PUBERTY NOW AND PUBERTY THEN.   The age when puberty occurs has changed dramatically across the years. On the average, it is now at the youngest age for those in developed countries—about 12.8 years for American females. It has decreased from the upper to the lower teens in the space of a century or so. The decrease is thought to parallel improvements in nutrition. For any individual, the onset of puberty is determined by heredity, nutrition, exercise, and stress. Given that we are about as nourished (and as stressed) as we can get, further age decreases are probably unlikely.

There are wide variations in the onset of puberty as our little description of Bill and Gene pointed out. It may occur as early as 10 years for some and as late as 15 years for others. The pubertal period only lasts about 3 years, so that some individuals start and finish puberty while some of their same-aged peers have not yet even begun (Santrock, 1987). Some effects of early maturation on the adolescent are shown in Table 10-5. Most of these effects disappear in later adolescence.

TABLE 10-5
SOME EFFECTS OF EARLY MATURATION ON ADOLESCENTS *from Santrock, 1987.*

Early Maturing Males

- Perceive themselves more positively; have higher self-esteem
- Rated more attractive, composed, and socially sophisticated by peers and adults
- Less satisfied with their bodies and their weights
- May be less flexible in identity formation
- Less often chosen as leaders early on, more often later

Early Maturing Females

- More satisfied with their figure development early on
- Less satisfied with their figure development later when late maturers catch up
- Less prestige in elementary school; more prestige in junior high with peers
- May be less flexible in identity formation
- More popular with boys; date more
- More independence granted them early on
- Lower grades and achievement scores
- More trouble at school

Working through Adolescence

Some psychologists have proposed that there are developmental tasks that need to be accomplished in the various life periods—complex behaviors that are learned by most individuals during these times. According to Havinghurst (1972) such developments during adolescence include:

- *The development of new and more mature relationships with peers of both sexes.* Most of you will recall that this was a time when you wanted to be close to someone of the other sex, and there wasn't much information about how to do this. It was also the time when you formed your first intimate friendships. We'll deal with this more below.

- *The development of a clear social role, either instrumental (masculine), expressive (feminine), or both (androgynous).* Actually, your gender identity which underpins this social role was long since formed (Chapter 7), but some finishing touches occur during this time, such as continued refinement in how to interact socially with your peers.

- *The acceptance of your physique and the effective use of your body.* So much growth takes place during adolescence that your new body took some getting used to. Occasionally, it may have embarrassed you.

- *The achievement of emotional independence from parents and other adults.* Many of you probably found that adolescence was a time when you no longer wanted to be with your parents all of the time. Typically, you may have felt both good and bad about that at the same time. As time passed you felt better and better about making your own decisions and leading your own life.

- *Preparation for marriage and family life.* This task may have begun to interest you when you began to attend showers or bachelor parties for someone who was getting married or who was going to have a baby.

- *Preparation for a career.* A lot of you worked part-time. You found out that the job that you were doing would not be one you would want forever. Maybe this started you thinking about what you would like to do.

- *The development of values and ethics.* During high school, one of the authors recalls hanging out one night with some friends who needed gas for their cars. They liberated it from the local school buses—just a little at a time—and were never detected. He decided that he would be unavailable to hang out with them anymore. No doubt most of you have had comparable experiences. During this time, many moral decisions have to be made, and they aren't easy.

- *The development of socially responsible behavior.* Perhaps this was the time when you learned that it paid off to be at work on time, to get school assignments done early, and to keep your area of your home clean.

That these tasks of adolescence may be enduring features is suggested by how many of them are still relevant today, quite a few years after Havinghurst proposed them.

Others have proposed that adolescence is a time of identity formation.

Other Tasks of Adolescence

"WHO AM I ANYWAY?"   Consider the following telephone conversation:
"Hi Don? George. Want to get a Coke? I'll pick you up."
George and Don are seniors in high school. It's a Wednesday evening about 8 P.M. during the school year. Don might respond with:

1. "Sounds great. I don't want to study anyway." Or:
2. "Well, George, I'd like to but I've got this trigonometry test tomorrow. I'd better study. Can I take a rain check?"

Each of these endings provisionally tells us something about Don's development during adolescence. While we shouldn't make too much out of one little interaction, let's indulge in a generalization or two. If, on these occasions, Don's

Many adolescents work. During this time they establish good work habits. They also get a taste for what they don't like about the jobs they do.

response is always like the first one, we might conclude that he is not much of a scholar. Maybe he has decided that he doesn't want much more education. Would you guess that he has thought about what he wants to be (as they say) "when he grows up"? The second response seems to indicate an interest in doing well in school subjects. Perhaps the Don of this response is contemplating college, or a specific career. One of the things that occurs during some part of adolescence is that you figure out who you are and what you want to do.

How Did You Become You?   Adolescence has been thought of as the time when you begin to separate from your family, as your relationships with your parents and your siblings change. The adolescent establishes an "identity." We can think of this identity as a collection of self-descriptions that an individual has learned to apply. These self-descriptions are taught us throughout our lives by people asking such questions as "What are you doing?" or "How do you feel?" We learn to reply, "I'm thinking," or "I'm fine." A full collection of these "I" statements describes in our own words who we are. Eventually, we even reflect upon these statements about ourselves and in doing so contemplate who we are. At the beginning of adolescence there may be little such self-reflection. There are several ways of conceptualizing this change.

Identity versus Confusion?   In Erik Erikson's stages of psychosocial development, adolescence is thought to be comprised of two opposing tendencies—identity or identity confusion. With appropriate development a synthesis occurs between these two tendencies.

For Erikson, identity is achieved by investing oneself in an enduring set of commitments. These commitments involve an ideological stance defined by a set of values, an occupational stance defined by educational and career goals, and an interpersonal stance defined by sexual orientation. Essentially this means trying different behaviors over several years before an enduring style results.

In fact, for Erikson the process of identity formation continues throughout life. However, most identity formation is thought to occur toward the end of adolescence, say from 18 to 21 years. The new experiences of going to college and starting employment probably contribute to this in large measure.

Erikson's view of adolescence may not be all that correct. Most adolescent boys don't show much of an identity crisis during adolescence (Douvan & Adelson, 1966; Offer & Offer, 1969). Adolescent girls may find it more difficult to find identity than boys do, but for them, too, there is little sense of crisis (Douvan & Adelson, 1966).

The other great task of adolescence Erikson considered to be the development of intimacy. By this he didn't mean sexual intimacy, rather, he meant "true and mutual psychosocial intimacy." Necessarily, the development of intimacy awaited the development of identity. Failure to develop the ability to relate well with other humans would lead to a sense of isolation.

A TIME FOR MODELING AND SELF-REINFORCEMENT.   When a person learns to self-reinforce, there may be less dependence on external sources of reinforcement, because the individual can self-reinforce in the absence of external reinforcement. This ability may mean that greater delays to external reinforcement can be tolerated. The development of self-reinforcement processes and toleration of greater delays to reinforcement describe two major differences between children and adults. Adults are much less dependent on immediate, external reinforcement than children, and adults can self-reinforce. Behaviorally speaking then, two tasks of adolescence are to become less dependent on external reinforcement and to utilize more self-reinforcement because longer—adult-length—delays to reinforcement must be tolerated.

One process by which the foregoing occur is through modeling the behavior of others, especially if you see that what they do is reinforced. When you emit the behavior they do in the same situation, this may produce a different kind of reinforcement called **vicarious reinforcement** (Bandura, 1977), which is reinforcement that enhances performance based on the observation of others reinforced for the same behavior in the same situation. It is also often true that if you do what others do when they're reinforced, you, too, may be directly reinforced as they were.

vicarious reinforcement

Enhancement of performance by observing others being reinforced for the same performance.

WOMEN AND ADOLESCENT THEORY.   We saw above that women have been understandably indignant when psychological theory either ignored their development or considered their development—when different—to be somehow deviant from that of men, as though men's development was the standard (Kimmel & Weiner, 1985). A more important task than identity development for women during adolescence is the development and maintenance of intimate relationships with others (Chodorow, 1974; Gilligan, 1982). Unlike boys who must detach from their mothers, girls do not need to detach from their mothers to establish an identity for themselves.

"So, What Else Is Happening?"

The notable sexual developments of puberty bring with them the capability of reproduction as a part of sexual behavior. What are the facts about sexual behavior during adolescence?

Prior to adolescence there is often exploration of body parts under the guise of some game (for example, playing doctor). These encounters are often homosexual, especially for boys. But adolescence marks the time of the first serious sexual encounters with others, and for most the earlier homosexual encounters don't affect later sexual preference.

"BIRDS DO IT; BEES DO IT."   Most adolescents discover masturbation early in adolescence. About 33 to 50 percent of boys and 18 to 37 percent of girls have masturbated by the time they are 13 years old; by the time they are 18 to 19 years old, about 80 percent or more of boys and 59 percent of girls report that they have masturbated (Hass, 1979; Sorenson, 1973). By the time they get to college, women have caught up with men in this practice (Sarrel & Sarrel, 1981). While clearly common, considerable embarrassment still surrounds masturbation. Though no longer considered sinful, the practice may not be helpful to those who are withdrawn and otherwise emotionally disturbed (Chilman, 1983).

Figure 10-3
Percent of American teens from ages 13 to 18 who have had intercourse. *Data from Coles & Stokes, 1985.*

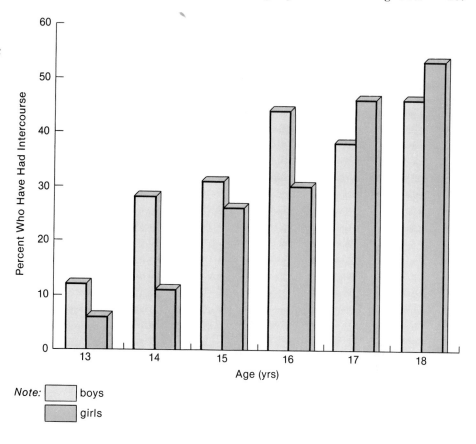

GETTING IT TOGETHER.   There comes a day for most everyone when full sexual relations with another occur. By age 18 about half of each sex has lost its virginity. Girls tend to be ambivalent about their first experience while boys tend to be glad (Coles & Stokes, 1985); however, girls don't remain ambivalent. Rates of nonmarital adolescent intercourse have been higher each time they have been sampled in the past (Zelnick & Kantner, 1980). Adolescents who engage in nonmarital intercourse are more likely to do so if they are going steady, date frequently, consider themselves in love, or are older (Chilman, 1983).

Growing Up Hard

Teenage problems have increased as the world gets more crowded and less forgiving and there is less familial control. Teens express the difficulties of the adolescent transition to young adulthood in several ways.

status offenses

Acts that are illegal because of age; for example, drinking alcohol.

DELINQUENCY.   If we use arrest figures to define delinquency, about 4 to 5 percent of children from 10 to 17 years qualify as delinquent annually. Boys outnumber girls about 3 to 1. About 60 percent of the offenses are misdemeanors, usually **status offenses,** that is, acts that are illegal because of age (for example, being in possession of alcohol). Delinquency is thought to occur for several reasons. First, it is at least partly social—there are rewards from the delinquent group for behavior that matches their own. Second, delinquency may be imbedded in your character. For example, you have been a good imitator of a delinquent parent. Third, delinquency may be a way to express unmet needs in your life, such as the absence of a parent or the presence of unrelenting poverty (Kimmel & Weiner, 1985).

Figure 10-4
Suicide rates by age, sex, and race in the United States. Notice how much more at risk males are than females. Finally, note the rise in the frequency of suicide for older white and Afroamerican males. *Data from U.S. National Center for Health Statistics, 1988.*

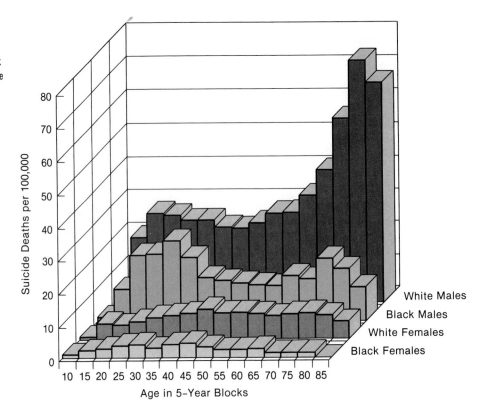

SUICIDE. Suicide is on the rise and has been among young men and women since the 1960s. It rises more sharply during the teen years for white males than for any other group. Suicide increases correspond with a time when there are more people of that age than ever before. Easterlin (1980) suggests that it is a function of the increased stressors on the current generation of teens because there are numerically so many more of them. Some reasons for suicide include increasingly difficult family problems, familial instability, broken social relationships, and failure in problem solving (Kimmel & Weiner, 1985). We deal more with suicide in Chapter 15 (Box 15-7).

RUNNING AWAY. More than 150,000 young people run away and are arrested annually. Many more who run are not arrested—perhaps as many as a million each year. These young people are at risk for many problems including violence, prostitution, and drug abuse. Problems at home and at school are often the causes of running away (Kimmel & Weiner, 1985).

SUBSTANCE ABUSE. Substance abuse can take several forms. At one end of the spectrum are the many young women who are bulimic or anorexic. **Bulimia nervosa** involves binging on food and then vomiting or using laxatives to purge the food from the body. It seems to involve food addiction as well as distortions of body image. **Anorexia nervosa** involves not eating and then purging whenever eating does occur. Suicide is not uncommon among anorexics. Young women for whom thinness is an ideal (cheerleaders; dancers) and even young men for whom weight goals are important (wrestlers) are susceptible to bulimia. Others of us who can't put down the potato chips until the bag is gone, may be on the same addictive continuum.

However, the major substances that are abused by adolescents are alcohol and drugs. Over 90 percent of high school students have tried alcohol at some time

bulimia nervosa

Bingeing food and then purging it to control weight yet satisfy food addiction.

anorexia nervosa

Self-imposed starvation with purging of food when eating does occur.

Tracey Gold, a successful entertainer, was an anorexic behind the scenes. In fact only about 50 percent of anorexics are currently saved through the treatment of their disorder.

in their lifetimes and over 60 percent have tried other illicit drugs (mostly marijuana) (Johnston et al., 1985). Most are recreational users, but a small yet significant number are psychologically or physically addicted, using on a daily basis. Fortunately, there has been some decrease in the use of these substances in the last few years (Figure 10-5).

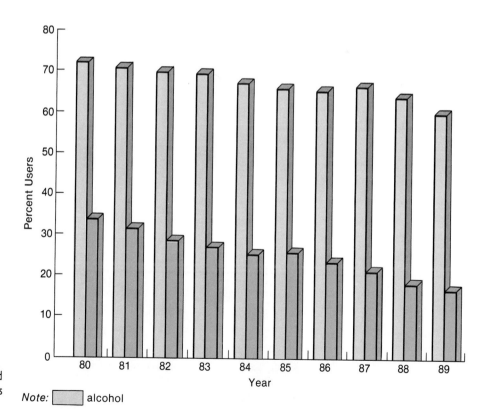

Figure 10-5

Percent of high school seniors who had used marijuana or alcohol in the 30 days previous to when they were surveyed. *Data from U.S. Department of Health and Human Services, 1990.*

Adolescent Cognitive Development

Recall that Piaget proposed that thinking changed qualitatively around the beginning of adolescence. This new stage of thinking was called the stage of formal operations (Table 10-2). Piaget thought that the adolescent was capable of abstract, scientific thought, while the preadolescent thought in concrete terms. An example describes the difference.

In Piaget's pendulum problem, the subject is asked what makes the pendulum go faster or slower. Subjects are shown pendulums of various lengths and weights and are asked to experiment with them. Children often combine a long string with a light weight and then a short string with a heavy weight. On the other hand, adolescents usually vary one aspect of the problem at a time keeping the other aspects constant—good scientific behavior. The younger children do not arrive at an accurate generalization; the adolescents do.

Remember, however, that we can conceptualize this type of change not as a qualitative one, but as the successive employment of ever more accurate rules, which can be taught (Siegler, 1986). Additionally, others have shown that we all don't inevitably end up thinking logically. Usually we think illogically! Logical thinking is much more likely by those who have experienced formal educations in math and science, and even then it doesn't occur all of the time. In general, however, it is fair to say that the adolescent is considering more abstract ideas.

WHAT ARE ADOLESCENTS THINKING?   Keating (1980) proposed that adolescents think about five different kinds of things, all of which children don't think about:

- *Possibilities.* Abstract thinking, for example, about UFOs, life and death, love, the universe.
- *Hypotheses.* These are generated and can actually be tested, or they can be tested in imagination.
- *The future.* The ability to plan shows up.
- *Thoughts.* These may reflect on their own behavior; diaries are kept.
- *Beyond old limits.* Old beliefs are challenged, new ones contemplated; all of it is endlessly discussed.

Are these people capable of thinking about anything? Yes, they are and they do: about the future, about other worlds, about all sorts of abstract things that children don't think about. Such thinking is one of the hallmarks of adolescent development.

Box 10–1

RISKY BUSINESS

Adolescents take risks. Perhaps this is partly due to the increased hormonal flow and the way that they egocentrically think they are invincible. The main risk to adolescents is their own behavior (Landers, 1988). Here are some prime examples of risky practices and absence of knowledge from a recent survey of eighth and tenth graders:

Motor vehicle accidents account for more than 70 percent of accidental deaths among 15- to 24-year-olds. But:

56 percent don't wear seat belts.

92 percent don't wear a helmet when they bicycle.

42 percent don't wear a helmet when they ride a motorcycle.

17 percent had used alcohol when boating or swimming in the past year.

30 to 45 percent had ridden in the past month with a driver who was under the influence of drugs or alcohol.

What about other violent ways to die? Homicide is the leading cause of death among Afroamerican males ages 15 to 24. And:

60 percent of the boys and 20 percent of the girls had used a gun in the past year.

50 percent of the boys and 25 percent of the girls had been in one fight during the past year.

13 to 14 percent reported being robbed or attacked at school or on the school bus.

Suicide ranks right up there as the second leading cause of death among 15- to 24-year-olds. But:

Over 50 percent of the children surveyed said it would be hard to talk to a school counselor about a suicidal friend.

Nearly 66 percent would find it hard to tell someone in the suicidal friend's family.

A bright spot in this survey was the teens' knowledge of AIDS (Acquired Immune Deficiency Syndrome)—more than 90 percent knew that AIDS could be transmitted through sexual intercourse and sharing syringe needles. But:

33 percent or more did not know what the early signs of sexually transmitted diseases are.

All of this has led researchers to suggest vigorous educational campaigns in the high school curriculum to promote an understanding of the dangers of high-risk behavior.

ADOLESCENT EGOCENTRISM.   Adolescents also fail to distinguish between their own points of view and those of others, so-called egocentrism. This is another characteristic of the way they think. Elkind (1967) has suggested four kinds of adolescent egocentrism:

1. *The imaginary audience.* Adolescents who exhibit this type of egocentrism believe that others are preoccupied with their appearance and behavior.
2. *The personal fable.* This type of thinking is exhibited when the adolescent gives evidence of being unique or having a special existence that no one else can know, obviously, because it is unique.
3. *Pseudostupidity.* This is when adolescents behave stupidly on purpose believing that such behavior will not be understood for how smart it is.
4. *Apparent hypocrisy.* This is the feeling that you don't have to abide by someone else's rules.

The egocentrism of adolescence is surmounted through the development of intimacy with others, which helps the adolescent understand other points of view.

Adolescent Social Development

A great deal happens to social development during adolescence. In the most general terms, new relationships emerge, and old relationships evolve.

PARENTS.   One relationship that undergoes substantial changes during adolescence is that between adolescent and parents. While these changes often result in increased tension and conflict, the conflict is not nearly so great as the media make it out to be (Santrock, 1987). The adolescent wants to be independent. Parents want further socialization to rules and regulations. Successful adolescent development occurs when these events are both perceived to occur by each side. The normal increase in conflict may be positive in the promotion of identity development and independence (Montemayor, 1983; Santrock, 1987).

chumship
A special preadolescent friendship.

CHUMS.   Prior to adolescence, children's friendships tend to be rather superficial because children are self-centered. The exception that happens along toward adolescence is the **chumship** (Sullivan, 1953). The chumship usually occurs when the preadolescent has started to become sensitive to the feelings and needs of other people. Chums may be chosen because they are intriguing or unique in some way, perhaps having a different family background, because they are complementary to one another. Chumships may last months, and they promote the development of adolescent friendships (Kimmel & Weimer, 1985).

FRIENDS FOR LIFE?   After the chumship, adolescent friendships develop. For the first time in life there may be important things to confide and to discuss that can't be discussed with just anyone. Parents no longer seem a good audience for these private matters and the adolescent's sensitivity to others continues to develop through the exchange of intimate information (Kimmel & Weimer, 1985). However, adolescent friendships are often of the order of a few months, rather than a lifetime, because of the different rates of social, cognitive, and physical development among adolescents.

Having survived adolescence, you become a young adult. What does this change mean?

Adult Development

Literally oodles of research has been accomplished with children and quite a bit with respect to adolescent development, too. Such is not the case with adult development. Both Piaget and Freud, for example, stopped their theorizing at the end of adolescence (Levinson, 1986). As Levinson has said, "The study of adult development is in its infancy" (Levinson, 1986). How might adult development be conceptualized? Before we examine this next period of the life cycle, let's look at a couple of ways of conceptualizing adult development.

Theories of Adult Development

Developmental psychologists have divided adult development into seven stages (Levinson et al., 1978); or eight (Gould, 1978). The data that these theorists use to compose their theories come primarily from extensive interviews with people at the various stages. Levinson's model originally was for men only (he and his colleagues called their book, *The Seasons of a Man's Life*) but more recently he has added women to the mix (Levinson, 1985, 1986; Roberts & Newton, 1987).

Levinson postulates a series of four eras which make up the life cycle, with transitions between these eras (Table 10-6). Each of these eras is comprised of different developmental tasks. Adults within a stage have a life structure which is observed through choice behavior, for example, choosing to marry. Within stages things are pretty calm and stable; transitions, on the other hand, are marked by

TABLE 10-6

A CAPSULE DESCRIPTION OF LEVINSON'S STAGES OF ADULT DEVELOPMENT *from Levinson, 1978.*

1. Preadulthood (Era 1) (Ages 0–22)
   Rapid growth and development; separation from mother; development of identity.
2. Early Adult Transition (Ages 17–22)
   Modification of relationships with family; formation of place in adult world.
3. Early Adulthood (Era 2) (Ages 17–45)
   Great energy; great stress; aspirations are formed and pursued; attempts to establish a place in society; developmental choices in marriage, family, work, lifestyle.
4. Midlife Transition (Ages 40–45)
   Beginning changes in the character of living; new individuation.
5. Middle Adulthood (Era 3) (Ages 40–65)
   Diminished physical capacity (usually without lifestyle restriction); "senior member" of your world; development of next generation; administrative.
6. Late Adult Transition (Ages 60–65)
   Preparation for final stage.
7. Late Adulthood (Era 4) (Age 60 and above)

instability and turmoil. We'll loosely use Levinson's model to structure our discussion of adulthood.

Getting into Adulthood

Most theories of adult development include a transition period that extends from the nebulous end of adolescence to the nebulous beginning of young adulthood. During this time several tasks define the eventual young adult. This is still a time of identity formation, further separating from family, behaving independently, and making decisions alone.

The young adult will usually be living away from parents. Often the transition from home occurs in fits and starts. The young adult lives away to go to college—but lives at home during the summer. Or the young adult lives at home to go to college but works away during the summer. There are many permutations, but over a few years the young adult lives less and less at home.

During this time, the young adult may also establish a career focus; this may involve college or vocational training or actual work experience. Work possibilities are explored. With the advent of some kind of work also comes the possibility of financial independence from parents.

This is also a time of the continuing development of intimate social relationships with others, which may or may not become relatively permanent.

Early Adulthood

Early adulthood exists when one has become more independent. Levinson considers that this period is marked by the adoption of the "dream"—sort of a fantasy of what you would like to be. It may also include a mentor—an unrelated person older by perhaps a decade in whom you can confide, bounce ideas off, and get advice from. The young adult may begin to vigorously pursue the dream (a million dollars earned before age 30).

It is in this stage that many young adults marry, start a family, and attempt to get into separate housing for their family. This sort of traditional progression no longer describes everyone in this stage, however, and the average age for marriage has risen steadily each year as you saw earlier.

"Thirty Something"

By the time one gets to the thirties, some reassessment may occur. Perhaps the dream has been unobtainable. Goals may be made more realistic, the dream modified, but still pursued. It may be a time for making it at work, for solidifying friendships, for investing in family development, and for creating a place in the community.

Larger changes may also occur including redirection in terms of work, divorce, and remarriage. So again, it should not be considered that this progression describes everyone. Bee (1987), for instance, has complained that it certainly didn't describe her. She didn't marry until she was 32, at which time she inherited two stepchildren. So much for uniform progression through adulthood!

Not much seems to happen to most of us during this time in terms of general health. Most of the health dollars are spent on getting young children through the diseases of childhood. The rest of us can eat, drink, and be merry, because tomorrow we'll still feel pretty good. And during this period, too, we stay intellectually pretty sharp.

Starting at around 40 years of age we begin to transition into our middle years—the midlife period.

The Middle Years

midlife period

The period of life from about 40 to 64 years of age.

The period from about ages 40 to 64 is the **midlife period.** Turning 40 is, at least superficially, a trying time in America. It's often celebrated with a party for the "lucky" individual, at which celebrants tease the person with tales of vanishing sexual prowess, graying or vanishing hair, paunches, cellulite, face and breast lifts, tummy tucks, and other age-related occurrences. Laughter is both genuine and forced. This is very much like passing from adolescence, again. During this time men may seek younger women to prove they're still virile. Women may seek other men to learn if they are still "desirable."

It may also be the time when the first signs of physical deterioration appear: "tennis elbow" where that never happened before; having to hold the newspaper farther away to accommodate the eyes to the print; puffing after walking upstairs; lower back pain; and finding out that your children, now young adults, run faster, see better, and have more stamina than you do.

There are other common midlife occurrences as well: One's children slowly and painfully become young adults with all the stressors that that transition produces within the family; one's wife may seek to leave the role of housewife and mother and become a student or an employee; one's husband may discuss leaving his job to start his own business; one's parents may require assistance; both spouses

ARLO & JANIS reprinted by permission of NEA, Inc.

may feel like getting away from everything and going anywhere. Anything, except more of the same.

Clearly, it's a time for adjustment. Many people who have never had to diet before in their lives begin now—often because their physicians warn them of impending disaster. Women may begin to worry seriously about breast and uterine cancer; men may begin to worry about heart attacks. Some may drink less because they can't tolerate the resulting hangovers; and they may smoke less because it interferes with their jogging or their racquetball. The huge business in spas and community recreation programs, testifies at least in part to the attempt by the middle-aged to put off further aging and to look good. But many do not change. They appear trapped in their lives.

THE MIDDLE-AGED WOMAN.   Women may suffer middle age in a way that is discriminatory. First, they may no longer be desirable to younger men. On the other hand, their middle-aged male peers may be attractive to younger women who seek security, and in turn these same middle-aged men may find themselves more attracted to younger women.

Western society has dealt cruelly with the middle-aged woman by virtually ignoring her plight. If she has spent her married life nurturing a family, she earns no retirement pension. If she desires either to return to or start work, she finds that she has earned no experience in the eyes of industry, not even if she has volunteered in her community. The middle-aged woman of today, while more educated than her own mother, is less well-educated than her own adult daughter (U.S. Congress, House Select Committee on Aging, 1980). Both face the ubiquitous discrimination against women, but mother faces two additional difficulties: (1) She is not as well-equipped as her daughter either educationally or socially, and (2) her social structure is more rigid.

Since the major problems of the middle-aged woman are societal, little self-adjustment is possible that will solve these problems, except perhaps learning to tolerate frustration. The problems must be dealt with at the level of society, such as eliminating educational and job barriers that bar middle-aged adults from the marketplace. In the case of education there is a need for more adult-oriented classes, offered at convenient times, in convenient locations, for convenient lengths of time (U.S. Congress, House Select Committee on Aging, 1980). To adjust to the realities of midlife, the middle-aged woman will want not only more education but also more employment opportunity. At work she will want fairer treatment than she now receives.

One adjustment that can be made by both young and middle-aged women is to become more political, as many women have, because the issues that face women are essentially political. Of course, one way to behave politically is to support groups that represent a point of view with which you agree, for example, the National Organization for Women (NOW) and Nine to Five. By support we mean that you can contribute your time, energy, and money to such groups.

networking
The act of communicating successively with a chain of individuals to obtain or to pass information.

Women have also begun to exert influence through **networking,** a concept that emerged from the women's movement. Networks are loose associations of friends and acquaintances who have the same interests that you do. They may meet casually for lunch. Information is exchanged. It has been said that persons who know how to operate within the network system can obtain whatever information they seek, anywhere in the world, in just a few telephone calls (Naisbitt, 1982). Networks can be a successful way to organize at the local level, with considerable informal effect.

Women also face biological difficulties in midlife that men appear not to. Lately there have been a number of well-publicized cases of women who opted to become mothers near the age of 40 (for example, Susan Sarandon). Such decisions are not lightly taken, for they mean parenting through much of midlife. Infants of women who are late in their reproductive cycle are at increased risk for abnormality. The probability of abnormality increases with the age of the mother. Add to this the dilemma of the work place. When substantial numbers of women opt for pregnancy during their careers, this will force industry to respond more thoroughly to their needs; currently, not enough businesses willingly make provision for pregnancy leave and for day-care thereafter. Again, the problem has political overtones.

menopause
That period of a woman's life when her reproductive system slows and stops as evidenced by the cessation of menstruation.

Finally, women face the period of the late forties known as **menopause.** Menopause is rather poorly defined in terms of time because its onset and ending may not be easily discriminated. This is the period when a woman's reproductive capacity diminishes and then ceases. The period of the change from reproduction to nonreproduction—divided into premenopause, menopause, and postmenopause—is called the **climacteric.** It can begin as early as age 40 and can last as long as 20 years. Premenopause is signaled by decreased ovarian function and decreased production of estrogen. During menopause, menstrual flow may become irregular and less frequent until it finally stops. The menopausal period terminates when menstruation has not occurred for 12 months in a row, and this change may take up to 2 years to complete (Porcino, 1983).

climacteric
The period of a woman's life pre-, during, and post-menopause.

In addition to irregular and decreasing menses, other signs of menopause are hot flashes—flushing of the skin, perspiration, and increased pulse rate and temperature (seen in about 80 percent of women as frequently as hourly); maturation of the vagina—lowered elasticity, and possibly decreased lubrication during intercourse; and a potpourri of other events including weight gain, swelling of the breasts, water retention, heart palpitations, and frequent urination (Porcino, 1983).

Because they lived shorter lives, women in earlier times did not experience the postmenopausal period. Today's woman may live 25 years in this period (Porcino, 1983). Many women report that they feel better during this part of their lives than during any other—a kind of **postmenopausal zip.**

postmenopausal zip
For some women, a feeling of well-being and high energy after the completion of menopause.

Perhaps it's unnecessary to add that menopause seems to occur in a woman's life just when the other stressors mentioned above are present in greater-than-usual quantities. It's the time of life when one's parents (and in-laws!) may be aging poorly and in need of help; when one's children may be finishing the process of becoming adults, and not doing this smoothly; and when one's husband may be going through a midlife crisis of his own. While the biology of women affects each woman during midlife, we should not conclude that this time of life is automatically a crisis period for all.

THE MIDDLE-AGED MAN.   Crisis for middle-aged men is not universal. Midlife crisis seems to select only certain men. Others may thrive during midlife. Farrell and Rosenberg (1981) studied 300 men in depth and found four types of midlife experience. These experiences depended on a complex of interactions among the individual dynamics of the particular man, the dynamics of his family, and the dynamics of his social class. By "individual dynamics" the authors meant self-concept and emotional maturity. Social class was reflected in the man's educational level, his income, and his occupational status. Note that the types of men that follow are dependent on the current state of society—the men are its products. Thus, no immutable stages or types of person are denoted by Farrell and Rosenberg's findings.

The first type of man generally sails through midlife. This man behaved maturely as a young adult and handled problems of marriage and family relations well. He is satisfied over the past and the present, and confidently in control of his fate. His type often has adequate resources, both financial and familial. (It may be easier to conclude that you're a successful person if all the trappings that surround you strengthen that view.) A similar type of man might have experienced some failure on the way to midlife, but these failures have served to increase his sensitivity. While midlife is more of a struggle for this individual, it's perceived as a worthwhile struggle, not as a crisis. The problem-solving behaviors this man developed earlier in life serve him well in coping during this period.

A second type of man is also successful superficially in midlife, but his success is a facade for feelings of desperation, loss, and confusion. This man denies the existence of his problems rather than dealing with them as the first type of man did. This person keeps his life bearable by following rigid rules with respect to his family and himself. He may report that his work is satisfying but, when pressed for details, he presents evidence of boredom, conflict, and being left out. As long as the myth he has created survives, this man will traverse middle age without any crisis largely because our Western culture supports this type of behavior in men (Farrell & Rosenberg, 1981).

midlife crisis

Behavior problems that appear to be associated with the midlife period (for example, job dissatisfaction).

The third type of man experiences a **midlife crisis.** This man is confused and overwhelmed by the events of midlife. His crisis has its roots in early adulthood, during which his problems had been papered over. Farrell and Rosenberg found that this type of man was often still highly dependent on his parents, was only superficially intimate with his family, and often made major life commitments on the basis of compromise. They felt that such men were entering a period of more than just transitory decline. That is, their problems would continue to worsen and they would be unable to handle them successfully.

The fourth type of man also experiences a crisis during midlife, but it cannot really be designated a midlife crisis, per se. The reason is that this type of man has been in crisis all his life! Midlife is just one more period of discontent. This type of man is often deprived, neglected, and possibly brutalized as a child, the son of semiskilled or unskilled laborers. He may have attempted to escape the poverty of his childhood by marriage and employment only to fail there as well. He may be a drifter from job to job, a drinker, someone who loses friends. During the midlife

While children are the problem of their parents during the growing-up years, parents are the problem of their grown-up children during the parents' years beyond midlife.

period he is hostile, distrustful, isolated, bigoted, depressed, and unsuccessful at altering his life (Farrell & Rosenberg, 1981).

Thus, the problems of men during midlife would seem to revolve around earlier learned skills or the failure to learn such skills, that is, the failure to develop an understanding of themselves primarily. However, men in midlife may also be trapped by their society in roles that appear to fit the social stratum in which they live and work. Such traps—poverty, inadequate parents, patriarchy—may have precluded the development necessary for them to understand themselves, and, therefore, to deal with the stresses of midlife.

Beyond the Middle Years

"Mom just called," Dick said to his wife, Julie. "Dad's wandered off again. He's been gone a couple of hours. I'd better go over and see if I can find him."

"Dick, we're going to have to get them some help. One of these days your Dad is going to hurt himself. And your Mom just can't handle him on her own. Why do they always call you? Why don't they call your sister?"

"Julie, please don't start in on that again right now. It's all I can do to think about where he might have gone. Besides it's easy for you to talk. We don't have your mom and dad to complain about! We'll talk about it when I get back, okay?"

"You know," Dick mused, out loud, "none of this started until Dad retired last year. He really has been at loose ends since then."

This interaction may be familiar to some of you. The closer you are to age 40, the more likely you are to have parents who are beginning to age.

THE GRAYING OF THE DEVELOPED WORLD. The populations in developed countries are older now than they used to be! That is, the average age in the developed world is rising. There are at least two reasons for this: First, the birthrate has decreased in developed countries over the past years; and, second, people are living longer, due to better nutrition, sanitation, and medical care. In particular, they're surviving childhood, a condition that separates the developed and developing worlds. In the former, most deaths are of elderly people, while in the latter, most deaths are of children (Abrams, 1981). Because people are living longer, older people constitute a larger proportion of the population in developed countries. This is worrisome because the elderly require a disproportionate share of

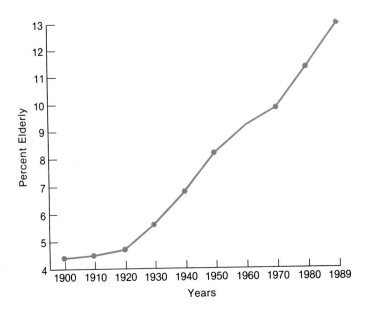

Figure 10-6
The percent of elderly (65 years or older) in the United States for selected years since 1900. *Data from U.S. Department of Commerce, 1990.*

health services and, therefore, account for a disproportionate share of the costs of such services to society in general.

SOME RESULTS OF PHYSICALLY AGING.   "Someone has said that if you want to know what it feels like to be old, you should smear dirt on your glasses, stuff cotton in your ears, put on heavy shoes that are too big for you, and wear gloves; then try and spend the day in a normal way" (Skinner & Vaughan, 1983, p. 38).

At least part of the meaning of the word *age* connotes biological changes in one's body. Your body does change, and the changes are not particularly desirable. As expressed in the above quote, your senses may become less acute. Eyesight may require correction for the first time, but serious eye degeneration is fairly rare. Hearing loss is quite common: About 29 percent of all people over 65 have a significant loss (Falk et al., 1981). Smell, taste, and touch may also deteriorate somewhat. Skin becomes less elastic. Also, to list a few general biological changes that occur with age, there is usually a decrease in muscle mass and in bone density; a decrease in the number of nerve cells (after age 25!); a decrease in the volume of cartilage (beginning between ages 20 and 30!); a decrease in nervous tissue of the heart and an increase of connective tissue resulting in lowered cardiac output; a decrease in the diameter of arteries and a stiffening thereof; and a decrease in the effectiveness of the immune system (Osness, 1981). As yet it is unknown whether some of these changes can be retarded or even stopped. Notwithtanding these changes, it's a myth that the majority of elderly people are ill. The majority are healthy.

There are at least two general kinds of disability that afflict the elderly: First, there are the *diseases of the "good life."* As we have previously discussed, these appear to be due to "living too well." In essence, by eating the wrong kinds of foods, by eating too much food in general, by not exercising regularly throughout life, by smoking tobacco, by drinking alcohol, by not successfully combatting stress, and by living in polluted environments, we produce these diseases. The diseases are familiar: cardiovascular disorders, and cancers of the lungs and other organs. Second, there are the *disabilities produced by prolonged wear and tear.* These can be worn-out joints, kidneys, tendons, teeth and gums, and occluded lenses of the eyes to mention a few. These disabilities seem to be due to us living long enough to outlast specific parts of our bodies. Some of these body parts can be cared for by advances in medical technology, for example, artificial hip sockets.

Cognitive Changes.   There are also changes in cognitive processing with advancing age. These are very individual, from the rapid senility produced by diseases (see below), to a professor still teaching well and debating students at 80 years of age.

Brain cells don't replicate after early development is complete. That is, there is no more cell division and replacement of nervous system cells that die. But another kind of development that appears to continue well into old age is the branching and connecting of existing nerves. New connections continue to be formed.

A general finding is that in reaction time experiments, older adults do less well than younger adults, which suggests that cognitive processing time increases with age. Yet with practice and motivation, older adults can decrease their reaction times. However, older adults never regain the speed of younger adults who also increase their speed with practice (Salthouse & Somberg, 1982).

Memory, too, is affected by aging but not in the way that is popularly thought. Older people are supposed to be able to remember ancient events well and recent events poorly. This is a myth (Perlmutter, 1987; Perlmutter et al., 1980). The kind of memory that seems to deteriorate in older adults is episodic memory—memory for events. This is memory that requires cognitive effort and speed, and is irrelevant to one's own experience. Semantic memory—memory for words and their meanings—is much more resistant to change with aging (Whitbourne & Weinstock, 1986).

Intelligence as measured by IQ tests seems to be rather stable with aging. There is a slight drop after age 60 but this is rather individual also and may be associated with health problems and poor attentional focus (Field et al., 1988; Stankov, 1988). The several years before death are associated with a large drop in IQ called the **terminal drop** (Berg, 1987).

terminal drop

A large decrease in IQ seen in the several years before death.

Diseases of Old Age.   It goes without saying that the diseases of lifestyle mentioned previously, the major causes of death in the United States, afflict the elderly the most. Cardiovascular diseases and cancer are the two most likely to occur. Space does not permit a comprehensive list of all the diseases of aging, so we'll present just one—Alzheimer's disease.

Alzheimer's disease

A disease of the elderly in which progressive pathological changes take place in the brain producing senility and eventual death.

senility

Loss of mental faculties associated with aging.

Alzheimer's disease involves the progressive deterioration of the cells of the brain. Its effect is to produce the symptoms of **senility**—a loss of mental faculties associated with aging. There is no known cause at this writing. A virus, changes in brain chemistry, and excessive aluminum in the body have all been postulated (Porcino, 1983). Alzheimer's attacks women three times as often as men, and it afflicts some 2 million people (5 to 6 percent) over age 65. Three stages are observed: First, there is difficulty in remembering, primarily recent events, and there is less spontaneity of personality. This phase may last 2 to 4 years. Second, problems of remembering increase and intellectual impairment is noted, for example, in abstract reasoning. Personal habits may also deteriorate during this time, which may extend from 2 to 12 years. In the final stage, the individual is mute and unresponsive and loses weight rapidly, usually dying from a secondary cause (for example, pneumonia) within a year. The effect of this disease in which a loved one progressively deteriorates is very strong on a family forced to observe and unable to help (Porcino, 1983).

BECOMING A SENIOR CITIZEN.   Old age is the period from 65 years onward. There are several major adjustments common to old age, including retirement, various infirmities, and sex. Let's dispel a couple of myths. First, the majority of older people are healthy. This does not conflict with data which show that health-care costs for the elderly are more expensive than for other age groups. Some elderly do get sick, and because of their age recovery can take longer. And more are in need of chronic care than those of younger ages. This makes their health-care bill higher than for young people. But still, the majority are healthy. Second, 95 percent are in the community, not in nursing homes—another myth. Only about 5 percent are in nursing homes (Cicirelli, 1981). Yet this latter figure is economically alarming. Given the increasing number of people who will be classified as elderly as the average age of the population advances, the 5 percent of elderly in nursing homes will come to represent more people and a greater societal cost.

The majority of the elderly prefer to remain independent. And they are happiest if they feel in control of their lives (Berghorn & Schafer, 1981). But if they require help, they prefer it to come from their adult children (Cicirelli, 1981). This presents a major problem, since adult children may want to help—as Dick wanted to help his father—but may not be able to to the extent necessary. Adult children also do not identify the problems of their parents correctly: Their parents are most worried about crime and personal safety, while their adult children consider their parents' most pressing problems to be home and health care.

Helping one's parents is stress producing. Cicirelli (1981) notes the following: (1) that the degree of negative feelings toward parents by their children is a function of the degree of their dependency on their children; (2) that the degree of negative feelings toward parents is a function of the amount of services provided by the adult children; (3) that, regardless of how attached adult children are to their parents, helping one's parents engenders physical and emotional fatigue, at least partly due to feelings that one cannot satisfy the demands of the elderly, no matter what; and, (4) that adult children feel the loss of personal freedom, impatience, frustration, and irritation. Thus, the interactions between adult child and aging parent may be difficult. As yet, there are no solutions.

Retirement.   People haven't always retired. Little more than 100 years ago only 25 percent of American men over 65 were retired. Today the proportion is 75 percent (Skinner & Vaughan, 1983). Retirement often involves a major change in lifestyle. Because it involves major changes it can be stressful. Let's face it, there are those who never liked the work they were doing before they retired (Terkel, 1974). Yet, without being aware of it, they may have depended a great deal for social activity on the people with whom they worked. The work itself might not have been rewarding, but interacting with one's colleagues might have been (Skinner & Vaughan, 1983). They may miss the camaraderie of coffee breaks, lunch, a squeezed-in shopping trip, the bowling league, the company outings. As with the loss of any social relationship, termination of these activities may lead to feelings of depression. The retiree who liked his job may be in even greater difficulty—not only are there the losses of social relationships but also the loss of rewards from doing the job itself. This person may no longer feel useful.

Self-adjustment is possible in these cases. Retirement can sometimes be gradually prepared for across several years. During this time the potential retiree can develop new friendships with those who may share common interests—interests that will displace the termination of the job, for example, fishing or golfing.

Major changes, such as moving far away to a retirement community, may not be favorable under all circumstances because they may increase stress. In addition to the stress of moving, one may leave behind powerful sources of reward, such as family, friends, known locales, and activities. Thus, while the novelty of a new place may provide short-term rewards, in the long term there may be a net loss of rewards with resultant depression. Yet *age homogeneity*—the fact that everyone in

Many people when they retire now move to communities that contain people primarily of their own ages and interests, and where the weather is warmer in the winter.

a retirement community is about the same age—and the resulting uniformity of interests among the residents may make moving to a retirement community very positive (Longino, 1981). It is certain that most such moves are self-selected.

Many successful retirees turn former hobbies into serious pursuits. The retiree who liked to build furniture may now build furniture for profit as well as fun. Yet, the time cannot be totally filled with avocations for many people. Skinner and Vaughan (1983) suggest volunteer work as a way to find new sources of reward. In essence, some individuals may need to **retire from retirement.** For the retiree who liked work, new sources of similar work could be sought possibly on a part-time basis, or the essence of the work could be abstracted and carried on without formal employment. For example, college professors could continue to write books if writing were a part of their work they especially enjoyed.

retiring from retirement
The supplementary addition of work or volunteer activities to the schedule of a retired person.

You may be thinking, "What does this have to do with me? I'm only 23!" Yet it is never too early to think ahead—to find out now what it is you might want to be doing later, when you are free. Activities you begin now may help later. Learn a lifetime sport that you can modify as you age. Take some tennis, bowling, or golf lessons and concentrate on learning to play well enough across the years to enjoy your outings. When you eventually slow down, play doubles instead of singles, play 9 holes instead of 18, or bowl a few lines instead of all night. Remember, these are skilled activities. You cannot expect to hit a tennis ball successfully without lessons and practice. In other words you must persevere long enough to experience the rewards of the activity, and these rewards usually don't occur until you become reasonably skilled at the activity.

But pursuing one sport will not fill your life. What are you going to do after you finish playing? What of intellectual activities? Music? Cards and games? Reading? Hobbies? The idea is to make a "well-rounded you" early in life. Then you will have activities to which you can turn when the boredom of later life strikes. *Boredom* is a major difficulty for old people, just as it is for children (Skinner & Vaughan, 1983). Successful self-adjustment will preclude boredom. Get in the habit now of doing things for yourself. The things you do for yourself take up time, and you will learn new things if you do them yourself. The good intentions of others to help you may be misguided because they may stop you from helping yourself and continuing to do so. This is a plight of older people (Skinner & Vaughan, 1983).

In other words, Dick really needs to think about whether he helps his parents' situation when he rushes to find his father after his mother calls. Not rushing right over may seem cruel. But what if Dick usually finds his dad at the billiard parlor, or at the corner store, and his dad is not really confused about anything, he just forgot to tell his wife where he was going? Maybe his father is asserting some independence. The problem might be better solved if Dick helped his father to remember to tell his wife that he was going out, or to call if he stayed longer than he thought he would. Maybe, if he'd waited, his dad would have shown up anyway, even if he had gotten a little confused, because he was given the time to work out his confusion. Perhaps his mother uses this behavior of her husband to get attention from her son. Each of these possible reasons for the behavior of Dick and his parents suggests a slightly different solution to the wandering of Dick's dad, and analyzing and dealing with the reasons should probably be guided by a professional. The point still stands, however, that each of us should be allowed to do as much as we can for ourselves throughout our lives and particularly as we age. As with other habits though, it doesn't hurt to begin early.

Sex and the Senior Citizen.   Yes, there *is* something to say about this. One of the world's great myths may be that sex is only for the young. It isn't, as many senior citizens could tell you. Kinsey's pioneering studies first noted this (Kinsey et al., 1948; Kinsey et al., 1953). He reported that there was a general decline in the

TABLE 10-7
SOME POSSIBLE SEX-RELATED CHANGES AS A FUNCTION OF AGE *From Dailey 1981.*

Men	*Women*
1. Longer to achieve an erection	1. Vaginal walls may become thinner
2. Erection may be slightly less hard	2. Normal lubrication of vagina may be less
3. May take longer for ejaculation to occur	3. May take longer to become aroused
4. Release of semen may be less forceful and orgasmic experience may be less intense	4. May be some diminution of orgasmic experience
5. Period of time until next erection may be longer	

frequency of sexual behavior with age, but the decline is no more rapid from 60 to 80 than it is from 30 to 60. He found that only one of five men was incapable of intercourse at 60 years of age. By age 80 this had risen to three of four. However, this also means that 25 percent of men may still be active this late in life. Many other investigators have corroborated Kinsey's results (for example, Freeman, 1961; George & Weiler, 1981; Masters & Johnson, 1970; Newman & Nichols, 1960).

We have noted above that women undergo changes in their *reproductive* functions during menopause. While these changes may alter sexual functioning somewhat, they do not eliminate it. There is no known physiological reason for a decline in sexuality (Koadlow & Tunnadine, 1980). We have listed the changes that appear to take place with age in Table 10-7. Some maintain that the change in elasticity of the vagina, mentioned above as an example, may only be a function of the reduced frequency of sexual intercourse (Masters & Johnson, 1966). None of the events in Table 10-7, either singly or in concert, precludes sexual relations.

Perhaps the worst aspect of sex for the senior citizen is that it is denied (Falk & Falk, 1981). First, it is denied by the young in a youth-oriented culture probably because it makes thinking about the care of the elderly easier. For example, it has been found that students grossly underestimate the frequency of intercourse of their parents (Pocs & Godon, 1977; as cited Dailey, 1981). That this denial actually makes the care of the elderly easier may also be a myth. Second, sex may be denied by those who are no longer capable of it themselves and, therefore, see such behavior as not normal—using themselves as referents. Third, it may be emotionally denied, essentially in the form of jealousy, particularly if there is competition for the limited resources that are available and one is not winning the competition. This may be a problem among elderly women when there are too few elderly men to go around (almost always the case) and some portion of the elderly men is no longer capable. Finally, the young may deny the sexuality of their parents because any natural explanation may put inheritance at risk. A single elderly parent might even remarry! And then what?

Death and Dying: The Final Adjustments

Eventually, of course, we all die—that appears to be inevitable. Death raises a lot of questions—when, where, and why, among them. It also seems to be something we fear. Let's have a brief look at some of the data that illuminate death.

WHO DIES AND WHEN THEY DIE. It is well known that, on the average, we will live longer than any generation of North Americans that has preceded us. Today the average American woman can expect to live until she's 78 and the average American man until he's 74. Notably, the death rate per 1,000 population has decreased

TABLE 10-8
THE TEN LEADING CAUSES OF DEATH IN THE UNITED STATES, 1900 AND 1988 *From Lerner, 1970; U.S. Department of Commerce, 1990.*

Cause of Death	Percent of All Deaths	Cause of Death	Percent of All Deaths
1900		**1988**	
1. Influenza and pneumonia	11.8	1. Diseases of the heart	35.3
2. Tuberculosis	11.3	2. Malignant neoplasms (cancer)	22.4
3. Gastritis, duodenitis, enteritis, etc.	8.3	3. Cerebrovascular diseases	6.9
4. Diseases of the heart	8.0	4. All accidents	4.5
5. Vascular lesions affecting the central nervous system	6.2	5. Pulmonary diseases	3.8
6. Chronic nephritis	4.7	6. Pneumonia and influenza	3.6
7. All accidents	4.2	7. Diabetes mellitus	1.9
8. Malignant neoplasms (cancer)	3.7	8. Suicide	1.4
9. Diseases of early infancy	3.6	9. Chronic liver disease	1.2
10. Diphtheria	2.3	10. Kidney diseases	1.0

almost by half in this century: In 1910 it was 14.7. In 1981 it was 8.6. Lately, too, the gap in the average life expectancy between men and women has narrowed, possibly reflective of the change in lifestyle for many women who are now employed outside the home.

The reasons for death other than by natural causes have shifted dramatically across this century (see Table 10-8). In the early part of the century, prior to the discovery of wonder drugs like penicillin, the major causes of death were bacterially caused communicable diseases. These have just about been eradicated. Where they may still be contracted, they can be successfully treated. Of major concern today are illnesses that are produced by viruses. Some of these have been conquered by vaccine, such as poliomyelitis, but there are many still that will affect us. Given rapid changes in the causal virus (for example, HIV), these may be very troublesome indeed.

WHY PEOPLE DIE AND WHERE THEY DIE. Generally speaking, traditional reasons for death include disease, accident, suicide, and nature (that is, old age). In the 1980s, notwithstanding the current healthier lifestyles of those who exercise frequently and eat correctly, the major cause of death in the United States was cardiovascular disease, such as heart disease and stroke, followed by cancer and accidents. However, there is a trend toward a decrease in the rate of deaths attributed to major cardiovascular diseases. In the 28 years depicted in Table 10-9 the rate of deaths due to cardiovascular diseases has decreased about 23 percent. Such a trend suggests that the healthier lifestyles of the population may have lowered the death rate due to this cause. Yet it's still the leading cause of death. On the other hand, the death rate due to cancer has increased about 24 percent in the same period of time, perhaps reflecting the continued poisoning of our environments and, ultimately, ourselves (Table 10-9). It may be that with major advances in medicine, fewer deaths will be attributed to natural causes now and in the future.

mortality
The death rate; the number of people who die relative to the population of people from which they come.

Mortality may also relate to socioeconomic status (Lerner, 1970). If we roughly divide the population into three strata—middle, blue collar, and poverty classes—we can note some differences in mortality among them. The poverty group has the highest overall mortality rate and much of that appears due to communicable diseases of infancy, young childhood, and young adulthood. Either absence of private medical care or lack of personal care—for example, failure to

TABLE 10-9
DEATH RATES (PER 100,000 POPULATION), 1960–1988, FOR CARDIOVASCULAR DISEASES AND CANCERS

Year	Cardiovascular	Cancer
1960	515.1	149.2
1970	496.0	162.8
1980	436.4	183.9
1985	409.6	193.3
1988	394.4	197.3

use available services—could account for this. Lerner (1970) notes that this group has historically always led the death rates.

The white-collar middle class have access to and utilize private medical facilities and they fare very well during infancy, childhood, and young adulthood. However, their mortality rate increases dramatically to more than the other two groups during midlife. The degenerative diseases probably account for this, due to an overrich lifestyle.

The blue-collar group seems to have the best mortality rate. They escape the mortality rate of the poverty group during early infancy, childhood, and young adulthood, and of the middle-class degenerative diseases during midlife. The former may be due to access to adequate medical care, the latter to the absence of an overly rich lifestyle.

Finally, where people die has shifted dramatically over the years. In 1949 some 49.5 percent of people died in institutions. Most of these—nearly 40 percent—died in hospitals. By 1958, approximately 61 percent were dying in institutions, nearly 48 percent of these in the general hospital (Lerner, 1970). Currently, 62 percent die in hospitals or medical centers (National Center for Health Statistics, 1987).

DEFINING DEATH. Death has been examined about as much as love. Poets, playwrights, and philosophers have all expressed points of view. We would have no need to define death if recent medical developments—people who seem to die and then are resuscitated—hadn't occurred. *Biological death* is defined as the state in which all the biological indicators that describe life are *permanently* absent. Such death is irreversible, by definition. Where biological indicators of life exist (we won't try to define exactly when they begin and what they are), it's possible to define two kinds of life: **physical life** and **psychological life.** With modern technology, an individual can be physically alive but psychologically dead. Individuals "living" in such a condition, in which the brain shows none of its usual activity, are called **brain dead** or **clinically dead.** In this condition, a mechanical life-support system is usually necessary for physical life to continue. Necessary for psychological life, as a boundary condition, is a functioning brain.

In essence, if our brains stop functioning and our bodies stop functioning, we are biologically dead. However, it's possible that such an occurrence is gradual. The body's shutting off of itself when death occurs may take several minutes. (There are records of individuals whose vital signs seemed entirely missing upon cursory analysis, but who were still biologically alive because they recovered later.) If death is the absence of all our normal functions, and such functions are necessary for us to report our feelings, then death can neither be felt nor reported on. What then do we fear?

physical life

The functioning of the body in the absence of clinical signs that the brain is functioning; usually necessitates mechanical life support; synonymous with brain dead or clinically dead.

psychological life

The state in which the brain is functioning.

brain dead or **clinically dead**

The absence of clinical signs that the brain is functioning.

Box 10-2

Death Anxiety: How Much Do You Have?

Fear of death and dying has been measured on a number of scales. We have produced a classic example for you to assess your fear of death.
(Circle one: T = true; F = false)

1. I am very much afraid to die.	T	F
2. The thought of death seldom enters my mind.	T	F
3. It doesn't make me nervous when people talk about death.	T	F
4. I dread to think about having to have an operation.	T	F
5. I am not at all afraid to die.	T	F
6. I am not particularly afraid of getting cancer.	T	F
7. The thought of death never bothers me.	T	F
8. I am often distressed the way time flies so very rapidly.	T	F
9. I fear dying a painful death.	T	F
10. The subject of life after death troubles me greatly.	T	F
11. I am really scared of having a heart attack.	T	F
12. I often think about how short life really is.	T	F
13. I shudder when I hear people talking about a World War III.	T	F
14. The sight of a dead body is horrifying to me.	T	F
15. I feel that the future holds nothing for me to fear.	T	F

From Templer & Ruff, 1971.

Score yourself on the Death Anxiety Scale in the following manner: Count 1 for each statement where your answer (T or F) agrees with the following list: 1–T; 2–F; 3–F; 4–T; 5–F; 6–F; 7–F; 8–T; 9–T; 10–T; 11–T; 12–T; 13–T; 14–T; 15–F. Total your count. Most people score between 4.5 and 7 (Templer & Ruff, 1971). If you score 10 or above, you score higher on death anxiety than all but about 16 percent of the population. If this worries you, you may wish to talk to a professional about it.

death anxiety
The fear of dying or death.

FEAR OF DEATH.   The fear of death is called **death anxiety.** Why do we have such anxiety?

What we really fear is the absence of a condition we have grown to know and love—life. Most of us lead lives that contain positive occurrences. The proposed absence of any of these occurrences is aversive to think about. Even if our lives are not totally full of wonderful events, they may be at least okay. Even if they are not okay, our lives are not bad. Even those who are seriously ill engage in this kind of rationalization: Life could be worse than it is (Taylor, 1983). A kind of solace is gained thereby: Life is better than nonlife. It has to be, doesn't it? Well, doesn't it?

MAKING ADJUSTMENTS TO DYING AND DEATH.   There is plenty of anecdotal evidence to suggest that what we think may at least partially influence the likelihood that we will die. For example, Trelease (1975) has commented on the possibility that some Alaskan Indians know when they're about to die and that they don't die until their business in life is finished. As a priest he was called to pray for Indian people who thought they were dying. They would ask him to gather about them people to whom they had final things to say: Old scores would be righted, debts forgiven, and so forth. Sometimes it would take days for him to gather the requested individuals and to bring himself and them to the remote area where the dying person was. Inevitably, he reports that the person would be alive, waiting patiently. Final prayers would be said, the dying person would see all the people with whom there was some business, and then a few hours later death would occur. It would seem that these people knew they were about to die, but in some sense could hold off that outcome long enough to finish their business.

There is now some scientific evidence, too, which suggests that how we behave may relate to how we die. Animals that have learned not to respond to shocks, for example, are more likely to grow tumors in response to injections of tumor cells than animals that have learned to escape the shocks (Visintainer et al., 1982). Apparently, the animals' histories with the shocks relate to the functioning of their immune systems in some way, which lowers the likelihood that the tumor is rejected. In other words, the animal's disease-fighting capability is changed by a psychological experience.

There seem to be parallels with humans, too (Maier & Laudenslager, 1985). Following the stress of bereavement, for example, immune functioning is decreased in humans (Bartrop et al., 1977). Children whose mothers leave them to enter the hospital to give birth react both behaviorally and physiologically in ways that suggest agitation and depression (Field & Reite, 1984). In monkeys, maternal separation is associated with suppressed immune function (Laudenslager et al., 1982). It's also known that where there is perceived loss of control over events (as there seems to be in bereavement and depression), there's an increased incidence of cancer in humans (Fox, 1978; Schmale, 1972; as cited by Visintainer et al., 1982).

What all this may mean is that during illness an acceptance of the inevitability of death and dying may actually lead to that condition. Such acceptance may be a helpless reaction, an outcome of which may be lowered immune functioning; this in turn could mean further illness or an exacerbation of the current illness.

The Process of Dying.   How do we feel knowing that we may die? Elisabeth Kübler-Ross (1969; 1975) interviewed terminally ill patients to determine whether a common process could be defined. She described five stages of dying: denial, anger, bargaining, depression, and acceptance. Kübler-Ross noted that the progression through these stages is not clean or inevitable. Let's take a brief look at each stage.

- *Stage 1: Denial.* In this stage the dying person refuses to believe he or she is dying, notwithstanding several congruent diagnoses. People need to be helped to face the inevitable here. Few remain in this stage.
- *Stage 2: Anger.* In this stage the dying person often becomes angry at what fate has dealt him or her and may lash out at his or her caretakers. It is important to understand and to help people at this stage understand that anger is natural. But, as with denial, anger, too, needs to be dealt with.
- *Stage 3: Bargaining.* This stage involves attempts to postpone the inevitable. Any treatment may be acceptable if the patient perceives that it will extend life. The patient may try to bargain with God or the physician.
- *Stage 4: Depression.* Kübler-Ross considers that this stage marks the beginning of acceptance, during which the patient exhibits a sort of preparatory grief. Dying people should be permitted the freedom to grieve during this stage.
- *Stage 5: Acceptance.* This stage is notable for its lack of anger and depression if the patient has had the time to work through the preceding stages. However, it is not a time of happiness, rather more one that is absent of feeling. The patient is prepared to die.

It should not be expected that everyone will exhibit these stages. As with the unique ways in which people live their lives, they are also unique in the ways that they process dying. This very uniqueness questions the generality of Kübler-Ross' findings (Kastenbaum, 1985). Moreover, Kübler-Ross' stages should not be used to suggest that those who progress through them have somehow done a better job of processing their own deaths than those who don't (Kalish, 1985).

grief
Strong emotional behavior
elicited by the loss of a
significant other, usually
through the death of that
person.

The Process of Grieving.   As with the eventual first-hand experience of death and dying, all of us will also experience the death of others who are close to us. A result of this occurrence will be **grief,** the anguish, heartache, sadness, and sorrow that one feels following the loss of a loved one.

We don't know exactly why people grieve. It's a normal, probably biological reaction to the loss of a significant other. It occurs in the primate species, so we're not unique. One biological (evolutionary) function it could serve would be to keep animals who live in social conditions behaving socially. For example, the grief process could keep mothers from separating from their children because grief produces such aversive feelings (Averill, 1968).

Grief is probably a reaction to severe stress. Indeed, there may be health effects of the loss of a significant person in our environment (Holmes & Rahe, 1967; Maier & Laudenslager, 1985; Osterweiss et al., 1984). Loss of a significant person is one of the most severe stressors we can experience.

Symptoms of Grief.   The study of grief in modern times was begun by psychiatrist Erich Lindeman (1944) as a part of a study of 101 bereaved persons, including 13 survivors of a tragic night in 1942 when 491 people perished in a fire in a Boston nightclub. The most prevalent feelings immediately after knowledge of the death of someone close are shock, numbness, and disbelief. Feelings of separation usually follow and are in turn followed sometimes by "hearing" the person's voice or "seeing" the deceased in dreams or perhaps walking down the street. Such illusions usually disappear when the deceased fails to return. For people who exhibit maladaptive behavior, the grief process can be a time when a greater amount of maladaptive behavior is exhibited. Immune system functioning lowered by grief can put susceptible individuals at risk. Eventually, the process terminates with resolution and acceptance of the death followed by reintegration (Ramsay, 1979). The length of the entire process varies widely across individuals from weeks to years. Bereavement and grief are discussed further in Chapter 15.

SUMMARY

- We can conceptualize life as a cycle from birth to death. During this life cycle our biology and common environmental events lead to common ways of behaving at particular stages of the cycle.

- Prenatal growth and development appear to be primarily genetic and hormonal. However, during this phase the developing embryo and fetus are susceptible to chemicals such as narcotics and alcohol that can pass the placental barrier. These substances can lead to birth defects.

- During the childhood stage of development there has been much study of children's thinking and morals. Piaget divided the development of children's thinking into four levels—sensorimotor, preoperational, concrete operational, and formal operational. Each level involved qualitatively different ways of thinking which Piaget demonstrated through children's behavior on problem-solving tasks. Since Piaget, it has seemed more parsimonious to consider the development of children's thinking in terms of the use of more and more complex rules, susceptible to learning and modification.

- The development of moral reasoning has also been studied in children. Kohlberg studied children's responses to moral dilemmas. He divided children's moral reasoning into three levels—preconventional, conventional, and postconventional or principled—with two stages at each level. With each advance in moral reasoning, morality becomes more and more internalized.

- The next stage of the life cycle—adolescence—has also been well studied. It is the time of puberty, the appearance of secondary sexual characteristics, and the development of reproductive capability during which children become adults, first physically and then cognitively. During this stage new relationships develop with members of the other sex, social roles are refined, and emotional independence from parents is achieved. Moreover, career preparation and preparation for marriage and family life begin, values and ethics are shaped, and socially responsible behavior emerges. Some theorists such as Erikson consider that adolescence is a time of identity development and the development of intimacy. Behaviorally speaking it is a time for modeling and self-reinforcement. Adolescence is also a time for taking risks which are associated with delinquency, suicide, running away, and substance abuse. Adolescent thought is characterized by greater abstraction and more complex rule use than thought in children.

- The least study has gone into the stages of the life cycle that characterize adult development. Nevertheless, theories have emerged that divide adulthood into a number of stages as well. Levinson's theory, for example, divides adulthood into seven stages—preadulthood (Era 1), early adult transition, early adulthood (Era 2), midlife transition, middle adulthood (Era 3), late adulthood transition, and late adulthood (Era 4). Each of the transitions among the eras is said to be marked by some turmoil while each of the eras themselves is supposed to be relatively tranquil. Each of the eras has its characteristic behaviors.

- Eventually the life cycle terminates with our deaths about which most of us are fearful. Many more deaths now owe to cardiovascular diseases and cancer than ever before, and more of us will die outside our homes than before. There even appears to be adjustment upon the knowledge of our certain death. Kübler-Ross has suggested that first we deny, and then we are angry, next we try in vain to bargain. When the inevitability sinks in, it is marked by depression, the beginning of acceptance. The final stage is the acceptance of one's inevitable death.

Box 10-3

SELF-ADJUSTMENT FOR STUDENTS:
CHANGING COMPLEX BEHAVIORS

It's one thing to change a simple behavior such as decreasing the frequency of swearing. For that you might focus mainly on the identification of antecedents (where and when does it occur) and consequences (what happens as a result of it). Complex behavior is another matter. To change complex behavior, in addition, you need to focus on the behavior itself. If your goal is to acquire some complex skills, it's helpful to consider task analysis, mastery criteria, behavioral chaining, and shaping.

TASK ANALYSIS
Task analysis means breaking down a skill into its component parts so it can be learned effectively

and so that the improvements in it can be accurately monitored. Let's consider learning to play golf as the complex skill. How would you go about breaking golf playing into its component parts?

Don't be afraid to guess at breaking a task into its components. There is no right or wrong way. What you want to end up with is a series of steps (that is, behaviors), the accomplishment of which allow you to perform the complex skill. It is helpful to choose as the first step what seems to be the simplest behavior of the complex skill. This behavior is most likely to produce some naturally reinforcing consequences (success!) because it is the

Continued

TABLE 10-10

BEHAVIORAL PROGRESSION AND MASTERY CRITERIA FOR LEARNING GOLF *From Simek & O'Brien, 1981.*

Step	Shot	Mastery Criterion
1	10-inch putt	4 putts consecutively holed
2	16-inch putt	4 putts consecutively holed
3	2-foot putt	4 putts consecutively holed
4	3-foot putt	4 putts consecutively holed
5	4-foot putt	2 holed, 2 out of 4 within 6 inches
6	6-foot putt	4 consecutively within 6 inches
7	10-foot putt	4 consecutively within 12 inches
8	15-foot putt	4 consecutively within 15 inches
9	20-foot putt	4 consecutively within 18 inches
10	30-foot putt	4 consecutively within 24 inches
11	35-foot chip 5 feet off green, 7-iron	4 out of 6 within 6 feet
12	35-foot chip 15 feet off green, wedge	4 out of 6 within 6 feet
13	65-foot chip	4 out of 6 within 6 feet
14	25-yard pitch	4 out of 6 within 10 feet
15	35-yard pitch	4 out of 6 within 15 feet
16	50-yard pitch	4 out of 6 within 15 feet
17	75-yard shot	4 out of 6 within 30 feet
18	100-yard shot	4 out of 6 within 40 feet
19	125-yard shot	4 out of 6 within 45 feet
20	150-yard shot	4 out of 6 within 54 feet
21	175-yard shot	4 out of 6 within 66 feet
22	200-yard shot (if within your range)	4 out of 5 within 90 feet
23	Driver	

simplest. Secondly, it is important to proceed from the simple to the complex.

As an example, we describe a program by Simek and O'Brien (1981) which taught novices to play golf. They started with putting—actually very short putts—as the first response, for the reasons detailed above. As short putts were successfully made, the length of the putt required as the next step increased. You can see from Table 10-10 that Simek and O'Brien's program proceeded from longer and longer putts to short chip shots, to longer chip shots, to short pitch shots, to longer pitch shots, to middle-length iron shots, then eventually to hitting fairway woods, and finally to swinging a driver. We'll see below how this program fared.

MASTERY CRITERIA

A second important component of a program to develop a complex skill is to set some mastery criteria for each step of the program. Mastery criteria are performance requirements for practicing a skill such that if the criteria are met, the behavior has been learned. Again there are no rules for developing mastery criteria except for those of experience. Obviously the criteria have to be sufficient to make it likely that you are sufficiently accomplished on the current step and that you can successfully begin on the following step. Simek and O'Brien kept their students on the short putts and at a particular step until the students were able to sink four putts in a row at that particular distance. At longer putts the students had to putt to within a certain distance of the hole on consecutive putts, the remaining distance being a putt they had already mastered.

It is important in a program to develop complex behavior that you not proceed to the next step until the mastery criteria of the present step are met. The reason is that you may not sufficiently develop the skills at one step, some or all of which may be necessary to the mastery of a following step.

FAILING MASTERY

What if you can't seem to get by a particular step? It's possible that you lack a skill necessary to the accomplishment of that step. It's time for further task analysis. This usually means the insertion of more steps in your program—steps that precede the step in the program you can't seem to get past—along with their accompanying mastery criteria.

If you are bored while learning a complex skill, one possibility may be that the steps are too small and too many. In that case, carefully remove a few. But remember, if you can't make any further progress, you've probably removed too many. Of course, an important second reason for boredom is that there is insufficient reinforcement for your behavior.

How did Simek and O'Brien's novices do? Well, they were compared with six other novices who had eight traditional lessons from a golfer who was a teacher. Simek and O'Brien's six students spent their eight lessons on the task analyzed program, meeting the mastery criteria at each step. They beat the traditionally taught students by an average of 17 strokes in an 18-hole round of golf.

BEHAVIORAL CHAINING

Where different behaviors must be put together to accomplish a task, procedures to establish a behavioral chain can be used. A behavioral chain is a sequence of stimuli and responses in which an antecedent stimulus leads to a behavior, which in turn produces a consequence, which in its turn is also the antecedent stimulus for the next behavior. Consider the behavioral chain involved in making an omelette:

Step 1. Break three eggs into a mixing bowl; add a little milk or water.

Step 2. Whisk eggs until frothy.

Step 3. Pour frothy egg mixture in heated and oiled omelette pan.

Step 4. Cook egg mixture until just barely firm on the heated side.

Step 5. Add whatever ingredients you want to one side of cooked egg mixture (chilis, red peppers, mushrooms).

Step 6. Fold half of cooked egg mixture without ingredients on it over other half of egg mixture. Leave in pan only long enough to heat added ingredients.

Step 7. Serve.

Learning what the consequence is of each step of the recipe leads you to the next step. For example, the good omelette maker has to know when the eggs are sufficiently whisked to meet (but not exceed) the criterion of being frothy (Step 2), and when the mixture is just firm on the heated side and not firm on the top side (Step 4). Each of these conditions signals the end of one step and the beginning of the next.

Behavioral chaining can take place in three different ways: The entire sequence is gone through repeatedly from beginning to end until mastery is achieved—called total task presentation; or where each step or link in the chain is mastered separately either starting at the beginning and working toward the end (forward chaining) or starting at the end and working toward the beginning (backward chaining).

Any complex task can be thought of as a behavioral chain. Essentially, completing a task analysis is completing the job of separating a behavioral chain into its links.

SHAPING

When you look at Table 10-10 you can see that the behavioral progression in the first ten steps essentially involved the same response—putting. However, the amount of swing in the golf club was gradually increased. This exemplifies a procedure called shaping. Shaping involves a gradual change in the behavioral requirement needed to produce reinforcement. It is used to develop behaviors that don't exist in your (or someone else's) repertoire. You begin with a response that resembles the terminal behavior that you want. Eventually, a golfer has to take a complete swing at a ball resting on a

Continued

tee with a driver. While most of us can visualize how this should look, when we do it we really have no idea whether what we did matches how it should have been done. The solution is to start with components of the eventual response (say a swing with a putter through an arc of a few degrees) and progress in small steps to the final behavior.

Shaping can be used to modify the form (topography) of a behavior, the force of a behavior, the amount of a behavior, and the speed with which a behavior is performed. It's an important strategy for any self-adjustment project whose ultimate goal involves substantial behavioral change from its starting point. Shaping is so very common in everyday life—learning to drive with a manual shift, learning to dance the latest dance, forming a good clay pot on a potter's wheel—that we take its existence for granted. In learning these behaviors, shaping inevitably occurs whether we're conscious of it or not. It is much better to understand how to set up the process yourself to maximize your learning.

You might be wondering how shaping differs from chaining. In chaining, you take a series of steps and link them together. As you add new links, you don't discard old links. All components (or links) of the chain are important. In shaping, a behavior gradually changes over trials (in its form, force, amount, or speed).

Important rules of thumb for you to keep in mind while shaping include: start small, meet each mastery criterion before moving up a step, and keep progressive steps small.

Finally, throughout all of these procedures, don't neglect your management of consequences. Positive consequences are vital to keep you engaging in the steps of your program to develop complex behavior.

MEMORY BOOSTER

■ IMPORTANT TERMS

Be prepared to define the following terms (located in the margins of this chapter). Where appropriate, be prepared to describe examples.

Ovum Stage	Climacteric
Embryonic Stage	Postmenopausal Zip
Fetal Stage	Midlife Crisis
Attachment Behavior	Average Age In The Developed World
Puberty	Terminal Drop
Sex Hormones	Alzheimer's Disease
Menarche	Senility
Vicarious Reinforcement	Retiring From Retirement
Status Offenses	Mortality
Bulimia Nervosa	Physical Life
Anorexia Nervosa	Psychological Life
Chumship	Brain Dead
Midlife Period	Death Anxiety
Networking	Grief
Menopause	

■ **QUESTIONS FROM IMPORTANT IDEAS IN THIS CHAPTER**

1. Briefly describe the four levels of Piaget's theory of cognitive development in children. Briefly state three ways in which subsequent research has led us to modify Piaget's theory.

2. In two or three sentences, summarize Siegler's information processing account of child cognitive development.

3. Briefly describe several developmental tasks that teenagers need to experience.

4. What environmental stressors also may be present during menopause based on the woman's time of life?

5. What kind of man usually has a crisis during middle age? What kinds of men do not have crises during middle age?

6. Briefly describe four eras of adulthood, and the kinds of behaviors and tasks that characterize these eras.

7. Describe the three stages of Alzheimer's disease.

8. Suggest four reasons why the sexuality of elderly people may be denied.

9. What sequence seems to describe the progression toward our acceptance of death, and how valid a description is this sequence?

10. What functions might grief serve?

Living in Today's Society and Environment: Violence, Prejudice, and Pollution

---

CHAPTER OUTLINE

LEARNING OBJECTIVES

After reading this chapter, you should be able to:

- Discuss several causes of violence and aggression in today's society.
- Take steps to prevent violence and aggression.
- Discuss the differences between terms like *stereotypes, prejudice, discrimination, sexism,* and *racism.*
- Evaluate the extent to which you may be prejudiced.
- Discuss ways to decrease prejudice and discrimination.
- Discuss the "tragedy of the commons" as it relates to the depletion of our natural resources.
- Discuss different types of pollution and their effects on human behavior.
- State how crowding affects behavior in terms of crime, aggression, withdrawal, and altruism.

In the chapters thus far, we have focused largely on adjustment at the individual level. We've looked at strategies that you can follow to cope with stress, stick to an exercise program, be liked by your date, and a host of other topics. But now consider the following:

On Violence

- Thirty-five percent of a sample of San Francisco women reported being victims of either attempted or completed rape by acquaintances or dates (Russell, 1984).
- Almost 4 million children each year in the United States are abused by their parents (Pedrick-Cornell & Gelles, 1982).

On Prejudice

- Men outnumber women 9 to 1 as narrators of television commercials (Bretl & Cantor, 1988).
- Desegregation in schools in the United States has led to improvements in Afro-American reading achievement and to more Afro-Americans attending and succeeding in college, but, unfortunately, racial attitudes have not been much affected by desegregation (Stephan, 1986).

On Pollution

- Working in high levels of noise, such as close to a busy airport, can cause ulcers and other stress-related illnesses (Colligan & Murphy, 1982).
- There is strong evidence that childhood exposure to even low-level doses of lead (such as from auto fumes or chewing lead paint) can impair children's IQs (Needleman & Gatsonis, 1990).

All of the above problems are society- or planet-wide. Each of us can take some steps at the individual level to solve such problems. But these problems also require collective adjustment at the societal level. Government programs, mass media campaigns, large-scale industrial applications, and the like are required if we are to make serious headway in their resolution. In this chapter, we focus on the problems of violence, prejudice, and pollution. And we examine adjustment strategies at both individual and societal levels.

Violence in Today's Society

Did you know that, each year, approximately 6 million Americans are victimized by violent crimes (Widom, 1989)? That reported rapes of females in the United States occur at a rate of approximately one every six minutes (Doyle, 1989)? That unreported rapes may occur ten times as often as reported rapes (Koss et al., 1988)? That the most common concern of the elderly is not home and health care but rather concern for crime and personal safety (Berghorn & Schafer, 1981)? And, as described in Chapter 10, that violence within families is a towering problem in the United States? Ours is, indeed, a violent society, and violence is a problem to be coped with. Let's briefly consider some of the causes of violence and aggression, and some steps that we can take to prevent it.

Some Causes of Violence and Aggression

aggression

Behavior (verbal or physical) that is directed toward the goal of harming or injuring another living being who is motivated to avoid such treatment.

Aggression is behavior (verbal or physical) that is directed toward the goal of harming or injuring another living being who is motivated to avoid such treatment (Baron, 1977). The dictionary meaning of *violence* is "a use of force so as to injure or damage; a rough injurious act." You can see that violence is a somewhat broader term, and can refer to damage to property as well as injury to individuals. For our purposes, however, we will use the terms interchangeably.

LEARNING.   There is little doubt that aggressive tendencies can be selectively bred into animals (Lorenz, 1974). Pit bull terriers, for example, were bred for fighting, which is one of the reasons that they have been banned in some cities in Canada and the United States. Most psychologists, however, believe that aggression is largely learned in humans. Many of the aggressive tendencies of adults are likely learned as children. You may recall from Chapter 3, for example, an experiment by Albert Bandura and his colleagues in which children learned to be aggressive by watching an adult beat up a Bobo doll. And there is considerable evidence that boys raised by fathers who practice wife abuse are likely to be abusive to their own wives later in life (McCall & Shields, 1986); that children who were victims of child abuse themselves are likely to abuse their own children (Kaufman & Zigler, 1987); and that physical abuse of a male child by his father is also highly predictive of that male being physically abusive in a dating relationship (Alexander et al., 1991).

There is also an established link between the learning of aggression and all the violence viewed on television (Singer, 1989). Perhaps that's not so surprising

After reviewing hundreds of studies that examined the effects of violence on television, the National Institute of Mental Health (1982) concluded that "violence on television does lead to aggressive behavior by children and teenagers who watch the programs."

when we consider that the average American child will watch more than 20,000 televised shootings before becoming an adult (Liebert, 1986); that some 95 percent of televised cartoons and 80 percent of TV dramas contain violence (Oskamp, 1984); and that the average American child spends more time watching the television set than attending school (Liebert & Poulos, 1975). In one study, for example, a group of seven- and eight-year-old boys who watched a violent television program were much more aggressive later during a game of floor hockey than were boys who had watched a television program that did not contain violence (Josephson, 1987). Study after study leads to the same conclusion: If we see others act violently and get away with it, and/or if we anticipate rewards for behaving aggressively, then aggression is more likely to occur.

FRUSTRATION.   Some researchers have suggested that aggression is a response to frustration. After all, if a soft drink machine takes your money but doesn't give you the soft drink, don't you feel frustrated? And aren't you likely to give the machine a kick? In the 1930s, a group of psychologists at Yale University proposed the **frustration-aggression hypothesis**—the theory that frustration always results in aggressive behavior and all aggressive behavior is caused by frustration (Dollard et al., 1939). But the theory didn't hold up in all cases. As we just described, for example, children can learn to be aggressive simply as a function of watching someone else be aggressive (that is, modeling).

frustration-aggression hypothesis

The theory that frustration always results in aggressive behavior, and all aggressive behavior is caused by frustration.

Leonard Berkowitz (1962, 1989) revised the theory of the Yale psychologists to suggest that frustration leads to anger, and that anger may be followed by aggression only if suitable environmental cues are present. In one experiment, for example, college students were given an opportunity to administer electric shocks to a colleague who tormented them. They were more likely to do so when in the presence of aggressive cues such as a rifle and a revolver, than when neutral objects (such as badminton racquets) were present (Berkowitz & LePage, 1967). Other studies have supported this "weapons effect," and have provided one of the arguments offered by Berkowitz and others calling for a ban of the sale of handguns in the United States (Berkowitz, 1981).

AVERSIVE STIMULATION.   Aggression is also a reaction to aversive stimulation. If two rats, for example, are placed in a small cage and administered a brief electric shock, they will fight each other (Ulrich & Azrin, 1962). Aggression by animals in such circumstances appears to occur as an unlearned response to pain. Humans also show aggressiveness in response to aversive stimulation, such as excessive

Studies have demonstrated a "weapons effect." Individuals are more likely to be aggressive if they are frustrated in the presence of aggressive cues, such as guns, than when in the presence of neutral objects (such as tennis racquets).

heat, although their reactions are more than likely learned. If you're cooped up in a hot stuffy room, for example, do you become irritable? Are you likely to react aggressively? Probably you would. Consider that violent crimes are more likely on hotter days than cooler days, and during hotter seasons than cooler seasons (Anderson, 1989). Drivers of cars without air conditioning in Phoenix, Arizona, are more likely to honk at a stalled car on hotter days than on cooler days (Kenrick & MacFarlane, 1986). And pitchers in major league baseball games are more than twice as likely to hit the batters with a pitch for games played outdoors in 90-degree weather as compared to games played in cooler temperatures (Reifman et al., 1988). Such studies have led Berkowitz (1988, 1989) to propose that aversive stimulation may be a more basic cause of aggression than frustration.

Preventing Violence and Aggression

We must recognize up front that aggression has many causes and that there is no simple solution to preventing it. At the same time, we must not throw up our hands in a "there's nothing we can do about it" gesture. Let's look at some of the options that might make a difference.

TEACH CHILDREN TO BE COOPERATIVE.   As indicated above, ample evidence exists that many sources of aggression stem from childhood learning experiences. An important step that we, as adults, can take then, is to avoid modeling aggressive actions to children. We should not rely on physical punishment or verbal abuse to discipline children. And we should avoid modeling aggressive and violent encounters with other adults. We should use rewards in positive ways to strengthen cooperative, nonaggressive behavior. What if we see children themselves showing aggressive behavior? How should we react? Some research has indicated that, rather than punishing an aggressive child, we should ignore the child's aggressive behavior and reward the child's cooperative, nonaggressive behavior (Hamblin et al., 1969). Moreover, we must remember that children who are physically abused by their parents tend to physically abuse their own children (Kaufman & Zigler, 1987). In general, if we minimize the causes of specific undesirable alternative behavior and take care to provide prompts and rewards for desirable behavior, then the undesirable behavior may not occur (Martin & Pear, 1992).

TALK TO CHILDREN ABOUT TV VIOLENCE.   What about the violence on television? We're not likely to stop our children from watching television, and it's hard to imagine having much effect on the television moguls who do the network programming. One possibility is to teach our children that aggression is not the best way to handle conflict, and that the violence that they see on television is unrealistic. For example, we can help them to recognize that, unlike an hour of the Teenage Mutant Ninja Turtles, an hour or so in the real world is not filled with 28 karate kicks, 37 head butts, and an assortment of punches and weapons attacks. An experiment conducted with a group of children in Illinois supports this approach. Eron and Huesmann (1984) taught 170 children that the world is not like it is portrayed on television, and that aggression is wrong and is not an effective way of solving problems. In a follow-up two years later, these children were less affected than untrained children by the television violence that they observed. This suggests that you should discuss with your children the frequent violence seen on television, and explain to them both your feelings about it and its inaccurate portrayal of the real world.

ENCOURAGE THE PASSAGE OF LAWS AGAINST VIOLENCE.   Still another possibility is to write your Congress members and encourage them to pass laws that will make a difference. Laws that can make a difference are those that have an immediate impact on perpetrators of violence and those that make violence less likely. For example, in a study in Minneapolis, overnight arrests of men who beat their wives was a relatively effective strategy for decreasing this offense (Sherman & Berk, 1984). In Jamaica in 1974, the passing of strict gun control and other anticrime laws led to a 25 percent drop in robberies and a 37 percent decrease in nonfatal shootings the following year (Diener & Crandall, 1979). The right laws and their enforcement *can* make a difference.

Violence against Women

Violence against women deserves special attention. The fact is that 89 percent of violent crimes are conducted by men (Kenrick, 1987), and that a great deal of the violence in our society is done by men against women. We've already commented on the high frequency of rape in the United States. And an additional 2 million women each year in the United States suffer from physical abuse from their spouses (Pedrick-Cornell & Gelles, 1982). Clearly, extra measures are needed to deal with this problem.

Prevention of rape and violence against women in our society is not just a problem for the women to deal with. It is also a problem of changing certain societal values in general, and certain attitudes of men in particular. First, we need to engage in wide-ranging consciousness-raising regarding movies, magazines, videos, and television programs that have a violent and sexual theme. We must educate everyone concerning the data presented in Chapter 7 of the dangers of exposure to pornography involving sexual violence. Its effects tend to be associated with (1) male aggression against females, (2) general acceptance of sexual violence against women, and (3) acceptance of myths regarding female sexual desires. As expressed by Susan Brownmiller (1984), acceptance of pornography involving sexual violence is nothing more than "propaganda against women."

rape myths
Inaccurate beliefs (usually held by males) about why rape occurs and what happens during rape.

Second, we need to educate men about various **rape myths** (see Box 11-1). Many men apparently need to learn that women do *not* enjoy rape, and that being roughed up is *not* sexually stimulating to most women. Studies have indicated that male college students who are briefed on such rape myths are much less accepting of erotic rape stories and pornographic films that portray women as enjoying a mixture of violence and sex (Donnerstein & Berkowitz, 1981; Malamuth & Check, 1984). How can such information be communicated to men everywhere? One possibility is to organize a series of public conferences. For example, in Ottawa, Canada, the first national men's conference aimed at ending male violence was recently held. The goal of the conference was to encourage all men—not just abusers—to accept responsibility for the "epidemic" of male violence in today's society (Cox, 1991). Repetition of such conferences in other locales, and the coverage of them by the media, are valuable consciousness-raising activities.

Third, we need to encourage victims of abuse to pursue legal action against their assailants. Many victims fear taking this approach, especially battered wives. But where husbands have been arrested or presented with court orders that call for their arrest if they harm their wives again, the likelihood of continued battering greatly decreases (Bardon, 1982). The laws affecting violence against women are slowing improving, and women must be encouraged to use them.

Fourth, women should be encouraged to learn ways to prevent violence from men. Consider, for example, the problem of *acquaintance rape* or *date rape*— forcible rape by an acquaintance, often while on a date. Studies by Charlene Muehlenhard and her colleagues have led to several strategies for women to prevent acquaintance rapes (Muehlenhard, 1988; Muehlenhard & Linton, 1987). They suggest the following:

1. If it's your first date, meet your date in a public place or in a group so that you can examine his behavior in relative safety.

Box 11-1

RAPE MYTHS

Rape myths are inaccurate beliefs (usually held by males) about why rape occurs and what happens during rape. Here are some of the more common rape myths.

1. *Myth:* Rape only happens in dark alleys and in deserted places.
   Fact: It happens more often in or near the victim's home.
2. *Myth:* Provocative dressing produces rape.
   Fact: Most rape victims are not provocatively dressed.
3. *Myth:* The rape victim is a certain type—she's emotional, tearful, uncontrolled.
   Fact: There's not one "type" of rape victim. Psychologically, the word *type* does not apply here. However, the authorities who deal with rape victims say that rape victims react in two general ways: One is emotionally expressive, the other is highly controlled. The former is more likely to be believed by the police.
4. *Myth:* She asked for it.
   Fact: No means no, it does not mean anything else. Men don't die from incomplete sexual satisfaction.

5. *Myth:* Women enjoy being raped.
   Fact: Rapists know differently, and women know differently.
6. *Myth:* The rapist is a monstrous maniac.
   Fact: He's more likely the man next door, who looks just like any ordinary guy.
7. *Myth:* Only females should deal with rape victims.
   Fact: Only people of considerable sensitivity should deal with rape victims; biological sex is irrelevant.
8. *Myth:* Women cry rape when it isn't.
   Fact: In New York, out of 2,000 rape cases, there were a total of just 5 in which women falsely accused men of rape; that's about one quarter of one percent, the same as false reports of other crimes such as robbery. Moreover, it is estimated that for every one reported rape, there are three to ten unreported rapes. So it might be concluded that women more frequently don't cry rape when it is rape, then cry rape when it isn't.

From Doyle, 1989; O'Reilly, 1984.

2. Share some of the expenses on dates. This sets the stage for equal input to all decisions, and may lessen the expectation of your date to "get what he paid for."
3. Clearly express your desires regarding intimacy early in the evening. For example, you might say, "I would enjoy holding and kissing you, but please don't interpret it as a come-on for something more." A lack of clear communication on your part along with ambiguous messages will lead some men to believe that "she says no but she really means yes."
4. If all else fails, holler loudly, "This is rape and I'm calling the cops," and push, kick, or claw your assailant. Beal and Muehlenhard (1987) reported that the combination of these responses will stop most men from making unwanted advances.

Finally, women who have been raped or abused should be encouraged to seek professional counseling.

In this section, we have dealt with just some aspects of the problems of violence. We must also recognize that considerable violence in our society is expressed by the members of one group who have been prejudiced against the members of another group, such as violence by whites against Afro-Americans during the early days of the civil rights movement, or by Nazis against Jews during World War II. While it's an oversimplification to say that prejudice causes violence, the two have nevertheless gone together throughout recorded history. Let's now take a look at some of the problems associated with prejudice and discrimination.

Prejudice and Discrimination in Today's Society

Harold Brown slammed down the newspaper in disgust. "It says here that the government's going to raise welfare payments again. Don't they realize that they're supporting a bunch of no-good, lazy, shiftless bums? I don't get handouts like that."

Harold's children listened intently as they always did when their dad got emotional.

"I sure wish you wouldn't talk that way in front of the children," his wife replied.

"I'm just sick and tired of the policies of this bunch. They're just paying those bums for doing nothing, nothing at all."

How many times in their lifetimes might Harold Brown's children hear him make such statements? How many times might this happen collectively in nations such as ours? And what would be the result? Would these children be more likely to be prejudiced against people on welfare than children whose fathers did not speak out on this issue? In this section we examine the associated problems of prejudice and discrimination, and we discuss steps that we can all take to reduce prejudice and discrimination in today's society.

Stereotypes, Prejudice, and Discrimination

Central to our understanding of terms like *prejudice* and *discrimination* is an appreciation of our tendency to put ourselves into groups. Often, we divide our world into "us" and "them" according to sex (males vs. females), race (black vs.

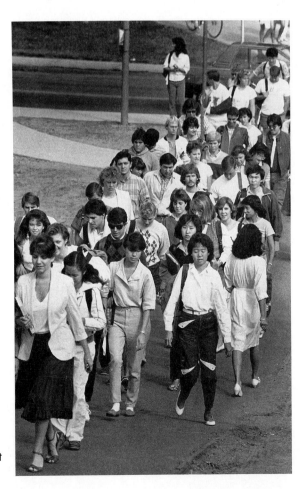

Is America the great racial melting pot that it was once thought to be?

Box 11-2

ARE YOU PREJUDICED?

To be dogmatic is to express opinions strongly, usually without reference to evidence. Being dogmatic does not automatically make you prejudiced. However, you are more likely to be prejudiced if you score high on a dogmatism scale than if you obtain a low score. Complete the following scale, then score yourself according to the guidelines below.

Short Dogmatism Scale

Answer each statement by circling a number. Agree very much = +3; Agree on the whole = +2; Agree a little = +1; Disagree very much = −3; Disagree on the whole = −2; Disagree a little = −1.

1. Fundamentally, the world we live in is a pretty lonely place.
   +3   +2   +1   −1   −2   −3

2. It is often desirable to reserve judgment about what's going on until one has a chance to hear the opinions of those one respects.
   +3   +2   +1   −1   −2   −3

3. A person who thinks primarily of his own happiness is beneath contempt.
   +3   +2   +1   −1   −2   −3

4. In the history of mankind there have probably just been a handful of really great thinkers.
   +3   +2   +1   −1   −2   −3

5. Most people just don't know what's good for them.
   +3   +2   +1   −1   −2   −3

6. Once I get wound up in a heated discussion I just can't stop.
   +3   +2   +1   −1   −2   −3

7. The worst crime a person can commit is to attack publicly the people who believe the same thing he does.
   +3   +2   +1   −1   −2   −3

8. In this complicated world of ours the only way we can know what is going on is to rely upon leaders or experts who can be trusted.
   +3   +2   +1   −1   −2   −3

9. In the long run the best way to live is to pick friends and associates whose tastes and beliefs are the same as one's own.
   +3   +2   +1   −1   −2   −3

10. While I don't like to admit this even to myself, I sometimes have the ambition to become a great person like Einstein, or Beethoven, or Shakespeare.
    +3   +2   +1   −1   −2   −3

From Schulze, 1962.

Scoring: To obtain a dogmatism score for your responses to the scale, sum your totals. Remember, each minus is subtracted. A positive score is correlated with dogmatism, so the higher a positive score you obtain the more dogmatic you probably are. Scores near zero are non-dogmatic.

white), age (young vs. old), and so forth. Social psychologists refer to these categories as *in group* and *out group* (Baron & Byrne, 1987). Members of the in group share a common identity and a sense of belonging, while members of the out group are perceived as being different from the in group in some important way (Myers, 1990).

Do you belong to various groups? And what do you think about other groups? Have you ever found yourself saying, for example, that "professors are absent-minded"? "Men are aggressive"? "English people are reserved"? or "Women are emotional"? If so, you have shown a **stereotype**—an oversimplified generalization about the characteristics of members of a group. Stereotypes usually emphasize a

stereotype

An oversimplified generalization about the characteristics of members of a group.

potential difference between the in group and the out group. And we tend to stereotype members of various groups so that our own group will be seen as superior. For example, attractive women may perceive themselves as happier and more sociable than less attractive women; while less attractive women may perceive attractive women as more snobbish and likely to get a divorce. Stereotypes are usually misinformed because they consider all of the members of the stereotyped group to have the same characteristics, and they ignore the tremendous diversity within all groups. While there may be a slight basis for some stereotypes, any group (such as professors, men, English people, or women) is more remarkable for differences among its members than for the similarities among them.

prejudice

A negative attitude that consists of stereotyped beliefs against members of a group, negative feelings toward them, and a tendency to act negatively toward them.

Prejudice is built on stereotypes, but it involves more than just oversimplified beliefs about the characteristics of members of a group. To be **prejudiced** against a group is to hold *stereotyped beliefs* against its members, to *feel* negatively toward them, and to be inclined to *act* negatively toward them. These three components—holding certain beliefs, harboring certain feelings, and showing a tendency to act—are also the defining characteristics of an *attitude* (Myers, 1990). And to be prejudiced is essentially to hold a negative attitude toward a group. If an individual expresses the stereotype "honkys are hypocritical," harbors negative feelings toward "honkys," and avoids places where "honkys" hang out, then the speaker has exhibited an anti-"honky" prejudice.

discrimination

Any behavior that has as its result the denial of rights or privileges to another human.

Discrmination is any behavior that has as its result the denial of rights or privileges to another human. It is more likely to be defined by the laws of the land. Discrimination exists, for example, when one class of people have access to rewarding resources (for example, good schools) while another class of people do not. To state that women are not mechanically inclined is a *stereotype*, to express contempt for women who want to be mechanics is *prejudice*, and to exclude women from auto maintenance courses is *discrimination*. Prejudice may not result in overt discrimination, but discrimination always is correlated with prejudice.

Sexism and Racism

sexism

A negative attitude toward members of a given gender, and/or institutionalized discriminatory practices that place members of that gender in an inferior role.

Sexism and racism usually include both prejudice and discrimination. **Sexism** refers to a negative attitude toward members of a given gender, and/or institutionalized discriminatory practices that place members of that gender in an inferior role. **Racism** refers to a negative attitude toward people of a given race, and/or institutionalized discriminatory practices against members of that race. Suppose, for example, that an airline company required that all its inflight cabin attendants be female and a minimum height of 5 ft 8 in. Because on-the-job effectiveness is not determined by one's sex, and because the height requirement would tend to exclude most Asians and Hispanics, the company's hiring practices could be labeled both sexist and racist. Racism is also typically accompanied by the belief that one's own race is superior.

racism

A negative attitude toward people of a given race, and/or institutionalized discriminatory practices against members of that race.

As illustrated by the above example, sexism can exist against males, but it is much more commonly a problem for females. During the past few decades, however, prejudice against women has decreased considerably. During the 1930s, for example, approximately 30 percent of Americans sampled indicated that they would vote for a female President. By 1988, that number had increased to almost 90 percent (Myers, 1990). And we just don't hear anyone anymore saying that women shouldn't get equal pay for equal work. As expressed by Andy Rooney (1991), "Few men are silly enough to think that and if by any chance they are, they wouldn't be dumb enough to say it." While blatant prejudice against women is largely a thing of the past, subtle prejudices and inequalities based on sex still exist. Consider, for example, that 26 percent of American college students recently agreed that "the activities of married women are best confined to the home and family" (Astin et al.,

1987), that women are underrepresented (by a ratio of 1 to 3) in prime-time television (Gerbner et al., 1986), and that they are outnumbered 9 to 1 as narrators of television commercials (Bretl & Cantor, 1988). Although women have come a long way from the second-class citizenship they once held, there is still work to do to achieve the goal of true equality between the sexes. (Also see section on Sexism in Chapter 7.)

Is racism common in America? There is no doubt that racism was common at various times in U.S. history against Hispanics in the American Southwest, Chinese in California, and Native Americans and Afro-Americans throughout the country (Aronson, 1990). But during the past several decades, fewer and fewer people have expressed racist attitudes. For example, researchers at the National Opinion Research Center reported that, during the early 1940s, only 30 percent of white Americans sampled believed that white and Afro-American students should go to the same schools. By 1985, that number had risen to almost 90 percent. While the results of such surveys indicate that Americans are becoming less racist, other studies suggest that current racism may simply be more subtle. For example, in one recent survey, approximately 75 percent of white Americans thought that there should *not* be laws against marriages between Afro-Americans and whites (National Opinion Research Center, 1988), but 57 percent of whites expressed that they would feel unhappy if their child married an Afro-American (Life, 1988).

Thus, the good news is that blatant racist attitudes in the United States have plummeted in recent years. The bad news is that subtle prejudice and discrimination still exist against Afro-Americans (Myers, 1990), Native Americans (Trimble, 1988), and Hispanics (Ramirez, 1988). As described later in this chapter, much more needs to be done. But before looking at ways to reduce prejudice and discrimination, let's examine some of their causes.

The Development of Prejudice and Discrimination

There is little question that prejudice is learned early in life through well-known socialization practices involving the family, society's institutions (for example, schools), and peer groups.

FAMILY INFLUENCE.   Parents and other significant adults are imitated by children. In our earlier example, Harold Brown can expect his children to grow up prejudiced against those on welfare, just because he himself has that opinion and has expressed it in their presence. They may further develop opinions with respect to others by modeling his actions, even in the absence of any verbal behavior. Children tend to behave and believe as their parents do. Parents may also directly condition certain verbal responses by their children, both knowingly and unknowingly. For example, they may laugh at a particular behavior that is "cute." Perhaps this behavior seems innocuous at the time—for example, labeling of strangers or of those who look different (for example, "Look at that funny man"). Later, however, it may be called stereotyping.

INSTITUTIONAL INFLUENCE.   Society's institutions also assist in the socialization process. The media can have a strong impact on prejudicial attitudes because of the way certain groups are portrayed. For example, in the not-too-distant past, newspapers consistently reported the race of a criminal if he or she was Afro-American, but made no mention of race when the criminal was white. This could easily have given readers the impression that most criminals are Afro-American.

In addition to formal academic training, schools presumably teach children to play together and to get along well in groups. However, more often than not, there is little conscious thought given by such institutions to their role in the development of prejudice. For example, teachers might unknowingly influence children to behave ethnocentrically because of practices like putting children into groups. *Ethnocentrism* is the belief that one's own group is superior to other groups. Investigators have suggested that prejudice and discrimination may be one of the products of group formation (Tajfel & Turner, 1985). In one study for example, a third-grade school teacher in Riceville, Iowa, told her class that, "The blue-eyed people are smarter than the brown-eyed people . . . blue-eyed people are cleaner than brown-eyed people. They are more civilized" (Weiner & Wright, 1973). She forced the brown-eyed children to sit at the back of the room and allowed the blue-eyed children to sit up front. Blue-eyed children were also given additional privileges. Almost immediately, the blue-eyed children began ridiculing and teasing the brown-eyed students, and refused to associate with them. There was even a fight because one boy called another "brown eyes." The next day, the teacher reversed the situation. She told the class that she had lied and that it was really the brown-eyed children who were better and brighter. As might be predicted, the brown-eyed children readily adopted this prejudice and began teasing the blue-eyed children. Fortunately, on the third day, the teacher explained that the exercise had been an experiment. Both the teacher and the students found it valuable to discuss how it felt to be the object of prejudice and discrimination. Unfortunately, teachers often do group children in various ways unknowingly.

Often institutional biases go unnoticed. For years, for example, people paid little attention to the portrayal of the Native American in films and television programs as a stereotyped savage (Trimble, 1988). (The Academy Award–winning movie *Dances with Wolves* offers a far different portrayal.) Recognizing such institutional biases is a first step toward correcting them.

PEER INFLUENCE.   Children also learn from their peers. For example, there is typically more discussion of sexual behavior at the peer level than either in school or at home. It is in this way that children's opinions about other children are molded by their friends. The first groups will form, and children will be included and excluded. The same socialization processes will be at work inside the group. Children will model other children who have status and will be socially reinforced by children who attend to them when they say specific things ("I think Joey stinks. I'll bet he never takes a bath!").

COMPETITION.   Economic considerations may also play a role in the development of prejudice and discrimination. Consider, for example the attitudes of many white Americans toward Chinese immigrants in the 1800s. When workers were needed to help build the railroads in the American West, newspaper articles emphasized the strong family life, honesty, and industriousness of Chinese people. But when many whites moved west looking for jobs after the U.S. Civil War, popular writings did an about-face, suggesting that the Chinese were dishonest and inferior (Martin, 1991). As another example, researchers have found that whites who showed the greatest racial prejudice against Afro-Americans were those who were in direct competition with Afro-Americans for jobs (Maykovitch, 1975). In such situations, the development of prejudice against a minority may have monetary benefits for members of the majority.

AUTHORITARIAN PERSONALITY.   Prejudice is highly correlated with a personality characteristic called authoritarianism. This characteristic was first studied after World War II by a group of California psychologists concerned with anti-Semitism, or prejudice against Jews (Adorno et al., 1950). They wanted to try and understand the personality characteristics of a culture that would allow something like the Holocaust to occur. What they discovered was **authoritarianism**—a tendency to be traditional and conventional, to be submissive to established authority, and to be hostile and aggressive to minority groups (Altemeyer, 1988). The researchers dis-

authoritarianism

A tendency to be traditional and conventional, to be submissive to established authority, and to be hostile and aggressive to minority groups.

Prejudice is everywhere and affects every group.

covered that individuals who showed authoritarian tendencies displayed prejudice not only against Jews but also against other minority groups.

The original research on authoritarian personality was criticized on several grounds, including the possibility that the California researchers were somewhat biased by their own strongly held democratic values (Brown, 1965). But subsequent research by Bob Altemeyer in Canada and the United States using an improved measure of authoritarianism confirmed and extended many of the original conclusions. First, some people do demonstrate strong authoritarian tendencies. Between 1973 and 1988, for example, average scores by University of Manitoba students on Altemeyer's test for authoritarianism rose 20 percent (Altemeyer, 1988). In 1986, Altemeyer sampled the views of senators and legislators in Minnesota, California, Mississippi, and Connecticut. Some of those politicians held authoritarian views akin to fascism, while others strongly opposed authoritarianism (Altemeyer, 1988). Interestingly, those views were not split along party lines. Distinct authoritarian and nonauthoritarian views were held by both Democrats and Republicans. Second, there is substantial evidence that authoritarian characteristics are highly correlated with prejudice. In South Africa, for example, those who most strongly support apartheid tend to have authoritarian attitudes (Van Staden, 1987). However, authoritarianism should not be thought of as a cause of prejudice. Rather, both are behavior patterns that are most likely caused by the various socialization practices discussed above.

What Sustains Prejudice and Discrimination?

There are a number of reasons why discrimination and prejudice are sustained in a society. First, people may be more comfortable with other people who think as they do, and they may act in ways to promote such uniform thinking. For example, members of a group can be subtly rewarded for adherence to the "party line." On the flip side of the coin, members of a group can be subtly punished for utterances and actions that don't fit the party line. Perhaps that's why those in the in group are more likely to use stereotypes (when describing members of the out group) when in the presence of in group members than when alone (Wilder & Shapiro, 1991).

Another possibility is that the cohesion within a group can be enhanced by blaming the out group when things go wrong—a practice known as **scapegoat-**

scapegoating
The practice of belittling or blaming the behavior or characteristics of another individual or group so as to enhance by contrast the characteristics or behavior of oneself or one's own group.

ing. According to Aronson (1980), in early times a "scapegoat" was literally a goat. Centuries ago, a religious leader while reciting the sins of his congregation would place his hands on the head of a goat. The goat was then chased into the wilds, symbolically taking the sins of the people with it. One theory suggests that a group might resort to scapegoating when its members appear to be frustrated by events beyond their control (Dollard et al., 1939). If people are unable to deal directly with a cause of frustration, they seek a safer target—a scapegoat. In the case of prejudice, the scapegoat may be a minority group that is clearly distinguishable from a more powerful majority (because of highly visible characteristics such as skin color, accent, and name) and hence is safe to attack. In our opening scenario to this section on prejudice and discrimination, for example, Harold Brown, perhaps frustrated by uncontrollable tax increases and inflation, used welfare recipients as scapegoats. Blaming a scapegoat may have the effect of relieving one's frustrations, and thereby maintaining one's prejudices against the scapegoat.

self-fulfilling prophecy
The tendency to have expectations, and to act in a way that confirms those expectations.

Our prejudices may also be maintained through a process referred to as the **self-fulfilling prophecy**—the tendency of our expectations to cause us to act in a way that confirms those expectations. If we have expectations about the way members of a particular group should act, we are likely to treat them in a way that will confirm those expectations. Consider a fascinating experiment performed in some northern California schools in the 1960s. At the end of an elementary school year, Robert Rosenthal and his colleagues tested all the children in a particular school with a new intelligence test. Then in conferences at the start of the fall term with individual teachers, the investigators casually would say, "By the way, in case you're interested in who did what on those tests we're doing for Harvard . . . ," and they would drop the names of several children in the teacher's class who supposedly did very well on the test. The implication was that those children would be expected to do well in the current year. This was done in the same casual manner with all of the teachers in all of the grades. In reality, however, the children whose names were mentioned were drawn randomly, independent of their performance on the intelligence test. The investigators then retested all the children at the end of the year. Children who were thought by their teacher to be "spurters" (those children the investigators had claimed to show strong intellectual potential) gained more IQ points than those who had not been so labeled (see Figure 11-1) (Rosenthal & Jacobson, 1968a; 1968b).

What accounts for this phenomenon? The teachers appeared to behave in a way that confirmed their expectations—the self-fulfilling prophesy (Rosenthal,

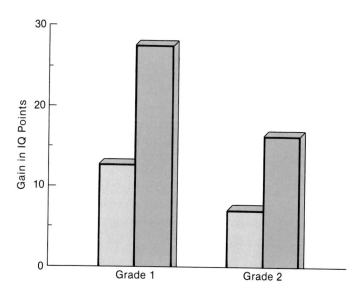

Figure 11-1
Light grey bars are "spurters." Dark grey bars are "non-spurters."

1973). Perhaps they were emotionally warmer toward "brighter" students and gave them more feedback. Perhaps they also unconsciously grouped the children according to their supposed intellectual level, thereby influencing the development of prejudice between the groups. Thus, if we have expectations that certain groups will show certain stereotypes, we are likely to behave in a way to confirm those expectations, and our stereotypes will be maintained.

Getting Rid of Prejudice and Discrimination

You can see that prejudice is developed and maintained from a variety of causes. It is not surprising, then, that there is no simple way of reducing it. Let's examine some steps that we all can take and support.

PREJUDICE-PROOF OUR CHILDREN.   One way to control prejudice or discrimination is to stop it before it begins. Our children need to become critical thinkers. We need to have them develop inquiring minds and to be skeptical about broad generalizations that characterize stereotypes. We need to teach them to question statements that are made only on the basis of authority, to require justification for statements that are value laden, to evaluate what is said to them, and to experience things for themselves. If our children learn these skills, they may be less likely to act in a prejudiced way. Consider, for example, an experiment that examined the way in which sixth graders react to disabled persons. An experimental group of students was first given training in critical thinking in which they were encouraged to look for several possible solutions to problems, and to select a solution that seemed most appropriate. The experimental group and a control group of untrained sixth graders were then asked to consider a variety of problems concerning persons with disabilities. In one task, for example, the sixth graders were required to select a partner (either a picture of a boy with no apparent disability or a boy in a wheelchair) to perform a variety of activities, such as a wheelchair race, a game of soccer, and a game of checkers. The choices made suggested that the students trained in critical thinking saw people as individuals. They frequently chose the boy in the wheelchair for the wheelchair race, rarely chose him for the soccer game, and showed little or no preference for either boy for the checkers game. The control group, on the other hand, tended to choose the boy with no apparent disability more often for all tasks (Langer et al., 1985).

ENCOURAGE CONTACT BETWEEN GROUPS.   One way to reduce prejudice is to encourage contact with the out group. This was one of the hoped-for outcomes of the U.S. Supreme Court decision in 1954 which ruled that separate schools for Afro-Americans and whites were inherently unequal. Unfortunately, desegregation has not always had the desired effect. While studies have shown that achievement by Afro-American children tends to increase in integrated schools, white children in the same schools have shown an increase in prejudice towards Afro-American schoolchildren about as often as they have shown a decrease (Amir & Sharan, 1984; Stephan, 1986).

If increasing contact between two groups will sometimes reduce prejudice and sometimes not, what are the conditions where prejudice reduction does occur? At least three sets of such conditions have been identified. First, the people from the different groups should encounter each other on an *equal status* basis, so that individuals in neither group are disadvantaged by the situation (Brewer & Miller, 1988). But this has not always occurred in desegregated schools. If Afro-American children from an academically inferior school are suddenly bused to an integrated school and are expected to compete with white children at the same grade level who have had better academic training, then they are not contacting each other with equal status.

Prejudice is reduced between interracial group members when those members must help one another in order for their group to be successful.

jigsaw method
A method of reducing prejudice; involves distributing bits of information to members of a small interracial group; each must then contribute and cooperate in order for the group to solve a problem.

Second, tasks assigned to the different groups should require that their members *cooperate* to solve common goals (Johnson & Johnson, 1989). Aronson and Bridgeman (1979), for example, reported positive results with the **jigsaw method.** They assigned children to small interracial learning groups that were given problems to be solved and lessons to be learned. Each child in a group received only one part of the information necessary to solve the problem or complete the lesson. Each child was then responsible for communicating his or her part of the puzzle to the rest of the group. When the children were forced to help one another in order for the group to be successful, to teach and to learn from one another, and to pay attention to each other, prejudice was broken down, and the minority children achieved higher self-esteem and gained more academically.

Third, members of different groups need to get to know each other *as individuals* (Cook, 1979). If Afro-American, Hispanic, and white children at an integrated school hang out in their respective groups before, during, and after classes, then between-group prejudice is likely to persist. For prejudice to be reduced, individuals from each group must enjoy unique one-on-one experiences.

MAKE THE MASS MEDIA A ROLE MODEL.   Previously we described examples of how films have perpetuated stereotypes in their portrayal of the Native American, and how prime-time television has portrayed stereotypes in their underrepresentation of women in certain roles. We must continue to examine the mass media for examples of stereotyping and prejudice that have gone unnoticed. Are you aware, for example, that in photographs of people in magazines and newspapers, about two thirds of the photo of a male is typically devoted to the face, while less than half the photo of a female is devoted to the face (Archer et al., 1983), and that this phenomenon even exists in *Ms.* magazine (Nigro et al., 1988)? What stereotypes does this sex bias perpetuate? Dane Archer and his colleagues (1983) suggest that individuals whose faces (rather than bodies) are featured in photos are likely to be seen as more intelligent. We must demand that the mass media be sensitive to the perpetuation of prejudice, and that it provide positive and equitable exposure of both sexes and all minorities.

TAKE A PERSONAL STANCE.   On an interpersonal level, we must remember that prejudicial statements are often uttered because of the attention that they usually receive. Even arguing against a prejudiced person in an effort to convince the person of the error of his or her ways is a form of attention. Probably the best way to react to an instance of prejudice is to actively ignore it. Purposely change the subject or walk away from the person making the prejudicial utterance. Don't laugh, for example, when people tell ethnic jokes. Ethnic jokes, in particular, tend to make the group that hears them more cohesive, to separate it from the group about whom the joke is told. In these jokes there is an attempt to lower the self-esteem of the group being disparaged, and by implicit comparison, to raise the self-esteem of the group telling/listening to the joke (Martineau, 1972). In terms of the learning concepts described in Chapter 3, treat prejudicial statements and ethnic jokes as operant behaviors to be decreased, and put them on extinction.

The problems of prejudice and discrimination require solutions directed to both individuals and to society as a whole. Let's now turn to another problem that requires both individual and societal adjustments, the problem of preserving and living with Mother Earth.

Preserving and Living with the Environment

Mark and John have just arrived at a lake they haven't fished before, about an hour's drive from the city in which they live. Because of the easy access, a great deal of unsupervised camping and recreation takes place there. While unloading their fishing gear, they hear the incessant buzzing of motorcycles roaring up and down the nearby hill. "Jeez," said Mark, "look at all the garbage floating in the water. I'm not sure I wanna eat fish from a place like this!"

"People who come here must really be pigs. I can't understand why people trash an area like this."

"That's for sure. Somebody oughta do something about it."

What *does* lead people to pollute an area like the one Mark and John were fishing? Where does the responsibility for such acts lie? And what of industry's lack of consciousness to these same problems? Does industry pollute on purpose? Is it

Because no one person is responsible for public properties, they often look like this area.

possible to get rid of the several kinds of pollution we now live with—the pollution of the air we breathe, of the soils in which we grow our food, and of our bodies from the other kinds of pollution? And what about our lifestyles? Are we consuming resources that will mean our children will live less well? Are we overpopulating? Does it always seem crowded wherever you go?

And what about your personal concern for the environment? Do you throw beer cans from your car as you travel? Do you clean up a campsite you've visited to make it cleaner for the next occupant? If you smoke out of doors, where do you throw your cigarette butts? Have you ever carved your initials on a tree or spray-painted a slogan on a building? What are your feelings about such matters? To measure your attitudes toward the environment, we encourage you to complete the questionnaire in Box 11-3.

In this section, we'll examine examples of environmental pollution, and we'll review some strategies to promote conservation. We'll also look at one of the results of overpopulation—crowding and its effects on behavior.

The Tragedy of the Commons

commons

Public ground; historically, often town squares where townspeople could graze their cows.

Environmental problems are frequently problems of **commons**—public lands shared by everyone, areas that no one owns. The name derives from the common ground in a seventeenth- or eighteenth-century English township wherein the people in the town could graze their cows freely (Hardin, 1968). The opportunity to use the common enabled an individual farmer to graze a couple of extra cows, and to experience the short-term gains of having more fattened cows to market. This was all right only as long as all the farmers in the township collectively didn't graze any more cows on the common than it could handle. However, individual farmers typically grazed more cows than this number. The long-term effect was a common permanently ruined from the extra grazing, which adversely affected the group, but only at a later time. The discovery that people behave similarly in all commons has been labeled the **tragedy of the commons.**

tragedy of the commons

The despoliation of a resource by overuse because of short-term reinforcers for individual behavior (as in grazing extra cows on a common), even though, collectively, the overuse leads to long-term punishers (loss of the resource) for a group or society.

In the tragedy of the commons, or the commons dilemma, short-term consequences—rewards—lead to the overuse of some resource. The short-term consequences affect individual behavior a great deal (individual farmers profit directly from having more cows on the common). But the delayed consequences—punishers—in the form of absence of a valuable resource, affect a group. Because they're delayed so long, the punishers don't affect the individual now (it takes years of overgrazing for the commons to be ruined). Environments in which this happens are often environments that don't belong to anyone in particular—they belong to everyone in general. Perhaps because they belong to everyone and no one, no group specifically assumes responsibility for them until, too late, they're irrevocably changed.

LOSS OF A RESOURCE. Let's consider another natural resource, fish, and the "commons" in which they're found, the oceans. Perhaps because the oceans belong to no one specifically, the behavior of humans on the oceans is largely unregulated. Nations have only recently begun to regulate parts of the oceans that are international. For several hundred years, and even today within limits, the guiding doctrine has been that of the "freedom of the seas" (Anand, 1983). Thus, the oceans qualify as giant, international commons. Who speaks for the oceans?

The fish in the oceans are a resource within commons just as the grass is in the township. As with the grass, if the fish are harvested at a rate that does not exceed their ability to replenish themselves, they may be used indefinitely. But there has been no way to regulate the harvest in international waters. Whales are a case in point. Several species of whale have been so successfully hunted that there is international worry that they may be hunted out of existence. It's the old tragedy

Box 11-3

ENVIRONMENTAL CONCERN SCALE

Circle one opinion for each statement.

SA = Strongly agree; A = Agree; NS = Not sure;
D = Disagree; SD = Strongly disagree.

1. The federal government will have to introduce harsh measures to halt pollution, since few people will regulate themselves.　　SA　A　NS　D　SD

2. We should not worry about killing too many game animals because in the long run things will balance out.　　SA　A　NS　D　SD

3. I'd be willing to make personal sacrifices for the sake of slowing down pollution even though the immediate effects may not seem significant.　　SA　A　NS　D　SD

4. Pollution is *not* personally affecting my life.　　SA　A　NS　D　SD

5. The benefits of modern consumer products are more important than the pollution that results from their production and use.　　SA　A　NS　D　SD

6. We must prevent any type of animal from becoming extinct, even if it means sacrificing some things for ourselves.　　SA　A　NS　D　SD

7. Courses focusing on the conservation of natural resources should be taught in the public schools.　　SA　A　NS　D　SD

8. Although there is continual contamination of our lakes, streams, and air, nature's purifying processes soon return them to normal.　　SA　A　NS　D　SD

9. Because the government has such good inspection and control agencies, it's very unlikely that pollution will become excessive.　　SA　A　NS　D　SD

10. The government   SA   A   NS   D   SD
    should provide
    each citizen with
    a list of agencies
    and organiza-
    tions to which
    citizens could
    report grievances
    concerning pol-
    lution.
11. Predators such as   SA   A   NS   D   SD
    hawks, crows,
    skunks, and
    coyotes which
    prey on farmers'
    crops and poul-
    try should be
    eliminated.
12. The currently   SA   A   NS   D   SD
    active antipollu-
    tion organiza-
    tions are more
    interested in
    disrupting soci-
    ety than they are
    in fighting pollu-
    tion.

13. Even if public   SA   A   NS   D   SD
    transportation
    were more effi-
    cient than it is, I
    would prefer to
    drive my car to
    work.
14. Industry is trying   SA   A   NS   D   SD
    its best to de-
    velop effective
    pollution tech-
    nology.
15. If asked, I would   SA   A   NS   D   SD
    contribute time,
    money, or both
    to an organiza-
    tion like the
    Sierra Club to
    improve the
    quality of the
    environment.
16. I would be will-   SA   A   NS   D   SD
    ing to accept an
    increase in my
    expenses of $100
    next year to
    promote the
    wise use of natu-
    ral resources.

From Weigel & Weigel, 1978.

Scoring: On Items 1, 3, 6, 7, 10, 15, and 16, score yourself with a 4 for each Strongly agree, 3 for each Agree, 2 for each Not sure, 1 for each Disagree, and 0 for each Strongly disagree. Sum these items. On Items 2, 4, 5, 8, 9, 11, 12, 13, and 14, score yourself with a 0 for each Strongly agree, 1 for each Agree, 2 for each Not sure, 3 for each Disagree, and 4 for each Strongly disagree. Sum these items and add the two totals together to produce a grand total. The higher your score, the greater your environ-

mental concern. For comparison, a sample of New Englanders averaged 44.2. Reflecting their greater concern for the environment, a sample of Sierra Club members averaged 54.5. Thus, if you score about 52–53, your concern for the environment would exceed all but about 16 percent of the population at large. On the other hand, if you scored around 35–36, your concern for the environment would be lower than about 84 percent of the population.

once again. The International Whaling Commission, which began in 1946 and now represents over 40 signatory countries, has enacted regulations to control the numbers and kinds of whales harvested. Indeed, this commission asked for zero quotas in the Pacific Basin after 1986. Only three nations, specifically Japan, the former USSR, and Norway, formally objected, but Japan agreed to end whaling entirely by 1988. These are countries whose populations use many parts of the whale for food and for whom whaling is a major industry. Thus, it's in the best short-term interests of such countries to harvest as many whales as they can. In the long term, if the figures of the International Whaling Commission are correct, soon there will be no whales of some species left to harvest. Therefore, these countries may force themselves out of the whale business, but not before they ruin the resource for everyone else, including themselves. This represents a huge loss, since biological extinction is irreversible. Once gone, a species is gone forever.

reversed commons dilemma

The despoliation of a resource by pollution because of short-term reinforcement of convenience for the individual or business that pollutes; the long-term punishment is the loss of the resource to a group or society.

A REVERSED COMMONS DILEMMA.   Sports arenas and stadiums, movie theaters and city streets, streams, rivers, and oceans, and the air around us face a **reversed commons dilemma.** Often the problem in such areas is not the depletion of a resource but the ruining of the environment. This behavior is convenient for the individual in the short term, and negative to the group in the long term (Hardin, 1968). There may be lower personal cost to dropping a hot dog wrapper on the street than carrying it to a trash can. It may be easier to leave your garbage in a wilderness area than to pack it out yourself. The long-term consequences, however, are a spoiled wilderness and a street littered with garbage.

Industries often behave similarly when it is cheaper in the short term to dump industrial waste into a public stream, or expel it into the atmosphere, than to dispose of it in some other way. (Who speaks for the stream or the air when jobs may be at stake?) The long-term consequences may not be seen for years, and when they're eventually recognized, the costs may be averaged over society at large and may not be charged to the businesses that were the original polluters. Indeed, before much of today's modern technology, some industries might not have known they were polluting. In such conditions it's easy for a business not to worry too much about pollution. It's also easy under such conditions to rationalize that nature will always recover.

Given the scenario of the tragedy of the commons, many resources may be permanently lost. Whales are but a case in point. Any of our natural resources might be lost, even those that are *renewable*—wilderness, flora and fauna, potable water, breathable air. Other resources, such as the earth's elements (for example, iron and coal) are finite or *nonrenewable resources*. The only question is *how* finite? How long can they last?

Industries often pollute the environment when it is cheaper for them in the short term to dump industrial waste into a public stream or to expel it into the atmosphere than to dispose of it in some other way.

MANAGING COMMONS.   Is it possible to manage our endangered commons? Hardin and others (Crowe, 1969; Hardin, 1968; Hardin & Baden, 1977) believe that it is, but not with what is called a *technological fix* (Lloyd, 1980). A technological fix involves the use of technology to solve a problem. But the dilemmas of the commons are not technological ones. They're dilemmas produced by humans behaving individually, the sum total of whom produces a societal problem. The solutions—if there are any—are social, that is, educational, moral, political. Solutions for these types of problems have been called *cognitive fixes* and *structural fixes* (Lloyd, 1980). A cognitive fix involves information campaigns, education, and communication. A structural fix involves actual societal changes on a grand scale at many levels.

Society must make it more costly for individuals in the short term to mistreat the commons than it is rewarding in the short term. And society must impose those costs upon all of its members indiscriminately.

Environmental Pollution

LITTERING.   Littering may be considered a minor problem. Superficially an aesthetic problem, litter can also lead to injury and the spread of disease (Osborne & Powers, 1980).

If there were only one or two people in the United States they could throw away all of their garbage and it wouldn't foul the environment much. But there are 250 million Americans and a single act of littering by each of us produces a considerable problem.

How can the problem be solved? A variety of studies of technological and cognitive fixes have been made (Geller, 1980; Osborne & Powers, 1980). These include studies on the effectiveness of education, studies on the effectiveness of prompts to behave correctly (for example, Geller et al., 1976), rewards for picking up litter (or not littering in the first place), even lotteries for picking up litter (Powers et al., 1973). Fines can also be given for littering. However, they affect too few of the people who litter and generally produce resentment, so they have been largely ineffective (Osborne & Powers, 1980). Environmental prompts such as antipollution signs have helped little and only under limited circumstances. Rewarding people for picking up litter or not littering in the first place is inherently costly and has yet to be tried on a large scale.

Educating our young about littering is an often futile task. Kids see adults littering our commons. Why should they be different? A 30-minute videotape watched at school will not change their behavior sufficiently in the real world, where it counts. An extensive education program at all age levels, using popular media (television, radio), and effective spokespersons (movie stars), coupled with school education might help indoctrinate children to the idea that they must help keep their country beautiful. But such a cognitive fix is not likely to happen.

A structural fix in the form of a collective economic adjustment may be the only short-term solution. Governments can make it economically feasible to pick up (or not throw down) litter. The best examples of structural fixes for the litter problem are the bottle deposit bills that exist in many areas of North America (Osborne & Powers, 1980). When the value of the material involved in soft-drink and beer containers is sufficiently high, people will collect the containers from roadsides; others will not discard them to begin with, but will recycle them. Of course, the litter problem is broader than beverage containers, which constitute only a portion of the total amount of garbage strewn along our highways. But the point still stands: When it becomes worthwhile to save litter for recycling, people will do it.

What can you do in the meantime? Become a recycler. In some stages mandatory recycling—a structural fix—is already a reality. Become a person who respects the environment and who hates to see it fouled. Set better examples for others than you currently do. The individual actions of many individuals who set appropriate examples for their children and their peers may eventually ease the problem.

NOISE.   *Noise pollution* is "any sound that is physiologically arousing and harmful, subjectively annoying, or disruptive of performance" (Glass & Singer, 1972, p. 15). In general it is a stressor, although its effects might not be seen immediately during the noise itself (Sigal, 1980). High levels of noise can impair memory functioning (Cohen & Lezak, 1977), cause ulcers and other stress-related illnesses (Colligan & Murphy, 1982), interfere with academic learning of children (Cohen et al., 1981), and decrease the chances that people will offer to help a student who has dropped a pile of books (Mathews & Canon, 1975). Noise can act as a punisher; that is, it can suppress the response that produces it (Azrin & Holz, 1966; Herman & Azrin, 1964). Most local governments have ordinances against noise, but they're not necessarily enforced, particularly if the noise is industrial and the industry provides jobs in the community.

AIR AND WATER.   These substances are also part of our natural commons. They belong to all humans in general and to no one individual specifically. As such there are no international agencies to regulate their use effectively. The results of the accident at Chernobyl and the Canadian–American dispute over acid rain suggest the difficulties.

There is little research into the psychological effects of air and water pollution. Known physiological effects of air pollution run the gamut from upper respiratory irritation due to exposure to smog, to potential cancers from long-term exposure to certain chemicals used in manufacturing. It's clear that we cannot live without supplies of both clean air and water.

The immediate payoff of a job in an industry that pollutes air and/or water is a powerful reward for a person who needs that job to survive. Such persons are not likely to be concerned with the long-delayed collective welfare of subsequent generations. As individuals, therefore, we may be trapped into supporting the continued despoliation of our planet (see Platt, 1973).

We also seem to be blindly proceeding down the path of further pollution of

Drawing by Dedini; © 1985 The New Yorker Magazine, Inc.

"Polycyclic aromatic hydrocarbons are falling upstate, while simple showers of sulfur and nitrogen are blanketing the central counties. Toxic air pollutants will be prevalent in all areas and may endanger some lower forms of aquatic life. For the rest of us, enjoy the sun and the weekend."

our ground water supplies. Every area of the United States, for example, is discovering that industries—which may not even be in existence any longer—have caused serious soil and water pollution near their plants. The information void is great here because areas such as underground aquifers are difficult to study. Yet the U.S. government must locate a place for nuclear wastes and the current thinking involves an underground location. Will our offspring curse us for this? Prudence would seem important.

Little personal adjustment suggests itself here. Strong collective action (structural fixes) will probably be required. As usual, the fight will pit industry (with the threat of lost jobs and higher costs to the consumer) against the public as represented by government or more frequently by special interest groups.

A PERSONAL CODE. John has just helped a local legislator post hand bills promoting the legislator's reelection. He has tacked one to each telephone pole in the precinct. He knows the legislator has no plans to take these down afterward. He also knows that the weather strips them from their locations and they become a major source of litter. "What am I gonna do?" he wonders. "If I tell him, he'll be angry, and I'll lose the advantages of my association with him. If I don't tell him, how am I gonna live with myself?"

It may be that families and schools must return to the teaching of personal morality and ethics as part of a cognitive fix. Essentially missing from the behaviors of individuals and industries who pollute are consciences that foster thinking about the effects of one's own behavior on others. People who pollute appear to think only of themselves.

Conservation

Conservation is the act of saving a resource. Sometimes, such as in times of national crisis, governments force their people to conserve through rationing. Conservation is always forced by costs: Those resources that are the most scarce are usually the most valuable (for example, diamonds), they cannot be purchased frequently or in quantity by most people. They are, therefore, conserved. In the United States in 1974, conservation became a major public issue during the oil embargo. People drove less because the cost of gasoline rose; it was also personally costly to wait in line for gasoline and people feared their supply of gasoline would run out altogether. The major collective actions taken were structural fixes: Automobile manufacturers were forced to produce smaller, more fuel-efficient automobiles. Industries reacted by switching from burning oil to burning coal. Countries searched for more oil, found more oil, and produced more oil, all because it was profitable to do so. Public and private use of alternative sources of energy (for example, solar) received government subsidy. The effect of these structural fixes was to drive oil prices to their lowest point in many years.

As a result of the lower oil prices, however, people began to drive more and to conserve less. Larger cars once again increased in popularity (although not as large as the gas guzzlers of the 1960s). The speed limits on major highways rose once again. Research into alternative energy sources was placed on the back burner. Less research went into the efficient extraction of oil (for example, from tar sands). And the government engaged in a war in the Middle East in 1991, a war that was popular in part because it ensured America's access to Middle East oil reserves. We can extract a rule from this example: People will conserve when it's necessary to conserve; they will stop conserving if it's not necessary.

Wait a minute, you say. This is a rather economic and pessimistic view of humankind isn't it? What about those people who are going to conserve anyway? If we're correct, such people will try to conserve, but they'll conserve less as time passes because individual short-term rewards exist for not conserving (for example, more travel), while the long-term costs once again will be borne by the group as a whole. Sound familiar?

One day the problem of world oil scarcity will return. With a nonrenewable resource such as oil, the piper eventually has to be paid. The only question is *when*, and, most importantly, will such payment destroy an unprepared society? No one knows.

conservation ethic
The view that we must protect, conserve, and recycle the earth's resources.

CONSERVATION AS PROGRESS.   It's problems of this sort that have lead to a **conservation ethic** in the United States and elsewhere. Such an ethic, while important, is not widespread at the present since the United States, while containing only a fraction of the earth's people, uses fully half of its energy resources.

The conservation ethic maintains, first, that excessive use of the earth's resources will eventually exhaust them. Second, such excessive use comes at the expense of poisoning ourselves and our environments, irrevocably. Third, we're using resources that belong to all humans and to future generations, not just to those who live in the developed nations. One day the earth may be uninhabitable. In the extreme, this view is against technological fixes as the panacea for our environmental problems. The conservation ethic involves the sparing use of the earth's resources, recycling them as many times as possible, the cleaning up of polluted environments, and the belief that humans are a part of nature, not separate from it. Were this ethic to become truly widespread, it would constitute a cognitive fix.

growth ethic
The view that growth is good, and that stagnation or lack of growth is not good; leads to uncontrolled resource utilization.

GROWTH AS PROGRESS.   Contrast the foregoing with the prevailing ethic, the metaphor of growth. According to this **growth ethic,** any system, including a society, stagnates if it is not continually growing. This is primarily the ethic of American business. It involves maximum exploitation of the earth's resources, a throwaway society, pollution control where forced, and the belief that humans—reluctantly a part of nature—can to a great extent control nature.

In this view, humanity can solve the problems it creates through technological fixes. The view is optimistic about the future. Scarce earth resources do not mean that humans cannot find the material elsewhere, for example, the other planets. In this view it would be shortsighted and stagnating not to develop the resources of other worlds.

As in many cases where there are such opposing views, it is probably best that neither prevail. Rather, we should abstract the best features of each ethic to help with our adjustment to our environment and to our survival.

Crowding and Behavior

It is well known that when animals are crowded in closed colonies they become aggressive with one another, infant mortality rises, normal social behavior breaks down, subsequent learning is impaired, exploratory behavior is reduced, and the number of animals in the colony decreases (Calhoun, 1962; Freedman, 1975; Goeckner et al., 1973).

How is it with humans? We're very successful breeders, and in some parts of the world the combination of too many people and the absence of food has led to famine and disease. Elsewhere there is sufficient food for just about everyone but it's still crowded. Are there behavioral effects from such crowding? Can we adjust to crowded conditions?

CROWDING AND CRIME.   Superficially it would seem that there is more crime in areas where there are many people, for example, big cities. As city population size gets smaller, both violent and property crimes—per 100,000 people—decrease (see Table 11-1). But when examined in greater depth these figures don't argue for a relation between population density and crime. The size of a city does not

TABLE 11-1
CRIME RATE[a] AND CITY POPULATION, 1984

Population	Violent Crime	Property Crime
250,000 or more	1,288	7,303
100,000–249,999	756	6,707
50,000–99,999	549	5,349
25,000–49,999	390	4,826
10,000–24,999	287	4,028
fewer than 10,000	251	3,695

[a] *These are offenses known to the police per 100,000 people.*

necessarily relate to its population density. A city can be either spread out or concentrated in a relatively small area. Thus, of two cities with the same population, the one with the smallest area will have the higher population density. Further, population density will vary greatly within cities. In some neighborhoods (for example, Queens in New York), density may be near what it is in rural neighborhoods around the country, while in other neighborhoods of the same city it may be very high (Manhattan). So the data of Table 11-1 cannot be used to directly correlate crime with population density.

The study of the effects of population density on crime is made more difficult by other variables—variables potentially important to behavior—such as average income in the area, ethnicity of the area, and average years of education of the population in the area. When all these variables are controlled for, there is no relation observed between population density and crime (Freedman, 1975) or other problems such as alcoholism and suicide (Galle et al., 1974), or juvenile delinquency (Galle et al., 1972; Winsborough, 1965).

A much more important variable that relates to crime is income level. There is much more crime in low-income areas regardless of population density (Freedman, 1975).

CROWDING AND AGGRESSION.   Crowding does have an effect on aggression, but it appears to be related to gender and the type of work a person does. If tasks are individual ones (remembering, calculating, doing puzzles, and so forth), there is absolutely no effect from population density on performance (Freedman et al.,

In crowded environments, people are likely to draw into themselves, and are less likely to come to the aid of another person.

1971). However, if a task is social—involving others—we see a different picture. In this case, the population density relates to aggression by sex. That is, where population density is high, males tend to react competitively while females tend to react more cooperatively. Where population density is low, males react less competitively and females react less cooperatively (Freedman et al., 1972; Ross et al., 1973).

CROWDING AND WITHDRAWAL.   There is ample evidence both in the laboratory and in the field that people actively draw into themselves in crowded areas. Children interact less (Hutt & Vaizy, 1966); college students disclose less (Sundstrom, 1975), are less talkative and less sociable (Baum et al., 1975; Baum & Valins, 1977; Valins & Baum, 1973); and people are less willing to make eye contact (Baum & Greenburg, 1975) if population density is high.

altruistic behavior

Behavior in aid of another person for which there is no apparent reward.

CROWDING AND ALTRUISM.   **Altruistic behavior** is behavior in aid of someone else where there is no overt reward. What happens to altruistic behavior when there is crowding? The answer is not simple.

The first time social scientists seriously examined altruism and crowding was after the Kitty Genovese murder in New York in the 1960s. Returning from work one night, Kitty was attacked by a knife-wielding killer. Her cries for help were ignored while she was repeatedly stabbed. Her attacker left her screaming in pain, then returned to stab her some more. Eventually it was proved that 38 people had heard her cries. No one came to help. Why? Is there a relation between population density and the absence of altruism?

Laboratory studies suggest that there is. College students who believed they were alone were more likely to offer help to a perceived epileptic undergoing a seizure than if they believed that several people were aware of the problem (Darley & Latane, 1968). Other work, however, suggests that city dwellers are less likely to help because they fear for their own safety rather than having a different personal norm for helping (Holahan, 1977; House & Wolf, 1978).

CROWDING AS ANOTHER PROBLEM OF COMMONS.   Crowding is the outcome of an endangered commons. The immediate rewards of the dense urban environment for the individual—rewards for sexual behavior, the rewards involved in a supply of labor within a family, the rewards of increased welfare payments or tax deductions—may only be counteracted in the long term by the collective punishment of crowding (and the absence of sufficient food and space).

SUMMARY

- Most psychologists agree that violence and aggression by humans is largely learned. Children learn aggression by observing aggressive adults, by watching violence on television, and because aggressive acts are often rewarded. Aggression is also correlated with frustration and anger, especially when suitable environmental cues are present. Aggression is also a reaction to aversive stimulation.

- There are several steps that we can take to prevent violence and aggression, including teaching our children to be cooperative, explaining to children that the violence that they see on television is not the best way to handle conflict and that it is an inaccurate portrayal of the real world, and by encouraging passage of laws that may have an immediate impact on perpetrators of violence and that make violence less likely.

- A number of steps must also be taken to prevent rape and violence against women in our society. We need to engage in wide-ranging consciousness-raising regarding the effects of violent and sexual themes in movies, in magazines, and on television. We need to educate men about various rape myths such as the myth that women enjoy a mixture of violence and sex. We need to encourage victims of abuse to pursue legal action against their assailants. And women should be encouraged to learn a variety of ways to prevent violence from men, such as ways to prevent date rape.

■ The terms *stereotype, prejudice, discrimination, racism,* and *sexism* are all related. A stereotype is an oversimplified generalization about the characteristics of members of a group. To be prejudiced against a group is to hold stereotyped beliefs against its members, to feel negatively toward them, and to be inclined to act negatively toward them. Discrimination is any behavior that has as its result the denial of rights or privileges to another human. Sexism is essentially prejudice and/or discrimination toward members of a given gender, while racism is essentially prejudice and/or discrimination against members of a given race. While sexism against women and racism against Afro-americans in America has decreased considerably during the last 50 years, subtle prejudices still exist.

■ Prejudice is learned by children through modeling by parents and other family members, institutionalized practices in schools and by the media, and interactions with peers. Economic considerations may also play a role in the development of prejudice and discrimination, especially in competitive situations where the development of prejudice against a minority may have monetary benefits for members of the majority.

■ Some individuals display authoritarianism—a tendency to be traditional and conventional, to be submissive to established authority, and to be hostile and aggressive to minority groups. Those who display an authoritarian personality also tend to be highly prejudiced.

■ Prejudices are maintained by several processes, including modeling and social reinforcement among members of a prejudiced group against members of some other group. They are also maintained by scapegoating—the tendency to blame others when things go wrong—and by the self-fulfilling prophecy—the tendency of our expectations to cause us to act in a way that confirms expectations.

■ We can help to get rid of prejudice and discrimination by teaching our children not to accept stereotypes about groups, by encouraging contact between groups in a way that will enable their members to cooperate on an individual and equal status basis, by demanding that the mass media not perpetuate prejudice, and by taking a personal stance against those who exhibit prejudice.

■ Our environment can be thought of as a common—a public area subject to despoliation if it is either overused or otherwise mistreated by people. Such misuse appears due to the immediate payoff affecting the behavior of individuals in the common versus the long-delayed punishment to the group if the common is used up or spoiled. Endangered commons seem impervious to technological fixes. They may only be amenable to cognitive and structural fixes such as education and economic sanctions.

■ The conservation ethic calls for the judicious use of resources, and the protection and preservation of the environment. In this ethic, humans are viewed as a part of nature who live and die within nature's bounds. The growth ethic defines progress in terms of growth, and involves the rapid use of resources without much thought of protecting and preserving the environment.

■ Crowding, one type of environmental problem, can heighten aggression and withdrawal and decrease altruistic behavior. Crowding *per se,* however, does not increase crime. Crime is much more related to socioeconomic class and educational level.

Box 11-4

SELF-ADJUSTMENT FOR STUDENTS: REVIEW YOUR PROGRAM AND EVALUATE PROGRESS

We assume that you have completed the self-adjustment boxes at the end of preceding chapters. First, you picked a specific problem for your self-adjustment project. Next, you took steps to build your commitment to stick to the project. You then figured out how to observe, record, and graph instances of the problem. Next, after analyzing some of the possible causes of the problem, you took steps to design a program. Specifically, you decided how you might capitalize on stimulus control, how

A contract for the Self–Adjustment Project of _____

My self–adjustment project concerns the problem of:
_____
_____
_____

My specific goals for my self–adjustment project are:
_____
_____
_____

Short–term goals for my self–adjustment project include:
_____
_____
_____

Strategies that I will follow to observe, record, and graph my behavior include:
_____
_____
_____

Steps that I will take to minimize the causes of the problem include:
_____
_____
_____

The details of my treatment plan include:

1 Steps to manage the situation _____
_____
_____

2 Steps to manage consequences _____
_____
_____

3 Steps to deal with or change complex behavior _____
_____
_____

Continued

Figure 11-2
Outline of self-adjustment program: A behavioral contract.

Rewards that I can earn for sticking to my project include:
_____
_____
_____

Rewards that I can earn for successfully completing my project include:
_____
_____
_____

Other steps that I will take to increase and maintain my commitment to the project include:
_____
_____
_____

I, ____(your name)____ , promise to explain all aspects of my project
to ____(name of supporter)____ . I also agree to report my progress
to ____(name of supporter)____ during each day of my project until my
long-term goal is achieved.

Date _____

Signed _____   Signed _____
       (your signature)   (supporter's signature)

to incorporate rewards into your program, and whether or not you needed to take specific steps (such as task analysis, shaping, or chaining) because of the complexity of the behavior that you would like to change. It's time now to summarize all of your program's components, put the program into effect, and evaluate progress.

COMPONENTS OF SELF-ADJUSTMENT PROGRAM

Review the first seven steps that you took in the development of a self-adjustment program (see the self-adjustment box at the end of Chapters 4 through 10). Outline the components of your program in the preceding behavioral contract (see Figure 11-2).

EVALUATING PROGRESS

An important part of successful self-adjustment is to frequently monitor progress toward goal attain-ment. Your *long-term goal* is the overall outcome that you hope to achieve upon successful comple-tion of your program (see Box 4-4). *Short-term goals* are specific progress goals or checkpoints along the way to help you monitor progress. If a long-term goal, for example, is to obtain an "A" in this course, then a short-term goal might be to study the course material for a minimum of three hours during the next weekend. Another short-term goal might be to complete a certain number of the study questions (located at the end of each chapter) each day. Ideally, for each day of your project, you should have a short-term goal that is precisely stated and realistic, that moves you in the direction of your long-term goal. For some proj-ects, such as preparing and practicing for a job in-terview, all of the short-term goals could be pre-pared at one time. For other projects (such as get-ting an "A" in this course) it may be more

Continued

reasonable to set short-term goals for the next few days. When they are reached, you can set another series of short-term goals for the next few days, and so on.

Another important component of evaluating progress is to monitor your performance using your self-observation system. One of the best ways to motivate yourself to persist with your project is to obtain frequent feedback on your progress. Ideally, the feedback will be positive—you will be meeting your short-term goals and obtaining rewards for doing so. Occasionally you might encounter a relapse, or progress toward a goal may not be satisfactory. We discuss specific strategies that you can use to deal with such situations in the self-adjustment box at the end of the next chapter. For now, if progress is not satisfactory, you might focus on the adequacy of your short-term goals, Remember, they are not etched in stone, and they may need to be readjusted occasionally.

MEMORY BOOSTER

■ IMPORTANT TERMS

Be prepared to define the following terms (located in the margins of this chapter). Where appropriate, be prepared to describe examples.

Aggression	Scapegoating
Frustration-Aggression Hypothesis	Self-Fulfilling Prophecy
Rape Myth	Jigsaw Method
Stereotype	Commons
Prejudice	Tragedy of the Commons
Discrimination	Reversed Commons Dilemma
Sexism	Conservation Ethic
Racism	Growth Ethic
Authoritarianism	Altruistic Behavior

■ QUESTIONS FROM IMPORTANT IDEAS IN THIS CHAPTER

1. Describe evidence indicating that aggression in humans is likely learned as children.
2. How and why did Berkowitz revise the frustration-aggression hypothesis?
3. List three steps that we can take to prevent violence in society.
4. Describe several steps that can be taken to prevent violence against women.
5. Discuss several factors that contribute to the development of prejudice and discrimination.
6. Describe some steps that could be taken by society and by individuals to reduce prejudice.
7. What is it that people do that produces the tragedy of the commons? Why do they do it?
8. What are technological, cognitive, and structural fixes? Why are cognitive and structural fixes necessary to solve the commons dilemma?
9. What is the effect of crowding on crime rate, aggression, and withdrawal? How is crowding the outcome of a commons problem?

12

CAREER PLANNING AND WORK

CHOOSING A CAREER

Assess Yourself Again!
Obtain Career Information

GETTING A JOB

Preparing a Resumé
Preparing a Cover Letter
Getting to the Interview Stage
Preparing for Job Interviews
Having a Successful Interview
Repeating the Process

SURVIVING IN THE WORLD OF WORK

Some Tips on Starting Your New Job
Two Months Later: What Is Your Job?

Getting Ahead: Communicating
    Effectively
Getting Ahead: How to Manage Your
    Boss

WOMEN IN THE WORK PLACE

SUMMARY

SELF-ADJUSTMENT FOR STUDENTS: RELAPSE PREVENTION

MEMORY BOOSTER

365

LEARNING OBJECTIVES

After reading this chapter, you should be able to:

- Describe how vocational interest tests are developed.
- Prepare a resumé.
- Describe steps that you can take to obtain a job interview.
- Improve your skills for taking job interviews.
- Describe strategies for starting a new job on the "right foot."
- Contrast different performance appraisal systems.
- Describe the characteristics of effective communication.
- Describe some facts and fictions about women in the work place in the United States.

If you ask people in various occupations how they chose particular college majors and subsequent careers, a surprising number say things like: "I liked the professor." "It sounded glamorous." "I wanted to take as many classes as possible with my girlfriend." "To make my parents happy." Hardly the sorts of foundations on which careers should be built! Perhaps it is not surprising that many people detest their work and stay on the job strictly for their paychecks.

There are a number of reasons why you should spend considerable time and energy examining career options early in your college experience. First, unless you win a lottery or marry a rich person, you will spend more of your waking hours on career-related activities than on any other activity for the rest of your life. Therefore, why not earn your living by doing what you enjoy? Second, your choice of occupation is an important determinant of whether or not you might face the unpleasant experience of being unemployed. In very bad recessions, while less than 10 percent of workers in some fields have been out of work, as many as 75 percent of workers in other occupations have been unemployed (Schertzer, 1985). Third, your choice of occupation will permeate every other aspect of your life—where you live, how often you move, with whom you associate during and after work, your socioeconomic status, and even your emotional and physical health. As expressed by David Campbell (1974), "If you don't know where you're going, you'll probably end up somewhere else."

In this chapter, we offer guidelines for choosing an occupation and obtaining a job. Important steps include examining career options, preparing a resumé and a cover letter, obtaining interviews, and performing successfully during interviews. But finding work that you enjoy is only the first step. Maintaining a successful career is something else again. And surviving in the work place involves a variety of skills in addition to the work itself. We're talking about things like starting off on the "right foot," understanding the performance appraisal system, communicating and cooperating with co-workers, learning to understand your boss, and managing your boss effectively. These topics are also addressed in this chapter.

Choosing a Career

In 1945, hundreds of thousands of American soldiers returned home from World War II. Approximately a year later, the birth explosion known as the **baby boom** began. Estimates of the length of the baby boom range from 8 to 15 years (Mencke & Hummel, 1984). When the products of this boom—the baby boomers—began graduating from college in the late 1960s, there were excellent job opportunities

Enjoying your work is an important outcome of careful career selection.

baby boom

The birth of unusually large numbers of babies following World War II as a function of hundreds of thousands of American soldiers returning home; estimates of the length of this period range from 8 to 15 years.

for college graduates in virtually every area and occupational field imaginable. By the late 1970s, however, things had changed. During the 1980s, keen competition for jobs was a stressful fact of life for the majority of college graduates. One in five college graduates took jobs not usually requiring a college degree (*Occupational Outlook Handbook*, 1986–1987). Projections for the job market for college graduates to 1995 show a slight improvement (Sargent, 1986). Nevertheless, the number of college graduates entering the labor force through 1995 is projected to continue to exceed the number of openings in jobs requiring four or more years of college education (Sargent, 1986). The U.S. Bureau of Labor Statistics' projections to 1995 predict a surplus of about 200,000 college graduates entering the job market. This implies that about one college graduate out of every nine will not be able to find a college-level job when entering the job market. These statistics do not mean that you should drop out of college. There is clear evidence that the chances of having no job at all decline as one's education level increases. Moreover, on average, college graduates have a higher level of income than persons who are not college graduates. Nevertheless, you should carefully choose your college major, minor, and elective courses in a way that will increase the number of specific vocational options that might be available to you. The first step in this process is to conduct a careful self-examination.

Assess Yourself Again!

Perhaps your mother wants you to be a doctor. Perhaps you father wants you to be a lawyer. But what career would *you* most enjoy? Some people enjoy their work so much that it doesn't seem like work to them. How can you find such a career? Your first step is to assess the current strengths and activities you enjoy. Selecting a career that maximizes the opportunity to perform activities that you already enjoy is a step in the direction of selecting a career that will give you considerable enjoyment throughout your life. If you don't particularly enjoy small talk and socializing

Box 12-1

Interest Checklist

Below are 115 activities listed in 23 groups. Read each activity and place a check next to those that you would like as jobs or hobbies. Check an activity even if you are interested in only part of it. If you have not done an activity, but think that you would like to, given the opportunity, check that one also. If you are not interested in the activities in any one group, leave a blank. Work quickly, not spending too much time thinking about any one kind of work. (Scoring is at the end of the Box.)

A

_____ Sketching and painting portraits, landscapes, still life or figures on canvas
_____ Creating, designing and painting posters, signboards, showcards, charts, diagrams, labels, and illustrations for advertising copy, books, and magazines
_____ Modeling or carving various objects from wood, clay, plaster, or stone
_____ Sketching rooms and planning the arrangement of furniture, wall decorations, and color schemes
_____ Creating and drawing to scale patterns for new types and styles of clothes

B

_____ Playing a musical instrument
_____ Singing various types of songs
_____ Creating and composing musical compositions or arranging a melody for orchestral use
_____ Conducting an orchestra
_____ Studying musical theory and techniques, melody, and harmony

C

_____ Writing magazine articles, plays, short stories, poems or books
_____ Translating from one language to another
_____ Reporting news for a newspaper or magazine
_____ Writing or editing news items for a newspaper, periodical, or book
_____ Doing literary research for historical publications

D

_____ Acting in a play or dramatic production
_____ Announcing radio programs
_____ Dancing for the entertainment of others
_____ Making a living by playing football, baseball, hockey, or other sports
_____ Entertaining others by juggling, sleight-of-hand, pantomime, or magic

E

_____ Developing advertising campaigns
_____ Applying the principles of accounting, statistical analysis, contracts, credit, marketing conditions, and applied psychology to the problems of business
_____ Drawing up legal documents such as contracts, partnerships, deeds, and wills
_____ Conducting lawsuits
_____ Working up sales methods

F

_____ Figuring out arithmetic problems using multiplication, division, squares, and square roots
_____ Copying long lists of numbers and checking to be sure they are copied right
_____ Finding mistakes in answers to arithmetic problems
_____ Doing addition and subtraction
_____ Working with fractions and decimals

G

_____ Keeping business records, such as sales slips, receipts, bills, attendance records, and amount of goods purchased or work done
_____ Typing letters and reports
_____ Taking dictation in shorthand or on a stenotype machine
_____ Receiving, checking, counting, grading, examining, and storing supplies
_____ Sorting, indexing, and assembling papers and other written records

H

_____ Being a salesclerk, selling or taking tickets, handling money, or making change
_____ Answering the telephone
_____ Giving people information such as street directions or location of merchandise in stores
_____ Preparing lists of prospects and contacting them in order to make sales
_____ Attempting to interest prospective buyers by showing sample articles or displaying a catalog

I

____ Teaching school

____ Talking to individuals or families and assisting them in solving their personal or financial problems

____ Interviewing and advising individuals concerning their schooling, jobs, and social problems

____ Studying social and economic conditions in order to help individuals or groups solve problems of general welfare

____ Enforcing laws involving fire and crime prevention, traffic, sanitation, or immigration

J

____ Planning a balanced diet (planning a menu or a meal)

____ Mixing foods to obtain new flavor

____ Going to some trouble to make foods look attractive

____ Learning the right way to season foods

____ Selecting meals and vegetables in a grocery store for freshness and quality

K

____ Playing games with children

____ Telling stories to children

____ Looking after children to see that they are kept neat and clean

____ Taking care of children when they are sick

____ Helping children dress or undress

L

____ Giving first aid treatment

____ Setting tables and serving food or drinks

____ Acting as a hostess or headwaiter in a dining room

____ Caring for people's hair and fixing their nails

____ Waiting on other people and caring for their clothes

M

____ Studying the soils, weather, climate, and so on in which plants and animals live and grow best

____ Plowing, planting, cultivating, or harvesting crops

____ Trying out various methods of growing plants to find the best way

____ Breeding, raising, and caring for livestock such as cattle, sheep, hogs, and chickens

N

____ Catching fish with nets, hooks, harpoons, spears, or guns

____ Cleaning fish

____ Steering ships and plotting a course with the aid of a compass or sextant

____ Standing watch on a ship to look out for rocks, lighthouses, buoys, or other ships

____ Observing activity of fish to determine their habits and food requirements

O

____ Using a trap to catch animals

____ Acting as a guide for hunting parties

____ Chopping or sawing down trees and trimming branches from trees using an ax or saw

____ Moving or piling up stacks of logs and loading and fastening logs with chains

____ Caring for forests by looking out for fires or tree diseases

P

____ Designing machinery and mechanical or electrical equipment

____ Developing and executing plans for the construction of buildings or bridges

____ Using drafting tools to prepare detailed plans and drawings for buildings or machines

____ Doing research in a chemical, physical, or biological laboratory

____ Drawing maps

Q

____ Taking apart mechanical things such as bicycles, automobile engines, pumps, typewriters, or guns and putting them back together again

____ Examining mechanical equipment for wear or damaged parts to see what needs to be done

____ Following complicated directions and diagrams to put parts of machines together

____ Tuning up motors to see that they are running right

____ Greasing and oiling machines

R

____ Repairing electric stoves, refrigerators, vacuum cleaners, fans, and motors

____ Studying the theory of electricity, including direct and alternating current, volts, amperes, ohms, and so on   *Continued*

_____ Wiring, splicing, soldering, and insulating electrical connections
_____ Building and testing radio sets
_____ Changing fuses, repairing electric irons, wiring lamps, fixing light plugs and short circuits

S

_____ Working on scaffolds and climbing around on buildings while assembling large pieces with a hammer, rivets, or welding equipment
_____ Painting, plastering, puttying, or paperhanging
_____ Working with hand tools such as saws, plumb lines, rulers, and squares
_____ Bending, threading, and fitting pipes, fixing drains and faucets
_____ Doing carpentry, plumbing, floor-laying, or roofing

T

_____ Assembling or repairing instruments such as watches, locks, cameras, fountain pens, or field glasses
_____ Examining, inspecting, and separating objects according to quality, size, color, or weight
_____ Cutting and shaping glass or stone for jewelry and similar small articles
_____ Cutting, shaping, and rolling dough for breads and pastries
_____ Cutting, sewing, or repairing clothing, shoes, or other articles from cloth, leather, or fur

U

_____ Running lathes, drill presses, and other machine shop equipment
_____ Making calculations to determine angles, curves, or shapes of small metal or wooden parts
_____ Pushing levers and buttons or turning handwheels to start, stop, slow down, or speed up machines
_____ Operating heavy equipment to move dirt or rocks
_____ Making parts and tools from metal

V

_____ Doing freehand lettering or copying sketches on wood, metal, canvas, or film
_____ Making photographic copies of drawings, records, or pictures for books or newspapers
_____ Setting type by hand or machine for printing, or working with sizes, styles, and spacing of type or proofreading
_____ Using soft crayon to copy maps, charts, posters, and drawings
_____ Cutting designs or letters into metal, stone, or glass using hand tools or engraving wheels

W

_____ Observing formulas, timing, temperature, and pressure directions
_____ Handling or pouring hot metals, or plating metals
_____ Operating furnaces, boilers, ovens, and other equipment
_____ Grinding, mixing, or separating chemicals
_____ Measuring, mixing, or cooking foods for canning

SCORING

Scoring: To score the checklist in Box 12-1, first list the letters (A) through (W) vertically on a scoring sheet. Next, count the number of checks in each group of activities (e.g., the number of checks in the activities under the letter (A)), and record that number beside the appropriate letter on your scoring page. Finally, those letters with the highest numbers beside them indicate the kinds of activities in which you are most interested.

with people, for example, then you should be cautious about choosing a career that requires a great deal of such activity, such as working in the public relations field.

One way of getting in touch with the activities that you most enjoy is to think back over the last few days and jot down, in two columns, those things that you most enjoyed and those things that you least enjoyed. Do you like to solve problems of financial management? Write reports? Take apart electrical appliances? Work in the garden? Work to solve other people's problems? Think in terms of simple action verbs and make a list of those skills that you enjoy most.

vocational interest test

A test designed to help a person select a career.

Another possibility is to take a formal **vocational interest test.** Vocational interest tests all follow essentially the same strategy (Lowman, 1991). First, in creating the tests, the designers collect many answers to many questions from people in different career fields. Next, they prepare many questions for you, the testee, to assess the activities that you enjoy and the skills that you possess. In analyzing your answers, they compare your answers to those given by people in various career fields on whom the test has been standardized. To the extent that you enjoy the same activities and have many of the same skills as people in a particular area, then you will obtain a high score in that particular career field.

Strong–Campbell Interest Inventory

A popular vocational interest test.

A popular vocational interest test is the **Strong–Campbell Interest Inventory.** A total of 70 occupations are represented on the inventory grouped into six general occupational themes, such as "investigative" (including occupations like design engineer, physicist, and social scientist), "social" (occupations like teacher, psychologist, and counselor), and "enterprising" (occupations like realtor, political campaigner, and business executive). Your answers to the items help you determine if your interests are "very dissimilar," "dissimilar," "average," "similar," or "very similar" to those of people in particular occupations. Another interest checklist was developed by the Occupational Analysis and Industrial Services Division of the U.S. Department of Labor. Various items and job categories were taken from the *Dictionary of Occupational Titles* and listed in 23 groups. This checklist is provided for your interest in Box 12-1.

Another strategy is to ask yourself what you really want from a job. For example, Renwick and Lawler (1978) conducted a survey of work satisfaction using readers of *Psychology Today* as the subjects. A total of 23,008 readers returned the 77-item questionnaire entitled, "How Do You Like Your Job?" The top 18 items ranked in order of importance are listed in Table 12-1.

You might use the items listed in Table 12-1 to help you identify factors that are important for you in selecting a career. Note that, for the persons surveyed, the amount of pay received ranked twelfth on the list.

TABLE 12-1
JOB FEATURES CONSIDERED IMPORTANT *From Renwick & Lawler, 1978.*

Items are ranked on the basis of average responses from 1 (most important or most often satisfying) to 18 (least important or least often satisfying).

1. Chances to do something that makes you feel good about yourself
2. Chances to accomplish something worthwhile
3. Chances to develop new things
4. Opportunity to develop your skills and abilities
5. The amount of freedom you have on your job
6. Chances you have to do things you do best
7. The resources you have to do your job
8. The respect you receive from people you work with
9. Amount of information you get about your job performance
10. Your chances of taking part in making decisions
11. The amount of job security you have
12. Amount of pay you get
13. The way you are treated by the people you work with
14. The friendliness of people you work with
15. Amount of praise you get for a job well done
16. Amount of fringe benefits you get
17. Chances for getting a promotion
18. Physical surroundings of your job

Box 12-2

Where Are the Jobs?

What are the fastest growing occupations between now and the year 2000? How many jobs will the fastest growing occupations actually provide during the next decade? You're probably thinking, "I'm just in the first year of college. I haven't even chosen a major and you're asking me about jobs to the year 2000!"

While it may seem that we're jumping the gun a little, it's never too early to be narrowing down your choices for possible careers. Table 12-2 lists the 40 occupations with the largest projected job growth between 1988 and the year 2000. Table 12-3 provides projections for the 12 fastest growing occupations during that same period. It's important to note that these two projections are different. For example, while medical secretaries represent the fourth fastest growing occupation, they are thirty-ninth on the list for the total number of jobs to be provided. The 11 most rapidly declining occupations are listed in Table 12-4.

Thus, when considering job opportunities over the next decade, you may want to choose an occupation that is expected to employ a large number of people. Alternatively, you may want to be in on the ground floor of an occupation that is growing rapidly, even though there are currently relatively few job openings.

Obtain Career Information

You have now analyzed some of your strengths and interests. You have identified some of the things that you would like from a career. Obtaining personal information on your interests, abilities, and values is an important first step in career planning. You have some idea of what you hope will be out there by way of a career. You now must find out the realities of what might be available.

VISIT A CAREER RESOURCE CENTER.   Chances are very good that your university has a career resource center. It may have career vocational counselors who will undoubtedly have a great deal of information. Check them out. Let them know about your self-assessment, and ask them to recommend information on careers that would enable you to capitalize on your strengths and interests.

OBTAIN CAREER INFORMATION FROM THE LIBRARY.   Most libraries carry several basic references to help you in career planning (for example, Isaacson, 1986; Kent, 1989). A very useful source is the *Occupational Outlook Handbook*. This valuable piece of career material is written for adults, high school students, and college students, and is published every two years by the U.S. Bureau of Labor Statistics (Government Printing Office, Washington, D.C., 20402). It forecasts where "tomorrow's" jobs will be in more than 850 occupations in 30 industries.

TALK TO YOUR PROFESSORS.   As practicing psychologists and professors, we know a great deal about job opportunities for psychologists in academic settings and in our local communities. Similarly, most professors in most disciplines stay on top of local job opportunities in their areas of expertise. Most of them would be more than happy to spend an hour with you over a cup of coffee and talk about the pros and cons of a career in their particular discipline.

TABLE 12-2
FORTY OCCUPATIONS WITH LARGEST PROJECTED JOB GROWTH, 1988–2000*

Occupation	1988 Employment (in thousands)	2000 Employment (in thousands)	Percent Change 1988–2000
Salespersons, retail	3,834	4,564	19
Registered nurses	1,577	2,190	39
Janitors and cleaners	2,895	3,450	19
Waiters and waitresses	1,786	2,337	31
General managers and top executives	3,030	3,509	16
General office clerks	2,519	2,974	18
Secretaries, except legal and medical	2,903	3,288	13
Nursing aides, orderlies, and attendants	1,184	1,562	32
Truck drivers, light and heavy	2,399	2,768	15
Receptionists and information clerks	833	1,164	40
Cashiers	2,310	2,614	13
Guards	795	1,050	32
Computer programmers	519	769	48
Food counter, fountain, and related workers	1,626	1,866	15
Food preparation workers	1,027	1,260	23
Licensed practical nurses	626	855	37
Teachers, secondary school	1,164	1,388	19
Computer systems analysts	403	617	53
Accountants and auditors	963	1,174	22
Teachers, kindergarten and elementary	1,359	1,567	15
Maintenance repairers, general utility	1,080	1,282	19
Child-care workers	670	856	28
Gardeners and groundskeepers, except farm	760	943	24
Lawyers	582	763	31
Electrical and electronics engineers	439	615	40
Carpenters	1,081	1,257	16
Store clerks, sales floor	1,164	1,340	15
Food service and lodging managers	560	721	29
Home health aides	236	397	68
Cooks, restaurants	572	728	27
Physicians	535	684	28
Teacher's aides and educational assistants	682	827	21
Clerical supervisors and managers	1,183	1,319	12
Blue collar supervisors	1,797	1,930	7
Electrical and electronic engineer technicians	341	471	38
Dining room and cafeteria attendants and bar helpers	448	578	29
Financial managers	673	802	19
Automotive mechanics	771	898	16
Medical secretaries	207	327	58
Social workers	385	495	29

* *From Statistical Abstract of the United States, 1990, based on moderate trend projections.*

OBTAIN PART-TIME OR SUMMER WORK EXPERIENCE. Many companies set up work experience programs for students. A part-time or summer position that is somewhat related to your chosen occupation is an excellent way of determining if the day-to-day work experience measures up to your expectations. Obviously, you have to separate your summer position from the realities of a full-time position in

TABLE 12-3
TWELVE FASTEST GROWING OCCUPATIONS,
1988–2000*

Occupation	Percent Growth in Employment
Medical Assistants	70
Home health aides	68
Radiological technologists and technicians	66
Medical secretaries	58
Securities and financial services salesworkers	55
Travel agents	54
Computer systems analysts	53
Computer programmers	48
Human service workers	45
Correction officers and jailers	41
Electrical and electronics engineers	40
Receptionists and information clerks	40

* *From Statistical Abstract of the United States, 1990, based on moderate trend projections.*

that field. Working as a nurse's aide in a hospital is just not the same as working in that hospital as a doctor. Nevertheless, from both firsthand experience and direct observation, you can gain a good understanding of what it would be like to work in that particular career. If it's not possible to obtain part-time or summer work in your chosen field, then you should seriously consider volunteer work. Sometimes volunteer work leads to paid part-time or summer positions. At the very least, it provides you with additional experiences that will enable you to more knowledgably focus your career choice.

TABLE 12-4
ELEVEN MOST RAPIDLY DECLINING OCCUPATIONS,
1988–2000*

Occupation	Percent Growth in Employment
Electrical and electronic equipment assemblers, precision	−44
Electrical and electronic assemblers	−44
Farmers	−23
Stenographers	−23
Telephone and cable TV line installers and repairers	−21
Sewing machine operators, garment	−14
Crushing and mixing machine operators and tenders	−14
Textile draw-out and winding machine operators	−13
Machine feeders and offbearers	−13
Hand packers and packagers	−12
Packaging and filling machine operators and tenders	−11

* *From Statistical Abstract of the United States, 1990, based on moderate trend projections.*

INTERVIEW PERSONS IN CAREERS OF INTEREST.   A useful way of obtaining information about a particular occupation is to interview someone working in that area. An interview can give you firsthand information about what it's like to actually work in that particular occupation. Because such individuals are likely to be quite busy, you may have to make several calls before obtaining a half hour or an hour for a potential interview. When you call, explain your situation and ask for their cooperation. Make sure that you are well-prepared ahead of time with a number of specific questions. Asking vague, wishy-washy questions will probably be a waste of your time and theirs.

Getting a Job

First, the bad news. Getting a job is not easy. Moreover, some of the traditional approaches just aren't particularly successful. For example, the want ads typically contain only about 20 percent of the vacancies that actually exist. The other 80 percent of the opportunities are never advertised (Mencke & Hummel, 1984). Second, many of the positions that are advertised in want ads are actually filled before the newspaper ever goes to press (Mencke & Hummel, 1984). Third, there are so many people sending out resumés to companies (some companies receive approximately 250 unsolicited resumés per day) that very few of such people are granted an interview, let alone offered a job (Bolles, 1990). Now, the good news. There are jobs available, and there are a number of steps that you can take to increase your chances of successfully obtaining a job (Lott & Lott, 1989).

Preparing a Resumé

resumé

A summary statement that describes one's assets, experiences, education, and potential in a way that will maximize the possibility of being hired for a particular job.

Most potential employers will expect to see a resumé. The old saying, "Haste makes waste" was never truer than in writing a **resumé** and a cover letter. Many students make the mistake of assuming that quantity will override quality in preparation of resumés and cover letters. That's simply not the case. The failure of a student to attend carefully to the preparation of a thoughtful, accurate, and neatly typed resumé and cover letter will signify, to many potential employers, an individual who will fail to attend to important and significant job details. A resumé allows you to sell yourself and your strengths in a creative and positive way. It should display your assets, experiences, and potential in a way that will maximize the possibility of the employer giving you serious consideration for a position. Most libraries, book stores, and career development centers have books on how to write resumés (e.g., Jackson, 1990). While the content varies somewhat from occupation to occupation and position to position, the major components are described below. These are illustrated with reference to the sample resumé shown in Box 12-3.

IDENTIFYING INFORMATION.   As you can see in Box 12-3, Scott's resumé begins with his name, address, and telephone number where he can be contacted. Some people put their name at the top of the resumé. Others put "Resumé of" and then their name.

PERSONAL DATA.   Most states have passed laws against employers requiring personal information on marital status, sex, age, and the like. If you decide to include this information, then you might list date of birth, place of birth, marital status, number of children, height, weight, and health status. Like it or not, some personal characteristics, such as age, may have an effect on whether or not you will be considered for a position. One solution is to list personal information at the end of your resumé so that your statements about experience and education will be seen first.

Box 12-3

RESUMÉ

RESUMÉ

Scott K.

CAREER OBJECTIVE:	To be employed as a teacher of Business Education courses, and to combine this with coaching basketball at the high school level.
ADDRESS:	51 Munson Avenue Tamsden, Manitoba Canada
PHONE:	(207) 289-2938
BIRTHDATE:	April 11, 1967

EDUCATIONAL BACKGROUND:

1990–1992	Currently pursuing a *Bachelor of Education* degree, in the Business-Teacher-Education Program Balsted University (In-Depth Marketing Major). Expected graduation date: June 1992
1986–1990	*Bachelor of Commerce* (Hons.) Balsted University (Finance Major)

EMPLOYMENT:

1988, 1989, 1990, 1991 (summers)	Recreation Technician II City of Tamsden Parks and Recreation Department responsibilities included supervision at a number of inner-city playgrounds; organizing games and activities for children; and supervision and maintenance of wading pool and park facilities
1989, 1990, 1991 (summers)	Instructor Balsted University week-long Basketball School for High School Level basketball players (boys and girls)
1987 (summer)	Front Desk Clerk Advance Automotives responsibilities included filling out work orders and purchase orders, filing, making appointments, answering telephones, operating the cash register
1986 (summer)	Cook and Cashier Dairy Queen Restaurant
1985 (summer)	Cook and Cashier Wendy's Restaurant

CAREER OBJECTIVE. As you can see in Box 12-3, Scott listed his career objective right at the start of his resumé. Often this information is placed after the Personal Information section. While the career objective should be a fairly specific, narrow statement, it is necessary to walk the fine line between an objective that is so narrow that the employer might screen you out of a particular position and one that

BASKETBALL PLAYING AND COACHING EXPERIENCE:

Member of Men's Varsity Basketball Team at Balsted University, 1989–1990, 1990–1991, and 1991–1992 seasons
—placed 3rd in Canada in 1989–1990
—ranked #1 in Canada going into the 1991 National Playoffs

Completed: (a) National Coaching Certification Program for Level I Basketball, 1990; and (b) course on Psychology of Coaching at Balsted University, 1987

Head Coach of Boys Varsity Basketball Team at Tamsden Junior High School (ages 14–15) in 1986–1987 and 1987–1988
—record of 33 wins and 15 losses
—organized and managed two successful 8-team tournaments

Member of Men's Junior Varsity Basketball Team at Balsted University, 1987–1988 and 1988–1989 seasons

Member of Boys' Varsity Basketball Team at Tamsden High School during all three years as a high school student
—leading scorer on team and city all-star during senior year

EXTRA-CURRICULAR ACTIVITIES AND INTERESTS

Have been active in a number of sports and have a keen interest in various sports and physical fitness. Highlights include:
—Provincial Wrestling Champion in weight class four years in a row
—Member of several Provincial championship teams, including Bantam football (1982), Midget soccer (1983), and Juvenile soccer (1985)
—Head Coach of Boy's Varsity Soccer Team at Tamsden Junior High School (1985)
—Head Coach of Girls' Varsity Soccer Team at Vincent High School (1990)

REFERENCES:

Mr. Joe DeCush	Mr. Brian Dillis	Ms. Janice Hurt
372 Fontling Road	87 Elm Point Road	22 Westparke Bay
Tamsden, Manitoba	Tamsden, Manitoba	Tamsden, Manitoba
R2R OS8	R3H 7P7	R4A 2K1
(207)648-9804 (home)	(207)257-5088 (home)	(207)882-2399 (home)
(207)784-1709 (business)	(207)474-8795 (business)	(207)662-2894 (business)
Mr. DeCush is a Business Education teacher at Tamsden High School and one of my former coaches.	Mr. Dillis is the Physical Education Department Head at Tamsden High School, and one of my former coaches. He served as my adviser during my two years of coaching basketball.	Ms. Hurt is one of my teachers in the Business Education program at Balsted University. She is also serving as my supervisor during my student teaching.

is so vague that it could mean almost anything. Note that Scott stated his career objective without using the first person or personal pronoun.

EDUCATIONAL BACKGROUND. As indicated in Box 12-3 under Educational Background, Scott listed his degrees (beginning with the most advanced), major subjects, schools, and dates of attendance. Since he was applying for a job while finishing up his Bachelor of Education degree, he indicated the expected graduation date.

EMPLOYMENT EXPERIENCE.   Some people use the descriptor "experience" for this section since it enables them to list positions for which they were not compensated, such as internships or volunteer positions. Titles of the various positions are important because they communicate levels of responsibility. As indicated by Scott's resumé in Box 12-3, most recent jobs are listed first. If you have a great deal of employment experience, it is important that you emphasize career-related jobs. This is also an opportunity for you to use words which emphasize work-related accomplishments, such as *organized, developed, supervised,* and so on. Your employment description should showcase your accomplishments, skills, and responsibilities to as great an extent as possible. Note that in Scott's resumé he included a separate section for "Basketball Playing and Coaching Experience." Such a listing signified the importance for Scott of the opportunity to coach basketball as a career objective.

EXTRACURRICULAR ACTIVITIES AND INTERESTS.   This subsection may be more important for some positions than for others. In general, most employers are not likely to be interested in whether or not you are an Alfred Hitchcock enthusiast. However, there may be some extracurricular activities and interests that clearly complement your career objectives, such as was the case with Scott's resumé (see Box 12-3). Often, the extracurricular activities section enables you to highlight your leadership qualities in various social, civic, and/or community organizations.

REFERENCES.   This is an optional category and many people do not list references on their resumé. Instead, they mention their availability in a cover letter. Whether or not you decide to include references may depend in part on how much additional information you want to place in your resumé. Remember, it's typically recommended that resumés be no longer than two pages.

OPTIONAL CATEGORIES.   Depending upon your level of training and accomplishments, there are several additional optional categories that you may want to add, including professional licenses, professional affiliations, special skills, and publications.

After you have prepared a sample resumé, show it to others who have had an opportunity to examine resumés (professors or employers who are personal acquaintances). Ask for feedback. Check for misspelled words, poor grammar, and typographical errors. Check all dates for accuracy. We recommend that you have the final copy prepared by an excellent typist on a good quality typewriter or printer. Additional copies can then be reproduced by offset printing. Avoid cheap photocopies that look like cheap photocopies.

Preparing a Cover Letter

Some people follow a "mass-mailing" strategy—sending a cover letter and resumé to hundreds of potential employers. For obvious reasons, the cover letter and resumé are likely to be of a standard form. Researchers suggest that a positive employer response to such a mailing might vary from 1 response in 212 resumés mailed to 1 in 1,000 (Mencke & Hummel, 1984). You can see that mass-mailings are an ineffective strategy.

One way to maximize your chances is to pay even more attention to the preparation of your cover letter than you did to the preparation of your resumé. It is the cover letter that must first catch the attention of a potential employer. Experts in this area (Mencke & Hummel 1984; Schertzer, 1985; Beatty, 1989; Yate, 1991) recommend that the cover letter contain the following components. First, it should be addressed to a specific person by name. While this may take some research on your part, it demonstrates some initiative in problem-solving ability, a characteristic that the mass-mailing campaigner has obviously not shown. Next, you should ensure that the first paragraph will attract the reader's interest. One way to do this is to name a person whom the prospective employer knows. Another strategy is to mention an article published by the employer, or a particular product of the company with which you are familiar. The second paragraph should communicate to the employer that you have taken the trouble to do some research on the company. It might be something about their training program, the growth of the company, or the company organization. Demonstrating that you have taken the trouble to find out something about the company will place you even higher on the totem pole of comparison to mass-mailing campaigners. The third paragraph should be used to elaborate on how your experience and/or education especially qualifies you for the position for which you are applying. This paragraph provides an overview of what you have to offer, and acts as an introduction to your resumé. You should indicate your enthusiasm, your willingness to work, and your interest in the job. In the final paragraph, you should make an appropriate request for further contact. You might ask for an application form, for an interview, or you might indicate a particular time when you will be in the area and where you can be reached by phone.

As was the case with your resumé, the cover letter should be prepared carefully, with correct spelling and grammar, and be neatly typed on standard-sized white paper.

Getting to the Interview Stage

We have already suggested that checking the want ads and conducting a mass-mailing campaign with resumés and cover letters are not the best approaches to being granted an interview for a job. What are the best approaches?

SEEK HELP FROM FAMILY MEMBERS, RELATIVES, AND FRIENDS. The best way to obtain an interview is from personal contacts. Brainstorm a list of all of your family members, relatives, and friends who may be connected in any way with the career field of your choice. Let them know about the kind of job you're looking for. Ask them to let you know if they hear of an opportunity.

ASK YOUR INSTRUCTORS. As we indicated previously, most professors stay on top of career opportunities in their respective disciplines. Ask them for their help. This can be especially important if you worked for them on an internship or a summer research or volunteer position.

FOLLOW UP ON SUMMER POSITIONS. If you followed our previous advice, you will have worked in your career field in a summer job or on a part-time basis in some capacity. If you have done a good job and people liked your work, then talk to people in that organization about your career aspirations.

REGISTER WITH A COLLEGE PLACEMENT CENTER. More and more colleges are developing placement centers to help their students procure positions following graduation. At the very least, the placement center will be able to supply you with general information on career opportunities in your field. It may also alert you to company representatives who will be visiting your college to interview prospective graduates for future positions. Be prepared to complete various forms, obtain letters of recommendation, and generally complete a file that the placement center will maintain concerning your status. On many campuses, hundreds of recruiters from both government and private companies interview graduating students two or three times a year.

REGISTER WITH THE STATE EMPLOYMENT OFFICE.   Every state has employment offices located in major cities. They both register potential employees and accept orders for workers from prospective employers. They will also typically provide vocational interest testing and counseling services for workers. There is no fee for use of a state employment service.

REGISTER WITH A COMMERCIAL PLACEMENT OFFICE.   There are some private placement offices that will help you find a job for a fee. Before entering into any agreement with a commercial agency, find out who pays the fees. Such fees typically start at approximately 5 percent of the first year's salary, and can increase considerably from there. We recommend using commercial placement offices as a last resort.

Preparing for Job Interviews

A job interview is an opportunity to perform. To perform well in any endeavor, you have to practice and be well-rehearsed. In general, interviewers will expect you to (1) be pleasant, friendly, knowledgeable, and to show a positive attitude toward working; (2) have some knowledge and understanding about their company or agency; (3) answer questions clearly and concisely that show how your skills are suitable to the job; and (4) ask some pertinent questions of the interviewer. The style of the interviewer can vary from highly structured to very loose, from warm and friendly to aloof and cold, and from highly skilled in communication to very unskilled. Some interviewers will expect you to do most of the talking, while others will prefer very brief remarks. The length of an interview is generally about 30 minutes, although interviews for high-level positions can last much longer.

In many instances, interviewers seem to be primarily concerned with ruling out undesirable candidates (Yate, 1991). Factors that might lead to a negative evaluation include lack of knowledge of the company or agency; inability to answer questions clearly and concisely; acting passively and unenthusiastically during the interview; talking about personal problems or family problems; criticizing your former employer or the people you worked with; overemphasizing your limitations or weaknesses; acting too aggressively by pushing and pressuring the interviewer; and lying about previous jobs (contradictions often show up on reference checks).

Preparing for an interview can be divided into five areas. First, you should learn as much as you can about the company or agency. *The Wall Street Journal Index,* for example, provides a great deal of information on a wide range of companies. You may be able to obtain a copy of a company's annual report or advertising brochures, or you may be able to talk to people who work with the firm. The more that you can find out about the company or agency, the more that you will be able to match your skills to its needs. Second, you should learn as much as possible about the interview process for that particular company or agency. How long will the interview last? Can you talk to other students who have been interviewed by that company (or that person) during the preceding year? Perhaps placement officials at your college placement center can give you some information about the interviewing process of a particular company or agency. Third, prepare a list of probable questions and think about how you would answer those questions. Questions frequently asked during job interviews are listed in Table 12-5.

The fourth step is to list the questions that you want to ask the interviewer. Besides providing you with personal information that might help you to decide whether or not you might want to accept a job with that company, asking questions of the interviewer also signifies your interest in the job and the company. Some questions that you may want to ask include: (1) Can I see a written job description?

TABLE 12-5
QUESTIONS OFTEN ASKED DURING JOB INTERVIEWS

1. What led you to choose this particular career or academic major?
2. Why do you want to work for this company?
3. What are your qualifications that will help you be successful in this position?
4. Describe previous work experience relevant to this position.
5. What are the most important personal considerations for you in your future career planning, and how does this position fit in?
6. What do you expect to be doing five years from now?
7. What are your career goals?
8. If you are married, how does your spouse view the possibility of your working for our company?
9. How do you usually go about making decisions?
10. What do you consider to be your strongest attributes for this position?
11. What do you consider to be your most obvious weaknesses for this position?
12. Were you ever fired from a job? Why?
13. Have you ever quit a job? Why?
14. What are your views on salary for this position?
15. What are your financial goals five years from now?
16. Why should this company hire you?
17. Do you have any questions you want to ask?

(2) What is company policy on overtime, vacation time, and sick leave? (3) What is the probationary period for new employees and how are they evaluated at the end of that time? (4) Do you have written information available concerning salary schedules, pay raises, and retirement plans? (5) What is the next step in the hiring process and when will I hear about the results of the interview? Finally, the last step of preparing for an interview is to practice. Set up a mock interview situation with a friend. Choose a setting structured somewhat like a formal office. Brief your friend on the questions to be asked and have your friend play the role of the interviewer. Practice the interview like a full dress rehearsal. Practice your initial greeting, your body language and attentiveness during the interview, and especially the clarity of your answers to the questions. Also, ask your friend to surprise you by asking questions that are not on the list you provided.

Having a Successful Interview

Previously we mentioned factors that might lead you to be evaluated negatively in an interview. What contributes to a positive evaluation? While we've alluded to some important factors, the following are further suggestions for conducting yourself well during job interviews (also, see Yate, 1991; Biegeleison, 1991).

The body language that you display during a job interview can greatly influence how interviewers will react to you. You should begin the interview with a smile, eye contact, and a firm handshake.

Most important is to stay relaxed. Many people feel stress during a job interview, and understandably so. Remember and use the relaxation procedures described in Chapter 4. In particular, you may want to practice centering and coping self-statements just before entering the interview. When you go to an interview, go alone. You don't want your employer to think that you are not mature enough to handle the job. Absolutely be on time. Also, dress conservatively and neatly. A neat, well-groomed appearance helps create a good first impression. First impressions are also strongly influenced by a firm handshake, eye contact, and a smile. After initial introductions, remain standing until you are invited to sit. During the interview, maintain an attentive posture. Make frequent eye contact while answering questions and speak in a clear voice. Both communication and interpersonal skills are extremely important during the interview. When answering questions, keep your responses short and to the point. If you have a great deal more to say on an answer, ask the interviewer, "Would you like me to explain that further?" Finally, do not prolong the interview unnecessarily. When the interviewer thanks you for applying for the position and coming to the interview, simply ask about the next step of the hiring process.

Repeating the Process

It will be the rare person who gets a job for every interview. Prepare yourself to repeat the process. Immediately after an interview, debrief yourself. A good friend could listen to you at this time. Visualize the interview. What seemed to be the good points? What aspects of the interview seemed doubtful to you? Now is the time to consider what you should have said if you were surprised by some question. Rehearse the better answer you have just thought of. Interviewing is a skill, and like most skills it can be learned through experience. Don't despair.

If you do repeat the process a number of times without successfully obtaining employment, you may wish to seek professional help with your job search.

Surviving in the World of Work

Let's suppose that you worked hard at school, demonstrated creative job hunting, were rewarded with several interviews and job offers, and you're about to start this great new job. There are a number of things that you can do to ensure that your work experience will be a success.

Some Tips on Starting Your New Job

How can you ensure that you start off on the "right foot"? Deutsch (1984) described six tips for starting a new job. First, you should "dress for success," but be conservative. Individualistic styles might be acceptable after you have firmly established your value to the company or agency. Until that time, however, dress to fit in.

Second, capitalize fully on the employee orientation program. Your first few days will be a blur of new faces, new names, and new procedures. Approach the orientation period as though you were cramming for very important final exams. You've probably developed a number of very effective memory aids. Use them.

Third, try to determine the company's working style right from the start. That is, some agencies and work settings operate very formally. In other settings, everyone is "laid back" and informal. Adapt to the style of the company.

Fourth, develop friendly relations with your coworkers but do so carefully. Remember the tips on disclosure and developing friendships in Chapter 8.

Fifth, keep an ongoing record of your work activities. Write down each facet of your daily work. List projects assigned to you and the dates on which you completed them. Over a period of time, it may seem that your job stays relatively

Do you "dress for success"?

the same. Nevertheless, a running record of your work activities and dates completed will likely surprise you in terms of how your responsibilities expand over time. Not only is this type of self-monitoring a useful self-motivational strategy, it can provide an extremely valuable record when you ask the boss for a raise a year down the road. It can provide an objective record of why you are more valuable to the company than when you started. You will be surprised at the new challenges, new skills learned, and changed responsibilities that occur during that time.

The last tip to remember before starting work is simply a reminder to "go all out." At the beginning of each day, remind yourself to "do your best." At the end of each day, ask yourself, "Did I do my best?" As expressed by Hegarty (1982), "A major key in obtaining job satisfaction is to give more than you get." That is, if you try to be as valuable as possible to the firm, you will become more valuable to them. This increases the chance of benefits accruing to both you and the firm.

Two Months Later: What Is Your Job?

You have been working with the firm for several weeks now. What exactly is your job? It is extremely important that you know the organization for which you work, its goals, your own particular duties and responsibilities, and how they fit in with the goals of the organization. You undoubtedly know your job at a general level. For example, you might be responsible for "customer relations" or for "taking inventory." In today's competitive employment environment, however, that level of generality is simply not good enough. To help you evaluate your knowledge of your current position, we encourage you to self-assess using the questionnaire in Box 12-4.

performance appraisal
A regularly scheduled, formal evaluation of an employee's performance on a particular job; commonly used as one of the conditions for promotion or dismissal.

PERFORMANCE APPRAISALS.   Many organizations evaluate a new employee's performance after the first three months, the first six months, and after one year by completing formal **performance appraisals.** Thereafter, performance appraisals

---

Box 12-4

A Checklist for Assessing Knowledge of the Components of Your Job

Items	Yes	No	Don't Know	If No, How Can I Change It?	Priority for Action
Does a written program description for the company exist?	☐	☐	☐	☐	☐
Is the description quite detailed?	☐	☐	☐	☐	☐
Does the description include a statement of:					
1. philosophy of the organization and/or rationale for the agency?	☐	☐	☐	☐	☐
2. goals?	☐	☐	☐	☐	☐
3. guidelines for prioritizing goals?	☐	☐	☐	☐	☐
4. an organizational chart?	☐	☐	☐	☐	☐
5. delivery model and/or program components?	☐	☐	☐	☐	☐
6. job descriptions for staff that indicate:					
a. measurable performance criteria?	☐	☐	☐	☐	☐
b. performance standards?	☐	☐	☐	☐	☐
c. feedback mechanisms?	☐	☐	☐	☐	☐
d. frequency of feedback guidelines?	☐	☐	☐	☐	☐
Is the description congruent with the goals and philosophy of the agency?	☐	☐	☐	☐	☐
Can I verbalize:					
1. the goals of the organization?	☐	☐	☐	☐	☐
2. performance criteria?	☐	☐	☐	☐	☐
3. standards for performance?	☐	☐	☐	☐	☐
Are there specific outcome measures of my performance that are:					
1. objective?	☐	☐	☐	☐	☐
2. reliable?	☐	☐	☐	☐	☐
3. quantitative?	☐	☐	☐	☐	☐

commonly occur on a yearly basis. Szilagyi and Wallace (1983) identified the following five levels at which performance can be evaluated in organizations:

1. Corporate or organizational outcomes (such as profits)
2. Unit or division outcomes (such as production levels per division)
3. Individual task outcomes (such as the number of units sold by a salesperson)
4. Individual behavior (such as the number of house calls made by a salesperson)
5. General behavioral characteristics (such as attitudes or aptitudes as measured by various paper and pencil tests and/or by supervisor ratings).

Szilagyi and Wallace (1983) also identified five possible sources of performance appraisal, including (1) supervisors, (2) peers, (3) the employees to be appraised (self-appraisal), (4) subordinates of the person to be appraised, and (5) people outside the immediate organization, such as clients. The one thing that you can be sure of is that you *will* be appraised at work. The most frequently used form

Has my "expected" level of performance been defined in
terms of behaviors needed to meet that level?   ☐ ☐ ☐ ☐ ☐

Can I verbalize expected outcome measures of my
performance?   ☐ ☐ ☐ ☐ ☐

Can I state the relationship of the desired outcome measures
of my performance to organizational goals?   ☐ ☐ ☐ ☐ ☐

Does my supervisor agree that the desired outcome measures
of my performance are complementary to the mission of
the organization?   ☐ ☐ ☐ ☐ ☐

Are my work behaviors defined so that they can be reliably
recorded by means of a checklist with a series of yes/no
decisions?   ☐ ☐ ☐ ☐ ☐

If my work behaviors are not readily amenable to supervisory
observation, can I use some form of self-evaluation?   ☐ ☐ ☐ ☐ ☐

Have I conducted a formal self-evaluation comparing my
actual levels of performance to the desired outcome
measures?   ☐ ☐ ☐ ☐ ☐

Have I prioritized all of my relevant work behaviors in terms
of their importance to the desired outcomes?   ☐ ☐ ☐ ☐ ☐

Does my supervisor agree with the prioritization?   ☐ ☐ ☐ ☐ ☐

of appraisal is the appraisal of general behavioral characteristics or "traits" (Szilagyi & Wallace, 1983). A sample of such a rating form is shown in Table 12-6.

"trait" performance appraisals

Performance appraisals based on how an employee exemplifies general personality traits or global characteristics on the job.

"Trait" performance appraisals are based on trait personality theories such as those described in Chapter 2. These types of forms have two main advantages. First, they can be developed very quickly. You don't have to be a genius to brainstorm a set of words that, at least superficially, appear to identify exemplary employees (as illustrated in Table 12-6). Second, they can be used to evaluate employees across a wide variety of jobs. Unfortunately, they suffer from the same problems that characterize the trait personality theories; that is, they are extremely global and do not reliably describe any particular behaviors of an employee in a work setting. For that reason, they're not especially useful for bringing about an improvement in an employee's behavior. If you tell employees that they need to show more leadership or more initiative, that could be interpreted to mean almost anything.

TABLE 12-6
A SAMPLE OF A GENERAL RATING FORM TO APPRAISE WORKERS *From Szilagyi & Wallace, 1983.*

Name _____   Date _____

Birthdate _____   Time in current position (Years) _____

Section I Personal Qualifications

FACTORS

		3 Better than Average	2 Average	1 Less than Average
Ratings on these factors measure salesperson's personal qualifications (ability) and character traits (habits) solely in respect to the requirements of the job. Circle appropriate rating.				
Appearance	Cleanliness, neatness, appropriate dress.	☐	☐	☐
Manners	Politeness, courtesy, tactfulness.	☐	☐	☐
Intelligence	Capacity and power to comprehend, rationalize, exercise good judgment.	☐	☐	☐
Education	Sufficient for requirements of job, either formally or self-acquired.	☐	☐	☐
Physical condition	Health, energy, stamina.	☐	☐	☐
Industry	Works steadily, conscientiously, and productively.	☐	☐	☐
Perserverance	Persists in tasks despite difficulties and obstacles.	☐	☐	☐
Loyalty	Close self-identification with the company; fidelity to its interests.	☐	☐	☐
Self-reliance	Relies upon self rather than others to accomplish tasks; stands on own feet.	☐	☐	☐
Self-confidence	Adequate self-confidence.	☐	☐	☐
Leadership	Inspires confidence and trust; others turn to him or her for help and guidance.	☐	☐	☐
Initiative	Produces new ideas, methods, or devices.	☐	☐	☐
Enthusiastic	Shows enthusiasm.	☐	☐	☐
Cooperative	Works well with other employees. Accepts assignments in other work areas.	☐	☐	☐
	SCORE	☐	☐	☐

behavioral performance appraisals

Performance appraisals based on whether or not an employee shows specific behaviors in his or her daily work.

In recent years, there has been a trend toward the use of **behavioral performance appraisals** that focus more on specific behaviors that employees are expected to show in their daily work. For example, Table 12-7 lists some of the job responsibilities and standards of performance on a behaviorally based appraisal system for evaluating the supervisor of a sheltered workshop for mentally retarded persons. In the organization where this appraisal system was used, supervisors were evaluated monthly in terms of the extent to which they showed the minimum frequency of behaviors that characterized their listed responsibilities (Hazen & Martin, 1985).

Another behaviorally based measure of job performance is referred to as a **behavioral observation scale.** With this type of assessment, commonly occurring behaviors required of an employee are listed as items on the scale. An example of a behavioral observation scale for a public affairs manager is shown in Table 12-8. A supervisor evaluating a public affairs manager would indicate the frequency with which the manager typically showed each of the behaviors. The five points on the Likert Scale are commonly anchored to specific percentages. For example, a "4" might mean that the employee had been observed to show a particular behavior on 90 to 100 percent of the opportunities, a "3" on 80 to 89 percent of the opportunities, a "2" on 70 to 79 percent of the opportunities, a "1" on 60 to 69 percent of the opportunities, and a "0" for less than 60 percent of the time.

behavioral observation scale

A behaviorally based measure of job performance that lists commonly occurring behaviors required of an employee, and rates the extent to which the employee shows those behaviors.

TABLE 12-7

ITEMS FROM A BEHAVIORAL APPRAISAL FORM FOR EVALUATING SUPERVISORS OF SHELTERED WORKSHOPS

Responsibilities	*Standards of Performance and/or Minimum Frequency of Occurrence*
Keeps up-to-date records of overtime and vacation of employees.	Updates overtime daily and vacation records monthly.
Provides the contract manager with production data for billing purposes.	Keeps up-to-date records of production shipments and ensures an accurate account is listed on the shipping invoice twice weekly.
Supplies the director of the workshop with client attendance records.	Completes and sends monthly attendance statistics by the fifth of each month.
Orders supplies.	Ensures stationery and housekeeping supplies are checked and ordered weekly.
Evaluates performance of staff on a regular basis.	Does staff assessments on all workshop employees and discusses the assessment results with them in an individual interview on a monthly basis.
Ensures quality control of production.	Conducts spot checks of production at least four times daily to ensure staff are keeping the error rate of clients at no more than 5 percent.
Ensures that staff keep client files up to date.	Checks client files to ensure that staff have updated training summary sheets on a monthly basis.

Which performance appraisal system is likely to be most useful? That depends in part on the function of the performance appraisal. Performance appraisals are used to decide on promotion or perhaps separation, to give feedback to employees in order to bring about performance improvement, to provide a basis for merit pay increases, to determine the need for employee-retraining programs, to evaluate the success of existing employee-training programs, and to be a source of information for various business decisions such as budgeting and work scheduling. In most cases, the behaviorally based measures of job performance are most useful for these functions. If you do not have such a system at your place of work, we encourage you to design one to monitor your own performance (see Table 12-7). Not only will it help to motivate you during the year, it can prove extremely helpful during your performance appraisal when you discuss the more global categories with your supervisor.

Besides having an updated record of your self-appraisal, you should ensure that all other assignments have been up to date prior to the performance review. Throughout the review, try to be as specific as possible. Also, once the review is over, you and your supervisor will likely be expected to sign the copy of the review provided by your supervisor.

Getting Ahead: Communicating Effectively

In the chapters describing developing friendships (Chapter 8), and assertiveness training (Chapter 15), we provided numerous guidelines to help you communicate effectively. In this section we want to review additional areas of communication that are important in work settings. In most jobs you will have information to share, opinions to express, decisions to make, and you will both give and receive criti-

Table 12-8

A Behavioral Observation Scale for Assessing a Public Affairs Manager *Latham, 1982.*

Interactions with the Public

1. Identifies community and special interest groups or organizations that can influence directly or indirectly company operations.	Almost Never	0	1	2	3	4	Almost Always
2. Directs the public to the local superintendent for questions, support, or assistance so that the superintendent is looked upon favorably by the community.	Almost Never	0	1	2	3	4	Almost Always
3. Asks for and listens openly to criticisms of the company.	Almost Never	0	1	2	3	4	Almost Always
4. Can explain the company's rationale for engaging in policies that irritate or concern local residents.	Almost Never	0	1	2	3	4	Almost Always
5. Follows up on complaints lodged against the company to see if the company's explanation is understood.	Almost Never	0	1	2	3	4	Almost Always
6. Can explain the basis for controversial company actions without irritating or offending the listener.	Almost Never	0	1	2	3	4	Almost Always
7. Knows the opinions of each member of the city council on issues that do or could impact the company.	Almost Never	0	1	2	3	4	Almost Always
8. Knows the mayor(s) on a first name basis.	Almost Never	0	1	2	3	4	Almost Always
9. Can formulate a response compatible with the company's philosophy during a crisis situation (e.g., 22 people injured minutes ago).	Almost Never	0	1	2	3	4	Almost Always
10. Develops and implements surveys on community attitudes that do or could impact region operations.	Almost Never	0	1	2	3	4	Almost Always
11. Insures that opinion makers in the community (e.g., members of the Chamber of Commerce) are invited to functions that may be of interest to them.	Almost Never	0	1	2	3	4	Almost Always
12. Knows the county commissioners on a first name basis.	Almost Never	0	1	2	3	4	Almost Always
13. Uses NEWSLINE or region newspaper to explain both sides of an issue factually without offering an opinion.	Almost Never	0	1	2	3	4	Almost Always
14. Provides information and background to region and corporation on need to support political candidates.	Almost Never	0	1	2	3	4	Almost Always

cism. Communicating assertively without guilt or anxiety, and honestly and directly without hidden agendas, can help you to get things done in the best possible way (Cawood, 1983; LaRouche & Ryan, 1984; Yate, 1991). The components listed below do not exhaust the subcategories of effective communication. They are nevertheless among the more important to attend to in the work environment.

DEVELOPING LISTENING SKILLS. A few years ago, the Sperry Corporation (now Unisys, after merging with Burroughs), a company that is known for its computers, farm equipment, and flight controls, launched a multimillion-dollar advertising campaign to combat inefficient and ineffective listening. According to one of their ads, most people in business spent half of their time at work listening, but they did so at only a 25-percent efficiency level. Their brochure further claimed that knowing how to listen could double the efficiency of American business.

What are some of the potential barriers to effective listening? Those listed by Sperry included daydreaming, listening primarily for facts instead of for ideas and central themes, judging physical aspects of the speaker (such as dress and hairstyle) before understanding what was being said, focusing on the speaker's delivery or mannerisms instead of content, and becoming personally antagonized by emotion-laden words. Many listeners "hear what they want to hear" rather than hearing what the speaker is saying. As expressed by Hegarty (1982), they listen *against* as opposed to listening *to*. That is, they listen to obtain ammunition for an argument rather than listening to understand what the speaker is saying.

What are some of the components of effective listening? As with all aspects of effective communication, body language is important. Making eye contact while maintaining a relaxed posture is a good start. Remaining still and refraining from making distracting and impatient gestures (such as cleaning your fingernails with your thumbnail) help. Facial expression is also important. If you find yourself frowning or opening your mouth to impatiently make a counterargument, then you're engaging in evaluative rather than nonevaluative listening. You're jumping to conclusions prematurely. According to Cawood (1983), one of the most effective ways to demonstrate that you've heard the other person is to reflect back the content of their statements in your own words. The idea here is to convey the other person's meaning without being obvious and without merely repeating the other person's words (which is likely to make them feel patronized). Common lead phrases for you to do so include, "You seem to be saying that . . . " or "What I understand you to be saying is. . . . " This type of paraphrasing will make it easier for you to practice nonevaluative listening and to stop yourself from prematurely jumping to conclusions and interrupting with counterarguments, personal decisions, and suggested solutions.

GIVING INFORMATION AND INSTRUCTIONS.   There are a number of reasons why information and/or instructions will *not* have the desired effect on a listener. (1) Many people are very poor listeners. (2) Sometimes the spoken message is inconsistent with our nonverbal signals. For example, we have probably all seen a spouse question a mate about some activity while speaking with stiff mannerisms, clenched teeth, and a frown, and at the same time saying, "No I'm not mad. I just want to know what you were doing." (3) Sometimes we forget to mention time frames for our directive. For example, a parent might tell a child to "take out the garbage." The child assumes that that means anytime in the next few days. The parent assumes that it means anytime within the next hour. (4) Sometimes we assume that one explanation or interpretation of complex material is sufficient. That's a mistake that we, as professors, must constantly guard against. Having taught a particular course for several years, we know the material well. It's very easy to assume that the students will easily understand it when we explain it to them once. (5) Sometimes our information or instructions might not be effectively received by the listener because we (knowingly or unknowingly) allow sarcasm or sexism to creep into our message. You can counteract all of these problems to some extent by increasing the effectiveness with which you dispense information and give instructions.

The first step for giving instructions or information effectively is to ensure that you have the attention of the listener. Select or arrange the setting to minimize distractors. Next, make sure the spoken message is consistent with your body language. Give your instructions with an erect but relaxed posture. Maintain eye contact. Project your voice energetically so that the instructions can be heard. When giving directives, don't end your sentences on an upward pitch that makes them sound like questions. When giving information, be specific and provide a clear description of the details. When giving instructions to coworkers or staff whom you supervise, tell them what you expect them to do in observable and measurable terms. What is it that you want to happen as a result of the instructions? Make sure that this is clearly understandable by your coworkers or employees. Limit the instructions to a reasonable number at any one time. Finally, if you want to be

Body language and eye contact are two important components of effective communication.

doubly sure that the information or instructions are appropriately received, ask for feedback. If appropriate, ask that the information be repeated or paraphrased in the words of the listener.

GIVING CRITICISM.   Sooner or later in the work environment, you will be a supervisor, a manager, a person in charge. That means occasions will arise where it will be both appropriate and necessary for you to give constructive criticism to one of your supervisees. At some point, you might also have to give constructive criticism to a colleague.

Giving criticism to an individual in a way that changes his or her behavior in the desirable direction without at the same time causing resentment and undesirable side effects is very difficult. As expressed by Hegarty (1982), "Constructive criticism is almost always destructive." Nonetheless, there are a number of things that you can do to increase the chances that your criticism will be accepted in the best possible way. But first, let's identify several things that you should *not* do when giving constructive criticism. Don't give criticism when you're angry. An angry, sarcastic, or sneering tone will greatly increase the chances that the recipient will become angry and will be unreceptive to what you say. If possible, don't criticize in public. Don't begin with generalities and undesirable personality traits (for example, don't say, "That was dumb" or "That was incompetent" or "You have a terrible attitude"). Speaking in generalities almost never helps, and it usually harms. Don't create an atmosphere of "me against you." Rather, try to create an atmosphere of "us against the problem" (Deutsch, 1984). Don't blame, moralize, or threaten. If you start out by saying, "You never listen to me," you've greatly increased the chances that they *won't* listen to you. Finally, don't bring up old history. This is often seen in arguments where one spouse criticizes another (for example, "Last week you said . . . ."; "Oh yeah, what about last month when you . . . ").

constructive criticism

A practice of identifying particular behaviors that are unsatisfactory and at the same time identifying alternative desirable behaviors to take the place of the unsatisfactory ones.

Constructive criticism begins with effective timing (Cawood, 1983). Choose a time for constructive criticism when both you and the recipient are relaxed and not under pressure or stressed out. Our previous guidelines for using positive reinforcement suggested that you should try to reinforce desirable behavior immediately after it occurs. Constructive criticism is a different ball of wax. You should *not* be using constructive criticism as a punisher to decrease behavior. (But punishers, of course, *should* occur immediately after an undesirable behavior.) Rather, constructive criticism is an instructional tactic. If a particular undesirable behavior is interfering with productivity at work, you may have to deal with it immediately. If not, choose a time to deal with it when the employee is likely to be most receptive.

Provide clear verbal cues to the recipient about the topic of discussion, and do so by emphasizing the potential for improvement, not the problem (for example, "I want to talk about how we can improve the taking of inventory"). Then, as clearly, objectively, and specifically as possible, identify the relevant problem behavior, explain briefly why it's a problem, and identify specific desirable alternative actions. Or at the least, ask the individual how it can be improved. For example, suppose that your company has a policy of assigning new staff members to experienced staff members, so that the experienced staff members can "show them the ropes." And suppose further that you have the responsibility of making the assignments. Unfortunately, one experienced staff member considers this program to be a nuisance. That person answers questions asked by new staff members with a curt yes or no, rather than voluntarily explaining procedures in detail. Before assigning a new staff member to this disgruntled veteran employee, you might say to him when you're alone, "I want to talk to you about the most effective way of training our new employees. When you answer their questions with a brief yes or no, they're less likely to understand our procedures and are more likely to make mistakes. If they make mistakes, the company's profits go down and that can reflect on all of our salaries. I'd like you to go out of your way to answer their questions in sufficient detail so that they will fully understand our procedures here at work."

When giving constructive criticism, stick to the main point and keep it limited. Finally, end on a positive note and then allow the person a chance to respond. In the above example, you might follow up with "You know your job really well, and I know it will benefit the company and all of us if we maximize the effectiveness of our training program for new staff." Ending on a positive note helps create the atmosphere of "us against the problem" and minimizes the possibility that the constructive criticism will turn into a destructive confrontation.

DISAGREEING WITHOUT BEING DISAGREEABLE.   Suppose that you and someone at work disagree. You decide that you have to work something out. But you dread having a confrontation. What do you do? Guidelines for having a confrontation include most of the guidelines listed above for giving criticism. Timing is important. You should focus clearly on the problem, explain why it's a problem, and discuss alternatives. You should avoid blaming, moralizing, threatening, bringing up old history, and arguing in generalities. In many respects, having a confrontation that does not become disagreeable involves a combination of the skills of listening, giving information, and giving criticism. You have to go beyond giving criticism in the sense that you need to genuinely listen to what the other person is saying, what his or her reasons are for the actions, and you need to judge the reasonableness of those actions. You may want to use statements like, "I understand your position, now please let me explain mine," or "I can see that we agree to disagree, now let's see if we can find some middle ground," or "We don't want to create a 'no-win' situation here, so let's see if we can come up with an alternative that we can both live with." At all costs, remain calm and try to diffuse any situation in which the other person becomes angry. Always try to explain your position in a polite, noncritical way. Always try to identify compromises that will allow the other person to "save face." Finally, remember your body language. Glaring at someone without breaking eye contact, standing with your arms folded high on your chest or with hands on your hips, standing with feet wide apart in a tense manner, or raising your eyebrows can all signal confrontation, not compromise. Besides saying it in words, your body language can also communicate, "I understand and respect what you say, but I see things differently. Let's try to work it out."

ACCEPTING CRITICISM.   Sooner or later you will be on the receiving end of criticism in the work environment. If you have an unreasonable boss (and, as described later in this chapter, there are many of those), this may happen more often than you would like. Also, the person criticizing you might not be as knowledgeable about how to give criticism as you are. Nevertheless, learning to be responsive to constructive criticism from others is an important skill to learn, and it can help you function in an increasingly effective fashion throughout life, not just in the world of work.

The first step in learning to accept criticism is to learn to distinguish between well-meaning constructive criticism offered by others and destructive attempts at manipulation. From some people, you will encounter sarcasm ("You call *that* a report?"), baiting remarks ("I'll bet you don't finish your report on time"), overgeneralizations ("You're never on time"), and sexist or hostile remarks designed to get a reaction out of you ("What can you expect from a woman?"). For such people, their rewards include getting a reaction out of you, making you angry, seeing you lose control, or generating an argument. If you respond to their manipulation attempts, then they win and they're more likely to repeat them. In most situations your best strategy is to ignore them. Accepting their challenge can be costly, both emotionally and from a time management perspective. If you can't ignore them, then practice responding assertively in the manner described in Chapter 15. Alternatively, simply smile and make a disarming comment ("That sweater looks very nice on you").

When the criticism is relevant to your functioning competently, listen attentively until it is expressed fully. Maintain eye contact and a relaxed position, and avoid confrontational body language. When the criticism is completed, ask nonthreatening questions to clarify your understanding of the concern. If you understand fully, paraphrase to demonstrate understanding in the same way that you do when practicing good listening skills. Avoid making lengthy explanations or justifications for your previous behavior. Once you understand the criticism clearly, recognize the mistake (for example, "With my 20–20 hindsight, I can see now that that was not the best way to handle the situation"). Finally, discuss alternative ways of dealing with the situation in the future. If your critic has not offered guidelines for corrective action, then ask that this be done. Alternatively, make suggestions and request confirmation. When you have had a chance to implement a new course of action, draw it to your supervisor's attention and request feedback. As was the case with our guidelines for giving criticism, this final step for receiving criticism helps to make it an "us against the problem" situation rather than a "you against me" one.

You might be thinking, "That's all well and good on paper. But when people criticize me, I get so upset that I want to strike back at them. How do I control that?" If you have trouble handling criticism emotionally, read the procedures in Chapter 5 for dealing with stress. The progressive muscle relaxation techniques, centering, and coping self-statements can all be used to help you deal with criticism. If those don't work, then ask your critic to postpone things for a while. You might say something like, "I'm sorry but this really upsets me. Would it be all right if I talked to you about it tomorrow morning?" By the next morning, you will have had a chance to review your coping strategies, and perhaps to come up with a solution to the problem.

positive strokes or **"warm fuzzies"**

Terms from transactional analysis that refer to things that you do and say to others which will make them feel good about themselves, such as giving a compliment or a pat on the back.

GIVING COMPLIMENTS.   "Different strokes for different folks" is a popular expression. It implies that not everyone finds the same events to be rewarding. Sincere praise, however, is a reward for just about everyone almost all the time. In the jargon of transactional analysis, **positive strokes,** or **"warm fuzzies,"** are what you do and say to others so that they will feel good about themselves (Berne, 1964). A compliment, a smile, a special look, praise, a pat on the back, all of these are positive strokes. Although it's nice to make people feel good by giving them positive strokes, that's only a part of the story. You must also be alert to their behavior just before you "stroke" them. Whenever you give someone a warm fuzzy (dispense positive reinforcement), it follows some behavior. According to the principle of positive reinforcement, that behavior will be strengthened or maintained. Let's suppose that you work in a busy place. Nobody has much time to talk to his or her colleagues. One colleague in particular seems to make more than his share of mistakes. To try and make him feel better, you give him a warm fuzzy each time he makes a mistake. After a month or so of this routine, you might have made him feel better fairly often. But you might also have unknowingly influenced him to make more mistakes. Therefore, one rule for giving compliments is to give them when things are going well and people are working effectively. The advice of Blanchard and Johnson (1982) for managers is, "Catch a worker doing something good today."

general praise

Compliments such as "good!" "well done!" and so forth that are general in nature and do not identify specific behaviors.

prescriptive praise

Praise that identifies a particular aspect of behavior that is desirable or which indicates improvement.

Another rule for giving compliments is to be specific. Let them know exactly what aspect of their work behavior it is that you're complimenting. Comments like, "Good!" "Well done!" "That was great!" are examples of **general praise. Prescriptive praise** identifies that aspect of an employee's performance which was desirable or which indicated improvement. In other words, you don't just tell people that they "did good." You tell them *what* they did well. Prescriptive praise is especially useful when you want to encourage an employee to concentrate on a particular component of a skill or task.

Another rule is to be sincere. One way of doing this is to tell them how good you feel about what they did right, and to explain how it might improve the overall performance of the organization. Sincere compliments are almost always effective. Insincere compliments are almost always detected.

Try not to water down the effects of the compliment. This can happen if you pair compliments with criticism (for example, "That was a good job, but . . . "). If you consistently pair praise for good performance with criticism for bad performance, the praise may eventually lose much of its effectiveness. Be constantly on the lookout for desirable behaviors in employees and colleagues to praise. Also, when you spot an inappropriate behavior, consider providing some corrective instruction. But be wary of continually praising one thing and criticizing several others in the same interaction. Also, do not use praise as "sugar coating" for asking a favor. If you consistently approach a particular typist in the typing pool with the statement, "You're the fastest typist we've got, I wonder if you would quickly type this up for me," the typist may become resentful and unresponsive to both your praise and your requests.

Getting Ahead: How to Manage Your Boss

Some bosses may seem impossible to deal with. Lombardo and McCall (1984) asked 73 highly successful executives in large industrial corporations about their experiences with intolerable bosses. They reduced the total descriptions of undesirable attributes to a *"rogues gallery"* of nine different types of intolerable bosses. Examples include the *Attilas*—dictators who do not allow anyone else to make decisions; *heelgrinders*—who frequently belittle and humiliate their employees; *snakes in the grass*—who just generally can't be trusted; and *slobs*—whose appearance and prejudices make them intolerable to employees. Some day, you may encounter such bosses. Hopefully, however, your boss will be a reasonable person trying to do a job. In many jobs, the key to improving your work life will lie in your relation to your boss rather than in the job itself. The above guidelines on communicating effectively will help you to improve that relationship. In this section, we describe several additional considerations for "managing your boss."

a golden rule for managing your boss

The rule that suggests you should "try to make your boss look good."

"readers"

A category of people who prefer to see reports on problems or projects before talking about them; identified by Drucker.

"listeners"

A category of people who prefer to hear about projects and talk about them first, and then have memos to refer to; identified by Drucker.

WHAT IS YOUR BOSS'S JOB?   What is reality from your boss's point of view? To whom is your boss responsible? What work objectives have been imposed on your boss from those above? Pamela Newman, a management consultant, suggests that a **golden rule** to remember when managing your boss is to *make the boss look good* (Newman, 1978). The more you understand about the boss's job, the easier it will be for you to follow the golden rule.

To learn as much as you can about your boss's responsibilities, talk to his or her colleagues and/or assistants. Check out some of the magazines and newsletters that the boss subscribes to. Sit in on meetings with the boss as often as possible. Extra effort on your part to determine what it is that your boss has to do, organize, coordinate, manage, and evaluate will usually pay dividends in the long run.

WHAT COMMUNICATION STYLE DOES YOUR BOSS PREFER?   Peter Drucker, a frequent contributor to *Management Review,* suggests that most people can be divided into "readers" and "listeners" (Drucker, 1977). **"Readers,"** like John F. Kennedy, like to see reports on problems or projects before talking about them. If your boss is a reader, show him or her a written description of your project first, then start to talk. **"Listeners,"** like Ronald Reagan, like to hear about projects and talk about them first, and then have memos to refer to. If your boss is a listener, don't send a memo. Go in and talk about it first, and then follow up with a written report. If you learn to work with your boss in the preferred communication style, then you will work more effectively.

COMMUNICATE YOUR TIME MANAGEMENT TO YOUR BOSS.   Do you remember guidelines on time management in Chapter 1? Critical aspects include identifying long-term objectives, preparing daily to-do lists, and prioritizing so that you complete the high-priority activities first. If you have a lot of independence in your job, you should frequently share your long-term objectives and prioritization outcomes with your boss. As we indicated in that chapter, it's easy to fall into the trap of concentrating on doing the job right, rather than on doing the right job. Make sure that you and your boss agree on which job is the right one. Most bosses don't like surprises.

DO YOUR HOMEWORK BEFORE MEETINGS WITH YOUR BOSS.   A sound old rule states: It takes 10 minutes of preparation time for each minute of interview time (Drucker, 1977). Always prepare ahead of time when meeting with the boss. Most managers feel that they don't have enough time and that they spend too much time with their subordinates. Doing your homework before meetings will help ensure that your boss does not see *you* as a "time waster."

GIVE YOUR BOSS FEEDBACK.   Like everyone else, your boss likes to be "stroked," to receive "warm fuzzies." When your boss does something that you like, give him or her a well-deserved compliment. Just as Blanchard and Johnson (1983) suggested that bosses should "catch a worker doing something good today," so too an employee should try to "catch a boss doing something good today."

Also, provide feedback when your boss delegates additional tasks to you without consideration of your prior responsibilities. You might encounter a boss who will clearly outline your duties for the next week or so. Then, two or three days later, the boss will give you five or six additional jobs to perform without recognizing the time needed to complete the previously assigned tasks. In such a situation, you should (1) acknowledge the importance of the newly assigned jobs; (2) provide a brief update on your progress on the previously assigned jobs; (3) indicate that you would be happy to perform the newly assigned jobs but that it would mean that the previously assigned jobs will be completed *X* amount of time late; and (4) ask the boss if that's what she or he would prefer.

Women in the Work Place

Women now constitute 50 percent of the American work force (Rukeyser et al., 1988). And experts estimate that eight of every ten adult women will be working outside of the home by the year 2000 (Matthews & Rodin, 1989). Clearly women constitute a major force in the work place. In spite of their prominent role, they have been the subject of numerous abuses as well as of erroneous overgeneralizations about their performance on the job (see Box 12-5).

Some progress has been made toward equality for women in the work place during the past 20 years. Much, however, remains to be done. In career planning, women must be encouraged to move into a broader range of occupations in order to maximize opportunities for advancement, higher earnings, and job satisfaction (Van Fossen & Beck, 1991). Vocational counselors need to help young women develop more elaborate, strategic plans for selecting alternative careers, meeting career goals, and recognizing and surmounting anticipated barriers to those goals (Granrose, 1985). It is also important for women to be realistic in coordinating childbearing and career plans.

For women to get ahead on the job, all of the previous guidelines for surviving in the work place are applicable. Several additional guidelines, however, need to be noted. In her book, *Taking Stock: A Women's Guide to Corporate Success*, Sharie Crain (1977) described a number of stereotypes that male bosses hold concerning female employees. One is that female employees simply want to do their job from nine to five and then go home to their family, rather than make sacrifices for their careers. One way of counteracting this stereotype is to communicate clearly to your boss your goals and expectations with respect to working overtime, traveling on company business, taking courses, and even relocating to another city. Another commonly held stereotype is that "it's the woman's job to make coffee" and to do other such "caretaking" tasks. Both men and women are more likely to hand out potentially demeaning jobs to female employees than to male ones. Getting coffee is not in and of itself a humbling experience. It's demeaning only if it's a case of **gender-role stereotyping.** If the boss sometimes gets coffee for you, and you sometimes get coffee for the boss, depending upon who's busy at the time, then that would be a perfectly reasonable arrangement. It's important to keep things in proper perspective and not to overreact. Don't respond immediately to the task itself. Wait until it's clear that the task is *not* normal treatment for men in the same position. If being asked to perform a task is clearly a case of gender-role stereotyping, then follow the guidelines described previously for immediately confronting a negative behavior.

gender-role stereotyping
Having expectations or making assumptions about an individual based on gender, rather than on the basis of ability and/or job characteristics of a particular position.

Box 12-5

SOME FACTS AND FICTIONS ABOUT WOMEN IN THE WORK PLACE

During the past decade, the earnings gap between men and women has decreased. That's *fact*, but progress is extremely slow. In 1983, women who worked full-time earned 67 percent of men's earnings. In 1988, they earned 70 percent of men's earnings. Moreover, in a number of occupations, there has been little or no progress in wage equity between women and men performing the same job (Rukeyser et al., 1988). In managerial and professional occupations, for example, women earned 69.1 percent of men's salaries in 1983. By 1988, women earned 69.8 percent of men's incomes in those occupations (*Statistical Abstract of the United States*, 1990).

Male and female managers are about equally accessible to their employees (for guidance, direction, and so forth on the job). This is *fiction*. One study indicated that female managers were approximately *twice as accessible* to their employees as were their male counterparts (as reported in Duetsch, 1984). In general, the female managers were more likely than the male managers to leave their offices to see if their employees needed them, and to encourage their employees to seek them out.

During the past 15 years, women have made dramatic strides in entering nontraditional occupational fields (those labeled as jobs for men based on tradition rather than job content). This is largely *fiction*. Although the number of women entering nontraditional fields has increased during the last decade, women continue to be concentrated in low-skilled, lower paying jobs and clustered in the "pink collar"

jobs (Couchman & Peck, 1987). During the late 1980s, 98 percent of all secretaries, 97 percent of all child-workers, 95 percent of all registered nurses, 91 percent of all sewing machine operators, and 85 percent of all restaurant servers were women (Van Fossen & Beck, 1991). On the other hand, women make up less than 2 percent of the corporate officers of *Fortune 500* companies (Morrison & Von Glinow, 1990).

Women will be the major source of new workers in the American economy during the 1990s. That's *fact*. Women are expected to comprise two of every three entrants into the work force until 1995 (Choate & Linger, 1986).

Career plans of the majority of college women in the 1980s were altered by child rearing. That's *fiction*. Research indicated that child rearing plans were altered because of career plans more often than the reverse (Granrose, 1985).

Female workers are more likely than male workers to take unscheduled breaks on the job (to talk on the telephone, socialize at work, repair makeup, and the like). That's *fiction*. Researchers observed male and female workers in various organizations to assess the time spent in unscheduled breaks as well as in scheduled breaks (such as coffee time). On the average, male workers spent 11 percent of their working time in nonwork activities (scheduled and unscheduled) while female workers spent 8 percent of their workday in scheduled and unscheduled breaks (as reported in Deutsch, 1984).

Another potentially difficult issue for women is sexual harassment. Although sexual harassment can be a problem for men, it's much more likely to be encountered by women. Guidelines on sexual harassment issued by the U.S. Equal Employment Opportunity Commission (as described by Deutsch, 1984) stipulate that sexual harassment is a form of illegal sex discrimination. In addition to a physical act against an employee, it can include verbal abuse, unwelcome sexual advances, and any conduct that creates an "intimidating, hostile, or offensive working environment." The key phrases are that the alleged conduct be *sexual in nature* and *unwelcome* (Deutsch, 1984). An important first step for women in dealing with potential sexual harassment is to have a clear understanding in their own minds as to what is considered acceptable and unacceptable behavior on the part of a boss or male employee. Following the guidelines for responsible assertiveness, you should clearly indicate to the potential offender your full understanding of your job responsibilities, the extent to which you appreciate his support and behavior as a boss or coworker, and the behavior that is unacceptable. If you cannot bring yourself to confront the individual, you might consider clearly explaining your concerns in a personal letter. If it later becomes necessary for you to file a complaint, such a letter might constitute valuable evidence. Additional information on sexual harassment can be obtained from Working Women's Institute, 593 Park Avenue, New York, NY 10021.

SUMMARY

■ An important first step in choosing a career is to conduct a careful self-examination to enable you to identify those things that you're good at and enjoy doing. Choosing an occupation that gives you an opportunity to capitalize on your strengths and values will greatly increase your chances of earning a living by doing something that you will enjoy.

■ After your self-assessment, you need to obtain information on alternative careers that might be suitable for you. Useful activities include visiting a career resource center, obtaining career information from such sources as the *Occupational Outlook Handbook*, talking to your professors, obtaining part-time or summer work experience in potential career areas, and interviewing people in various occupations.

■ After you have made some career choices, you must prepare a' resumé and cover letter, and then identify potential employers. Valuable activities to locate job opportunities include seeking help from family members, relatives, and friends; talking to your instructors; following up on summer positions; registering with a college placement center; and registering with the state employment office.

■ After obtaining suitable job opportunities, you must prepare for the interview. Appropriate steps include learning about the company and its interview process, preparing a list of potential questions and answers, preparing a list of questions you want to ask, and practicing interviewing with a friend.

■ After obtaining a job, you should take steps to start off on the right foot, and to make yourself as valuable as possible to the firm. You should learn everything you can about the organization in which you work, the details of your own particular duties and responsibilities, and how they fit in with the goals of the organization. You should know precisely what it is that you are expected to do and exactly how your performance will be assessed.

■ An important component of surviving in the work place is to learn to communicate effectively. Subskills of effective communication include developing listening skills, giving information and instructions, giving criticism, disagreeing without being disagreeable, accepting criticism, and giving compliments.

■ Another strategy for surviving in the work place is to learn to deal with your boss. You should learn about the boss's responsibilities in order to put yourself in a more valuable position with her or him, use the boss's preferred style of communication, keep your boss informed of your ongoing projects and objectives, prepare ahead of time for meetings with the boss, and give the boss feedback about his or her behavior.

■ Special issues confronting women in the work place are job discrimination and sexism. All of us have a role in working toward the day that women will be treated equally.

Box 12-6

SELF-ADJUSTMENT FOR STUDENTS:
RELAPSE PREVENTION

By now, you will hopefully have achieved some success in your program of self-adjustment. Hopefully, you have not yet experienced a *relapse*—a return to the unwanted behavior at approximately the same rate that it occurred before your program was initiated. Unfortunately, however, relapses are common in self-adjustment programs (Marlatt, 1982). A strategy in preventing relapses is to recognize their possible causes and to take steps to minimize them. Some of the more common reasons for relapse in self-adjustment programs, and possible ways to avoid them, are described below.

A DRASTIC SHORT-TERM CHANGE IN LIVING CONDITIONS

John faithfully followed his exercise program for a month and a half but then didn't exercise for two weeks straight while on a motor-home trip. The complete change in routine, the duties each night in the campground, and other factors took their toll. Unfortunately, after returning from his vacation, he had adapted to "life without exercise" and found it difficult to reinitiate his program.

   If you anticipate a short-term change in living conditions, include a continuation of your self-adjustment as part of your planning. Possibilities include temporarily changing your support group (so that you will receive support in the new environment), modifying your adjustment program so that you continue at least part although not necessarily all of your program in the new environment, and signing a contract with your support group to provide extra reinforcers for you contingent upon

successful maintenance of self-adjustment when you return to the old environment.

FAILURE TO INCORPORATE EVERYDAY REWARDS INTO YOUR PROGRAM

Many people begin self-adjustment programs with a great deal of enthusiasm. The extra work involved in recording and graphing, charting progress, maintaining a contract with friends, and rearranging the environment don't seem all that burdensome at first. But to ensure long-term success, it's important that successful self-adjustment be tied in with naturally occurring everyday rewards. Consider, for example, the problem of structuring a fitness program so that exercising leads to natural rewards in daily activities. Some people ride their exercise bike or run in place on their mini-trampoline while watching their favorite television program. Another person we know loves watching movies on his VCR and rents movies a minimum of four nights a week. He signed a contract with his wife that he would watch a movie on the VCR only if he first walked to the rental store to pick up the movie—a distance of approximately one and one-half miles. How can you incorporate natural daily rewards into the support of your successful self-adjustment?

NEGATIVE SELF-TALK ABOUT HOW DIFFICULT IT IS TO STICK TO THE PROGRAM

When people attempt to change, they are bound to encounter stumbling blocks, In such situations, negative self-talk can exacerbate the problem and may lead to a relapse. For example, people who have difficulty dieting often say things to themselves like "I'm famished" or "I'll never make it to dinner so I'll have a little snack to tide myself over." That type of self-talk is a cue to eat.

What kinds of negative self-talk might you experience that could lead to a relapse? For each example that you can think of, identify desirable alternative self-talk that might have the opposite effect. Dieters, for example, when a little bit hungry, might tell themselves things like "I'm a little bit hungry, but I'm not starving. The people in Ethiopia—*they're* starving" or "Feeling a little bit hungry will give me a chance to build my character and prove that I have some willpower."

Failure to Recognize Setback Situations

Many smokers claim that smoking helps them to relax, especially if they are feeling a little anxious or are under stress. For a smoker who is trying to quit, a situation where that person might experience stress is a likely situation for a setback, a situation where the person will want a cigarette. Many overweight people eat when they are emotionally upset. When such individuals attempt to diet, becoming emotional is likely to cause a setback. A common cause of relapses in self-adjustment programs is a failure to recognize setback situations—situations where one is at high risk for returning to earlier unwanted behavior patterns. A strategy for you to prevent relapse is to identify your own setback situ-

ations and to take steps to cope with them. If becoming emotionally upset could cause you to experience a relapse, for example, you might practice the emotion control strategies described in Chapters 4 and 15. If drinking alcoholic beverages in social situations is likely to cause a relapse, then try experimenting with available nonalcoholic wines and beers. The more that you can recognize setback situations before they are encountered, the better are your chances for coping with them.

Overreaction to Occasional Setbacks

Leroy, after two weeks of no smoking, smokes a cigarette at a party. Francis, following ten days of successful dieting, has a triple topping sundae at the ice cream parlor. Very few people achieve successful self-adjustment without experiencing an occasional setback. But remember that a setback is not a relapse. A relapse means returning to the unwanted behavior at the same rate that it originally occurred. A common mistake of many people on self-adjustment programs is to dwell on the few occasions when they experience setbacks, rather than emphasizing the many occasions when they have stuck to their program. If you suffer a setback, chalk it up to a bad day. But don't dwell on it. Instead, review the previous days of that particular week when you followed your self-adjustment program. Use your successes to set new goals and to make a renewed commitment to stick to your program.

MEMORY BOOSTER

■ IMPORTANT TERMS

Be prepared to define the following terms (located in the margins of this chapter). Where appropriate, be prepared to describe examples.

Baby Boom	Constructive Criticism
Vocational Interest Test	Positive Strokes or ''Warm Fuzzies''
Strong–Campbell Interest Inventory	General Praise
Resumé	Prescriptive Praise
Performance Appraisal	A Golden Rule for Managing Your Boss
''Trait'' Performance Appraisals	''Readers''
Behavioral Performance Appraisals	''Listeners''
Behavioral Observation Scale	Gender-Role Stereotyping

■ QUESTIONS FROM IMPORTANT IDEAS IN THIS CHAPTER

1. Describe the steps typically followed in the development of vocational interest tests.
2. What factors might lead to a negative evaluation on a job interview?
3. What can you do to make a job interview a success?
4. Briefly describe the different kinds of performance appraisal systems.
5. What are some barriers to and some components of effective listening?
6. Describe four important components of giving instructions effectively.
7. Constructive criticism: How should you give it? And how should you accept it?
8. What are some facts and fictions about women in the work place?

chapter

13

PSYCHOLOGICAL DISORDERS

CHAPTER OUTLINE

After reading this chapter, you should be able to:
- Define the characteristics of abnormal behavior.
- Describe three models of abnormal behavior.
- Explain how the major categories of abnormal behavior are diagnosed.
- Differentiate among several subtypes of anxiety disorder, two major types of mood disorder, and several subtypes of somatoform disorder.
- Describe the usual features of schizophrenic behavior.
- Differentiate among several subtypes of dissociative disorder.
- Describe the major features of antisocial personality disorder.
- Summarize, in a general way, causes of the various psychological disorders.

Morton doesn't want to get out of bed in the morning. He never feels like going to work. When he gets home at night he only wants to be by himself. He goes to bed early, but he's still exhausted when he gets up in the morning. He knows he feels depressed but he can't seem to do anything about it. It's as though a heavy weight is grinding him down. He knows he should find help but he doesn't really believe that anyone can make him feel much better for very long. Lately, he's thought about going to sleep and never waking up—ever.

In the above example, personal adjustment is obviously necessary, yet Morton is unable to help himself. Most people would agree that his behavior is "abnormal." In this chapter we define what is meant by abnormal behavior. Such behavior has always been of interest to society in general because it is usually very upsetting. We also discuss how serious behavior problems are classified, and we define and illustrate examples of some of the most serious psychological problems.

Defining Abnormal Behavior

exhibitionism

Public display of the genitals (usually by males) to unwitting and unwilling observers.

Do you know abnormal behavior when you see it? A behavior that is rare may appear different and in that sense, abnormal. Consider for example **exhibitionism,** or in common language, *flashing.* One reason flashing may be considered abnormal behavior is because it is statistically unlikely in most people's experience. The statistically low probability of abnormal behavior helps to define it, but low probability is insufficient by itself to complete the definition. A particular behavior such as flashing may occur fairly frequently in a particular population (such as to females sitting in parks in large cities) and we would still want to call it abnormal. And there are many low-probability behaviors that we would not want to call abnormal.

A second reason a behavior may be considered abnormal is because it is startlingly inappropriate to the situation in which it occurs. Baring the genitals during a medical examination doesn't faze the doctor who asks you to do it. Flashing the cashier in the checkout line of your local supermarket has quite a different effect.

A third reason we recognize abnormal behavior concerns our desire to see it stopped. Behavior that we call abnormal usually occurs in circumstances where it will be punished. Exhibiting one's genitals in the park, in front of the bus stop, or in

Different environments and occasions where somewhat similar behaviors are and are not considered abnormal.

front of the schoolyard will attract official attention, eventually. (Exhibitionism has always been a male problem behavior. Women have not been known to be flashers.) In other circumstances, however, exhibitionism may be rewarded. In our liberated society, it is not abnormal for male go-go dancers, displaying considerable anatomy, to dance in bars. The patrons of such performances are primarily female and they reward such behavior with their presence, and their dollars. Under these conditions exhibitionism is not abnormal.

A fourth reason we call behavior abnormal is if it occurs too frequently for the norms implicit to our society. This is particularly the case for behaviors that may be self-damaging if performed excessively, such as substance abuse. You may not be thought abnormal for getting a little loaded at a fraternity party. However, your behavior is abnormal if you get drunk or high on a daily basis.

Fifth, behavior is also judged to be abnormal if it is perceived by ourselves and others to be maladaptive. By maladaptive behavior we mean behavior that appears to be voluntarily generated which interferes with our social functioning. Excessive use of drugs such that their effects interfere with our daily functioning, or aspects of our personalities that lead us to behave in particular ways would qualify under this definition of abnormal behavior.

Finally, our own behavior may be extremely distressing to us personally, and, yet, we may feel powerless to change it. We may be extremely troubled without anyone else knowing—a personal definition of abnormal behavior. We may perceive that we don't feel good or that we are experiencing thoughts that we cannot control or that our behavior is crazy and we are unable to stop it. Such feelings are often associated with depression and with the anxiety disorders (about which more below).

In sum, we are likely to define a behavior as abnormal if it is statistically unlikely, if it occurs too frequently for a society's norms, if it is startling due to its occurrence in inappropriate circumstances, if we find it socially unacceptable and want it stopped, if it is maladaptive, and if we find it personally troubling.

Now that we know what abnormal behavior is, let's see how much of it exists and how much of a problem it is for our society.

Mental Illness: A Substantial Problem

Did you know that in 1981 there were more than 200,000 people in mental hospitals in the United States? That's approximately one in 1,000 people. This means that there is a fair chance that you know someone who has problem behavior serious enough to require hospitalization. Another measure of the extent to which we are touched by abnormal behavior is evident in a tally of state and county mental hospitals, private mental hospitals, general hospitals with psychiatric units, Veterans Administration hospitals, and free-standing psychiatric outpatient service units in the United States, all of which provide services for people with problem behavior. In 1987, there were about 5,000 such facilities. There is probably one or more of these institutions fairly close to where you live.

It is estimated that anywhere from a fifth to one third of the American population has sought help at some time in their lives for a psychological problem (Regier et al., 1984; Robins et al., 1984). The kinds of behavioral difficulties that people report the most and how often these difficulties occur in the population are shown in Figure 13-1. You can see that problems stemming from substance abuse and dependence are most frequent. These are followed by difficulties with general and specific fears (phobias, panic) and by emotional difficulties such as depression. We'll define and discuss these terms below. The figures show that abnormal behavior is a substantial problem for our society.

Today we are likely to call those who exhibit abnormal behavior "mentally ill." Are they really ill? Why do we use these particular words to describe them? In order to understand why we use these particular words to describe people who behave abnormally, we need to look briefly at history. There we will see that the cultural context has a great deal to do with our choice of words—indeed, our very thinking—about the causes and treatments of abnormal behavior.

Mental Illness: What Is It?

A Little History

Throughout history, people have answered this fundamental question in very different ways. Ten thousand years ago, if you suffered from what we now call a psychological disorder, other members of your culture might have removed a portion of your skull to release the evil spirits causing your problem.

Figure 13-1

The prevalence of selected psychological disorders in the United States. You can do some arithmetic here yourself. Consider that the American population is 250 million and multiply the percentage of each of the bars by the population size. You can see that each of these computations results in large numbers. *From Robins et al., 1984.*

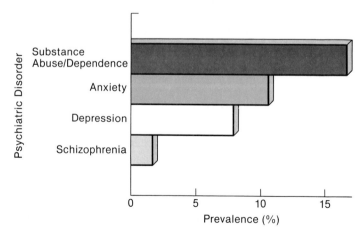

In ancient Greece, people would have assumed you had an imbalance in what they believed were the main elements of the body: blood, phlegm, and bile. Your problem would have been treated with a special diet, rest, and warm mineral baths to induce relaxation.

If you acted crazily in medieval Europe, fellow citizens might have assumed you were engaging in sacrilegious witchcraft or were possessed by demons, and "cured" you with exorcism and other "remedies" aimed at purging you of those evil spirits. Moreover, considerable sexuality pervaded these actions. According to the *Malleus Maleficarum,* the authoritative text of the time on the detection and purging of witches, a witch was to be "stripped, with her pubic hair shaved, before presentation to the judges, so that demons could not have a place to hide" (Zax & Cowan, 1976, pp. 40–41).

With the Reformation and the rise in arts and sciences and their attendant humanism, people who exhibited unusual behavior were gradually treated more humanely. In nineteenth-century America, the deplorable conditions prevailing in mental asylums and other institutions were reported by Dorothea Dix. By this time people were thought less often to be possessed by spirits. The nineteenth century was also the time of Louis Pasteur, a French chemist. Pasteur's research showed that there were microscopic entities that could grow in foods and other substances. His work led to the **germ theory of medicine.** People who were ill exhibited *symptoms* of their illness. Treatment of the symptoms alone was not sufficient to produce a cure; the physician had to treat the underlying cause. The body came to be known as a place where wars between germs and germ fighters occurred. If the germ fighters (for example, white blood cells; antibodies) won, the person got better, or was *cured.* If the germ fighters lost, the person stayed *sick* or *ill.*

So how does the germ theory of medicine apply to the psychology of abnormal behavior? As you can see from the above, the treatment of abnormal behavior historically follows from what people think causes the abnormal behavior—too much bile, loss of soul, or possession by spirits, for instance. According to the germ theory of medicine—which provides a context within which to view abnormal behavior—abnormal behavior is conceptualized as an illness to be cured.

From the germ theory of medicine have evolved several modern ways to view abnormal behavior. We'll examine three of these ways to set the context for our discussion of the kinds and varieties of abnormal behaviors and the current methods of treatment of abnormal behavior.

germ theory of medicine

The theory that disease is constituted by the intrusion of pathological substances (for example, bacteria, or viruses) into the body which produce overt symptoms of distress.

The Intra-psychic Model of Abnormal Behavior

It was Freud who first sought to understand and to treat abnormal behavior by applying the germ theory of medicine. However, Freud made some changes to fit his own thinking about the reasons for abnormal behavior. We now call Freud's adaptation of the germ theory of medicine, the **intra-psychic model of abnormal behavior** (Craighead et al., 1976). Recall that Freud thought personality disturbances were responsible for abnormal behavior (Chapter 2). These disturbances, he believed, were the result of happenings within (intra-) the mind (psyche). Any abnormal behavior was merely a symptom of the underlying problem in the personality, just as your scratchy throat is a symptom of an infection in your body. And because it was only a symptom, the abnormal behavior itself was not treated directly. In the same way that a physician would not treat someone's pneumonia symptoms but would treat the underlying disease, Freud sought to treat the underlying personality disturbance.

intra-psychic model of abnormal behavior

Abnormal behavior model in which behavior is a symptom of an underlying (hypothetical) personality system.

The Biological Model of Abnormal Behavior

A second adaptation of the germ theory of medicine is to seek the causes of abnormal behavior in human biology such as in the physiological systems of the body, in the systems that produce and use hormones and other chemicals, and in the functioning of the nervous systems, including the brain. Current work in the biological model of abnormal behavior involves a search of genetic structures for genetic abnormalities which may relate to abnormal behavior (Kennedy et al., 1988; Sherrington et al., 1988), and in the manufacture of drugs which produce temporary changes in our nervous systems. Like the germ theory of medicine, this model looks on abnormal behavior as symptomatic of other problems—in this case biological problems.

Socio-behavioral Models of Abnormal Behavior

Socio-behavioral models of abnormal behavior consider abnormal behavior to be related to the same events that are assumed to cause all behavior and that these events are found in three different domains: our biology and its expression; our lifelong history of experience (past environments); and what is happening in our current environments, including what is going on within our skins, that is, what we sense, think, and feel (Bandura, 1977; Skinner, 1974). This model borrows from the germ theory of medicine its belief in the importance of biology to behavior. The emphases on past and present environments come from experimental psychology which has shown how important these two domains are to behavior, and from psychologists like Freud who understood the importance of past experiences.

So, what should we believe about how to conceptualize the reasons for abnormal behavior? Personality? Biology? Biology, learning history, and current environment? It turns out to be a matter of emphasis. All behavior can be thought of as the result of interactions between our biology and the past and present environments in which it is expressed. Thus, both our biology and our past and present environments are responsible for behavior, including abnormal behavior. How much each of these domains is responsible for behavior is another story and the subject of research and controversy.

Given this interactional approach we can expect to see explanations of and treatment for abnormal behavior rooted in both biology and environment. In the next chapter we'll see how this interactional approach is applied to helping people who exhibit abnormal behavior. But before we do that, we need to explore how abnormal behavior is classified and then to explore some of the major types of abnormal behavior.

Classifying Abnormal Behaviors

When you visit your physician with a sore throat, you are generally quite relieved when the doctor says, "It looks as though you have a streptococcus infection. I'll prescribe some penicillin for you." Related to curing the strep infection are two important outcomes of your visit: First, the doctor can accurately identify what's wrong with you; and second, she or he can prescribe an effective course of treatment, known to work, say, 99 percent of the time. Effective treatment follows identification and labeling of your physical problem.

But what does this have to do with abnormal behavior? In the same way, psychologists and psychiatrists would like to examine you and say, "It sounds as though you are agoraphobic," and then have some specific treatment in mind for your agoraphobia—a fear of getting into places from which you cannot easily escape or in which you can't get help—which would work 99 percent of the time.

Unfortunately, in the real world, diagnosing and treating psychological disorders isn't that easy. And it isn't that easy for two main reasons: The first is that in psychology, we don't yet have as good a model to explain behavior as medicine has, for example, to explain infectious diseases. This is why, in the foregoing section, we could only generally say that biology, past experiences, and present environments explain abnormal behavior. As yet psychology is not advanced enough as a science to say how much of each of these three domains contributes to any particular abnormal behavior.

The second reason is that, because we don't know how each of these domains contributes to any particular abnormal behavior, we cannot easily categorize the behavior as belonging to one category of abnormality rather than another. When an individual utters statements that are obviously lies which reflect his or her beliefs, but which are not true (that is, they are delusions), is the individual schizophrenic? Or is the person in the manic phase of bipolar disorder? These behaviors can be observed in both these categories. Which one should they belong to?

So what has been the solution? One solution is a standard reference, a kind of dictionary or manual that helps define varieties of abnormal behavior. Such definitions are arrived at by consensus, in the absence of a complete model of abnormal behavior. This dictionary or manual is called the *Diagnostic and Statistical Manual of Mental Disorders* and is published by the American Psychiatric Association.

The *DSM's*

Actually there have been four of these manuals, called *DSM's* for short: *DSM-I, DSM-II, DSM-III,* and *DSM-III-R* (R is for *Revised*), and a fifth is planned. These manuals define mental "illnesses" or "disorders" for the American health professions. Each disorder is meticulously described, both what behaviors should be observed to diagnose a particular disorder, and what should not be observed, for example, if the particular constellation of behaviors should fit wholly in another category, or if the behaviors partially overlap with another category, as in our example above.

The *DSM* is useful to the practicing psychiatrist and psychologist because it aids in the classification and identification of the patient's psychological disorder. Once such identification is made, then the kind of treatment the patient requires should follow.

WHY SO MANY *DSM's*? You may wonder why there have been continued revisions of these manuals, and one answer is fairly obvious. The field keeps developing and "new" disorders are defined. A less obvious answer is the fact that the health professionals behind these revisions do not always agree on the precise definitions and classifications of some of these disorders, and the revisions reflect changes in the thinking of the committees who rewrite the manuals. As an example, in the beginning editions, the manuals gave intra-psychic explanations for particular disorders. Subsequent editions were more behavioral because intra-psychic explanations of behavior became less popular.

DSM-III-R

Diagnostic and Statistical Manual of Mental Disorders (3rd ed., rev.); a publication of the American Psychiatric Association which contains the most current psychiatric disorders, and which is used for diagnostic purposes by psychiatrists and psychologists.

The current **DSM-III-R** provides essential and correlated features of particular psychological disorders along with ages of onset, course of the disorders, impairments, complications, predisposing factors, prevalence, sex ratios, familial patterns and requirements for differential diagnosis. Moreover, the system in the *DSM-III-R* is multiaxial, meaning that a clinician evaluates each client according to not just one but five different factors or axes (hence, multiaxial).

MYTHS AND LABELS. There are those who believe that there is little to be gained from labeling and categorization like that in the *DSM's*, and a great deal to be lost (Szasz, 1960; 1987). One difficulty with labels is the extra baggage they always seem to carry. Once labeled as schizophrenic, for example, you may always be considered schizophrenic even if you are currently well. It is true that many schizophren-

TABLE 13-1
A SUMMARY OF THE *DSM-III-R* CLASSIFICATION OF ABNORMAL BEHAVIORS *Adapted from the DSM-III-R.*

Major Clinical Syndromes

Disorders Usually First Evident in Infancy, Childhood, or Adolescence

This category contains problem behavior that usually appears before biological maturation. It includes disorders such as childhood autism, attention deficit disorder, gender identity disorder, mental retardation, and the disorders of elimination (encopresis; enuresis).

Organic Mental Disorders

This category contains problem behavior associated with tissue damage in the brain either chemically induced or from unknown causes. Cocaine dependence is an example of the former, and Alzheimer's disease is an example of the latter.

Psychoactive Substance Use Disorders

Problem behavior falls in this diagnostic category if alcohol or drugs are used maladaptively to the extent that such use interferes with individuals' lives.

Schizophrenia

This is a disorder of thought in which the individual's total behavior is grossly disorganized. Verbal behavior in particular is often fragmented, delusional, and hallucinatory.

Delusional (Paranoid) Disorder

The individual's verbal behavior is delusional, most often paranoid, that is, suspicious (without good reason). While this paranoia is also a symptom of schizophrenia, individuals diagnosed with delusional disorder do not usually have other symptoms of schizophrenia.

Psychotic Disorders Not Elsewhere Classified

This is a category in which individuals are classified if their symptoms fit the psychotic disorders but the six months' presence of the problem behaviors necessary to define a psychotic disorder is not met.

Mood Disorders

These are disorders of the emotions, and principally refer to the set of emotional feelings called depression, and to the temporal swings between depression and mania called bipolar disorder.

Anxiety Disorders

These are disorders characterized by fear/anxiety that result in physiological changes such as sweaty hands, dizziness, or heart palpitations, and the escape and avoidance of situations where the fear is likely to occur. The fears are strong enough that they interfere with the individual's life. The fears run the gamut from very specific ones (called phobias) to diffuse anxiety that may pervade all of an individual's life.

Somatoform Disorders

Individuals who are characterized as having a somatoform disorder feel physically ill in the absence of organic signs that they are ill. Chronic pain where no physical cause for pain can be found, constitutes an example of a somatoform disorder.

Dissociative Disorders

These individuals usually have a loss of memory, or the inability to identify themselves. Or they may exhibit several distinct personalities in which one personality may not be aware of the others (multiple personality). Consequently, these are disorders of consciousness.

Sexual Disorders

The sexual disorders are classed three different ways: (1) those in which the problem is perceived to be a gender identity disorder (Chapter 7); (2) the paraphilias in which unusual stimuli control sexual arousal (for example, the fetishes); and (3) sexual dysfunctions where the major problem is the inability to perform sexually (for nonorganic reasons). We examined sexual dysfunctions in Chapter 7.

Sleep Disorders

The sleep disorders include insomnia (not being able to sleep), sleepwalking, and sleep terrors.

Factitious Disorders

Individuals so diagnosed feign illness or psychological symptoms.

TABLE 13-1 (Continued)

Impulse Control Disorders

This category covers a wide range of behaviors, all of which are characterized by poor self-control. Self-control problems may be exhibited in pathological gambling or stealing (where survival is not involved). They may also be exhibited in fire setting, hair pulling (trichotillomania), and uncontrollable outbursts of swearing, tantrums, and violent activity (intermittent explosive disorder).

Adjustment Disorder

These are disorders that are abnormal reactions to changes in daily life. They are characterized by an individual's failure to react appropriately to identifiable life stressors (for example, loss of employment) that have occurred in the past three months. Reactions may encompass the entire range of emotional and psychotic behaviors but at less than the full-blown intensity required for diagnosis in another category.

Psychological Factors Affecting Physical Condition

Individuals diagnosed in this category have experienced life stressors which appear to relate to a physical condition, such as in stress-induced hypertension.

TABLE 13-2
THE MULTIAXIAL SYSTEM OF DIAGNOSIS OF THE *DSM-III-R*

One way the *DSM-III-R* encourages clinicians to make a careful, sensitive, and accurate diagnosis is by assessing each case according to not one but five key factors (axes).

Axis I: Major Clinical Syndromes

The clinician first decides where the client is located in the 16 major categories of Table 13-1. This is accomplished through observation, formal assessment, and interview. For example, the clinician may decide that the individual is schizophrenic and provides a number code that equates to schizophrenia. A particular type of schizophrenia may also be subcoded—that is, given a further identifying number.

Axis II: Personality and Developmental Disorders

This axis is coded in two distinct ways. Number codes on this axis either modify and provide additional information on the category selected in Axis I, or they indicate a major personality or developmental disorder (such as mental retardation).

Axis III: Physical Disorders and Conditions

Individuals who have psychological disorders also sometimes have accompanying physical conditions (for example, diabetes) which may or may not be related to their psychological problems. Such conditions are coded on this axis to foster understanding of any physical conditions that might contribute to an individual's psychological problem, and affect treatment.

Axis IV: Severity of Psychosocial Stressors

Psychological problems almost always respond negatively to stress. This is *not* to say that psychological problems are caused by stress, but many seem to be worsened by it. On this axis the stress in an individual's environment is rated (from 1 = None to 6 = Catastrophic) so that some feeling can be gained as to how much of a particular psychological problem may be stress related, and how well treatment might proceed in the presence of such stressors. Catastrophic stressors include events such as a devastating natural disaster in which loved ones are killed or your home is destroyed.

Axis V: Global Assessment of Functioning Scale

On this axis a rating of the individual's overall function is attempted in regards to both current function and the best function the individual has shown the previous 12 months. The individual is rated on a scale which runs from being nearly free of symptoms and functioning well, to serious impairment, impaired understanding of reality, and whether or not the individual is a danger to self or others.

ics don't get well while others cycle in and out of periods where their behavior looks more or less schizophrenic. In the jargon of the trade, a well schizophrenic is a schizophrenic, *in remission.* This means that you're still considered to be schizophrenic but that you're not currently exhibiting schizophrenic behavior. You can imagine the effect of such a label on someone who is actually never going to act

Box 13-1

In his delightful book, *Pure Types Are Rare: Myths and Meanings of Madness*, in which he challenges current psychiatric thinking, Silverman (1983) describes an encounter he had as a fledgling graduate student. In his words:

> I recall a silent, scowling, middle-aged patient . . . who spent most of the day in the same armchair in a corner of the dayroom [in the mental hospital] within view of the television set and who communicated mainly by gestures and grunts. He was called *catatonic schizophrenic*, and though the immobility and mutism that characterizes this disorder was certainly not as blatant in this case as in my textbook illustrations, it sufficed for me, until I happened on the ward late one evening to find him chatting amiably with his roommate.

"The catatonic speaks," I said bursting into my supervisor's office the next morning. "He just doesn't talk around us."

"We know that." He grinned at me.

"Then he's not catatonic, is he?" I was truly puzzled.

"He's catatonic enough." He shrugged. "Pure types are rare. Besides, what else would we call him?" (Silverman, 1983, p. 3)

A catatonic schizophrenic in a typical attitude. Such a position may be held for a long time.

The point is that so-called textbook cases may be just that: found primarily in textbooks.

schizophrenically again (and such people do exist), when they apply for employment or otherwise have to identify their health history. This is particularly a problem when a psychological label encompasses a wide range of behavior, as it does in schizophrenia.

The theoretical opinions and labels of psychiatrists count heavily in the diagnosis of abnormal behavior, because the criteria for psychiatric classification are arrived at by consensus—and in the world of mental health, a psychiatrist's opinions are more equal than others' opinions. Our own opinion (we're licensed, practicing psychologists as well as teachers) is that people do act crazy—put in your own adjective/adverb: different, funny, strange, weird—on occasion. Some act crazy on many occasions. Sometimes they need help to not act crazy. But, from the perspective of a practical model of adjustment, we assume that such people behave differently not because their behavior is driven by underlying entities as in the germ theory of medicine, but because their behavior is a result of their social-behavioral history, their current situation, and their genes.

Some Major Psychological Disorders

In the material that follows, we'll look at some of the major psychological disorders classified in the *DSM-III-R* and at some of the current explanations for their occurrence. It would take an entire book—a *DSM* in itself—to examine all abnormal behavior, so we will start with some psychological disorders that practicing psychologists regularly encounter and proceed to others that are more rare. You may well know someone who has had to cope with one or more of the disorders below.

Anxiety Disorders: Problems with Fears

A great number of people are afraid of various events in their lives (see Figure 13–1). They may be uncomfortable camping because they are afraid of being mauled by bears. Or they are afraid of skiing down a steep hill. These are ordinary fears in the sense that we all have some of them. Interestingly, these types of fears may not stop us from engaging in the feared behaviors: We camp in an area frequented by bears, but we're a little uncomfortable (and we hang up our food); or we ski down a steep hill to avoid being called "chicken" by our acquaintances. If the experiences are good, we may be a little less afraid of similar situations in the future.

But there are individuals whose lives are changed by such fears because their fear stops them from behaving in a way that is important to their lives. There are a wide range of such fears from those highly specific to particular objects or events (snakes, blood, airplanes) to a generalized anxiety over everything. If such fears incapacitate an individual in some way, these fears are classed as anxiety disorders.

There are several subclassifications of anxiety disorder. The most important ones follow.

panic

A dreadful experience in which a person feels chest pain, heart palpitations, choking, and/or other sensations that occur suddenly and lead one to attempt to escape the situation in which these changes occur.

PANIC.   The mythical god, Pan, was said to sleep by the roadside. If disturbed by passersby he would let out a bloodcurling scream, so frightening that it scared some to death. Intense fright has become known as **panic** (Barlow, 1988). Today any four or more of the following symptoms that occur in a brief period of time (less than ten minutes) define panic: shortness of breath (or smothering), choking, palpitations or racing of the heart, chest pain or discomfort, sweating, faintness, dizziness (lightheadedness), depersonalization (feeling detached from one's body), nausea or abdominal distress, numbness or tingling sensations, flushes or chills, trembling or shaking, fear of dying, and fear of going crazy or doing some-

There are many events that are fearful to some people (the photo shows an example). Whether or not such fears interfere with a person's life depends largely on how often an individual must confront the anxiety-provoking situation. A fear of snakes, for example, wouldn't affect your life too much if you lived in a large city. But consider how incapacitated you would be in a large city if you were afraid of small, enclosed spaces such as elevators.

thing uncontrolled (American Psychiatric Association, 1987). You can see that experiencing these events together would be very distressing—especially since attacks of panic are typically sudden, unexpected, and forceful.

Panic is first usually reported by individuals in their twenties and typically lasts for years (if untreated). A person who experiences panic may go through periods of time free of panic alternating with periods of frequent panic attacks. Individuals with panic disorder are more likely to attempt to commit suicide than those with no psychological disorder (Johnson et al., 1990).

PANIC AND AGORAPHOBIA. Consider 31-year-old Dennis, an insurance salesman (Oltmanns et al., 1986). He experienced a panic attack while Christmas shopping with his wife. He suddenly felt sick; his hands trembled uncontrollably; his vision blurred; he felt weak; and he felt chest pressure that led him to believe he was going to smother. He became very fearful and escaped to their car where his wife eventually found him. His panic attacks—two or three per year—were unpredictable. Because some attacks had occurred while driving, Dennis would only drive in the right-hand lane so that he could easily pull onto the road's shoulder if necessary. He dreaded long bridges where pulling over would be problematic. Other attacks had occurred at social occasions which he subsequently avoided. Dennis lived many years with this problem before he sought professional help.

You can see from Dennis' example that panic can become associated with other events. For Dennis driving was among these events. A very common theme in this disorder is the fear of any situation from which there is perceived to be no escape. Such fear is called **agoraphobia.** Individuals with agoraphobia and panic will often not go into places where they perceive that help will not be available should they panic. In a sense, agoraphobia is a fear of panic; agoraphobics feel an intense, disabling dread at the thought of having a panic attack especially away from the safety of home or a trusted person. People with agoraphobia commonly avoid anxiety-provoking situations such as crowded city streets, restaurants, malls, shops, subways, bridges, and expressways. Normal life becomes a struggle for many, some of whom will go outside only with a trusted companion. A portion of agoraphobics become totally housebound in their efforts to avoid any situation that they fear may cause panic. Dennis' panic and agoraphobia ruined his marriage and his social life before he sought treatment.

agoraphobia
Fear of public or open places in which a person feels that there is no escape or help should a panic attack occur.

SOCIAL PHOBIA. Individuals with social phobias have a great fear of situations in which they may be scrutinized by others (Leibowitz et al., 1985). More specifically, these individuals fear they will be embarrassed or humiliated by their own actions in public, or by the judgment of others. For individuals with a social phobia, common activities like eating in a public restaurant, using public restrooms, and writing or speaking in front of others can provoke severe anxiety. Alcoholism and depression are often seen with social phobia (Leibowitz et al., 1985).

SIMPLE PHOBIA. We can all relate to simple phobias because most of us have some. These are fears that exist to highly specific stimuli, like the fear of particular animals, of the sight of blood, of closed spaces, or of flying. The main features of such phobias are heightened fear when confronted with the phobic stimulus (for example, the small enclosed space of an elevator) and the escape and avoidance of such stimuli (you take the stairs instead of the elevator—whether your destination is three flights up or thirty).

POST-TRAUMATIC STRESS DISORDER. Samuel Pepys, seventeenth-century English diarist, witnessed the Great Fire of London in 1666. This fire produced substantial loss of life and property, destruction, and disorganization in that city. Pepys chronicled it all. Six months after the fire, he wrote, "[I]t is strange to think how to this very day I cannot sleep a night without great terrors of fire; and this very night

---

Box 13-2

FLEEING, FIGHTING, FAINTING, FREEZING, AND SURVIVAL

Some of what appear to be phobic responses, for example, escaping from a fear-producing situation, may actually be very adaptive ways in which we automatically cope with life-threatening events. From the perspective of survival, these "phobic" responses are anything but disordered.

FLEEING AND FIGHTING

We are not all that many generations away from a time when it was important to be fearful of being eaten by a wild animal. While today's threats to our well-being are different (at least in our own society), our physical responses to stress and fear are not. Most animals (us included) will flee a threat but, if cornered, will fight. Both of these responses which could be thought of as "phobic" appear to promote survival.

FAINTING

Fainting is not often described as a survival response, but it may very well be one. A response to attack, injury, and blood loss that produced the lowered blood pressure and heart rate of a faint would surely have been adaptive in minimizing shock and increasing survival chances if one had been at-

tacked and were bleeding. Perhaps this response is still present in people who faint at the sight of blood (Barlow, 1988).

FREEZING

Some animals faint so completely that they appear to be paralyzed with fear. This is called *tonic immobility*, a paralysis of the limbs in the absence of nerve damage (Gallup, 1974). While this has not been thought to be a response of humans, reports from women who have been brutally raped suggest otherwise (Suarez & Gallup, 1979). These women report a sudden inability to move, tremors of the limbs, an inability to vocalize, numbness to pain, feeling cold, and a just-as-sudden recovery of the ability to move, and the ability to attack their attacker at the termination of the act. This sequence of behaviors closely parallels those observed in animals. Barlow notes wisely that recognition of the possibility of tonic immobility in humans would prevent tragic and erroneous interpretations by authorities who lean toward acquiescence as the alternative explanation for not fighting a rapist (Barlow, 1988). Tonic immobility may be adaptive in preventing further physical injury in an already violent encounter.

---

could not sleep to almost two in the morning through thoughts of fire" (quoted in Daly, 1983, p. 66). Pepys was almost assuredly suffering post-traumatic stress disorder (PTSD).

If you or someone you know has been raped, served in combat, or survived some other trauma such as work-related exposure to toxic substances (Schottenfeld & Cullen, 1985), you probably don't require a definition of this disorder. This is fear caused by very traumatic experience. Individuals with PTSD continually relive their trauma either through dreams or repeated intrusive thoughts. These individuals also experience psychological numbing, or a reduced responsiveness to the world. Sufferers of PTSD attempt to avoid any reminders of their original trauma and often feel intense anxiety in any situations associated with the traumatic event. Some Vietnam vets, for example, have felt they must avoid war movies, and women who have been raped are sometimes afraid to walk on streets similar to one where their attack occurred. While PTSD can occur immediately after a trauma, sometimes symptoms of this disorder don't surface until months or years after the initial, terrifying event.

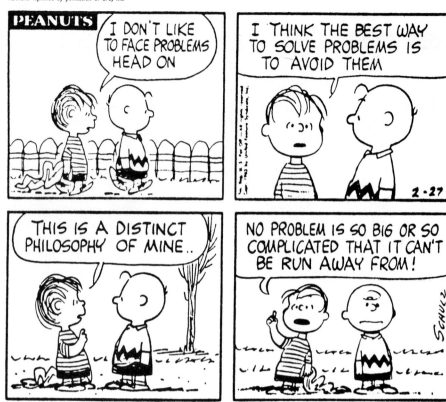

GENERALIZED ANXIETY DISORDER.   Individuals suffering from generalized anxiety disorder experience continuous, diffuse anxiety that attaches to at least two—and generally more—specific life circumstances. In generalized anxiety disorder, an individual feels an ongoing sense of anxiety and dread—worrying about finances, anxious that a loved one may die or be injured, or anticipating various catastrophes. An individual with this disorder feels restless, is easily fatigued, and may have shortness of breath, palpitations, trouble swallowing, and nausea or diarrhea. Other physical signs of this disorder include muscular tension, autonomic hyperactivity (pounding heart, dizziness, sweating), irritability, edginess, and trouble concentrating. These feelings can be disruptive and clearly are unpleasant, but generalized anxiety is rarely incapacitating. Most individuals with this disorder just go through life being anxious. As such, generalized anxiety disorder often is not brought to the attention of a psychologist or psychiatrist. Instead, many people suffering generalized anxiety visit their physicians who prescribe mild tranquilizers.

OBSESSIVE-COMPULSIVE DISORDER (OCD).   One night while lying in bed you wonder, "Have I locked all the doors and windows?" To reduce your worry you check them all and find that you did. You relax and go to sleep. Fairly normal, right?

On the other hand, let's say that within minutes after checking everything once, you think that you may have missed a window, and you begin to worry again. Once more you get up, and find that everything is securely locked. Still pretty normal, right?

But what if this cycle repeats itself over and over again? What if hours later you still find yourself repeatedly checking all of your doors and windows because you are convinced you may have left one open, and you are afraid. And what if this happens every night? You cannot sleep at night because you spend all of your time

Box 13-3

THE SEVERITY OF OBSESSIVE-COMPULSIVE RITUALS

To appreciate just how debilitating obsessive-compulsive rituals can be, note the following case summaries:

1. Cleaning Ritual:

A 30-year old male presented with fears of being contaminated by touching various objects he considered dirty. He had to cover various "dirty objects" with paper towels before he was able to touch them. If, however, he did happen to touch his laundry, his bed, door handles in public restrooms, his shoes, the gas cap on his car, or other "dirty" objects, he experienced vague feelings of dirtiness and discomfort, and he would engage in extensive washing of his hands, along with any clothing he believed had come into contact with the object. The patient kept one hand "clean" at all times and refused to place this hand in his trousers pocket or to use it to shake hands. As a result of these OCD [obsessive-compulsive disorder] symptoms, the patient was unable to work full time because of avoidance behaviors, and his social life dwindled because he spent several hours each day engaged in cleaning.

2. Checking Ritual:

A 50-year-old female patient engaged in repetitive checking behaviors when she was not sure whether she had performed an action correctly. As an example, she would plug and unplug electrical appliances 20 times or more to be sure that she actually took the plug out of the socket. She would do the same with light switches, turning them on and off repeatedly to ensure that she had in fact turned them off. She stared at the address on envelopes for up to several minutes to ensure that she had seen her name on the envelope. She counted money over and over, and her arithmetic required so many recalculations that she totally avoided financial paperwork and could no longer work in her previous job as a bookkeeper. The patient was no longer able to read because she continually returned to sentences she had already read because she was not sure she had actually seen them.

From Baer & Jenike, 1986, p. 5.

You can see that such behavior would very much interfere with normal functioning. While such rituals may seem silly when they are read silently like this, and it may seem as though it would be easy to instruct the individual simply to stop, doing so makes them feel extraordinarily anxious. Most don't stop without treatment.

---

checking. (Not so normal now.) You're afraid to go to sleep, each morning you're exhausted, and you become more and more run down until you lose your job because of poor performance.

This is called **compulsive behavior**—behavior that is repeated over and over again, eventually eating up the time that an individual needs to spend on other important things like going to work, sleeping, and socializing. The most common compulsive behaviors are those that involve cleaning rituals (for example, excessive hand washing) or checking rituals (for example, repeatedly checking that appliances are turned off or that doors are locked). Individuals with these compulsions are called "cleaners" and "checkers" in the jargon of the trade.

Compulsive behavior often occurs in response to **obsessional behavior** which is recurrent thoughts, impulses, or ideas that intrude in an individual's mind. These invasive, recurring thoughts are often horrific to the individual experiencing them (for example, repeated thoughts of killing one's own child). While most people experience an occasional horrific thought (about a frustrating boss, teacher, or sibling, for example), those fleeting thoughts don't constitute obsessional behavior. Similarly, like many people you may recognize elements of compulsive behavior in your own actions, such as checking your car door two or three times to be

compulsive behavior

Overt behaviors that are repetitively performed and which the individual cannot easily suppress; they usually involve rituals (for example, repeated hand washing) that the individual thinks will avoid perceived aversive stimulation (for example, contamination).

obsessional behavior

Recurring, persistent, or disturbing thoughts which resist the individual's attempts to suppress them.

Howard Hughes, movie mogul, millionaire, playboy—and sufferer from obsessive-compulsive disorder. Hughes became heavily preoccupied with dirt and germs, terrified that he would be contaminated by other people and by touching ordinary everyday objects like a spoon or a piece of paper. Hughes' solution was to isolate himself in a penthouse suite in a Las Vegas hotel where the environment was designed to be as sterile as possible. Unlike most people with OCD, Howard Hughes had sufficient wealth to construct an entire staffed, private world that catered to his disorder. His protectors had detailed procedural manuals to follow with respect to his food and other objects brought to him. Everything was to be handled through layers of Kleenex. Hughes is reported to have demanded that three copies of any newspaper be brought to him. He could then select the middle one which was unlikely to have been touched by anyone else.

sure it's locked. But such actions don't indicate a disorder unless they interfere with your normal life.

Obsessive-compulsive disorder (OCD), the label for this combination of behaviors, was once thought to be rare. Now it is thought that as many as 2 percent of Americans are afflicted—4 to 6 million people. The problem usually begins in late adolescence, although there is now some evidence of these behaviors in children (Rapoport, 1989). Children who exhibit obsessive-compulsive behaviors often become adults who exhibit obsessive-compulsive behaviors.

Interestingly, OCD sufferers know that they are behaving illogically, that there is no compelling reason for carrying out their time-consuming ritual behavior. This awareness, however, does not enable people with OCD to stop their compulsive actions. Historically, this was called the *neurotic paradox* (Mowrer, 1950).

THE CAUSES OF ANXIETY.   In Chapter 4 we discussed an important cause of a simple anxiety reaction—the presentation of an aversive stimulus. But an anxiety disorder is much more complex than a simple, single anxiety reaction. With anxiety disorders, as with most of the psychological disorders we will discuss, their causes cannot be easily indicated. Moreover, it is rare that a single cause can be isolated. Rather, there are usually a collection of potential factors associated with the disorder. You will further see that the potential causes divide themselves into the various domains of the models that are used to explain abnormal behavior.

For the anxiety disorders, some biological factors appear to be indicated. For example, anxiety disorders tend to run in families (Noyes et al., 1987; Torgersen, 1983), while individuals with obsessive-compulsive disorder show changes in the brain in the same area that is associated with diseases of repetitive motion like Parkinson's and Sydenham's chorea (Rapoport, 1989). They also show signs of central nervous system dysfunction such as problems in fine-motor coordination (Hollander et al., 1990). Also biologically, as discussed in Chapter 3, our history as a species may make us more likely to develop fears to some stimuli (snakes; blood) rather than others—so-called *preparedness* (Seligman, 1971; McNally, 1987).

It is also possible to conceptualize anxiety responses as conditioned fear responses developed via reflexive learning and the avoidance and escape of anxiety-producing events as developed by operant learning (McAllister et al., 1986), particularly to those stimuli we are prepared to fear (see Chapters 3 and 4). The evidence of a role for experience seems especially clear with respect to post-traumatic stress disorder, which develops as a function of exposure to environmental events. Yet, not every phobic can recall an earlier traumatic event (Marks, 1987). However, in all of the anxiety disorders, there may be a case for observational learning. For example, children may acquire the fears of their parents and their peers simply by observing how those individuals deal with (or fail to deal with) traumatic events.

At the same time though, the field must explain how it is that some individuals can be exposed to traumatic events and not become anxious or phobic while others may be exposed to events that are fairly ordinary and become phobic of them. A speculative answer is that the anxiety disorders are due to all three of the factors we mentioned above: genetic susceptibility including a particular biology, learning experiences both general and specific, and the current environment. Notably, this will be a conclusion you will see again.

Mood Disorders: Problems with Emotional State

Consider these words: *feeling down, blue, dejected, low, unhappy, sorrowful, melancholy, despairing, gloomy, heavyhearted, dispirited, sad.* Quite a number of them, aren't there? Why so many words to describe one set of feelings? Possibly because it is with words like these that people have struggled to describe an overwhelmingly bleak and debilitating emotional state—a state that is not, unfortunately, uncommon in human experience. **Depression** is one of the mood disorders, prolonged emotional states that color your perception of the world. We'll look at two types of mood disorder, major depression and bipolar disorder.

depression
A disturbance of mood of long-standing duration characterized by dejection, sadness, and lethargy.

MAJOR DEPRESSION.   Consider the case of Leslie, a 38-year-old overweight, married woman (Atwood & Chester, 1987). Leslie felt that her husband was worthless—he made too little money, lacked ambition, and failed to satisfy her sexually. Leslie looked sad—she walked slowly and sighed frequently. She accomplished little during her days, sometimes not getting dressed for a week at a time because she didn't have the energy. And, she reasoned, who would care if she did anyway?

Many people suffer from depression. Several famous people who have been described as sufferers are shown below.

She felt that there was no place worth going and no one worth seeing. Her husband fed these feelings because he long since had accepted her argument that he had failed her. Life weighed heavily upon her. She felt trapped by people who had failed her.

As with Leslie, individuals who experience major depression feel worthless, unable to accomplish even the smallest task. Sometimes their sleep patterns are seriously disturbed, either shortened or lengthened. Some depressed individuals may have no interest in food whatsoever, while others may have increased appetites. Most feel chronically fatigued and hopeless, with no energy and no interest in pleasurable activities. Concentration on any activity is difficult. Seriously depressed individuals may not speak much, and they are often indecisive. They are more likely than individuals without psychological disorders to attempt suicide (Johnson et al., 1990). Leslie came to therapy thinking that her problem was her indecisiveness about getting a divorce (Atwood & Chester, 1987). Major depression may arise slowly over weeks in unnoticed fashion; eventually it interferes with life.

Blue Monday Is Not Depression.   The fact that you don't like Mondays and would rather stay in bed than go to work or school doesn't mean you are depressed. People who are depressed have episodes that, if untreated, can last for months. The blues we all feel occasionally are usually normal reactions to life's stresses—reactions that we find are gone in a day or two. Even grief is a normal reaction. Although the sadness and the sudden emptiness produced by a loss of a loved one are severe, for most of us grief resolves in a matter of weeks or months, and it does so seemingly automatically. Depression does not necessarily resolve automatically.

BIPOLAR DISORDER: RIDING THE MOOD PENDULUM.   Henry was admitted to a psychiatric hospital because he had not come out of his room at home for two months (Atwood & Chester, 1987). He seemed passive, tearful, and hopeless. However, this was not the Henry that the hospital staff eventually had trouble with. Henry, who was 250 pounds and 6 feet, 3 inches tall would get angry every few months and destroy hospital property. His behavior seemed to vacillate back and forth. On the one hand, there were periods when he felt the world had rejected him and during which, to avoid humiliation, he would withdraw. On the other hand, during his up or manic periods, he could hold a job, live on his own, and to all appearances be successful and ambitious. However, Henry's manic periods would end with rage toward his mother and family, leading to property destruction which necessitated further hospitalization.

Henry is an individual whose moods vacillate back and forth across the months. An individual who is depressed for a long period of time and returns to normal between depressions is labeled as **unipolar.** Individuals like Henry alternate between periods of depression and **mania** and have **bipolar disorder.** During mania such individuals may exhibit a much greater than ordinary amount of energy. They may sleep very little but never feel tired, talk incessantly, claim to feel fantastic, be intolerant of interruptions in their speech, seem self-confident beyond belief, and even claim to know things they can't possibly know. Finally, they may focus heavily on activity in one area such as their occupation, their sexual relations, their politics, or their religion. Manic individuals can feel so sociable that they call at any time of the night without understanding the feelings of those friends they have dragged out of bed (American Psychiatric Association, 1987).

Mania usually begins abruptly and it may last from only a few days to months. Manic individuals may have to be protected from themselves because their high activity rates and impaired judgments put themselves and others in physical danger. When mania ends, it is usually followed by deep depression. For Henry, after his

unipolar depression
Depression wherein the mood swing includes feelings of inadequacy, personal withdrawal, increased sleeping, and diminished work productivity and attention.

mania
An agitated state characterized by abnormally high energy, inflated self-esteem, and extreme activity.

bipolar disorder
Depression in which mood swings include both depressed mood and a manic phase; during manic phase the individual may exhibit considerable self-esteem, unbridled socializing, decreased sleeping, increased productivity, and expanded attention.

Composer George Frederich Handel composed prolifically during what were probably periods of near mania. He completed the *Messiah* in only three weeks of virtually continuous composition and a month later completed another long work.

mania, he was no longer invigorated, he had no ambition, no initiative, and no energy. He became the avoidant, passive little boy, fearful of the world, and over-powered by it, which characterized his depressive periods (Atwood & Chester, 1987).

THE CAUSES OF DEPRESSION.   Mood disorders such as these are seen usually in early adulthood, although we know now that children can and do experience depression. Moreover, the likelihood of major depression is one in four in the lifetime of a woman, while it is one in ten in the lifetime of a man (*Science*, August 15, 1986, p. 723). Why this difference? No one knows but we suspect that it is related to women's traditional gender role in which they are subordinated to men. Interestingly, bipolar disorder is seen about equally often in each sex.

Although many studies have examined depression, we are still unable to say what causes this mood disorder. Researchers have, however, identified several key factors, that relate to depression.

Heredity.   Both unipolar and bipolar depression tend to run in families. If, for example, your mother was clinically depressed, you stand a statistically greater chance of experiencing depression than if your mother had no history of depression. But this doesn't mean that heredity *causes* depression—many children of depressed parents live their lives free of the disorder.

The Brain's Chemistry.   Researchers have searched for differences in brain chemistry that may help to explain depression. These brain-chemistry models concern either surpluses or deficits of particular chemicals (such as sodium) or hormones (such as steroid and thyroid) that relate to brain function. While these

Box 13-4
Are You Depressed?

Please read each of the statements below and indicate the extent of your agreement or disagreement with each item by placing the appropriate number in the spaces provided. The numbers mean:

1 I disagree completely.
2 I disagree slightly.
3 I am neutral about this statement.
4 I agree slightly.
5 I agree completely.

There are no right or wrong answers. Please respond to each item. Scoring for this inventory can be found below.

_____ 1. Much unhappiness is externally caused or created by outside persons and events.

_____ 2. People who sincerely try to find the meaning of life are likely to find it if they keep at it.

_____ 3. Considering the blatant and widespread sexism in our society, it is unlikely that any concerned woman can be truly happy.

_____ 4. Everyone needs the love and approval of those persons who are important to them.

_____ 5. Some people could not be happy living in a small town or a large city because some of the things they need are not available there.

_____ 6. Most people spend so much time at things they *have to* do that they have little time left to do the things they *want to* do.

_____ 7. There are some people in this world who can truly be described as rotten.

_____ 8. Because parents or society taught acceptance of certain traditions, one must go on accepting these traditions.

_____ 9. It is natural to get upset by the errors and stupidities of others.

_____ 10. Incompetence in anything whatsoever is an indication that a person is inadequate or valueless.

_____ 11. If things are not the way one would like them to be, it is a catastrophe.

_____ 12. The racial problems in this country are terrible, and it is horrible that solutions have not been found.

_____ 13. A person should try and excel at some things.

_____ 14. Given the kind of home life some people have had, it is almost impossible for them ever to be happy.

_____ 15. Punishing oneself for all errors will help prevent future mistakes.

_____ 16. What others think of you is most important.

_____ 17. Persons living in slum conditions are almost certain to feel depressed or miserable.

_____ 18. Love and success are two basic human needs.

_____ 19. There is invariably a right, precise, and perfect solution to human problems and it is catastrophic when this perfect solution isn't found.

_____ 20. Avoiding life's difficulties and self-responsibilities is easier than facing them.

_____ 21. Because a certain thing once strongly affected one's life, it should indefinitely affect it.

_____ 22. The main goal and purpose of life is achievement and success.

_____ 23. The political situation in our country is awful; our leaders should lead more honest lives than they do.

_____ 24. One should try to change if other persons dislike him or her.

_____ 25. Failure at something one really wants to do is terrible.

_____ 26. Depending on others is better than depending on oneself.

_____ 27. People really can't help it when they feel angry, depressed, or guilty.

_____ 28. An adult must be approved of or loved by almost everyone for almost everything he or she does.

_____ 29. Because a person was once weak and helpless, he or she must always remain so.

_____ 30. One should blame oneself severely for all mistakes and wrongdoings.

From Muñoz, 1977.

Scoring the Personal Beliefs Inventory

The Personal Beliefs Inventory is easily scored. Simply add your score for each item and get a total for all 30 items. This total must be between 30 and 150. Then divide by 30. This will give you an average score for each item somewhere between 1 and 5. Muñoz found that a sample of clinically depressed patients produced an average score of 2.93, while the average score for a nondepressed group was about 2.60 (Muñoz, 1977). Thus, if your average score is around 2.5, you can infer that you are not depressed.

brain-chemistry models are intriguing, no single one can, alone, fully explain depression (Whybrow et al., 1984).

The Environment.   The environment is thought to be implicated in depression. People with depression may learn that their behavior is ineffective in producing environmental change (called *learned helplessness*) and that this feeling of ineffectiveness is akin to depression (Seligman, 1975). Or depression could be the result of extinction for behavior that is ordinarily rewarded either because the behavior is inappropriate or because the reward has lost its potency (Lewinsohn & Hoberman, 1982). And it has been suggested that an individual's negative and irrational thinking causes depression. It is well known that depressed individuals are negative about themselves, their experiences, and their futures (Beck et al., 1979; Ellis & Harper, 1975). Leslie's reaction to her husband is a case in point: "She would think: 'Poor me, I'm married to such a boring, useless person. Other women are married to romantic, interesting men' " (Atwood & Chester, 1987; p. 7). She further thought no one cared what she did. And she worried about all of her physical imperfections. This type of very low self-esteem is typical of depressive thinking.

Our summary with respect to the causes of depression is very similar to that for the anxiety disorders. First, biology is implicated a couple of ways: There appears to be a genetic component, and there may be changes in the brain either as a cause or as a result of depression. Secondly, there are roles for one's past experiences and for the current environment, especially if the current environment contains stress and negative thinking.

Somatoform Disorders

Physicians are not infrequently visited by patients with multiple complaints about their bodies—the way they hurt, the way they sound, the way they feel, the way they aren't working right. Often the doctor can find nothing physically wrong. Moreover, the patient usually relates that these problems have been around a long time, and multiple doctors have been consulted over the years. Possibly these patients exhibit a somatoform disorder.

This group of disorders is characterized by physical complaints for which there is no independent evidence of an organic or physiological nature. For example, in *somatoform pain* disorder, an individual may complain of being in severe pain, but physical examinations fail to turn up physiological reasons for the pain reported. **Hypochondriasis** describes an individual who repeatedly interprets relatively normal body symptoms as indicative of serious physical disorder (Meyer, 1989). Often hypochondriacal individuals have a history of experience with others who are ill. **Conversion disorder** is diagnosed when individuals exhibit a specific loss of physical function that appears to relate to psychological conflict in their lives. A limb may be "paralyzed," or the individual may be "blind" or may have no feeling in one hand (that is, glove anesthesia). On the other hand, *somatization disorder* may be diagnosed when the individual has chronic multiple somatic complaints that are often vague and exaggerated.

THE CAUSES OF SOMATOFORM DISORDERS.   There does not seem to be any role for genetics in the somatoform disorders (Torgersen, 1986). It is possible, however, that brain function is implicated in conversion disorder (Davison & Neale, 1990). Interestingly, conversion disorder is seen less now in developed countries than it is in third world countries, suggesting socio-cultural factors. Where conversion disorder is seen in developed countries it is more likely to be associated with the lower socioeconomic classes where religion is strong and fundamentalist (Proctor, 1958). People who become hysterical easily also seem to be more susceptible to somatoform disorders (Nemiah, 1985).

hypochondriasis
Psychological disorder characterized by a patient's enduring belief that he or she has a serious illness in the absence of supportive physical evidence.

conversion disorder
Psychological disorder characterized by loss of body function (such as paralysis of a limb) in the absence of supportive physical evidence.

People with hypochondriasis may be hypersensitive to what is going on in their bodies (Barsky et al., 1988). They appear to be more sensitive to noise, heat/cold, and hunger as examples. How do individuals become hypochondriacs? No one knows, but given that hypochondriacal individuals are supersensitive to their body's sensations, a plausible account involves learning to identify subtle body sensations. This could occur via childhood and other experiences in which one learns to respond to questions such as, "Don't you feel well?" with reference to a particular body sensation (Lipowski, 1988). Notably, hypochondriacs do not fear getting sick; they are convinced that they are already sick (Meyer, 1989). It is thought that a great many people who have this problem never see a psychologist. The obvious reason, of course, follows from the fact that they are convinced that they are physically sick. Why see a psychologist?

Schizophrenic Disorders: Problems with Thoughts

Margaret's schizophrenic behavior appeared when she was in high school. She reported to school officials that her psychology teacher was inserting obscene thoughts into her head (Oltmanns et al., 1986). Even after seeing the school counselor, Margaret still felt that the obscene thoughts were neither her own nor under her control. She was very agitated by the fact that school officials did not report her psychology teacher to the police. After this and some other incidents her parents had Margaret admitted to a private psychiatric facility.

An examination of Margaret's verbal behavior upon the occasion of a subsequent hospital admission showed it to contain auditory hallucinations, delusional thinking, and formal thought disorder. Some of these behaviors can be seen in a sample from her intake interview:

PSYCHIATRIST: Do you ever hear voices saying things about you?

MARGARET: I had a dream once about the television one night at school. Walter Cronkite said John Lennon was dead. Sometimes I dream about television. I'm not a fairy am I?

PSYCHIATRIST: No.

MARGARET: Fairies don't go to heaven, do they?

PSYCHIATRIST: What do you mean by a fairy?

MARGARET: I had a dream once that there was a small red door in our kitchen, and I walked through the door with my brother, and I said to my brother, "I'm going to the bathroom." I was going to run away from the house . . . and there was a dog barking outside, a police dog. So I suppose I was arrested.

PSYCHIATRIST: Were you?

MARGARET: Yes, they did arrest me, didn't they?

PSYCHIATRIST: I don't know. What do you remember about it?

MARGARET: I don't know . . . (laughs) . . . My brother says he's under arrest for my dinner.

PSYCHIATRIST: For your dinner? What does that mean? It sounds kind of silly.

MARGARET: Yeah . . . I almost got mad. I'm not jealous of my brother, you know. He's very happy. I heard two voices talking one night. It sounded like two saints in my bedroom saying, "She's going to have the baby tonight." I think my counselor delivered a baby of mine. Do you think I caused John Lennon's death by committing adultery? (Oltmanns et al., 1986, pp. 247–248)

schizophrenia

Psychological disorder in which a patient shows disconnected verbal behavior, delusions, hallucinations, and maintenance of extreme body postures.

You can see that Margaret's train of thought jumps around, that she reports hearing voices talking about her, and that her emotions are inappropriate to the interview situation. Because of these symptomatic behaviors Margaret was diagnosed as schizophrenic. Schizophrenia is the most widely used diagnosis in mental hospitals—about half of all people admitted are so diagnosed. **Schizophrenia** means literally split (schiz) mind (phrenia), but should be understood as meaning a separation of thought from logic and a separation of thought from emotion.

Schizophrenics such as Margaret report being controlled by God or by inner voices (Oltmanns et al., 1986). They may also report a different reality from normal people, even when they are in symptom-free periods. During these times they appear to be more sensitive to their inner experiences which may contain rotated and distorted images of the environment in which color is strong (Hurlburt, 1990). Possibly the more schizophrenic they are the more such images appear as their only reality. (See Table 13-3.)

WHAT HAPPENS TO SCHIZOPHRENICS?   Most individuals become schizophrenic during adolescence or early adulthood, but onset in midlife and later is possible. Ciompi (1980) studied 228 patients diagnosed as schizophrenic, and the majority of these patients had been schizophrenic for 35 years. About half the patients had *acute onset* (that is, all at once), and about half had *insidious onset* (that is, symptoms appeared gradually). In the midcourse of the disorder, for about half, the schizophrenia remained continuously present. For the other half, it was episodic. In the late course of the disorder, for about half, the result was moderate to severe disability. For the other half, it was mild disability or full recovery. This study suggests that the course and outcome of schizophrenia vary widely across patients (Warner, 1985).

Our case example, Margaret, was a schizophrenic whose schizophrenic behaviors were episodic. Antipsychotic medication, which we'll discuss more fully in the next chapter, would usually help decrease her delusional behavior and her

TABLE 13-3
SOME KEY FEATURES OF SCHIZOPHRENIA *Adapted from Kraepelin, 1919.*

These features of schizophrenia were first identified many years ago but are still used today.

1. *Hallucinations.* These are reactions to events occurring within the body. More than likely hallucinations involve a failure to discriminate the source of the event as coming from within the body (Bentall, 1990). Patients may complain of hearing voices whispering unpleasant things. Some patients feel that their own thoughts are being broadcast aloud. Others feel that they have to perform whatever actions the voices specify. Still others may claim to see people who are not present.

2. *Delusions.* Delusions are statements that patients make that are not true. *Delusions of paranoia* are those statements that imply that the patients harbor unreasonable suspicions—believing that they are being spied on, for example, or that others are plotting against them. There may be *delusions of guilt* in which the patient believes he or she has led a sinful life. There are often *delusions of grandeur:* The patient says that he is a famous personality, inventor, performer, or politician. In *thought transference*, the patient may claim to know the thoughts of other people.

3. *Thought Problems.* The patient may be unable to say much about any subject, so-called *poverty of thought.* The patient may lose the logical ordering of thought and may jump from subject to subject, so-called *loose associations.* The patient may be *incoherent*, that is, not understandable. And finally, the patient may not be able to continue a particular line of discourse and simply stops—evidence of *thought blocking*.

Periods of very little speech in which the patient must be pressed to say even a word or two may alternate with periods in which the patient may talk incessantly. Some of the patient's speech may contain *neologisms*—nonsense words that sound like regular words, but which are not.

4. *Emotional Problems.* The schizophrenic patient often shows emotional *blunting*, that is, neither joy nor sadness but a kind of indifference to former close relations. There may be *inappropriate emotion*—the patient may laugh uncontrollably when nothing is funny. There may also be *sudden shifts of emotion* for no apparent reason.

5. *Other Problems.* Schizophrenics will often brook no interference with themselves—they are very *negative*. They appear to shut themselves off from the world (*autism*), they have no drive to work, and their judgment is impaired.

hallucinations in a few weeks. However, for a variety of reasons when outside of the hospital, Margaret would not take her medication consistently. Usually this discontinuation of medication would lead to a subsequent relapse within months of the discontinuation (Oltmanns et al., 1986).

THE CAUSES OF SCHIZOPHRENIA.   There is no known single cause of schizophrenia. However, we can point to a number of events that are related to this disorder's occurrence.

Inheritance.   There is some evidence that heredity plays a role in the occurrence of schizophrenia. People who have schizophrenic relatives are at greater risk than people with no schizophrenic family members. The risk rises the closer the affected relative. Naturally, then, it is highest for children whose (biological) parents are both schizophrenic, and for identical twins whose twin brother or sister is schizophrenic. If an identical twin is diagnosed as schizophrenic, there is close to a 50 percent chance of the other twin developing this disorder. Since about 50 percent of identical twins in this situation will not develop schizophrenia, however, it seems clear that heredity alone cannot account for this disorder.

The Brain's Chemistry.   There has been much speculation that chemical changes of some kind in the brain may cause schizophrenia. Chemical change theories have focused on neurotransmitters—those substances responsible for the transmission of signals from one nerve to another. There is a variety of evidence for chemical change theories. First, the schizophrenic-like behavior of those who occasionally ingest too much of various street drugs such as angel dust (PCP) or lysergic acid (LSD) or the hallucinations induced by wild mushrooms like psilocybin used by certain Native American cultures in their religious rituals look very much like the behaviors exhibited by those who are schizophrenic. Second, such drugs are known to interact with normally occurring neurotransmitters. Third, there are drugs that reduce schizophrenic symptoms in the short term and these are also related to the action sites of neurotransmitters. Another possibility is that normal neurotransmitters are chemically changed in the schizophrenic into hallucinogenic drugs such as mescaline, LSD, and psilocybin. Many of these hallucinogenic drugs are similar in their chemical structures to the neurotransmitters with which they are known to interact. Indeed, that's how the effects of such drugs are produced.

And there are more such chemical change theories that involve hormones, proteins, and slow-acting viruses. The very existence of so many of these brain chemistry theories testifies to the inadequacy of any one of them as a complete explanation of schizophrenia.

The Brain's Structure.   There is some evidence that injuries to the limbic system of the brain (which regulates emotional behavior) exist in many chronic, institutionalized schizophrenics (Gray et al., 1991; Stevens, 1982), and some cerebral atrophy (that is, shrinking of the brain), too (Weinburger et al., 1982). However, it is impossible to know whether these conditions lead to schizophrenia or are an outcome of it. Further, these changes do not exist in all schizophrenics.

The Brain's Functioning.   There is some evidence that schizophrenics don't filter environmental stimulation very well. In daily life, each of us is constantly surrounded by an enormous number of (potential) stimuli. Fortunately, we are able to automatically filter out most of these stimuli so that we can do just a few important things at a time: completing a sentence in conversation, for example, while bringing our car to a stop at an intersection.

Schizophrenics may be unable to selectively filter the stimuli around them; bombarded by the demands of unrelated stimuli, schizophrenics would find it difficult to focus on and complete any single thought, conversation, or task. Remember how Margaret's train of thought jumped around during her interview? This type of disordered thinking may reflect the scattered attention of the schizophrenic and may illustrate the loss of "filtering" ability that most of us have normally. Thought of in this manner, a schizophrenic's withdrawal may be a self-protective response, providing at least minimal retreat for a person overwhelmed by a world in which all stimuli leap forward to demand immediate attention.

The Environment.   There is also some evidence that implicates the environment, including family communication patterns, family emotions, and stress, particularly life event stress such as deaths of close relatives, job loss, and divorce. Schizophrenics are more likely to have grown up in families where communication was poor, where emotions were impoverished (for example, with cold, demanding parents), and where abuse occurred.

And environmental stressors are known to trigger schizophrenic episodes in those already predisposed to schizophrenia. When Margaret, who was in the hospital recovering from a schizophrenic episode, learned that her father was divorcing her mother, she immediately became more schizophrenic—talking openly about people interfering with her thoughts, threatening another patient with bodily harm, refusing food. This worsening of her behavior lasted for several days. The mystery here is that many children grow up in the atypical environments we've described, and may even have schizophrenic relatives, yet they don't develop schizophrenia.

Another group of disorders seems to produce behaviors similar to schizophrenia; however, some of these disorders involve known changes in the central nervous system. These are the organic mental disorders.

Organic Mental Disorders

organic dementias
Disturbances of thought and other behavior because of a physical change in the nervous system, usually the brain.

Shelley has been admitted to a psychiatric facility at 23 years of age. Shelley is of near average intelligence but didn't finish high school. After dropping out, she supported herself by cashiering for a local supermarket. Now she can't remember her name. She seems bewildered, as though she is waiting for instructions to do something; when she is instructed, she stares as though she is still waiting. Over the preceding months, Shelley has become withdrawn—less and less communicative with her family. She seems unable to remember past events. Her normally good judgment seems to be gone. Soon she is soiling and unable to feed herself. Across the months in the institution to which she is committed, staff report that Shelley occasionally follows instructions on workshop tasks and completes her work. At other times she is combative with the other residents or cries uncontrollably. Infrequently she will have several days in a row where she answers to her name, and wants to know where she is and why she can't go home. These periods appear spontaneously. However, they are rare events and last only a day or two. For the most part Shelley looks bewildered and is unresponsive to those around her. Shelley's diagnosis is **organic dementia**. Physical examinations reveal no known physical cause of her behavior changes. It is assumed that there has been substantive change in brain function.

A progressive change in behavior and function such as Shelley's is extremely troubling and not infrequently these changes occur, as they did for her, in the absence of any ascertainable physical pathology. Such massive changes in behavior are taken to mean that there is global brain dysfunction, hence the use of the word *organic*. The word *dementia* refers to the deterioration of cognitive function. The prognosis in a case such as Shelley's is not good. At the very least she faces lifelong institutionalized care.

There are a number of organic dementias that result from known organic changes in the brain—Alzheimer's disease seen in elderly individuals is one such type. The first sign of Alzheimer's is often the loss of the capacity to remember recent events. The affected individual may be aware of these changes and be distressed by them. As the disease progresses, however, individuals with Alzheimer's become less aware of the loss of function. As with Shelley they lose other cognitive functions as well as memory, eventually becoming mute and uncommunicative. During this deterioration they eventually fail to recognize their own families. Occasionally they may be combative. Unfortunately, there is no known cause of Alzheimer's disease and no known cure. Alzheimer's disease ends with the death of the affected individual. The prolonged period of the disease which can involve more than ten years means that there is correspondingly prolonged anguish and suffering for loved ones who can only helplessly watch the deterioration of someone they remember but who no longer remembers them.

As the last in our sample of *DSM-III-R*'s Axis 1 psychological disorders, we examine a collection of disorders characterized by selective losses of consciousness and depersonalization—the dissociative disorders.

Dissociative Disorders

While checking into a hotel in a major city, you suddenly realize that you've got someone else's wallet with his or her credit cards, and you've lost your own. You check with the manager about how to make payment and turn in the wallet. She looks at the driver's license in the wallet you give her and it has a picture on it that resembles you. You claim that it isn't you; you don't know who it is. She follows you out to the car you came in and finds out that it is registered in the same name as that on the driver's license. You don't recognize the name and don't know where you got the car from. Several other employees of the hotel all seem to think you are the person who owns the wallet and the car. But you don't recognize what must be your own name nor any of your documents. In fact you don't recall where you live. The hotel manager calls the paramedics.

Later it's found that you've never had any prior psychiatric problems. But several highly stressful events appear to have preceded your crisis. The day before your son was arrested on drug dealing charges, and you have had considerable ongoing marital problems. You're not intoxicated, and a medical exam shows nothing abnormal for your age. What has happened to you? Does this sound pretty spooky? It would be utterly bewildering to have lost most of your knowledge of yourself and your environment, wouldn't it?

PSYCHOGENIC AMNESIA.   You've all read of people who have disappeared, only to be found somewhere else with another name, and who do not recognize relatives and friends they have left behind. As did the person above, these people exhibit what is called a dissociative disorder. Dissociative disorders involve sudden disruptions or alterations of normal consciousness (Meyer, 1989) and there are several varieties. We'll look at two. Our case example above would be called **psychogenic amnesia**—a temporary loss of the ability to recall personal information. Usually this is a selective memory loss, although the media often portray the loss as complete. Frequently stressful events also appear to precede the disorder. Psychogenic means that there is no organic cause that can be pointed to. This condition is quite rare, but when it is seen, it occurs most often in adolescents and young adults who are female. Recovery from this disorder is usually fairly rapid.

psychogenic amnesia
A temporary loss of the ability to recall personal information; a selective memory loss.

MULTIPLE PERSONALITY.   Individuals with multiple personality disorder appear to have more than one distinct personality. Frequently there is selective amnesia among the personalities—one personality may not know of the existence of another. Individuals with multiple personalities show up in therapy because there are parts of their lives that don't make sense to them. Perhaps they have been accused of behaving in a way quite unlike their normal behavior. Or they have memory problems. Consider the case of Paula (Oltmanns et al., 1986). She would wake up every two or three weeks with a terrific headache as though she had a hangover, but she didn't drink. Paula was worried that occasionally the back seat of her car was replete with empty beer and whiskey bottles. She didn't know how they got there. She seemed to have severe memory problems, complaining that she lost parts of days. She often could not remember details. After having gone to bed, she would wake up driving her car. She had been sexually abused as a child by her father but could recall no details. Unknown to Paula or to her therapist, her other personality ("Sherry") called Paula's therapist to talk about Paula. Not wanting to violate Paula's right to confidentiality and without knowing the relationship between Sherry and Paula, the therapist refused to see Sherry. Then he told Paula of the call. Eventually during this therapy session, Sherry emerged along with several other distinct personalities. Sherry seemed to know about most of the other personalities, while Paula knew of none of them. Sherry seemed to be wantonly sexual; Paula was not. The initial dissociation appeared to trace to a time when Paula was raped by her father and another man. Paula psychologically disappeared from this trauma and Sherry was left with it.

While multiple personality disorder is rare, its dramatic features appear to capture the attention of the media and this may make it seem less rare. However, from 1817 through 1980, fewer than 200 cases had been reported (Boor, 1982; Winer, 1978). Most clinicians never see a true case in an entire career (Meyer,

Kenneth Bianchi and Angelo Buono known as the "Hillside Stranglers" were convicted of raping, torturing, and killing 11 young women in the Los Angeles area. Bianchi, who was tried in Washington State for the murder of two other women, pleaded not guilty by reason of insanity. He claimed to have a multiple personality and the defense produced psychiatrists to testify on his behalf. However, the prosecution hired Martin Orne, a scientific skeptical psychologist to test (and trap) Bianchi. Bianchi was hypnotized (supposedly) in order to reach his other "personality." Orne showed that Bianchi was faking hypnosis by putting him under and asking him to do two incompatible things: respond one way if he was feeling his hand touched in a particular area, and respond again when his hand was touched in another area, *which he would not feel.* Bianchi did not respond when his hand was touched in the other area. A truly hypnotized subject would have responded because instructional control over a hypnotized subject is virtually absolute. Bianchi was faking, and it could be inferred that he was therefore also faking the multiple personality that he claimed had committed murder. Both men are serving life sentences without the possibility of parole.

1989). Multiple personality disorder is observed in females anywhere from three to nine times as often as in males (Reid & Wise, 1989).

As it did with Paula, and as is the case with the other dissociative disorders, this dissociative disorder appears to follow from extremely stressful or traumatic events, particularly during childhood (Sanders & Giolas, 1991). In fact, child abuse, particularly sexual abuse, is thought to be a predisposing factor. Also, people who have multiple personality disorder seem easily able to go into spontaneous hypnotic trances (Sarason & Sarason, 1989).

Because multiple personality disorder is so rare it has received little scientific study. This makes it difficult to separate it from good acting, or from the case where someone simply has several normal "selves" that are a function of different environments. Do you act differently on Friday night than you do on Thursday? Do you act differently in a bar than you do in church? There are many normal ways in which our general behavior differs from time to time and place to place. Perhaps multiple personalities are only an extreme form of these different behavior patterns and not really distinct personalities at all (Sarason & Sarason, 1989).

With our excursion through the dissociative disorders, we bring our sample of the *DSM-III-R*'s Axis 1 disorders to a close. Next we look briefly at one type of Axis 2 disorders—the personality disorders.

Personality Disorders

Each of us responds to life's situations in a variety of ways—some of them adaptive and productive, others maladaptive and unproductive. Individuals are diagnosed with one of the personality disorders when they show chronic, pervasive, inflexible, maladaptive patterns of perceiving and responding to the environment. To qualify as a personality disorder, such perceptions and responses must be sufficiently maladaptive to cause disruption in functioning and personal distress (Meyer, 1989).

There are three groups of personality disorders. The first involves odd or eccentric behavior that may have overtones of *paranoia* such as continual suspiciousness; overtones of schizophrenia such as flat emotional expression (called *schizoid*); social isolation; and peculiarities of thought, appearance, and behavior (called *schizotypal*). Perhaps you've known someone who was the town hermit; someone who functions around the borders of a town, doesn't talk except in grunts, doesn't socialize, seems indifferent to praise, and barely acknowledges those who offer greetings. Such an individual could be diagnosed with schizoid personality disorder (Reid & Wise, 1989).

The second group of personality disorders involves dramatic, emotional, and erratic responding in four areas: the *antisocial* personality who is manipulative, exploitive, guiltless, and dishonest (more below on this character); the *borderline* personality who is chronically angry, intense, and has unstable moods and poor personal relationships; the *histrionic* personality who is seductive, requires immediate gratification, and has rapidly changing moods; and the *narcissistic* personality who is self-absorbed.

The third group of personality disordered individuals are anxious and fearful and this group also divides four ways: those who are *avoidant*—easily hurt and embarrassed, they stick to routines to avoid anxiety-provoking experiences; those who are *dependent*—wanting others to make decisions and who fear being abandoned; those who are *obsessive-compulsive*, in this case, perfectionistic, preoccupied with details, and indecisive; and those who have a *passive-aggressive* personality marked by resentment over demands and suggestions, procrastination, and deliberate inefficiency.

Many of these patterns of behavior can be recognized by the time of adolescence or early adulthood. Individuals with personality disorders will usually have trouble with employment and social relations on a continuing basis, but they don't require hospitalization for the most part. Take, for example, an individual who has been in a particular job for years and who is known to colleagues as someone who is always complaining about being passed over for promotions, who complains about the difficulty of the jobs given when everyone else thinks the jobs are about the same in difficulty, who may hold up projects because of being the last finished, and who feels that being last occurs because the job he or she did was the hardest. This person is often not moved around in a company because no one else wants to work with him or her, and this person may be frequently released from employment. Such an individual might be diagnosed with a passive-aggressive personality disorder (Reid & Wise, 1989).

Unfortunately, individuals with personality disorder are often the last to accept the fact of their behavior's effect on others. This makes them very difficult to deal with clinically.

To get a further flavor for the personality disorders, we examine one important subcategory, the antisocial personality, in more detail.

ANTISOCIAL PERSONALITY DISORDER. Do you remember the kid who frequently skipped school, was frequently in fights, and always seemed to be in trouble? Such a person may also have been a habitual liar, thief, and destroyer of property. Such a collection of behaviors in a young person has been labeled a *conduct disorder* (American Psychiatric Association, 1987). The behaviors that comprise a conduct disorder are extremely resistant to change even with the most intensive therapy (Kazdin, 1987).

What happens to such children? They may grow up to be adults who are

Garry Gilmore, murderer executed in 1977, seemed to fit the prototype of the antisocial personality.

classed as having an antisocial personality disorder. We describe the antisocial personality in some detail because this problem appears to be the best defined of the personality disorders, and because it is fairly common among those who are in trouble with the law. As the name of this disorder implies, antisocial adults are continually at odds with society—in maladaptive, often violent ways harmful to themselves and others. These adults have trouble holding a consistent job because they are repeatedly absent without reasonable explanation. They tend to be irritable and aggressive—possibly spouse and child beaters. In addition, they are often liars, impulsive, reckless, irresponsible, lack remorse, and have difficulty maintaining monogamous relationships (American Psychiatric Association, 1987).

People with antisocial personality disorder are frequently institutionalized as criminals but typically appear incapable of feeling any guilt or sorrow over their crimes. Continually drawn to violent conflict, antisocial adults are much more likely than normal to die prematurely and violently. Garry Gilmore, who was executed for murder in Utah in 1977, may be a prototypical case of antisocial personality disorder. Gilmore was in trouble with the law for car theft by the time he was 15. Above average in intelligence, he was often truant at school and was accused of stealing from his classmates. On parole from prison he was abusive to the children of the woman he was living with. He used alcohol and drugs from an early age. On parole from 11 years in the penitentiary for armed robbery, Gilmore killed two people in cold blood. Gilmore's case became notorious because he demanded to be executed before the normal course of appeals was concluded, and because at the time no one had been executed in the United States in the prior 11 years. Gilmore seemed to have no remorse or guilt over what he had done. The state of Utah met his request.

SUMMARY

- Abnormal behavior is recognized by a number of criteria: because of its startling nature due to low level of occurrence, because of its inappropriateness of time and place, because it may exceed society's norms for acceptable frequency, because we want it stopped, because we or others perceive it to be maladaptive, and/or because it is personally distressing to us. Anywhere from a fifth to a third of us will seek professional help at least once in our lifetimes for a psychological problem.

- The reason that we call individuals who have psychological problems mentally ill follows from the germ theory of medicine. Two offshoots of that model, the intra-psychic and the biological models of abnormal behavior, are currently used to describe and explain abnormal behavior. A third model of behavior, the socio-behavioral model, considers that abnormal behavior—like all behavior—is a function of our heredity (and within that domain, our biology), our lifetime of learning experiences, and our current environments.

- Abnormal behaviors are classified and categorized in the *Diagnostic and Statistical Manual of Mental Disorders* (3rd ed., revised) into major psychological disorders. Several of these major categories and their apparent causes include anxiety disorders, mood disorders, somatoform disorders, schizophrenic disorders, organic mental disorders, and dissociative disorders. Very generally, the causes for these disorders seem to run the gamut from being vulnerable by reason of heredity or sex, from having abnormal biology (the specifics of which are usually unknown but are not infrequently associated with the central nervous system), to experiences in our learning histories as children and adults, and to our current environments which may contain lots of stress. These are all disorders that are coded on Axis 1 of any diagnosis based on the *DSM-III-R*. On Axis 2, personality disorders are maladaptive, enduring ways of behaving that have some of the features of the foregoing major psychological disorders.

By now you've had some experience attempting to self-adjust a problem behavior. You could have done one of several things: (1) attempted to increase a desirable behavior; (2) attempted to decrease an undesirable behavior; (3) attempted to get a behavior to occur only at the right time and place; or (4) attempted to develop a complex skill. We hope that you've had considerable success. But more than likely, you've had some success and some failure. How can you improve the results of this project and how can you make the next self-adjustment you attempt more likely to succeed? Here are some tips on how to trouble-shoot and problem solve.

AREAS TO TROUBLE-SHOOT AND PROBLEM SOLVE

Biting Off Too Big a Chew. Many people want to accomplish too much in their first self-adjustment and this guarantees failure. A goal to become a nuclear physicist is fine, but not as the result of a single project, especially not if you've never had a course in physics nor even had college algebra. Be realistic. Bite off a very small chew for your project; that is, narrowly construe what it is that you can accomplish in the time you've got. Success will be much more likely. Let's say that you want to make up a new, prettier, or more handsome you. This makeover may have 20 or more different components. Start with one. Perhaps this is the time to stop biting and start growing nails, or to start brushing your teeth after every meal instead of once a day. Think small here and success will be more likely.

Specification of the Target Behavior. If you have difficulty knowing when your target behavior has occurred or whether a particular instance of behavior was the target behavior, then the target behavior is not specified precisely enough. Under these circumstances you should redefine the target behavior. Usually this means more "unfuzzifying." Remember, someone else should be able to use your definition and count as instances of the target

behavior exactly what you counted and nothing else. Don't worry about being too narrow in your definition. The problem usually is being too broad, too all inclusive. You can always expand the target behavior definition carefully after you meet your initial goals.

Problems with Consequences. What if your target behavior didn't increase or decrease as it was supposed to? More than likely you have a problem with the consequences for it. They are probably not functioning as you hoped they would. There are several possibilities here.

First, maybe the consequences were simply nonfunctional as reinforcers or punishers. Choose again and rethink the guidelines for selecting reinforcers in Box 9–4. Often there is simply not a large enough variety of reinforcers. Increase the variety of consequences available in your program so that when one doesn't work another one will. Also, chosen consequences may not be powerful enough. Choose stronger ones if you can.

Second, the scheduling of consequences may be wrong. There are at least two things to think about here: First, recall that to be most successful, consequences must be immediately applied upon the occurrence of the target behavior; and second, they must be appropriately scheduled. For most self-adjustment projects, this means every time the target behavior occurs. Within this framework reinforcer and punisher amounts should be small so that in the reinforcement case you won't satiate quickly and in the punishment case you won't simply avoid the entire project.

Third, have you short-circuited the reinforcement process (Martin & Pear, 1992)? This is where you reinforce even though you haven't met your criterion for reinforcement, that is, the reinforcement is essentially free—you didn't meet your weekly goal but you went out Friday night anyway. This is problematic only where you are unable to control yourself. As we have mentioned, a way

Continued

around this is to give the control of the adjustment contingencies to someone else. Let that person decide whether your target behavior has occurred and whether to dispense the appropriate consequence.

Problems with Contracts.   Often behavioral contracts are not as clearly worded as they should be. Were there arguments between you and the contract mediator? Arguments are usually a sign of lack of clarity. Clarify the contract with respect to target behavior definitions, to measurement of the target behavior, and to reinforcement processes. Did you find the contract to be fair to you? Don't sign it until you feel that it is. Did the contract reflect positive change in your behavior? Make sure that it does. Did the mediator carry out her or his part of the contract? If not, get another mediator.

Developing Complex Behavior.   The problems encountered here both overlap with the above and are exclusive to this area. We mentioned some of these in Box 10–3. If the target behavior doesn't result from your program, do more task analysis. Often the program steps will not be small enough—insert some more based on your task analysis. If you're bored, then either the program steps are too small or the reinforcement program is inadequate. If you can't get to the next step, do more task analysis and insert more steps. These intervening steps may need to raise the skill level at that particular step more thoroughly, that is, you may need to raise the criteria for accomplishing the step.

Relapses.   A relapse is the fact that you stop behaving on your program. These are going to happen, so remember that they are normal. But they don't need to signal failure. Having fallen off the wagon is only a bad deal if you don't climb back on again. Indeed, you should watch out for what is known as the *abstinence violation effect*, essentially the horrible feelings of guilt you experience for not meeting your program goals, which lead you to tell yourself that you are a total failure. You're not. To be aware of this effect is to be forearmed against it. Take personal responsibility for the relapse to get yourself in the proper frame of mind to pick back up where you left your program. Analyze why the relapse occurred. Were there reinforcers available outside the program for the absence of the target behavior? Or for other nonprogrammed behaviors? Was the reinforcement in your program not immediate, not strong enough, and not scheduled frequently enough? Did you encounter some rare events that you hadn't planned for? Insert whatever program corrections you think you need and start again. Ensure that your revised program contains some provision for relapse.

Did It All Fail?   If it did, you may have problems in your analysis of the causes of your target behavior. Reanalyze why it is that your target behavior is (or is not) occurring. Examine all of your initial premises. Wipe the slate, and start again. If the problem behavior seems too tough, it may be a signal that professional help is needed for this one (see Box 15-8).

MEMORY BOOSTER

■ IMPORTANT TERMS

Be prepared to define the following terms (located in the margins of this chapter). Where appropriate, be prepared to describe examples.

Exhibitionism	Compulsive Behavior
Germ Theory of Medicine	Obsessional Behavior
Intra-Psychic Model of Abnormal Behavior	Depression
DSM-III-R	Unipolar Depression
Panic	Mania
Agoraphobia	Bipolar Disorder

Hypochondriasis

Conversion Disorder

Schizophrenia

Organic Dementia

Psychogenic Amnesia

■ QUESTIONS FROM IMPORTANT IDEAS IN THIS CHAPTER

1. Describe six reasons that might lead us to judge behavior as abnormal.
2. Briefly describe three models of abnormal behavior. What are the implications of each model for treatment of abnormal behavior?
3. Briefly describe the five axes upon which diagnosis of a psychological disorder rests in the *DSM-III-R.*
4. In general terms, what are the common features of the anxiety disorders (see Table 13-1)?
5. What is the difference between unipolar depression and bipolar depression?
6. What are the general features of the somatoform disorders?
7. Briefly describe four key behavior patterns that characterize schizophrenia.
8. In what ways are the dissociative disorders also disorders of consciousness?
9. Briefly describe three major clusters of personality disorders.
10. In what three domains do the causes for abnormal behavior appear to be located?

TREATMENT
OF PSYCHOLOGICAL
DISORDERS

CHAPTER OUTLINE

LEARNING OBJECTIVES

After reading this chapter, you should be able to:

- Differentiate between the goals of insight, behavior, cognitive behavior and pharmaco-therapies.
- Describe the major features of Freudian psychoanalysis, modern psychoanalysis, Rogers' nondirective therapy, the behavior therapies, cognitive behavior therapies, and pharmaco-therapy.
- Describe the similarities and differences between Ellis' rational-emotive therapy, Beck's cognitive therapy, and Azrin's operant therapy for the treatment of depression.
- List the major pharmaceuticals used to treat abnormal behavior and the psychological disorders each is applied to.
- Describe the most common psychotherapeutic treatments for the anxiety disorders, the mood disorders, and schizophrenia.

Consider the following:

Ms. B was a 48-year-old housewife who would not eat solid food because she was afraid she would choke to death on a piece of it (Spitzer et al., 1983). She kept her fear at bay by eating only soft foods. Her fear of choking caused her to eat very slowly, so that simple meals lasted as long as two hours, and she could no longer eat with her family. Ms. B's fear stemmed from an incident involving one of her children who had choked for a few seconds on a piece of food 15 years earlier. Ms. B's anxiety had risen over this incident and over the following year she had become more and more convinced that she herself could choke to death on solid food. She even felt that she could choke to death several hours after eating if any piece of food still remained in her throat. Ms. B has a long-standing simple phobia. How can she be helped?

Mrs. K, age 73, was found on a beach, delirious, barely breathing, with an empty pint of whiskey in her hand (Oltmanns et al., 1986). She was taken to the hospital and there she seemed confused about who or where she was and about how she got into her current state. Later, when Mrs. K became conscious of her surroundings, she was guilt-ridden and ashamed. In therapy, Mrs. K related that she had tried to commit suicide and had failed. Guilt and shame are common reactions to failed suicide. Further exploration by her therapist brought to light that Mrs. K felt responsible for the death of her husband months earlier from cancer and Alzheimer's disease. Mrs. K had nursed him faithfully for years in their home. Unfortunately, he had died the day after she reluctantly put him in the hospital. Discussions with the residents and manager of the retirement hotel where Mrs. K lived showed that she had secluded herself more and more frequently in her room during the months preceding her suicide attempt, that she had begun daily trips to a nearby liquor store, and that she frequently smelled of liquor. Mrs. K was diagnosed as having experienced a major depression episode. How can she be helped?

Mr. R was taken by the police from a commercial airline. Upon admission to the hospital, among other things, he claimed that he was Jesus Christ and that his food contained ground-up corpses (Spitzer et al., 1983). His speech was difficult to follow and he indicated that he was continually hearing voices. The hospital discovered that Mr. R had been released a few days earlier from a mental hospital. They found further that he had a long history of delusional behavior, hallucinations, and disorganized speech. He was diagnosed as having chronic schizophrenia. Can Mr. R be helped?

In the foregoing examples, you can see evidence of three kinds of abnormal behavior, all labeled differently. The question in each case is, can these unfortunate people be helped? If so, how can they be helped? In the present chapter we look at some of the ways that psychology and psychiatry attempt to help people who exhibit abnormal behavior. In doing so, we look at the major types of psychotherapy—procedures for producing behavior change in people exhibiting abnormal behavior. Finally, we see how the various therapies for abnormal behavior are applied to specific instances of abnormal behavior, particularly to individuals who have anxiety disorders, mood disorders, and schizophrenia, as do our example cases above.

Given space limitations we will necessarily omit many specific techniques. We present descriptions of the techniques, along with a synopsis of the outcomes of some of the work in several problem areas. Unlike many of the preceding chapters, however, we do not expect you to be able to apply these techniques for treating problems of adjustment. Seriously abnormal behaviors require expert attention.

Let's start with a glimpse at the history of modern psychological treatment and then discover who is treated and what professionals do the treatment.

Treatments, Clients, and Providers

TREATMENTS.   Modern psychological treatment began with Freud in the early part of the twentieth century. Freud's mentor Joseph Breuer treated a young woman (Anna O) who in current terms had a somatoform disorder—analgesia and paralysis of the right arm, headaches, and coughing fits, all with no physical basis. Breuer noted that Anna was helped by talking about emotional events in her past. During such talks her physical problems would go away. Freud applied this knowledge to his own cases and psychoanalysis was born. Psychoanalysis is one type of psychotherapy. Eighty years later there exist a large number of psychotherapeutic techniques, most of which trace to the current models we have for explaining abnormal behavior (Chapter 13). We'll examine several of these below in some detail. They can be divided into the general categories of insight therapies, behavior therapies, cognitive behavior therapies, and psychopharmacological therapies.

CLIENTS.   But first let's briefly examine for what disorders help is most often provided. From the last chapter you may recall that substance use/abuse disorders are currently the most prevalent disorders, followed respectively by anxiety disorders, mood disorders, and schizophrenia. In the mental health system, however, help is most often sought for schizophrenia, and then for mood disorders, anxiety disorders, and substance use/abuse disorders. This makes sense when you consider that schizophrenia is most dysfunctional and therefore most likely to come to the attention of the mental health system. The order of this list would be different if the list was composed by private practitioners where clients tend to be self-selected and affluent. In such a list, anxiety and mood disorders would be most prevalent.

People come to psychotherapy for a variety of general reasons. First, they may be personally troubled, feel unable to help themselves, and subsequently reach out for help. Secondly, someone they know may exert pressure to get them into psychotherapy. Third, some individuals' behaviors may bring them into contact with the legal system, which, in turn, seeks the help of the mental health system. In the last two cases, the individuals involved are often unaware that their behaviors are cause for concern. Do people who seek professional help for their behaviors all have diagnosable psychological disorders? Not really. Many who seek professional

Box 14-1
MENTAL HEALTH AND YOU

Here is a list of factors associated with the likelihood of being diagnosed with a psychological disorder. Just because you fit in the most risky area on each factor does not mean that you do now or ever will need help. All these factors do is describe conditions that are present in those who have been diagnosed with psychological disorders.

1. *Age.* Someone who is younger is more likely to be diagnosed with a psychological disorder than someone who is older. In fact over half of the people admitted to mental health facilities are between 18 and 44 years old (Rosenstein & Millazo-Sayre, 1981).
2. *Marital status.* If you're married or widowed your chances of being diagnosed with a psychological disorder are less than if you're single, divorced, or separated.
3. *Education.* People with less education are more likely to be diagnosed with a psychological disorder than people with more education.
4. *Personal income.* The lower your personal income the greater the likelihood of being diagnosed with a psychological disorder.
5. *Employment status.* If you are unemployed you have a greater likelihood of being diagnosed with a psychological disorder.
6. *Friends.* If you have few or no social contacts you have a greater likelihood of being diagnosed with a psychological disorder.
7. *Quality of social relationships.* If your relationships with friends and relatives are very unsatisfying, you have a greater likelihood of being diagnosed with a psychological disorder.
8. *Marital satisfaction.* The lower your degree of satisfaction with your marriage, the greater the likelihood of being diagnosed with a psychological disorder.

help for problem behavior may only want to improve their marriages or other relationships, break bad habits, or gain more self-control.

provider-of-treatment

A mental health professional who can provide psychological services, especially psychotherapy.

PROVIDERS.   This is the term used by insurance companies that pay for services for people to see mental health professionals. It is shorthand for **provider-of-treatment**. Mental health providers can be divided into psychologists, psychiatrists, and others. To be called a psychologist requires a doctoral degree of some kind (Ph.D, Psy.D., Ed.D.), all of which require five to seven years of training beyond the bachelor's degree. The training is usually a combination of psychological theory, research, and application. Application often takes the form of a one- or two-year internship in mental health settings. Moreover, in the United States you cannot advertise yourself as a psychologist unless you are licensed or certified to do so by a state's business regulation agency.

Psychiatrists are physicians who have received a medical degree (M.D.) and have a four-year residency in psychiatry beyond the M.D. degree. Their medical training is the same as it is for all physicians who receive the M.D. degree. Their residency provides their psychiatric specialty. Such residencies occur in mental hospitals and other institutions where populations of people exhibit seriously abnormal behavior.

Other mental health providers are social workers, psychiatric nurses, and counselors. These individuals often work in concert with psychologists and psychiatrists, and the roles of all of these providers blur considerably. Social workers provide the interfaces among institution, client, family, and community, while psychiatric nurses are most likely to be found providing client care in psychiatric institutions. Counselors typically work in schools and human service agencies of various kinds and provide vocational, marital, rehabilitation, and drug counseling.

TABLE 14-1
MENTAL HEALTH PROVIDERS

The types of providers listed in this table provide the majority of mental health professional services in the United States.

Provider	Education/Degree	Activities
Psychologist	Ph.D., Psy.D., Ed.D. (B.A. + 5–7 years)	Assessment Diagnosis Therapy
Psychiatrist	M.D. (B.A. + 8 years)	Diagnosis Therapy
Social worker	M.S.W. (B.A. + 2 years)	Therapy Community interface
Psychiatric nurse	B.S., B.A., M.A. (B.A. + 0–2 years)	Therapy Patient care
Counselor	M.A. (B.A. + 2 years)	Therapy

Ph. D. = Doctor of Philosophy; Psy.D. = Doctor of Psychology; Ed.D. = Doctor of Education; M.D. = Medical Doctor; M.S.W. = Master of Social Work; B.A. = Bachelor of Arts; B.S. = Bachelor of Science; M.A. = Master of Arts.

Now you know who provides treatment and for what problems treatment is most likely to be received. Next we'll look at what constitutes psychotherapeutic treatment. There are many types of psychotherapy and categorization into the various types tends to be somewhat arbitrary. We'll focus on insight therapies, behavior therapies, cognitive behavior therapies and pharmaco-therapies.

Psychotherapy: A Definition

psychotherapy

Any therapy used by a psychologist/psychiatrist to change a client's behavior or to provide insight into the causes of the client's behavior.

Psychological methods of treating abnormal behavior are collectively called **psychotherapy.** Thus, psychotherapy is a general term that refers to any therapy practiced by a psychologist or psychiatrist. All psychotherapies consist of interactions between a client and a therapist. These interactions differ based on the type of psychotherapy, from talking with the therapist about your problems, or practicing desirable behavior patterns under the guidance of the therapist, to counting the negative ways you talk about yourself and the world. All of these specific instances are psychotherapies, even though they differ from one another. Their common denominator is that they attempt to change either the client's problematic behavior or the client's awareness of the causes for the problematic behavior through talking and other activities. In addition, drugs and other biomedical treatments play a helping role in many psychotherapies.

Kinds of Psychotherapy

While the aim of all psychotherapies is to help clients behave normally, in a very general way, the immediate goals of various therapies are different. Insight therapies focus on techniques that lead the client to understand the reasons for problem behavior and the reasons for the feelings such behavior produces. To accomplish this, insight therapies rely a great deal on talk between client and therapist. On the other hand, the focus of the behavior therapies is the direct change of problem behavior, while the focus of cognitive behavior therapies is the direct change of faulty thinking. Therefore, these therapies emphasize implementation of procedures to directly change problem behavior and/or faulty thinking. And finally, pharmaco-therapies focus on direct change in biological function through medication. We'll begin our look at these types of psychotherapies with a discussion of insight therapies. To help give you the flavor of the different therapies we'll describe them as though you are the client.

Insight Therapies: Now Do You Understand?

psychoanalysis

The psychotherapy first developed by Freud in which the client talks repeatedly with a therapist until insight is gained by the client into her or his problems.

PSYCHOANALYSIS: THE TALKING CURE.   As we mentioned above, **psychoanalysis** was the first psychotherapy. In this therapy, talking about your problems and your past is all important. Remember that Freud believed that current abnormal behavior is rooted in early abnormal experience. When early experiences produced conflict between a pleasure seeking id, the ideals of the superego, and the realities of society, the ego would defend the individual against feelings of guilt and anxiety. Ego defense mechanisms distorted one's true desires and impulses, and buried true impulses in the unconscious.

As a psychotherapeutic method, psychoanalysis is structured to get you to converse in an uninhibited fashion. If you do talk uninhibitedly, you will say things that you didn't know you would. The psychoanalyst's goal is to make you aware of unconscious impulses that may show up in your uninhibited talk. A way to get these unconscious impulses to surface is to provide a nonthreatening audience, a person to whom you can feel safe presenting your fears, losses, inadequacies, hurts, traumas, emotions, aggressive impulses, sexual thoughts—everything. The idea is to talk eventually about inner desires and conflicts that are important to you but of which you are unaware. Psychoanalysis contains several procedures to get you to talk about these unconscious desires and conflicts.

Free Association.   One psychoanalytic procedure to get you to talk without inhibition is to have you practice *free association.*   In one version the therapist verbalizes single words across regular, brief intervals. You say the first word that

During traditional psychoanalysis the client reclines so that relaxation is likely. The therapist assumes a position behind the client so that there is unlikely to be inhibiting eye contact or any body language messages. In other words, the situation is arranged to be as comfortable and as uninhibiting to the client as possible. While this picture may be true for traditional psychoanalysis, there are a great many other varieties of psychotherapy for which it may not be true. As examples, psychotherapy may occur with more than one client at a time (group therapy); or where therapy demands that the client actively rehearse or practice some new behavior, the psychotherapy may not even occur in the therapist's office.

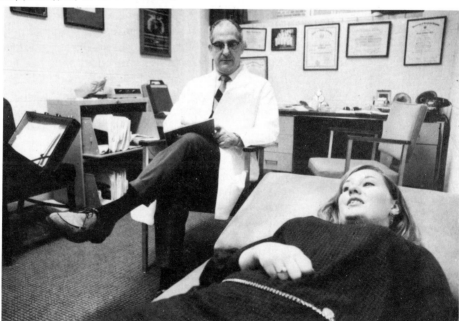

comes to mind, *without thinking about it.* (*Therapist:* "dog"; *Client:* "cat"; *Therapist:* "mother"; *Client:* "bitch"). Hypothetically, the associations that result will be free of conscious control and therefore reflect associations of which you are unaware (that is, unconscious). You and the therapist then interpret these associations.

Dream Analysis.   Psychoanalysts believe that dreams, too, offer access to the unconscious mind. In psychoanalysis, dreams are thought to represent events that are not under conscious control, so they may provide a window to events of which you are unaware. Thus, your memory (even incorrect memory) of a dream is of interest to the psychoanalyst. What you believe you remember of a dream, and the way you recount that dream, can sometimes provide both you and the therapist with surprising insights.

Insight.   Throughout the client–therapist interactions in psychoanalysis, the psychoanalyst guides the client toward insight into deep personal problems. Insight implies that the client recognizes the real reasons for his or her emotions, motives, and behaviors. Often insight occurs suddenly in therapy, almost as a kind of "aha" phenomenon:

"After months of talking about her husband as a demanding, overbearing man who was always gloomy, Rose Francis, aged 50, remarked to her therapist: 'You know, I guess I really don't like him'" (Sarason & Sarason, 1989, p. 488). She was plainly surprised that she had said this. After this point in her therapy, she understood her husband's worries and concerns in a new way (Sarason & Sarason, 1989).

Transference.   Consider the situation: Here you are in therapy, week after week, telling your therapist your innermost thoughts and feelings. Eventually you will feel that you know your therapist very well (even if your therapist doesn't share much personal information with you); and your therapist will certainly know you very well! You are also physically close to your therapist every few days. These are the conditions for the development of a close relationship. Not surprisingly, in these circumstances clients often develop strong feelings toward (or against) their therapists. Moreover, there may be a transfer of feelings to the therapist, feelings the client has about other people who are the subjects of discussion. This transfer of feelings is called **transference.**

transference
The transfer of feelings that the client has about others to the therapist.

Let's imagine that a young woman in therapy with an older male psychoanalyst says, "You disgust me. I can feel your eyes on my body every session. You're no better than any other man." If we further postulate that this young woman is troubled by early sexual experiences with her father, such feelings about the therapist are taken, in psychoanalysis, as evidence of transference (here negative transference) of feelings about her father to the therapist, that the client and therapist then interpret.

Resistance.   The psychoanalyst will notice that certain topics are missing from your discussions. Perhaps each time you start to talk about your relationship with your mother, you break off or otherwise abbreviate the discussion, or you start on other topics. In psychoanalysis this unaware omission of certain topic areas is known as *resistance,* and the therapist will lead the discussion in a direction that attempts to analyze these areas. Why don't you want to talk about your mother?

Psychoanalysis can take a long time. It is necessary for patient and therapist to explore conflicts from childhood because childhood is where Freud thought personality development occurred and where it could have been disturbed. Thus, it is not uncommon for traditional psychoanalysis to require several sessions per week for several years. As such, traditional psychoanalysis is expensive and has become rare.

MODERN PSYCHOANALYSIS.   Today, psychoanalysis is more likely to reflect the changes that have been brought to it by Freud's students and others. The focus of modern psychoanalysis is more on the conscious aspects of behavior, the client's current living conditions, and the client's current social relations, rather than on uncovering unconscious impulses. The therapeutic process is accelerated because not as much time is spent in the past and on unconscious processes, although the historical causes of behavior remain important (Davison & Neale, 1990), and because the new psychoanalyst is likely to be more direct in focusing on good therapist–client intercommunication.

CLIENT- (PERSON-) CENTERED THERAPY.   A second type of insight therapy has been called *person-centered* because the focus is on you as a person in therapy. The goal is still understanding by you of the whys and wherefores of your behavior, but the focus of therapy shifts to your understanding of yourself as a person. All psychotherapies are really client-centered because they all intend to make you, the client, well. But some therapies, more than others, consider getting well to be your job, not the therapist's.

nondirective therapy

A client-centered therapy in which the therapist provides a nonpunitive, empathic, reflective, all-accepting audience; the client is expected to talk freely, a behavior thought to promote insight and personal growth.

Carl Rogers' **nondirective therapy** exemplifies the person-centered approach. Contrary to the Freudians, Rogers thought that the conscious thoughts and feelings of the client were the most important to deal with. Moreover, labels and diagnoses were unimportant to him.

Rogers thought that people's behavior became problematic for them when there was an incongruence between the way they saw themselves (their ideal self) and the way that others saw them (their real self). He thought that healthy people were aware of their own behavior, its effect on themselves and others. A good understanding of one's own behavior would lead to less reliance on the opinions of others for growth and development.

Rogers' therapeutic focus was on the kind of environment the therapist should provide for the client. First, he thought, the therapist must show the client *unconditional positive regard*. This is the unconditional acceptance of the client, faults and all. Second, the therapist must be fully *empathic* with the client, attempting to see and feel things the client's way. Third, the therapist must strive for *authenticity,* that is, for a real, not a professional relationship with the client. And fourth, the therapist must provide a mirror-like *reflection* of the client by actively listening to what the client says, essentially encouraging more discourse but not indicating which way the discourse should go. It is the total environment which the therapist presents that makes it likely that the client will explore troubling thoughts and feelings.

Rogers believed that personal growth occurred automatically through the increase in self-knowledge and self-acceptance which resulted from such a therapeutic environment (Rogers, 1951, 1961, 1970). In the sense that all the therapist does in Rogerian psychotherapy is to provide the appropriate environment (not a small accomplishment), the client heals herself or himself. It is in this way also that Rogers' nondirective therapy is client-centered—the client sets the pace and direction of therapy.

The therapeutic program in client-centered therapy is ambitious—about as ambitious as psychoanalysis—and that is, the total reconstruction of the client's personality. With each insight the client becomes more aware of who she or he is and with this awareness hopefully comes self-actualization. Such a broad focus is much less characteristic of the behavior therapies, the next type of psychotherapy we will consider.

Box 14-2

"I Hear What You're Saying":
Carl Rogers in Action

To get a flavor of unconditional positive regard, empathy, authenticity, and reflection at work read the following excerpt from a therapy session of Carl Rogers. He is interacting with a 28-year-old male client.

> Client: I just ain't no good to nobody, never was, never will be.
>
> CR: Feeling that now, hm? That you're just no good to yourself, no good to anybody. Never will be any good to anybody. Just that you're completely worthless, huh?—Those really are lousy feelings. Just feel that you're no good at all, hm?
>
> Client: Yeah. (Muttering in low, discouraged voice) That's what this guy I went to town with just the other day told me.
>
> CR: This guy you went to town with really told you that you were no good? Is that what you're saying? Did I get that right?

> Client: M-hm.
>
> CR: I guess the meaning of that if I get it right is that here's somebody that —meant something to you and what does he think of you? Why he's told you that he thinks that you're no good at all. And that just really knocks the props out from under you. (Client weeps quietly.) It just brings the tears. (Silence of 20 seconds)
>
> Client: (Rather defiantly) I don't care though.
>
> CR: You tell yourself that you don't care at all, but somehow I guess some part of you cares because some part of you weeps over it.

Can you infer instances of unconditional positive regard, empathy, authenticity, and reflection?

From Meador & Rogers, 1984, p. 167.

Behavior Therapies: Old Habits Die Hard

In psychoanalytic and client-centered therapies you talk with and listen to the therapist to increase your self-awareness and self-knowledge. Your increased self-awareness and self-knowledge lead to your insight into the causes of your behavior. In contrast to psychoanalysis and client-centered therapy, the behavior therapies place much less emphasis on self-awareness, self-knowledge, and insight as therapeutic goals. Rather the goal of the behavior therapies is behavior change, particularly the change of your problematic actions and thoughts. In seeing a psychotherapist for behavior therapy, therefore, you not only talk about your problems, but you also take direct action to change your behavior patterns. Behavior therapists believe that much abnormal behavior is learned behavior, a result of interactions among your biology, your history of experiences, and your current environment.

behavior therapies

Psychotherapies in which the focus is directly on changes in behavior through techniques from experimental psychology.

The **behavior therapies** are based on the principles of operant and reflexive learning that were discussed in Chapter 3, and the biology which supports these principles. Let's look first at some behavior therapies built upon operant learning principles.

POSITIVE REINFORCEMENT.   Remember that a great deal of our behavior is affected by its consequences. This is the central fact of operant conditioning. Using this fact, the behavior therapist influences a client's behaviors by scheduling consequences for him or her. Specifically the therapist attempts to reinforce the client's desirable behavior and withholds reinforcement for the client's undesirable behavior. Let's see how this happens.

In a classic case (Isaacs et al., 1960), a therapist was conducting a group therapy session with several clients. One client, a chronically schizophrenic man, had been mute for years. The therapist was pulling something out of his pocket when a pack of chewing gum fell to the floor. He noticed the man's eyes on the gum. This was the first sign of interest that the man had shown in the proceedings. Behavior therapists know that events and objects in which people show interest usually function as positive reinforcers for them. So the therapist designed a program using chewing gum as a positive reinforcer. Across the first two weeks of this program, the therapist simply held up a stick of gum before the client. When the client's eyes made contact with the therapist's eyes, he was given the gum. During the next two weeks, the therapist held up the gum, waited for eye contact, and said "Say gum, gum." He accepted any vocalization from the client as a response after which the client received the gum. During the next two weeks the therapist held up the gum as before but waited for vocalizations that were closer to the sound of the word *gum*. During the sixth week, the therapist held up the gum, looked at the man, said "Say gum, please," and the man clearly and distinctly said, "Gum, please," and the therapist gave him the gum. Thereafter, the man spoke increasingly often with the therapist, who continued to reinforce him for speaking. Interestingly, the man did not speak with other hospital staff who treated him as though he were still mute, until they too were taught to wait for him to speak before interacting with him.

This example not only illustrates how *positive reinforcement* works, but also illustrates the principles of *stimulus control* and *shaping*. The man discriminated the conditions for the reinforcement of speaking (the presence of the therapist with the gum) and the conditions for the nonreinforcement of speaking (the absence of the therapist with the gum). He spoke only in the environment where speaking was reinforced. This is evidence of stimulus control. Eventually, of course, the behavior therapist's work with the hospital staff, getting them to prompt speech and then to reinforce this client's speaking, and to withhold their attention until he did speak, resulted in the *generalization* of speaking to many environments. Generalization of treatment gains is an important goal of therapy for all clients. The principle of shaping is seen in the successive changes of the reinforcement contingencies in this client's program across the weeks until the target behavior occurred. In this study the shaping steps were to (1) reinforce an attentional response—eye contact; (2) reinforce an attentional response only when it occurs with a vocalization; and (3) reinforce an attentional response only when it occurs with vocalizations approximating the target phrase ("Gum, please").

TOKEN ECONOMIES. Where reinforcement involves tangible objects like the piece of gum above, a symbol of the reinforcement called a token can be given instead. The client then exchanges the token at some later time for actual reinforcers in what is called a **token economy.** In the token economy, behaviors that are functional to the client's recovery are reinforced. Institutionalized schizophrenics, for example, may receive tokens for keeping their rooms clean; for maintaining proper hygiene; for working daily in the institution; for attending and engaging in occupational therapy, physical therapy, and psychotherapy; for talking rationally; and so on (Ayllon & Azrin, 1968; Glynn, 1990; Kazdin, 1977; Paul & Lentz, 1977). The schizophrenics exchange their tokens at regular times for luxuries—cigarettes, cosmetics, and privileges are examples—that are important to them. In several ways token economies work similarly to larger economies like those of countries (Hursh, 1980).

token economy

A miniature economic system, often employed in institutions, to strengthen desirable behavior and weaken undesirable behavior.

SOCIAL SKILLS TRAINING. When someone says, "How are you?" you usually reply, "Fine thanks, how are you?" And the person replies with something like, "I'm great. Isn't it a beautiful day today?" Then, perhaps you respond with, "Yes, but I think it's going to be hot this afternoon." Most of us take this ordinary social interaction for granted. But what of individuals who do not initiate such an interaction or who do not respond appropriately when such an interaction starts? The behavior of these individuals is abnormal in the sense that it is lacking or incorrect

Most of us take the greeting ritual for granted, but for individuals who lack the behaviors to engage someone with a greeting, behavior therapy involving social skills training may be necessary to help them overcome this and other social deficits.

in a social situation. From the perspective of the behavior therapist the behavior of such individuals can be corrected by training them in the specific and general social skills which they lack. This process is called *social skills training* (Morrison & Bellack, 1984). While social skills training contains many specific procedures, in the most common variety, the behavior therapist reinforces the client's approximations to desirable social behavior and withholds reinforcement for the client's undesirable social behavior. Increasing social-information processing (for example, teaching the client to evaluate the social situation before speaking), and reducing anxiety generated by social interactions are useful additional components of social skills training packages (Heinssen & Glass, 1990).

Assertiveness Training.   Afraid to say no? Afraid to speak up with your point of view for fear of retaliation? Or are you too aggressive or too quick to anger? Assertiveness training may help. Assertiveness training is one kind of social skills training. Behaving assertively is behaving in such a way that you do not provoke aggression while still taking a stand—clearly, a social skill. The behavior therapist teaches where and how to be assertive by positively reinforcing the client's appropriate assertive behaviors and by withholding reinforcement (or by mildly punishing) aggressive behavior. The client may also be taught to correctly interpret when others are attempting to be assertive. Behavioral rehearsal (discussed below) is employed to involve the client in the practice of the newly acquired assertiveness skills. We deal more with assertiveness training in Chapter 15.

BEHAVIORAL REHEARSAL.   What better way to try out your therapeutically new behaviors than to practice them in front of a small, yet rewarding audience (your behavior therapist)? When engaging in **behavioral rehearsal** the client practices sequences of behavior scripted and portrayed by the behavior therapist. Then the behavior therapist acts as director by leading the client through the behavioral sequences, prompting the client when necessary, and reinforcing improvements in the client's performance. Behavioral rehearsal is frequently a component of social skills training because it helps people to hone their new skills in a nonthreatening environment.

behavioral rehearsal

The practicing of a particular way of behaving (for example, assertively) prior to the situation in which the behavior will eventually be tried.

The development of responsibly assertive behavior may be helpful for those who lack this skill. In the photo a young woman asserts her right to question an auto mechanic about her bill.

modeling

A procedure in which a sample of a given behavior is shown to an individual to induce that person to imitate the behavior.

MODELING.   Just as a fashion model displays or "models" clothes, in the context of behavior therapy, the therapist can display or model behavior, called **modeling,** which a client then tries to copy. The therapist observes the client's attempts and reinforces those responses that are good copies.

We'll have a further look at more operant and observational learning-based therapies later when we discuss applications of psychotherapeutic treatments to specific psychological disorders. Before that point, let's look at some reflexive learning–based behavior therapies. Two of these therapies have been of great importance—the first, aversion therapy, in application to the addictive disorders such as alcoholism, and the second, systematic desensitization, in application to the anxiety disorders such as simple phobias.

AVERSION THERAPY.   What if every time you had an alcoholic drink you found out that you couldn't stop until either the alcohol was gone or you were senseless? Seem farfetched? It is to many who can drink alcohol socially. But to many others, this outcome is not farfetched. What if after smoking for ten years, you decide to quit, but after a week without a cigarette you can no longer stand it, and you start smoking again? Does this seem farfetched? In fact, many smokers try repeatedly to stop and cannot. Or what if you're addicted to the thrills of gambling? Again, you try to stop and you cannot.

counterconditioning

The procedure of pairing a stimulus (e.g., a crowded environment) that elicits an undesirable response (e.g., fear) with a stimulus that elicits an opposite response (e.g., relaxation). Eventually, the first stimulus loses the capacity to cause the undesirable response.

What can be done about undesirable reinforcers—those in which we tend to overindulge or that harm us? A behavior therapy technique called *aversion therapy,* which is based on the principle of **counterconditioning,** may help. In application to the problem of undesirable reinforcers, counterconditioning involves the repeated association of the undesirable reinforcer with a powerful aversive event.

Here is an example of how aversion therapy can work: Let's say that you are an alcoholic and you've agreed to an aversion therapy program. You check into a clinic and are taken to a bar that looks just like the real thing. You are given an injection of disulfiram. After waiting a few minutes to let the drug get into your system, the "bartender" says, "What'll you have?" You indicate your favorite beverage, it's poured, and you immediately drink it. An instant later, you're violently ill. More drinks are poured and each time the alcohol makes you sick. This scene is

TABLE 14-2
A SCHEMATIC ILLUSTRATION OF THE
PROCEDURE OF COUNTERCONDITIONING

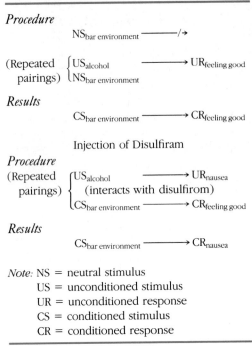

Procedure

$$NS_{bar\ environment} \longrightarrow /\rightarrow$$

(Repeated pairings) $\left\{ \begin{array}{l} US_{alcohol} \longrightarrow UR_{feeling\ good} \\ NS_{bar\ environment} \end{array} \right.$

Results

$$CS_{bar\ environment} \longrightarrow CR_{feeling\ good}$$

Injection of Disulfiram

Procedure

(Repeated pairings) $\left\{ \begin{array}{l} US_{alcohol} \longrightarrow UR_{nausea} \\ \quad \text{(interacts with disulfirom)} \\ CS_{bar\ environment} \longrightarrow CR_{feeling\ good} \end{array} \right.$

Results

$$CS_{bar\ environment} \longrightarrow CR_{nausea}$$

Note: NS = neutral stimulus
US = unconditioned stimulus
UR = unconditioned response
CS = conditioned stimulus
CR = conditioned response

repeated on several subsequent occasions. Soon you start to get nauseous when you smell the alcohol before you drink it; possibly even the thought of alcohol makes you queasy. Even the bar doesn't seem the welcome place it once did. What has happened?

Prior to aversion therapy treatment, alcohol used to produce pleasant body sensations. Now it makes you feel bad. Not only that but conditions that are associated with drinking now also make you feel bad. Reflexive learning has taken place. The process is called counterconditioning because the former conditioned reflexes (the smell of alcohol being pleasing and making you feel good, for instance) have been "reconditioned," that is, counterconditioned, and now are conditioned illness reflexes much like the unconditioned reaction produced by the disulfiram when it is consumed with the alcohol.

Aversion therapy has been applied to deviant sexual behavior (Fuastman, 1976); nicotine addiction (Tiffany et al., 1986); and alcohol addiction (Volger et al., 1977).

Aversion therapy procedures are generally used as a last resort because of their impact on the client, and clients are always volunteers for such procedures. Do aversive conditioning procedures work? Take alcoholics as an example. One year after aversion therapy, which included returning for several booster sessions, 63 percent of the 625 clients in one study were still abstaining from alcohol use, while three years later approximately one third were still abstaining (Wiens & Menustik, 1983). These are good numbers when compared with other methods.

SYSTEMATIC DESENSITIZATION.   You've just had a serious automobile accident, and you're deathly afraid of another—so afraid that you won't drive anymore. But there's no other way to get to work. You'll lose your job. What can you do?

Systematic desensitization, developed by Joseph Wolpe (1958), is designed to counter the avoidance of fearful situations such as in the example above. As does aversion therapy, systematic desensitization works via counterconditioning. However, in systematic desensitization, the direction of the counterconditioning is reversed. A conditioned fear reflex exists—thinking about getting back into the car produces fear. The behavior therapist gets rid of the conditioned fear reflex by counterconditioning the events leading to the fear reflex so that these events lead to a relaxation reflex instead. Let's see how this occurs. (Detailed steps for applying systematic desensitization in a self-adjustment project are described in Chapter 15.)

First, client and therapist construct a *fear hierarchy*. A fear hierarchy consists of about a dozen scenes that involve the feared event. The scenes are developed to produce varying degrees of fear and are commonly arranged from least feared to most feared. Perhaps the least fearful scene you could tolerate after your automobile accident is to imagine yourself sitting in an automobile parked in your driveway. The most fearful scene might involve imagining yourself in your automobile at the moment of another crash. In between might be scenes of driving on roads of varying surfaces, speeds, traffic densities, and other similarities to your recent crash (see Table 14-3).

After the hierarchy is constructed, you are to become relaxed. If you don't know how to relax yourself, and most people do not, the behavior therapist teaches this skill.

Now comes the critical part. While you are fully relaxed, the therapist presents the first scene in the fear hierarchy (sitting in your car in your garage), and asks you to imagine it and to hold the scene in your imagination for ten seconds or so in the absence of fear. You imagine the scene, helped by the therapist's descriptions of it. If fear starts to occur, you signal with a raised finger and the therapist withdraws the scene. When this happens, you may need to be more deeply relaxed, and you and the therapist work toward this outcome. If no fear occurs, a brief pause is taken, you relax some more and the next scene in the hierarchy is presented. Across several sessions you and the therapist work your way up the hierarchy scene by scene, at a rate of approximately three or four scenes per session.

Sometimes the hierarchy is not scaled correctly and a particular scene may be too fear provoking where it is, so it is moved. Sometimes it is necessary to go back over already finished scenes. Eventually, however, you and your therapist find yourselves finished with the most frightening scene. Now you can imagine the most feared event of all without fear. At this point it may be possible for you to encounter real examples of the formerly feared objects or events and interact with them

TABLE 14-3
A Sample Fear Hierarchy for a Driving Phobia

You in your automobile:
 1. in the garage; engine off.
 2. in your driveway; engine off.
 3. parked on the quiet road in front of your home; engine off.
 4. parked on a busier neighborhood street; engine off.
 5. parked on the verge of a busy two-lane highway; engine off.
 6. backing out of your garage into your driveway and stopping.
 7. backing out of your garage into the street and parking.
 8. driving around the quiet block on which you live.
 9. driving to your nearest market and back on fairly quiet streets.
10. driving to work on busy city streets.
11. driving back from work on busy city streets.
12. driving on a freeway with very little traffic and moderate speed.
13. driving on a freeway with moderate traffic and moderate speed.
14. driving on a freeway with heavy traffic and moderate speed.
15. driving on a freeway with heavy traffic and high speed.

fearlessly. Counterconditioning has occurred with respect to the fear reflex. The events that used to produce fear now produce relaxation.

A very positive aspect of systematic desensitization is that getting rid of your fear can occur with relatively little fear on your part. This makes it a clinically useful technique, because if you are scared by a particular form of treatment, you may not return for further help. However, as you can see, systematic desensitization depends critically on how well you can imagine. For those who don't have good imagining skills, systematic desensitization may not be as effective as other methods, such as actual exposure (*in vivo* desensitization), which we'll discuss below.

Because systematic desensitization involves changes in your biological state (from fearful to relaxed) and imagination (cognition), it appears to fit into more than one therapeutic category. It has some of the features of cognitive therapy which work primarily with thoughts and images (cognitions) and some of the features of techniques that attempt to change your behavior by changing your biological state, both of which we examine below.

***IN VIVO* DESENSITIZATION.**   Psychologists have known for some time that the way to eliminate fears of all kinds is to actually expose the client to the feared object or event (Barlow, 1988). The assumption in systematic desensitization—which, you saw, uses imagination of the feared object or event—is that through generalization, you will be able to approach the feared objects or events in real life and those objects or events will no longer elicit anxiety. But what if generalization does not occur? That is, what if you cannot get back in your car and drive it after the systematic desensitization we described above? Then actual exposure to the feared objects and events may be necessary.

In a useful variant of systematic desensitization, you and your therapist construct a fear hierarchy that is desensitized in real life (*in vivo*). That is, real objects and events that can be controlled by the therapist are used in the desensitization process. Consider for a moment that you are deathly afraid of heights (acrophobic) and that you want to get rid of this fear so that you can hike more places or so you can go above the main floor in buildings. You and your therapist could construct a hierarchy that has you look down from greater and greater heights where there is less and less constraint against falling. Then with your therapist you could actually ascend the buildings or other structures in the hierarchy, starting, for example, on the balcony of a one-story building, successfully accomplishing that feat while remaining relaxed and without fear, and thereafter repeating this process in higher and higher locations.

In vivo desensitization may be more effective than systematic desensitization because it does not rely on how well you imagine the feared objects and events. However, you may have to be more motivated to engage in the actual—although graded—confrontation of the feared objects and events in *in vivo* desensitization.

Participant modeling is also a real-life, gradual approach procedure. Essentially, it is a variant of *in vivo* desensitization with modeling and guidance by the therapist added but without the relaxation component. So it, too, can be used to eliminate phobic behavior. In *modeling with guidance,* the therapist manually guides you through a particular skilled activity, such as the movements involved in approaching and grasping a snake if you are fearful of snakes.

The therapist may demonstrate how a snake reacts by handling the snake in front of a client who fears these reptiles. Then, in a series of gradual steps, the client models or copies the behavior of the therapist and handles the snake. These steps might involve first touching the snake with gloved hands while the therapist holds it, then touching it without gloves, then holding it after being handed it, then picking it up alone, and so forth, all of which the client may watch the therapist do fearlessly a number of times.

This series of pictures shows examples from films of a young boy interacting fearlessly with a dog. The films were shown to a young girl who was apprehensive about dogs. Viewing the films and being gradually exposed to dogs in more and more threatening situations enabled the formerly apprehensive girl to act fearlessly with the dogs.

Even simply watching peers behave fearlessly may be sufficient to accomplish fear reduction and behavior change. Children fearful of dogs have observed fearless peers interact with big dogs and have been more able themselves to interact with the dogs thereafter (Bandura, 1969).

Cognitive Behavior Therapies: Get It in Your Head

Does what you carry in your head relate to the way you feel? Cognitive behavior therapists believe that the way you talk to yourself about yourself and your life, may have a great deal to do with how you feel. People who feel really badly about their lives are often diagnosed as depressed. Does depression have something to do with how we talk to ourselves? Cognitive behavior therapists believe this to be true. In turn, is how we talk to ourselves learned? All behavior therapists believe this to be true. Then, if what we say to ourselves is learned, given the underlying premise of all the behavior therapies, it ought to be possible to unlearn and change what we say to ourselves. If we can change how we talk to ourselves, perhaps we can affect how we feel. It is in this sense that cognitive behavior therapists attempt *cognitive restructuring* to "change your head."

As illustrations of cognitive restructuring, we'll look at two therapies that are in wide use today to deal with depression.

rational-emotive therapy
Ellis' therapy in which the patient's irrational beliefs (that cause emotional problems) are challenged and changed to rational beliefs.

ELLIS' RATIONAL-EMOTIVE THERAPY. In **rational-emotive therapy** (RET), developed by Albert Ellis, the client is thought to have constructed an irrational, personally catastrophic world. Ellis was originally trained in psychoanalysis, but he noted that clients' insights into their problems did not solve those problems. The people Ellis saw seemed to be more troubled by their current lives—not the distant past. Further, they would frequently make irrational, catastrophic statements about their lives ("If I don't go to work tomorrow, I'm going to be dismissed"). Ellis sharply challenges these irrational statements of gloom and doom ("Wrong," he might counter. "If you call in and say you don't feel well, not many employers would fire you for that").

Ellis contends that depression results from holding irrational beliefs about yourself and the world which are illustrated in absolutist thinking (for example, "I must be loved by every significant person in my life"). The RET therapist tries to pin down your irrational ideas, challenges you to validate them, shows that they cannot be validated, chops up these ideas, and shows you how they lead to your depres-

Box 14-3

Albert Ellis at Work

The following excerpt is from the initial therapy session with a 25-year-old single woman who worked as a computer programmer (Ellis, 1989). Early in the session the woman states that she is depressed because she thinks that she has no purpose in life and that she should have such a purpose. Ellis challenges her by stating that most humans live happy lives without purpose. She reacts emotionally to his initial challenges because she perceives that he is treating her abruptly and because she doesn't think that this is the way her therapy should proceed.

Client: I'm upset because I know, I—the role that I envisioned for myself being when I walked in here and what I [Laughs, almost joyously.] and what I would do and should do—

Ellis: Yeah?

Client: And therefore you forced me to violate that. And I don't like it.

Ellis: And isn't it awful that I didn't come out greatly! If I had violated that beautifully, and I gave him the right answers immediately, and he beamed, and said "Boy, what a bright woman this is!" then it would have been all right.

Client: [Laughing good-humoredly.] Certainly!

Ellis: Horseshit! You would have been exactly as disturbed as you are now! It wouldn't have helped you a bit! In fact, you would have gotten nuttier! Because then you would have gone out of here with the same philosophy you came in with: "That when I act well and people pat . . . me on the head and say, 'What a great woman am I!' then everything is rosy!" It's a nutty philosophy! Because even if I loved you madly, the next person you talk to is likely to hate you. So I like brown eyes and he likes blue eyes or something. So you're dead! Because you really think: "I've got to be accepted! I've got to act intelligently!" Well, why?

Client: [Very soberly and reflectively.] True.

Ellis: You see?

Client: Yes.

Ellis: Now, if you will learn that lesson, then you've had a very valuable session. Because you don't have to upset yourself. As I said before, if I thought you were the worst shit who ever existed, well that's my opinion. And I'm entitled to it. But does it make you a turd?

Client: [Reflective silence.]

Ellis: Does it?

Client: No.

Ellis: What makes you a turd?

Client: Thinking that you are.

Ellis: That's right! Your belief that you are. That's the only thing that could ever do it. And you never have to believe that.

---

sion. Then you are taught to replace such ideas with more rational ones (for example, "Not everyone has to love me, but life *is* better when people love me"). You may also do homework assignments in RET in which you take risks ("Call in tomorrow, say you're sick"). You learn then that the former irrational beliefs ("I'll be fired!") are not supported by the outcomes of your risky behavior ("My boss just said, 'I hope you feel better soon!'") (Ellis & Bernard, 1985; Haaga & Davison, 1986). Finally you are taught to watch for subsequently occurring irrational ideas.

Beck's cognitive therapy

Beck's therapy for depression in which individuals restructure their way of thinking about the world via reality checking, testing maladaptive assumptions, counting automatic dysfunctional thoughts, and substituting more appropriate ones.

BECK'S COGNITIVE THERAPY.   A cognitive restructuring therapy similar to RET is Aaron **Beck's cognitive therapy,** which is also applied to depression. Beck also believes that what you say to yourself affects how you feel. Beck noted that depressed individuals have automatic, dysfunctional thoughts ("I'm a crummy lover"). If you were his client you would note such thoughts and how you feel after having them. You would also look for the events that precipitate such thoughts. Then you would evaluate how reasonable the thought was (Was there evidence to support it? Are there other ways to interpret it? Is the negative outcome your fault? If it is, is that so bad?).

In essence, in Beck's cognitive therapy you are taught to engage in a kind of hypothesis testing called *reality checking*. Then you're taught to substitute more

Box 14-4

Aaron Beck at Work

The following is an excerpt from the cognitive therapy of a woman who attempted to commit suicide and still wanted to at the time of the session. She had found out that her husband was unfaithful (Beck, 1976, pp. 289–291).

Beck: Why do you want to end your life?

Client: Without Raymond, I am nothing. . . . I can't be happy without Raymond. . . . But I can't save our marriage.

Beck: What has your marriage been like?

Client: It has been miserable from the beginning. . . . Raymond has always been unfaithful. . . . I have hardly seen him in the past five years.

Beck: You say that you can't be happy without Raymond. . . . Have you found yourself happy when you are with Raymond?

Client: No, we fight all the time and I feel worse.

Beck: You say that you are nothing without Raymond. Before you met Raymond, did you feel you were nothing?

Client: No, I felt I was somebody.

Beck: If you were somebody before you knew Raymond, why do you need him to be somebody now?

Client: [Puzzled.] Hmmm . . .

Beck: Did you have male friends before you knew Raymond?

Client: I was pretty popular then.

Beck: Why do you think you will be unpopular without Raymond now?

Client: Because I will not be able to attract any other man.

Beck: Have any men shown an interest in you since you have been married?

Client: A lot of men have made passes at me, but I ignore them.

Beck: If you were free of the marriage, do you think that men might be interested in you—knowing that you were available?

Client: I guess maybe that they would be.

Beck: Is it possible that you might find a man who would be more constant than Raymond?

Client: I don't know. . . . I guess it's possible.

Beck: You say that you can't stand the idea of losing the marriage. Is it correct that you have hardly seen your husband in the past five years?

Client: That's right. I only see him a couple times a year.

Beck: Is there any chance of getting back together with him?

Client: No . . . He has another woman. He doesn't want me.

Beck: Then what have you actually lost if you break up the marriage?

Client: I don't know.

Beck: Is it possible that you'll get along better if you end the marriage?

Client: There is no guarantee of that.

Beck: Do you have a real marriage?

Client: I guess not.

Beck: If you don't have a real marriage, what do you actually lose if you decide to end the marriage?

Client: [Long pause.] Nothing, I guess.

reasonable thoughts for the dysfunctional ones. Finally, you are taught to identify and *test maladaptive assumptions.* These are demonstrably incorrect assumptions about the world that may make you feel bad ("If I fail to do something perfectly, the result is not good enough").

Beck also challenges the common feeling of depressed individuals that they don't get anything accomplished. His clients have to keep weekly activity schedules on an hourly basis. These written records usually show clients that they accomplished far more than they would have guessed (Haaga & Davison, 1986; Sacco & Beck, 1985).

BECK'S THERAPY AND RET.   Does Beck's cognitive therapy sound a little like rational-emotive therapy? There are similarities. Both therapies attempt to change how you view yourself by having you examine how you talk about yourself. Both attempt *cognitive restructuring,* changing how you talk to yourself—especially what you believe about yourself, in the form of either irrational beliefs or negative beliefs. The major differences in the two therapies are the ways in which the cognitive changes are produced. Ellis' school of therapy challenges the client as you saw above (Box 14-3) in the attempt to point out the irrationality of the client's beliefs. Beck's school of therapy involves a gentler questioning from which the negativeness, inconsistencies, and illogic in a client's thinking become evident (Box 14-4).

COGNITIVE RESTRUCTURING AND PSYCHOANALYSIS.   Does cognitive restructuring sound like psychoanalysis? It might, a little, because the focus in cognitive restructuring is also on talk, but cognitive behavior therapies such as RET or Beck's cognitive therapy are really very different from psychoanalysis. Recall that in psychoanalysis, your talk is considered symptomatic of personality problems. In the cognitive behavior therapies, your talk *is* the problem, not a symptom of a problem. In psychoanalysis, the goal is your insight into the reasons for your behavior. In the cognitive behavior therapies, the goal is your changed behavior with the result that you feel well. Yet the fact that you learn specifically what it is about the way you think that makes you feel bad also suggests insight.

Other Therapies

GROUP THERAPY.   Most therapies can be administered in a group setting of six to eight people, and receiving therapy in such a group has some advantages. Among other advantages, group therapy is a better use of therapist time; it is less expensive for each client; it permits each client to see that her or his problems are not unique; it provides a forum in which a client can directly try out new social skills (Curran & Monti, 1982); and it provides an environment intermediate to individual therapy and the world outside the therapy environment. However, group therapy can have its dark side, too: The group's interactions may not mirror the protected environment of some individual therapies, with the result that a participant in the group may occasionally be emotionally hurt.

The social dynamics of a therapy group are those of any developing relationship. There is the opportunity for self-disclosure ("Last night my wife and I had a terrible row"), for the development of a sense of belongingness and support from the group ("You all have helped me a great deal"), for the clarification of your own norms ("I have really slowed down sexually, has that happened to any of you?"), for discovering that others have similar problems ("Yes, it has") and similar solutions ("My husband and I actually schedule regular times to be alone together"), and for the development of self-understanding through social learning ("I didn't realize I affected people that way").

family therapy

Psychotherapy applied to the family as a unit, usually focusing on family processes such as communication, relationship enhancement, and discipline.

FAMILY THERAPY.   Each of us is a member of a number of social groups. For example, we may be part of a family or we may be married. The problems created by the dynamics of group interaction may lead us to search for help. Many psychologists believe that the problems you experience in a group are group problems, not individual problems, and that these problems need to be resolved by the group, not by the individual. Thus, in **family therapy,** the client is the family, not an individual in the family (Foley, 1989). During family therapy, the family works together—sometimes being seen altogether in their own home—to resolve their common difficulties.

Family problems often revolve around the family's inability to solve problems; the fact that the family is not well organized with individual and collective responsibilities not well spelled out; the possibility that the family is too rigidly organized; the possibility that the family is overclose to one another; the possibility

The family therapist often wants to observe family interactions in the home because this is where the family behaves together most of the time and where family problems may be seen firsthand.

that the family lacks emotional ties and communication; and the family's failure to agree on child-rearing practices (Sarason & Sarason, 1989).

MARITAL THERAPY. Is the institution of marriage in trouble? In one way, it is: Divorces constitute over 40 percent of marriages in any year. And this percent has increased steadily across the years. In another way marriage is not in trouble: Over 90 percent of Americans, for example, will marry at least once during their lifetimes (Glick, 1984*a*), suggesting that the institution of marriage continues to be important to us. Couples seek **marital therapy** when a marital relationship has soured and they wish to save it but also (less frequently) when they wish to enhance the marital relationship.

marital therapy
Psychotherapy applied to a couple, usually as a method of saving the marriage, but also to enhance the relationship.

Marital therapists often like to see both partners together so that the partners' interactions can be observed firsthand. Marital therapy most often focuses on increasing the following: communication, the appropriate expression of feelings, the amount of help each partner gives to the other, and the enjoyment the partners get out of shared experiences (Bornstein & Bornstein, 1986).

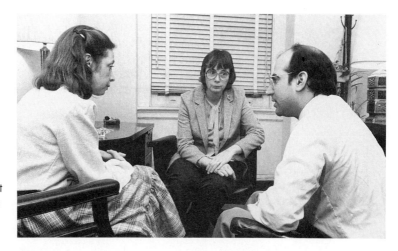

A lot more about the marital relationship is likely to be observed by the marital therapist when clients who require marital therapy are seen together than when they are seen individually.

Box 14-5

Communication Training in Marital Therapy

Married partners Steve and Elaine have created lists of positive and negative partner behaviors. Their therapist wants them to use the lists to help them learn to talk through what they really appreciate about each other. This exercise is actually behavioral rehearsal at increasing effective communication.

Elaine: (to Steve) You're a kind person, and that's something I really think is unique about you.

Steve: (nods head)

Therapist: Elaine, can you be more specific for Steve? What is it that makes him kind? What does he do that allows you to conclude he's a kind person?

Elaine: Well, he's different than other men . . .

Therapist: No, I want you to tell him directly. Talk to Steve, not to me.

Elaine: Okay, you're different than most other men, or at least different than how I think other men are. You're soft-spoken and sincere. You may not always have a lot to say, but when you do say something it's usually kind and gentle. I really don't think you would ever go out of your way to hurt anyone or anything.

Steve: Hmmm, I don't know what to say. I mean, I don't know what to say right now.

Therapist: (to Steve) That's okay. (to Elaine) That was very good, but I wonder if you could give Steve a recent example of a situation where you saw him being kind as you just spoke about it.

Elaine: Yeah, I think so. Last week when my mom called to tell us about my Aunt Audrey's illness, you were really very nice [Elaine then goes into details which are omitted]. . . . That's something that I really appreciate about you . . .

Therapist (to Steve) How does it feel to hear that kind of thing from Elaine?

Steve: It really feels good. We don't say those kinds of things to one another or, if we do, I guess we don't always hear them.

Therapist: Yes, but when you do say them or your partner hears them it sure makes a difference doesn't it?

Steve: Sure does. (reaches over, holds Elaine's hand, and speaks to her) Thank you.

From Bornstein & Bornstein, 1986, pp. 114–115.

ECLECTICS: DOING WHATEVER WORKS. A lot of psychologists don't like to be called psychoanalysts, client-centered therapists, behavior therapists, or cognitive therapists. They see that some procedures work best with some individuals, and other procedures work better with others. These therapists are the eclectics. To be eclectic means to not be held to any one theoretical approach but to take what appears to be most valid from each. An eclectic therapist wants to do what works, and may decide to use a number of different approaches to the same problem (say depression) because experience has shown that certain individuals react better to one approach than another (Lazarus, 1971).

Changing Behavior by Changing Your Biological State

In some psychotherapies, your own behavior produces a change of biological state, which subsequently allows desirable behavior to occur. We'll look briefly at two general kinds of state-changing therapies. One kind focuses on changes in muscle tension and the other focuses on cognitive quieting (which we define below). These therapies are taught to clients by their therapists as methods of dealing with fear and stress.

Progressive Muscle Relaxation

You saw that in systematic desensitization you needed to be relaxed in order to visualize a feared event without fear. Relaxation is a biological state that is incompatible with the state that we feel as fear. It is also difficult to feel stressed when you are relaxed.

One way to produce relaxation is to tense and relax various muscle groups in your body as we showed you in Chapter 5, and to focus concurrently on the feelings associated with the release of tension in your muscles. Therapists often give their clients tape-recorded instructions to help accomplish this after initial demonstrations in the therapy setting.

Autogenics: Imagine That!

Autogenics are self-suggestions, and autogenic training is another way that you can relax yourself. Autogenics are less a technique for relaxing your muscles than they are a technique to produce *cognitive quieting*—essentially a state in which you are not talking to yourself about anything—and a sense of well-being. Autogenics can be helpful if you tend to talk to yourself in ways that make you uptight ("I simply must get this done today, or I'll be in big trouble!")?

In autogenics the therapist first suggests various body conditions to you (for example, that one of your limbs is heavy and warm). Eventually you take over the suggestions yourself. The entire procedure takes some time to learn well, and it needs to be practiced an instruction at a time several times a day. After reaching proficiency with the self-instructions singly ("I am at peace"), single self-instructions are combined into groups of instructions so that a number of self-suggestions are made at one time ("Neck and shoulders, arms and legs, hands and feet heavy and warm"). People who are very practiced with autogenics claim that they can totally relax in just a few seconds. Autogenic relaxation may reflect changes in the autonomic nervous system (Lehrer & Woolfolk, 1986), moreso than in the muscles as is the case with progressive muscle relaxation.

Meditation: Stuff of the East

Meditational exercises may also produce relaxation and a sense of well-being. While the procedures in meditation may be somewhat different from autogenics, the effects may be common. Usually there is a mantra phrase of some kind ("Ohmmmmm"), to function much like the self-suggestions in autogenics. There may also be exercises to clear the imagination of activity by maintaining a specific focus on a thought, a sensation, a word, or some mental state (Sarason & Sarason, 1989).

Pharmaco-Therapy: Doing It with Drugs

Pharmaco-therapy is one of the most direct expressions of a belief in the biological model of abnormal behavior. Recall that the biological model of abnormal behavior is grounded in the belief that there is something wrong with the individual physically—most often with the individual's brain and the chemical substances (that is, neurotransmitters) that are thought to aid in the transmission of impulses along nerves—and it is this physical problem that leads to abnormal behavior.

Pharmaco-therapy is the treatment of abnormal behavior by the administration of drugs and is the primary form of treatment which results from the biological model of abnormal behavior. Given our laws, behavior-controlling medications can be dispensed only by prescription by licensed medical practitioners. Psychiatrists are licensed medical practitioners, remember? Clinical psychologists often recommend medication, too, through the physicians with whom they are associated in clinics and hospitals.

COMMONLY PRESCRIBED BEHAVIOR-CONTROLLING DRUGS. Drugs are prescribed to control problem behavior observed in three broad classes of disorder—depression, schizophrenia, and anxiety. For depression alone there are three classes of drugs that attempt to keep the client's mood on an even keel. Where the depression is unipolar, that is, does not cycle from depression to mania and back, either tricyclic antidepressants or monoaminoxidase inhibitors are used. Where the depression is bipolar, that is, the individual cycles from depression to mania and back, lithium carbonate is prescribed because it appears to prevent the onset of mania. For schizophrenia, major tranquilizers, such as the phenothiazines (called neuroleptics), are prescribed. And for anxiety, the prescription is for anxiolytics—minor tranquilizers—such as the benzodiazepines. The most common of these minor tranquilizers is diazepam, known in the trade as Valium or Librium.

There is also a recent movement to use antidepressants to treat panic and obsessive-compulsive disorder (Rapoport, 1989), suggesting the possibility of a closer relationship between depression and anxiety than previously thought. Some clients suffering from panic attacks respond best to exposure therapies, when they are concurrently given tricyclic antidepressants (Roy-Byrne & Katon, 1987).

Clients are ideally never just prescribed drugs without also receiving psychotherapy of some kind. Not infrequently, however, this ideal is not met. Given the heavy emphasis on the medical model for disease in our country, it is all too easy to try drugs first (for any disorder). Because drugs may quiet an agitated client (possibly because the client is overdosed and stuporous), doctors can incorrectly view the case as solved and the drug treatment a success. Also, staff difficulties are eased by the cessation of abnormal behavior when clients are drugged. The chain of events—agitated client/agitated staff/drug dispensed/quiet client/calm staff—can lead easily to abuse because it provides staff with immediate reinforcement for drug dispensing.

DEPENDENCE, ADDICTION, AND SIDE EFFECTS.   For those of you who may be taking tranquilizers (for which there are about 50 million prescriptions written each year), you should be cautious. Most of you will *not* be taking the major tranquilizers prescribed for hospitalized mental patients. You should be cognizant, however, of the possibility that even the minor tranquilizers may produce psychological dependency, if not outright addiction, even when taken at the prescribed doses. Psychological dependency means that the substance may be difficult to give up for psychological reasons, but when the attempt is made to quit, there are no physical signs of withdrawal. Physical symptoms upon giving up the drug are the classic signal that the drug is addicting.

For clients who are taking behavior-controlling drugs in an institution, there are two major concerns. A first concern about these drugs is their effectiveness, which is usually good in the short term, perhaps due to the client being simply slowed down physically by the drug. It is the long term that is the problem. Long-term use can lead to vegetative-like states or to **tardive dyskinesia.** Tardive dyskinesia involves uncontrolled body movements (often of lips and tongue). The risk of tardive dyskinesia rises with the age of the client. About 10 to 20 percent of clients in mental hospitals and about 40 percent of schizophrenics in or out of hospitals show some evidence of tardive dyskinesia that is linked to drug treatment (Sarason & Sarason, 1989).

A second major concern of pharmaco-therapy is the side effects that drugs often produce—lethargy, drowsiness, drunken-like behavior, inability to concentrate, insomnia, confusion, and, as mentioned above, dyskinesia. It also may be

tardive dyskinesia

Involuntary movements of the face, tongue, trunk, and limbs as a side effect of prolonged use of antipsychotic drugs.

difficult to participate in therapy if you are lethargic, confused, or unable to concentrate.

Psychosurgery and Electroconvulsive Therapy

psychosurgery

The surgical procedure of separating the frontal lobes from other parts of the brain to reduce emotional behavior.

electroconvulsive shock therapy

The passage of a brief electric current across the brain to produce a convulsion. Used as a treatment for life-threatening depression where nothing else works.

Psychosurgery and **electroconvulsive therapy** (ECT) are drastic treatments that are used when a client's problem behaviors are resistant to all other forms of treatment and the client is of great danger to self or others. Such behaviors occur in extreme depression in which the client may be suicidal, and in the uncontrollable rages that can accompany mania. Both psychosurgery and ECT directly change brain function and thus clearly result from holding to the biological model of abnormal behavior.

In one type of psychosurgery, the prefrontal lobotomy, the frontal lobes of the cortex of the brain are surgically separated from the emotion-regulating centers of the brain that supply it. Psychosurgery has been largely abandoned due to the unpredictable outcomes it produces and to the availability of calming drugs. Some recipients become calm and tractable after lobotomies, some show no changes, some become lethargic and vegetative, and still others become childlike and immature.

Psychosurgery seems gruesome and it is unfortunate that it has ever been associated with psychological practice, if, for no other reason than the Frankenstein-like images which it conveys. Yet, when it was first presented, psychosurgery was considered a sufficient medical advance to produce a Nobel prize for its creator, a Portugese psychiatrist named Monitz.

In ECT, a brief electric current is passed across the brain which produces a momentary convulsive seizure. Electroconvulsive shock treatment is still used—about 80,000 cases per year (Sackheim, 1985)—but now only on individuals who are extremely depressed and suicidal and for whom nothing else has worked. Moreover, ECT has undergone considerable standardization. Recipients now are given a general anesthetic and a muscle relaxant so that they essentially awake after treatment with no knowledge of it. After three treatments per week for several weeks depressed clients often improve and this improvement occurs in the absence of any known brain damage (Scovern & Killman, 1980; Weiner, 1984).

Now let's examine how the major disorders are treated today in the United States. We'll give you several brief sketches and tell you how the cases we presented to you at the beginning were treated. Given that we've already detailed

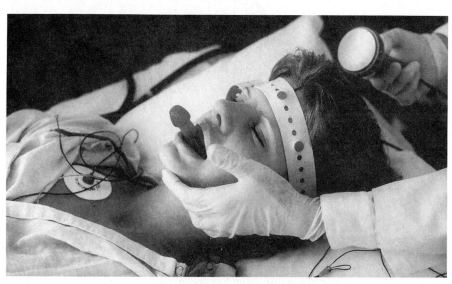

Electroconvulsive therapy is used currently where clients are extremely depressed and unresponsive to any other therapy. Its standardization in terms of the use of muscle relaxants and general anesthetics means that it is less horrifying to the client and those who are observing. Specifically why ECT works is not known.

some of the kinds of treatments, we'll refer back to those you have already read about.

Treatment of Psychological Disorders

Anxiety Disorders

AGORAPHOBIA AND PANIC.   Practice, practice, practice. It's a fact. The most successful way to treat agoraphobia—the debilitating fear of finding yourself in a locale from which you cannot escape or in which you cannot get help—is to gradually expose yourself to the feared environment (Marks, 1987). Barlow and his colleagues do that by having the agoraphobic practice taking a feared route toward a feared destination (Barlow, 1988). Often only a few sessions are required for significant improvement. Antidepressant drugs may assist here if the client also has mood problems, if the medication is taken together with the exposure routines (Telch et al., 1985).

SIMPLE AND SOCIAL PHOBIAS.   Let's take Ms. B's case as an example of treatment of a simple phobia. Recall that Ms. B. could not eat solid food—and had not done so for 15 years—because she was afraid of choking (Spitzer et al., 1983). How was she helped?

Professor Gallagher and his controversial technique of simultaneously confronting the fear of heights, snakes and the dark.

Ms. B's therapist tried *in vivo* desensitization. After explaining treatment to her, Ms. B began to eat solid foods a little at a time in the relaxed environment of the therapist's office. During each session she would choose the food for the following session—a slightly more difficult food for her to eat. Between sessions she would practice at home with foods that she was able to eat in her treatment sessions. She began with one-half a peanut at the beginning, progressed to carrots and apples, and then went on to sandwiches by the sixth session.

There were two other components to her therapy. One was educational. The therapist explained the anatomy of the esophagus and the body's natural defenses against choking when he became aware that Ms. B had misconceptions about how swallowing worked. She expressed great relief at this information. The second component involved the use of a timer to speed up Ms. B's rate of eating.

A three-year follow-up telephone call found Ms. B to be eating normally. She would still occasionally find herself worrying about choking, however. She reported a relapse at one year which she successfully treated herself using the same *in vivo* desensitization procedures (Spitzer et al., 1983).

Mood Disorders

In the section on cognitive restructuring, we have already shown you how Ellis' rational-emotive therapy and Beck's cognitive therapy are applied to the behaviors of depressed individuals. There are other behavior therapies used to treat depression as well; here is one.

AZRIN'S OPERANT REINFORCEMENT METHOD. Nathan Azrin believes that depressed people don't produce much behavior that can be reinforced. For example, if they don't go outside they may miss a beautiful sunset. His approach is therefore designed to increase the frequency of behaviors that will produce reinforcement. His clients first identify four attainable behavioral goals (for example, losing ten pounds to feel more attractive). Next, from lists, the client identifies positive attributes that apply to him or herself ("I'm a good listener"); items that are pleasurable (foods liked in the past); recreational activities liked in the past (walking, reading); and people liked. The client then practices making positive self-statements; engages in a daily and weekly schedule of rewarding activities using the above lists (including a brief daily Happy Talk period); identifies traumatic events that could happen to anyone, but would be unlikely to happen to him or herself per se (becoming blind)—used to induce a contrast effect; identifies nondepressing attributes of traumatic events ("I'm overweight, but my breasts are bigger because of it"); engages in social skills training where there are social skills deficits, job seeking where there is unemployment-related depression, and study scheduling where there is academic difficulty; and corrects any depressive response with multiple positive statements (Azrin & Besalel, 1981; Hoberman & Lewinsohn, 1985).

COMBINED COGNITIVE RESTRUCTURING AND PHARMACO-THERAPY. Drugs are commonly used to treat depression with some success. As we noted above, the drugs used are the tricyclic antidepressants (for example, Imipramine) for major depression and lithium salts (lithium chloride) for bipolar depression. Dosages of these have to be very carefully monitored because drugs can produce undesirable side effects. Lithium, for example, is toxic to the kidneys. These drugs are used in combination with the psychotherapies for depression that we have already discussed.

Psychologists are always interested in which therapeutic technique is best for a particular problem behavior. Often it is difficult to tell because there isn't comparative research available. However, researchers have compared cognitive restructuring therapy (such as that of Beck's) with the use of antidepressants in the treatment of depression. The antidepressants tend to reduce depression more quickly while cognitive behavior therapy tends to produce less relapse (Roth et al., 1982; Simons et al., 1986). Thus, in the case of depression, the preferred treatment at this time appears to be a combination of cognitive restructuring therapy and antidepressant medication (Agras, 1987).

Let's see how Mrs. K's major depression episode was handled. Recall that she attempted to commit suicide feeling despondent over her inability to prevent her husband's death from cancer and Alzheimer's disease (Oltmanns et al., 1986). Mrs. K's family wanted her to live with them, but Mrs. K's therapist wisely decided that Mrs. K valued her independence. Mrs. K agreed that she wanted to go back to her hotel residence, although she later told her therapist that this was, in part, because that locale would give her another chance at suicide. Mrs. K's therapist was a middle-aged woman who specialized in gerontology—the study of aging—and whose warmth and empathy won Mrs. K over. It took several weeks of discussions to get around to the major issue—Mrs. K's guilt feelings over her husband's death. Her self blame included thoughts that she was living well because of her husband's earnings, that he had died among strangers due to her selfishness, that she was really no good to anybody, and that she was especially no good because she couldn't cope with her husband's death while all the other widows at the hotel were doing fine. At this point her therapist uncovered the fact that Mrs. K had experienced episodes of depression all of her life and these episodes also contained the same pattern of self-blame. The exaggerations and distortions in Mrs. K's statements led her therapist to believe that Beck's cognitive restructuring therapy would apply well. Thirty therapy sessions later, Mrs. K was taking a more active interest in social functions in her community. She also had stopped drinking alcohol.

Schizophrenia

Schizophrenia is typically treated with a combination of therapeutic procedures including various behavior therapies, family therapy, and pharmaco-therapy.

BEHAVIOR THERAPY.   Schizophrenics can be differentially reinforced for talking appropriately and for withholding inappropriate verbal behavior such as delusional and hallucinatory statements (Ayllon & Haughton, 1964; Wince et al., 1972). They can learn that normal behavior produces social attention and other reinforcers and that these reinforcers will not occur if problem behavior does. In a successful outcome the schizophrenic client shows a suppression of abnormal verbal behavior and increases in normal behavior.

Schizophrenics who are hallucinating can sometimes be taught that the auditory sensations they hear are of their own making—that they are hearing their own bodies (Burns et al., 1983). They then can be taught to ignore their own inner talk until it goes away.

Token Economies.   Previously we mentioned that a symbol of a reinforcer could work to strengthen and maintain behavior and that these symbols commonly take the forms of tokens. Token economy programs in which tokens are earned for functional behavior (self-care; work) and exchanged for privileges have been successfully used with schizophrenics (Paul & Lentz, 1977). As the client proceeds through the various levels of these programs, more and more freedom and responsibility are earned until the client approximates living outside the institution.

For those schizophrenics who—at this state of our knowledge—will continue to require some community support, the group home which contains a token economy program is an extension of the psychiatric hospital. Group home programs that employ token economies have been successful at getting schizophrenics back into the community and maintaining them at normal functioning levels (Fairweather et al., 1969).

Social Skills Training.   There has also been considerable success in teaching schizophrenic clients social skills and in demonstrating the importance of social skills for effective communication and assertiveness (Bellack et al., 1984; Kelly & Lamparski, 1985; Morrison & Bellack, 1984). Other studies have demonstrated the effectiveness of behavioral treatments for teaching both social skills and job-finding skills for schizophrenic clients (Bellack et al., 1984; Bellack & Hersen, 1978; Jacobs et al., 1984). Such findings have led to the argument that behavior therapy can make a significant contribution to the treatment, management, and rehabilitation of schizophrenic clients (Bellack, 1986).

FAMILY THERAPY.   Where the schizophrenia is episodic rather than chronic, clients are treated, where possible, as outpatients. In these cases family therapy is indicated. The family is taught to help manage the behavior of their schizophrenic relative. Such programs essentially attempt to change the ways in which the family reacts to schizophrenic behavior (for example, Anderson et al., 1986; Atkinson, 1986).

PHARMACO-THERAPY.   Schizophrenic behavior can be managed with pharmaco-therapy, using the phenothiazines (for example, Thorazine) which are major tranquilizers (Klein & Davis, 1969; but see Paul & Lentz, 1977). No one knows why these tranquilizers work. One possibility is that schizophrenics may be overwhelmed by environmental stimulation. Perhaps the tranquilizer makes such stimulation tolerable through a general quieting effect. The fact that drugs do have an effect in some cases suggests that there may be some physical basis to schizophrenic behavior, but after one hundred years of research no one yet knows what the physical basis is.

The most likely treatment for schizophrenia today is a combination of pharmaco-therapy (in the form of tranquilizers) and some form of psychotherapy. The nature of the latter will usually reflect the orientation of the staff of the institution.

As an example of some of the problems of dealing with schizophrenia let's look at Mr. R who, you'll recall, was taken from an airplane after exhibiting bizarre verbal behavior (Spitzer et al., 1983). Mr. R's history was to be hospitalized and medicated for abnormal behaviors which included drunkenness, property destruction, and carrying a concealed weapon. Whenever his behavior led to his arrest he would usually be found incompetent to stand trial and be remanded to psychiatric hospitalization. After a few weeks in the hospital, Mr. R usually would become lucid enough to gain his freedom (". . . if I don't talk supernatural I can pass a psychiatric exam. . ."), although some schizophrenic behavior, such as speech that contains very little information and inappropriate emotions, always would be present. Mr. R's relatives don't help him because he once set his grandmother's house on fire when he thought (erroneously) the she had withheld some money of his. After he gains his freedom, the downward cycle of drinking, violence, and increasingly bizarre behavior usually begins again, posing an as yet unsolvable problem for his family and community. Mr. R is a schizophrenic who is not particularly helped by medication. Attempts to hospitalize him for longer periods of time have failed (Spitzer et al., 1983).

Psychotherapy: How Good Is It?

After reading all about the various techniques that comprise psychotherapy, you might wonder about its effectiveness. At one level psychotherapy must be fairly effective, because clinical psychologists and psychiatrists have plenty of business.

But perhaps that's only because they are among the few possible choices for help, and because the stress of living today is producing more people who require help.

At a second level, is there evidence that psychotherapy is better than no treatment at all? The answer is yes—there is a clear positive effect of psychotherapy—but we need to modify this conclusion somewhat. A positive therapeutic effect may not occur for everyone. The positive outcome is an average (Smith et al., 1980). Smith and colleagues concluded that the average client who received psychotherapy was better off than 75 percent of people who were not treated, and for fear and anxiety alleviation, clients who received psychotherapy were better off than 83 percent of those who were untreated.

At a third level, we can ask whether some psychotherapies are better than others. In one sense, the answer is "yes." Certain behavior therapies, for example, are more effective than insight therapies for the treatment of simple phobias. In another sense, however, this may be an unanswerable question. How would you compare a therapy whose goal is insight with a therapy whose goal is change in a specific behavior? Would this be like comparing apples and oranges? There are some answers here but they are pretty complex.

SUMMARY

- While the most frequently occurring psychological disorders are substance abuse/dependence, anxiety disorders, mood disorders, and schizophrenia, respectively, the disorders most seen in the mental health system are schizophrenia, mood disorders, anxiety disorders, and substance abuse/dependence, respectively.

- You're more at risk for a psychological disorder if you are younger rather than older, are unmarried rather than married, are less educated rather than more educated, are unemployed rather than employed, earn a smaller rather than a larger income, have few friends rather than many friends, have unsatisfactory rather than satisfactory social relationships, and have an unsatisfactory rather than a satisfactory marriage. But these are just risk factors—you can have them all and not have a psychological disorder.

- Providers of mental health services are psychologists, psychiatrists, and others such as social workers, psychiatric nurses and counselors. All have at least a Bachelor's degree. Psychologists have Ph.D.s, Psy.D.s, or Ed.D.s, while psychiatrists have M.D.s which make them medical doctors.

- Psychotherapy refers to a varied array of treatments provided by mental health professionals, the aims of which are to either provide insight into the reasons for behavior, or to change behavior. They can be divided into insight, behavior, cognitive behavior and pharmaco-therapies.

- The first psychotherapy was Freud's psychoanalysis, a talk therapy in which the patient seeks insight into problem behavior, and eventual personality change. Psychoanalysis is rare now because it takes years to complete. In its modern form the focus is much more on the here and now and less on one's history.

- The client- or person-centered psychotherapies focus on the client as a person. In Rogers' nondirective therapy, the client is seen as healing on his or her own within the therapeutic environment presented by the therapist.

- The behavior therapies are a collection of psychotherapies that stand in contrast to psychoanalysis and the client-centered therapies because they are derived from experimental psychology. The behavior therapies include such techniques as positive reinforcement, aversion therapy, systematic desensitization, and modeling. All behavior therapies focus on specific problem behaviors or sets of behaviors that need to be changed.

■ The cognitive behavior therapies follow from the behavior therapies. Their focus, however, is on the client's verbal behavior, especially self-talk, as the cause of abnormal behavior and emotional upset. Cognitive restructuring therapies seek to change the way clients think about themselves in relation to their world.

■ Other psychotherapies take place in groups, either of strangers who have similar problems, in which case the focus is on dealing with the group's common problem; or of related individuals (families; marrieds), in which case the inter-relations within the group are the source of the problem behaviors.

■ Some psychotherapies change behavior by attempting to change the client's biological state (without drugs). These generally have the individual practice either exercises involving muscular effort or exercises involving cognition. When these procedures produce relaxation (the changed biological state) the individual can be exposed, for example, to fearful stimuli without raising anxiety levels. Systematic desensitization is the most well known of these procedures.

■ Pharmaco-therapy is the final way that abnormal behaviors are commonly treated today. Pharmaceuticals directly produce biological state change in the client. While medications appear to produce immediate positive effects, in many cases there is considerable concern over the mechanisms of their actions, their immediate side effects, and their long-term side effects.

■ The anxiety disorders are treated with gradual exposure to the feared stimuli either in imagination (systematic desensitization) or in real life (in vivo desensitization). Minor tranquilizers are often prescribed to increase the likelihood of exposure to the feared stimuli during treatment and during behavioral rehearsal.

■ Depression is treated with cognitive restructuring therapy in which the client attempts to restructure how the world is viewed and how she or he fits into it under the guidance of the therapist. There are behavior therapy components here as well that include exercises in behaving differently and checking the outcomes of so doing. It is very common for those who are depressed to be on medication concurrently with the application of these other therapies.

■ Schizophrenia is treated with behavior therapy for social skills development, talking normally, work adjustment, and self-care. In acute cases it is also treated as a family problem via family therapy. It is very common for those behaving schizophrenically to be on tranquilizing medication concurrently with these other therapies.

■ Psychotherapy is effective for the majority (but not all) of the people who are exposed to it.

Box 14-6

SELF-ADJUSTMENT FOR STUDENTS: MAKE IT LAST

You've nearly finished your self-adjustment project, and hopefully you have made some good gains. Now what? Obviously, you should do whatever will make your gains endure or even improve. How do you go about that?

RELAPSE AWARENESS

First, recall our discussion of relapse in Chapter 13. Remember that relapse is normal. If you have one, recall that the world doesn't end as a result of a relapse. You need only to analyze why the relapse occurred and to start again.

The way to make your self-adjustment last—and to prevent relapse—is to plan for it to last. In essence this means planning for three kinds of generalization. Each of these kinds of generalization should be a formal aspect of any good self-adjustment program.

PLAN FOR STIMULUS GENERALIZATION

Stimulus generalization involves producing your target behavior in new environments, similar to those in which your program occurred, until your target behavior occurs automatically in any new environment.

Usually you will have conducted your self-adjustment project in a few specific environments (for example, your dorm, apartment, or home). First, identify where you have conducted your project. It is likely that these environments (let's call them your *project environments*) are partially in control of your adjusted behavior. Let's take a weight loss project as an example. Perhaps you have conducted your weight loss project in your apartment, and in your college's cafeterias and restaurants. Now you are under the control of the project environments and you stick to low-calorie, high fiber, nonfat foods when you eat in the project environments. But what about when you go home for vacation? Or to a restaurant on a weekend? Or to a banquet? Or on an airplane? What then? You are no longer in the project's environ-

ments. You hope that in these new environments you will still select low-calorie, high-fiber, nonfat foods. Well, hope usually won't do it.

Bring Your Adjusted Behavior under the Control of New Environments. To accomplish generalization of your behavior to new environments, expand your self-adjustment program so that it includes new environments. You could do this one environment at a time. Isolate the one most likely to disrupt your program first and commit (see our earlier section on commitment in Box 5-2) to carrying out your program in that environment. Perhaps this means buying a salad or other low-calorie, nonfat foods during trips to fast food restaurants that you visit weekly with your friends. After you are successful in carrying out your program in this new environment, add another, get successful in it, and then add a third new environment. Continue to add new environments until your behavior is appropriate in all of them. At this point, just possibly, still other environments that you have not yet experienced will now control appropriate eating behavior with little more work on your part. You've achieved wide-spread stimulus generalization.

CHANGE RELATED RESPONSES

Changing related responses involves the changing of responses that complement those that you worked on explicitly during your self-adjustment program. Let's say that your weight loss program involved primarily selecting appropriate foods, and that you have succeeded in doing just that anywhere you eat. How else might you help yourself lose weight? One way might be to increase the amount of water that you drink daily—to make you feel a bit more full. When you are successfully choosing appropriate foods in a variety of environments, you could begin to increase your daily water intake. Once that behavior was well established, you could add another set of behaviors such as a mild exercise program or you could take smaller portions of food when they are offered to you.

Strengthening each of these new behaviors would increase the likelihood that your original self-adjustment program gains would last.

PLAN GENERALIZATION OVER TIME

Generalization over time means that your target behavior(s) will occur at times other than when you are formally programming them.

Engage Natural Reinforcers. Generalization across time depends on the continued effectiveness of consequences for your adjusted behavior. If you used non-natural, arbitrary reinforcers to produce your adjusted behavior, it is time to bring your behavior under the control of natural reinforcers. (Arbitrary reinforcers are ones that you or someone else scheduled; natural reinforcers are those that nature schedules.) Often this process itself occurs naturally. For example, your arduous weight loss program may make it more likely that the way you look stimulates others to look at you, perhaps even to comment on how good you look. This is naturally rewarding to most everyone. A leaner you may also feel better, actually be healthier, and have more energy, all of which may function as natural reinforcers which contribute to the maintenance of your adjusted behavior. Where natural reinforcers are not forthcoming, you can behave in ways that make them more likely. For example, compliments can be sneakily solicited. (Sneaky prompt: "Wow, I feel great." Likely response: "You should, you look great!") Soliciting natural reinforcement may mean sensitizing important people in your world to your accomplishments. Let them know what you've accomplished. Most often they'll respond favorably.

Continue to Schedule Non-natural Reinforcement. It is possible that natural reinforcers by themselves may be insufficient to maintain your new behaviors. This outcome calls for you to schedule intermittently some of the same consequences that helped your adjustment in the first instance. To continue with our weight loss example, let's suppose that one of your reinforcers was an article of new clothing in a smaller size dependent on a given amount of weight loss. You could continue to schedule such an outcome for maintenance of your program gains. One month in which there were no weight gains or in which there was further weight loss could lead to purchase of a second article of clothing. You get the idea: Continue to schedule some of the reinforcers that stimulated your behavior change in the first place. They can assist in maintenance of your program gains.

For your own self-adjustment project list the arbitrary consequences contained in your program in one column of Table 14-4. In the second column, list as many natural consequences for your target behavior as you can.

It is possible, that, hard as you try, there is no way that you can change yourself—and you're miserable because of it. Perhaps professional help should be sought. We'll deal with this possibility in the next chapter.

TABLE 14-4
ARBITRARY AND NATURAL CONSEQUENCES OF MY TARGET BEHAVIOR

Arbitrary Consequences	*Natural Consequences*
1. _____	1. _____
2. _____	2. _____
3. _____	3. _____
4. _____	4. _____
5. _____	5. _____

MEMORY BOOSTER

■ IMPORTANT PEOPLE

You should know who these persons are and why they are important:

Sigmund Freud   Albert Ellis
Carl Rogers   Aaron Beck
Joseph Wolpe   Nathan Azrin

■ IMPORTANT TERMS

Be prepared to define the following terms (located in the margins of this chapter). Where appropriate, be prepared to describe examples.

Provider-of-Treatment   Counterconditioning
Psychotherapy   Rational-Emotive Therapy
Psychoanalysis   Beck's Cognitive Therapy
Transference   Family Therapy
Nondirective Therapy   Marital Therapy
Behavior Therapies   Tardive Dyskinesia
Token Economy   Psychosurgery
Behavioral Rehearsal   Electroconvulsive Shock Therapy
Modeling

■ QUESTIONS FROM IMPORTANT IDEAS IN THIS CHAPTER

1. In a sentence or two each, what are the objectives for the client of insight therapies, behavior therapies, cognitive behavior therapies, and pharmaco-therapies?
2. In a sentence or two each, indicate how free association, dream analysis, and transference might be used by a psychoanalyst to help a patient achieve the goal of psychoanalysis.
3. In two or three sentences, explain how Carl Rogers' non-directive therapy is "client-centered."
4. Describe how counterconditioning is involved in aversion therapy and in systematic desensitization.
5. How are cognitive restructuring therapies similar to and different from other behavior therapies and psychoanalysis?
6. In a sentence or two each, briefly describe six approaches to changing your behavior by changing your biological state.
7. Consider the approaches to treating depression by Albert Ellis, Aaron Beck, and Nathan Azrin. How are the goals of each of these approaches similar and different?
8. Are there some disorders for which the best treatment might be a combination of some form of psychotherapy and some form of pharmaco-therapy? Justify your answer.
9. How effective is psychotherapy?

RESOLVING HARMFUL EMOTIONS (ANXIETY, ANGER, LONELINESS, AND GRIEF)

CHAPTER OUTLINE

After reading this chapter, you should be able to:

- Describe several strategies for overcoming anxiety.
- Apply systematic self-desensitization to overcome any fears that you might have.
- Apply several strategies for controlling anger.
- Describe the basic components of the LADDER technique for increasing assertiveness.
- Differentiate among transient, situational, and chronic loneliness.
- Describe three ways in which loneliness can be ameliorated.
- Differentiate between bereavement and grief.
- Describe several adjustment strategies that facilitate the normal grief process.

Perhaps you can't do some very simple things in your life because you're afraid to. Maybe you can't speak up for yourself—you're afraid of what might happen if you do. Or perhaps you're afraid to be in the desert because you might encounter a snake or a scorpion, so you turn down invitations to go camping.

Perhaps you've noticed that you get angry a lot with your spouse, your children, your colleagues, and your friends. Have any of these individuals begun to avoid you because of it? What should you do?

Perhaps you find yourself alone most of the time, and this gives you an aching feeling in the gut—you feel quite badly about it—but no one seems to notice or to care.

Perhaps you've just broken up with someone with whom you've had a fantastic relationship. Now, however, he or she doesn't want to see you anymore; or perhaps this person is moving away—the relationship is over. This breakup makes you feel terrible. Or perhaps your sister or brother has just been killed in an automobile accident. You're distraught. How can you possibly live without her or him?

In each of the preceding scenarios we experience emotions that are unpleasant—emotions that we'd like to experience less—anxiety, anger, the emptiness of being lonely, the bottomless sadness of the loss of someone you love. These are emotions that we'd like to resolve as quickly as possible—emotions that can be particularly troublesome.

People who experience severe emotional problems should seek professional help (severe psychological problems and their treatment are discussed in more detail in Chapters 13 and 14). Cases of milder though still troublesome problems of anxiety, anger, loneliness, and grief, however, can be self-adjusted. In this chapter, we describe specific steps that you can take to overcome problematic anxiety, anger, loneliness, and grief.

Can You Self-Adjust Harmful Emotions?

When should you attempt to self-adjust for these harmful emotions and when should you seek professional help? There are no hard and fast rules, but here are some guidelines.

You should attempt to self-adjust in the following situations:

- The problem is a mild one.
- You feel reasonably sure that you can handle it.
- You can define the problem objectively.
- There is self-adjustment suggested for it in a book such as this.
- You've tried to self-adjust this particular problem before and succeeded.

You should seek professional help in these situations:

- The problem seems overwhelming to you.
- You feel certain that you cannot handle it.
- You cannot define what is wrong with you.
- There is no self-adjustment suggested for your problem in a book such as this.
- You've tried to self-adjust this particular problem more than once and failed.

Adjusting Anxiety

fear
The label given to cognitive appraisal of a danger.

anxiety
The label given to the unpleasant emotion we experience as a consequence of cognitive appraisal of a danger.

phobia
Intense, irrational, and incapacitating anxiety of a particular stimulus or class of events.

As we explained in Chapter 4, emotions include three components: the immediate body reactions (both internal physiological arousal and observable expression) during the experience of emotion, the ongoing display of emotional behavior, and the labels given to emotions. Anxiety and fear are the labels given to the emotional experience when we encounter impending danger or aversive events. But what's the difference between anxiety and fear? Beck and Emery (1985) suggest that fear is a label for the cognitive appraisal of a danger, while anxiety is a label for the consequence of the appraisal (Beck, 1991). That is, people use the term **fear** when they're talking about danger (for example, "I'm afraid of dogs"). Having made such an appraisal—perhaps in the presence of a dog—the consequence of the appraisal is **anxiety.** As we described in Chapter 1, when the appraisal generates intense, irrational, and incapacitating anxiety, we refer to it as a **phobia.**

What Are You Afraid Of?

We have included a copy of the Fear Survey Schedule (Box 15-1) to help you ascertain your own fears. You may already have a very good idea of some of them; for example, you may not be able to go into your garden for fear of encountering a snake. But in other cases, you may not be quite as aware of your fears, perhaps because you don't encounter the fear-generating stimulus very often (for example, the sight of blood).

Many fears are typical, but some can be handicapping.

Box 15-1

MEASURE YOUR OWN FEAR (FEAR INVENTORY)

The items in this survey refer to things and experiences that may cause fear or other unpleasant feelings. Circle the number in the column that describes how much you are disturbed by a particular item at this point in your life. Scoring is found below.

0 = Not at all; 1 = A little; 2 = A fair amount; 3 = Much; 4 = Very much.

1. Noise of vacuum cleaners	0	1	2	3	4	32. Sudden noises	0	1	2	3	4
2. Open wounds	0	1	2	3	4	33. Dull weather	0	1	2	3	4
3. Being alone	0	1	2	3	4	34. Crowds	0	1	2	3	4
4. Being in a strange place	0	1	2	3	4	35. Large open spaces	0	1	2	3	4
5. Loud noises	0	1	2	3	4	36. Cats	0	1	2	3	4
6. Dead people	0	1	2	3	4	37. One person bullying another	0	1	2	3	4
7. Speaking in public	0	1	2	3	4	38. Tough-looking people	0	1	2	3	4
8. Crossing streets	0	1	2	3	4	39. Birds	0	1	2	3	4
9. People who seem insane	0	1	2	3	4	40. Sight of deep water	0	1	2	3	4
10. Falling	0	1	2	3	4	41. Being watched working	0	1	2	3	4
11. Automobiles	0	1	2	3	4	42. Dead animals	0	1	2	3	4
12. Being teased	0	1	2	3	4	43. Weapons	0	1	2	3	4
13. Dentists	0	1	2	3	4	44. Dirt	0	1	2	3	4
14. Thunder	0	1	2	3	4	45. Crawling insects	0	1	2	3	4
15. Sirens	0	1	2	3	4	46. Sight of fighting	0	1	2	3	4
16. Failure	0	1	2	3	4	47. Ugly people	0	1	2	3	4
17. Entering a room where other people are already seated	0	1	2	3	4	48. Fire	0	1	2	3	4
						49. Sick people	0	1	2	3	4
18. High places on land	0	1	2	3	4	50. Dogs	0	1	2	3	4
19. Looking down from high buildings	0	1	2	3	4	51. Being criticized	0	1	2	3	4
20. Worms	0	1	2	3	4	52. Strange shapes	0	1	2	3	4
21. Imaginary creatures	0	1	2	3	4	53. Being in an elevator	0	1	2	3	4
22. Strangers	0	1	2	3	4	54. Witnessing surgical operations	0	1	2	3	4
23. Receiving injections	0	1	2	3	4	55. Angry people	0	1	2	3	4
24. Bats	0	1	2	3	4	56. Mice	0	1	2	3	4
25. Journeys by train	0	1	2	3	4	57. Blood					
26. Journeys by bus	0	1	2	3	4	a. human	0	1	2	3	4
27. Journeys by car	0	1	2	3	4	b. animal	0	1	2	3	4
28. Feeling angry	0	1	2	3	4	58. Parting from friends	0	1	2	3	4
29. People in authority	0	1	2	3	4	59. Enclosed places	0	1	2	3	4
30. Flying insects	0	1	2	3	4	60. Prospect of a surgical operation	0	1	2	3	4
31. Seeing other people injected	0	1	2	3	4	61. Feeling rejected by others	0	1	2	3	4
						62. Airplanes	0	1	2	3	4

63. Medical odors	0	1	2	3	4	78. Becoming nauseous	0	1	2	3	4
64. Feeling disapproved of	0	1	2	3	4	79. Spiders (harmless)	0	1	2	3	4
65. Harmless snakes	0	1	2	3	4	80. Being in charge or responsible for decisions	0	1	2	3	4
66. Cemeteries	0	1	2	3	4						
67. Being ignored	0	1	2	3	4						
68. Darkness	0	1	2	3	4	81. Sight of knives or sharp objects	0	1	2	3	4
69. Premature heart beats (Missing a beat)	0	1	2	3	4	82. Becoming mentally ill	0	1	2	3	4
70. a. Nude men	0	1	2	3	4	83. Being with a member of the other sex	0	1	2	3	4
b. Nude women	0	1	2	3	4	84. Taking written tests	0	1	2	3	4
71. Lightning	0	1	2	3	4	85. Being touched by others	0	1	2	3	4
72. Doctors	0	1	2	3	4						
73. People with deformities	0	1	2	3	4	86. Feeling different from others	0	1	2	3	4
74. Making mistakes	0	1	2	3	4	87. A lull in conversation	0	1	2	3	4
75. Looking foolish	0	1	2	3	4						
76. Losing control	0	1	2	3	4						
77. Fainting	0	1	2	3	4						

Adapted from Wolpe, 1982.

SCORING THE FEAR SURVEY SCHEDULE

The Fear Survey Schedule (FSS) has no standard scoring. However, you can get a fair estimate of your overall "fear level" by making the following two comparisons. Total your score by adding all the numbers you circled together. Divide this total by 89. The result is a mean score for the FSS. In one study, the mean score on the FSS for two groups of teens was 1.94 (Cautela, 1972). If your score is approximately 2.0 or less, your fears are pretty normal compared to this group. Another way to compare yourself with other FSS-takers is the following: Count the number of items on which you scored a 1 or a 2. Divide these by 89 and multiply by 100 to get a percentage. Count the number of items on which you scored 2 or 3 (yes, you do count the 2s again). Divide these by 89 and multiply by 100. Count the number of items on which you scored 3 or 4 (yes, you do count the 3s again). Divide these items by 89 and multiply by 100. You should now have three percentages—one for items scored 1 or 2, one for items scored 2 or 3, and one for items scored 3 or 4. Males score about 70 percent of the items 1 or 2; about 26 percent 2 or 3; and about 1 percent 3 or 4 (Spielberger, 1978). Men: Did you score a higher percentage of items at 3 or 4 than this? Females score about 52 percent of the items 1 or 2; about 44 percent 2 or 3; and about 4 percent 3 or 4 (Spielberger, 1978). Women: Are your percents much different than these? Particularly, do you score a higher percentage of items at 3 or 4? Finally, for men and women, of the items on which you have scored 3 or 4, are there particular themes that connect them? For example, are they indicative of a fear of animals in general, or insects, or heights? If your scores seem quite different from these casual norms, you may want to consult a professional in your student health service or in your community. Or, as in the case of Barb described below in this chapter, you may want to try to self-adjust your fear.

Methods for Controlling Anxiety Problems

systematic desensitization

A behavior therapy technique developed by Joseph Wolpe to help clients overcome phobias and extreme anxiety; includes constructing a fear hierarchy, learning deep muscle relaxation, and systematically imagining fear-producing items from the fear hierarchy while in a relaxed state.

systematic self-desensitization

Essentially the same procedure as systematic desensitization, but in which the client progresses through the various desensitization stages without the help of a therapist.

fear hierarchy

A list of items that cause anxiety with the items ranked from those that produce the least anxiety to those that produce the most anxiety; the items are typically organized around some theme, such as fear of flying.

SYSTEMATIC SELF-DESENSITIZATION.   Do you remember Barb's problem from Chapter 1? She had an irrational fear of riding in airplanes—so much so that she canceled her reservation to visit a friend in another city. That was back in 1976. Barb decided that it was time to take a stand. No more trip cancellations. Beginning on August 11 of that year, she started a program to overcome her fear. A little over two weeks later, on August 26, Barb took her first plane trip, and enjoyed it immensely. She has successfully enjoyed flying many times since. How did she overcome her anxiety? By using systematic self-desensitization.

Systematic desensitization is a behavior therapy technique to overcome extreme or irrational fears of particular objects or events. Recall that the procedure is based on counterconditioning (see Chapters 3 and 14) in which a conditioned stimulus loses its ability to elicit a conditioned response if that conditioned stimulus is paired with a stimulus that elicits an incompatible response. Wolpe's systematic desensitization procedure helps people combat fear by teaching them to perform relaxation responses while imagining situations that normally produce fear or anxiety. As you read in Chapter 14, systematic desensitization can be divided into three major steps: (1) constructing a fear hierarchy, (2) learning deep muscle relaxation, and (3) carrying out the actual therapy steps for the desensitization process. **Systematic *self*-desensitization** is essentially the same procedure, except that the client progresses through the various desensitization stages without the help of a therapist. We will describe the three major steps of this approach as they were followed by Barb. (For details of Barb's case, see Roscoe et al., 1980; or Martin & Pear, 1992.)

Constructing a Fear Hierarchy.   A **fear hierarchy** is a list of items that cause anxiety, with the items ranked from those that produce the least anxiety to those that produce the most. The items are typically organized around some theme, such as Barb's fear of flying. Barb's fear hierarchy is shown in Table 15-1.

To prepare a fear hierarchy concerning a particular fear, you should put each item of the hierarchy on a 3 × 5 index card. On the front of each index card,

Figure 15-1

A sample index card for a fear-producing situation

Front Side

> Talking to the travel agent, making reservations.

Back Side

> 1. Phoning the travel agent—dial number, call answered.
>
> 2. Giving particulars of destination, dates of trip.
>
> 3. Writing down flight numbers and times.
>
> 4. Marking calendar with dates, flight times, and flight numbers.

describe a particular item in a brief phrase. On the back of the card, list additional prompts that will help you to realistically imagine yourself actually experiencing the item. A sample index card used by Barb is shown in Figure 15-1.

When you have from 10 to 20 fear-producing items on index cards, arrange them in order starting with the item that produces the least anxiety and ending with the item that produces the most anxiety. Then, to ensure that the steps between

TABLE 15-1
EXAMPLE OF A FEAR-OF-FLYING HIERARCHY

1. The plane has landed and stopped at the terminal. I get off the plane and enter the terminal, where I am met by friends.
2. A trip has been planned, and I have examined the possible methods of travel and decided "out loud" to travel by plane.
3. I have called the travel agent and told him of my plans. He gives me the times and flight numbers.
4. It is the day before the trip, and I pack my suitcase, close it, and lock it.
5. It is ten days before the trip, and I receive the tickets in the mail. I note the return address, open the envelope, and check the tickets for the correct dates, times, and flight numbers.
6. It is the day of the flight, I am leaving home. I lock the house, put the bags in the car, and make sure that I have the tickets and money.
7. I am driving to the airport for my flight. I am aware of every plane I see. As I get close to the airport, I see several planes—some taking off, some landing, and some just sitting on the ground by the terminal.
8. I am entering the terminal. I am carrying my bags and tickets.
9. I proceed to the airline desk, wait in line, and have the agent check my tickets and then weigh and check my bags.
10. I am in the lounge with many other people, some with bags also waiting for flights. I hear the announcements over the intercom and listen for my flight number to be called.
11. I hear my flight number announced, and I proceed to the security checkpoint with my hand luggage.
12. I approach the airline desk beyond the security checkpoint, and the agent asks me to choose a seat from the "map" of the plane.
13. I walk down the ramp leading to the plane and enter the door of the plane.
14. I am now inside the plane. I look at the interior of the plane and walk down the aisle, looking for my seat number. I then move in from the aisle and sit down in my assigned seat.
15. The plane is in flight, and I decide to leave my seat and walk to the washroom at the back of the plane.
16. I notice the seat-belt signs light up, so I fasten my seat belt and notice the sound of the motors starting.
17. Everyone is seated with seat belts fastened, and the plane slowly moves away from the terminal.
18. I notice the seat-belt signs are again lighted, and the pilot announces that we are preparing to land.
19. I am looking out the window and suddenly the plane enters the clouds and I cannot see out the window.
20. The plane has stopped at the end of the runway and is sitting, waiting for instructions to take off.
21. The plane is descending to the runway for a landing. I feel the speed and see the ground getting closer.
22. The plane has taken off from the airport and banks as it changes direction. I am aware of the "tilt."
23. The plane starts down the runway, and the motors get louder as the plane increases speed and suddenly lifts off.

each item are sufficiently small (no "jump" in anxiety level from one item to the next should be too large), you should:

1. Rate each item on a scale from 0 to 100 where 100 means that the situation elicits the maximum amount of anxiety (almost extreme panic) when encountered in the natural environment, and 0 means that the situation produces absolutely no emotion when encountered in real life. This value is referred to as the number of **subjective units of discomfort (suds)** elicited by the situation.

2. After giving each index card a suds rating, recheck the ranking to ensure that each item in the hierarchy has a higher suds ranking than the item below it and a lower ranking than the number above it. If necessary, change the order of some of the items to be consistent with your suds ratings.

3. Use your suds ratings to ensure that distances between items in the hierarchy are approximately 5 to 10 suds. Construct new items and insert them between any items that are greater than 10 suds apart.

4. Number each of the cards in order, starting by numbering the card causing the least anxiety as "1."

subjective units of discomfort (suds)

A measure or value attached to the *subjective units of discomfort* that are elicited or aroused when one imagines a particular fear-producing situation; ranging from 100 (the situation in real life elicits extreme panic) to 0 (the situation in real life elicits essentially no fear).

Learning Deep Muscle Relaxation. This step involves learning to relax all of the muscles in the body and to recognize the feeling of relaxation. You need to learn to relax the body in stages: relaxing one arm, the other arm, the head, the neck, the shoulders, the stomach, the abdomen, the legs, and then all the muscles at the same time. The best way to do this is to follow the guidelines for learning deep muscle relaxation that we presented in Chapter 4. After completing the program of muscle relaxation described in Chapter 4, you should be able to relax totally in a matter of minutes. When you accomplish that goal, you are ready to begin the next phase of your self-desensitization program. If possible, do not make any contacts with the actual fear-producing stimuli until your self-desensitization program is complete.

Barb was able to master the relaxation exercises more quickly than recommended by the general guidelines outlined in Chapter 4. She first practiced the exercises with a prerecorded tape of instructions while lying on her bed. After four sessions (spread over two days, relaxation was then practiced in a number of other settings (for example, in the living room and while riding in a car as a passenger). She acquired increased skill at relaxing easily in these other settings. After four days of considerable practice, she felt ready for the next step of the program.

Implementing the Self-Desensitization Program. Now that you have constructed your fear hierarchy and are able to relax completely within minutes, you are ready to start your program. This is done according to the following steps:

1. Find a quiet, private place that is free of distractions (preferably the same place in which your relaxation practice sessions were conducted).

2. Place your stack of cards containing descriptions of the feared items within easy reach. The cards should be in order, with the least fear-producing card on top and the most fear-producing card on the bottom.

3. Take several minutes to relax completely, as you have been practicing prior to this session.

4. When you are in a state of complete relaxation, take the card on top of the deck and look at the brief phrase that describes the situation that would normally cause some slight anxiety. Now turn the card over and look at the prompts to help you to visualize the situation clearly and vividly. After looking at the prompts, close your eyes and try to imagine that you are actually in that situation, as prompted by your card. After about 10 seconds, put the card down and relax totally. Relax for about 30 seconds, and during this time completely forget about the scene that you have just imagined. Think only of the muscles and how completely relaxed you feel, while breathing deeply.

5. Now pick up the same card again, and then close your eyes and imagine that situation for at least 10 seconds. Put the card in a separate pile, and relax

completely for another 30 seconds. During this time, do not think of the scene that you were just imagining while in a relaxed state. After the 30 seconds are up, consider the amount of anxiety you felt while imagining this scene the second time. If you were able to imagine the scene with approximately five or fewer suds, then you are ready to proceed to Card 2. If you felt more than five suds of anxiety, you should repeat the above routine once or twice more. If you felt less than five suds of anxiety, then relax for two minutes and repeat the procedure with the second card.

6. If you have great difficulty in imagining a scene, or in relaxing while imagining it, or if you feel more than ten suds of anxiety, immediately stop imagining and induce deep muscle relaxation for a minute or two. Then repeat visualization of the item for only 3 to 5 seconds rather than a full 10 seconds.

7. If Step 6 doesn't work, go back to the previous item and imagine that item for 20 seconds on two successive presentations of the item. Then again try the item that caused the difficulty.

8. If you still have problems with a particular item, try to construct three new items with smaller steps between them to correct the difficulty encountered with the troublesome item. Proceed through the new items exactly as described.

9. In general, you should be able to proceed through one to four items per session. However, it is all right to go as slowly as one item per session, if necessary. On the other hand, if you do not feel anxiety, you should not hesitate to go through as many as four items per session, or perhaps more.

10. Each session should begin with an item that was completed successfully in the previous section.

11. Sessions should not last more than about 20 minutes. Sessions might be conducted as frequently as twice per day and no less frequently than twice per week.

12. If you experience difficulties that do not yield to the corrective procedures in Steps 6 to 8, cease self-desensitization attempts and seek professional help.

It is important to keep track of your progress. Thus, at the end of each session, you should record on a separate sheet of paper the name and number of the particular items you imagined successfully, the number of exposures to each item successfully imagined, the suds ratings of the items completed in that session, and the date of the session. We also recommend that you graph your data in a way that is meaningful to you. To understand your progress better, you should also indicate the suds rating of the item when you first prepared your anxiety hierarchy and the final suds rating, which, ideally, is less than five. In addition, if in real life you experience the actual situation represented by a successfully completed item, assess your suds rating in the real situation and compare it with your rating when imagining the situation. This will give you some indication of the success of your generalization to the natural environment.

The results of Barb's program are presented in Table 15-2. The success of her program was informally confirmed by her husband, who accompanied her on her first flight following its completion. He reported that during the flight Barb behaved in a "normal" manner: socializing with other passengers, eating meals, moving freely about the aisle of the plane, and looking out the window during take-offs and landings.

EXPOSURE METHODS. In systematic desensitization, you desensitize your fear in your imagination as described above. The assumption is that, through stimulus generalization, you will subsequently be able to approach the feared stimulus in real life and the stimulus will no longer elicit anxiety. Recall from Chapter 14 that a variation of systematic desensitization is called ***in vivo* desensitization.** With this procedure you desensitize a fear in "real life," or *in vivo,* rather than desensitizing the fear in your imagination. The steps for *in vivo* desensitization are similar to those described above, but rather than progressing through a hierarchy of imagined fear situations, you actually approach the fear-producing stimuli. *In vivo* de-

***in vivo* desensitization**

Application of the desensitization procedure in the "real world"; an individual progresses through a hierarchy of fear items by actually experiencing the items rather than by imagining them.

participant modeling

A behavior therapy procedure for overcoming fear; an individual with a fear observes a model gradually approaching the feared stimulus, and then imitates the model.

flooding

Exposure of client to feared stimuli across long time periods (for example, hours), often *in vivo*.

sensitization has been used to overcome fears of darkness, birds, small animals, and a variety of other situations for which it is relatively easy to arrange for controllable real-life encounters.

Another approach that involves gradual exposure to the anxiety-eliciting situation is called **participant modeling** (see Chapter 14). With this approach, the individual with the fear observes a model gradually approaching the feared stimulus. If an individual had a fear of dogs, for example, that individual might observe a model approach to within 15 feet of a dog. The individual would then be encouraged to imitate the model. At the next step, the model might approach to within 12 feet of the dog. Again, the individual is encouraged to imitate the model. The procedure continues in this gradual way until both the model and the person with the fear come into contact with the feared stimulus. As with *in vivo* desensitization, this approach is especially useful for overcoming fears of stimuli that are easy to control in terms of distance and position.

Another exposure method is known as **flooding.** It is conducted with the aid of a therapist and resembles forced reflexive extinction. The therapist attempts to put the patient in the presence of the feared stimulus very early during the therapy and to maintain exposure for long periods of time, such as an hour or more per

TABLE 15-2

FEAR-OF-FLYING DATA RECORDED BY BARB[a]

SESSION (AND DATE)	TASK		ORIGINAL SUDS RANKING[b]	SUDS RANKING OF ITEMS IMMEDIATELY AFTER DESENSITIZATION OF THOSE ITEMS	Suds Ranking of Items When Encountered in the Natural Environment	
					CONTACT 1 (OUTBOUND FLIGHT: AUG. 26)	CONTACT 2 (RETURN FLIGHT: SEPT. 6)
1 (Aug. 11)	Prepare hierarchy and do suds ranking on all items					
2 (Aug. 13)	Prepare cards					
3 (Aug. 14)						
4 (Aug. 15)	Learn deep muscle relaxation					
5 (Aug. 16)						
6 (Aug. 17)						
7 (Aug. 18)	Item	1	0	0	0	0
		2	5	0	5[c]	—[d]
		3	6	0	6[c]	—[d]
		4	10	0	0	0
		5	13	0	0	—[d]

TABLE 15-2 (Continued)

Session (and Date)	Task	Original Suds Ranking[b]	Suds Ranking of Items Immediately After Desensitization of Those Items	Suds Ranking of Items When Encountered in the Natural Environment	
				Contact 1 (Outbound Flight: Aug. 26)	Contact 2 (Return Flight: Sept. 6)
8 (Aug. 19)	6	17	0	0	0
	7	23	0	1	0
	8	27	0	0	0
	9	29	0	0	0
	10	30	0	0	0
	11	35	0	1	0
9 (Aug. 20)	12	38	0	0	0
	13	43	0	0	0
	14	46	0	0	0
10 (Aug. 21)	15	50	0	0	0
	16	60	0	0	0
	17	70	0	0	0
11 (Aug. 22)	18	75	0	0	0
	19	80	0	—[d]	—[d]
	20	90	0	1	0
12 (Aug. 23)	21	97	3	3	0
	22	99	9	9	10
	23	100	6	(25)5[e]	0

[a] *For the descriptions of the items listed in the table, see the corresponding item numbers in Table 15-1.*
[b] *The original suds ranking was done during Session 1.*
[c] *These items were encountered in the natural environment prior to desensitization training.*
[d] *These items were not encountered in the natural environment.*
[e] *When the plane suddenly moved from the end of the runway after having been stopped, the client was unprepared and a suds ranking of 25 resulted. However, she was able to recover her composure during the actual situation and reduce her anxiety to a suds ranking of 5.*

session. Although the feared object or stimulus may be presented in imagination, it is more usually presented *in vivo*. Studies have shown that various exposure methods (including participant modeling and flooding) have been at least as effective, and sometimes more effective, than systematic desensitization in imagination (Leitenberg, 1976). Indeed, some research has suggested that practice in the feared situation might account for the effectiveness of systematic desensitization (Leitenberg, 1976). Systematic desensitization nevertheless has been demonstrated to be an effective procedure for overcoming a number of anxiety disorders (Turner et al., 1985). Moreover, a number of studies have demonstrated that systematic self-desensitization, following methods like those described in this chapter, can be an effective approach to overcoming phobias (Baker et al., 1973; Krop & Krause, 1976; Rosen et al., 1976; Wenrich et al., 1976).

CENTERING AND COPING SELF-STATEMENTS TO DEAL WITH ANXIETY-CAUSING SELF-TALK. As indicated in Chapter 4, certain types of statements can become conditioned stimuli which elicit anxiety. As a student, you might have found yourself thinking such things as, "What if I fail this test?" "What if she asks me a question in class? Everyone will think I'm stupid." "How come I'm the last to leave the exam?

Everyone else must really know their stuff!" Not only are such statements not likely to help you in any way, the anxiety that they cause can interfere with your problem-solving ability (Holroyd et al., 1978). As we described in Chapter 4, an effective strategy for counteracting such irrational statements includes centering and practicing coping self-statements. Centering, as you may recall, is a relaxation strategy in which you breathe very low down in your abdomen. Alternative coping self-statements might include, "I won't think about the consequences of failing—I'll concentrate on what I can do to be successful" or "Just because they finished before me doesn't mean that they got everything correct. My only concern is to finish within the allotted time." Other examples are provided in Chapter 4. It's useful to write out specific coping statements that deal with various situations in advance, so that they will be readily available when you need them. For example, if you have a high frequency of anxiety-evoking thoughts related to taking exams, you might write out specific coping self-statements to counteract feelings of anxiety that might occur: (1) the night before, while studying; (2) on the way to the classroom, just before taking the exam; (3) when you first read the exam questions; (4) later during the exam, when you see other students leave.

Adjusting Anger

anger
An emotional experience caused by the withdrawal or withholding of rewards.

As we learned in Chapter 4, the withdrawal or withholding of rewards causes emotional behavior that we label as **anger.** A vending machine that takes our money but doesn't produce the goods, being kept waiting in the doctor's office, having the ticket line close just before you get to the window to buy your ticket, pens that stop writing in the middle of a quiz—all of us have experienced such anger-causing events.

The various ways that we learn to display anger are not always problematic. For example, the increase in the vigor of behavior that often accompanies the emotional arousal of anger (Amsel & Roussel, 1952) might help you to unscrew that sticky top on the pickle jar. However, anger is problematic for many individuals and is a contributing factor to physical and verbal aggression (Hazaleus & Deffenbacher, 1986), child abuse (Nomelini & Katz, 1983), personal injury and property damage (Hazaleus & Deffenbacher, 1986), ineffective problem solving (Ellis, 1976), and various health problems (Gentry et al., 1982). According to self-reports of individuals questioned by Averill (1983), most people become mildly to moderately angry at least several times a week, and in some cases, several times a day. What are some of the things that make you angry? To help you decide, you may want to complete the Annoyance List in Box 15-2.

Methods for Controlling Anger

catharsis
A term in Freudian theory in which pent-up emotions are released; technically, becoming aware of id impulses that were previously buried in the unconscious.

How should you control your anger? Should you "bottle it up" inside of you? Or should you "let it all hang out"? Freud and others have suggested that release of pent-up emotions, or **catharsis,** is a healthy practice. Many people seem to feel that it is especially bad to "bottle up" anger and keep it inside. On the other hand, a number of studies have shown that not only does expressing anger not always get rid of it, it may prolong it and make it more intense (Averill, 1982; Ebbesen et al., 1975; Tavris, 1984). Moreover, considering that anger is often a response to the perceived misdeeds of friends or loved ones (Averill, 1983), we should remember the Chinese proverb, "By controlling the anger of a minute, you may avoid the remorse of a lifetime." As we indicated in Chapter 4, the way we express anger depends upon our operant-learning experiences. It's therefore reasonable to suppose that people who show frequent angry outbursts are perfectly capable of learning a calmer, cooperative way of solving the problem that caused their anger in the first place. Research on strategies to effectively deal with anger has focused

Box 15-2
THE ANNOYANCE LIST

Below is a list containing types of people and various daily occurrences. If the situation or person described is annoying to you, place a check next to the statement. See below for scoring.

_____ 1. A person telling me how to drive

_____ 2. A person acting in an affected manner

_____ 3. Getting a telephone busy signal

_____ 4. To see reckless driving

_____ 5. To hear a loud talker

_____ 6. To see an adult picking his nose

_____ 7. A person telling me to do something when I am just about to do it

_____ 8. A person continually criticizing something

_____ 9. A person being sarcastic

_____ 10. To wait for someone to come to the phone

_____ 11. To know a person is staring at me

_____ 12. To have my thoughts interrupted

_____ 13. A person putting his hands on me unnecessarily

_____ 14. A person adjusting my TV set

_____ 15. A person giving me a weak handshake

_____ 16. A person picking his teeth

_____ 17. A person who "can't leave the party"

_____ 18. A person continually trying to be funny

_____ 19. Being asked almost constantly to do something

_____ 20. To be evaluated critically by a relative stranger

_____ 21. To hear a person use "shock words"

_____ 22. To have to walk on slippery sidewalks

_____ 23. To listen to politicians make promises

_____ 24. To hear a person talking during a musical number

_____ 25. To hear "loud" music

_____ 26. To be unable to find a bus seat

_____ 27. A person watching me work

_____ 28. To hear a person swear

_____ 29. To see overaffectionate demonstration between members of the same sex

_____ 30. To hear disparaging remarks about a member of a minority group

_____ 31. A man frequently referring to his girlfriends

_____ 32. A woman frequently referring to her boyfriends

_____ 33. Too much discussion of sex on a date

_____ 34. To have to kiss an unattractive relative

_____ 35. To see public lovemaking

_____ 36. A person talking a great deal and not saying anything very important

_____ 37. To listen to a sales pitch

_____ 38. To have "too many" TV commercials

_____ 39. A person interrupting me when I am talking

_____ 40. To see a person spit

_____ 41. To have a hostess repeatedly urging me to take some food I do not want

_____ 42. Not being able to find the rattle in the car

_____ 43. To discover that the library book is not there

_____ 44. To see colors that clash

_____ 45. To see an untidy room

_____ 46. To find a hair in my food

_____ 47. To have a hole in my stocking or sock

_____ 48. The classmate who talks too much

_____ 49. Not to be listened to

_____ 50. To be given impractical suggestions

Adapted from von Haller Gilmer, 1973.

SCORING THE ANNOYANCE LIST

There are no specific cut-off points or score ranges for this checklist. Its main function is to help you identify daily events that typically make you angry. Some research has suggested that on average people find approximately 15 to 20 of these items annoying (Aero & Weiner, 1981). If you have checked more than 15 to 20 items, it's possible that you experience a fairly high level of daily stress. If this is true, you might want to reexamine the stress adjustment procedures in Chapter 5.

Withdrawal or withholding of rewards causes anger.

on relaxation techniques, coping self-statements, and responsible assertiveness training.

RELAXATION STRATEGIES.   John was an introductory psychology student who frequently had a problem controlling his anger. He had experienced significant consequences for his anger, such as damage to interpersonal relationships, physical assaults, and property damage. Deciding that he needed help, he enrolled in a program being researched by Jerry Deffenbacher at Colorado State University. The program consisted of six, weekly one-hour, small-group sessions that took place in a small classroom. During the first few sessions, along with some other students who also had problems with anger, John learned the progressive muscle relaxation procedure described in Chapter 5. He also learned to relax through deep breathing (much like the centering procedure described in Chapter 5). During the next four sessions, John imagined specific scenes that had caused him to experience anger in the past. When he became aware of the internal cues of anger arousal caused by a particular scene, he then practiced actively relaxing the anger away. Across sessions, the intensity of anger elicited by the scenes was increased from moderate to very high. John also completed homework assignments that emphasized *in vivo* application of relaxation coping skills for anger reduction. By the end of the six-week treatment program, John felt much less general and situational anger, and showed much less verbal and physical antagonism and much greater constructive coping when provoked. These results were maintained at five-week and one-year follow-ups.

The research of Deffenbacher and his colleagues has clearly demonstrated the value of relaxation strategies for helping clients learn to control anger (Deffenbacher et al., 1986; Hazaleus & Deffenbacher, 1986). But, like all of the adjustment procedures in this book, for them to help you, you have to practice them. The program followed by John is a good model. To use relaxation to help you deal with anger, first become skillful with the relaxation procedures. Next, make a list of anger-producing situations and arrange them in order from those that cause minimal anger to those that cause maximum anger. Then, beginning with the first item on the list, imagine that particular situation. When you experience bodily cues indicating that you are beginning to feel angry, then practice the muscle relaxation procedures. Rehearse each item in this way on two or three occasions, and then go on to the next item. As with desensitization of a fear, you might work at the rate of one or two items per day. After you have worked through all of the items, then begin practicing with the procedures as you encounter anger-provoking situations *in vivo*.

COPING SELF-STATEMENTS.   Ebbe Ebbesen and his colleagues were working in San Diego when a number of engineers and technicians were laid off by their aerospace company. The layoffs came as a complete surprise to the employees and occurred two years prior to a previously announced contract-termination date. This seemed like a good time to study anger. During interviews, Ebbesen and his colleagues asked some of the laid-off employees questions about the company and the company supervisors (for example, "Are there aspects of the company you don't like?"). This gave them a chance to talk about their anger. The employees were then given a questionnaire to determine if this opportunity to vent expressions of hostility increased or decreased their anger. Contrary to the view that catharsis makes one feel better, expressing their anger during the interview did not cause them to feel less angry. Those who expressed anger toward the company exhibited even more hostility on the questionnaire than did a control group who had not been given an opportunity to vent their anger (Ebbesen et al., 1975).

Studies like the above have indicated that talking about something that makes you angry can make you even angrier. This has important implications for controlling anger. Namely, you should practice alternative coping self-statements that can have the opposite effect (Ellis & Bernard, 1985; Meichenbaum, 1986). Some coping self-statements can be of a general sort to help you to react to feelings of anger in any situation. Examples might include:

- "First, I'll relax, then I'll deal with the problem."
- "Feeling relaxed is a lot more comfortable for me than feeling angry."
- "I'm not going to let it get to me."
- "I can handle this if I stay relaxed and stay in control."

In other situations, it may be necessary to tailor specific coping self-statements to counteract particular irrational and anger-provoking thoughts (Novaco, 1975; 1979). For example, if your boss tells you that he's dissatisfied with some aspect of your work, your first tendency might be to react with an angry retort. Alternatively, you might say to yourself, "He's probably having a bad day. I know he generally appreciates my work." As another example, a new employee at a store where you are shopping might be extremely slow in managing the cash register. Instead of angrily berating the employee (which will probably worsen his performance), you might say to yourself, "He's probably doing the best that he can do. I know that I would be upset if customers yelled at me. Besides, a few more minutes won't make any difference." When you're developing your coping self-statements, try to think of the situation from the point of view of the person who is irritating you. There are often valid reasons for the other person's irritating behavior. Verbalizing those will help you to control your anger.

Responsible Assertiveness to Prevent Anger

Joan is picking up her car which she left this morning for a tune-up.
"That'll be $250, lady."
"Two hundred fifty dollars!" thought Joan to herself. "How could it be that much? It seems a lot." "Will you take a check?" she asked aloud.
"No problem, lady."

Marcia is standing in the express line at the check-out counter. The man in front of her has just placed 15 items on the revolving tray. The sign clearly says 8 items or less.

"Hey, can't you read?" Marcia shouts at the man, "You're not supposed to be in this line unless you have 8 or fewer items."

"Mind your own business, lady."

Marcia shouts at the clerk, "How are we supposed to get express service if you allow people to put more groceries on here than the sign says?"

Perhaps you've found yourself in situations similar to these. Joan was too fearful. Marcia was angry and aggressive. Do you allow people to use you because you can't say no? Do you find yourself behaving one way and then later wishing you'd behaved another way?

Do you go over such scenes and figure out what you should have done? Many of us are unwilling victims of others who run roughshod over our feelings, who compel us to do things against our wills. How can we stop this from happening? In cases such as Joan's, nonassertive individuals often feel anger, at themselves for not speaking up and at the individual with whom they should have been assertive. Assertion training has proven to be an effective way of dealing with anger in some cases (Rimm et al., 1974; Rosenthal & Rosenthal, 1985). If your own failure to behave assertively in certain situations leads to feelings of anger or to aggressive behavior, then we encourage you to practice the LADDER technique described on page 487 to help adjust your anger. The LADDER technique can be used concurrently with systematic self-desensitization. Together you can learn to relax in the face of heretofore anger-producing situations and at the same time to be responsibly assertive.

As before, if your anger doesn't progressively diminish we suggest that you seek professional help.

ASSERTIVENESS VS. NONASSERTIVENESS.   Webster's first definition of the verb *assert* is "to state or affirm positively, assuredly, plainly, or strongly" (*Webster's Third New International Dictionary*, 1968). Inherent in the definition is the fact that an assertion is verbal. In dealing with assertive behavior we'll be dealing primarily with the way we talk to people, and the way they talk to us. We'll learn how to speak positively, and assuredly, but contrary to the definition, we'll learn how to do so in terms that do not provoke strong reactions from our listeners. We'll call assertion that does not provoke unwanted feelings or aggression on the part of the listener, **responsible assertion.**

responsible assertion
Verbal behavior assertive of one's rights in a situation, and that does not provoke unwanted feelings or aggression.

Researchers have identified specific verbal behaviors that differentiate between assertive and nonassertive persons. Assertive persons speak more loudly and make more requests of others than do nonassertive persons (Eisler et al., 1973). Assertive persons also use fewer words to get their message across (Galassi et al., 1975) and take less time to deliver a message than do nonassertive persons (Eisler et al., 1973). Finally, assertive individuals are more likely to make "I" statements to express their feelings (for example, "I would really appreciate it if you would blow your smoke in the other direction because it bothers my asthma"). There are also differences in nonverbal behaviors between assertive and nonassertive people. For example, assertive people are more likely to maintain eye contact during conversation, to stand erect with their heads up, and to match their expressions with what they are saying, than are nonassertive people (Williams & Long, 1979).

assertion training
Training that enables one to behave assertively, such as using the LADDER technique.

Assertion (or assertiveness) **training** refers to a behavior change procedure in which a client is taught to take positive assertive action in various situations. Since first introduced by Salter in 1949, assertion training has developed into a popular movement as evidenced by numerous paperback books, training groups, courses, and so on. In spite of this popularity, there is still considerable disagreement on how assertion should be defined and measured. There are at least 20 distinct definitions in current use in major journals (St. Lawrence, 1987).

Here's another definition of assertive behavior (Alberti & Emmons, 1986; p. 7): "Assertive behavior promotes equality in human relationships, enabling us to act in our own best interests, to stand up for ourselves without undue anxiety, to express honest feelings comfortably, to exercise personal rights without denying the rights of others." In essence, developing your skills in assertion is a way to improve your communication skills.

WHY BE ASSERTIVE? Popular current media reports on assertion training claim that it is particularly helpful to improve the well-being of individuals who are passive, lacking in self-confidence, unable to make decisions, and excessively inhibited. It can be especially helpful for individuals who experience anxiety in a variety of social situations. Considerable research supports such claims. For example, in a study of professional women, assertive women reported higher sexual satisfaction than nonassertive women (Whitly & Poulsen, 1975). Bugental and Love (1975) observed that mothers in families with children having no notable problems were much more verbally assertive when showing approval or disapproval than were mothers of children in disturbed families. Orenstein and colleagues (1975) found that people who rated themselves high on assertiveness also reported fewer anxieties. Morgan (1974) reported the same relation with respect to social anxieties. Although such studies indicate potential benefits of assertiveness, they are correlational in nature and do not necessarily demonstrate that learning assertiveness will improve other behaviors. Other research, however, has reported such findings. For example, assertiveness training has helped people to control their anger (Rimm et al., 1974), reduce their anxiety (Percell et al., 1974), decrease marriage problems between distressed couples (Fenesterheim, 1972), and to learn to control excessive blushing when dealing with others (Gibbs, 1965). Additional clinical benefits of assertion training have also been reported (for references, see Walker et al., 1981).

ARE YOU ASSERTIVE ENOUGH? How assertive are you? To find out, complete the Assertiveness Inventory in Box 15-3.

According to authors of the inventory there is no meaning to a total score on the inventory because assertiveness does not exist as a general quality, although it was first defined as such (Alberti & Emmons, 1986; Salter, 1949).

If you answered Questions 1, 4, 6, 7, 10, 12, 14, 16, 18, 19, 22, 24, 25, 27, 28, 30, and 35 with a 0 or a 1 and Questions 2, 5, 9, 11, 15, 17, and 21 with a 3 or a 4, then you are probably in need of help in being more assertive. Look at your responses to each of these questions and make a list of the particular situations in which you have trouble behaving assertively.

aggression

Behavior that verbally or physically abuses a person or property and causes physical or psychological damage thereto.

ASSERTION VS. AGGRESSION. There is an important difference between behaving assertively and behaving aggressively. **Aggression** has long been defined as "any form of behavior directed toward the goal of harming or injuring another living being who is motivated to avoid such treatment" (Baron, 1977). In assertion, one exerts one's rights as a human without subsequent offense. In aggression, while the aggressive behavior is often an expression of one's rights, it is likely to be reciprocated and be counterproductive. That is, aggression begets aggression. The difference in the two types of behavior is often subtle and hard to discriminate.

For Box 15-3, if you answered Questions 3, 8, 13, 20, 23, 26, 29, 31, 32, 33, and 34 with a 3 or a 4, you probably behave fairly aggressively toward others. You might want to decrease these and other such behaviors that constitute aggressive responses.

DEVELOPING RESPONSIBLE ASSERTION. Before we begin this task, it's necessary to talk about your rights as a human. For many individuals who have trouble being assertive, the reasons may lie in the childhood training they received from significant adults in their lives. These constitute the "mistaken traditional assumptions"

Box 15-3

ASSERTIVENESS INVENTORY

The following questions will help you assess your assertiveness. Draw a circle around the number that describes how you behave in the particular situation. Be as honest as you can about yourself.

0 = No, never; 1 = Somewhat, sometimes; 2 = average; 3 = Usually, a good deal of the time; 4 = Nearly always, entirely.

1. When a person is highly unfair, do you call it to his or her attention?   0 1 2 3 4

2. Do you find it difficult to make decisions?   0 1 2 3 4

3. Are you openly critical of others' ideas, opinions, behavior?   0 1 2 3 4

4. Do you speak out in protest when someone takes your place in line?   0 1 2 3 4

5. Do you often avoid people or situations for fear of embarrassment?   0 1 2 3 4

6. Do you usually have confidence in your own judgment?   0 1 2 3 4

7. Do you insist that your spouse or roommate take on a fair share of household chores?   0 1 2 3 4

8. Are you prone to "fly off the handle"?   0 1 2 3 4

9. When a salesman makes an effort, do you find it hard to say "No" even though the merchandise is not really what you want?   0 1 2 3 4

10. When a latecomer is waited on before you are, do you call attention to the situation?   0 1 2 3 4

11. Are you reluctant to speak up in a discussion or debate?   0 1 2 3 4

12. If a person has borrowed money (or a book, garment, thing of value) and is overdue in returning it, do you mention it?   0 1 2 3 4

13. Do you continue pursuing an argument after the other person has had enough?   0 1 2 3 4

14. Do you generally express what you feel?   0 1 2 3 4

15. Are you disturbed if someone watches you at work?   0 1 2 3 4

16. If someone keeps kicking or bumping your chair in a movie or a lecture, do you ask the person to stop?   0 1 2 3 4

17. Do you find it difficult to keep eye contact when talking to another person?   0 1 2 3 4

---

that guide the behavior of many of us (Davis et al., 1982). Most of us learn at least a few of these. The resultant behaviors are often incompatible with behaving responsibly and assertively. We present these mistaken traditional assumptions for you in Box 15-4.

From your responses to the Assertiveness Inventory, choose the situation in which you feel you are the least assertive. Our goal will be to improve your

18. In a good restaurant, when your meal is improperly prepared or served, do you ask your waiter/waitress to correct the situation?   0   1   2   3   4

19. When you discover merchandise is faulty, do you return it for an adjustment?   0   1   2   3   4

20. Do you show your anger by name-calling or obscenities?   0   1   2   3   4

21. Do you try to be a wallflower or a piece of the furniture in social situations?   0   1   2   3   4

22. Do you insist that your property manager (mechanic, repairman, etc.) make repairs, adjustments, or replacements which are his/her responsibility?   0   1   2   3   4

23. Do you often step in and make decisions for others?   0   1   2   3   4

24. Are you openly able to express love and affection?   0   1   2   3   4

25. Are you able to ask your friends for small favors or help?   0   1   2   3   4

26. Do you think you always have the right answer?   0   1   2   3   4

27. When you differ with a person you respect, are you able to speak up for your own viewpoint?   0   1   2   3   4

28. Are you able to refuse unreasonable requests made by friends?   0   1   2   3   4

29. Do you have difficulty complimenting or praising others?   0   1   2   3   4

30. If you are disturbed by someone smoking near you, can you say so?   0   1   2   3   4

31. Do you shout or use bullying tactics to get others to do as you wish?   0   1   2   3   4

32. Do you finish other people's sentences for them?   0   1   2   3   4

33. Do you get into physical fights with others, especially with strangers?   0   1   2   3   4

34. At family meals, do you control the conversation?   0   1   2   3   4

35. When you meet a stranger, are you the first to introduce yourself and begin a conversation?   0   1   2   3   4

Adapted from Alberti & Emmons, 1986.

assertiveness in that situation. Do not expect your improved assertiveness in a single situation to transfer very much to other situations. If you employ this same exercise for a number of nonassertive situations, however, it may result in some transfer to a novel situation.

In this book, to help you develop an improved assertiveness style, we rely on the LADDER approach, developed by Davis and colleagues. This method involves

---

Box 15-4

SOME MISTAKEN TRADITIONAL ASSUMPTIONS ABOUT LIFE—AND YOUR TRUE LEGITIMATE RIGHTS

Mistaken Traditional Assumptions	*Your Legitimate Rights*
1. It is selfish to put your needs before others' needs.	1. You have a right to put yourself first, sometimes.
2. It is shameful to make mistakes. You should have an appropriate response for every occasion.	2. You have a right to make mistakes.
3. If you can't convince others that your feelings are reasonable, then they must be wrong, or maybe you are going crazy.	3. You have the right to be the final judge of your feelings and accept them as legitimate.
4. You should respect the views of others, especially if they are in a position of authority. Keep your differences of opinion to yourself. Listen and learn.	4. You have a right to your own opinions and convictions.
5. You should always try to be logical and consistent.	5. You have a right to change your mind or decide on a different course of action.
6. You should be flexible and adjust. Others have good reasons for their actions and it's not polite to question them.	6. You have a right to protest unfair treatment or criticism.
7. You should never interrupt people. Asking questions reveals your stupidity to others.	7. You have a right to interrupt in order to ask for clarification.
8. Things could get even worse, don't rock the boat.	8. You have a right to negotiate for change.
9. You shouldn't take up others' valuable time with your problems.	9. You have a right to ask for help or emotional support.
10. People don't want to hear that you feel bad, so keep it to yourself.	10. You have a right to feel and express pain.
11. When someone takes the time to give you advice, you should take it very seriously. They are often right.	11. You have a right to ignore the advice of others.
12. Knowing that you did something well is its own reward. People don't like showoffs. Successful people are secretly disliked and envied. Be modest when complimented.	12. You have a right to receive formal recognition for your work and achievements.
13. You should always try to accommodate others. If you don't, they won't be there when you need them.	13. You have a right to say no.
14. Don't be antisocial. People are going to think you don't like them if you say you'd rather be alone instead of with them.	14. You have a right to be alone, even if others prefer your company.
15. You should always have a good reason for what you feel and do.	15. You have a right not to have to justify yourself to others.
16. When someone is in trouble, you should help him or her.	16. You have a right not to take responsibility for someone else's problem.
17. You should be sensitive to the needs and wishes of others, even when they are unable to tell you what they want.	17. You have a right not to have to anticipate others' needs and wishes.
18. It's always good policy to stay on people's good side.	18. You have a right not to always worry about the goodwill of others.
19. It's not nice to put people off. If questioned, give an answer.	19. You have a right to choose not to respond to a situation.

Adapted from Davis et al., 1982.

writing a script for a situation requiring assertiveness, practicing the flow of the situation with the script, and then practicing it without the script. Finally, prepared by this rehearsal, the person goes into the actual situation.

Ladder. We use the acronym/mnemonic device "LADDER" to help you remember the six steps of this method. The acronym is formed from the first letter of the descriptor for each step.

1. **L**ook *at the situation*. What are your rights in it? What do you need from it? Objectively define what your goal is in the situation. In doing this be sure to specify *who* the interaction is with, *when* it usually occurs, *what* its subject matter is, *how* you usually react, your *fears* of what will happen if you are assertive, and your *goal*.

   For example, Joan thought her automobile repair bill was too high, but she never did anything about it. She often acted nonassertively. She wrote the following: "I fear picking up my car from the mechanic [*who*], after some work has been done [*when*], because the bill always seems a lot higher than I think it should be [*what*]. Most of the time, I just don't say anything [*how*] because I'm afraid maybe he'll swear at me or keep my car or something [*fears*]. I'd like to be able to have him go over the bill with me and explain the various costs [*goal*]."

2. **A**rrange *a time*. This is the time (mutually agreed upon) to discuss the problem with the person who is involved. (Exclude this step when you choose to be spontaneously assertive.)

   Joan wrote the following: "Excuse me, Mr. White, do you have a minute right now so we could discuss my bill?" And, if the reply is negative, she prepared herself to say, "Well, when would it be convenient for you? It's important to me to get it straightened out in my mind as soon as possible."

   Then she rehearsed this, first silently, and then aloud in front of a mirror.

3. **D**efine *the problem*. Specify the situation as objectively as possible.

   Joan wrote: "The problem is that I meekly accept without comment the bill that is presented to me by the mechanic wherever I get my automobile repaired."

4. **D**escribe *your feelings*. Use "I" statements of your own feelings that do not blame anyone else, for example, "I am dismayed."

   For this, Joan wrote: "I'm very uncomfortable when the bill is presented to me and it's not explained. It leaves me feeling that I might have been cheated."

5. **E**xpress *your request*. Use only one or two simple, specific sentences to do this.

   Joan wrote: "I'd very much appreciate it if you could explain the charges on the repair bill. I'm particularly interested in why the work was necessary."

6. **R**einforce. Let the listener know what good may come of complying with your request.

   Joan wrote: "It's important for me to have confidence in the people I deal with. And it might help me to take better care of my car."

Now let's see how the LADDER approach might apply to Marcia's case. Having finished with the store manager who interceded between Marcia and the man with the extra groceries, Marcia realized that her behavior was aggressive, not assertive. It certainly evoked aggression! In addition to starting to count the number of times she behaved aggressively, Marcia reviewed the LADDER method with respect to the incident in the grocery store.

First, she *looked at* the situation. She thought, "It really burns me up when someone takes advantage of everyone else like that guy did. However, I shouldn't put him down. That was wrong. All I want is for the store to make that kind of thing less likely to happen again. Now let's see . . . what can I do?"

Second, in consideration of *arranging a time* to work out the problem, she realized that she needed to contact the store's manager. If she did not get satisfaction there, she could go higher in the chain of command. She thought, "I'll call the store manager and determine a time when we can talk about this."

Third, she *defined the problem*. "I hate to be taken advantage of," she mused, "and this is a classic example of it. In a nutshell, the problem is that people use the express line when they have too many groceries. They shouldn't do that."

Fourth, she thought about her *feelings* in the matter. "I feel used by this man, and it amazes me that the store isn't enforcing its own rules."

Fifth, she thought about *making a simple request.* "What I would like, is to not ever have anyone do that to me again. But that's wishful thinking. How about, 'I'd really appreciate it if the store would enforce its rules about using the express line?' "

Finally, she thought about how to *reinforce* the store manager. She realized that she was a regular customer. "All I have to do is suggest that I will continue being a steady customer, because, for the most part, the store is nicely run."

BODY ASSERTION.   Not all assertion is verbal. The way in which you present yourself can be an important component of behaving assertively. Make eye contact with your listener, but not so much as to make that person uncomfortable (see Chapter 8). Keep your eyes (and therefore your body) on a level with the listener (or a bit above for more power). Maintain an open, friendly countenance and stance. Gesture if you feel like it, but don't be dramatic. Cultivate an inflected voice—it makes you more interesting (see Chapter 8). Check in a mirror that your expression is congruent with the rest of your demeanor. Practice enough so that your delivery is fluent but not stilted or rehearsed. Listen to people who talk with a minimum of disfluencies—they sound more confident than those whose speech is loaded with "uhs," "ums," and so on.

FEAR OF ASSERTION.   If you're afraid to assert yourself, then you will need to review the procedures in Chapter 5 for relaxation. Practice the brief relaxation strategies described there. While relaxed, visualize going through your assertion script. Visualize the worst possible outcome, but visualize handling it well. Stay relaxed the entire time. Stop the imaging if you feel your relaxed state slipping away. Regain the relaxed state and proceed. Present to yourself all the parts of the script while relaxed, until you feel no fear while reviewing it.

SAYING NO.   Some people know how to do this intuitively. However, many of us do not. Women may have particular problems with this, given the male myth that when women say no they really mean yes (Phelps & Austin, 1975).

It may seem easier in the short term not to say no. But over the long term, not having said no, you may find yourself overburdened or compromised in some way. Guidelines for learning to say no include:

1. Practice saying no. As in other assertions, much is gained by reviewing potential situations (before they occur if possible) and writing out the script in LADDER format. Practicing will make you feel less guilty on the first real occasion that you use this new skill.
2. Keep it simple. You don't have to apologize for saying no.
3. You can give reasons, but make sure they reflect your feelings accurately. If they do not, then you may be trapped into negotiations.
4. You can express understanding, but again, don't fake it.

Adjusting Loneliness

Jan is unhappy. Her best friend, Marie, just moved out of town with her family because her husband got another job. Jan and Marie and their spouses spent almost every Friday evening together. Usually they had a few drinks and then went to a movie or out to eat. Sometimes the four of them just stayed at home and talked. On most major holidays their entire families got together to celebrate. Jan and Marie are about the same age and many aspects of their lives, and their likes and dislikes, are similar. They frequently met for lunch or to go shopping or to go to an art museum, and they talked often on the telephone. In short, they are very similar people who enjoyed one another's company a great deal.

Loneliness and grief—two emotions most of us will experience in our lives.

Now Jan is very lonely because Marie has moved away. The parting was tearful. Jan has other close friends, but none quite as close as Marie. What will happen to Jan's feelings? Is this likely to be a temporary condition? Can she do anything to ameliorate her feelings of loneliness? Or must she just wait it out?

Are there enough lonely people out there to warrant including a section on loneliness in a book on adjustment? Perhaps not surprisingly, the answer is yes. In surveys of a number of different populations, a fair proportion of the respondents answer that they're lonely now or have been lonely in the past. For example, 75 percent of freshmen at UCLA stated that they had been lonely at least occasionally since they arrived on the campus; and 40 percent indicated their loneliness was moderate to severe (Cutrona, 1982). Weiss (1982) estimated that between 50 and 60 million Americans feel extremely lonely at some time during any given month. Certain groups may be more at risk for loneliness than others (for example, widows, widowers). Loneliness may also contribute to suicidal behavior (Margulis et al., 1984). So, the problems of the lonely may be severe, and there appear to be substantial numbers of people who feel that they're lonely.

What Is Loneliness?

loneliness
A set of emotional feelings related to the absence of intimacy, a perceived dissatisfaction with social relationships, or insufficient social reinforcement.

There are a number of ways of defining **loneliness** (Peplau & Perlman, 1982; Perlman 1989). One way to define loneliness is as a response to the *absence of intimacy*: "I really miss you," John wrote to his wife. "I miss having you here to talk to when I come home. I miss holding you close, the smell of your hair when you come out of the shower, your warm body snuggling against me at night—you've been gone almost a month, I hope you never have to go on another business trip again, ever."

A second way to define loneliness is through a *perceived dissatisfaction* with one's social relationships: "I really don't want to go out with Charlie anymore," complained Frances while having coffee with her friend, Donna. "All we ever do is go drinking with his buddies. And the conversations never change. The same dumb jokes. Same talk about football. I mean, that's all we ever do. I need a change. I need to meet some new people. And you know what really burns me? Every time someone takes a drink, *someone* in the group hollers out, "It don't get no better than this!' "

Third, loneliness may be due to insufficient *social reinforcement*: "I wonder what the boss thinks about that project I handed in," thought Bert to himself. "It sure would be nice to know what he thinks of my work." Later while driving home in the car, Bert mused out loud, "Let's see, when I walk in the door, Carla's immediately going to start talking about her day at work and how much she loves her job. Sure wish she'd notice me for a change. I wonder if she'll say anything about how I vacuumed the carpet and scrubbed the kitchen floor? I wonder if she'll notice my new haircut?"

The three approaches to defining loneliness appear to be closely related because the socially rewarding processes in each may be similar.

transient loneliness
Loneliness lasting from a few minutes to a few hours.

situational loneliness
Loneliness because significant others are lost due to their physical separation.

chronic loneliness
Loneliness that has been present for two or more years.

Young (1982) has distinguished three variants of loneliness: transient, situational, and chronic. **Transient loneliness** lasts for a brief time—from a few minutes to a few hours—and has been experienced by almost everyone at one time or another. Because the symptoms of transient loneliness are not severe, not much attention has been devoted to it. **Situational loneliness** results from an important event—such as death of a spouse, a first-year college student moving away from home for the first time, or a divorce. In this kind of loneliness significant others are lost for uncontrollable reasons. The distinction between the first two categories and the category of **chronic loneliness** is based on time. Individuals who have been lonely for two or more years consecutively define the last category. Thus Jan, whose best friend Marie has just moved away, is situationally lonely. Categorizing loneliness in this manner may imply the possibility of dealing differentially with it.

Loneliness may relate to a number of behaviors in the emotional, motivational, and cognitive domains. It's described as an unpleasant experience, possibly related to depression (Young, 1982). Lonely people may describe themselves as unhappy, tense, restless, pessimistic, possibly even hostile (Peplau & Perlman, 1982). Contradictory effects may be seen in personal motivation: Lonely people may report both more and less motivation, depending on how long they have been lonely. They may report being quite active immediately after becoming lonely, and later report considerable weariness. Lastly, lonely people may report a lowered ability to concentrate; they may be highly focused on their interpersonal relationships (Peplau & Perlman, 1982).

Causes of Loneliness

Margulis and others (1984) postulated four antecedents to loneliness: the absence of a social partner who can help the lonely person achieve goals and objectives; a belief that this unavailability is enduring; thoughts of another; and desire for another. If any of these conditions exists, a person may report feeling lonely. Personal characteristics may also be related: Those who are shy, introverted, less willing to take social risks, have low self-esteem or are self-deprecating, or have poor social skills may be more likely to report being lonely (Peplau & Perlman, 1982). However, personal factors may not produce loneliness unaided. Cultural and situational factors may also conspire. Our own culture, which emphasizes rugged individualism for males, may help to spawn loneliness (Peplau & Perlman, 1982).

ABSENCE OF SOCIAL PARTNER.   Jeff is destitute. His wife recently left him for another man. He's been drinking a lot and he feels terrible. He hasn't cleaned the apartment for three weeks. It's Friday night and he doesn't know what to do. He has a couple of drinks while he thinks over his situation. Many drinks later he's sound asleep in the chair in which he began. The apartment is still not clean. Jeff hasn't fed himself; he's a mess; and his life's a mess.

For most of us, people exist whom we feel we cannot do without. They satisfy our needs and, by so doing, we're attracted to them, perhaps even attached or bonded to them socially. Their absence may mean that our needs will go unfulfilled. These needs may be very simple (a sexual relationship) or mundane (someone to talk to), or very complex (a marital relationship). If the social partner is responsible for fulfilling a great many of these needs, that person's absence may be felt very strongly. In fact, Margulis and colleagues (1984) call this latter kind of relationship a profound rather than a mundane one. **Profound relationships** are those in which the partners satisfy a great many needs for one another. **Mundane relationships** are much more casual and their absence, therefore, may be less strongly felt. Jeff has had a profound relationship with his wife of seven years.

profound relationships

Relationships in which the partners satisfy a great many needs for one another.

mundane relationships

Relationships in which the partners satisfy only a few needs for one another.

This person is in a crowd but may be lonely.

While absence of a specific social partner may cause loneliness, as in Jeff's case, the overall number of social contacts may be important. This factor may be more the cause of transient loneliness, and there may be wide individual differences. Contacts that make one person feel crowded for space and overburdened with attention may make another person lonely. Timing of social contacts may also be important. For young people, not having a date on Friday night may cause transient loneliness, while staying home alone during the week might be welcomed. Quality of social contacts may also be important. Many college students when they first leave home, for example, are surrounded by hundreds of other students during the day, but they lack the intimacy and social contact provided by the family and friends back home. Thus, they may feel lonely.

BELIEF OF ENDURING LOSS.   Before he passed out, Jeff began to think that this time his wife truly would not be back. When she left him before, she had always returned. But each time she was away longer than before. Each time his drinking had been the major reason for her leaving. "This time," he said to himself, "I've done it. She's gone for good."

Jeff has come to realize that the rewards formerly available in terms of his relationship with his wife no longer exist, and that this state of affairs will likely continue for an unendurable time. As long as Jeff believes that this time is longer than can be tolerated, he'll be lonely. Such a belief may lead to grief, as discussed below.

THOUGHTS OF PARTNER.   In his dazed condition, Jeff blearily realizes that he needs to stop thinking so much about his wife. Every time he tries to stop, however, she pops back into his mind. When he awakens in the morning, he misses her. When he goes into the bathroom about the time his wife would be making herself up, she's not there. When his usual breakfast doesn't appear on the table, he thinks once more of her.

The partner's absence or unavailability itself may instigate thoughts and/or desires for the partner directly. Also, where the absent partner helped reach certain goals, the failure to reach these goals may also provoke thoughts of the partner.

CONTINUING DESIRE FOR PARTNER.   Jeff drags himself to work. He doesn't look good; he doesn't feel good. He doesn't have many friends at work. He still misses his wife terribly, and every night he still drinks himself to sleep. The desire for his partner may continue to exist as long as there's no change in Jeff and as long as there's no one to take his wife's place.

How then can these separate individuals—Jan and Jeff—cope with their loneliness?

Amelioration of Loneliness

Peplau and Perlman (1982) have suggested three ways to cope with loneliness: First, the lonely person's social relationships must be changed; second, the lonely person's social needs must be changed; and third, the lonely person's perception of the social problem must be altered.

CHANGING SOCIAL RELATIONSHIPS.   Jan has no problem with this. It's summertime and she and her family have visitors who take up their social time. She also has other friends and invites them over more frequently. In essence, she doesn't have to change social relationships as much as she needs to shift the emphasis from one relationship to another.

Jeff is another story. Jeff's primary social relationships occur in the bars in which he drinks. He sees none of these people when he isn't drinking. Jeff decides that he cannot help himself alone. He attends a meeting of Alcoholics Anonymous

TABLE 15-3
TACTICS FOR OVERCOMING LONELINESS

1. Use the strategies that will help friendships form: Be a good listener, be where people are, have interesting things to talk about, disclose things about yourself at about the rate you are disclosed to, listen for those disclosures that people make to you.
2. Invite people to join in your activities.
3. Learn new activities.
4. Set up a self-desensitization program to overcome fears of being alone, going out alone, initiating contact with others.
5. Self-monitor your frequency of giving compliments to others.

(AA). There he meets many people who disclose similar problems. There's much in common to discuss. Maybe they can help him.

ALTERING SOCIAL NEEDS AND DESIRES. Jan doesn't need to worry about this. She's generally well self-adjusted. When her husband goes fishing on a Friday evening, and there's no one to socialize with, she catches up on some letter writing. While he's gone, she also decides to have a two-hour soak in the bathtub. This always makes her feel relaxed.

Jeff is another story. He's afraid to go out alone, unless he's had a few drinks. Yet he's unhappy staying home, unless he's drinking. His AA meetings are helping him understand that the alcohol is part of his problem. He also realizes that there are changes he must make in himself, either with or without professional help. He decides wisely to seek professional help, considering himself too much of a basket case to help himself alone.

Along with other things they're working on, Jeff's psychologist teaches him to relax himself (see Chapter 5). Then he conducts systematic desensitization, basing the hierarchy on a fear of being alone. Jeff also practices his relaxation daily, usually when he gets home from work and the urge for a drink is strong.

ALTERING PERCEPTION OF THE PROBLEM. Jan sees the problem immediately. She knows that it really isn't a problem. While she dearly loves Marie as a friend, she knows that they must live their own lives. Both she and Marie will form new friendships, and their own friendship will change somewhat due to the distance separating them. Each of these events, Jan understands, is pretty inevitable. "Life goes on," she thinks.

Jeff is another story. He has many perceptions about himself and about life that are inaccurate. He thinks he has to drink to feel good. He thinks he has to be around others to feel good. He thinks he's a crummy lover. His loneliness may be overcome only if these and other feelings are successfully dealt with. Because of these perceptions, he is not likely to adjust on his own. He needs help.

Jan and Marie have been separated about six weeks and Jan has all but gotten over her loneliness. She still tends to mope a little on Friday nights, but she's involved other friends in some of the things she and Marie used to do. She raised her rate of entertaining somewhat; she and Marie have talked on the telephone and written one another, and they have plans to meet in a city they both like in a few months. In addition, Jan and her family plan to visit with Marie and her family over Christmas. Jan has found a couple of other women who like to have lunch together. Thus, Jan's adjustment to life without Marie is progressing normally.

Jeff has been in therapy and going to AA meetings for about a year. He's had several setbacks that occurred when he started drinking again. He's adjusted to the fact that his wife is gone. He even feels that he can now spend some time by himself and enjoy it. He met another lady through his AA meetings. They're proceeding very slowly. Jeff and his therapist are working on Jeff's self-concept, and Jeff is doing homework exercises in relaxation and social skills development.

Adjusting Bereavement

Fred's dad has just died. Fred is inconsolable. He and his dad fished and went to ballgames together. His dad also babysat Fred's two children. And when there was handiwork to be done at Fred's home, his dad would often help. In short, Fred and his dad were very close. When Fred thinks about his dad, he often feels like crying, although he tries to stop himself from crying in public. He's numb. He's unable to sleep. He has no appetite. He's disinterested in work. Everyone in his family is avoiding him because his temper seems very short. He's confused about feeling like crying—after all American men don't do that very often, do they? He's getting tired of the platitudes that his father's many friends seem to repeat with each phone call. His daily consumption of cigarettes has risen. Will he ever feel better? How long will it take? What is normal behavior in this type of situation? In this section we try to answer these questions and suggest what is normal grieving and how to adjust to it where possible.

Defining Bereavement and Grief

bereavement

The state of being deprived of a significant other by that person's death; the reaction to this loss.

grief

Strong emotional behavior elicited by the loss of a significant other, usually through the death of that person.

The French root of the word *bereavement* means to rob (Jeter, 1983). **Bereavement** is the loss of a significant other and the reaction to this loss. When we say, for example, "the children were bereaved of their mother," we imply that they were deprived of hope and joy, and made desolate through their loss. As we mentioned in Chapter 10, **grief** is one component of this entire response pattern. It's the anguish, heartache, sadness, and sorrow that one feels following loss of a loved one. Grief has been separated from bereavement for study (Brasted & Callahan, 1984; Ramsay, 1979).

With grief, it's less a matter of *if* you will experience it and more a matter of *when*. It's estimated that between 5 and 9 percent of the general population will experience bereavement in any one year (Osterweiss et al., 1984). The only people who may avoid such occurrences are those who die young. Each year in the United States there are approximately 800,000 individuals who are widowed. Moreover, approximately 400,000 young people (under the age of 25 years) die each year (Osterweiss et al., 1984). Sooner or later, the situation will arise for all of us in which someone significant to us dies. And we will grieve that person's absence.

While grief is caused by the death of someone significant to us, it can also be caused by any significant loss. It may be produced by divorce, for example, where there is loss of a spouse (but not the death of the spouse); or by moving one's residence, when significant friends are left behind (Brasted & Callahan, 1984; Ramsay, 1979). (Note the parallel to conditions that generate loneliness above.) For the most part, however, grief has been studied in humans following bereavement itself.

GRIEF AND DEPRESSION.   While there are some commonalities, the constellation of feelings and behaviors that comprise grief are not the same as clinical depression. Freud (1917) first made this useful distinction. Freud thought that people who were depressed felt emptiness within, while those who were grieving felt emptiness without. Moreover, in depression there may be strong feelings of worthlessness that are not observed in grief (Ramsay, 1979). However, there are anywhere

Public displays of grief and mourning— including displays by those who are famous (upper photo)—are manifestations of the effects of bereavement.

from 10 to 45 percent of the bereaved who have sufficient symptoms to be classified as depressed up to one year after bereavement (Bornstein et al., 1973; Clayton et al., 1972; Clayton et al., 1974).

CONSEQUENCES OF BEREAVEMENT. Some of the consequences of bereavement relate to age, health, and sex. For example, males seem more at risk than females for increased mortality following bereavement (for example, Thompson et al.,

---

Box 15-5

Some Consequences of Bereavement for Adults

1. A significant increase in mortality for males under the age of 75. This consequence also relates to whether the man remarries, if his bereavement is the loss of his spouse.

2. Suicide increases in the first year for older widowers and for single men who have lost their mothers.

3. Cardiovascular disease, infectious diseases, and death from accidents increase among widowers; among widows, death from cirrhosis rises.

4. If the bereaved smokes, drinks, or uses other substances, their use goes up. Bereavement also produces some new users.

5. Depressive symptoms are common during the first year.

6. In prepaid health programs, use of the program's services rises in the year following bereavement, but regular medical services are not sought out.

7. Those most at risk are the previously ill (physical or mental), substance abusers, and those without social supports.

1984). Young people seem more at risk than older people. Bereavement doesn't seem to produce any specific diseases, but for those who already have chronic illnesses, these illnesses may be exacerbated. Among the elderly, reports of health problems increase as does use of medication (Thompson et al., 1984). Further among the elderly, indicators of mental health stress rise significantly (Gallagher et al., 1983). Finally, those without social support systems already in place may be more at risk. Note that the foregoing applies to adults, not children. (There may also be risks for children, about which more below.)

SYMPTOMS OF GRIEF.   Recall from Chapter 10 that the study of grief in modern times was done by psychiatrist Erich Lindeman (1944) as a part of a study of 101 bereaved persons, including 13 survivors of a tragic night in 1942 when 491 people perished in a fire in Boston's Cocoanut Grove nightclub. Research by Lindeman and others suggests that many people go through five stages of grief: (a) shock and numbness, as evidenced by incoherence and physical signs (fainting, etc.), and leading to a feeling of being emotionally drained; (b) denial and disbelief, as evidenced by refusal to acknowledge the death of the individual; (c) perception that the individual is still around, as indicated by "hearing" the person's voice or "seeing" the deceased in dreams or perhaps walking down the street; (d) feelings of separation, indicated by statements that the deceased is finally gone; and (e) resolution and acceptance, indicated by the grieving person returning to normal activities (Ramsay, 1979).

Phases or Components?   While Lindeman suggested that most people pass through stages of grief, more recent researchers have provided evidence that there is no strict route through grief. The experience of grief may differ slightly for everyone who undergoes it. Current thought is that there may be phases to the overall process, but caution is necessary. Phases may not progress in a standard fashion in each grieving individual. Instead they may overlap or may not all be seen (Osterweiss et al., 1984). This has led some to talk of components of grief, rather than phases (see Brasted & Callahan, 1984; Ramsay, 1979).

pathological grief

Grief that is abnormal in some way, usually because it has not resolved and appears therefore to be stalled.

unacceptable grief

Another term for pathological grief.

PATHOLOGICAL GRIEF. Where grieving does not correctly resolve, the individual appears to be mired in the grieving process. Occasionally, too, there may be an absence of grief or grief may even be delayed. These occurrences are usually signals that the grief process is **pathological,** that is, not normal. (Because the amount of grief or its onset may not constitute a problem for everyone, Gauthier and Marshall (1977) suggest the term **"unacceptable grief"** rather than pathological grief.) For such individuals professional help may be necessary. Whether grief becomes unacceptable appears to relate to the suddenness of the loss (Ramsay, 1979); the absence of a support group for the bereaved; the failure of the support group to stop supporting grieving and begin supporting adaptive behavior (Gauthier & Marshall, 1977); the bereaved's previous state of health, particularly mental health (Osterweiss et al., 1984); the age of the bereaved; and whether the bereaved attended the funeral (Zisook & DeVaul, 1983). Pathological grief may also relate to the age of the deceased. People have a much harder time accepting the death of children than they do the death of an adult (Ramsay, 1979).

Guide to Normal Grieving

Most of you will adjust automatically to the fact that you have lost someone important to you. In other words, the grief you feel, and the way you behave during this process will be culturally acceptable. However, the following information—digested now during a time when you feel no grief—may help you to adjust to the process when grief finally does occur.

ALLOWING A TIME AND PLACE TO GRIEVE. At first, Fred knew that he was too emotional to function well in public, so he stayed home. There, if he felt like crying, he went to his bedroom and let himself go. During these times his wife held him if he wanted that. Fred had felt that he needed to be able to let out some of his emotions. He also thought that he wouldn't feel so much like crying in public if he had already cried in private. He stayed away from sleeping pills and tranquilizers during this time, figuring that if he was in a drugged state it could dull his feelings and somehow slow down the process of grieving (see Ramsay, 1979).

Fred dealt with his initial grief more or less on his own. In some societies, a death is a time for a communal event, such as a wake. Such an event can help people deal with the loss of a loved one by identifying a traditional time and place to grieve.

A wake is a party at which the deceased is celebrated. It is another manifestation of public grieving.

SELF-REDUCTION OF EMOTIONAL RESPONSES.   When Fred was in public and felt that he was going to burst into tears, he tried thought stopping (see Chapter 1). He shouted "no!" to himself. When the urge to cry passed he thought of his "peace" scene, the one he uses whenever he meditates. For Fred this is a scene where he's taking a nap as a child. It's a summer day and he can hear bees buzzing around the flowers outside the open window of his room. When he thinks of this scene, he feels himself start to relax. In fact, almost inevitably when Fred imagines his peace scene, he recites the first few statements from his relaxation mantra. For Fred, this has to do with his limbs feeling heavy and warm. When he was in public where he couldn't completely relax for a long period of time, Fred used his relaxation mantra for just a minute or so.

Fred let himself cry early in the grief process. Later on, when he felt that he shouldn't be crying when he thought about his dad, he used thought stopping, his peace scene, and relaxation.

CARRYING ON WITH LIFE.   Fred's boss was very understanding. He suggested that Fred rest a few days and then come in one morning just for a half a day. Fred did this. The following day he was back full-time. He still felt emotional, but it became a little easier each day to relax through those periods.

At home, Fred still had to take his oldest son to little league. And there was the lawn to mow. Fred noticed that involving himself in routine household chores helped keep his mind off his father's death, so he increased the amount of time he spent on these tasks. His children, momentarily unhappy at the loss of their grandfather, soon were asking for the attention that they always received from their father. Fred found that he enjoyed these activities with his children even more now—his children seemed so alive and vital. Finally, Fred felt that it would be nice to relax with some fishing. He called one of his father's fishing partners. They hit it off well.

DESENSITIZATION TO THE LOSS.   Soon after the loss it may be too painful to examine closely one's relations with the deceased. However, if this doesn't become easier with the passage of time—especially a long time—then special techniques or help may be needed.

Whenever Judy's husband starts to talk about their son who died eight months before, she becomes enraged. She wasn't able to cry much during and after the funeral. She wasn't able to bring herself to see her son in the mortuary. Talk of her son is so upsetting to her that she runs to the bedroom or out of the house rather than talk to her husband. Judy decides she had better do something to help herself, but she doesn't want to see anyone professionally. She remembers a class in which she learned about systematic self-desensitization, a technique in which strong anxiety attached to life events can be neutralized. She decides to start doing this.

First she constructs a hierarchy of items that relate to her son and his death. The hierarchy includes such items as:

- Remembering how strong Bobby was at the end of his illness when it was clear he would die.
- Feeling extremely guilty that she didn't spend enough time with him.
- Feeling that she was forced to choose between her job and her son, and that she chose the job.
- Feeling extremely angry with her son for having died and then feeling guilty about feeling angry.
- Feeling that God had unnecessarily taken her child.

Constructing such a hierarchy is not an easy task (Ramsay, 1979). The last item, for example, gave Judy horrendous problems just to think about, let alone write down, because it attacked the roots of her faith. Nevertheless, she felt that it

---

Box 15-6

A SUMMARY OF RISK FACTORS POTENTIALLY RELATING TO UNRESOLVED GRIEF IN YOUTH

Risk of unresolved grief is greater if:

1. Loss occurs either before child is five years old or during early adolescence.
2. Loss of mother occurs before girls are eleven years old or loss of father before boys are adolescents.
3. The child has preexisting behavioral problems: The more severe they are, the greater the risk.
4. A poor (especially a conflicting) relationship existed with the deceased.
5. The parent who survives is psychologically dependent on the grieving child.
6. A social support system is absent, or the surviving adult is incapable of using one if it exists.
7. The child's environment is unstable; for example, there are multiple caretakers and disruption in familiar routines.
8. Parental remarriage occurs and there is a negative relationship with the new parent.
9. There was a lack of prior knowledge of death.
10. The death is unanticipated.
11. The death is the suicide or murder of a sibling or parent.

---

had to be done. In spite of heavy emotions, she persists with the task until the hierarchy contains about a dozen items which are arranged in order, from those that produce the least anguish to those that are the most upsetting.

From the class that she took on desensitization, she knows that she must now begin thinking about the items on the hierarchy while in a relaxed state. Judy decides to incorporate her morning shower into the routine.

During her morning shower, she feels very relaxed. The hot water streaming over her feels very good. First she thinks about the item on the list that produces the least anxiety. She only holds the thought as long as she feels relaxed in the shower. If the thought becomes too painful she stops it and lets herself think again how wonderful the shower is. In this way each day, thinking about only one item per day, she gradually works her way through all the items on the list. She doesn't hurry the process, preferring not to make herself upset and exhausted with the task.

Several weeks later her husband says, "You know, I was thinking about Bobby today. I remember when he used to come in from playing in the mud. We wouldn't know whether to be angry because he was so dirty or glad because he looked so cute."

"I thought of that the other day myself," replied Judy. "I sure miss him. I couldn't say that until now. Do you want to talk about it a little? It would sure help me sort out my feelings."

Bereavement in Youth

Some young people are also going to experience bereavement, perhaps not in numbers as great as adults, but still in significant quantities. For example, as many as 5 percent of children in the United States may lose one or both parents by the time they are 15 years old (Kliman, 1979). Probably the most serious of losses for a child are those of a parent or a sibling.

Box 15-7

Suicide: Problem and Prevention

Razors pain you;
Rivers are damp;
Acids stain you;
And drugs cause cramp.
Guns aren't lawful;
Nooses give;
Gas smells awful;
You might as well live.

Dorothy Parker
"Resume," 1926

How Often Does It Happen? (Stillion et al., 1989)

Is there a problem? More than we'd like to think. Here are a few discouraging facts:

Suicide was the eighth leading cause of death in 1986 in the United States (30,904 deaths in that year).

What these statistics fail to portray is that many suicides go unrecognized as such—they may be reported as accidents—and there may be ten times as many actual suicides (Hirschfeld & Davidson, 1988).

Suicide occurs about four times as often in males as it does in females in the United States (see Figure 10-4).

Among males, suicide occurs nearly twice as often among white males as it does among Afro-American and all other minority males (see Figure 10-4).

Suicide rates increase with age for males, while they remain low and relatively unchanged for females (see Figure 10-4).

Though half the rate of white males, suicide rates for minority males are still four times those of minority females (see Figure 10-4).

Ten Myths About Suicide (Schneidman et al., 1961)

1. *People who talk about suicide don't commit suicide.* Wrong! The majority who do so have talked about it.

2. *Suicide occurs without warning.* After the fact it is usually easy to see warning signals that were overlooked.

3. *Improvement after a suicide crisis means that the suicide risk is over.* It doesn't. Nearly half of Schneidman and colleagues' clients committed suicide within 90 days of the initial crisis they were helped through.

4. *Suicide and depression are synonymous.* There are major components of depression that relate to many suicides—particularly feelings of hopelessness and no expectations for the future. But there are also suicides by individuals who are not depressed but who may be psychotic, agitated, or anxious.

5. *All suicidal persons are mentally ill.* Schneidman and associates found that many of their clients' suicide notes were quite rational, referring to pain, age, and ambivalence about life—not the pictures of people who were mentally ill, in the sense of being out of touch with reality.

6. *Suicide is the result of a single process.* It isn't. Rather, it's a complex phenomenon.

7. *Suicide is immoral.* Not necessarily. Such a conclusion depends on the times and places in which we live, that is, our cultures.

8. *Suicide can be controlled by legislation.* It is very difficult to legislate the private behavior of human beings. It is thought that penalties against suicide serve only to make attempts more lethal and to make the person who fails to succeed less likely to seek help.

9. *The tendency to suicide is inherited.* If children of parents who have committed suicide also commit suicide is that act inherited, or is it an instance of modeled behavior? It is just as easy to conclude the latter as the former.

10. *Suicide is the curse of the poor and the disease of the rich.* All socioeconomic groups contribute their share to suicide statistics.

Grief may not be expressed much in young children for two reasons. First, grief appears to require understanding. Very young children (younger than three years) appear not to grieve; it is unlikely that they as yet understand the permanent, irreversible nature of death. Understanding of the nature of death—its three components: irreversibility, nonfunctionality, and universality—does not appear to occur until between five and seven years of age (Speece & Brent, 1984). Interestingly, this is about the time children are thought by Piaget to make a transition from the

Factors Associated with Adult Suicide

1. *An accumulation of negative life events.* These include declining health, financial problems, reduced career opportunities, loss of significant others (separation, divorce, death), often with very little time among the events, and often with a history of negative life events earlier in life as well as temporally proximate to the suicide.

2. *Depression.* Suicide is much more prevalent (that is, 30 times more!) among adults with a diagnosis of depression than those without such a diagnosis or in comparison with those with other psychiatric diagnoses.

3. *Alcoholism.* Alcoholism goes hand-in-glove with suicide, raising the risk to some 58 to 85 times that of nonalcoholics (Roy & Linniola, 1986). Many more alcoholic suicides are males than females, the typical case being a middle-aged male between 45 and 55 years, with a 25-year drinking history and currently drinking. It is well known that alcohol and depression are often related. It is also possible that alcoholic males are more likely candidates for suicide than females both because males are more likely to be alcoholics than females and because females are socialized to reach out for help, while males are socialized to go it alone (Stillion et al., 1989).

Prevention (Health and Welfare, Canada, 1987)

1. *Change societal conditions that relate to suicide.* This means active cooperation of media and mental health professionals to prevent modeling—a known effect of publicized suicides; making suicide instruments less lethal and/or harder to obtain; working to decrease the stigma involved in seeking help if you have suicidal thoughts or impulses; and educating more professionals in both risk assessment and therapeutic intervention.

2. *Educate to improve peoples' abilities to cope.* Teach understanding and toleration of failure experiences; teach specific coping strategies such as problem-solving techniques, positive coping self-statements, the development of a sense of humor, realistic goal-setting, relaxation techniques, and all the others that we have mentioned that are relevant to stress reduction.

3. *Educate for suicide prevention.* This means that public schools must participate in the development of programs in order to educate children, and they have done so to some extent. These programs usually present facts, signs, symptoms, referral sources, and some coping skills development (Stillion et al., 1989).

Intervention for the Untrained

If you get suicide signals from a friend or acquaintance, what should you do?

1. Determine the seriousness of the attempt (or the would-be attempt) through thoughtful, empathetic questioning. It is particularly important to determine the *level of lethality*. In general, specific plans involving specific times, places, methods, and the availability of instruments indicate a much higher level of lethality than the absence of these plans. It is important to be supportive and understanding.

2. Don't leave the person alone for any reason or for any amount of time.

3. Seek qualified professional help as soon as possible. In doing so, determine who would be most acceptable to your friend. This help is as much for you as it is for your friend.

preoperational stage of thinking to the concrete-operational stage. However, there is as yet no validation of this potential relationship between the child's conception of death and these modes of thinking (Speece & Brent, 1984). Second, grief may require social attachments to be lost and grieved over. Very early in life children may not react to the loss of their principal care givers if regular care is provided by a surrogate. In these cases there may as yet be no social attachment in the infant's life.

IMMEDIATE REACTIONS.   In large part, children who grieve are likely to act similarly to adults immediately after the death of a significant person. They are stunned, angry, fearful; they don't sleep well; and they may lose their appetites. They may also show behavior of an earlier developmental period. For example, children under five years may show bowel and/or bladder disturbances and those in school may become withdrawn (Osterweiss et al., 1984).

INTERMEDIATE REACTIONS.   No conclusions are possible regarding medical outcomes, although these cannot be ruled out. Intermediate behavioral reactions appear to include an increased chance of depression, and an increased chance of school-related difficulties.

LONG-TERM REACTIONS.   Here the data are the weakest, but they seem to imply an increased risk of physical and mental health problems later in life (Osterweiss et al., 1984). For example, the risk of depression may increase by a factor of two or three (Lloyd, 1980). There is even an increased chance of becoming involved with the criminal justice system if one is bereaved in youth (Markesun & Fulton, 1971).

Helping Children Adjust to Bereavement

A number of factors appear to facilitate children's adjustment to bereavement. Primarily they need to be treated in an open, honest, and supportive manner. This may be difficult, particularly when the child's reaction may not seem normal to the adult, and the adult, too, may be upset with grief. If the death is anticipated, the child should be included in family discussions of the event, discussed in vocabulary that the child can understand. If possible, and the child desires it, contact should be maintained with the dying person. This is especially so if the dying person can show the child his or her acceptance of death. Children should be reassured that they are not going to suffer the same fate as the deceased. Being evasive, suggesting that the deceased's death was preventable, and sheltering or otherwise overprotecting surviving children may place them at risk (Krell & Rabkin, 1979).

Professional help might be sought when the following behaviors are observed in the child: persistent fear that she or he will die; hopes of a reunion with the deceased, perhaps expressed as a desire to die also; persistent blame and guilt; overactivity; compulsive caregiving; and accident proneness (Bowlby, 1980). Note the emphasis in the foregoing on the *persistent* nature of these occurrences as an indicator of pathology.

SUMMARY

- People who experience severe emotional problems should seek professional help. Many individuals, however, can learn to deal with milder emotional problems. In this chapter we described specific steps to overcome problematic anxiety, anger, loneliness, and grief.

- One strategy for overcoming anxiety is systematic self-desensitization. The three major steps of this procedure include constructing a fear hierarchy (a ranking of fear-producing situations from those that are the least feared to those that are the most feared), learning deep muscle relaxation (the alternate tensing and relaxing of one's muscles to achieve a relaxed state), and carrying out the actual therapy steps of self-desensitization (listing items of the fear hierarchy on index cards and systematically using the cards to imagine the anxiety-producing items while in a relaxed state). *In vivo* desensitization is a procedure in which fear-producing items are encountered in real life rather than desensitizing them in one's imagination. Participant modeling requires that an individual with a fear observe a model who gradually approaches the feared stimulus. The individual with the fear is encouraged to imitate the model in a step-by-step fashion. Two other strategies for countering fear are centering and coping self-statements. Centering involves controlled breathing to help you relax and to eliminate potential anxiety-evoking thoughts. Coping self-statements involve alternative thoughts that counteract the fear or anxiety.

- The withdrawal or withholding of rewards causes emotional behavior that we label as anger. One way to cope with anger is to learn to relax in the presence of situations that normally evoke an angry response. Because talking about something that makes you angry can cause you to become even angrier, practicing coping self-statements instead can help you to counteract particular irrational and anger-provoking thoughts. Assertion training teaches you to express your feelings in a direct and honest way without becoming aggressive and without putting others down. It is an effective anger-coping strategy when anger comes from not speaking up in situations where you believe that others are taking advantage of you.

- Responsible assertion includes both verbal and nonverbal behavior that produces a positive change toward you by a listener without counteraggression. As with any other adjustment, it is necessary to strengthen such behavior via practice. One practice routine follows the LADDER technique: **L**ook at the situation, **a**rrange a time to discuss the problem, **d**efine the problem, **d**escribe your feelings, **e**xpress your wishes, and **r**einforce the listener. This is done by writing rehearsal statements in the form of a script. Saying no is dealt with similarly. Often, responsible assertiveness is undermined by verbally aggressive behavior. Such behavior should be decreased in frequency while responsibly assertive behavior is increased.

- The problems of loneliness can be severe, and there appear to be substantial numbers of people who feel lonely at any given time. Almost everyone has felt transient loneliness at some time or another—loneliness that lasts from a few minutes to a few hours. Situational loneliness results from an important event such as the death of a loved one or a close friend moving away. Chronic loneliness is loneliness that lasts for two or more years consecutively. Loneliness can be caused from the absence of a social partner, a belief of an enduring loss of that partner, frequent thoughts of the absent person, and a continuing desire that the partner will return. The overall number of social contacts and timing and quality of social contacts are also important contributors. Strategies to cope with loneliness include changing social relationships, altering social needs and desires, and changing one's perception of the problem. Strategies such as those for developing friendships reviewed in Chapter 8, as well as self-desensitization to overcome fears of being alone, can also be helpful.

- Bereavement refers to the loss of a loved one as well as the effects of that loss. One effect of bereavement is grief, feelings of sorrow and sadness. During the normal process of grief, one is unlikely to need professional help to get through it; it is a fact of life that nearly everyone experiences. Biological structure and environment, together, lead to adjustment to loss, which results in grief. However, awareness may assist in the process. That process may be facilitated if one allows oneself to grieve, if one exposes oneself to the facts of the loss producing the grief until such events are rendered relatively neutral, and if one attempts to carry on. Children should be actively supported during their time of grief by being included in honest discussions, and where possible by visiting with the dying person. They should not be overprotected during this time.

Box 15-8
BEYOND SELF-ADJUSTMENT:
SEEKING PROFESSIONAL HELP

At the beginning of this chapter we suggested some considerations to keep in mind if you were contemplating self-adjustment for emotional problems. What about *any* personal problems you might have? When is it a good idea to try to self-adjust and when is it a better idea to seek professional help?

Actually, the guidelines given at the beginning of the chapter apply here as well. Let's restate the guidelines for seeking professional help, and examine them a bit more fully.

REASONS FOR SEEKING PROFESSIONAL HELP

The Problem Seems Overwhelming. If the problem seems overwhelming to you, seek professional help because the problem is probably already interfering with your daily life. Don't be afraid to ask for advice here from your friends. Do they see you as overwhelmed?

You Feel Certain That You Cannot Handle It. If you have the feeling that you cannot cope with your problem and that you feel helpless to deal with it, seek professional help. Feelings of helplessness may indicate your lack of motivation, and your difficulty in seeing a way out of your dilemma.

You Cannot Define What Is Wrong with You. What if you just feel really bad, both mentally and physically? Your emotions seem all screwed up. People are treating you differently and you don't know why. You feel out of synch and left out. If you cannot figure out what is producing all of these feelings and they persist, seek professional help.

Books Such as This Say Don't Self-Adjust. You've taken some of the surveys in this or another self-help book and you're off the end of the scale. The book says that you shouldn't self-adjust your problem. Seek professional help. Everything may still be all right because this and other books make the decision to seek help a liberally based one. It is better to find out that we (and you) were wrong—you don't need help—than to *not* find out that we were right.

You've Tried Before and Failed. This is often a good indicator that you need professional help. However, there is no reason why you shouldn't try again to self-adjust. Perhaps the prior program you tried was ill-advised or your motivation was insufficient. However, if you fail again, then the fact that you have been motivated to try a couple of times and have not succeeded suggests first that you consider the problem important to deal with, and second, that you have been unable to do so successfully. Seek professional help under these circumstances.

PROFESSIONAL SERVICES

Locating Therapists. Now that you've decided to seek professional help, where is it? One place to start is with your telephone book's yellow pages. But where to look? The headings *Psychologists, Psychotherapists,* and *Psychiatrists* (the last of which will shunt you to Physicians and Surgeons) will get you many listings. The laws of most states do not permit someone to call him or herself a psychologist or psychiatrist in printed material such as the telephone book without first being licensed or certified to do so.

The above listings will show you mostly individuals or groups of individuals who are in private practice. Therapists can also be located in many community agencies such as: community mental health centers, hospitals, social services agencies, and schools. So searching your community or your telephone book for these listings will also pay off.

What Kind of Therapist Do You Want? This is a big question. Because there are so many persuasions of therapist, and there are good ones and bad ones of each, it is important to shop around. Some of your friends may have had experiences that will be valuable for you. What you want is someone who is effective for you regardless of the specific academic degree, someone with whom you feel good, someone who exudes some confidence, someone who has empathy for your problem. You will be sharing intimate secrets—can you feel good about doing that with this person? If the therapist's sex is important to you, be sure to factor that in. Good therapists cross theoretical boundaries. If you don't like what you feel during the preliminary interview or you don't like what is happening to you in therapy, don't stay. Find someone else. Evaluate carefully if you feel like escaping each time when therapy gets difficult. It may not be your therapist. Therapy is hard work for both participants, and it is easy to run away from it.

Remember that you, your insurance company, or both are paying for this experience. You have every right to inquire as to qualifications, fees, theoretical approach, projected length of therapy, and so on.

Insurance. Insurance policies are not without restrictions. Either read your policy or call your insurance company ahead of time. Often insurance companies may know specialists in your particular problem area. They may also have restrictions on which problems they will cover, which therapists they will reimburse, how many sessions they'll pay for in the resolution of a particular problem, and what proportion of the therapy they'll cover.

Therapy costs from about $25 to $100 per session (50 minutes). However, if you cannot afford the cost and you have no insurance, many community agencies charge fees based on your ability to pay.

Most colleges have counseling centers that are fully staffed with qualified professionals, making that a good place for students to try. In addition, teaching hospitals attached to universities and departments of psychology in colleges and universities often contain clinics or individuals who are also in private practice.

Results of therapy. Miracles should not be expected. At a frequency of one session per week, therapy for many problems ranges from several weeks to several months. For the most part, therapy is slow, and no one is going to do the job for you. In some respects, a good therapist is a friend and guide who will help you help yourself.

■ **IMPORTANT PERSONS**

You should know who this person is and why he is important:

Joseph Wolpe

■ **IMPORTANT TERMS**

Be prepared to define the following terms (located in the margins of this chapter). Where appropriate, be prepared to describe examples.

Fear	Assertion Training
Anxiety	Aggression
Phobia	Loneliness
Systematic Desensitization	Transient Loneliness
Systematic Self-Desensitization	Situational Loneliness
Fear Hierarchy	Chronic Loneliness
Subjective Units of Discomfort (SUDS)	Profound Relationships
In vivo Desensitization	Mundane Relationships
Participant Modeling	Bereavement
Flooding	Grief
Anger	Pathological Grief
Catharsis	Unacceptable Grief
Responsible Assertion	

■ **QUESTIONS FROM IMPORTANT IDEAS IN THIS CHAPTER**

1. List three main phases of systematic desensitization. Describe each in a paragraph or less.
2. Using an example, describe how one might use centering and coping self-statements to counteract anxiety from irrational self-talk.
3. Describe the steps that you might follow in using relaxation strategies to cope with anger.
4. Does "venting your anger" cause you to feel more or less angry? Justify your answer.
5. Identify specific verbal and nonverbal behaviors that differentiate between assertive and nonassertive persons.
6. Describe three general ways in which a person must change in order for loneliness to be ameliorated.
7. Briefly describe each of five classic stages or components of grief.
8. What self-adjustment procedures might be employed to facilitate the grief process?

REFERENCES

ABRAMS, D. B., & WILSON, G. T. (1983). Alcohol, sexual arousal, and self-control. *Journal of Personality and Social Psychology, 45,* 188–198.

ABRAMS, M. (1981). Demographic trends. In D. Hobman (Ed.), *The impact of aging: Strategies for. care.* New York: St. Martin's Press.

ADAMS, G. R. (1982). Physical attractiveness. In A. G. Miller (Ed.), *In the eye of the beholder: Contemporary issues in stereotyping.* New York: Praeger.

ADAMS, P. R., & ADAMS, G. R. (1984). Mt. St. Helen's ashfall: Evidence for a disaster stress reaction. *American Psychologist, 39,* 252–260.

ADER, R., & COHEN, N. (1982). Behaviorally conditioned immunosuppression and murine systemic lupus erythematosus. *Science, 215,* 1534–1536.

ADER, R., & COHEN, N. (1985). CNS-immune system interactions: Conditioning phenomena. *Behavioral and Brain Sciences, 8,* 379–426.

ADLER, A. (1931). *What life should mean to you.* Boston: Little, Brown.

ADORNO, T. W., FRENKEL-BRUNSWICK, E., LEVINSON, D. J., & SANFORD, R. N. (1950). *The authoritarian personality: Studies in prejudice.* New York: Harper & Row.

AERO, R., & WEINER, E. (Eds.) (1981). *The mind test: 37 classic psychological tests you can now score and analyze yourself.* New York: William Morrow.

AGRAS, W. S. (1987). Presidential address: Where do we go from here? *Behavior Therapy, 18,* 203–217.

ALBERTI, R. E., & EMMONS, M. L. (1986). *Your perfect right: A guide to asser-tive living* (5th ed.). San Luis Obispo, CA: Impact Publishers.

ALBRECHT, S., BAHR, H. S., & GOODMAN, K. L. (1983). *Divorce and remarriage: Problems, adaptations, and adjustments.* Westport, CT: Greenwood Press.

ALEXANDER, P. C., MOORE, S., & ALEXANDER, E. R., III (1991). What is transmitted in the intergenerational transmission of violence? *Journal of Marriage and the Family, 53,* 657–668.

ALLEN, K. E., HART, B. M., BUELL, J. S., HARRIS, F. R., & WOLF, M. M. (1964). Effects of social reinforcement on isolate behavior of a nursery school child. *Child Development, 35,* 511–518.

ALLEN, R. J. (1983). *Human stress: Its nature and control.* Minneapolis, MN: Burgess Publishing.

ALLPORT, G. W. (1937). *Personality: A psychological interpretation.* New York: Holt.

ALLPORT, G. W. (1961). *Pattern and growth in personality.* New York: Holt, Rinehart, & Winston.

ALLPORT, G. W., & ODBERT, H. S. (1936). Trait names: A psycholexical study. *Psychological Monographs, 47,* 2–11.

ALTEMEYER, B. (1988). *Enemies of freedom: Understanding right wing authoritarianism.* New York: Jossey-Bass.

AMERICAN CANCER SOCIETY REPORT (1986). New York: Author.

AMERICAN LUNG ASSOCIATION (1989). *Freedom from smoking in 20 days.* New York: Author.

AMERICAN PSYCHIATRIC ASSOCIATION (1987). *Diagnostic and statistical manual of mental disorders* (3rd ed., rev.). Washington, DC: Author.

AMERICAN PSYCHOLOGICAL ASSOCIATION (1985). *Ethical principles in the conduct of research with human participants.* Washington, DC: Author.

AMIR, Y., & SHARAN, S. (1984). *School desegregation: Cross-cultural perspectives.* Hillsdale, NJ: Lawrence Erlbaum.

AMSEL, A., & ROUSSEL, J. S. (1952). Motivational properties of frustration: Effect on a running response of the addition of frustration to the motivational complex. *Journal of Experimental Psychology, 43,* 363–368.

ANAND, R. P. (1983). *Origin and development of the law of the sea: History of international law revisited.* The Hague: Martinus Nijhoff.

ANDERSON, C. A. (1989). Temperature and aggression: The ubiquitous effects of heat on the occurrence of human violence. *Psychological Bulletin, 106*(1), 74–96.

ANDERSON, C. M., REISS, D. J., & HOGARTY, G. E. (1986). *Schizophrenia and the family: A practitioner's guide to psychoeducation and management.* New York: Guilford Press.

ARCHER, D., IRITANI, B., KIMES, D. B., & BARRIOS, M. (1983). Face-ism: Five studies of sex differences in facial prominence. *Journal of Personality and Social Psychology, 45,* 725–735.

ARGYLE, M., & DEAN, J. (1965). Eye contact, distance, and affiliation. *Sociometry, 28,* 289–304.

ARNETZ, B. B., WASSERMAN, J., PETRINI, B., BRENNER, S. O., LEVI, L., ENEROTH, P., SALOVAARA, H., HJELM, R., SALOVAARA, L., THEORELL, T., & PETTERSON, I. L. (1987). Immune function in unemployed women. *Psychosomatic Medicine, 49,* 3–12.

ARON, A., DUTTON, D. G., ARON, E. N., & IVERSON, A. (1989). Experiences of falling in love. *Journal of Social and Personal Relationships, 6,* 243–257.

ARONSON, E. (1980). *The social animal* (3rd ed.). San Francisco, CA: W. H. Freeman.

ARONSON, E., & BRIDGEMAN, D. (1979). Jigsaw groups and the desegregated classroom: In pursuit of common goals. *Personality and Social Psychology Bulletin, 5,* 438–446.

ARRICK, C. M., VOSS, J., & RIMM, D. C. (1981). The relative efficacy of thought-stopping and covert assertion. *Behavior Research and Therapy, 19,* 17–24.

ASTIN, A. W., GREEN, K. C., & KORN, W. S. (1987). *The American freshman: Twenty year trends.* Los Angeles: Higher Education Research Institute, UCLA.

ASTRACHAN, A. (1986). *How men feel.* New York: Anchor Press.

ATKINSON, J. (1986). *Schizophrenia at home: A guide to helping the family.* London: Croon Helm.

ATWOOD, J. D., & CHESTER, R. (1987). *Treatment techniques for common mental disorders.* Northvale, NJ: Jason Aronson.

AVERILL, J. R. (1968). Grief: Its nature and significance. *Psychological Bulletin, 70,* 721–748.

AVERILL, J. R. (1969). Autonomic response patterns during sadness and mirth. *Psychophysiology, 5,* 399–414.

AVERILL, J. R. (1982). *Anger and aggression.* New York: Springer-Verlag.

AVERILL, J. R. (1983). Studies on anger and aggression: Implications for theories of emotion. *American Psychologist, 38,* 1145–1160.

AXELROD, S., & APSCHE, J. (Eds.) (1983). *The effects of punishment on human behavior.* New York: Academic Press.

AYLLON, T., & AZRIN, N. H. (1968). *The token economy: A motivational system for therapy and rehabilitation.* New York: Appleton-Century-Crofts.

AYLLON, T., & HAUGHTON, E. (1964). Modification of symptomatic verbal behavior of mental patients. *Behavior Research and Therapy, 2,* 87–97.

AZRIN, N. H., & BESALEL, V. A. (1981). An operant reinforcement method of treating depression. *Journal of Behavior Therapy and Experimental Psychiatry, 12,* 145–151.

AZRIN, N. H., & HOLZ, W. C. (1966). Punishment. In W. K. Honig (Ed.),

Operant behavior: Areas of research and application. New York: Appleton-Century-Crofts.

BACHOP, M. W. (1989). Current research on psychoanalytic ideas. *Contemporary Psychology, 34,* 466–467.

BAER, L., & JENIKE, M. A. (1986). Introduction. In M. A. Jenike, L. Baer, & W. E. Minichello (Eds.), *Obsessive-compulsive disorders.* Littleton, MA: PSG Publishing.

BAHR, H. S. (1981). Religious intermarriage and divorce in Utah and the mountain states. *Journal for the Scientific Study of Religion, 20,* 260.

BAILEY, J. M., & PILLARD, R. C. (1991). A genetic study of male sexual orientation. *Archives of General Psychiatry, 48,* 1089–1096.

BAKER, B. L., COHEN, D. C., & SAUNDERS, J. T. (1973). Self-directed desensitization for acrophobia. *Behavior Research and Therapy, 11,* 79–89.

BAKER, L. J., DEARBORN, M., HASTINGS, J. E., & HAMBERGER, K. (1984). Type A behavior in women: A review. *Health Psychology, 3,* 477–497.

BALDWIN, J. D., & BALDWIN, J. I. (1986). *Behavior principles in everyday life* (2nd ed.). Englewood Cliffs, NJ: Prentice Hall.

BAMMER, K., & NEWBERRY, B. H. (1983). *Stress and cancer.* Toronto: C. J. Hogrefe.

BANDURA, A. (1965). Influence of models' reinforcement contingencies on the acquisition of imitative responses. *Journal of Personality and Social Psychology, 1,* 589–595.

BANDURA, A. (1969). *Principles of behavior modification.* New York: Holt, Rinehart, & Winston.

BANDURA, A. (1974). Analysis of modeling processes. In A. Bandura (Ed.), *Psychological modeling: Conflicting theories.* New York: Lieber-Atherton.

BANDURA, A. (1977). *Social learning theory.* Englewood Cliffs, NJ: Prentice Hall.

BANDURA, A. (1982). Self-efficacy mechanism in human agency. *American Psychologist, 37,* 122–147.

BANDURA, A. (1986). *Social foundations of thought and action: A social-cognitive theory.* Englewood Cliffs, NJ: Prentice Hall.

BANDURA, A., ROSS, D., & ROSS, S. (1963*a*). Imitation of film-mediated aggressive models. *Journal of Abnormal and Social Psychology, 66,* 3–11.

BANDURA, A., ROSS, D., & ROSS, S. (1963*b*). Vicarious reinforcement and imitative learning. *Journal of Abnormal and Social Psychology, 67,* 601–607.

BARDON, J. C. (1982, February 27). Battered wives: How law can help. *The New York Times.*

BARLOW, D. H. (1988). *Anxiety and its disorders.* New York: Guilford Press.

BARON, L., & STRAUSS, M. A. (1984). Sexual stratification, pornography, and rape in the United States. In N. M. Malamuth & E. Donnerstein (Eds.), *Pornography and sexual aggression.* Orlando, FL: Academic Press.

BARON, R., & BYRNE, D. (1987). *Social psychology: Understanding human interaction* (5th ed.). Boston: Allyn & Bacon.

BARON, R. A. (1977). *Human aggression.* New York: Plenum.

BARSKY, A. J., GOODSON, J. D., LANE, R. S., & CLEARY, P. D. (1988). The amplification of somatic symptoms. *Psychosomatic Medicine, 50,* 510–519.

BARTROP, R. W., LAZARUS, L., LUCKHURST, E., KILOH, L. G., & PENNY, R. (1977). Depressed lymphocyte function after bereavement. *The Lancet, 1,* 834–836.

BATCHELOR, W. S. (1988). AIDS 1988: The science and limits of science. *American Psychologist, 43,* 853–858.

BAUM, A., GATCHEL, R. J., & SCHAEFFER, M. A. (1983). Emotional, behavioral and physiological effects of chronic stress at Three-Mile Island. *Journal of Consulting and Clinical Psychology, 51,* 565–572.

BAUM, A., & GREENBURG, C. J. (1975). Waiting for a crowd: The behavioral and perceptual effects of anticipated crowding. *Journal of Personality and Social Psychology, 32,* 667–671.

BAUM, A., HARPIN, R. E., & VALINS, S. (1975). The role of group phenomena in the experience of crowding. *Environment and Behavior, 7,* 185–198.

BAUM, A., & VALINS, S. (1977). *Architecture and social behavior: Psychological studies in social density.* Hillsdale, NJ: Lawrence Erlbaum.

BAUMEISTER, R. F. (1984). Choking under pressure: Self-consciousness and paradoxical effects of incentives on skillful performance. *Journal of Personality and Social Psychology, 46*(3), 610–620.

BAUMEISTER, R. F., & STEINHILBER, A. (1984). Paradoxical effects of supportive audiences on performance under pressure: The home field disadvantage in sports championships. *Journal of Personality and Social Psychology, 47*(1), 85–93.

BEACH, F. A. (1956). Characteristics of masculine sex drive. In *Nebraska*

Symposium on Motivation (vol. 4). Lincoln: University of Nebraska Press.

BEAL, G., & MUEHLENHARD, C. (1987, November). Getting sexually aggressive men to stop their advances: Information for rape prevention programs. Paper presented at the Annual Meeting of the Association for Advancement of Behavior Therapy, Boston.

BEATTY, R. H. (1989). *The perfect cover letter*. New York: John Wiley.

BECK, A., RUSH, J., SHAW, B., & EMERY, G. (1979). *Cognitive therapy of depression*. New York: Guilford Press.

BECK, A. T. (1976). *Cognitive therapy and the emotional disorders*. New York: International Universities Press.

BECK, A. T. (1991). Cognitive therapy: A 30-year retrospective. *American Psychologist, 46,* 368–375.

BECK, A. T., & EMERY, G. (1985). *Anxiety disorders and phobias: A cognitive perspective*. New York: Basic Books.

BECK, D. F., & JONES, M. A. (1973). *Progress on family problems: A nationwide survey of clients' and counselors' views on family agency services*. New York: Family Service Association of America.

BECKNELL, J. C., JR., WILSON, W. R., & BAIRD, J. C. (1963). The effect of frequency of presentation on the choice of nonsense syllables. *Journal of Psychology, 56,* 165–170.

BEE, H. L. (1987). *The journey of adulthood*. New York: Macmillan.

BELLACK, A. S. (1986). Schizophrenia: Behavior therapy's forgotten child. *Behavior Therapy, 17,* 199–214.

BELLACK, A. S., & HERSEN, M. (1978). Chronic psychiatric patients: Social skills training. In M. Hersen & A. S. Bellack (Eds.), *Behavior therapy in the psychiatric setting*. Baltimore: Williams & Wilkins.

BELLACK, A. S., & HERSEN, M. (1978). *Behavioral assessment*. New York: Pergamon Press.

BELLACK, A. S., TURNER, S. M., HERSEN, M., & LUBER, R. F. (1984). An examination of the efficacy of social skills training for chronic schizophrenic patients. *Hospital and Community Psychiatry, 35,* 1023–1028.

BELSKY, J. (1985). Exploring differences in marital change across the transition to parenthood: The role of violated expectations. *Journal of Marriage and the Family, 47,* 1037–1044.

BEM, S. (1977). Beyond androgyny: Some presumptuous prescriptions for a liberated sexual identity. In J. Sherman & F. Denmark (Eds.), *Psychology of women: Future directions for research*. New York: Psychological Dimensions.

BEM, S. L. (1983). Gender schema theory and its implications for child development: Raising gender aschematic children in a gender schematic society. *Signs, 8,* 598–616.

BEM, S., & LENNEY, E. (1976). Sex typing and the avoidance of cross-sex behavior. *Journal of Personality and Social Psychology, 33,* 48–54.

BEM, S. L. (1985). Androgyny and gender schema theory: A conceptual and empirical integration. In T. B. Sonderegger (Ed.), *Nebraska symposium on motivation 1984: Psychology and gender*. Lincoln: University of Nebraska Press.

BEM, S. L. (1987). Gender schema theory and the romantic tradition. In P. Shaver & C. Hendrick (Eds.), *Sex and gender* (*Review of Personality and Social Psychology* vol. 7). Newbury Park, CA: Sage.

BENNETT, N. G., BLANC, A. K., & BLOOM, D. E. (1988). Commitment and the modern union: Assessing the link between premarital cohabitation and subsequent marital stability. *American Sociological Review, 53,* 127–138.

BENOWITZ, N. L., HALL, S. M., HERNING, R. I., JACOB, P., JONES, R. T., & OSMAN, A. L. (1983). Smokers of low-yield nicotine cigarettes do not consume less nicotine. *New England Journal of Medicine, 309,* 139–142.

BENTALL, R. P. (1990). The illusion of reality: A review and integration of psychological research on hallucinations. *Psychological Bulletin, 107,* 82–95.

BERG, S. (1987). Intelligence and the terminal decline. In G. L. Maddox & E. W. Busse (Eds.), *Aging: The universal human experience*. New York: Springer.

BERGER, M. (1971). Trial marriage: Harnessing the trend constructively. *The Family Coordinator, 20,* 38–43.

BERGHORN, F. J., & SCHAFER, D. E. (1981). The quality of life and older people. In F. J. Berghorn, D. E. Schafer, & associates (Eds.), *The dynamics of aging: Original essays on the processes and experiences of growing old*. Boulder, CO: Westview Press.

BERKOWITZ, L. (1962). *Aggression: A social psychological analysis*. New York: McGraw-Hill.

BERKOWITZ, L. (1981, June). How guns control us. *Psychology Today,* pp. 11–12.

BERKOWITZ, L. (1988). Frustrations, appraisals, and aversively stimulated aggression. *Aggressive Behavior, 14,* 3–11.

BERKOWITZ, L. (1989). Frustration-aggression hypothesis: Examination and reformulation. *Psychological Bulletin, 106,* 59–73.

BERKOWITZ, L. (1990). On the formation and regulation of anger and aggression: A cognitive-neoassociationistic analysis. *American Psychologist, 45*(4), 494–503.

BERKOWITZ, L., & LePAGE, A. (1967). Weapons as aggression-eliciting stimuli. *Journal of Personality and Social Psychology, 7,* 202–207.

BERNARD, J. (1974). *The future of motherhood*. New York: Dial Press.

BERNARD, M. E. (1991). *Using rational emotive therapy effectively: A practitioners' guide*. New York: Plenum.

BERNE, E. (1964). *Games people play*. New York: Grove Press.

BERSCHEID, E., & WALSTER, E. (1974). A little bit about love. In T. L. Huston (Ed.), *Foundations of interpersonal attraction*. New York: Academic Press.

BESSELL, H. (1984). *The love test*. New York: Warner.

BIDDLE, W. (1986). The deception of detection. *Discover, 7*(3), 24–33.

BIEGELEISON, J. I. (1991). *Make your job interview a success* (3rd ed.). New York: Prentice Hall Press.

BLAIR, S. N., GOODYEAR, N. N., GIBBONS, L. W., & COOPER, K. H. (1984). Physical fitness and incidence of hypertension in healthy normotensive men and women. *Journal of the American Medical Association, 252,* 487–490.

BLANCHARD, E. B., & EPSTEIN, L. H. (1977). The clinical usefulness of biofeedback. In M. Hersen, R. M. Eisler, & P. M. Miller (Eds.), *Progress in behavior modification* (vol. 4). New York: Academic Press.

BLANCHARD, K., & JOHNSON, S. (1982). *The one-minute manager*. New York: William Morrow.

BLISS, E. C. (1976). *Getting things done: The ABCs of time management*. New York: Bantam Books.

BLOOD, R. O., & WOLFE, D. M. (1960). *Husbands and wives*. New York: Free Press.

BLUM, K. (1984). *Handbook of abusable drugs*. New York: Gardiner Press.

BLUMSTEIN, P., & SCHWARTZ, P. (1983). *American couples.* New York: William Morrow.

BOGARDUS, C., LILLIOJA, S., RAVUSSIN, E., ABBOTT, W., ZAWADZKI, J. K., YOUNG, A., KNOWLES, W. C., JACOBOWITZ, R., & MOLL, P. P. (1986). Familial dependence of resting metabolic rate. *New England Journal of Medicine, 315,* 96–100.

BOLLES, R. (1967; 1975). *Theory of motivation* (1st ed.; 2nd ed.). New York: Harper & Row.

BOLLES, R. N. (1990). *What color is your parachute? A practical manual for job hunters and career changers* (2nd ed.). Berkley, CA: Ten Speed Press.

BOOR, M. (1982). The multiple personality epidemic. *Journal of Nervous and Mental Disease, 170,* 302–304.

BOOTH-KEWLEY, S., & FRIEDMAN, H. S. (1987). Psychological predictors of heart disease: A quantitative review. *Psychological Bulletin, 101,* 343–362.

BORNSTEIN, P. E., CLAYTON, P. J., HALIKAS, J. A., MAURICE, W. L., & ROBINS, E. (1973). The depression of widowhood after thirteen months. *British Journal of Psychiatry, 122,* 561–566.

BORNSTEIN, P. H., & BORNSTEIN, M. T. (1986). *Marital therapy: A behavioral communications approach.* New York: Pergamon Press.

BOUCHARD, C., TREMBLAY, A., NADEAU, A., DESPRES, J. P., THERIAULT, G., BOULAY, M. R., LORTIE, G., LeBLANC, C., & FOURNIER, G. (1989). Genetic effect in resting and exercise metabolic rates. *Metabolism, 38,* 364–370.

BOWLBY, J. (1980). *Loss: Sadness and depression—Attachment and loss* (vol. III). New York: Basic Books.

BOZETT, F. W. (1988). Gay fatherhood. In P. Bronstein & C. P. Cowan (Eds.), *Fatherhood today: Men's changing role in the family.* New York: John Wiley.

BRADY, J. V. (1958, October). Ulcers in "executive" monkeys. *Scientific American, Vol 199,* 95–100.

BRAMWELL, S. T., MASUDA, M., WAGNER, N. N., & HOLMES, T. H. (1975). Psychosocial factors in athletic injuries: Development and application of the social and athletic readjustment rating scale. *Journal of Human Stress, 1,* 6–20.

BRANDSMA, J. M., MAULTSBY, M. C., & WELSH, R. J. (1980). *The outpatient treatment of alcoholism: A review and comparative study.* Baltimore: University Park Press.

BRANNON, R. (1976). The male sex role: Our culture's blueprint of manhood, and what it's done for us lately. In D. David & R. Brannon (Eds.), *The forty-nine percent majority.* Reading, MA: Addison-Wesley.

BRASTED, W. S., & CALLAHAN, E. J. (1984). A behavioral analysis of the grief process. *Behavior Therapy, 15,* 529–543.

BRAY, G. A. (1969). Effect of caloric restriction on energy expenditure in obese patients. *Lancet, 2,* 397–398.

BREGMAN, E. O. (1934). An attempt to modify the emotional attitudes of infants by the conditioned response technique. *Journal of Genetic Psychology, 45,* 169–198.

BREHM, S. S. (1985). *Intimate relationships.* New York: Random House.

BRENNER, M. H. (1973). *Mental illness and the economy.* Cambridge, MA: Harvard University Press.

BRETHERTON, I. (1985). Attachment theory: Retrospect and prospect. *Monographs of the Society for Research in Child Development, 50*(1, Serial No. 209).

BRETL, D. J., & CANTOR, J. (1988). The portrayal of men and women in U.S. television commercials: A recent content analysis and trends over fifteen years. *Sex Roles, 18,* 595–609.

BREWER, M. B., & MILLER, N. (1988). Contact and cooperation: When do they work? In P. A. Katz & D. Taylor (Eds.), *Towards the elimination of racism: Profiles in controversy.* New York: Plenum.

BRICKMAN, P., COATES, D., & JANOFF-BULMAN, R. (1978). Lottery winners and accident victims: Is happiness relative? *Journal of Personality and Social Psychology, 36,* 917–927.

BRIDGES, K. M. B. (1932). Emotional development in early infancy. *Child Development, 3,* 324–334.

BROGAN, N., & KUTNER, N. (1976). Measuring sex-role orientation: A normative approach. *Journal of Marriage and the Family, 38,* 31–39.

BROWN, J. D. (1991). Staying fit and staying well: Physical fitness as a moderator of life stress. *Journal of Personality and Social Psychology, 60,* 555–561.

BROWN, R. (1965). *Social psychology.* New York: Free Press.

BROWN, R. (1973). Development of a first language in the human species. *American Psychologist, 28,* 97–106.

BROWN, S. A., GOLDMAN, M. S., & CHRISTIANSEN, B. A. (1985). Do alcohol expectancies mediate drinking patterns of adults? *Journal of Consulting and Clinical Psychology, 53,* 512–519.

BROWNELL, K. D. (1989, June). When and how to diet. *Psychology Today,* pp. 40–46.

BROWNELL, K. D., & WADDEN, T. A. (1991). The heterogeneity of obesity: Fitting treatments to individuals. *Behavior Therapy, 22,* 153–177.

BROWNMILLER, S. (1975). *Against our will: Men, women, and rape.* New York: Simon & Schuster.

BROWNMILLER, S. (1984, November). Comments in debate on "The place of pornography," *Harper's,* 31–45.

BRYAN, J. H., & WALBEK, N. H. (1970). Preaching and practicing generosity: Children's actions and reactions. *Child Development, 41,* 329–353.

BRYSON, J. B., & BRYSON, R. (1978). Preface. *Psychology of Women Quarterly, 3,* 6–8.

BUGENTAL, D. B., & LOVE, L. (1975). Nonassertive expression of parental approval and disapproval and its relationship to child disturbance. *Child Development, 46,* 747–752.

BUIE, J. (1987, November). 12-step program can boost therapy. *APA Monitor,* p. 12.

BUMPASS, L. L., & SWEET, J. A. (1972). Differentials in marital instability: 1970. *American Sociological Review, 37,* 754–766.

BURNS, C. E. S., HEIBY, E. M., & THARP, R. G. (1983). A verbal behavior analysis of hallucinations. *The Behavior Analyst, 6,* 133–143.

BURNS, D. D. (1989). *The good feeling handbook.* New York: William Morrow.

BURTON, D. (1986). *The American Cancer Society's "fresh start": 21 days to stop smoking.* New York: Simon & Schuster (Pocket Books).

BUSCAGLIA, L. (1982). *Living, loving, and learning.* New York: Fawcett Columbine.

BUSS, D. M. (1985). Human mate selection. *American Scientist, 73,* 47–51.

BUZAS, H. P., & AYLLON, T. (1981). Differential reinforcement in coaching skills. *Behavior Modification, 5,* 372–385.

BYRNE, D. (1971). *The attraction paradigm.* New York: Academic Press.

BYRNE, D., & KELLEY, K. (1984). Introduction: Pornography and sex research. In N. Malamuth & E. Donnerstein (Eds.), *Pornography and sexual aggression.* Orlando, FL: Academic Press.

CALHOUN, J. B. (1962). Population density and social pathology. *Scientific American, 206,* 139–148.

CAMPBELL, D. (1974). *If you don't know where you're going, you'll probably end up somewhere else.* San Francisco: Argus.

CAMPBELL, D. T., & SPECHT, J. C. (1985). Altruism: Biology, culture and religion. *Journal of Social and Clinical Psychology, 3*(1), 33–42.

CANTOR, N. (1990). From thought to behavior: "Having" and "doing" in the study of personality and cognition. *American Psychologist, 45,* 735–750.

CARGAN, L., & MELKO, M. (1982). *Singles: Myths and realities.* Beverly Hills, CA: Sage.

CARTER, E. A., & McGOLDRICK, M. (1988). Overview: The changing family life cycle—A framework for family therapy. In E. A. Carter & M. McGoldrick (Eds.), *The changing family life cycle: A framework for family therapy* (2nd ed.). New York: Gardner Press.

CARTER, H., & GLICK, P. C. (1976). *Marriage and divorce: A social and economic study.* Cambridge, MA: Harvard University Press.

CASH, T. F., WINSTEAD, B. A., & JANDA, L. H. (1986). The great American shape-up. *Psychology Today, 20*(4), 30–37.

CASTRONIS, M. (1976). Jog in the pool—No pain! *The Journal of Physical Education, 74*(1), 8.

CATTELL, R. B. (1966). *The scientific analysis of personality.* Chicago: Aldine.

CATTELL, R. B. (1973). *Personality and mood by questionnaire.* San Francisco: Jossey-Bass.

CATTELL, R. B. (1983). *Structured personality-learning theory.* New York: Praeger.

CATTELL, R. B., EBER, H. W., & TATSUOKA, M. M. (1970). *Handbook of the 16 Personality Factor Questionnaire (16PF).* Champaign, IL: Institute for Personality and Ability Testing.

CAUTELA, J. R. (1972). The use of the *Fear Survey Schedule* and the *Reinforcement Survey Schedule* to survey possible reinforcing and aversive stimuli among juvenile offenders. *Journal of Genetic Psychology, 121,* 255–261.

CAUTELA, J. R. (1983). The self-control triad: Description and clinical applications. *Behavior Modification, 7,* 299–315.

CAWOOD, D. (1983). *Assertiveness for managers: Learning effective skills for managing people.* Vancouver, Canada: International Self-Counsel Press.

CENTERS FOR DISEASE CONTROL. (1987). Recommendations for prevention of HIV transmission in health-care settings. *Morbidity and Mortality Weekly Reports, 36*(Suppl. 2).

CENTERS FOR DISEASE CONTROL. (1988). *AIDS weekly surveillance* report for June 6 (Center for Infectious Diseases). Atlanta: Author.

CHECK, J. V. P., & MALAMUTH, N. M. (1983). Sex-role stereotyping and reactions to depictions of stranger versus acquaintance rape. *Journal of Personality and Social Psychology, 45,* 344–356.

CHECK, J. V. P., MALAMUTH, N. M., ELIAS, B., & BARTON, S. A. (1985). On hostile ground. *Psychology Today, 19*(4), 56–61.

CHELUNE, G. J., ROBINSON, J. T., & KOMMOR, M. T. (1984). A cognitive interactional model of intimate relationships. In V. Derlega (Ed.), *Communication, intimacy, and close relationships.* Orlando, FL: Academic Press.

CHILMAN, C. S. (1983). *Adolescent sexuality in a changing American society* (2nd ed.). New York: John Wiley.

CHOATE, P., & LINGER, J. K. (1986). The shape of things to come. *Vocational Education Journal, 61*(7), 26–29.

CHODOROW, N. (1974). Family structure and feminine personality. In M. Z. Rosaldo & L. Lamphere (Eds.), *Women, culture, and society.* Stanford, CA: Stanford University Press.

CHRISTY, S. (1990). Women, work, and the workplace. In L. L. Lindsey, (Ed.) *Gender roles: A sociological perspective.* Englewood Cliffs, NJ: Prentice Hall.

CICIRELLI, V. G. (1981). *Helping elderly parents.* Boston: Auburn House.

CIOMPI, L. (1980). Catamnestic long-term study on the course of life and aging of schizophrenics. *Schizophrenia Bulletin, 6,* 606–618.

CLARKE, A. C. (1952). An examination of the operation of residential propinquity as a factor in mate selection. *American Sociological Review, 17,* 17–22.

CLAYTON, P. J., HALIKAS, J. A., & MAURICE, W. L. (1972). The depression of widowhood. *British Journal of Psychiatry, 120,* 71–78.

CLAYTON, P. J., HERJANIC, M., MURPHY, G. E., & WOODRUFF, R. A. (1974). Mourning and depression: Their similarities and differences. *Canadian Psychiatric Association Journal, 19,* 309–312.

CLINE, V. (1970). *Minority report of the U.S. Commission on Obscenity and Pornography.* New York: Bantam Books.

Coaching Theory Level III. (1989). National Coaching Certification Program, Ottawa, Canada.

COHEN, R., DE JAMES, P., NOCERA, B., & RAMBERGER, M. (1980). Application of a simple self-instruction procedure on adult exercise and studying. Two case reports. *Psychological Reports, 46,* 443–451.

COHEN, S. (1980). After-effects of stress on human performance and social behavior: A review of research and theory. *Psychological Bulletin, 88,* 82–108.

COHEN, S., EVANS, G. W., KRANTZ, D. S., STOKOLS, D., & KELLY, S. (1981). Aircraft noise and children: Longitudinal and cross-sectional evidence on adaptation to noise and the effectiveness of noise abatement. *Journal of Personality and Social Psychology, 40,* 331–345.

COHEN, S., EVANS, G. W., STOKOLS, D., & KRANTZ, D. (1986). *Behavior, health, and environmental stress.* New York: Plenum.

COHEN, S., & HOBERMAN, H. M. (1983). Positive events and social supports as buffers of life change stress. *Journal of Applied Social Psychology, 13,* 99–125.

COHEN, S., & LEZAK, A. (1977). Noise and attentiveness to social cues. *Environment and Behavior, 9,* 559–572.

COHEN, S., & WILLIAMSON, G. M. (1991). Stress and infectious disease in humans. *Psychological Bulletin, 109,* 5–24.

COLEMAN, J. C., & GLAROS, A. G. (1983). *Contemporary psychology and effective behavior* (5th ed.). Glenview, IL: Scott Foresman.

COLEMAN, M., & GANONG, L. H. (1985). Love and sex role stereotypes. Do macho men and feminine women make better lovers? *Journal of Personality and Social Psychology, 49,* 170–176.

COLES, R., & STOKES, G. (1985). *Sex and the American teenager.* New York: Harper & Row.

COLLIGAN, N. J., & MURPHY, L. R. (1982). A review of mass psychogenic illness in work settings. In N. J. Colligan, J. W. Pennebaker, & L. R. Murphy (Eds.), *Mass psychogenic illness.* Hillsdale, NJ: Lawrence Erlbaum.

COLP, R. (1985). Changes in American sexual attitudes during the past century. In Z. Defries, R. C. Friedman, & R. Corn (eds.), *Sexuality: New perspectives.* Westport, CT: Greenwood Press.

CONTRATTO, S. (1984). Mother: Social sculptor and trustee of the faith. In M. Lewin (Ed.), *In the shadow of the past.* New York: Columbia University Press.

COOK, S. (1979). *Social science and school desegregation: Did we mislead the Supreme Court?* Boulder, CO: Institute of Behavioral Science, University of Colorado.

COOPER, K. H. (1968). *Aerobics.* New York: Bantam Books.

COOPER, K. H. (1970). *The new aerobics.* New York: Bantam Books.

COOPER, K. H. (1978). *The aerobics way.* New York: Bantam Books.

COOPER, K. H. (1982). *The aerobics program for total well-being: Exercise, diet, emotional balance.* New York: Bantam Books.

COOPER, K. H. (1985). *Running without fear.* New York: Bantam Books.

COUCHMAN, G. M., & PECK, C. J. (1987). Training for women over 35. *Vocational Education Journal, 62*(3), 13.

COX, B. (1991, October 20). Macho values cited in violence. *The Winnipeg Free Press,* p. A3.

COX, F. D. (1979). *Human intimacy: Marriage, the family, and its meaning.* St. Paul MN: West Publishing.

COZBY, P. C. (1972). Self-disclosure, reciprocity and liking. *Sociometry, 35,* 151–160.

CRAIGHEAD, W. E., KAZDIN, A. E., & MAHONEY, M. J. (1976). *Behavior modification: Principles, issues, and applications.* Boston: Houghton Mifflin.

CRAIK, F. I. M., & TULVING, E. (1975). Depth of processing and the retention of words in episodic memory. *Journal of Experimental Psychology: General, 104,* 268–294.

CRAIN, S. (1977). *Taking stock: A woman's guide to corporate success.* Chicago, IL: Contemporary Books.

CROWE, B. L. (1969). The tragedy of the commons revisited. *Science, 166,* 1103–1107.

CUPACH, W. R., & METTS, S. (1986). Accounts of relational dissolution: A comparison of marital and non-marital relationships. *Communication Monographs, 53,* 311–334.

CURLEE-SALISBURY, J. (1986). Perspectives on Alcoholics Anonymous. In N. J. Estes & M. E. Heinemann (Eds.), *Alcoholism: Development, consequences, interventions* (3rd ed.). St. Louis: Mosby.

CURRAN, J. P., & MONTI, P. M. (Eds.) (1982). *Social skills training: A practical handbook for assessment and training.* New York: Guilford Press.

CUTRONA, C. E. (1982). Transition to college: Loneliness and the process of social adjustment. In L. A. Peplau & D. Perlman (Eds.), *Loneliness: A sourcebook of current theory, research, and therapy.* New York: John Wiley.

DAILEY, D. (1981). Sexual expression and aging. In F. J. Berghorn, D. E. Schafer, & associates (Eds.), *The dynamics of aging: Original essays on the processes and experiences of growing old.* Boulder, CO: Westview Press.

DALY, R. J. (1983). Samuel Pepys and post traumatic stress disorder. *British Journal of Psychiatry, 4,* 211–223.

DANSEREAU, D. F. (1985). Learning strategy research. In J. W. Segal, S. F. Chipman, & R. Glaser (Eds.), *Thinking and learning skills* (vol. 1). Hillsdale, NJ: Lawrence Erlbaum.

DARLEY, J. M., & LATANE, B. (1968). Bystander interventions in emergencies: Diffusion of responsibilities. *Journal of Personality and Social Psychology, 8,* 377–383.

DARWIN, C. (1872). *The expression of emotions in man and animals.* New York: Philosophical Library.

DAVIES, D. L. (1962). Normal drinking in recovered alcoholic addicts. *Quarterly Journal of Studies on Alcohol, 23,* 94–104.

DAVIS, M., ESHELMAN, E. R., & McKAY, M. (1980; 1982). *The relaxation and stress reduction workbook* (1st ed.; 2nd ed.). Oakland, CA: New Harbinger Publications.

DAVISON, G. C., & NEALE, J. M. (1990). *Abnormal psychology* (5th ed.). New York: John Wiley.

DAVITZ, J. R. (1969). *The language of emotion.* New York: Academic Press.

DAY, W. (1983). On the difference between radical and methodological behaviorism. *Behaviorism, 11,* 89–102.

DEAUX, K. (1984). From individual differences to social categories: Analysis of a decade's research on gender. *American Psychologist, 39,* 105–116.

DEFFENBACHER, J. L., DEMM, P. M., & BRANDON, A. D. (1986). High general anger: Correlates and treatment. *Behavior Research and Therapy, 24*(4), 481–489.

DeLONGIS, A., COYNE, J. C., DAHOF, G., FOLKMAN, S., & LAZARUS, R. S. (1986). Relationship of daily hassles, uplifts, and major life events to health status. *Health Psychology, 1,* 119–136.

DeLONGIS, A., FOLKMAN, S., & LAZARUS, R. S. (1988). The impact of daily stress on health and mood: Psychological and social resources as mediators. *Journal of Personality and Social Psychology, 54*(3), 486–495.

DeLUISE, M., BLACKBURN, G. L., & FLIER, J. S. (1980). Reduced activity of the red cell sodium potassium pump in human obesity. *New England Journal of Medicine, 303,* 1017–1022.

DEMBROSKI, T. M., MacDOUGALL, J. M., WILLIAMS, B., & HANEY, T. L. (1985). Components of Type A, hostility, and anger: Relationship to angiographic findings Reply. *Psychosomatic Medicine, 47,* 219–233.

DEMENT, W. C., & KLEITMAN, N. (1957). The relation of eye movements during sleep to dream activity: An objective method for the study of dreaming. *Journal of Experimental Psychology, 53,* 339–346.

DENZIN, N. K. (1984). *On understanding emotion.* San Francisco: Jossey-Bass.

DERLEGA, V. (1984). Self-disclosure and intimate relationships. In V. Derlega (Ed.), *Communication, intimacy, and close relationships.* Orlando, FL: Academic Press.

DERLEGA, V. J. (1988). Self-disclosure: Inside or outside the mainstream of social psychological research? *Journal of Social Behavior and Personality, 3,* 27–34.

DERMER, M., & THIEL, D. L. (1975). When beauty may fail. *Journal of Personality and Social Psychology, 31,* 1168–1176.

DEUTSCH, A. R. (1984). *How to hold your job: Gaining skills and becoming promotable in difficult times.* Englewood Cliffs, NJ: Prentice Hall.

DIAMOND, M., & KARLEN, A. (1980). *Sexual decisions.* Boston: Little, Brown.

DIENER, E. (1984). Subjective well being. *Psychological Bulletin, 95,* 542–575.

DIENER, E., & CRANDALL, R. (1979). An evaluation of the Jamaican anti-crime program. *Journal of Applied Social Psychology, 9,* 135–146.

DION, K., BERSCHEID, E., & WALSTER, E. (1972). What is beautiful is good. *Journal of Personality and Social Psychology, 24,* 285–290.

DION, K. L., & DION, K. K. (1976). Love, liking, and trust in heterosexual relationships. *Personality and Social Psychology Bulletin, 2,* 187–190.

DOHRENWEND, B., PEARLIN, L., CLAYTON, P., HAMBURG, B., RILEY, M., & ROSE, R. (1982). Report on stress and life events. In G. R. Elliot & C. Eisdorfer (Eds.), *Stress and human health: Analysis and implications of research.* New York: Springer.

DOHRENWEND, B. P., & SHROUT, P. E. (1985). "Hassles" in the conceptualization and measurement of life stress. *American Psychologist, 40,* 780–785.

DOHRENWEND, B. S., DOHRENWEND, B. P., DODSON, M., & SHROUT, P. E. (1984). Symptoms, hassles, social supports and life events: The problem of confounded measures. *Journal of Abnormal Psychology, 93,* 222–230.

DOLEYS, D. M., MEREDITH, R. L., & CIMINERO, A. R. (Eds.) (1982). *Behavioral psychology in medicine and rehabilitation: Assessment and treatment strategies.* New York: Plenum.

DOLLARD, J., DOOB, L. W., MILLER, N. E., MOWER, O. H., & SEARS, R. R. (1939). *Frustration and aggression.* New Haven: Yale University Press.

DONNERSTEIN, E. (1984). Pornography: Its effect on violence against women. In N. M. Malamuth & E. Donnerstein (Eds.), *Pornography and sexual aggression.* Orlando, FL: Academic Press.

DONNERSTEIN, E., & BERKOWITZ, L. (1981). Victim reactions in aggressive erotic films as a factor in violence against women. *Journal of Personality and Social Psychology, 41,* 710–724.

DOUGLASS, M. E., & DOUGLASS, D. N. (1980). *Manage your time, manage your work, manage yourself.* New York: AMACOM (A division of American Management Associations).

DOUVAN, E., & ADELSON, J. (1966). *The adolescent experience.* New York: John Wiley.

DOYAL, L. (1990). Hazards of hearth and home. *Women's Studies International Forum, 13,* 501–517.

DOYLE, J. A. (1985). *Sex and gender.* Dubuque, IA: William C. Brown.

DOYLE, J. A. (1989). *The male experience* (2nd ed.). Dubuque, IA: William C. Brown.

DRISCOLL, R., DAVIS, K. E., & LIPITZ, M. E. (1972). Parental interference and romantic love: The Romeo and Juliet effect. *Journal of Personality and Social Psychology, 24,* 1–10.

DRUCKER, P. F. (1977, May). How to manage your boss. *Management Review,* pp. 8–12.

Drugs: Stirring the pot (1985). *Economist, 296,* 24–25.

DUBBERT, P., & WILSON, G. (1984). Goal-setting and spouse involvement in the treatment of obesity. *Behavior Research and Therapy, 22,* 227–242.

DUSH, D. M., HIRT, M. L., & SCHROEDER, H. (1983). Self-statement modification with adults: A meta-analysis. *Psychological Bulletin, 94,* 408–422.

DUTTON, D. G., & ARON, A. P. (1974). Some evidence for heightened sexual attraction under conditions of high anxiety. *Journal of Personality and Social Psychology, 30,* 510–517.

DUVALL, E. M., & MILLER, B. C. (1985). *Marriage and family development* (6th ed.). New York: Harper & Row.

D'ZURILLA, T. J. (1986). *Problem-solving therapy: A social competence approach to clinical interventions.* New York: Springer.

D'ZURILLA, T. J., & GOLDFRIED, M. R. (1971). Problem-solving and behavior modification. *Journal of Abnormal Psychology, 78,* 107–126.

D'ZURILLA, T. J., & NEZU, A. M. (1989). Clinical stress management. In A. M. Nezu & C. M. Nezu (Eds.), *Clinical decision making in behavior therapy: A problem solving perspective.* Champaign, IL: Research Press.

EASTERBROOKS, M. A., & GOLDBERG, W. A. (1985). Effects of early maternal employment on toddlers, mothers, and fathers. *Developmental Psychology, 21,* 774–783.

EASTERLIN, R. A. (1980). *Birth and fortune: The impact of numbers on personal welfare.* New York: Basic Books.

EBBESEN, E. D., DUNCAN, B., & KONECNI, V. J. (1975). Effects of content of verbal aggression on future verbal aggression: A field experiment. *Journal of Experimental Social Psychology, 11,* 192–204.

EHRENREICH, B. (1984, May 20). A feminist's view of the new man. *The New York Times Magazine.*

EISLER, R. M., MILLER, P. M., & HERSEN, M. (1973). Components of assertive behavior. *Journal of Clinical Psychology, 29,* 295–299.

EKMAN, P. (1972). Universal and cultural differences in facial expressions of emotions. In J. K. Cole (Ed.), *Nebraska symposium on motivation* (vol. 19). Lincoln: University of Nebraska Press.

EKMAN, P. (1980). Biological and cultural contributions to body and facial movement in the expression of emotion. In A. Rorty (Ed.), *Explaining emotions.* Berkeley: University of California Press.

EKMAN, P., LEVENSON, R. W., & FRIESEN, W. V. (1983). Autonomic nervous system activity distinguishes among emotions. *Science, 21,* 1208–1210.

EKMAN, P., SORENSON, E. R., & FRIESEN, W. B. (1969). Pan-cultural elements in facial displays of emotion. *Science, 164,* 86–88.

ELKIND, D. (1967). Understanding the young adolescent. *Adolescence, 13,* 1025–1034.

ELLIOT, G. R., & EISDORFER, C. (Eds.) (1982). *Stress and human health: Analysis and implications of research.* New York: Springer.

ELLIS, A. (1976). Techniques of handling anger in marriage. *Journal of Marriage and Family Counseling, 2,* 305–315.

ELLIS, A., & BERNARD, M. E. (Eds.) (1985). *Clinical applications of rational-emotive therapy.* New York: Plenum.

ELLIS, A., & HARPER, R. A. (1975). *A new guide to rational living.* Englewood Cliffs, NJ: Prentice Hall.

ELLIS, H. (1906). *Studies of the psychology of sex* (7 vols.). New York: Random House.

ENGLISH, H. B. (1929). Three cases of the "conditioned fear response." *Journal of Abnormal and Social Psychology, 34,* 221–225.

ENGSTROM, T. W., & MACKENZIE, R. A. (1967). *Managing your time.* Grand Rapids, MI: Zondervan.

EPSTEIN, S. (1983). The stability of confusion: A reply to Mischel and Peake. *Psychological Review, 90,* 390–393.

ERON, L. D., & HUESMANN, L. R. (1984). The control of aggressive behavior by changes in attitudes, values, and the conditions of learning. In R. J. Blanchard & C. Blanchard (Eds.), *Advances in the study of aggression* (vol. 1). Orlando, FL: Academic Press.

EYSENCK, H. J. (1947). *Dimensions of personality.* London: Routledge & Kegan-Paul.

EYSENCK, H. J. (1967). *The biological basis of behavior.* Springfield, IL: Charles C Thomas.

EYSENCK, H. J. (1982). *Personality, genetics, and behavior.* New York: Springer-Verlag.

EYSENCK, H. J. (1990). Genetic and environmental contributions to individual differences: The three major dimensions of personality. *Journal of Personality, 58,* 245–261.

FAIRWEATHER, G. W., SANDERS, D. H., MAYNARD, H., & CRESSLER, D. L. (1969). *Community life for the mentally ill: An alternative to institutional care.* Chicago: Aldine.

FALK, G., & FALK, U. (1981). Sexual behavior in old age: Last bastion of the Victorians. In G. Falk, U. Falk, & G. Tomashevich (Eds.), *Aging in America and other cultures.* Saratoga, CA: Century Twenty-One Publishing.

FALK, G., FALK, U., & TOMASHEVICH, G. V.

(Eds.) (1981). *Aging in America and other cultures*. Saratoga, CA: Century Twenty-One Publishing.

FARQUHAR, J. W. (1978). *The American way of life need not be hazardous to your health*. New York: W. W. Norton.

FARRELL, M. P., & ROSENBERG, S. D. (1981). *Men at midlife*. Boston, MA: Auburn House.

FAUST, M. S. (1977). Somatic development of adolescent girls. *Monographs of the Society for Research in Child Development, 42*(1, Serial No. 169).

FEIST, J., & BRANNON, L. (1988). *Health psychology: An introduction to behavior and health*. Belmont, CA: Wadsworth.

FELDMAN, P., & MacCULLOCH, M. (1980). *Human sexual behavior*. New York: John Wiley.

FENESTERHEIM, H. (1972). Assertive methods and marital problems. In R. D. Ruben, H. Fenesterheim, J. B. Henderson, & L. P. Ullman (Eds.), *Advances in behavior therapy* (vol. IV). New York: Academic Press.

FERGUSON, J. M. (1975). *Learning to eat*. Palo Alto, CA: Dell.

FESTINGER, L. (1951). Architecture and group membership. *Journal of Social Issues, 7*, 152–163.

FESTINGER, L., SCHACHTER, S., & BACK, K. (1950). *Social pressures in informal groups*. New York: Harper.

FIELD, D., SCHAIE, K. W., & LEINO, E. V. (1988). Continuity in intellectual functioning: The role of self-reported health. *Psychology and Aging, 3*, 385–392.

FIELD, T., & REITE, M. (1984). Children's responses to separation from mother during the birth of another child. *Child Development, 55*, 1308–1316.

FIELDING, J. E. (1985). Smoking: Health effects and control. *New England Journal of Medicine, 313*, 491–498, 555–561.

FLAXMAN, J. (1978). Quitting smoking now or later: Gradual, abrupt, immediate, and delayed quitting. *Behavior Therapy, 9*, 260–270.

FOLEY, V. D. (1989). Family therapy. In R. J. Corsini & D. Wedding (Eds.), *Current psychotherapies* (4th ed.). Itasca, IL: F. E. Peacock.

FOLKES, V. S. (1982). Forming relationships and the matching hypothesis. *Personality and the Social Psychology Bulletin, 8*, 631–636.

FOWERS, B. J., & OLSON, D. H. (1989). ENRICH Marital Inventory: A discriminant validity and cross-valida-

tion assessment. *Journal of Marriage and the Family, 15*, 65–79.

FOWLER, R. D. (1986, May). Howard Hughes: A psychological autopsy. *Psychology Today, 20*(5), 22–33.

FOX, E. L., & MATHEWS, D. K. (1981). *The physiological basis of physical education and athletics* (3rd ed.). New York: W. B. Saunders.

FREEDMAN, J. L. (1975). *Crowding and behavior*. San Francisco: W. H. Freeman.

FREEDMAN, J. L., KLEVANSKY, S., & ERLICH, P. (1971). The effects of crowding on human task performance. *Journal of Applied Social Psychology, 1*, 7–25.

FREEDMAN, J. L., LEVY, A., BUCHANAN, R. W., & PRICE, J. (1972). Crowding and human aggressiveness. *Journal of Experimental Social Psychology, 8*, 528–548.

FREEMAN, J. T. (1961). Sexual capacities in the aging male. *Geriatrics, 16*, 37–43.

FREIBERG, P. (1991, April). More high school seniors say "no." *The APA Monitor*, pp. 28–29.

FREUD, S. (1888–1939; reprinted 1963). In J. Strachey (Ed. and Trans.), *The standard edition of the complete psychological works of Sigmund Freud*. London: Hogarth Press.

FREUD, S. (1917; reprinted 1957). *Mourning and melancholia*. In J. Strachey (Ed. and Trans.), *The standard edition of the complete psychological works of Sigmund Freud* (vol. 14). London: Hogarth Press.

FRIEDMAN, M., & ROSENMAN, R. H. (1974). *Type A behavior and your heart*. New York: Alfred A. Knopf.

FROMME, D. K., JAYNES, W. E., & TAYLOR, D. K. (1989). Nonverbal behavior and attitudes toward touch. *Journal of Nonverbal Behavior, 13*, 3–14.

FRY, W. F., & ALLEN, M. (1975). *Make 'em laugh*. Palo Alto, CA: Science and Behavior Books.

FUASTMAN, W. O. (1976, November). Aversive control of maladaptive sexual behavior: Past developments and future trends. *Psychology, 13*(4), 53–60.

FUCHS, K., HOCH, Z., PALDI, E., ABRAMOVICI, H., BRANDES, J. M., TIMOR-TRITSCH, I., & KLEINHAUS, M. (1973). Hypnodesensitization therapy of vaginismus: Part I. *In vitro* method. Part II. *In vivo* method. *International Journal of Clinical and Experimental Hypnosis, 21*, 144–156.

FUENNING, S. I. (1981). *Physical fitness and mental health*. Lincoln: University of Nebraska Foundation.

FUNK, S. C., & HOUSTON, V. K. (1987). A critical analysis of the Hardiness Scale's validity and utility. *Journal of Personality and Social Psychology, 53*(3), 572–578.

GADPAILLE, W. (1972). Research into the physiology of maleness and femaleness. *Archives of General Psychiatry, 26*, 193–206.

GALASSI, J. P., & GALASSI, M. D. (1979). Modification of heterosocial skills deficits. In A. S. Bellack & M. Hersen (Eds.), *Research and practice in social skills training*. New York: Plenum.

GALASSI, J. P., KOSTKA, M. P., & GALASSI, M. D. (1975). Assertive training: A one-year follow-up. *Journal of Counseling Psychology, 22*, 451–452.

GALLAGHER, D. E., BRECKENRIDGE, J. N., THOMPSON, L. W., & PETERSON, J. A. (1983). Effects of bereavement on indicators of mental health in elderly widows and widowers. *Journal of Gerontology, 38*, 565–571.

GALLE, O. R., GOVE, W. R., & McPHERSON, J. M. (1972). Population density and pathology: What are the relations for man? *Science, 176*, 23–30.

GALLE, O. R., McCARTHY, J. D., & GOVE, W. R. (1974). Population density and pathology. Paper presented at the annual meeting of the Population Association of America, New York.

GALLUP, G. G., JR. (1974). Animal hypnosis: Factual status of a fictional concept. *Psychological Bulletin, 81*, 836–853.

GANELLEN, R. J., & BLAINEY, P. H. (1984). Hardiness and social support as moderators of the effects of life stress. *Journal of Personality and Social Psychology, 47*, 156–163.

GARBER, J., & SELIGMAN, M. E. P. (1980). *Human helplessness: Theory and applications*. New York: Academic Press.

GARCIA, J., & KOELLING, R. A. (1966). Relation of cue to consequence in avoidance learning. *Psychonomic Science, 4*, 123–124.

GAUTHIER, J., & MARSHALL, W. L. (1977). Grief: A cognitive-behavioral analysis. *Cognitive Therapy and Research, 1*, 39–44.

GAYTON, W. R., MATTHEWS, G. R., & NICKLESS, C. J. (1987). The home field disadvantage in sports championships: Does it exist in hockey? *Journal of Sport Psychology, 9*, 183–185.

GELLER, E. S. (1980). Applications of behavior analysis to litter control. In D. Glenwick & L. Jason (Eds.), *Behavioral community psychology: Pros-*

pects and progress. New York: Praeger.

GELLER, E. S., WITMER, J. F., & OREBAUGH, A. L. (1976). Instructions as a determinant of paper-disposal behaviors. *Environment and Behavior, 8,* 417–438.

GELLES, R. J., & CORNELL, C. P. (1990). *Intimate violence in families* (2nd ed.). Newbury Park, CA: Sage.

GENTRY, W. D., CHESNEY, A. P., GARY, H. E., HALL, R. P., & HARBURG, E. (1982). Habitual anger-coping styles: Effect of mean blood pressure and risk for essential hypertension. *Psychosomatic Medicine, 44,* 195–202.

GEORGE, L. K., & WEILER, S. J. (1981). Sexuality in middle and late life: The effects of age, cohort, and gender. *Archives of General Psychiatry, 38,* 919–923.

GERBNER, G., GROSS, L., MORGAN, M., & SIGNORIELLI, N. (1986). Living with television: The dynamics of the cultivation process. In J. Bryant & D. Zillman (Eds.), *Perspectives on media effects.* Hillsdale, NJ: Lawrence Erlbaum.

GERGEN, K. J., & GERGEN, M. M. (1981; 1986). *Social psychology* (1st ed; 2nd ed.). New York: Harcourt Brace Jovanovich.

GETTMAN, L. (1983, November). Testimony on HR 3525, "Permanent tax treatment of fringe benefits act of 1983." Ways and Means Select Revenues Subcommittee, August 1, 1983. *Employee Benefits Plan Review.*

GIBBS, D. N. (1965). Reciprocal inhibition therapy in a case of symptomatic erythemia. *Behavior Research and Therapy, 2,* 261–266.

GILLIGAN, C. (1982). *In a different voice: Psychological theory and women's development.* Cambridge, MA: Harvard University Press.

GLASS, D. C., & SINGER, J. E. (1972). *Urban stress: Experiments on noise and social stressors.* New York: Academic Press.

GLENN, N. D., & McLANAHAN, S. (1982). Children and marital happiness: A further specification of the relationship. *Journal of Marriage and the Family, 44,* 63–72.

GLENN, N. D., & WEAVER, C. N. (1981). The contribution of marital happiness to global happiness. *Journal of Marriage and the Family, 43,* 161–168.

GLENN, N. D., & WEAVER, C. N. (1988). The changing relationship of marital status to reported happiness. *Journal of Marriage and the Family, 50,* 317–324.

GLICK, P. C. (1984a). How American families are changing. *American Demographics, 6*(1), 20–25.

GLICK, P. C. (1984b). Marriage, divorce, and living arrangements: Prospective changes. *Journal of Family Issues, 5,* 7–26.

GLICK, P. C., & NORTON, A. J. (1977). Marrying, divorcing, and living together in the U.S. today. *Population Bulletin, 32,* 1–41.

GLYNN, S. M. (1990). Token economy approaches for psychiatric patients: Progress and pitfalls over 25 years. *Behavior Modification, 14,* 383–407.

GOECKNER, D., GREENOUGH, W., & MEAD, W. (1973). Deficits in learning tasks following chronic overcrowding in rats. *Journal of Personality and Social Psychology, 28,* 256–261.

GOLDIAMOND, I. (1965). Fluent and nonfluent speech (stuttering): Analysis and operant techniques for control. In L. Krasner & L. Ullmann (Eds.), *Research in behavior modification.* New York: Holt, Rinehart, & Winston.

GOLDING, J. M., POTTS, M. K., & ANESHENSEL, C. S. (1991). Stress exposure among Mexican Americans and non-Hispanic whites. *Journal of Community Psychology, 19,* 37–59.

GOLDMAN, M., & FORDYCE, J. (1983). Prosocial behavior as affected by eye contact, touch, and voice expression. *Journal of Social Psychology, 121,* 125–129.

GOULD, R. L. (1978). *Transformations: Growth and change in adult life.* New York: Simon & Schuster.

GRADY, D. (1986, July). Don't get jittery over caffeine. *Discover, 7,* 73–79.

GRANROSE, C. S. (1985). Plans for work careers among college women who expect to have families. *The Vocational Guidance Quarterly, 33*(4), 284–295.

GRAY, J. A., FELDON, J., RAWLINS, J. N. P., HEMSLEY, D. R., & SMITH, A. D. (1991). The neuropsychology of schizophrenia. *Behavioral and Brain Sciences, 14,* 1–84.

GREDEN, J. F., FONTAINE, P., LUBETSKY, M., & CHAMBERLIN, K. (1978). Anxiety and depression associated with caffeinism among psychiatric patients. *American Journal of Psychiatry, 135,* 963–966.

GREEN, K. A. (1971). *Better grades in college with less effort.* Woodbury, NY: Barron's Education Series.

GREEN, L. (1982). Minority students' self-control of procrastination. *Journal of Counseling Psychology, 29,* 636–644.

GREENSPOON, J. (1955). The reinforcing effect of two spoken words on the frequency of two responses. *American Journal of Psychology, 68,* 409–416.

GREENSPOON, J. (1976). *The sources of behavior: Abnormal and normal.* Monterey, CA: Brooks/Cole.

GRUDER, C. L. (1977). Choice of comparison persons in evaluating oneself. In J. M. Suls & R. L. Miller (Eds.), *Social comparison processes.* New York: Hemisphere.

GURIN, J. (1989, June). Leaner, not lighter. *Psychology Today,* pp. 32–36.

GURMAN, A. S. (1977). The patient's perceptions of the therapeutic relationship. In A. S. Gurman & A. M. Razin (Eds.), *Effective psychotherapy: A handbook of research.* Oxford, England: Pergamon.

HAAGA, D. A., & DAVISON, G. C. (1986). Cognitive change methods. In F. H. Kanfer & A. P. Goldstein (Eds.), *Helping people change: A textbook of methods* (3rd ed.). New York: Pergamon Press.

HALL, C. S. (1954). *A primer of Freudian psychology.* Cleveland: World Publishing.

HALL, C. S., LINDZEY, G., LOEHLIN, J. C., & MANOSEVITZ, M. (1985). *Introduction to theories of personality.* New York: John Wiley.

HALL, C. S., & VAN DE CASTLE, R. L. (1966). *The content analysis of dreams.* New York: Appleton-Century-Crofts.

HALL, R. G., SACHS, D. P., HALL, S. M., & BENOWITZ, N. L. (1984). Two-year efficacy and safety of rapid smoking therapy in patients with cardiac and pulmonary disease. *Journal of Consulting and Clinical Psychology, 52,* 574–581.

HAMAKER, C. (1986). The effects of adjunct questions on prose learning. *Review of Educational Research, 56,* 212–242.

HAMBLIN, R. L., BUCKHOLDT, D., BUSHELL, D., ELLIS, D., & FERRITOR, D. (1969, January). Changing the game from get the teacher to learn. *Transaction,* pp. 20–25, 28–31.

HAMILTON, E., WHITNEY, E., & SIZER, F. (1991). *Nutrition: Concepts and controversies* (5th ed.). St. Paul, MN: West.

HANEY, D. (1983, November 21). Girth control. *The Oregonian,* p. B1.

HARDIN, G. (1968). The tragedy of the commons. *Science, 162,* 1243–1248.

HARDIN, G. (1974). *Mandatory motherhood.* Boston Beacon Press.

HARDIN, G., & BADEN, J. (Eds.) (1977).

Managing the commons. San Francisco: W. H. Freeman.

HARRIS, B. (1979). What happened to Little Albert? *American Psychologist, 34*(2), 151–160.

HARRIS, B. V., & HARRIS, D. L. (1984). *Athlete's guide to sport psychology: Mental skills for physical people.* New York: Leisure Press.

HARRIS, C. S., & McREYNOLDS, W. T. (1977). Semantic cues and response contingencies in self-instructional control. *Journal of Behavior Therapy and Experimental Psychiatry, 8,* 15–17.

HARRIS, G., & JOHNSON, S. D. (1980). Comparison of individualized covert modeling, self-control desensitization, and study skills training for alleviation of test anxiety. *Journal of Consulting and Clinical Psychology, 48,* 186–194.

HARRIS, J. E. (1980). Memory aids people use: Two interview studies. *Memory and Cognition, 8,* 31–38.

HASS, A. (1979). *Teenage sexuality: A survey of teenage sexual behavior.* New York: Macmillan.

HATFIELD, E. (1984). The dangers of intimacy. In V. J. Derlega (Ed.), *Communication, intimacy, and close relationships.* Orlando, FL: Academic Press.

HATFIELD, E. (1988). Passionate and companionate love. In R. J. Sternberg & M. L. Barnes (Eds.), *The psychology of love.* New Haven: Yale University Press.

HATFIELD, E., & WALSTER, G. W. (1978). *A new look at love.* Menlo Park, CA: Addison-Wesley.

HAVINGHURST, R. J. (1972). *Developmental tasks and education* (3rd ed.). New York: McKay.

HAWKINS, R. C., & CLEMENT, P. (1980). Development and construct validation of a self-report measure of binge eating tendencies. *Addictive Behaviors, 5,* 219–226.

HAYDUK, L. A. (1978). Personal space: An evaluative and orienting overview. *Psychological Bulletin, 85,* 117–134.

HAYDUK, L. A. (1983). Personal space: Where we now stand. *Psychological Bulletin, 94,* 293–335.

HAYES, S. C., ROSENFARB, I., WULFERT, E., MUNT, E. D., KORN, Z., & ZETTLE, R. D. (1985). Self-reinforcement effects: An artifact of social standard setting. *Journal of Applied Behavior Analysis, 18,* 201–214.

HAYES-ROTH, B. (1977). Evolution of cognitive structure and processes. *Psychological Review, 84,* 260–278.

HAZALEUS, S. L., & DEFFENBACHER, J. L. (1986). Relaxation and cognitive treatments of anger. *Journal of Consulting and Clinical Psychology, 54,* 222–226.

HAZEN, A., & MARTIN, G. L. (1985). A performance appraisal system for the Vocational Training Department. Paper prepared for The Manitoba Developmental Centre, Portage la Prairie, Manitoba.

HEATON, T. B. (1990). Marital stability throughout the child-rearing years. *Demography, 27,* 55–63.

HEATON, T. B. (1991). Time-related determinants of marital dissolution. *Journal of Marriage and the Family, 53,* 285–295.

HEATON, T. B., & ALBRECHT, S. L. (1991). Stable unhappy marriages. *Journal of Marriage and the Family, 53,* 747–758.

HEBB, D. O. (1980). *Essay on mind.* Hillsdale, NJ: Lawrence Erlbaum.

HEFFERNAN, T., & RICHARDS, C. S. (1981). Self-control of study behavior: Identification and evaluation of natural methods. *Journal of Counseling Psychology, 28,* 361–364.

HEGARTY, C. (1982). *How to manage your boss.* New York: Ballantine Books.

HEIDER, E. R., & OLIVIER, D. C. (1972). The structure of the color of space in naming and memory for two languages. *Cognitive Psychology, 3,* 337–344.

HEINSSEN, R. K., JR., & GLASS, C. R. (1990). Social skills, social anxiety, and cognitive factors in schizophrenia. In H. Leitenbeg (Ed.), *Handbook of social and evaluation anxiety.* New York: Plenum.

HEINZELMANN, F., & BAGLEY, R. W. (1970). Response to physical activity programs and their effects on healthy behavior. *Public Health Reports, 85,* 905–911.

HERMAN, R. L., & AZRIN, N. H. (1964). Punishment by noise in an alternative response situation. *Journal of the Experimental Analysis of Behavior, 7,* 185–188.

HERMANN, C. P., OLMSTEAD, M. P., & POLIVY, J. (1983). Obesity, externality, and susceptibility to social influence: An integrated analysis. *Journal of Personality and Social Psychology, 45,* 926–934.

HIGBEE, K. L. (1988). *Your memory: How it works and how to improve it* (2nd ed.). Englewood Cliffs, NJ: Prentice Hall.

HILL, C. T., RUBIN, Z., & PEPLAU, L. A. (1976). Breakups before marriage:

The end of 103 affairs. *Journal of Social Issues, 32,* 147–168.

HILL, E. M., NOCKS, E. S., & GARDNER, L. (1987). Physical attractiveness: Manipulation by physique and status displays. *Ethology and Sociobiology, 8,* 143–154.

HINDE, R. A. (1981). The bases of a science of interpersonal relationships. In S. Duck & R. Gilmour (Eds.), *Personal relationships* (vol. I). New York: Academic Press.

HIRSCHFELD, R. M. A., & DAVIDSON, L. (1988). Risk factors for suicide. In A. J. Frances & R. F. Hales (Eds.), *Review of psychiatry* (vol. 7). Washington, DC: American Psychiatric Press.

HITE, S. (1976). *The Hite report.* New York: Macmillan.

HOBERMAN, H. M., & LEWINSOHN, P. M. (1985). The behavioral treatment of depression. In E. E. Beckham & W. R. Leber (Eds.), *Handbook of depression: Treatment, assessment, and research.* Homewood, IL: Dorsey Press.

HOCH,, Z., SAFIR, M. P., PERES, Y., & STEPLER, J. (1981). An evaluation of sexual performance—Comparison between sexually dysfunctional and functional couples. *Journal of Sex and Marital Therapy, 7,* 195–206.

HOCHSCHILD, A. R. (1989). *The second shift.* New York: Viking.

HOFFMAN, C., LAU, I., & JOHNSON, D. R. (1986). The linguistic relativity of person cognition: An English–Chinese comparison. *Journal of Personality and Social Psychology, 51,* 1097–1105.

HOLAHAN, C. J. (1977). Urban–rural differences in judged appropriateness of altruistic responses: Personal versus situational effects. *Sociometry, 40,* 378–382.

HOLLANDER, E., SCHIFFMAN, E., COHEN, B., RIVERA-STEIN, M., ROSEN, W., GORMAN, J. M., FYER, A. J., PAPP, L., & LIEBOWITZ, M. R. (1990). Signs of central nervous system dysfunction in obsessive-compulsive disorder. *Archives of General Psychiatry, 47,* 27–32.

HOLMES, T. H., & MASUDA, M. (1974). Life change and illness susceptibility. In B. S. Dohrenwend & B. P. Dohrenwend (Eds.), *Stressful life events: Their nature and effects.* New York: John Wiley.

HOLMES, T. H., & RAHE, R. H. (1967). The social readjustment rating scale. *Journal of Psychosomatic Research, 11,* 213–218.

HOLROYD, K. A., WESTBROOK, T., WOLF, M., & BADHORN, E. (1978). Performance, cognition, and physiological responding in test anxiety. *Journal of Abnormal Psychology, 87,* 442–451.

HOMME, L. E. (1965). Perspectives in psychology. XIV. Control of coverants: The operants of the mind. *Psychological Record, 15,* 501–511.

HONEYCUTT, J. M. (1986). A model of marital functioning based on an attraction paradigm and social-penetration dimensions. *Journal of Marriage and the Family, 48,* 651–667.

HORNEY, K. (1950). *Neurosis and human growth.* New York: W. W. Norton.

HORNSTEIN, G. A., & TRUESDELL, S. E. (1988). Development of intimate conversation in close relationships. *Journal of Social and Clinical Psychology, 7,* 49–64.

HORTASCU, N., & KARANCI, A. N. (1987). Premarital breakups in a Turkish sample: Perceived reasons, attributional dimensions and affective reactions. *International Journal of Psychology, 22,* 57–74.

HOUSE, J. S., & WOLF, S. (1978). Effects of urban residence on interpersonal trust and helping behavior. *Journal of Personality and Social Psychology, 36,* 1029–1043.

HUBER, J., & SPITZE, G. (1980). Considering divorce: An expansion of Becker's theory of marital instability. *American Journal of Sociology, 86,* 75–89.

HUGDAHL, K., & OHMAN, A. (1977). Effects of instruction on acquisition and extinction of electrodermal responses to fear relevant stimuli. *Journal of Experimental Psychology: Human Learning and Memory, 3,* 608–618.

HULL, J. G., VAN TREUREN, R. R., & VIRNELLI, S. (1987). Hardiness and health: A critique and alternative approach. *Journal of Personality and Social Psychology, 53*(3), 518–530.

HURLBURT, R. T. (1990). Sampling normal and schizophrenic inner experience. New York: Plenum.

HURSH, S. R. (1980). Economic concepts for the analysis of behavior. *Journal of the Experimental Analysis of Behavior, 34,* 219–238.

HUSTON, T. L., & LEVINGER, G. (1978). Interpersonal attraction and relationships. *Annual Review of Psychology, 29,* 115–156.

HUTT, C., & VAIZY, M. J. (1966). Differential effects of group density on social behavior. *Nature, 209,* 1371–1372.

HYDE, J. S. (1984). Children's understanding of sexist language. *Developmental Psychology, 20,* 697–706.

IMPERATO-MCGINLEY, J., PETERSON, R. E., GAUTIER, T., & STURLA, E. (1979). Androgens and the evolution of male-gender identity among male pseudohermaphrodites with 5a-reductase deficiency. *New England Journal of Medicine, 300*(22), 1233–1237.

ISAACS, W., THOMAS, J., & GOLDIAMOND, I. (1960). Application of operant conditioning principles to reinstate verbal behavior in psychotics. *Journal of Speech and Hearing Disorders, 25,* 8–12.

ISAACSON, L. E. (1986). *Career information in counselling and career development* (4th ed.). Boston: Allyn & Bacon.

IVANCEVICH, J. M., MATTESON, M., FREEDMAN, S. M., & PHILIPS, J. S. (1990). Work site stress management interventions. *American Psychologist, 45,* 252–261.

IZARD, C. E. (1971). *The face of emotion.* New York: Appleton-Century-Crofts.

IZARD, C. E. (1977). *Human emotions.* New York: Plenum.

IZARD, C. E. (1982). The psychology of emotion comes of age on the coat tails of Darwin. *Contemporary Psychology, 27,* 426–429.

JACKSON, T. (1990). *The perfect resumé.* New York: Doubleday.

JACOB, H. (1989). Another look at no-fault divorce and the post-divorce finances of women. *Law and Society Review, 23,* 95–115.

JACOBS, H. E., KARDASHIAN, S., KREINBRING, R. K., PONDER, R., & SIMPSON, A. P. (1984). A skills-oriented model for facilitating employment among psychiatrically disabled persons. *Rehabilitation Counseling Bulletin, 28,* 87–96.

JACOBSON, E. (1938). *Progressive relaxation.* Chicago: University of Chicago Press.

JAMES, J. E., STIRLING, K. P., & HAMPTON, B. A. M. (1985). Caffeine fading: Behavioral treatment of caffeine abuse. *Behavior Therapy, 16,* 15–27.

JAMES, W. (1890). *The principles of psychology.* New York: Holt, Rinehart, & Winston.

JANIS, I., & MANN, L. (1977). *Decision-making.* New York: Free Press.

JANIS, I., & WHEELER, D. (1978). Thinking clearly about career choices. *Psychology Today, 11*(12), 66–76, 121–122.

JANIS, I. L. (1982). Decision-making under stress. In L. Goldberger & S. Breznitz (Eds.), *Handbook of stress: Theoretical and clinical aspects.* New York: Free Press.

JEFFREY, R. W., & WING, R. R. (1983). Recidivism and self-cure of smoking and obesity: Data from population studies. *American Psychologist, 38,* 852.

JEMMOTT, J. B., ASHBY, K. L., & LINDENFELD, K. (1989). Romantic commitment and the perceived availability of opposite-sex persons: On loving the one you're with. *Journal of Applied Social Psychology, 19,* 1198–1211.

JEMMOTT, J. B., III, BORYSENKO, I. Z., BORYSENKO, M., MCCLELLAND, D. C., CHAPMAN, R., MEYER, D., & BENSON, H. (1983). Academic stress, power motivation, and decrease in salivary secretory immunoglobulin A secretion rate. *Lancet, 1,* 1400–1402.

JEMMOTT, J. B., III, & LOCKE, S. E. (1984). Psychosocial factors, immunologic mediation, and human susceptibility to infectious diseases: How much do we know? *Psychological Bulletin, 95,* 78–108.

JETER, K. (1983). Analytic essay: Family stress and bereavement. *Marriage and Family Review, 6,* 219–225.

JOHNSON, D. W., & JOHNSON, R. T. (1989). *A meta-analysis of cooperative, competitive, and individualistic goal structures.* Hillsdale, NJ: Lawrence Erlbaum.

JOHNSON, J., WEISSMAN, M., & KLERMAN, G. L. (1990). Panic disorder, comorbidity, and suicide attempts. *Archives of General Psychiatry, 47,* 805–808.

JOHNSON, M. A. (1989). Variables associated with friendship in an adult population. *Journal of Social Psychology, 129,* 379–390.

JOHNSON, P. J., & FIREBAUGH, F. M. (1985). A typology of household work performance by employment demands. *Journal of Family Issues, 6,* 83–105.

JOHNSON, W. G. (1971). Some applications of Homme's coverant control therapy: 2 case reports. *Behavior Therapy, 2,* 240–248.

JOHNSTON, L. D., BACHMAN, J. G., & O'MALLEY, P. M. (1985, January 4). News and Information Services Release, Institute of Social Sciences Research, University of Michigan, Ann Arbor.

JOHNSTON, L. D., O'MALLEY, P. M., & BACHMAN, J. G. (1988). *Illicit drug use, smoking, and drinking by America's high school students, college students, and young adults, 1975–1987.* Rockville, MD: National Institute on Drug Abuse.

JONES, E. (1953). *The life and work of Sigmund Freud* (vol. I). New York: Basic Books.

JONES, E. J., & GORDON, E. M. (1972). Timing of self-disclosure and its effects on personal attraction. *Journal of Personality and Social Psychology, 24,* 358–365.

Jones, M. C. (1924). The elimination of children's fears. *Journal of Experimental Psychology, 7,* 383–390.

Jones, S. E., & Yarbrough, A. E. (1985). A naturalistic study of the meanings of touch. *Communications Monographs, 52,* 19–56.

Josephson, W. L. (1987). Television violence and children's aggression: Testing the priming, social script, and disinhibition predictions. *Journal of Personality and Social Psychology, 53,* 882–890.

Jourard, S. M. (1959). Self-disclosure and other cathexis. *Journal of Personality and Social Psychology, 59,* 428–431.

Jourard, S. M., & Landsman, M. J. (1960). Cognition, cathexis, and the "dyadic effect" in men's self-disclosing behavior. *Merrill-Palmer Quarterly, 6,* 178–186.

Julien, R. M. (1988). *A primer of drug action* (5th ed.). San Francisco, CA: W. H. Freeman.

Jung, C. G. (1917, 1953). *On the psychology of the unconscious.* In H. Reid, M. Fordham and G. Adler (Eds.), *Collected works of C. G. Jung* (vol. 7). Princeton, NJ: Princeton University Press.

Jung, C. G. (1968). *Analytical psychology: Its theory and practice.* New York: Pantheon Books.

Kalish, R. A. (1985). *Death, grief, and caring relationships* (2nd ed.). Pacific Grove, CA: Brooks/Cole.

Kallmann, F. J. (1952a). Comparative twin study of the genetic aspects of male homosexuality. *Journal of Nervous and Mental Diseases, 115,* 283–298.

Kallmann, F. J. (1952b). Twin sibships and the study of male homosexuality. *American Journal of Human Genetics, 4,* 136–146.

Kallmann, F. J. (1953). *Heredity in health and mental disorder.* New York: W. W. Norton.

Kamerman, S. B., & Kahn, A. J. (1988). *Mothers alone.* Dover, MA: Auburn House.

Kanner, A. D., Coyne, J. C., Schaefer, C., & Lazarus, R. S. (1981). Comparison of two modes of stress measurement: Daily hassles and uplifts versus major life events. *Journal of Behavioral Medicine, 4*(1), 1–39.

Kaplan, H. I. (1985). History of psychosomatic medicine. In H. I. Kaplan & B. J. Sadock (Eds.), *Comprehensive textbook of psychiatry* (vol. IV). Baltimore: Williams & Wilkins.

Kaplan, H. S. (1974). *The new sex therapy: Active treatment of sexual dysfunctions.* New York: Brunner/Mazel.

Kaplan, H. S. (1977). Hypoactive sexual desire. *Journal of Sex and Marital Therapy, 3,* 3–9.

Kaplan, H. S. (1979). *Disorders of sexual desire.* New York: Brunner/Mazel.

Kaplan, J. I., & Sadock, B. J. (1981). *Modern synopsis of comprehensive textbook of psychiatry* (vol. III; 3rd ed.). Baltimore: Williams & Wilkins.

Karacan, I. (1977). Advances in the psychophysiological evaluation of male erectile impotence. *Weekly Psychiatry Update Series, 1,* 43.

Karol, R. L., & Richards, C. S. (1978, November). Making treatment effects last: An investigation of maintenance strategies for smoking reduction. Paper presented at the meeting of the Association of the Advancement of Behavior Therapy, Chicago.

Kassorla, I. (1980). *Nice girls do—And now you can too!* Los Angeles: Stratford Press.

Kastenbaum, R. (1985). Dying and death: A life-span approach. In J. E. Birren & K. W. Schaie (Eds.), *Handbook of the psychology of aging* (2nd ed.). New York: Van Nostrand Reinhold.

Kau, M. L., & Fischer, J. (1974). Self-modification of exercise behavior. *Journal of Behavior Therapy and Experimental Psychiatry, 5,* 213–214.

Kaufman, J., & Zigler, E. (1987). Do abused children become abusive parents? *American Journal of Orthopsychiatry, 57,* 186–192.

Kazdin, A. E. (1977). *The token economy: A review and evaluation.* New York: Plenum.

Kazdin, A. E. (1987). Treatment of antisocial behavior in children: Current status and future directions. *Psychological Bulletin, 102,* 187–203.

Keating, D. P. (1980). Thinking processes in adolescence. In J. Adelson (Ed.), *Handbook of adolescent psychology.* New York: John Wiley.

Keefe, F. J., & Blumenthal, J. A. (1980). The life fitness program: A behavioral approach to making exercise a habit. *Journal of Behavior Therapy and Experimental Psychiatry, 11,* 31–34.

Keesey, R., & Powley, T. (1986). The regulation of body weight. In M. R. Rosenzweig & L. W. Porter (Eds.), *Annual Review of Psychology* (vol. 37). Palo Alto, CA: Annual Reviews.

Keinan, G. (1987). Decision-making under stress: Scanning of alternatives and controllable and uncontrollable threats. *Journal of Personality and Social Psychology, 52*(3), 639–644.

Kelly, J. A., & Lamparski, D. M. (1985). Outpatient treatment of schizophrenics: Social skills and problem-solving. In M. Hersen & A. S. Bellack (Eds.), *Handbook of clinical behavior therapy with adults.* New York: Plenum.

Kennedy, J. L., Guiffra, L. A., Moises, H. W., Cavalli-Sforza, L. L., Pakstis, A. J., Kidd, J. R., Castiglione, C. M., Sjogren, B., Wetterberg, L., & Kidd, K. K. (1988). Evidence against linkage of schizophrenia to markers on chromosome 5 in a northern Swedish pedigree. *Nature, 336,* 167–170.

Kenrick, D. T. (1987). Gender, genes, and the social environment: A biosocial interactionist perspective. In P. Shaver & C. Hendrick (Eds.), *Sex and gender: Review of personality and social psychology* (vol. 7). Beverly Hills, CA: Sage.

Kenrick, D. T., & Funder, D. C. (1988). Profiting from controversy: Lessons from the person-situation debate. *American Psychologist, 43*(1), 23–34.

Kenrick, D. T., & MacFarlane, S. W. (1986). Ambient temperature and horn-honking: A field study of the heat/aggression relationship. *Environment and Behavior, 18,* 179–191.

Kent, G. E. (1989). *You're hired! Job search strategies for the '90s.* Toronto, Canada: Copp Clark Pitman, Ltd.

Kessler, J. W. (1966). *Psychopathology of childhood.* Englewood Cliffs, NJ: Prentice Hall.

Kiecolt-Glaser, J. K., Glaser, R., Williger, D., Stout, J., Messick, G., Shephard, S., Ricker, D., Romisher, S. C., Briner, W., Bonnell, G., & Donnerberg, R. (1985). Psychosocial enhancement of immunocompetence in a geriatric population. *Health Psychology, 4*(1), 25–42.

Kimmel, D. C., & Weiner, I. B. (1985). *Adolescence: A developmental transition.* Hillsdale, NJ: Lawrence Erlbaum.

Kimzey, S. L., Johnson, P. C., Ritzman, S. E., & Mengel, C. E. (1976, April). Hematology and immunology studies: The second manned Skylab mission. *Aviation, Space, and Environmental Medicine, 47*(4), 383–390.

King, K., Balswick, J. O., & Robinson, I. E. (1977). The continuing premarital sexual revolution among college females. *Journal of Marriage and the Family, 39,* 455–459.

KINSEY, A. C., POMEROY, W. B., & MARTIN, C. E. (1948). *Sexual behavior in the human male.* Philadelphia: W. B. Saunders.

KINSEY, A. C., POMEROY, W. B., MARTIN, C. E., & GEBHARD, P. H. (1953). *Sexual behavior in the human female.* Philadelphia: W. B. Saunders.

KIPNIS, D. (1971). *Character structure and impulsiveness.* New York: Academic Press.

KIRKENDALL, L. A., & ADAMS, W. J. (1971). *A reading and study guide for students in marriage and family relations.* Dubuque, IA: William C. Brown.

KLAUS, D., HERSEN, M., & BELLACK, A. S. (1977). Survey of dating habits of male and female college students: A necessary precursor to measurement and modification. *Journal of Clinical Psychology, 33,* 369–375.

KLEIN, D. F., & DAVIS, J. M. (1969). *Diagnosis and drug treatment of psychiatric disorders.* Baltimore: Williams & Wilkins.

KLEINKE, C. L., MEEKER, F. B., & STANESKI, R. A. (1986). Preference for opening lines: Comparing ratings by men and women. *Sex Roles, 15,* 585–600.

KLEINKE, C. L., & Walton, J. H. (1982). Influence of reinforced smiling on affective response in an interview. *Journal of Personality and Social Psychology, 42,* 557–565.

KLEINMUNTZ, B. (1982). *Personality and psychological assessment.* New York: St. Martin's Press.

KLEINMUNTZ, B., & SZUCKO, J. J. (1984). A field study of the fallibility of polygraph lie detection. *Nature, 308,* 449–450.

KLIMAN, G. (1979). Childhood mourning: A taboo within a taboo. In I. Gerber, A. Weiner, A. Kutscher, D. Battin, A. Arkin, & I. Goldberg (Eds.), *Perspectives on bereavement.* New York: Arno Press.

KLINTWORTH, G. K. (1962). A pair of male monozygotic twins discordant for homosexuality. *Journal of Nervous and Mental Diseases, 135,* 113–125.

KNOX, D., & WILSON, K. (1981). Dating behaviors of university students. *Family Relations, 30,* 255–258.

KOADLOW, E., & TUNNADINE, P. (1980). Sex. In B. Musgrave & Z. Menell (Eds.), *Change and choice: Women and middle age.* London: Peter Owen.

KOBASA, S. C. (1979). Stressful life events, personality, and health: An enquiry into hardiness. *Journal of Personality and Social Psychology, 37,* 1–11.

KOBASA, S. C., MADDI, S. R., & KAHN, S. (1982). Hardiness and health: A prospective study. *Journal of Personality and Social Psychology, 42*(1), 168–177.

KOCKOTT, G., DITTMAR, F., & NUSSELT, L. (1975). Systematic desensitization of erectile impotence: A controlled study. *Archives of Sexual Behavior, 4,* 493–500.

KOHLBERG, L. A. (1969). *Stages in the development of moral thought and action.* New York: Holt, Rinehart, & Winston.

KOHLBERG, L. A. (1981). *Essays on moral development. Vol. 1. The philosophy of moral development.* San Francisco: Harper & Row.

KOHLBERG, L., & ULLIAN, D. Z. (1974). Stages in the development of psychosexual concepts and attitudes. In R. C. VanWiele (Ed.), *Sex differences in behavior.* New York: John Wiley.

KOLATA, G. (1985). Obesity declared a disease. *Science, 227,* 1019–1020.

KOSS, M. P., DINERO, T. E., SEIBEL, C. A., & COX, S. L. (1988). Stranger and acquaintance rape. *Psychology of Women, 12,* 1–24.

KRAEPELIN, E. (1919). *Dementia praecox and paraphrenia.* Edinburgh: Livingstone.

KRANTZ, D. S., GRUNBERG, N. E., & BAUM, A. (1985). Health psychology. *Annual Review of Psychology, 36,* 349–383.

KRELL, R., & RABKIN, L. (1979). The effects of sibling death on the surviving child. *Family Process, 18,* 471–477.

KROP, H., & KRAUSE, S. (1976). The elimination of a shark phobia by self-administered systematic desensitization: A case study. *Journal of Behavior Therapy and Experimental Psychiatry, 7,* 293–294.

KUBLER-ROSS, E. (1969). *On death and dying.* New York: Macmillan.

KUBLER-ROSS, E. (1975). *Death: The final stage of growth.* Englewood Cliffs, NJ: Prentice Hall.

KUMAR, R., COOKE, F. C., LADER, M. H., & RUSSELL, M. A. H. (1977). Is nicotine important in tobacco smoking? *Clinical Pharmacology and Therapeutics, 21,* 520–529.

LAKEIN, A. (1973). *How to get control of your time and your life.* New York: Signet Books.

LANDERS, S. (1988, November). Survey verifies teen risk-taking. *APA Monitor, 19*(11), 30.

LANDIS, J. T. (1956). The pattern of divorce in three generations. *Social Forces, 34,* 201–207.

LANDIS, J. M., & SIMON, R. J. (1989). Women's and men's attitudes about a woman's place and role: the polls—a report. *The Public Opinion Quarterly, 53,* 265–276.

LANG, P. J., & MELAMED, B. G. (1969). Avoidance conditioning therapy of an infant with chronic ruminative vomiting. *Journal of Abnormal Psychology, 74,* 1–8.

LANGER, E. J., BASHNER, R. S., & CHANOWITZ, B. (1985). Decreasing prejudice by increasing discrimination. *Journal of Personality and Social Psychology, 49,* 113–120.

LANGER, E. J., JANIS, I. L., & WOLFER, J. A. (1975). Reduction of psychological stress in surgical patients. *Journal of Experimental Social Psychology, 11,* 155–165.

LAROUCHE, J., & RYAN, R. (1984). *Strategies for women at work.* New York: Avon Books.

LARSON, L. E., & GOLTZ, W. (1989). Religious participation and marital commitment. *Review of Religious Research, 30,* 387–400.

LATHAM, G. P. (1982). Behavior-based assessment in organizations. In L. W. Fredericksen (Ed.), *Handbook of organizational behavior management.* New York: Wiley.

LATHAM, G. P., & SAARI, L. M. (1984). Do people do what they say? Further studies on the situational interview. *Journal of Applied Psychology, 69,* 569–573.

LAUDENSLAGER, M.L., REITE, M., & HARBECK, R. J. (1982). Suppressed immune function in infant monkeys associated with maternal separation. *Behavioral and Neural Biology, 36,* 40–48.

LAUER, J., & LAUER, R. (1985). Marriages made to last. *Psychology Today, 16*(6), 22–26.

LAWSON, D. M., & RHODES, E. C. (1981, November). Behavioral self-control and maintenance of aerobic exercise: A retrospective study of self-initiated attempts to improve physical fitness. Paper presented at the meeting of the Association for the Advancement of Behavior Therapy, Toronto.

LAZARUS, A. (1971). *Behavior therapy and beyond.* New York: McGraw-Hill.

LAZARUS, R., & DELONGIS, A. (1983). Psychological stress and coping in aging. *American Psychology, 38,* 245–254.

LAZARUS, R. S. (1984*a*). On the primacy

of emotion. *American Psychologist, 39,* 124–129.

LAZARUS, R. S. (1984*b*). Puzzles in the study of daily hassles. *Journal of Behavioral Medicine, 7,* 375–389.

LAZARUS, R. S. (1991*a*). Cognition and motivation in emotion. *American Psychologist, 46,* 352–367.

LAZARUS, R. S. (1991*b*). *Emotion and adaptation.* New York: Oxford University Press.

LAZARUS, R. S., & FOLKMAN, S. (1984). *Stress, appraisal, and coping.* New York: Springer.

LEBOEUF, M. (1979). *Working smart: How to accomplish more in half the time.* New York: Warner Books.

LEBOW, M. D. (1981). *Weight control: The behavioral strategies.* New York: John Wiley.

LEBOW, M. D. (1989). *Adult obesity therapy.* New York: Pergamon Press.

LEBOW, M. D. (1991). *Overweight children: Helping your child to achieve lifetime weight control.* New York: Insight Books/Plenum.

LEBOW, M. D., GOLDBERG, P. S., & COLLINS, A. (1977). Eating behavior of overweight and nonoverweight persons in the natural environment. *Journal of Consulting and Clinical Psychology, 45,* 1204–1205.

LEHRER, P. M., & WOOLFOLK, R. L. (1985). The relaxation therapies. In R. M. Turner & L. M. Ascher (Eds.), *Evaluating behavior therapy outcome.* New York: Springer.

LEHRER, P. M., & WOOLFOLK, R. L. (1986). Are all stress-reduction techniques interchangeable, or do they have specific effects: A review of the comparative empirical literature. In R. L. Woolfolk & P. M. Lehrer (Eds.), *Principles and practices of stress management.* New York: Guilford Press.

LEIBOWITZ, M. R., GORMAN, J. M., FYER, A. J., & KLEIN, D. F. (1985). Social phobia. *Archives of General Psychiatry, 42,* 729–736.

LEITENBERG, H. (1976). Behavioral approaches to treatment of neurosis. In H. Leitenberg (Ed.), *Behavior modification and behavior therapy.* Englewood Cliffs, NJ: Prentice Hall.

LEMON, G. W. (1984). You are what you eat: Energy metabolism and nutrition for the coach and athlete. *Coaching Science Update, 5,* 35–40.

LERNER, M. (1970). When, why, and where people die. In O. Brim, Jr., H. E. Freeman, S. Levine, & N. Scotch (Eds.), *The dying patient.* New York: Russell Sage Foundation.

LEVANT, R. F., SLATTERY, S. C., & LOISELLE, J. E. (1987). Fathers' involvement in housework and child care with school-aged daughters. *Family Relations, 36,* 152–157.

LEVAY, S. (1991). A difference in hypothalamic structure between heterosexual and homosexual men. *Science, 253,* 1034–1037.

LEVENTHAL, H. (1982). The integration of emotion and cognition: A view from the perceptual monitor theory of emotion. In M. Clark & S. Feske (Eds.), *Affect and emotion.* Hillsdale, NJ: Lawrence Erlbaum.

LEVENTHAL, H., & TOMARKEN, A. (1986). Emotion: Today's problems. *Annual Review of Psychology, 37,* 565–610.

LEVINGER, G., & HUSTON, T. (1990). The social psychology of marriage. In F. D. Fincham & T. N. Bradbury (Eds.), *The psychology of marriage: Basic issues and applications.* New York: Guilford Press.

LEVINGER, G., & SNOEK, J. D. (1972). *Attraction in relationships: A new look at interpersonal attraction.* Morristown, NJ: General Learning Press.

LEVINSON, D. J. (1985). The life cycle. In H. I. Kaplan & B. J. Sadock (Eds.), *Comprehensive textbook of psychiatry/IV* (vol. 1, 4th ed.). Baltimore: Williams & Wilkins.

LEVINSON, D. J. (1986). A conception of adult development. *American Psychologist, 41,* 3–13.

LEVINSON, D. J., DARROW, C. M., KLEIN, E. G., LEVINSON, M. H., & McKEE, B. (1978). *The seasons of a man's life.* New York: Alfred A. Knopf.

LEWINSOHN, P. M., & HOBERMAN, H. M. (1982). Depression. In A. S. Bellak, M. Hersen, & A. E. Kazdin (Eds.), *International handbook of behavior modification and therapy.* New York: Plenum.

LEYENS, J. P., CAMINO, L., PARKE, R. D., & BERKOWITZ, L. (1975). Effects of movie violence on aggression in a field setting as a function of group dominance and cohesion. *Journal of Personality and Social Psychology, 32,* 346–360.

LIEBERT, R. M. (1986). Effects of television on children and adolescents. *Journal of Developmental and Behavioral Pediatrics, 7,* 43–48.

LIEBERT, R. M., & BARON, R. A. (1972). Some immediate effects of televised violence on children's behavior. *Developmental Psychology, 6,* 469–475.

LIEBERT, R. M., & POULOS, R. W. (1975). Television and personality development: The socializing effects of an entertainment medium. In A. Davids (Ed.), *Child personality and psychopathology: Current topics* (vol. II). New York: John Wiley.

LIEBERT, R. M., & SCHWARTZBERG, N. S. (1977). Effects of mass media. *Annual Review of Psychology, 28,* 141–173.

Life (1988, Spring). What we believe. Pp. 69–70.

LINDEMANN, E. (1944). Symptomatology and management of acute grief. *American Journal of Psychiatry, 101,* 141–149.

LINDEN, W. (1987). On the impending death of the Type A construct: Or is there a phoenix rising from the ashes? *Canadian Journal of Behavioral Science, 19,* 177–190.

LIPOWSKI, Z. J. (1988). Somatization: The concept and its clinical application. *American Journal of Psychiatry, 145,* 1358–1368.

LISSPERS, J., & OST, L. G. (1990). BVP-biofeedback in the treatment of migraine: The effects of constriction and dilation during different phases of the migraine attack. *Behavior Modification, 14,* 200–221.

LLOYD, C. (1980). Life events and depressive disorders reviewed: Events as predisposing factors. *Archives of General Psychiatry, 37,* 529–535.

LLOYD, K. E. (1980). Some reactions to a forthcoming energy shortage. In G. L. Martin & J. G. Osborne (Eds.), *Helping in the community: Behavioral applications.* New York: Plenum.

LOMBARDO, M. M., & McCALL, M. W. (1984, January). The intolerable boss. *Psychology Today, 18,* 44–48.

LONG, B. C., & HANEY, C. J. (1988*a*). Coping strategies for working women: Aerobic exercise and relaxation interventions. *Behavior Therapy, 19,* 75–83.

LONG, B. C., & HANEY, C. J. (1988*b*). Long-term follow-up of stressed working women: A comparison of aerobic exercise and progressive relaxation. *Journal of Sport and Exercise Psychology, 10,* 461–470.

LONGINO, C. F. (1981). Retirement communities. In F. J. Berghorn, D. E. Schafer, & associates (Eds.), *The dynamics of aging: Original essays on the processes and experiences of growing old.* Boulder, CO: Westview Press.

LONGINO, H. E. (1980). Pornography, oppression, and freedom: A closer look. In L. Lederer (Ed.), *Take back the night: Women on pornography.* New York: William Morrow.

LOPICCOLO, J., & LOBITZ, W. C. (1972). The role of masturbation in the treatment of orgasmic dysfunction. *Archives of Sexual Behavior, 2,* 163–171.

LoPiccolo, J., & LoPiccolo, L. (1978). *Handbook of sex therapy.* New York: Plenum.

Lorenz, K. (1974). *The eight deadly sins of civilized man.* New York: Harcourt Brace Jovanovich.

Lott, C. S., & Lott, O. C. (1989). *How to land a better job.* Lincolnwood, IL: V.G.M. Career Horizons.

Lowman, R. L. (1991). *The clinical practice of career assessment: Interests, abilities, and personality.* Hyattsville, MD: American Psychological Association.

Lowther, R., Martin, G. L., & Nicholson, D. (1978). Developing good sitting posture and programming generalization over different settings with profoundly handicapped girls. *Journal of Practical Approaches to Developmental Handicap, 2,* 17–23.

Lubin, B., Larson, R. M., & Matarazzo, J. D. (1984). Patterns of psychological test usage in the United States: 1935–1982. *American Psychologist, 39,* 451–454.

Luborsky, L., McLellan, A. T., Woody, G. E., O'Brien, C. P., & Auerbach, A. (1985). Therapist success and its determinants. *Archives of General Psychiatry, 42,* 602–611.

Luria, A. (1961). *The role of speech in the regulation of normal and abnormal behaviors.* New York: Liveright.

Lutzker, J. R., & Lutzker, S. Z. (1977). A two-dimensional contract: Weight loss and household responsibility performance. In E. E. Abramson (Ed.), *Behavioral approaches to weight control.* New York: Springer.

Lykken, D. T. (1981). *A tremor in the blood: Uses and abuses of the lie detector.* New York: McGraw-Hill.

Machung, A. (1989). Talking career, thinking job: Gender differences in career and family expectations of Berkeley seniors. *Family Studies, 15,* 35–58.

Mackenzie, R. A. (1975). *New time management methods for you and your staff.* New York: The Dartnell Corp.

Macklin, E. (1972). Heterosexual cohabitation among unmarried college students. *The Family Coordinator, 21,* 463–472.

Macklin, E. D. (1987). Nontraditional family forms. In M. B. Sussman & S. K. Steinmetz (Eds.), *Handbook of marriage and the family.* New York: Plenum.

MacLusky, N., & Natfolin, F. (1981). Sexual differentiation of the central nervous system. *Science, 211,* 1294–1303.

Maddi, R. (1980). *Personality theories: A comparative analysis* (4th ed.). Homewood, IL: Dorsey Press.

Mager, R. F. (1972). *Goal analysis.* Belmont, CA: Fearon Publishers.

Maier, S. F., & Laudenslager, M. (1985). Stress and health: Exploring the links. *Psychology Today, 19,* 44–49.

Malamuth, N. M. (1984). Aggression against women: Cultural and individual causes. In N. M. Malamuth & E. Donnerstein (Eds.), *Pornography and sexual aggression.* Orlando, FL: Academic Press.

Malamuth, N. M., & Check, J. V. P. (1984). Debriefing effectiveness following exposure to pornographic rape depictions. *Journal of Sex Research, 20,* 1–13.

Malamuth, N. M., & Donnerstein, E. (1982). The effects of aggressive-pornographic mass media stimuli. In L. Berkowitz (Ed.), *Advances in experimental social psychology* (vol. 15). Orlando, FL: Academic Press.

Maletzky, V. N. (1974). Behavior recording as treatment: A brief note. *Behavior Therapy, 5,* 107–111.

Malott, R. W., & Whaley, D. L. (1983). *Psychology.* Holmes Beach, FL: Learning Publications.

Malt, B. C., & Smith, E. E. (1984). Correlated properties in natural categories. *Journal of Verbal Learning and Verbal Behavior, 23,* 250–269.

Mandler, G. (1984). *Mind and body: Psychology of emotion and stress.* New York: W. W. Norton.

Margulis, S. T., Derlega, V. J., & Winstead, B. A. (1984). Implications of social psychological concepts for a theory of loneliness. In V. J. Derlega (Ed.), *Communication, intimacy, and close relationships.* Orlando, FL: Academic Press.

Markesun, E., & Fulton, R. (1971). Childhood bereavement and behavior disorders: A critical review. *Omega, 2,* 107–117.

Marks, I. (1987). Behavioral aspects of panic disorder. *American Journal of Psychiatry, 144,* 1160–1165.

Marlatt, G. A. (1982). Relapse prevention: A self-control program for the treatment of addictive behaviors. In R. B. Stuart (Ed.), *Adherence, compliance, and generalization in behavioral medicine.* New York: Brunner/Mazel.

Marlatt, G. A., Baer, J. S., Dononovan, D. M., & Kivlahan, D. R. (1988). Addictive behaviors: Etiology and treatment. *Annual Review of Psychology, 39,* 223–252.

Marlatt, G. A., & Parks, G. A. (1982). Self-management of addictive disorders. In P. Karoly & F. H. Kanfer (Eds.), *Self-management and behavior change: From theory to practice.* New York: Pergamon Press.

Marlatt, G. A., & Rohsenow, D. J. (1981). The think-drink effect. *Psychology Today, 15,* 60–62, 64, 66, 68–69, 93.

Martin, D. G. (1991). *Psychology: Principles and applications.* Scarborough, Ontario: Prentice Hall, Canada.

Martin, G. L. (1982). Thought stopping and stimulus control to decrease persistent disturbing thoughts. *Journal of Behavior Therapy and Experimental Psychiatry, 13*(3), 215–220.

Martin, G. L., & Lumsden, J. A. (1987). *Coaching: An effective behavioral approach.* St. Louis, MO: Times Mirror/Mosby.

Martin, G. L., & Pear, J. J. (1992). *Behavior modification: What it is and how to do it* (4th ed.). Englewood Cliffs, NJ: Prentice Hall.

Martin, M. J., & Pritchard, M. E. (1991). Factors associated with alcohol use in later adolescence. *Journal of Studies on Alcohol, 52,* 5–9.

Martin, R. A., & Lefcourt, H. M. (1983). Sense of humor as a moderator of the relation between stressors and moods. *Journal of Personality and Social Psychology, 45,* 1313–1324.

Martineau, W. H. (1972). A model of the social function of humor. In J. H. Goldstein & P. E. McGhee (Eds.), *The psychology of humor: Theoretical perspectives and empirical issues.* New York: Academic Press.

Maslow, A. H. (1954; 1970). *Motivation and personality* (1st ed.; 2nd ed.). New York: Harper & Row.

Mason, J. W. (1971). A re-evaluation of the concept of "nonspecificity" in stress theory. *Journal of Psychiatric Research, 8,* 323–333.

Mason, J. W. (1975). A historical view of the stress field. Part II. *Journal of Human Stress, 1,* 22–36.

Masters, J. C., Burrish, T. G., Hollon, S. D., & Rimm, D. C. (1987). *Behavior therapy: Techniques and empirical findings* (3rd ed.). Orlando, FL: Harcourt Brace Jovanovich.

Masters, W. H., & Johnson, V. E. (1966). *Human sexual response.* Boston: Little, Brown.

Masters, W. H., & Johnson, V. E. (1970). *Human sexual inadequacy.* Boston: Little, Brown.

Masters, W. H., & Johnson, V. E. (1979).

Homosexuality in perspective. Boston: Little, Brown.

Mathews, K. E., Jr., & Canon, L. K. (1975). Environmental noise level as a determinant of helping behavior. *Journal of Personality and Social Psychology, 32,* 571–577.

Mathews, V. D., & Mihanovich, C. S. (1963). New orientations on marital maladjustment. *Marriage and Family Living, 25,* 300–304.

Matsumoto, D. (1987). The role of facial response in the experience of emotion: More methodological problems and a meta-analysis. *Journal of Personality and Social Psychology, 52,* 769–764.

Matthews, K. A. (1988). Coronary heart disease and Type A behaviors: Update on and alternative to the Booth-Kewley and Friedman (1987) quantitative review. *Psychological Bulletin, 104,* 373–380.

Matthews, K. A., & Rodin, J. (1989). Women's changing work roles: Impact on health, family, and public policy. *American Psychologist, 44,* 1389–1393.

Maurer, D., & Vogel, V. H. (1973). *Narcotics and narcotic addiction.* Springfield, IL: Charles C. Thomas.

Maykovitch, M. K. (1975). Correlates of racial prejudice. *Journal of Personality and Social Psychology, 32,* 1014–1020.

McAdams, D. P. (1990). *The person: An introduction to personality psychology.* San Diego: Harcourt Brace Jovanovich.

McAllister, W. R., McAllister, D. E., Scoles, M. T., & Hampton, S. R. (1986). Persistence of fear-reducing behavior: Relevance for the conditioning theory of neurosis. *Journal of Abnormal Psychology, 95,* 365–372.

McCall, G., & Shields, N. (1986). Social and structural factors in family violence. In M. Lystad (Ed.), *Violence in the home: Interdisciplinary perspectives.* New York: Brunner/Mazel.

McCarthy, J. (1985). The medical complications of cocaine abuse. In D. Smith & D. Wesson (Eds.), *Treating the cocaine abuser.* Center City, MN: Hazelden.

McCrae, R., & Costa, P. T., Jr. (1986). Clinical assessment can benefit from recent advances in personality psychology. *American Psychologist, 41*(9), 1001–1003.

McCrae, R., & Costa, P. T., Jr. (1987). Validation of the 5-factor model of personality across instruments and observers. *Journal of Personality*

and *Social Psychology, 52*(1), 81–90.

McCrae, R. R., & Costa, P. T., Jr. (1989). The structure of interpersonal traits: Wiggins's circumplex and the Five Factor model. *Journal of Personality and Social Psychology, 56,* 586–595.

McFall, R. M. (1970). Effects of self-monitoring on normal smoking behavior. *Journal of Consulting and Clinical Psychology, 35,* 135–142.

McFall, R. M., & Dodge, K. A. (1982). Self-management and interpersonal skills learning. In P. Karoly & F. H. Kanfer (Eds.), *Self-management and behavior change: From theory to practice.* New York: Pergamon Press.

McGill, M. E. (1985). *The McGill report on male intimacy.* New York: Holt, Rinehart, & Winston.

McGovern, K. B., McMullen, R. S., & Lo-Piccolo, J. (1975). Secondary orgasmic dysfunction. I. Analysis and strategies for treatment. *Archives of Sexual Behavior, 4,* 265–275.

McLanahan, S., & Bumpass, L. (1988). Intergenerational consequences of family disruption. *American Journal of Sociology, 94,* 130–152.

McNally, R. J. (1987). Preparedness and phobias: A review. *Psychological Bulletin, 101,* 283–303.

Meador, B. D., & Rogers, C. R. (1984). Person-centered therapy. In R. J. Corsini (Ed.), *Current psychotherapies* (3rd ed.). Itasca, IL: F. E. Peacock.

Meichenbaum, D. (1986). Cognitive behavior modification. In F. H. Kanfer & A. P. Goldstein (Eds.), *Helping people change: A textbook of methods* (3rd ed.). New York: Pergamon Press.

Meltzoff, A. (1988). Infant imitation after a one-week delay: Long-term memory for novel acts and multiple stimuli. *Developmental Psychology, 24,* 470–476.

Mencke, R., & Hummel, R. L. (1984). *Career planning for the '80s.* Monterey, CA: Brooks/Cole.

Meyer, R. G. (1989). *The clinician's handbook* (2nd ed.). Boston: Allyn & Bacon.

Millenson, J. R. (1967). *Principles of behavioral analysis.* New York: Macmillan.

Mikhail, A. (1981). Stress: A psychophysiological conception. *Journal of Human Stress, 7,* 9–15.

Miller, A. G. (1970). Role of physical attractiveness in impression forma-

tion. *Psychonomic Science, 19,* 241–243.

Miller, B. C., McCoy, J. K., & Olson, T. D. (1986). Dating age and stage as correlates of adolescent sexual attitudes and behavior. *Journal of Adolescent Research, 1,* 361–371.

Miller, H. L., & Siegel, P. S. (1972). *Loving: A psychological approach.* New York: John Wiley.

Miller, L. C., Berg, J. H., & Archer, R. L. (1983). Openers: Individuals who elicit intimate self-disclosure. *Journal of Personality and Social Psychology, 44,* 1234–1244.

Miller, N. E. (1985). Rx: Biofeedback. *Psychology Today, 19*(2), 54–59.

Miller, R. L., & Gordon, M. (1986). The decline in formal dating: A study in six Connecticut high schools. *Marriage and Family Review, 10,* 139–156.

Mischel, W. (1968). *Personality and assessment.* New York: John Wiley.

Mischel, W. (1984). Convergences and challenges in the search for consistency. *American Psychologist, 39,* 351–364.

Mishra, P. K. (1983). Proxemics: Theory and research. *Perspectives in Psychological Researches, 6,* 10–15.

Mittelman, W. (1991). Maslow's study of self-actualization: A reinterpretation. *Journal of Humanistic Psychology, 31,* 114–135.

Modgil, S., & Modgil, C. (Eds.) (1985). *Lawrence Kohlberg: Consensus and controversy.* Philadelphia: Palmer Press.

Monat, A., & Lazarus, R. S. (1991). *Stress and coping: An anthology* (3rd ed.). New York: Columbia University Press.

Money, J. (1961). Sex hormones and other variables in human eroticism. In W. C. Young (Ed.), *Sex hormones and internal secretions* (vol. 2). Baltimore: Williams & Wilkins.

Money, J. (1965). *Sex research: New developments.* New York: Holt, Rinehart, and Winston.

Money, J. (1986). *Venuses penuses: Sexology, sexosophy, and exigency theory.* Buffalo, NY: Prometheus Books.

Money, J., & Ehrhardt, A. A. (1972). *Man and woman and boy and girl.* Baltimore: Johns Hopkins University Press.

Montemayor, R. (1983). Parents and adolescents in conflict: All families some of the time and some families most of the time. *Journal of Early Adolescence, 3,* 83–103.

Moore, M. (1982). Endorphins and exercise: A puzzling relationship. *The Physician and Sports Medicine, 10*(2), 198–207.

MORELAND, R. L., & ZAJONC, R. B. (1982). Exposure effects in person perception: Familiarity, similarity, and attraction. *Journal of Experimental Social Psychology, 18,* 395–415.

MORGAN, S. P., LYE, D. N., & CONDRAN, G. A. (1988). Sons, daughters, and divorce: Does the sex of children affect the risk of marital disruption? *American Journal of Sociology, 94,* 110–129.

MORGAN, W. G. (1974). The relationship between expressed social fears and assertiveness and its treatment implications. *Behavior Research and Therapy, 12,* 255–257.

MOROKOFF, P. (1978). Determinants of female orgasm. In J. LoPiccolo & L. LoPiccolo (Eds.), *Handbook of sex therapy.* New York: Plenum.

MORRISON, A. M., & VON GLINOW, M. A. (1990). Women and minorities in management. *American Psychologist, 45,* 200–208.

MORRISON, R. L., & BELLACK, A. S. (1984). Social skills training. In A. S. Bellack (Ed.), *Schizophrenia: Treatment, management and rehabilitation.* Orlando, FL: Grune & Stratton.

MOWRER, O. H. (1950). *Learning theory and personality dynamics.* New York: Arnold Press.

MUEHLENHARD, C. (1988). Misinterpreting dating behaviors and the risk of date rape. *Journal of Social and Clinical Psychology, 6,* 20–37.

MUEHLENHARD, C., & LINTON, M. (1987). Date rape and sexual aggression in dating situations: Incidence and risk factors. *Journal of Consulting Psychology, 34,* 186–196.

MUEHLENHARD, C. L., KORALEWSKI, M. A., ANDREWS, S. L., & BURDICK, C. A. (1986). Verbal and nonverbal cues that convey interest in dating. *Behavior Therapy, 17,* 404–419.

MUEHLENHARD, C. L., & MILLER, E. N. (1988). Traditional and nontraditional men's responses to women's dating initiation. *Behavior Modification, 12,* 385–403.

MUHLENKAMP, A. F., GRESS, L. D., & FLOOD, N. A. (1975). Perception of life change events by the elderly. *Nursing Research, 24,* 109–113.

MUÑOZ, R. F. (1977). A cognitive approach to the assessment and treatment of depression. *Dissertation Abstracts International, 38,* 2873B. (University Microfilms No. 77-26, 505, 154).

MURPHY, J. K., BRUCE, B. K., & WILLIAMSON, D. A. (1985). A comparison of measured and self-reported weights in a 4-year follow-up of spouse involvement in obesity treatment. *Behavior Therapy, 16,* 524–530.

MURRAY, J. B. (1991). Nicotine as a psychoactive drug. *Journal of Psychology, 125,* 5–25.

MURSTEIN,, B. I. (1980). Mate selection in the 1970s. *Journal of Marriage and the Family, 42,* 777–792.

MURSTEIN, B. I. (1986). *Paths to marriage.* Beverly Hills: Sage.

MYERS, D. G. (1986). *Psychology.* New York: Worth.

MYERS, D. G. (1990). *Social psychology* (3rd ed.). New York: McGraw-Hill.

NAISBITT, J. (1982). *Megatrends: Ten new directions transforming our lives.* New York: Warner Books.

NATIONAL CENTER FOR HEALTH STATISTICS. (1987). *Vital statistics of the United States, 1984, Vol. 11, Mortality,* Part A. DHHS Pub. No. (PHS) 87-1122. Public Health Service, Washington, DC: U.S. Government Printing Office.

NATIONAL INSTITUTE OF MENTAL HEALTH (1982). *Television and behavior: Ten years of scientific progress and implications for the 1980s.* Washington, DC: U.S. Government Printing Office.

NATIONAL OPINION RESEARCH CENTER (1988). *General social surveys, 1980–1987: Cumulative case book.* Storrs, CT: Roper Public Opinion Research Center, University of Connecticut.

NEEDLEMAN, H., & GATSONIS, C. (1990). Low-level lead exposure and the IQ of children. *Journal of the American Medical Association, 264,* 673–678.

NEIDHARDT, E. J., WEINSTEIN, M. S., & CONROY, R. F. (1985). *Managing stress: A complete self-help guide.* Vancouver: International Self-Council Press.

NEILL, J. (1987). "More than medical significance": LSD and American psychiatry, 1953–1966. *Journal of Psychoactive Drugs, 19,* 39–45.

NEMIAH, J. C. (1985). Somatoform disorders. In H. I. Kaplan & B. J. Sadock (Eds.), *Comprehensive textbook of psychiatry* (vol. IV). Baltimore: Williams & Wilkins.

NEWCOMB, M. D., & BENTLER, P. M. (1988). Impact of adolescent drug use and social support on problems of young adults: A longitudinal study. *Journal of Abnormal Psychology, 97,* 64–75.

NEWMAN, G., & NICHOLS, C. P. (1960). Sexual activities and attitudes in older persons. *Journal of the American Medical Association, 173,* 117–119.

NEWMAN, P. (1978, May–June). How to manage your boss. *Management Focus,* pp. 12–13.

NICKLAUS, J. (1974). *Golf my way.* New York: Simon & Schuster.

NIGL, A. J. (1984). *Biofeedback and behavioral strategies in pain treatment.* New York: Medical and Scientific Books.

NIGRO, G. N., HILL, D. E., GELBEIN, M. E., & CLARK, C. L. (1988). Changes in the facial prominence of women and men over the last decade. *Psychology of Women Quarterly, 12,* 225–235.

NISBETT, R. E., & ROSS, L. (1980). *Human inference: Strategies and shortcomings of social judgment.* Englewood Cliffs, NJ: Prentice Hall.

NOLLER, P., LAW, H., & COMREY, A. L. (1987). Cattell, Comrey, and Eysenck personality factors compared: More evidence for the five robust factors? *Journal of Personality and Social Psychology, 53,* 775–782.

NOMELINI, S., & KATZ, R. C. (1983). Effects of anger control training on abusive parents. *Cognitive Therapy and Research, 7,* 57–68.

NORMAN, W. T. (1963). Toward an adequate taxonomy of personality attributes: Replicated factor structure in peer nomination personality ratings. *Journal of Abnormal and Social Psychology, 66,* 574–583.

NOVACO, R. W. (1975). *Anger control.* Lexington, MA: Heath.

NOVACO, R. W. (1979). The cognitive regulation of anger and stress. In P. C. Kendall & S. D. Hollon (Eds.), *Cognitive behavioral interventions: Theory, research, and procedures.* New York: Academic Press.

NOYES, R., JR., CLARKSON, C., CROWE, R. R., YATES, W. R., & McCHESNEY, C. M. (1987). A family study of generalized anxiety disorder. *American Journal of Psychiatry, 144,* 1019–1024.

Occupational Outlook Handbook: 1986-87 (1986). U.S. Department of Labor, Washington, DC: Government Printing Office.

O'DONNELL, M. P., & AINSWORTH, T. H. (1984). *Health promotion in the workplace.* New York: John Wiley.

OFFER, D., & OFFER, J. (1969). *The psychological world of the teenager.* New York: Basic Books.

OHMAN, A., DIMBERG, U., & OST, L. G. (1984). Animal and social phobias: Biological constraints on learned fear responses. In S. Reiss & R. Bootzin (Eds.), *Theoretical issues in behavior therapy.* New York: Academic Press.

Olson, D. H. (1972). Marriage of the future: Revolutionary or evolutionary change? *The Family Coordinator, 21,* 383–393.

Oltmanns, T. F., Neale, J. M., & Davison, G. C. (1986). *Case studies in abnormal psychology* (2nd ed.). New York: John Wiley.

O'Reilly, H. J. (1984). Crisis intervention with victims of forcible rape: A police perspective. In J. Hopkins (Ed.), *Perspectives on rape and sexual assault.* New York: Harper & Row.

Orenstein, H., Orenstein, E., & Carr, J. E. (1975). Assertiveness and anxiety: A correlational study. *Journal of Behavior Therapy and Experimental Psychiatry, 6,* 203–207.

Orlando, V. P., & Hayward, K. G. (1978). A comparison of the effectiveness of three study techniques for college students. In P. D. Pearson & J. Hansen (Eds.), *Reading: Disciplined enquiry in process and practice.* Clemson, SC: National Reading Conference.

Osborne, J. G., & Powers, R. B. (1980). Controlling the litter problem. In G. L. Martin & J. G. Osborne (Eds.), *Helping in the community: Behavioral applications.* New York: Plenum.

Oskamp, S. (1984). *Applied social psychology.* Englewood Cliffs, NJ: Prentice Hall.

Osness, W. (1981). Biological aspects of the aging process. In F. J. Berghorn, D. E. Schafer, & associates (Eds.), *The dynamics of aging: Original essays on the processes and experiences of growing old.* Boulder, CO: Westview Press.

Oster, G., Huse, D. M., Delea, T. E., & Colditz, G. A. (1986). Cost effectiveness of nicotine gum as an adjunct to physician's advice against cigarette smoking. *Journal of the American Medical Association, 256,* 1315–1318.

Osterweiss, M., Solomon, F., & Green, M. (1984). *Bereavement: Reactions, consequences, and care.* Washington, DC: National Academy Press.

Oulette-Kobasa, S. C., & Pucetti, M. C. (1983). Personality and social resources in stress resistance. *Journal of Personality and Social Psychology, 45,* 836–850.

Overmier, J. B., & Seligman, M. E. P. (1967). Effects of inescapable shock upon subsequent escape and avoidance learning. *Journal of Comparative and Physiological Psychology, 63,* 23–33.

Paffenbarger, R. S., Jr., Hyde, R. T., Wing, A. L., & Hsieh, C. (1986). Physical activity, mortality, and longevity of college alumni. *New England Journal of Medicine, 314,* 605–613.

Paffenbarger, R. S., Jr., Hyde, R. T., Wing, A. L., & Steinmetz, C. H. (1984). A natural history of athleticism and cardiovascular health. *Journal of the American Medical Association, 252,* 491–495.

Paivio, A. (1986). *Mental representations: A dual coding approach.* New York: Oxford University Press.

Pam, A., Plutchik, R., & Conte, H. R. (1975). Love: A psychometric approach. *Psychological Reports, 37,* 83–88.

Parke, R. D., Berkowitz, L., Leyens, J. P., West, S. G., & Sebastian, R. J. (1977). Some effects of violent and nonviolent movies on the behavior of juvenile delinquents. In L. Berkowitz (Ed.), *Advances in experimental social psychology* (vol. 10). Orlando, FL: Academic Press.

Parker, N. (1964). Twins: A psychiatric study of a neurotic group. *Medical Journal of Australia, 2,* 735–742.

Passman, R. (1977). The reduction of procrastinative behaviors in a college student despite the "contingency fulfillment problems": The use of external control in self-management techniques. *Behavior Therapy, 8,* 95–96.

Patton, P. W., Corry, J. M., Gettman, L. R., & Graf, J. S. (1986). *Implementing health/fitness programs.* Champaign, IL: Human Kinetics Publishers.

Paul, G. L., & Lentz, R. J. (1977). *Psychosocial treatment of chronic mental patients: Milieu versus social learning programs.* Cambridge, MA: Harvard University Press.

Pauling, L. (1971). *Vitamin C and the common cold.* New York: Bantam Books.

Pauling, L. C. (1980). Vitamin C therapy of advanced cancer. *New England Journal of Medicine, 302,* 694.

Pavlov, I. P. (1927). *Conditioned reflexes: An investigation of the physiological activity of the cerebral cortex.* Trans. G. V. Anrep, London: Oxford University Press.

Payne, W. A., & Hahn, D. B. (1989). *Understanding your health* (2nd ed.). St. Louis, MO: Mosby.

Peck, E., & Senderowitz, J. (Eds.) (1974). *Pronatalism.* New York: Crowell.

Pedrick-Cornell, C., & Gelles, R. J. (1982). Elder abuse: The status of current knowledge. *Family Relations, 31,* 457–465.

Penney, A. (1982). *How to make love to each other.* New York: G. P. Putnam's Sons.

Peplau, L. A., & Perlman, D. (1982). Perspectives on loneliness. In L. A. Peplau & D. Perlman (Eds.), *Loneliness: A sourcebook of current theory, research and therapy.* New York: John Wiley.

Percell, L. P., Berwick, P. T., & Beigel, A. (1974). The effects of assertive training on self-concept and anxiety. *Archives of General Psychiatry, 31,* 502–504.

Perlman, D. (1989). Further reflections on the present state of loneliness research. In M. Hojat & R. Crandall (Eds.), *Loneliness: Theory, research, and applications.* Newbury Park, CA: Sage.

Perlmutter, M. (1978). What is memory aging the aging of? *Developmental Psychology, 14,* 330–345.

Perlmutter, M., Metzger, R., Miller, K., & Nazworski, T. (1980). Memory of historical events. *Experimental Aging Research, 6,* 47–60.

Pezzot-Pierce, T. D., LeBow, M. D., & Pierce, J. W. (1982). Increasing cost effectiveness in obesity treatment through use of self-help behavioral manuals and decreased therapist contact. *Journal of Consulting and Clinical Psychology, 50,* 448–449.

Phares, E. J. (1991). *Introduction to personality* (3rd ed.). New York: HarperCollins.

Phelps, S., & Austin, N. (1975). *The assertive woman.* San Luis Obispo, CA: Impact Publishers.

Pines, A. (1984, July–August). Ma Bell and the Hardy Boys. *Across the Board,* pp. 37–42.

Platt, J. (1973). Social traps. *American Psychologist, 28,* 641–651.

Pleck, J. H. (1983). Husbands' paid work and family roles: Current research issues. In H. Lopata & J. H. Pleck (Eds.), *Research in the interweave of social roles, Vol. 3, Families and jobs.* Greenwich, CT: JAI Press.

Plutchik, R. (1984). A psychoevolutionary theory of emotions. *Social Science Information, 21,* 529–553.

Pope, H., & Mueller, C. W. (1976). The intergenerational transmission of marital instability: Comparisons by race and sex. *Journal of Social Issues, 32,* 49–66.

Porcino, J. (1983). *Growing older, get-*

ting better: A handbook for women in the second half of life. Reading, MA: Addison-Wesley.

POWERS, R. B., OSBORNE, J. G., & ANDERSON, E. (1973). Positive reinforcement of litter removal in the natural environment. *Journal of Applied Behavior Analysis, 6,* 579–686.

PRATT, O. E. (1982). Alcohol and the developing fetus. *British Medical Bulletin, 38,* 48–52.

PREMACK, D. (1959). Toward empirical behavioral laws: Positive reinforcement. *Psychological Review, 66,* 219–233.

PREMACK, D. (1965). Reinforcement theory. In D. Levine (Ed.), *Nebraska Symposium on Motivation* (vol. 13). Lincoln, NE: University of Nebraska Press.

PRITIKIN, N. (1983). *The Pritikin promise: 28 days to a longer, healthier lifestyle.* New York: Pocketbooks, Division of Simon & Schuster.

PROCTOR, J. T. (1958). Hysteria in childhood. *American Journal of Orthopsychiatry, 28,* 394–407.

PURVIS, J. A., DABBS, J. M., & HOPPER, C. H. (1984). The "opener": Skilled user of facial expression and speech pattern. *Personality and Social Psychology Bulletin, 10,* 61–66.

RAGLAND, D. R., & BRAND, R. J. (1988). Type A behavior and mortality from coronary heart disease. *New England Journal of Medicine, 318*(2), 65–69.

RAINER, J. D., MESNIKOFF, A., KOLB, L. C., & CARR, A. (1960). Homosexuality and heterosexuality in identical twins. *Psychosomatic Medicine, 22,* 251–259.

RAMIREZ, A. (1988). Racism toward Hispanics: The cultural monolithic society. In P. A. Katz & D. A. Taylor (Eds.), *Eliminating racism: Profiles in controversy.* New York: Plenum.

RAMSAY, R. W. (1979). Bereavement: A behavioral treatment of pathological grief. In P. Sjoden, S. Bates, & W. S. Dockens (Eds.), *Trends in behavior therapy.* New York: Academic Press.

RAPOPORT, J. L. (1989). The biology of obsessions and compulsions. *Scientific American, 260*(3), 83–89.

RASCH, P. J. (1983). *Weight training.* Dubuque, IA: William C. Brown.

RATHUS, S. A., & NEVID, J. S. (1986). *Adjustment and growth: The challenges of life* (3rd ed.). New York: Holt, Rinehart, & Winston.

RAVUSSIN, E., LILLIOJA, S., KNOWLER, W. C., CHRISTIN, L., FREYMONA, D., ABBOTT, W. G., BOYCE, V., HOWARD, B. V., & BOGARDUS, C. (1988). Reduced rate of energy expenditure as a risk factor for body weight gain. *New England Journal of Medicine, 318,* 467–472.

REA, C. P., & MODIGLIANI, V. (1988). Educational implications of the spacing effect. In M. Gruneberg, P. E. Morris, & R. N. Sykes (Eds.), *Practical aspects of memory: Current research and issues.* Chichester, England: John Wiley.

REDER, L. M. (1985). Techniques available to author, teacher, and reader to improve retention of the main ideas of a chapter. In S. F. Chipman, J. W. Segal, & R. Glaser (Eds.), *Thinking and learning skills: Research and open questions* (vol. 2). Hillsdale, NJ: Lawrence Erlbaum.

REED, S. D. (1990). Behavioral medicine and behavior change. In F. H. Kanfer & A. P. Goldstein (Eds.), *Helping people change: A textbook of methods* (4th ed.). New York: Pergamon Press.

REED, T. (1980). Challenging some "common wisdom" on drug abuse. *International Journal of the Addictions, 15,* 359–373.

REGIER, D. A., MYERS, J. K., KRAMER, M., ROBINS, L. N., BLAZER, D. G., HOUGH, R. L., EATON, W. W., & LOCKE, B. Z. (1984). The NIMH epidemiologic catchment area program: Historical contact, major objectives, and study population characteristics. *Archives of General Psychiatry, 41*(10), 934–941.

REID, D. H., PARSONS, M. B., & GREEN, C. W. (1989). Treating aberrant behavior through effective staff management: A developing technology. In E. Cipani (Ed.), *The treatment of severe behavior disorders.* Washington, DC: American Association on Mental Retardation.

REID, W. H., & WISE, M. G. (1989). *DSM-III-R training guide.* New York: Brunner/Mazel.

REIF, A. E. (1981). The causes of cancer. *American Scientist, 69,* 437–447.

REIFMAN, A. S., LARRICK, R., & FEIN, S. (1988). The heat-aggression relationship in major league baseball. Paper presented at the American Psychological Association Convention.

REISSLAND, N. (1988). Neonatal imitation in the first hour of life: Observations in rural Nepal. *Developmental Psychology, 24,* 464–469.

RELMAN, A. (1982). Marijuana and health. *New England Journal of Medicine, 306,* 603–604.

RENWICK, P. A., & LAWLER, E. E. (1978). What you really want from your job. *Psychology Today, 11*(12), 53–65.

RENZETTI, C. M., & CURRAN, D. J. (1992). *Women, men, and society* (2nd ed.). Boston: Allyn & Bacon.

RICE, N. E., & GRUSEC, J. E. (1975). Saying and doing: Effects on observer performance. *Journal of Personality and Social Psychology, 32,* 584–593.

RIMM, D. C., HILL, G. A., BROWN, N. N., & STUART, J. E. (1974). Group assertive training in the treatment of expression of inappropriate anger. *Psychological Reports, 34,* 791–798.

ROBERT, M. (1990). Observational learning in fish, birds, and mammals: A classified bibliography spanning over 100 years of research. *The Psychological Record, 40,* 289–311.

ROBERTS, A. H. (1985). Biofeedback: Research, training, and clinical roles. *American Psychologist, 40,* 938–941.

ROBERTS, P., & NEWTON, P. M. (1987). Levinsonian studies of women's adult development. *Psychology and Aging, 2,* 154–163.

ROBERTS, R. N. (1979). Private speech in academic problem-solving: A naturalistic perspective. In G. Zevin (Ed.), *The development of self-regulation through private speech.* New York: John Wiley.

ROBERTS, R. N., & MULLIS, M. (1980, May). A component analysis of self-instructional training. Paper presented at the meeting of the Western Psychological Association, Honolulu.

ROBERTS, R. N., & THARP, R. G. (1980). A naturalistic study of children's self-directed speech in academic problem-solving. *Cognitive Research and Therapy, 4,* 341–353.

ROBINS, L. N., HELZER, J. E., WEISSMAN, M. M., ORVASCHEL, H., GRUENBERG, E., BURKE, J. D., & REGIER, D. A. (1984). Lifetime prevalence of specific psychiatric disorders in three sites. *Archives of General Psychiatry, 41,* 949–958.

ROBINSON, D. (1979). *Talking out of alcoholism: The self-help process of Alcoholics Anonymous.* London: Croom Helm.

ROBINSON, I., ZISS, B., GANZA, B., KATZ, S., & ROBINSON, E. (1991). Twenty years of the sexual revolution, 1965–1985: An update. *Journal of Marriage and the Family, 53,* 216–220.

ROBINSON, I. E., & JEDLICKA, D. (1982). Change in sexual attitudes and behavior for college students from 1965 to 1980: A research note. *Journal of Marriage and the Family, 44,* 237–240.

ROBINSON, I. E., KING, K., & BALSWICK, J. O.

(1972). The premarital sexual revolution among college students. *The Family Coordinator, 21,* 189–195.

ROBINSON, I. E., KING, K., DUDLEY, C. J., & CLUNE, F. J. (1968). Change in sexual behavior and attitudes of college students. *The Family Coordinator, 17,* 189–194.

ROBINSON, V. M. (1983). Humor and health. In P. E. McGhee & J. H. Goldstein (Eds.), *Handbook of humor research: Vol. 2. Applied studies.* New York: Springer/Verlag.

RODIN, J. (1981). Current status of the internal-external hypothesis for obesity: What went wrong? *American Psychologist, 36,* 361–372.

RODIN, J. (1986). Aging and health: Effects of the sense of control. *Science, 233,* 1271–1276.

ROGERS, C. R. (1951; 1970). *Client-centered therapy* (1st ed; 2nd ed.). Boston: Houghton-Mifflin.

ROGERS, C. R. (1961). *On becoming a person: A therapist's view of psychotherapy.* Boston: Houghton Mifflin.

ROGERS, C. R. (1980). *A way of being.* Boston: Houghton Mifflin.

ROHSENOW, D. J., BINKOFF, J. A., & NIAURA, R. S. (1988). Relevance of cue reactivity to understanding alcohol and smoking relapse. *Journal of Abnormal Psychology, 97,* 133–152.

ROLLINS, B. C., & CANNON, K. L. (1974). Marital satisfaction over the family life cycle: A reevaluation. *Journal of Marriage and the Family, 36,* 271–282.

ROONEY, A. (1991, October 2). Warriors must have an enemy. *The Winnipeg Sun,* p. 12.

ROSCH, E. (1974). Linguistic relativity. In A. Silverstein (Ed.), *Human communication: Theoretical perspectives.* New York: Helstead Press.

ROSCH, E. (1977). Classification of real world objects: Origins and representations in cognition. In P. N. Johnson-Laird & P. C. Wason (Eds.), *Thinking: Readings in cognitive science.* New York: Cambridge University Press.

ROSCOE, B., MARTIN, G. L., & PEAR, J. J. (1980). Systematic self-desensitization of fear of flying. In G. L. Martin & J. G. Osborne (Eds.), *Helping in the community: Behavioral applications.* New York: Plenum.

ROSE, S., & FRIEZE, I. H. (1989). Young singles' scripts for a first date. *Gender and Society, 3,* 258–268.

ROSEN, G. M., GLASGOW, R. E., & BARRERA, M., JR. (1976). A controlled study to assess the clinical efficacy of totally self-administered systematic desen-

sitization. *Journal of Consulting and Clinical Psychology, 44,* 208–217.

ROSEN, R. C., & BECK, J. G. (1988). *Patterns of sexual arousal.* New York: Guilford Press.

ROSENSTEIN, M. J., & MILAZZO-SAYRE, L. J. (1981). *Characteristics of admissions to selected mental-health facilities.* Rockville MD: U.S. Department of Health and Human Services.

ROSENTHAL, R. (1973). The Pygmalion effect lives. *Psychology Today, 7,* 56–63.

ROSENTHAL, R., & JACOBSON, L. F. (1968a). *Pygmalion in the classroom.* New York: Holt, Rinehart, & Winston.

ROSENTHAL, R., & JACOBSON, L. F. (1968b). Teacher expectations for the disadvantaged. *Scientific American, 218,* 19–23.

ROSENTHAL, T. L., & ROSENTHAL, R. H. (1985). Clinical stress management. In D. H. Barlow (Ed.), *Clinical handbook of psychological disorders: A step-by-step treatment manual.* New York: Guilford Press.

ROSS, M., LAYTON, B., ERICKSON, B., & SCHOPLER, J. (1973). Affect, facial regard, and reactions to crowding. *Journal of Personality and Social Psychology, 28,* 68–76.

ROTH, D., BEILSKI, R., JONES, M., PARKER, N., & OSBORN, G. (1982). A comparison of self-control therapy and anti-depressant medication in the treatment of depression. *Behavior Therapy, 13,* 133–144.

ROTHSTEIN, E. (1980, October 9). The scar of Sigmund Freud. *New York Review of Books,* pp. 14–20.

ROY, A., & LINNOILA, M. (1986). Alcoholism and suicide. In R. Maris (Ed.), *Biology of suicide.* New York: Guilford Press.

ROY-BYRNE, P. P., & KATON, W. (1987). An update on treatment of the anxiety disorders. *Hospital and Community Psychiatry, 38,* 835–886.

RUBENSTEIN, C. (1982). Psychology's fruit flies. *Psychology Today, 16*(7), 83–84.

RUBIN, L. B. (1983). *Intimate strangers.* New York: Harper & Row.

RUBIN, Z. (1970). Measurement of romantic love. *Journal of Personality and Social Psychology, 16,* 265–273.

RUBIN, Z. (1973). *Liking and loving: An invitation to social psychology.* New York: Holt, Rinehart, & Winston.

RUBIN, Z. (1974). From liking to loving: Patterns of attraction in dating relationships. In T. Huston (Ed.), *Foundations of interpersonal attraction.* New York: Academic Press.

RUBIN, Z., & MCNEIL, B. (1985). *Psychology: Being human* (4th ed.). New York: Harper & Row.

RUBONIS, A. V., & PICKMAN, L. (1991). Psychological impairment in the wake of disaster: The disaster-psychopathology relationship. *Psychological Bulletin, 109,* 384–399.

RUCH, L. O., & HOLMES, T. H. (1971). Scaling of life change: Comparison of direct and indirect methods. *Journal of Psychosomatic Research, 15,* 221–227.

RUKEYSER, L., COONEY, J., & WINSLOW, W. (1988). *Louis Rukeyser's business almanac.* New York: Simon & Schuster.

RUSHTON, J. P. (1975). Generosity in children: Immediate and long-term effects of modeling, preaching, and moral judgement. *Journal of Personality and Social Psychology, 31,* 459–466.

RUSSELL, D. E. H. (1984). *Sexual exploitation: Rape, child sexual abuse, and workplace harassment.* Beverly Hills, CA: Sage.

RUSSO, N. (1976). The motherhood mandate. *Journal of Personality and Social Psychology, 31,* 143–153.

SABATELLI, R. M. (1988). Exploring relationship satisfaction: A social exchange perspective on the interdependence between theory, research, and practice. *Family Relations, 37,* 217–222.

SACCO, W. P., & BECK, A. T. (1985). Cognitive therapy of depression. In E. E. Beckham & W. R. Leber (Eds.), *Handbook of depression: Treatment, assessment, and research.* Homewood, IL: Dorsey Press.

SACKETT, D. L., & SNOW, J. C. (1979). The magnitude of compliance and noncompliance. In R. B. Haynes, D. W. Taylor, & D. L. Sackett (Eds.), *Compliance in health care.* Baltimore: Johns Hopkins University Press.

SACKHEIM, H. A. (1985). The case for ECT. *Psychology Today, 19*(6), 35–40.

SADKER, M., & SADKER, D. (1985). Sexism in the schoolroom of the '80s. *Psychology Today, 19,* 54–56.

SADKER, M., SADKER, D., & BAUCHNER, J. (1984, April). *Teacher reactions to classroom responses of male and female students.* Paper presented at the Meeting of the American Educational Research Association, New Orleans, LA.

ST. JOHN-PARSONS, D. (1978). Continuous dual-career families: A case study. *Psychology of Women Quarterly, 3,* 30–42.

ST. LAWRENCE, J. S. (1987). Assessment of assertion. In M. Hersen, R. M. Eisler, & P. M. Miller (Eds.), *Progress in behavior modification* (vol. 21). Beverly Hills, CA: Sage.

SALTER, A. (1949). *Conditional reflex therapy.* New York: Farrar, Straus, & Giroux.

SALTHOUSE, T. A., & SOMBERG, G. L. (1982). Skilled performance: Effects of adult age and experience on elementary processes. *Journal of Experimental Psychology: General, 111,* 176–207.

SANDERS, B., & GIOLAS, M. H. (1991). Dissociation and childhood trauma in psychologically disturbed adolescents. *American Journal of Psychiatry, 148,* 50–54.

SANDERS, N. T. (1980). A comparison of two methods of training for the development of muscular strength and endurance. *Journal of Orthopaedic and Sports Physical Therapy, 1,* 210–213.

SANDLER, J., MYERSON, M., & KINDER, B. N. (1980). *Human sexuality: Current perspectives.* Tampa, FL: Mariner Publishing.

SANTROCK, J. W. (1987). *Adolescence: An introduction* (3rd ed.). Dubuque, IA: William C. Brown.

SARASON, I. G., & SARASON, B. R. (1989). *Abnormal psychology: The problem of maladaptive behavior* (6th ed.). Englewood Cliffs, NJ: Prentice Hall.

SARGENT, J. (1986). An improving job market for college graduates: The 1986 update of projections to 1995. *Occupational Outlook Quarterly, 30*(2), 3–7.

SARREL, L. J., & SARREL, P. M. (1981). Sexual unfolding. *Journal of Adolescent Health Care, 2,* 93–99.

SCHACHTER, S. (1971). *Emotion, obesity, and crime.* New York: Academic Press.

SCHACHTER, S. (1982). Recidivism and self-cure of smoking and obesity. *American Psychologist, 37,* 436–444.

SCHACHTER, S., & GROSS, L. P. (1968). Manipulated time and eating behavior. *Journal of Personality and Social Psychology, 10,* 98–106.

SCHACHTER, S., KOZLOWSKI, L. T., & SILVERSTEIN, B. (1977). Effects of urinary pH on cigarette smoking. *Journal of Experimental Psychology: General, 106,* 13–19.

SCHACHTER, S., & SINGER, J. E. (1962). Cognitive, social, and physiological determinants of emotional state. *Psychological Review, 69,* 379–399.

SCHANINGER, C. M., & BUSS, W. C. (1986). A longitudinal comparison of consumption and finance handling be-tween happily married and divorced couples. *Journal of Marriage and the Family, 48,* 129–136.

SCHERTZER, E. (1985). *Career planning: Freedom to choose* (3rd ed.). Lawrenceville, NJ: Houghton Mifflin.

SCHLIEFER, S. J., KELLER, S. E., CAMERINO, M., THORNTON, J. C., & STEIN, M. (1983). Suppression of lymphocyte stimulation following bereavement. *Journal of the American Medical Association, 250,* 364–377.

SCHMIED, L. A., & LAWLER, K. A. (1986). Hardiness, Type A behavior, and the stress–illness relation in working women. *Journal of Personality and Social Psychology, 51,* 1218–1223.

SCHNEIDMAN, E., FARBEROW, N., & LITMAN, R. (1961). The suicide prevention center. In N. Farberow & E. Schneidman (Eds.), *The cry for help.* New York: McGraw-Hill.

SCHOTTENFELD, R. S., & CULLEN, M. R. (1985). Occupation-induced post traumatic stress disorders. *American Journal of Psychiatry, 142,* 198–202.

SCHROEDER, D. H., & COSTA, P. T., JR. (1984). Influence of life event stress on physical illness: Substantive effects or methodological flaws? *Journal of Personality and Social Psychology, 46,* 853–863.

SCHULTZ, D. A., & WILSON, R. A. (1973). Some traditional family variables and their correlations with drug use among high school students. *Journal of Marriage and the Family, 35,* 628–631.

SCHULZE, R. H. K. (1962). A shortened version of the Rokeach Dogmatism Scale. *Journal of Psychological Studies, 13,* 93–97.

SCHWARTZ, B., & BARSKY, S. F. (1977). The home advantage. *Social Forces, 55,* 641–661.

Science, 1986, August 15, p. 723.

SCOTT, D. (1980). *How to put more time in your life.* New York: Rawson, Wade Publishers.

SCOVERN, A. W., & KILLMAN, P. R. (1980). Status of electroconvulsive therapy: Review of the outcome literature. *Psychological Bulletin, 87,* 260–303.

SELIGMAN, M. E. P. (1971). Phobias and preparedness. *Behavior Therapy, 2,* 307–321.

SELIGMAN, M. E. P. (1972). Phobias and preparedness. In M. E. P. Seligman & J. L. Hagar (Eds.), *Biological boundaries of learning.* New York: Appleton-Century-Crofts.

SELIGMAN, M. E. P. (1975). *Helplessness: On depression, development, and death.* San Francisco: W. H. Freeman.

SELYE, H. (1976). *The stress of life* (2nd ed.). New York: McGraw-Hill.

SELYE, H. (1980). The stress concept today. In I. L. Kutash, L. B. Schlesinger, et al. (Eds.), *Handbook of stress and anxiety.* San Francisco, CA: Jossey-Bass.

SELYE, H. (1982). History and present status of the stress concept. In L. Goldberger & S. Breznitz (Eds.), *Handbook of stress: Theoretical and clinical aspects.* New York: Free Press.

SEMANS, J. (1956). Premature ejaculation: A new approach. *Southern Medical Journal, 49,* 353–358.

SHAFFER, D. R., RUAMMAKE, C., & PEGALIS, L. J. (1990). The "opener": Highly skilled as interviewer or interviewee. *Personality and Social Psychology Bulletin, 16,* 511–520.

SHAW, G. A., & BELMORE, S. M. (1983). The relationship between imagery and creativity. *Imagination, Cognition and Personality, 2,* 115–123.

SHEKELLE, R. D., HULLEY, S. B., NEATON, J. D., BILLINGS, J. H., BORHANI, N. O., GERACE, T. A., JACOBS, D. R., LASSER, N. L., MITTLEMARK, M. B., & STAMLER, J. (1985). The MRFIT behavior pattern study: II. Type A behavior and incidence of coronary heart disease. *American Journal of Epidemiology, 122,* 559–570.

SHERMAN, L. W., & BERK, R. A. (1984). The specific deterrent effects of arrest for domestic assault. *American Sociological Review, 49,* 261–271.

SHERRINGTON, R., BRYNJOLFSSON, J., PETURSSON, H., POTTER, M., DUDLESTON, K., BARRACLOUGH, B., WASMUTH, J., DOBBS, M., & GURLING, H. (1988). Localization of a susceptibility locus for schizophrenia on chromosome 5. *Nature, 336,* 164–167.

SHERROD D. R. (1974). Crowding, perceived control, and behavioral aftereffects. *Journal of Applied Social Psychology, 4,* 171–186.

SHIPLEY, R. H. (1985). *Quit smart: A guide to freedom from cigarettes.* Durham, NC: J. B. Press.

SIEGEL, S. (1984). Pavlovian conditioning and heroin overdose: Reports by overdose victims. *Bulletin of Psychonomic Science, 22*(5), 428–430.

SIEGEL, S., HINSON, R. E., KRANK, N. D., & McCULLY, J. (1982). Heroin "overdose" death: The contribution of drug-associated environmental cues. *Science, 216,* 436–437.

SIEGLER, R. S. (1986). *Children's thinking.* Englewood Cliffs, NJ: Prentice Hall.

SIGAL, J. (1980). Physical environmental stressors. In M. S. Gibbs, J. R. Lachenmeyer, & J. Sigal (Eds.), *Community psychology: Theoretical and empirical approaches*. New York: Gardner Press.

SILVERMAN, I. (1983). *Pure types are rare: Myths and meanings of madness*. New York: Praeger.

SIMEK, T. C., & O'BRIEN, R. M. (1981). *Total golf: A behavioral approach to lowering your score and getting more out of your game*. Huntington, NY: B–Mod Associates.

SIMONS, A. D., MURPHY, G. E., LEVINE, J. L., & WETZEL, R. D. (1986). Cognitive therapy and pharmacotherapy for depression. *Archives of General Psychiatry, 43,* 43–48.

SIMPSON, J. A. (1987). The dissolution of romantic relationships: Factors involved in relationship stability and emotional distress. *Journal of Personality and Social Psychology, 53,* 683–692.

SIMPSON, J. A., CAMPBELL, B., & BERSCHEID, E. (1986). The association between romantic love and marriage: Kephart (1967) twice revisited. *Personality and Social Psychology Bulletin, 12,* 363–372.

SIMPSON, J. A., GANGESTAD, S. W., & LERMA, M. (1990). Perception of physical attractiveness: Mechanisms involved in the maintenance of romantic relationships. *Journal of Personality and Social Psychology, 59,* 1192–1201.

SINGER, D. (1989). Children, adolescents, and television. *Pediatrics, 83,* 445–446.

SIQUELAND, E., & LIPSITT, L. P. (1966). Conditioned head turning in human infants. *Journal of Experimental Child Psychology, 3,* 356–376.

SKINNER, B. F. (1938). *The behavior of organisms*. New York: Appleton-Century-Crofts.

SKINNER, B. F. (1948). *Walden II*. New York: Macmillan.

SKINNER, B. F. (1953). *Science and human behavior*. New York: Macmillan.

SKINNER, B. F. (1957). *Verbal behavior*. New York: Appleton-Century-Crofts.

SKINNER, B. F. (1974). *About behaviorism*. New York: Alfred A. Knopf.

SKINNER, B. F. (1987). Cognitive science and behaviorism. In B. F. Skinner (Ed.), *Upon further reflection*. Englewood Cliffs, NJ: Prentice Hall.

SKINNER, B. F. (1989). *Recent issues in the analysis of behavior*. Columbus, OH: Merrill.

SKINNER, B. F., & VAUGHAN, M. E. (1983). *Enjoy old age: A program of self-management*. New York: W. W. Norton.

SMITH, C., ELMIREZ, R., BERENBERG, J., & ASCH, R. (1983). Tolerance develops to the disruptive effects of delta 9-tetrahydrocannabinal on primate menstrual cycle. *Science, 219,* 1435–1455.

SMITH, D. G. (1976). The social content of pornography. *Journal of Communication, 26,* 16–33.

SMITH, E. E. (1988). Concepts and thought. In R. J. Sternberg & E. E. Smith (Eds.), *The psychology of human thought*. New York: Cambridge University Press.

SMITH, M., COLLIGAN, M., HORNING, R. W., & HURREL, J. (1978). *Occupational comparison of stress-related disease incidence*. Cincinnati: Cincinnati National Institute for Occupational Safety and Health.

SMITH, M. B. (1978). Psychology and values. *Journal of Social Issues, 34,* 181–199.

SMITH, M. L., GLASS, G. V., & MILLER, R. L. (1980). *The benefits of psychotherapy*. Baltimore: Johns Hopkins University Press.

SMITH, R. J. (1984). Polygraph tests: Dubious validity. *Science, 224,* 12–17.

SNIEZEK, J. A., & JAZWINSKI, C. H. (1986). Gender bias in English: In search of fair language. *Journal of Applied Social Psychology, 16,* 642–662.

SNOW, C. E. (1977). The development of conversation between mothers and babies. *Journal of Child Language, 4,* 1–22.

SNYDER, C. R., & SCHENKEL, R. J. (1975). The P. T. Barnum effect. *Psychology Today, 8*(10), 52–54.

SNYDER, S. H. (1984). Drug and neurotransmitter receptors in the brain. *Science, 224,* 22–31.

SOMMER, R. (1977, January). Toward a psychology of natural behavior. *APA Monitor,* 13–14.

SORENSON, R. C. (1973). *Adolescent sexuality in contemporary America*. Cleveland: World.

SPEECE, M. W., & BRENT, S. B. (1984). Children's understanding of death: Review of three components of a death concept. *Child Development, 55,* 1671–1686.

SPENCE, S. (1983). The training of heterosexual social skills. In S. Spence & G. Shepherd (Eds.), *Developments in social skills training*. New York: Academic Press.

SPIELBERGER, C. D. (1978). Fear Survey Schedule. In O. K. Buros (Ed.), *The eighth mental measurements yearbook* (Test No. 559). Highland Park, NJ: Gryphon Press.

SPITZER, R. L., SKODOL, A. E., GIBBON, M., & WILLIAMS, J. B. W. (1983). *Psychopathology: A case book*. New York: McGraw-Hill.

SPURR, J., & STEVENS, V. J. (1980). Increasing study time and controlling student guilt: A case study in self-management. *Behavior Therapist, 33,* 17–18.

STAATS, A. W. (1963). *Complex human behavior*. New York: Holt, Rinehart, & Winston.

STAATS, A. W. (1968). *Learning, language, and cognition*. New York: Holt, Rinehart, & Winston.

STAATS, A. W., STAATS, C. K., & CRAWFORD, H. L. (1962). First order conditioning of meaning and the parallel conditioning of a GSR. *Journal of General Psychology, 67,* 159–167.

STACHNIK, T. J. (1980). Priorities for psychology in medical education and health care delivery. *American Psychologist, 35,* 8–15.

STAINES, G. L., PLECK, J. H., SHEPARD, L. J., & O'CONNOR, P. (1978). Wives' employment status and marital adjustment: Yet another look. *Psychology of Women Quarterly, 3,* 90–120.

STANDING, L. (1973). Learning 10,000 pictures. *Quarterly Journal of Experimental Psychology, 25,* 207–222.

Statistical abstract of the United States, 110th ed. (1990). U.S. Department of Commerce, Bureau of Census, Washington, DC: Government Printing Office.

STECK, L., LEVITAN, D., McLANE, B., & KELLEY, H. H. (1982). Care, need, and conceptions of love. *Journal of Personality and Social Psychology, 43,* 481–491.

STEELE, C. M., CRITCHLOW, B., & LIU, T. J. (1985). Alcohol and social behavior II: The helpful drunkard. *Journal of Personality and Social Psychology, 48,* 35–46.

STEELE, C. M., & SOUTHWICK, L. (1985). Alcohol and social behavior I: The psychology of drunken excess. *Journal of Personality and Social Psychology, 48,* 18–34.

STEINEM, G. (1980). Erotica and pornography: A clear and present difference. In L. Lederer (Ed.), *Take back the night: Women on pornography*. New York: William Morrow.

STELMACK, R. M. (1990). Biological bases of extraversion: Psychophysiological evidence. *Journal of Personality, 58,* 293–311.

STEPHAN, W. G. (1986). The effects of school desegregation: An evaluation thirty years after *Brown*. In R. Kidd, L. Saxe, & M. Saks (Eds.), *Advances in applied social psychology*. New York: Lawrence Erlbaum.

STERN, G. S., McCANTS, T. R., & PETTINE, P. W. (1982). Stress and illness: Controllable and uncontrollable events' relative contributions. *Personality and Social Psychology Bulletin, 8*(1), 140–145.

STERNBERG, R. J. (1986). Triangular theory of love. *Psychological Review, 93,* 119–135.

STERNBERG, R. J., & GRAJEK, S. (1984). The nature of love. *Journal of Personality and Social Psychology, 47,* 312–329.

STEVENS, J. R. (1982). Neuropathology of schizophrenia. *Archives of General Psychiatry, 39,* 1131–1139.

STILLION, J. M., McDOWELL, E. E., & MAY, J. H. (1989). *Suicide across the life span–Premature exits*. New York: Hemisphere Publishing.

STOKOLS, D., NOVACO, R. W., STOKOLS, J., & CAMPBELL, J. (1978). Traffic congestion, Type A behavior, and stress. *Journal of Applied Psychology, 63,* 467–480.

STRAND, P. Z. (1970). Change of context and retroactive inhibition. *Journal of Verbal Learning and Verbal Behavior, 9,* 202–206.

STRASSBURG, D. S., ADELSTEIN, T. B., & CHEMERS, M. M. (1988). Adjustment and disclosure reciprocity. *Journal of Social and Clinical Psychology, 7,* 234–245.

STRAUSS, M. A. (1980). A sociological perspective on the causes of family violence. In M. R. Green (Ed.), *Violence and the family*. Boulder CO: Westview Press.

STRAUSS, M. A. (1991). Physical violence in American families: Incidence rates, causes, and trends. In D. D. Knudsen & J. L. Miller (Eds.), *Abused and battered: Social and legal responses to family violence*. New York: Aldine de Gruyter.

STUNKARD, A. (1980). *Obesity*. Philadelphia, PA: W. B. Saunders.

STUNKARD, A., SORENSON, T., HANIS, C., TEASDALE, T., CHAKRABORTY, R., SCHALL, W., & SCHUSLINGER, F. (1986). An adoption study of human obesity. *New England Journal of Medicine, 14,* 193–198.

SUAREZ, S. D., & GALLUP, G. G. (1979). Tonic immobility as a response to rape in humans: A theoretical note. *Psychological Record, 29,* 315–320.

SULLIVAN, H. S. (1953). *The interpersonal theory of psychiatry*. New York: W. W. Norton.

SUNDSTROM, E. (1975). An experimental study of crowding: Effects of room size, intrusion, and goal blocking on nonverbal behavior, self-disclosure, and self-reported stress. *Journal of Personality and Social Psychology, 32,* 645–654.

SWENSEN, C. H., ESKEW, R. W., & KOHLEPP, K. A. (1981). Stage of family life cycle, ego development, and the marriage relationship. *Journal of Marriage and the Family, 43,* 841–853.

SWENSEN, C. H., & TRAHAUG, G. (1985). Commitment and the long-term marriage relationship. *Journal of Marriage and the Family, 47,* 939–945.

SZASZ, T. (1961). *The myth of mental illness*. New York: Harper & Row.

SZASZ, T. (1989). *Law, liberty, and psychiatry: An inquiry into the social pressures of mental health practices*. Syracuse, NY: Syracuse University Press.

SZASZ, T. (1991). Noncoercive psychiatry: An oxymoron, reflections on law, liberty, and psychiatry. *Journal of Humanistic Psychology, 31,* 117–125.

SZASZ, T. S. (1960). The myth of mental illness. *American Psychologist, 15,* 113–118.

SZASZ, T. S. (1987). *Insanity: The idea and its consequences*. New York: John Wiley.

SZILAGYI, A. D., JR., & WALLACE, M. J., JR. (1983). *Organizational behavior and performance* (3rd ed.). Glenview, IL: Scott Foresman.

TAJFEL, H., & TURNER, J. (1985). The social identity of intergroup behavior. In S. Worschel & W. Austin (Eds.), *Psychology of intergroup relations* (2nd ed.). Chicago, IL: Nelson Hall.

TANNER, J. M., WHITEHOUSE, R. H., & TAKAISHI, M. (1965). Standards from birth to maturity for height, weight height velocity, and weight velocity: British children. *Archives of the Diseases of Childhood, 41,* 845–872.

TAVRIS, C. (1984). *Anger: The misunderstood emotion*. New York: Simon & Schuster/Touchstone.

TAYLOR, C. B., BANDURA, A., EWART, C. K., MILLER, N. H., & DeBUSK, R. F. (1985). Exercise testing to enhance wives' confidence in their husbands' cardiac capability soon after clinically uncomplicated acute myocardial infarction. *American Journal of Cardiology, 55,* 635–638.

TAYLOR, M. C., & HALL, J. A. (1982). Psychological androgyny: Theories, methods, and conclusions. *Psychological Bulletin, 92,* 347–366.

TAYLOR, S. E. (1983). Adjustment to threatening events. *American Psychologist, 38,* 1161–1173.

TAYLOR, S. E. (1986). *Health psychology*. New York: Random House.

TAYLOR, S. E. (1990). Health psychology: The science and the field. *American Psychologist, 45,* 40–50.

TEACHMAN, J. D., & POLONKO, K. A. (1990). Cohabitation and marital stability in the United States. *Social Forces, 69,* 207–220.

TELCH, M., AGRAS, W. S., TAYLOR, C. B., ROTH, W. T., & GALLEN, C. C. (1985). Combined pharmacological and behavioral treatment for agoraphobia. *Behavior Research and Therapy, 23,* 325–335.

TEMPLER, D. I., & RUFF, C. F. (1971). Death Anxiety Scale means, standard deviations, and embedding. *Psychological Reports, 29,* 173–174.

TERKEL, L. (1974). *Working: People talk about what they do all day and how they feel about what they do*. New York: Pantheon Books.

TEST, D. W., SPOONER, F., KEUL, P. K., & GROSSI, T. (1990). Teaching adolescents with severe disabilities to use the public telephone. *Behavior Modification, 14,* 157–171.

THOMPSON, J. K. (1986). Larger than life. *Psychology Today, 20*(4), 39–44.

THOMPSON, L., & WALKER, A. J. (1989). Gender in Families: Women and men in marriage, work, and parenthood. *Journal of Marriage and the Family, 51,* 845–871.

THOMPSON, L. W., BRECKENRIDGE, J. N., GALLAGHER, D., & PETERSON, J. (1984). Effects of bereavement on self-perceptions of physical health in elderly widows and widowers. *Journal of Gerontology, 39,* 309–314.

THORNDIKE, P. W., & HAYES-ROTH, B. (1979). The use of schemata in the acquisition and transfer of knowledge. *Cognitive Psychology, 11,* 83–106.

THORNTON, A. (1985). Changing attitudes toward divorce and separation: Causes and consequences. *American Journal of Sociology, 90,* 857–872.

THORNTON, A., & RODGERS, W. L. (1987). The influence of individual and historical time on marital dissolution. *Demography, 24,* 1–22.

TIFFANY, S. T., MARTIN, E. M., & BAKER, T. B. (1986). Treatments for cigarette smoking: An evaluation of aversive and counseling procedures. *Behavior Research and Therapy, 24,* 437–452.

TOBACYK, J., & MILLER, M. (1991). Comment on "Maslow's study of self-actualization." *Journal of Humanistic Psychology, 31*, 96–98.

TOBY, J. (1966). Violence and the masculine ideal: Some qualitative data. In S. K. Steinmetz & M. A. Strauss (Eds.), *Violence in the family*. New York: Harper & Row.

TOMKINS, S. S. (1981). The quest for primary motives: Biography and autobiography of an idea. *Journal of Personality and Social Psychology, 41*, 306–329.

TORGERSEN, S. (1983). Genetic factors in anxiety disorders. *Archives of General Psychiatry, 40*, 1085–1089.

TORGERSEN, S. (1986). Genetics of somatoform disorders. *Archives of General Psychiatry, 43*, 502–505.

TOUFEXIS, A. (1986, January). Dieting: The losing game. *Time*, pp. 52–58.

TRELEASE, M. L. (1975). Dying among Alaskan Indians: A matter of choice. In E. Kubler-Ross (Ed.), *Death: The final stage of growth*. Englewood Cliffs, NJ: Prentice Hall.

TRIMBLE, J. E. (1988). Stereotypical images, American Indians, and prejudice. In P. A. Katz & D. A. Taylor, (Eds.), *Eliminating racism: Profiles in controversy*. New York: Plenum.

TUPES, E. C., & CHRISTAL, R. E. (1961). *Recurrent personality factors based on trait ratings*. (USAF ASD Technical Report #61-97). Lackland Airforce Base, TX: U.S. Air Force.

TURKKAN, J. S. (1989). Classical conditioning: The new hegemony. *Behavioral and Brain Sciences, 12*, 121–179.

TURLA, P., & HAWKINS, K. L. (1983). *Time management made easy*. New York: E. P. Dutton.

TURNER, R. M., DiTOMASSO, R. A., & DELUTY, M. (1985). Systematic desensitization. In R. M. Turner & L. M. Ascher (Eds.), *Evaluating behavior therapy outcome*. New York: Springer.

TURNER, S. M., HOLTZMAN, A., & JACOB, R. G. (1983). Treatment of compulsive looking by imaginal thought-stopping. *Behavior Modification, 7*, 576–582.

TYRON, W. W., & CICERO, S. D. (1989). Classical conditioning of meaning—I. A replication and higher-order extension. *Journal of Behavior Therapy and Experimental Psychiatry, 20*, 137–142.

ULRICH, R. E., & AZRIN, N. H. (1962). Reflexive fighting in response to aversive stimulation. *Journal of the Experimental Analysis of Behavior, 5*, 511–520.

ULRICH, R. E., STACHNIK, T. J., & STAINTON, N. R. (1963). Student acceptance of generalized personality interpretations. *Psychological Reports, 13*, 831–834.

UPPER, D., CAUTELA, J. R., & BROOK, J. M. (1975). Behavioral self-rating checklist. Described in J. R. Cautela & D. Upper, The process of individual behavior therapy. In M. Hersen, R. M. Eisler, & P. M. Miller (Eds.), *Progress in behavior modification* (vol. 1). New York: Academic Press.

U.S. COMMISSION ON OBSCENITY AND PORNOGRAPHY (1970). *The report of the Commission on Obscenity and Pornography*. Washington, DC: U.S. Government Printing Office.

U.S. CONGRESS, HOUSE SELECT COMMITTEE ON AGING (1980). *The status of mid-life women and options for their future*. Washington, DC: U.S. Government Printing Office. Committee Publication No. 96-215.

U.S. CONGRESS, OFFICE OF TECHNOLOGY ASSESSMENT (1983, November). *Scientific validity of polygraph testing: A research review and evaluation—A technical memorandum* (p. 4). Washington, DC: U.S. Government Printing Office.

U.S. DEPARTMENT OF AGRICULTURE (1990). *Nutrition and your health: Dietary guidelines for Americans* (3rd ed.). Home & Garden Bulletin #232. Washington, DC: U.S. Government Printing Office.

U.S. DEPARTMENT OF COMMERCE (1990). *Statistical abstract of the United States, 1990*. Washington, DC: U.S. Government Printing Office.

U.S. DEPARTMENT OF HEALTH AND HUMAN SERVICES (1990). *The health consequences of smoking cessation: A report of the Surgeon General*. USDHHS, Public Health Service, Office of the Assistant Secretary for Health, Office on Smoking and Health.

U.S. DEPARTMENT OF HEALTH AND HUMAN SERVICES. Alcohol, Drug Abuse, and Mental Health Administration. (1990). *Drug use among American high school students and other young adults. National trends through 1987*. Washington, DC: U.S. Government Printing Office.

U.S. NATIONAL CENTER FOR HEALTH STATISTICS. (1988). *Vital statistics of the United States 1988*. Washington, DC: U.S. Government Printing Office.

VALINS, S. (1966). Cognitive effects of false heart-rate feedback. *Journal of Personality and Social Psychology, 4*, 400–408.

VALINS, S., & BAUM, A. (1973). Residential group size, social interaction and crowding. *Environment and Behavior, 5*, 421–440.

VAN FOSSEN, S., & BECK, J. (1991). Women opening doors to nontraditional occupations: A future with options. *Vocational Education Journal, 66*(4), 26–27.

VAN STADEN, F. J. (1987). White South Africans' attitudes toward the desegregation of public amenities. *Journal of Social Psychology, 127*, 163–173.

VISINTAINER, M., VOLPICELLI, J. R., & SELIGMAN, M. E. P. (1982). Tumor rejection in rats after inescapable or escapable shock. *Science, 216*, 437–439.

VOGLER, R. E., WEISBACH, T. A., & COMPTON, J. V. (1977). Learning techniques for alcohol abuse. *Behavior Research and Therapy, 15*, 31–38.

VON HALLER GILMER, B. (1973). Instructor's manual to accompany B. von Haller Gilmer, *Psychology*. New York: Harper & Row.

VYGOTSKY, L. S. (1965). *Thought and language*. Ed. and Trans. E. Hantmann and G. Vokar. Cambridge, MA: MIT Press.

VYGOTSKY, L. S. (1978). *Mind and society*. Cambridge, MA: Harvard University Press.

WADE, T. C., & BAKER, T. B. (1977). Opinions and use of psychological tests: A survey of clinical psychologists. *American Psychologist, 32*, 874–882.

WAHLER, R. G., WINKEL, G. H., PETERSON, R. F., & MORRISON, D. C. (1965). Mothers as behavior therapists for their own children. *Behavior Research and Therapy, 3*, 113–124.

WALKER, C. E., HEDBERG, A., CLEMENT, P. W., & WRIGHT, L. (1981). *Clinical procedures for behavior therapy*. Englewood Cliffs, NJ: Prentice Hall.

WALLACE, B., & FISHER, L. E. (1987). *Consciousness and behavior* (2nd ed.). Boston, MA: Allyn & Bacon.

WALLACE, I. (1971). *The writing of one novel*. Richmond Hill, Ontario: Simon & Schuster/Pocket Books.

WALLACE, J. (1985). The alcoholism controversy. *American Psychologist, 40*, 372–373.

WALLACH, M. A., & WALLACH, L. (1983). *Psychology's sanction for selfishness: The error of egoism in theory and therapy*. New York: W. H. Freeman.

WALLIS, C. (1983, June 6). Stress: Can we cope? *Time,* pp. 48–54.

WALSTER, E., WALSTER, G. W., PILIAVIN, J., & SCHMIDT, L. (1973). "Playing hard to get": Understanding an elusive phenomenon. *Journal of Personality and Social Psychology, 26,* 113–121.

WALTER, T., & SIEBERT, A. (1976). *Student success: How to be a better student and still have time for your friends.* New York: Holt, Rinehart, & Winston.

WARD, T., & LEWIS, S. (1987). The influence of alcohol and loud music on analytic and holistic processing. *Perception and Psychophysics, 41,* 179–186.

WARNER, R. (1985). *Recovery from schizophrenia.* Boston: Routledge & Kegan Paul.

WATSON, J. B. (1913). Psychology as the behaviorist views it. *Psychological Review, 20,* 158–177.

WATSON, J. B., & RAYNER, R. (1920). Conditioned emotional reactions. *Journal of Experimental Psychology, 3,* 1–14.

WAXMAN, S. R. (1990). Linguistic biases and the establishment of conceptual hierarchies: Evidence from preschool children. *Cognitive Development, 5,* 123–150.

WEBBER, R. A. (1980). *A guide to getting things done.* New York: Free Press.

Webster's new 20th century unabridged dictionary (1977). Buenos Aires: College World.

WEIGEL, R., & WEIGEL, J. (1978). Environmental concern: The development of a measure. *Environment and Behavior, 10,* 3–15.

WEINBURGER, D. R., DeLISI, L. E., PERMAN, G. P., TARGUM, S., & WYATT, R. J. (1982). Computer tomography in schizophreniform disorder and other acute psychiatric disorders. *Archives of General Psychiatry, 39,* 778–783.

WEINER, A. (1980). Self-Image Checklist. In R. Aero & A. Weiner (Eds.), *The mind test: 37 classic psychological tests you can now score and analyze yourself.* New York: William Morrow.

WEINER, M. J., & WRIGHT, F. E. (1973). Effects of undergoing arbitrary discrimination upon subsequent attitudes toward a minority group. *Journal of Applied Social Psychology, 3,* 94–102.

WEINER, R. D. (1984). Does electroconvulsive therapy cause brain damage? *The Behavioral and Brain Sciences, 7,* 1–53.

WEINGARTEN, K. (1978). The employ-ment pattern of professional couples and their distribution of involvement in the family. *Psychology of Women Quarterly, 3,* 43–52.

WEISS, J. M. (1977). Psychological and behavioral influences on gastrointestinal lesions in animal models. In J. D. Maser & M. E. P. Seligman (Eds.), *Psychopathology: Experimental models.* San Francisco: W. H. Freeman.

WEISS, R. S. (1982). Issues in the study of loneliness. In L. A. Peplau & D. Perlman (Eds.), *Loneliness: A sourcebook of current theory, research and therapy.* New York: John Wiley.

WEITZMAN, L. J. (1979). *Sex role socialization.* Palo Alto, CA: Mayfield Publishing.

WEITZMAN, L. J. (1985). *The divorce revolution.* New York: Free Press.

WENRICH, W., DAWLEY, H., & GENERAL, D. (1976). *Self-directed systematic desensitization.* Kalamazoo, MI: Behaviordelia.

"Where next with psychiatric illness?" *Nature, 336,* 95–96.

WHITBOURNE, S. K., & WEINSTOCK, C. S. (1986). *Adult development* (2nd ed.). New York: Praeger.

WHITE, L., & TURSKY, B. (Eds.) (1982). *Clinical biofeedback: Efficacy and mechanisms.* New York: Guilford Press.

WHITLY, M. P., & POULSEN, S. B. (1975). Assertiveness and sexual satisfaction in employed professional women. *Journal of Marriage and the Family, 37,* 573–581.

WHITNEY, E. N., & CATALDO, C. B. (1987). *Understanding normal and clinical nutrition.* St. Paul, MN: West.

WHORF, B. L. (1956). Science and linguistics. In J. B. Carroll (Ed.), *Language, thought, and reality: Selected writings of Benjamin Lee Whorf.* Cambridge, MA: MIT Press.

WHYBROW, P. C., AKISKAL, H. S., & McKINNEY, W. T. (1984). *Mood disorders: Toward a new psychobiology.* New York: Plenum.

WICKES, I. G. (1958). Treatment of persistent enuresis with the electric buzzer. *Archives of Diseases in Childhood, 33,* 160–164.

WIDOM, C. (1989). Does violence beget violence? A critical examination of the literature. *Psychological Bulletin, 106,* 3–28.

WIEBE, D. J. (1991). Hardiness and stress moderation: A test of proposed mechanisms. *Journal of Personality and Social Psychology, 60,* 89–99.

WIENS, A. N., & MENUSTIK, C. E. (1983). Treatment outcome and patient characteristics in an aversion therapy program for alcoholism. *American Psychologist, 38,* 1089–1096.

WILCOXIN, H. C., DRAGOIN, W. B., & KRAL, P. A. (1971). Illness-induced aversions in rat and quail: Relative salience of visual and gustatory cues. *Science, 171,* 826–828.

WILDER, D. A., & SHAPIRO, P. (1991). Facilitation of out group stereotypes by enhanced in group identity. *Journal of Experimental Social Psychology, 27,* 431–452.

WILHITE, S. C. (1988). Headings as memory facilitators. In M. Gruneberg, P. E. Morris, & R. N. Sykes (Eds.), *Practical aspects of memory: Current research and issues.* Chichester, England: John Wiley.

WILLIAMS, N. A., & DEFFENBACHER, J. L. (1983). Life stress and chronic yeast infections. *Journal of Human Stress, 9*(1), 26–31.

WILLIAMS, R. L., & LONG, J. D. (1979). *Toward a self-managed lifestyle* (2nd ed.). Boston: Houghton Mifflin.

WILSON, B. A. (1987). *Rehabilitation of memory.* New York: Guilford Press.

WINCE, J. P., LEITENBERG, H., & AGRAS, W. S. (1972). The effects of token reinforcement and feedback on the delusional behavior of chronic paranoid schizophrenics. *Journal of Applied Behavior Analysis, 5,* 247–262.

WINDLE, M., & MILLER-TUTZAUER, C. (1991). Antecedents and correlates of alcohol, cocaine, and alcohol–cocaine abuse in early adulthood. *Journal of Drug Education, 21,* 133–148.

WINER, D. (1978). Anger and dissociation: A case study of multiple personality. *Journal of Abnormal Psychology, 87,* 368–372.

WINSBOROUGH, H. H. (1965). The social consequences of high population density. *Law and Contemporary Problems, 30,* 120–126.

WOLF, M. (1984). *The complete book of nautilus training.* Chicago, IL: Contemporary Books.

WOLPE, J. (1958). *Psychotherapy by reciprocal inhibition.* Stanford, CA: Stanford University Press.

WOLPE, J. (1969; 1982; 1989). *The practice of behavior therapy* (1st ed.; 2nd ed.; 4th ed.). Elsmford, NY: Pergamon Press.

WOLPE, J., & LAZARUS, A. A. (1966). *Behavior therapy techniques: A guide to the treatment of neuroses.* New York: Pergamon Press.

WORTHY, M., GARY, A. L., & KAHN, G. M. (1969). Self-disclosure as an exchange process. *Journal of Personality and Social Psychology, 13,* 59–63.

WU, T. C., TASHKIN, D. P., DJAHED, B., & ROSE, J. E. (1988). Pulmonary hazards of smoking marijuana as compared with tobacco. *New England Journal of Medicine, 318,* 347–351.

YATE, M. (1991). *Knock 'em dead* (4th ed.). Holbrook, MA: Bob Adams, Inc. Publishers.

YODER, J. D., & NICHOLS, R. C. (1980). A life perspective comparison of married and divorced persons. *Journal of Marriage and the Family, 42,* 413–419.

YOUNG, J. E. (1982). Loneliness, depression, and cognitive therapy: Theory and application. In L. A. Peplau & D. Perlman (Eds.), *Loneliness: A sourcebook of current theory, research and therapy.* New York: John Wiley.

ZAJONC, R. B. (1968). Attitudinal effects of mere exposure. *Journal of Personality and Social Psychology Monograph Supplement, 9*(2), 1–27.

ZAJONC, R. B. (1984). On the primacy of affect. *American Psychologist, 39,* 117–123.

ZAMULA, E. (1989, June). Drugs and pregnancy: Often the two don't mix. *FDA Consumer Magazine,* DHHS Publication No. (FDA) 90-3174.

ZAX, M., & COWAN, E. L. (1976). *Abnormal psychology: Changing conceptions* (2nd ed.). New York: Holt, Rinehart, & Winston.

ZELNICK, M., & KANTNER, J. (1980). Sexual activity, contraceptive use, and pregnancy among metropolitan area teenagers: 1971–1979. *Family Planning Perspectives, 12,* 23–237.

ZEMAN, F. J. (1991). *Clinical nutrition and dietetics.* New York: Macmillan.

ZISOOK, S., & DEVAUL, R. A. (1983). Grief, unresolved grief, and depression. *Psychosomatics, 24,* 247–254.

ACKNOWLEDGMENTS

The authors and the publisher appreciate permission granted by the following individuals and organizations for use of illustrations, data, or text.

1: Laimute Druskis
3: Ken Karp
5: Marc Anderson
Box 1-2: Nicholls, S. (29 March 1989). *Winnipeg Free Press*. Reprinted with permission of The Canadian Press.
14: Michael Siluk/The Image Works
16: Royal Viking Line
19: Larry Murphy/University of Texas at Austin News & Information Service
Figure 1-1: Adapted from Allen, K. E., Hart, B., Buell, J. S., Harris, F. R., & Wolf, M. M. (1964). Effects of social reinforcement on isolate behavior of a nursery school child. *Child Development, 35,* 511–518. Reprinted with permission of The Society for Research in Child Development.
21: *Peanuts.* Reprinted by permission of United Features Syndicate, Inc.
23: Laimute Druskis
30: Laimute Druskis
Table 1-3: Reprinted with permission of the University of California Student Health Center.
36: Ken Karp
38: AP/Wide World Photos
Table 2-2: McRae, R., & Costa, P. T., Jr. (1986). Clinical assessment can benefit from recent advances in personality psychology. *American Psychologist, 41(9),* 1001–1003. Copyright © 1986 by the American Psychological Association. Adapted by permission of publisher and author.
Figure 2-1: Adapted from Eysenck, H. J. (1967). *The biological basis of behavior.* Springfield, IL: Charles C Thomas. Courtesy Charles C Thomas, Publisher, Springfield, IL.
42: Bob Daemmrich/The Image Works
Figure 2-2: Cattell, R. (1973). Reprinted with permission from *Psychology Today Magazine.* Copyright © 1973 (Sussex Publishers, Inc.).
45: Laimute Druskis
Figure 2-3: *Prentice Hall Transparencies for Psychology,* Series 1, 1985. Reprinted with permission of Prentice-Hall, Inc.
48: *Left*—Major Morris; *right*—Charles Gatewood
Figure 2-4: Charles G. Morris, PSYCHOLOGY: An Introduction, 7/E, © 1990, p. 479. Reprinted by permission of Prentice-Hall, Inc., Englewood Cliffs, NJ.
54: Van Bucher/Photo Researchers, Inc.
57: Ken Karp
58: Ken Karp

59: Bandura, A. (1986). *Social foundations of thought and action: A social cognitive theory.* Englewood Cliffs, NJ: Prentice-Hall, Inc.
60: Wahler, R. G., Winkel, G. H., Peterson, R. F., & Morrison, D. C. (1965). Mothers as behavior therapists for their own children. *Behavior Research and Therapy, 3,* 113–124.
62: Laimute Druskis
62: *Peanuts.* Reprinted by permission of United Features Syndicate, Inc.
Table 2-3: Adapted material from Maslow, A. H. (1970). *Motivation and personality* (2nd ed.). New York: Harper & Row. Copyright © 1954 by Harper & Row, Publishers, Inc. Copyright © 1970 by Abraham H. Maslow. Reprinted by permission of HarperCollins Publishers.
Box 2-4: "Self-Image Checklist" from *The Mind Test.* Copyright © 1981 by Rita Aero and Elliot Weiner. Published by William Morrow Co. All rights reserved. Used with permission.
Table 2-4: Upper, D., Cautela, J. R., & Brook, J. M. (1975). Behavioral self-rating checklist. Described in J. R. Cautela & D. Upper, The process of individual behavior therapy. In M. Hersen, R. M. Eisler & P. M. Miller (Eds.), *Progress in behavior modification* (vol. 1). New York: Academic Press. Reprinted with permission of publisher and author.
73: James Carroll
75: Photofest
Table 3-1: Baldwin, J. O., & Baldwin, J. I. (1986). *Behavior principles in everyday living* (2nd ed.). Englewood Cliffs, NJ: Prentice-Hall, Inc.
81: Los Angeles Police Department
83: John Isaac/United Nations
84: Len Rue, Jr./Monkmeyer Press
86: Toni Michaels/The Image Works
88: *Arlo & Janis.* Reprinted by permission of NEA, Inc.
90: Mimi Forsyth/Monkmeyer Press
93: Teri Leigh Stratford
96: Bandura, A., Ross, D., & Ross, S. (1963). Imitation of film-mediated aggressive models. *Journal of Abnormal and Social Psychology, 66,* 3–11. Copyright © 1963 by the American Psychological Association. Used with permission.
102: Arlington Child Development Center
103: Laimute Druskis
106: *The Family Circus.* Reprinted by permission of King Features Syndicate, Inc.
108: Ken Karp
110: Spencer Grant/Photo Researchers
113: Reuters/Bettman

Figure 4-3: Kimble, G., & Garmezy, N. (1963). *Principles of general psychology* (2nd ed.). Copyright © 1963 by John Wiley & Sons. Reprinted by permission of John Wiley & Sons, Inc., and author.

118: *Left* & *middle*—Teri Leigh Stratford; *right*—Steve Takatsuno

119: Peter Vandermark/Stock, Boston

121: From P. Ekman & W. V. Friesen, *Unmasking the Face*, Englewood Cliffs, NJ: Prentice Hall, 1975, p. 27.

126: Irene Springer

Figure 4-5: Millenson, J. R. (1967). *Principles of behavioral analysis*. New York: Macmillan. Copyright © 1967 by J. R. Millenson. Reprinted with permission of Macmillan Publishing Co.

136: Larry Fleming

138: AP/Wide World Photos

Figure 5-1: Lazarus, R. S., & Folkman, S. (1984). *Stress, appraisal, and coping*. New York: Springer.

141: *Left*—Laimute Druskis; *right*—Smithsonian Institution

Table 5-1: Holmes, T. H., & Rahe, R. H. (1967). The social readjustment rating scale. *Journal of Psychosomatic Research, 11,* 213–218. Reprinted with permission of Pergamon Press, Inc.

Ruch, L. O., & Holmes, T. H. (1970). Scaling of life change: Comparison of direct and indirect methods. *Journal of Psychosomatic Research, 15,* 221–227. Reprinted with permission of Pergamon Press, Inc.

Muhlenkamp, A. F., Gress, L. D., & Flood, N. A. (1975). Perception of life change events by the elderly. *Nursing Research, 24,* 109–113. Copyright © 1975 by the American Journal of Nursing Co. Used with permission. All rights reserved.

Table 5-2: Kanner, A. D., Coyne, J. C., Schaefer, C., & Lazarus, R. S. (1981). Comparison of two modes of stress measurement: Daily hassles and uplifts versus major life events. *Journal of Behavioral Medicine, 4,* 1–39. Reprinted with permission of Plenum Publishing Co. and author.

146: Ken Karp

148: *Hagar the Horrible*. Reprinted by permission of King Features Syndicate, Inc.

149: Alan Carey/The Image Works

Figure 5-2: Adapted from Selye, H. (1976). *The stress of life* (2nd ed.). New York: McGraw-Hill. Copyright © 1956 by McGraw-Hill, Inc. Reproduced with permission of McGraw-HIll, Inc.

151: Laimute Druskis

154: NASA

160: Peter Southwick/Stock, Boston

167: Mark Antman/The Image Works

169: *Left*—James Carroll; *middle*—Spencer Grant/Monkmeyer Press; *right*—Kopstein/Monkmeyer Press

Table 6-1: Cooper, K. H. (1982). *The aerobics program for total well being: Exercise, diet, emotional balance.* New York: Bantam Books. Copyright © 1982 by Kenneth H. Cooper, M.D., M. P. H. Used by permission of Bantam Books, a division of Bantam Doubleday Dell Publishing Group, Inc.

Box 6-2: O'Donnell, M. P., & Ainsworth, T. H. (1984). *Health promotion in the workplace.* New York: John Wiley.

Table 6-2: Cooper, K. H. (1982). *The aerobics program for total well being: Exercise, diet, emotional balance.* New York: Bantam Books. Copyright © 1982 by Kenneth H. Cooper, M. D., M. P. H. Used by permission of Bantam Books, a division of Bantam Doubleday Dell Publishing Group, Inc.

Table 6-3B: Reprinted with permission of the Metropolitan Life Insurance Co.

180: Laimute Druskis

184: *Hagar the Horrible.* Reprinted with permission of King Features Syndicate, Inc.

Table 6-4: Farquhar, J. W. (1978). *The American way of life need not be hazardous to your health.* New York: W. W. Norton.

187: Mark Antman/The Image Works

188: Larry Kolvoord/The Image Works

191: Michael Siluk/The Image Works

197: Shirley Zeiberg

204: Spencer Grant/The Picture Cube

205: Harriet Gans/The Image Works

Figure 7-3: Masters, W. H., & Johnson, V. E. (1965). The sexual response cycles of the human male and female. In F. A. Beach (Ed.), *Sex and behavior.* New York: Wiley. Reprinted with permission.

213: Ken Karp

Table 7-1: Robinson, I., Ziss, B., Ganza, B., Katz, S., & Robinson, E. (1991). *Journal of Marriage and the Family, 53,* 216–220.

217: John Chiasson/Gamma-Liaison

Figure 7-4: Feldman P., & MacCulloch, M. (1980). *Human sexual behavior.* New York: John Wiley. Reprinted by permission of John Wiley & Sons, Ltd.

221: *Wizard of Id.* Reprinted by permission of Johnny Hart and Creators Syndicate, Inc.

226: *Left*—Spencer Grant/The Picture Cube; *right*—Ken Karp

228: Jean Marc Barey/Agence Vandystadt/Photo Researchers

Box 7-5: Brogan, N., & Kutner, N. (1976). Measuring sex-role orientation: A normative approach. *Journal of Marriage and the Family, 38,* 31–39. Copyright © 1976 by the National Council on Family Relations, 3989 Central Ave., N.E., Suite 550, Minneapolis, MN 55421. Reprinted by permission.

234: *Top*—AP/Wide World Photos

234: *Bottom*—Bob David

235: Picasso reproduction = PH

241: Shirley Zeiberg

243: Junebug Clark/Photo Researchers

246: *Left*—Eugene Gordon; *right*—Photofest

248: *Downstown.* Reprinted by permission of Universal Press Syndicate.

Table 8-1: Jones, E. J., & Gordon, E. M. (1972). Timing of self-disclosure and its effect on personal attraction. *Journal of Personality and Social Psychology, 24,* 358–365.

Table 8-2: Miller, L. C., Berg, J. B., & Archer, R. L. (1983). Openers: People who elicit intimate self-disclosure. *Journal of Personality and Social Psychology, 44,* 1234–1244.

250: Shirley Zeiberg

258: Ken Karp

Table 8-4: Miller, B. C., McCoy, J. K., & Olson, T. D. (1986). Dating age and stage as correlates of adolescent sexual attitudes and behavior. *Journal of Adolescent Research, 1,* 361–371. Copyright 1986 by Sage Publications, Inc. Used with permission.

259: *But Beautiful* by Burke, J. & VanHeusen, J. Copyright 1947 (renewed) by Music Sales Corp. (ASCAP) and Bourne Co. (ASCAP) International copyright secured. All rights reserved. Used by permission.

Box 8-3: Rubin, Z. (1970). Measurement of romantic love. *Journal of Social Psychology, 16,* 265–273.

263: Shirley Zeiberg

265: Laimute Druskis

269: Spencer Grant/Photo Researchers

270: Rameshwar Das/Monkmeyer Press

272–275: Marriage readiness test adapted from Kirkendall, L. A., & Adams, W. J. (1971). *A reading and study guide for students in marriage and family relations.* Dubuque, IA: Wm. C. Brown Publishing.

276: *Left*—Spencer Grant/Photo Researchers; *right*—James Nachtwey

Figure 9-1: Data from Strauss, M. A. (1991). Physical violence in American families: Incidence rates, causes, and trends. In D. D. Knudsen & J. L. Miller (Eds.), *Abused and battered: Social and legal responses to family violence.* New York: Aldine de Gruyer.

Table 9-3: The first 20 items from Table 1 (without corresponding data) of Mathews, V. D., & Mihanovich, C. S. (1963). New orientations on marital adjustment. *Marriage and Family Living, 25,* 300–304.

284: *Top*—Rhoda Sidney

284: *Bottom left*—Eugene Richards; *bottom right*—M. E. Warren/Photo Researchers

286: John Robaton/United Nations

287: Office of Economic Opportunity

289: Drawing by M. Stevens; Copyright *The New Yorker Magazine,* Inc.

295: Ken Karp

Table 10-1: Zamula, E. (1989, June). Drugs and pregnancy: Often the two don't mix. *FDA Consumer Magazine,* DHHS Publication No. (FDA) 90-3174.

Table 10-3: Siegler, R. S. (1991). *Children's thinking* (2nd ed.). Englewood Cliffs, NJ: Prentice-Hall, Inc.

Figure 10-1: Siegler, R. S. (1976). Three aspects of cognitive development. *Cognitive Psychology, 8,* 481–520. Copyright © 1976 by Academic Press, Inc. Used with permission.

Table 10-4: Kohlberg, L. A. (1981). *Essays on moral development. Vol. 1. The philosophy of moral development.* San Francisco: Harper & Row.

302: James Carroll

Figure 10-2: Data from Tanner, J. M., Whitehouse, R. H., & Takaishi, M. (1965). Standards from birth to maturity for height, weight, height velocity, and weight velocity: British children. *Archives of the Diseases of Childhood, 41,* 845–872.

Table 10-5: Santrock, J. W. (1987). *Adolescence: An introduction* (3rd ed.). Dubuque, IA: Wm. C. Brown.

305: Laimute Druskis

Figure 10-3: Data from Coles, R., & Stokes, G. (1985). *Sex and the American teenager.* New York: Harper & Row.

309: PEOPLE Weekly © 1992 Jim McHugh

310: Rhoda Sidney

Table 10-6: Levinson, D. J., Darrow, C. M., Klein, E. G., Levinson, M. H., & McBee, B. (1978). *The seasons of a man's life.* New York: Alfred A. Knopf.

314: *Arlo and Janis.* Reprinted by permission of NEA, Inc.

317: J. Albert/The Image Works

321: Ken Karp

Table 10-7: Dailey, D. (1981). Sexual expression and aging. In F. J. Berghorn, D. E. Schaefer, and Associates (Eds.), *The dynamics of aging: Original essays on the processes and experiences of growing old.* Boulder, CO: Westview Press.

Table 10-8: Lerner, M. (1970). When, why, and where people die. In D. Brim, Jr., H. E. Freeman, S. Levine, & N. Scotch (Eds.), *The dying patient.* New York: Russell Sage Foundation.

Box 10-2: Templer, D. I. (1970). The construction and validation of a death anxiety scale. *Journal of General Psychology, 82,* 165–177. Reprinted with permission of the Helen Dwight Reid Foundation. Published by Hildref Publications, 1319 Eighteenth St., N.W., Washington, D.C. 20036. Copyright © 1970.

Templer, D. I., & Ruff, C. F. (1971). Death Anxiety Scale means, standard deviations, and embedding. *Psychological Reports, 29,* 173–174.

Table 10-10: Simek, T. C., & O'Brien, R. M. (1981). *Total golf: A behavioral approach to lowering your score and getting more out of your game.* Huntington, NY: B-Mod Associates.

334: Ewing Galloway

336: Teri Leigh Stratford

337: Okonewski/The Image Works

Box 11-2: Schulze, R. H. K. (1962). Short dogmatism scale. *Journal of Psychological Studies, 13,* 93–97. Copyright © 1962 by *Journal of Psychological Studies.*

341: Spencer Grant/Stock, Boston

346: UPI/Bettmann Newsphotos

349: Ken Karp

350: Rogers/Monkmeyer Press

Box 11-3: Weigel, R., & Weigel, J. (1978). Environmental concern: The development of a measure. *Environment and Behavior, 10,* 3–15. Reprinted by permission of Sage Publications, Inc.

354: Spencer Grant/Monkmeyer Press

356: Drawing by Dedini; Copyright © 1985 *The New Yorker Magazine,* Inc.

359: Reuters/Bettmann Newsphotos

367: Lorraine Rorke/The Image Works

Table 12-1: Renwick, P. A., & Lawler, E. E. (1978). What do you really want from your job? *Psychology Today, 11(12),* 53–55.

381: R. Sidney/Monkmeyer Press

Table 12-6: Szilagi, A. D., & Wallace, M. J. (1983). *Organizational behavior and performance* (3rd ed.). Glenview, IL: Scott-Foresman. Copyright © 1983, 1980 by Scott Foresman and Co. Reprinted by permission of HarperCollins Publishers.

Table 12-8: Latham, G. P. (1982). Behavior-based assessment in organizations. In L. W. Ferguson (Ed.), *Handbook of organizational behavior management.* New York: Wiley.

390: Rhoda Sidney

394: *Arlo and Janis.* Reprinted by permission of NEA, Inc.

401: Rhoda Sidney

403: *Left*—Charles Gatewood; *right*—Marc Anderson

Figure 13-1: Data from Robins, L. N., Helzer, J. E., Weissman, M. M., Orvaschel, H., Greunberg, E., Burke, J. D., & Regier, D. A. (1984). Lifetime prevalence of specific psychiatric disorders in three sites. *Archives of General Psychiatry, 41,* 949–958.

Table 13-1: American Psychiatric Association (1987). *Diagnostic and statistical manual of mental disorders* (3rd ed. rev.). Washington, D. C.: American Psychiatric Association.

410: Rhoda Sidney

411: Ed Lettau/Photo Researchers

414: *Peanuts.* Reprinted by permission of United Features Syndicate, Inc.

Box 13-3: Jewike, M. A., Baer, L., & Minichello, P. M. (Eds.) (1986). *Obsessive compulsive disorders.* Littleton, MA: PSG Publishing.

416: UPI/Bettmann Newsphotos

417: *Left*—New York Public Library Collection; *middle*—Library of Congress; *right*—AP/Wide World

419: Handel engraving PH

Box 13-4: Copyright © 1977 by Munoz, R. F., & Lewinsohn, P. M. Personal Beliefs Inventory (Form M-1).

Table 13-3: Kraepelin, E. (1919). *Dementia praecox and paraphrenia.* Edinburgh: Livingstone.

427: AP/World Wide

429: UPI/Bettmann Newsphotos

434: Ursula Markus/Photo Researchers

439: Van Bucher/Photo Researchers

Box 14-2: Meador, B. D., & Rogers, C. R. (1984). Person centered therapy. In R. J. Corsini (Ed.), *Current psychotherapies* (3rd ed.) Itasca, IL: F. E. Peacock. Reproduced by permission of the publisher, F. E. Peacock Publishing, Inc., Itasca, IL.

444: Laimute Druskis

445: Rhoda Sidney/Monkmeyer Press

449: Bandura, A., & Menlove, F. L. (1968). Factors determining vicarious extinction of avoidance behavior through symbolic modeling. *Journal of Personality and Social Psychology, 8,* 99–108. Copyright American Psychological Association. Used with permission of Albert Bandura, Ph.D.

Box 14-3: Ellis, A. (1989). Rational emotive therapy. In R. J. Corsini & D. Wedding (Eds.), *Current psychotherapies* (4th ed.). Itasca, IL: F. E. Peacock. Reproduced by permission of the publisher, F. E. Peacock Publishing, Inc., Itasca, IL.

Box 14-4: Beck, A. T. (1976). *Cognitive therapy and the emotional disorders.* Madison, CT: International Universities Press. Reproduced by permission of the publisher, International Universities Press, Madison, CT.

453: *Top*—Ursula Markus/Photo Researchers; *bottom*—Ken Karp

Box 14-5: Bornstein, P. H., & Bornstein, P. T. (1986). *Marital therapy: A behavioral communications approach.* Copyright © 1986. Reprinted with permission of Allyn and Bacon.

457: Will McIntyre/Photo Researchers

458: *The Far Side.* Reprinted by permission of Universal Press Syndicate, Inc.

467: Larry Fleming

469: Susan Rosenberg/Photo Researchers

Box 15-1: Wolpe, J. (1982). *The practice of behavior therapy* (3rd ed.). Elmsford, NY: Pergamon Press.

Box 15-2: Excerpt from *Psychology* by B. von Halmer Gilmer. Copyright © 1973 by B. von Halmer Gilmer. Reprinted by permission of HarperCollins Publishers.

480: Larry Fleming

Box 15-3: From *Your perfect right: A guide to assertive living* (5th ed.). Copyright by Robert E. Alberti & Michael L. Emmons. Reproduced by Prentice-Hall, Inc., with permission of Impact Publishers, Inc., P.O. Box 1094, San Luis Obispo, CA 93406. Further reproduction prohibited.

Box 15-4: Davis, M., Eshelman, E. R., & MacKay, E. R. (1982). *The relaxation and stress reduction handbook* (2nd ed.). Oakland, CA: New Harbinger Publications.

489: Ken Karp

489: *For Better or Worse.* Reprinted with permission of Universal Press Syndicate, Inc.

491: Spencer Grant/Monkmeyer Press

495: Reuters/Bettmann

Box 15-5: Osterweis, M., Solomon, F., & Green, M. (1984). *Bereavement: Reactions, consequences and care.* Washington, D.C.: National Academy of Sciences.

497: Michelle Vegnes/Jeroboam, Inc.

Box 15-6: Osterweis, M., Solomon, F., & Greene, M. (1984). *Bereavement: Reactions, consequences and care.* Washington, D.C.: National Academy of Sciences.

Box 15-7: "Resume," copyright 1926, 1928, renewed 1954. Copyright 1956 by Dorothy Parker, from *The Portable Dorothy Parker* by Dorothy Parker, Introduction by Brenden Gill. Used by permission of Viking Penguin, a division of Penguin Books, USA, Inc.

SUBJECT INDEX

Entries and page numbers in **boldface** indicate terms defined in the marginal glossary.

AA, 196
Abnormal behavior, 402, 430
  biological model of, 406
  classifying, 406, 408
  defining, 402–3
  intra-psychic model of, 405
  socio-behavioral models of, 406
Acquired Immune Deficiency Syndrome
  (AIDS), 222
Addiction, 456
Adjustment, 3, 32, 35
  disorder, 409
  and the other sex, 4
  problems of, 2, 6, 32
Adolescence, 301, 328
  and delinquency, 307
  modeling in, 306
  other tasks of, 304
  self-reinforcement in, 306
  working through, 304
Adolescent(s):
  effects of early maturation on, 303
  egocentrism, 311
  risk taking, 311
  and sexual intercourse, 307
  social development, 312
  thinking, 310
Adult development, 312, 329
  Levinson's stages of, 313
  theories of, 312
Adulthood:
  early, 312
  getting into, 313
  during the middle years, 314
  in the thirties, 314
Aerobic exercising, 159, 198
  beneficial effects of, 160
  frequency of, 171
  intensity of, 171
  length, of, 171
  types of, 171
Aerobic fitness, 168, 203
  importance of, 170

Aerobic fitness program:
  characteristics of, 171
Aerobic points system, 172, 203
  examples of, 172
Aggression, 336, 360, 364, **483,** 506
  and aversive stimulation, 337
  and frustration, 337
  and learning, 336
  prevention of, 338
Aging:
  physical changes from, 319
Agoraphobia, 412, 432
  treatment of, 457
Agreeableness, 40
Alarm (preparation) stage, 150, 162
Alcohol, 195–96, 199
  use by high school seniors, 308
Alternative food pattern, 186
Alzheimer's disease, 320, 332
Amino acids, 183, 203
Amphetamines, 191, 203
Anaerobic fitness, 169
Anal-retentive personality type, 48
Anal stage, 48
Analytical psychology, 52
Anatomy:
  female sexual and reproductive, 206
  male sexual and reproductive, 207
Androgyny, 231, 239
Anger, 125, 135, 360, **478,** 503, 506
  coping self-statements for, 481
  display of, 125
  methods for controlling, 478
  relaxation strategies for, 480
  responsible assertiveness for, 481
Anna O., 17
Annoyance List, 479
Anorexia nervosa, 308, 332
Antecedent, 237
Anus, 206
Anxiety, 126, 135, **469,** 505
  adjustment of, 469
  causes of, 416–17

Anxiety disorders, 408, 411–17, 463
  generalized, 414
  treatment of, 457
Anxiolytics, 456
Appraisal:
  primary, 140
  secondary, 140
Arbitrary inference, 111
Archetypes, 52, 72
Assertion:
  body, 488
  developing, 483 ff.
  fear of, 488
  versus aggression, 483
Assertion training, 482, 506
Assertiveness, 482
  Inventory, 484–85
  training, 444, 482
  why, 483
Attachment, 297
Attachment behavior, 297, 332
Authoritarianism, 345, 361, 364
Authoritarian personality, 345–46
Autogenics, 455
Autonomic nervous system, 115
  parts of, 116
Aversion therapy, 445
Aversive stimulation, 337
Avoidance learning of, 94, 97, 99
Azrin's operant reinforcement method for
  depression, 459

Baby boom, 367, 400
Bacterial vaginosis, 210
Barbiturates, 194
Baseline, 19
Beauty, 245
Beck's cognitive therapy, 450, 466
  and psychoanalysis, 452
  and rational emotive therapy, 451–52
Behavior, 3, 35, 238